CW00833102

REPORTING THE PARTITION OF PUNJAB 1947

Reporting the Partition of Punjab 1947

Press, Public and Other Opinions

RAGHUVENDRA TANWAR

MANOHAR
2006

First published 2006

ISBN 81-7304-674-3

Published by
Ajay Kumar Jain *for*
Manohar Publishers & Distributors
4753/23 Ansari Road, Daryaganj
New Delhi 110 002

Typeset by
Kohli Print
Delhi 110 051

Printed at
Lordson Publishers Pvt. Ltd.
New Delhi 110 007

Distributed in South Asia by
FOUNDATION BOOKS
4381/4, Ansari Rorad
Daryaganj, New Delhi 110 002
and its branches at Mumbai, Hyderabad,
Bangalore, Chennai, Kolkata

Contents

Preface

[I]t seems inevitable that good or bad right or wrong media tends to generate strong feelings in historians. . . .[1]

'What gives history its flesh and blood, is the men and motives behind policies and events. It is the inside knowledge that makes history human' commented an editorial of the *Pakistan Times*. It also said: 'Bare facts do not constitute history, nor are public statements by leaders, which are often facades to conceal the real forces at work.'[2] That bare facts do not constitute history is a view which many would be inclined to contest, but it is the second part of this interesting observation—that public statements often conceal more than they reveal, that is important in the context of the Punjab of 1947.

One result of this has been the wide disparity in the understanding of the partition of Punjab from the common perspective on the one hand and the form that has more broadly been presented in most histories on the other. This has happened because an important part of the writings available to us on the partition of Punjab (1947) have given far too much of attention to what the leaders on both sides were saying than to what they were actually doing. From this grew a trend—there were, of course, important exceptions—of understating, downsizing, downplaying a great part of the tragedy for what it was believed was the broader good of everyone concerned. As Gyanendra Pandey puts it: 'Indian historical writing has never escaped from this obligation to demonstrate oneness. Writings on partition bear the mark of it until today.'[3] In this sense, writings on the Partition of India have been shadowed by the story and success of the struggle for freedom. As Hansen also says: '. . . Partition has therefore been seen as an unfortunate departure from this otherwise glorious road to independence.'[4]

It has possibly been difficult as a result for the writers of history—of whatever school—to dwell on the 'ugly' chapter of the happenings of 1947, particularly those of Punjab, along with the distinguished story of victory upon victory that has come down to us as the story of the struggle for India's freedom. We therefore tend to present the Partition of India in what at times even appears to be nothing more than a disguise, a complex affair of negotiations, statements, charges and countercharges, heroes and villains, an affair where great minds took decisions for the greater good of the people and that if things did go a 'bit' wrong, they were not important enough to bother too much about. All the blood, the misery were just extra luggage. All this tutoring—the 'statement of facts'—has failed to alter the perceptions, and for the vast multitude of people even remotely connected or affected by the partition of Punjab it was much more than the fact that it was accompanied by the independence of India and the birth of Pakistan. For this vast majority of people who represented the actual execution of partition, it was not only a disaster in terms of the human lives last and the economic destruction or the division it caused among the people, more importantly, it also ended a way of life, a shared history.[5]

THE NEWSPAPER AS A SOURCE

Much can be said in favour of contemporary newspapers as a source for understanding what happened in Punjab in 1947 as can be said against them. A major reason which has prompted this study is the general consensus in recent research that:

> media effects have been identified to occur at a number of political economic and psychological levels . . . perhaps the most critical concern has focussed upon the capability of the media to shape the way people behave . . . especially among the potentially more malleable members of the public.[6]

Newman too has suggested that approaches to social science research detailed readings and examination of texts can help uncover embedded meanings.[7] It has become fairly accepted that a person's inner feelings and motives can best or more easily be understood by the text of what he or she may have said.[8] Extensive studies conducted during the period between the First and Second World Wars have also, for example, established the important role played by newspapers in shaping public opinion and behaviour.[9] The impact of the media has usually been seen to penetrate downwards through opinion makers.[10] Gunter, in fact makes out a strong case in favour of newspapers as a means to study situations similar to those of the Punjab in 1947, and refers to Max Weber who had pointed out almost a century earlier the need to study social and political issues on the basis of press coverage as well as public opinion.[11] Gunter goes on to point out that: 'a relationship is presumed to exist between the amount of coverage the media give to an event and how prominent it is in the public consciousness', and also that not only do people learn through the media but in fact it is the media that indicates to the people on the basis of the coverage it gives to an event, the importance that needs to be attached to it.[12]

As will be noticed, considerable emphasis has been given in this study to letters addressed to editors of various newspapers. This has been done to survey the opinions on specific issues. Coming from people of greatly divergent backgrounds, such letters have proved a valuable source. As Margaretta Jolly points out: 'the letter to the editor writer, as in most countries is not only articulate, [but also] reflective and expresses a general view held by many who do not or can not put it into words'.[13] In suggesting that 'letters (to editors and others) are records of the moment, they represent the ability of ordinary citizens to write and make history',[14] Jolly in fact underlines the significance of newspapers as an important source for reading minds, particularly in times that are disturbed. In this sense, she proceeds on the understanding that letters and opinion columns carrying topical articles are also in a way a representation of individual participation in political activity. In the same way they are also a kind of national forum for debate. Jolly points out the interesting example of the tremendous influence of letters to the editors and articles in newspapers in building up British public opinion, which forced the USA to enter the Second World War.[15]

In the case of Punjab in 1947, there was scarcely a day when the letters columns of leading newspapers were not carrying an interesting and alternate version of events that were important at a given time, and exhaustive theories in articles relating to the political options that needed to be considered. Or even just small local incidents involving say a corrupt policemen or may be just ordinary common issues like adulteration in ration supplies. Repeatedly one also notices the disgust of ordinary citizens with the role of provincial and national level political leaders. In sum, letters and articles carried by newspapers are known frequently to translate and interlink local issues—issues of the domestic sphere—into issues of the public sphere.

Newspapers, as Chandrika Kaul also suggests, are 'especially valuable in enabling the reconstruction of contemporary perspectives on events without the tendency towards teleology evident in subsequent historical accounts which aware of the outcome supply an artificial coherence to developments. Newspapers allow us to follow the manner in which contemporaries reacted to events as they unfolded over time.[16]

Of course at the same time it is also well known that newspapers do not always reproduce reality, on the contrary, they are known to sometimes add a 'spin', a kind of branded style to make the news more readable. Reality in the context of the newspapers is, as Darshnik Vyas has put it, little more than 'our cherished way of looking at the world'.[17] The newspaper's version, be it in the form of a news report, a letter, or even a photograph, is only a version and image of an incident which was considered necessary for recording and is therefore only a version: 'that didn't get away . . . just think how much more there is to history'. These are no doubt words that ring a challenge to any student of history: 'The image that should have been recorded could not or was not recorded.'[18]

Yes in this sense, therefore, newspapers cannot claim to be barometers of public opinion, but the fact remains that newspapers and their opinion are and were what politicians and public men have been known to more frequently respond to or attempt to influence.[19] Kaul suggests that 'newspapers did not simply mirror the opinion of their readers but also shaped it,' and that in times of crisis people, as a 1937 survey showed, turned more to their newspapers and other media for guidance than was normally the case.[20]

Developing this thesis, Kaul bases an important part of the view on studies by Lippman and Boyce and points out that news printed in newspapers was the result of a series of selections which enable a newspaper to evoke responses from its readers and it is this element that enables newspapers to create public opinion,[21] and above all, public opinion is what contemporaries perceived it to be.[22]

Many would say, and quite correctly, that a newspaper's coverage of crisis is therefore usually formulaic; 'So formulaic that iconic moments become symbols, their stereotyped references that become at best a rote memory.' The problem with the newspaper in this sense as a source is the presetting of agendas. Therefore, even as statements and objective reports are valuable sources to understand and reproduce events, it is the manner in which they are highlighted or understated and edited that frequently allows only half the truth to reach the unsuspecting reader.

While no such study is available of Punjab in particular, but other studies elsewhere have shown that newspaper readers of smaller towns prefer to read local news the most and national news the least.[23] Such studies have also shown that small town readers are interested in police stories, obituaries, stories that are local in character and impact, while those in larger towns preferred society columns, letters to editors and topical columns. Accepting and extending this argument, one can quite easily understand why even during the peak months of violence and anarchy in Punjab, newspapers, particularly the more widely read English ones, did not cut into the space of 'society' news, elite entertainment, and the like.

Research has also shown that the personal experiences of one person, if circulated through any medium—a photograph, a letter, a story—tend to make other individuals more receptive to similar stories involving other people and published by newspapers. Relatedly, Gunter suggests that media is capable of creating moods and feelings by the content it provides,[24] and that people read specific publications and stories because they expect to have certain needs satisfied by doing so.[25]

We can therefore proceed on the lines that given a choice people are more likely to read a newspaper which gives them not only 'news', but news that is packaged in a manner which suits their mental attitude—in other words, it is the editorial staff upon whom depends what and how much of an incident needs to be reported. The extensive and frequent reproduction from the editorials of 'rival newspapers', which will be noticed repeatedly in this work, is partly the result of this understanding.

THIS BOOK AND OF ITS SOURCES

This book is in a sense a limited chronicle of the partition of Punjab: limited because it focuses only on 1947, making in the process only peripheral and passing reference to the intricate and complex theories and versions that are abundantly available in the existing literature on the broader subject. Starting from about the end of 1946, it builds on the basis of detailed readings of a wide spectrum of news publications which appeared in the Punjab in 1947. While newspapers from all the four major languages of Punjab, namely English, Urdu, Punjabi and Hindi (about eighteen major ones in all) were researched, an overdrawing from the English press may in fact be noticed. This was because only two—and both English—of the long list of newspapers being published in Punjab were operating with a relatively good network of correspondents. Ironic as it may seem, vernacular dailies frequently if not always picked up leads and important stories from the English press. So much so that a note prepared in the form of a 'top secret' opinion on newspapers in India by the British Information Service even recorded how many Hindi dailies were picking up all major leads from the *Hindustan Times*.[26]

This in itself could have been ignored, however, a more serious problem with the regional language press based in Lahore and Amritsar was that almost without exception the Urdu and Punjabi newspapers were not only deeply committed to propounding the cause of the Muslim League or that of the Akalis', but a great deal of their effort as well as space, limited as it was, went towards framing and countering charges made against each other. The *Zamindar* (Urdu), for example, was widely popular, but naturally, as an assessment put it, 'it championed the Muslim interests (and did this) by the easiest method of criticising the prominent Hindu newspapers'.[27] Likewise, the *Khalsa*, not even remotely comparable with the *Zamindar* in popularity, was essentially an organ committed to 'watching Sikh Panthic interests'.[28]

But all this apart, the single most important reason for dependence on the English press remains the fact that once again, and without exception, every Punjabi and Hindi publication that had Lahore as its home before August 1947 was burnt down. The complete anarchy that prevailed in Amritsar and Lahore during August and September 1947 ensured among other things that practically nothing—machines, paper, or records—survived. In any case, papers that managed to pull through had ceased publication for the crucial months of August and September, and as a result are not available for the crucial context and events. To quote Gauba: 'all Hindu and Sikh papers had left Lahore (in panic) after the office of the *Tribune* was set on fire and the Editor of *Milap* was stabbed . . . Pakistan has come in for huge stocks of paper and machinery by the exodus of non-Muslim papers'.[29]

This study looks close to the surface so as to hear the marginalized voices, so as to restore a human dimension to a story that was essentially a story of human misery. To cite Pandey, there is an urgent need to focus on the 'little histories', the 'local intensities', the 'local voices', that have been erased not consciously perhaps but all the same.[30]

Much has already been written on the partition of Punjab. But surprisingly most of the accounts of the Punjab's partition have handled it as if it were little more than a political event, an achievement whose human dimension, of it if, at all, was only peripheral.

In this context in particular, this work is not therefore a story of the complex negotiations, the political intrigues, the political rhetoric that preceded the division of Punjab, nor even of how and why the partition of Punjab came about. It is in fact an attempt to focus on the 'little voices' that should have been heard but were swept away, of what transpired on the ground, the dusty lanes and by lanes of Punjab's villages and small towns, outside the secluded chambers where British officials conferred with Indian leaders deciding the future of people with whom both had nothing in common. In this sense it is also a story of the partition of Punjab which begins from where most other mainstream histories, if we may call them that, have ended. It starts from a time when Punjab's partition had become a certainty. It attempts to deal with the period of partition itself, because 'comparatively little attention has been paid by historians to the period of partition itself'.[31]

The work proceeds to reach the inner embedded meanings and motives, not only in the context of key players—both British and Indian—but also, and more pointedly, the ordinary, the kind who had no stake in the games and pulls of political power either way—the millions of ordinary souls who had not an inkling of what was happening and why it was happening.

It accepts and proceeds on the basic hypothesis of Gunter that 'behind immediately observable surface reality lie deep structures or unobservable mechanism. Only with effort can deep structures be exposed.'[32]

Texts, photographs, even mundane advertisements and classified columns, have been closely examined in an attempt to understand individual motives because individual motives appear to be crucially linked to broader and more important events. Much of what happened in Punjab has to be viewed in the context of the verbal and physical behaviour of the people, and it is this understanding that has led this study to the very fine print of regional news columns, to letters on a wide variety of issues from forlorn small towns which had nothing in common with the hyperactive worlds of Lahore and Amritsar. Finecombing of the Punjab High Court's (Lahore) daily proceedings, for example, reveals how one particular judge was extra liberal with cases relating to murder and arson which occurred in March 1947—bail in such cases was on discount. This naturally tells a story of its own.

The Tribune (Lahore), along with the *Civil & Military Gazette* was the leading opinion maker with a long and distinguished history of publication.[33] Gandhiji had once called it the 'best views paper in India'.[34] It had moved to Simla in August 1947. Just as the *Dawn* (Delhi/Karachi) and *Pakistan Times* (Lahore) represented the Muslim League's point of views, *The Tribune* usually found itself on the side of the Hindu and Sikhs, which in Punjab also meant the Congress. 'It exemplified the impact of many trends on the Punjabi press. . . . *The Tribune* was more widely quoted abroad than any other Indian newspaper cited even in the halls of Parliament. . . . It was the first English newspaper that recorded local events of minor national importance. . . . In 1945 it had . . . the largest circulation of an English newspaper in Punjab.'[35] Having moved in mid-August from Lahore to Simla in dramatic and violent circumstances it rebuilt from scratch.[36]

The Civil & Military Gazette (Lahore) was relatively fair and unbiased in its opinions on the Muslim versus Sikh and Hindu issues. By 1947 it had shed a considerable part of its 'pro-administration' and 'official' colour. It used photographs extensively to present stories. It was the only source in this part of the country for the Europeans news of home. In a sense it was the nearest to being a modern newspaper in the context of the present times. 'For more than forty years it has stood if not for disinterested journalism at least for sober policy . . . what takes *Pakistan Times* and *Dawn* a thousand words to express, F.W. Bustin of the *CMG* can say in a hundred. . .'[37] The (*CMG's*) significance in terms of pressure on the government and the impact on opinion making was far in excess of its circulation figures.[38] It remained relatively unaffected by the disturbances in 1947; as a result some of the most important press versions of the period of anarchy in Punjab, be they in Urdu, English, or Punjabi, are in some way or the other traceable to the *CMG*.

A special word needs to be said for the *Dawn*. Its importance like that of the *CMG* was far in excess of what its circulation figures tend to suggest. It rivalled *The Tribune* in importance and had as good a network of reporters. Even as their views differed intensely, between the two there was hardly any news that got away. It played in Punjab for the Muslim League the role that *The Tribune* played for the Congress and the Akalis. It was greatly fond of targetting Sardar Patel and held him responsible for many of its own problems. It was relatively much softer on Nehru. Started by Jinnah in Delhi, it remained the platform from where he and the League responded to others or initiated their point of view. It moved to Karachi in circumstances that were not as bad as those in which its rival *The Tribune* moved from Lahore to Simla. 'The editor Atlaf Hussain (was) a small and dynamic personality. All his writings . . . have a smell of gun powder.'[39]

The *Pakistan Times* started publication a few months prior to the partition of Punjab. With the Muslim League's main mouthpiece *Dawn* beginning to face problems in Delhi, the *Pakistan Times* rapidly became the flagbearer of the Muslim League's viewpoint. With the exit of *The Tribune* from Lahore in mid-August 1947, it provided the only competition to the well-entrenched *Civil & Military Gazette*.[40]

The Eastern Times was far less important. It was shoddily produced and yet it was popular among Muslim government employees, particularly in the Railways. It gave extensive coverage to the grievances of the employees. Almost every edition highlighted the imbalances between Muslims and the other communities in some department or the other, of the Railways in particular.[41]

The *Hindustan Times* was to Delhi what *The Tribune* had been in its heyday to Lahore. Owned by a leading business house, its pro-Congress and nationalist perceptive gave it considerable influence in the Congress and the government. For some reason, however, all its resources notwithstanding, its vision of Punjab remained almost distant, for example, even during the peak disturbances in March 1947 it spared a great deal of its space for articles and stories seeking a decrease in the nominal increase in income tax that had then been proposed in the budget. As things settled down it made up by sending teams of reporters into Punjab, amongest them Durga Das whose reports stood out for being not only informative but also sensitive and authentic. Being the 'counter point' to the *Dawn*, it was frequently accused of being pro-Hindu—pro-capitalist and pro-Congress.[42]

The *Statesman* was widely popular in Calcutta and Delhi.[43] A great part of this popularity coming from its editorials and editorial page articles. I.M. Stephens, its irrepressible editor, was perhaps the most influential journalist in India. At one stage the paper was even charged by influential quarters in London and Delhi as being one of the contributing factors for the failure of the Cabinet Mission (1946).[44] While it did not have much of a network of reporters in Punjab, some of its articles on Punjab, particularly the refugee movement and failures of planning, were outstanding.

Janvani (Hindi) a monthly published from the premises of the Kashi Vidyapeeth, Banaras, had the distinction of having Acharya Narendra Dev on its editorial board. Some of its articles and editorials were unsparing assessments of political events, leaders, and their policies. Naturally it was the platform from which many socialists shared their views.

Abhyudaya (Hindi, Allahabad), was founded by Madan Mohan Malviya in 1907. He edited it from 1909 to 1930 after which his son looked after it. The paper ceased publication in February 1948, that is, within a year of Malviya's death. Some of its articles and editorials, particularly on how corruption and lust for power had overrun the Congress, the control of food and cloth distribution channels by Congressmen, for example are 'eye openers'.

The *Indian Annual Register*, *The Pioneer* (Lucknow), the *Times of India* (Bombay), *The Leader* (Allahabad), the *Daily Milap* (Urdu, Lahore/Delhi), *Hindu Outlook* (Delhi, weekly), *Organiser* (Delhi, weekly), *Times* (London) and *Khalsa Samachar* (Punjabi, weekly, Amritsar) have also been referred to particularly for cross-checking major incidents and versions.[45]

The *Keesings Contemporary Archives* made it possible to access summarized newspaper versions of important events.[46] Since it compiled its reports from a cross-section of newspapers published in India and Britain, it was possible to cross-check dates and other specifics.

Besides newspapers and other such media publications, a large number of private papers and correspondence have also been used essentially to corroborate the leads picked up from newspapers, but often the other way round as well.

The papers of Jack Mortan,[47] and W.H.A. Rich[48] the SSPs of Lahore in 1946–7, A.J.V. Arthur,[49] the Deputy Commissioner of Multan, and of P. Brenden, Deputy Commissioner of Gurgaon, have proved exceedingly helpful in understanding the origin and nature of some of the incidents. The significance of Brenden's personal version of the killings in Gurgaon district, for example, lies in the fact that he has categorically and with great substance rejected the well-known version of F. Tuker (*While Memory Serves*) that the Meos made the first initiative in the major incidents. For Brenden it was clearly a case of Jat and Ahir offensive and Meo defence.[50]

Major General T.W. Rees', papers contain a report filed by him after he had relinquished charge of the Punjab Boundary Force. This is extremely important for understanding the kinds of problems faced by field officers during the peak days of the disturbances in the volatile districts of Amritsar and Lahore.[51]

O.H. Spate was contracted by the Ahmaddiya community to plead its case to the Punjab Boundary Commission in July 1947. His notes and diary entries provide a new and interesting dimension to the Commission's proceedings and point to Spate's belief that its very approach to the problem was incorrect, and also that Lahore was agog with rumours that both sides—India and Pakistan—were adopting all kinds of methods to sway the Commission's judgement.[52]

In a category apart are the versions and views recorded by British servicemen whose regiments were either based on duty in Punjab or happened to have been moving through Punjab during the disturbances. Lt. Col. John Peddie (7/14 Punjab Regiment) has recorded his shock and dismay at his government's decision to withdraw the British forces at a time when India needed them most.[53] Lt. Col. R.N.P. Reynolds (2/9 Gurkha) has recorded in extensive detail how the British and Indian officers and troops worked in harmony and under greatly challenging conditions without rest for days together.[54]

The Lloyd Jones Papers contain newsletters of the Assam Regiment and other Regimental documents. The Appendix to Newsletter-I is a note by Lt. Col. Lewis Collinson (2nd Battalion). Collinson was in fact only passing through Punjab and while waiting at Ambala for a train connection was suddenly directed on 21 September 1947 to take charge of Muslim Refugee Camp security with headquarters at Karnal. He has recorded in vivid detail some horrifying scenes, the inhuman conditions in the camps and most importantly his belief that many of the train attacks were in fact organized with the support of railway employees.[55]

The Stephens Papers also include a small booklet by Lionell Fielden. Fielden talks of Delhi in August 1947, particularly of the manner in which senior Congress party leaders had completely adapted 'living more or less under the conditions of luxury and splendour which they were apt to criticise under the British'.[56]

Personal reports by senior British functionaries have given an added insight into various issues and events. Francis Muddie, Governor of

West Punjab (took over on 15 August 1947), has recorded that the inexperience of the Superintendents of police and the deputy commissioners led to many of the problems and the fact that no plans had been drawn simply because there was no time.

I.M. Stephens, as noted, was editor of the *Statesman*, a position which gave him an extraordinary level of influence. He received a large number letters, articles and printed material on a host of problems, but what really stands out in our present context is his view that Mountbatten committed a great error by trying to push through the Partition of India in great haste, which left no time for planning[57] and contributed to the anarchy.[58] Lord Ismay's 'India Situation Report', written on 5 October 1947 is a frank admittance of the failure to predict the crisis, but more importantly, 'it would be difficult to find two people who agree as to how the trouble started, why it was not checked, what actually happened'.[59]

The Mridula Sarabhai Papers have been very useful in understanding and counter-checking various reports in newspapers relating to the abduction, recovery and resettlement of women.[60]

Transcripts of interviews recorded by the BBC with Field Marshal Auchinleck and Penderel Moon under the title of 'Plain Tales From The Raj', speak of the widespread corruption among officials including the British (Moon). Auchinleck has stated how the whole plan of transferring power in a short time was nothing but 'absurd absolutely'.[61]

Versions recorded in the form interviews, transcribed as oral history, have naturally to be handled with great caution—sometimes it is lapses in memory, at other times a version that may have been influenced by more contemporary and post developments. A great deal, of course, depends on the capability of the person who records it, even more on the kinds of questions he raises on the subject. In the 1970s the NMML provided for a project to record interviews with a large number of people. In the context of 1947 and the Punjab, these include among others, Bhimsen Sachar, Prabodh Chandra, Ishar Singh, Majhel, and Tek Chand, who were all key players in 1947.

I had approached these transcripts with great excitement, but soon realized that much had been left out. All the same, they provide some interesting insights. Sachar has talked of how Gopichand Bhargava beat him in the race to become East Punjab's first Premier only because he enjoyed Sardar Patel's 'solid backing', in 1947,[62] while Majhel as Minister for Civil Supplies, Relief and Rehabilitation, East Punjab, is honest enough to admit that no one had any idea how to handle the refugee crisis.[63] Prabodh Chandra was an important Congressman of West Punjab, and he hit hard on his party's leadership for ignoring the Muslims of Kashmir in particular.[64] Tek Chand recorded some interesting details on the killings in East Punjab and the condition of the refugee camps.[65]

A great deal of the correspondence between the Viceroy/Governor General, the Governors, Indian and Pakistani leaders and a number other people, personal reports, situation reports, proceedings of meetings up to mid-August 1947 has been available for many years in the monumental collection of 12 volumes known commonly as the *Transfer of Power* volumes, but there are a large number of other documents and correspondence relating to the post-August 1947 months that are also available under various heads—some as just Mountbatten Papers and others as Viceroy's Personal Reports. One fascinating file in the Mountbatten Papers deals with the plans and arrangements for the ceremonies of 15 August 1947 in Delhi and Karachi.[66] It is amazing to note the time and effort spared for all this even as Punjab was up in flames—truly there were two worlds.

The Viceroy's personal reports are a detailed treatise on a host of issues particularly relating to Punjab and the Sikhs, but as is well known, the more crucial and important notes of Mountbatten remain locked from public view.

Files of the Information Department and after August 1947 of the British Information Service have also proved very helpful, particularly for the cross-checking newspapers reports. The Information Department had prepared Fortnightly Appreciation reports of newspapers stories for its 'Confidential use', and frequently dealt with the important issues being debated by newspapers. In one case, for example, it dealt with the charge that districts that were managed by British superintendents of police and deputy commissioners had witnessed more violence.[67]

But coming back to the *Transfer of Power* volumes, they only seem to grow in importance. Volumes VIII to XII have been used for this work in many ways—to cross-check press versions with government versions and vice versa. Even though these volumes contain only select documents (possibly the more important are still hidden away), the meticulous, insightful, and brilliant notings on a variety of issues and situations by debatably the most disliked Englishman among the Muslim League—Sir Evan Jenkins, Governor of Punjab—are a treat to read. It is easy to come away from these volumes with an impression that possibly much, or at least a good deal, of the responsibility for all that happened in Punjab in 1947 rested not necessarily in Government House, Lahore and New Delhi but somewhere else. The significance of these volumes as well as their flaws has been noted by V.N. Datta: 'From these volumes it is apparent that politics for the Indian leaders had become a battlefield . . . leaders appear in these volumes as social climbers . . . looking for petty gains . . . while British officials look meticulously formal, imbibed [*sic*] with a lofty sense of duty.'[68] Since these volumes end with the transfer of power, the link between the press and official versions was maintained by following up reports in the files of the Viceregal Correspondences in the India Office Records at the British Library, London.

I must add here, of course, that volumes like the *Transfer of Power* and the other contemporary published works that have been used in this study more often to stress a point which may have been raised by a newspaper, the objective therefore being to substantiate an acceptable opinion, keeping the base of the argument put forth in line with the newspaper's version. In some cases, extended references have been drawn from the correspondence between the Governor of Punjab and Government House in Delhi from the *Transfer of Power* volumes but this too has been done with the objective of making the newspaper versions easier to grasp. I wish also to point out that while occasional references have been made to many of the important (popular) writings on the Partition of India that appeared in the decades that followed, in the references to published sources (secondary) the emphasis has remained on those that were essentially contemporary; in other words, recorded by people who saw things first-hand and possibly made their first notes in the heat of the moment. To name a few in this category: G.D. Khosla's *Stern Reckoning*; Penderal Moon's *Divide & Quit* and *Viceroy: Wavells Journal*; Tuker's *While Memory Serves*, C.N. Vakil's *The Economic Consequences of Divided India*; A.N. Bali's *Now It Can Be Told*; K.L. Gauba's *Inside Pakistan*; Taya Zinkin's *Reporting India*; the very accomplished historian B.R. Nanda's *Witness to Partition* (then written under the initial of J.). In the same category could also be added H.V. Hodson's *The Great Divide*; C.B. Birdwood's *India's Freedom Struggle: The Role of Muslims & Sikhs*, and the smaller, lesser-known recordings of Price Day, *Experiment in*

Freedom. A lot of what Durga Das recorded appeared in the *Hindustan Times* in late 1947 and the following years. Some of these recordings were later used to authenticate accounts in *From Curzon to Nehru*.

In a somewhat different category is another contemporary set of writings by people who discussed the problem of partition as they perceived it in the months leading to the actual crisis. Most of these are small booklets, often with great biases but very important all the same. Yusuf Meherally's *A Trip To Pakistan*; Shaukatullah Ansari's *Pakistan: The Problem of India*; Ziauddin Ahmad Sulerl's *Whither Pakistan* have contributed new and interesting angles to the debate.

I would also like to draw attention to another set of contemporary writings—versions recorded of disturbances by both sides, understandably from their respective perspectives. *The Sikhs in Action* was published by the West Punjab Government (1948), to be countered by the *Muslim League Attack on Sikhs and Hindus in Punjab* published by the Shiromani Gurudwara Prabandhak Committee. While D.M. Malik published *The Tragedy of Delhi* (1947), Prabodh Chandra contributed *The Rape of Rawalpindi*. Then there is an assessment of the Rashtriya Swayamsevak Sangh (RSS) and other Hindu and Sikh organizations by the Muslim League, *New Nazis*, by Azhar Husain Zaidi (1948 or 1949).

Reference has already been made to the unpublished memoirs and reports of British army officers who were in Punjab in 1947, but there are also a fairly large number of memoirs of such officers which have appeared in published form as parts of regimental and army histories. Byron Farwell gives a detailed account of what a Gurkha unit witnessed at Ambala station.[69] Charles Chenevix Trench relates how shocked British officers were with the: 'unseemly haste with which His Majesty's government and the last Viceroy shed their responsibility'.[70]

In a different category are the extensive writings of senior Indian public figures. I have made good use of the *Selected Works* of Jawaharlal Nehru, the *Correspondences* of Sardar Patel and Dr Rajendra Prasad and of course, of the many writings of Mahtama Gandhi. I have also drawn from Dr Lohia's *Guilty Men of India's Partition*—mainly his fascinating record of the historic meeting of the Congress Working Committee that debated the acceptance of the

3 June Plan, of how Maulana Azad sat sulking in a corner, of how the disillusioned Kriplani had to be woken up and, of course, of the heated exchange of words between Nehru and Lohia and to a lesser degree between Nehru and Patel on the one hand and Gandhi on the other.

In the context of the Punjab of 1947, the huge collection of documents, etc., dutifully recorded on microfilm and known as the All India Congress Committee Papers is not of much significance, but one does get some interesting views of the problems that followed partition, for example, Reel 123 deals generally with communications addressed to Kriplani and Jugal Kishore, about corruption, the misuse of power by influential Congressmen, allotment of houses and shops to displaced families.[71]

But having said all this I wish once again to emphasize that this study remains eventually a study of the Punjab of 1947 as seen through the columns of important newspapers, and the other sources have played a part which is merely supportive in nature and therefore limited and selective.

The major challenge in completing this book has been the absence of an established technique—a treaded path for chronicling press versions into a mould that could 'pass' as conventional history. Naturally, just as this was a handicap in many ways, in others it provided the freedom to walk a new path. The problem, or the challenge, has really been the overflow of information. But, then, considering that a newspaper's dimension is almost unlimited—there being no limit to what makes news and what does not—the problem as such was there all along. In a sense, I realized during the course of writing this the study that a newspaper is like a room which has a large number of windows and it is the reader's choice which window he chooses to look through. This applies to the casual reader. But for a student of history, there is always the temptation to open as many windows as possible in the hope that perhaps the next file, the next film, the next page will release more 'light'. This typical urge, which all those associated with history will understand, marked the beginning of my problems—being flooded with information of varying kinds I was overrun by once again the typical urge, the 'greed' to pack inasmuch as possible.

I tried to give all this mix of events, issues and the general situation a more readable form by fitting it all into a chronological framework. Shelly Bookspan has put it well:

I am aware of a school of historians which shuns narrative history as insubstantial, but I strongly believe that constructing a readable plausible narrative from disparate array of data is the most difficult interpretative task the historian has . . . if I have interwoven local and national events in such a way as their telling seems natural and not a product of intellectual strain. . . . I believe I have presented a successful interpretation.[72]

The first chapter seeks to provide a kind of 'compressed' version – a sequence of events or rather important events that preceded or even may have led to the first major outbreak of violence in the Punjab in March 1947, based, unlike the subsequent chapters, not on newspapers and private papers, etc., but more on acknowledged authoritative works. The chapter can be conveniently skipped by those who are familiar with the events of the time. The subsequent division of the book is essentially influenced by the significance of events placed in a chronological framework. For example, just as the second chapter deals with the disturbances of March and their impact, the third takes up from the 3 June Plan and focuses on the preparations, problems, apprehensions, the political pressure, the 'complete' confusion. The fourth chapter focuses on the announcement of the Boundary Commission Award and its implementation, the fifth deals with the immediate fallout—a period when the state simply broke down, became non-functional. The sixth and seventh chapters attempt to highlight the massive exercises of handling the largest ever population exchange the world has even known.

I did consider writing of a conclusion to end the book but found it exceedingly difficult. The few pages placed in the Postscript (Chapter VIII) were almost an afterthought, that had it not been for the great unhappiness that had come to prevail across the plains of Punjab, Delhi and its neighbouring areas in the months that followed the partition of Punjab, India would have been saved the shame and agony of Gandhi's assassination. Many would ask, where was the link between the killers of Gandhi and the partition of Punjab. And yet, I have not been able to break away from this nagging impression that had the exchange of population been foreseen and planned for, the extent and dimensions of Punjab's tragedy would have been dramatically limited. It was the all-pervasive atmosphere of blood, sadness and loss that possibly prompted a group of madmen to execute the killing of Gandhi—possibly believing that the great ill-will that pervaded the millions of displaced people would cover up for and absolve them.

ACKNOWLEDGEMENTS AND A FEW PERSONAL WORDS

The idea of such a study grew over many years, from listening to the stories told by family elders, of how the Muslims were forced out of East Punjab, the heavy hearts with which so many of them went, the case of my own village being a good one. And just as the story of Muslim existence in East Punjab came to an end, another one began. This story was as distressing—families coming to settle, broken and distraught, having left behind or lost everything, and having to start life afresh, from scratch. In the context of the region where I was born, the language, the culture, the dress of the displaced families who came from West Punjab, everything was different, and yet, the sheer will to survive, regain and rebuild saw, in a couple of decades, a reasonably sound assimilation with the population of the south-eastern regions, that is, the non-Punjabi speaking districts of Punjab (the present Haryana). The contribution of the displaced population (referred to in the main text as Refugees) to the economy, commerce and education of the south-eastern districts came in due course to be monumental.

Born into a prominent land-owning family in a village which was renowned for its Hindu Rajput and Muslim Rajput coexistence, a region where the Punjabi dialect had rarely been heard before August 1947 as fate would have it I married into a family which had suffered the bloodiest form of Punjab's partition. That the marriage was dramatic would be an understatement—it broke not only the rigid barriers of caste as practised by the Rajputs but, more importantly, the barriers of culture as well.

My mother-in-law, Swarn Anand (Satija), was the daughter of a leading medical practitioner of West Punjab (Khanewal) and was living until the beginning of August 1947 a life that most others could only dream about. As tension mounted in the plains the family, thinking it was only a matter of days before things settled down went, off to Manali for a few weeks taking along a handful of belongings. But as it turned out, the family would never return to Khanewal. Thus they entered free India virtually empty-handed.

My father-in-law, Dr P.N. Anand, was a fourth-year medical student at the Balak Ram Medical College, Lahore, when the disturbances pickedup pace in the first week of August 1947. He and his friends too had believed that it was only a matter of time before things settled down. They had to leave Lahore for Amritsar without the time even to collect their books and class notes. Such were the first-hand stories of the blood and brutality and from which grew the idea of this book.

Along with the stories of the pain and misery of the Muslim families who were uprooted from East Punjab and the millions who took their place, I had also heard from my father and his close friends, some of whom were important public figures in the Punjab in the 1940s, Rai Sahib Anant Ram (Unionist Party MLA, 1937) being one, stories that added to the list of questions relating to the manner in which the partition of Punjab was executed.

I was well committed to the study having already done considerable research, when the University Grants Commission of India, after a lengthy process selected me for its Research Award Fellowship (earlier designated as National Fellow) to work on the theme (February 2002). Academics across India who have interacted with the UGC are aware of the pitfalls, I too have had my share but on the whole the experience has been far better than I had expected. The Indian Council of Historical Research, New Delhi financed my source consultation visit to the United Kingdom, a visit that proved exceedingly rewarding.

Prof. Kapil Kumar has been a great support through the course of the study. I wish to record a special word of thanks for all he has done. I wish also to thank Prof. K.C. Yadav, my teacher, collegue and a dear friend. He has taken interest in all my work over the years.

It is difficult to remember the names of all the people particularly in the libraries, from whom I have taken help. I spent much time at the Nehru Memorial Museum & Library, New Delhi, where the staff was so helpful. I must thank the staff of the Reprographic Section for the supply of microfilms and prints of illustrations—particularly J.K. Joshi for all their help. I wish also to especially thank Kiran Hura and Kanchan Arya of the microfilm reading section. The NMML's microfilm repository is easily the richest and best managed in India, and for India-based newspapers possibly the best in the world. The Asiatic Library, Mumbai is truly a wonderful place particularly for rare out-of-print volumes. The staff were very helpful. I would also like to thank Dharam Singh Rautela, Senior Research Assistant in the manuscript section at the NMML, as well as Kishori Lal Sharma and Ram Sarup for help with the Urdu translations.

I wish particularly to thank the ever-active and smiling Dorian and Jill Jaber at the Oriental and India Office Records section of the British Library (London) for all their assistance. The Reading Room authorities at the Imperial War Museum Kennington (London), were very kind in giving me time and space even though I arrived without prior appointment. My thanks to the staff at the Library of the Centre for South Asian Studies, Cambridge.

I would also like to acknowledge the help of officials of the Punjab Civil Secretariat Library, Chandigarh, the National Archives of India and, of course, the extremely helpful staff at the State Central Library, Hyderabad, particularly Mr Joshi, the Assistant librarian.

I am very grateful to C.A. Bayly, Professor of Indian History St Catharine's College, Cambridge, for the time he spared to discuss the work and for guiding me to sources at the Imperial War Museum. I wish also to thank C. Pratt, Fellow Bursar, Fitzwilliams College, Cambridge, for his hospitality and all his help.

Prem Kumar has suffered many hours of discussion relating to this work—there are two reasons for this. One, his life-long experience as a journalist with, among others, the *Statesman* and the *Indian Express*—the latter's Chandigarh edition having been edited by him in the troubled days of the militancy in Punjab—led me to use him as a sounding board. The second, of course, is that being a dear friend he has shared with me his experiences as well as those of his family who were in Lahore in 1947. He also put me on to the *Statesman,* which proved very enriching. I tested some of my conclusions against his sharp mind and have benefited from his comments.

Prof. V.N. Datta, my teacher and a revered and respected friend, has taken great interest in this work and its progress, he guided me to important sources, particularly at the Centre for South Asian Studies, Cambridge, and even took personal interest in smoothening the way for me both in London and in Cambridge. I wish to record my very earnest gratitutde to Prof. Datta, his wonderful daughter Poonam and Mrs Kamla Datta for all the love, concern and care they have always shown.

I have always found it somewhat embarrassing to acknowledge the contribution and help of immediate family members—people who have always been taken for granted. My father (late) Kanwar Randhir Singh always believed that the partitioning of India on the basis of faith had distorted the face and character of India and undermined, indeed belittled the historical process through which India had moved over a thousand years. With all his feudal roots, he stood apart, an egalitarian to the core. That partition which saw some of his dearest friends departing for Pakistan, continued to stir in him until his last days the belief that 'perhaps we had not done enough to make them stay on in India'. I have been greatly influenced in this work by his views

I wish to record my deep sense of gratitude to my father-in-law, (Late) Dr P.N. Anand and my mother-in-law, Swarn Anand, for the interest they have taken in this work, the weekly words of encouragement, the walks down memory lane. It is to them and my wife Reicha that I wish to dedicate this work. This study could never have been completed without her.

Shriniwas, a master at computer typing. His earnestness and involvement in this work and never-complaining, ever-smiling attitude made things much easier. Finally I must thank Sidharth Chowdhury for his patience and asistance and of course Ramesh Jain making it possible.

October 2005 RAGHUVENDRA TANWAR

NOTES

1. Ann Marrie Plane, 'Historian Behind the Corner', *The Public Historian,* vol. 25, no. 3, Summer 2003.
2. *Pakistan Times*, 27 July 1947, NMML, New Delhi, microfilm.
3. Gyanendra Pandey, *Remembering Partition*, Cambridge 2001, p. 49.
4. Anders Bjorn Hansen, *Partition and Genocide: Manifestation of Violence in Punjab 1937–47*, New Delhi, 2002, p. 9.
5. Mushirul Hasan, *The Partition Omnibus*, Oxford, 2002, pp. xi–xii.
6. Barrie Gunter, *Media Research Methods, Measuring Audiences Reactions and Impact*, New Delhi, 2000, p. 56.
7. W.L. Newman, *Social Research Methods: Qualitative and Quantitative Approaches*, Boston, 1994, p. 61.
8. Gunter, *Media Research Methods*, p. 5.
9. Ibid., p. 10.
10. Ibid., p.12.
11. Ibid., p. 56.
12. Ibid., p. 196.
13. Margaretta Jolly, 'The Letter as a Propaganda', in Bertrand Taithe and Tim Thornton, *Propaganda: Political Rhetoric and Identity 1300–2000*, Surrey: Sutton, 1999, p. 251.

14. Ibid., p. 252.
15. Ibid., p. 242.
16. Chandrika Kaul, *Reporting the Raj: The British Press & India 1880–1922*, Manchester, 2003, p. 9.
17. Darshnik Vyas, 'Good Morning Kurukshetra', *Times of India*, 20 May 2004.
18. Susan D. Moeller, *Compassion Fatigue: How the Media Sell Disease Famine War and Death*, New York, p. 51.
19. Kaul, *Reporting The Raj*, p. 20.
20. Ibid.
21. Ibid.; W. Lippman, *Public Opinion*, New York, 1997, p. 224.
22. Ibid.; 'Public Opinion & Historians', *History* 63, June 1978, p. 225.
23. Gunter, *Media Research*, p. 106.
24. Gunter, *Media Research*, p.135; B. Zillmann and J. Byrant (eds.), *Selective Exposure to Communication*, New Jersey, 1985.
25. Gunter, *Media Research*, p. 135.
26. Note by D.D. Condon, Editor-in-Chief, British Information Service, New Delhi, September 1948, IOR L/1/1/321 File no. 104/1.
27. Emmet Davis, *Press and Politics in British Western Punjab 1836–1947*, Delhi, 1988, pp. 85–7.
28. Ibid., p. 84.
29. K.L.Gauba, *Inside Pakistan*, Delhi, 1948, pp. 179–80. (Accessible at the Royal Asiatic Library, Horniman Circle, Mumbai.)
30. Pandey, *Remembering Partition*, p. 65.
31. Ibid., p. 49.
32. Gunter, *Media Research*, pp. 7–8.
33. NMML, New Delhi.
34. Rangaswami Parthasarthy, *Journalism in India*, Delhi, 1989, p. 277.
35. Davis, *Press and Politics in British Western Punjab*, pp. 85–7.
36. IOR/L/1/1/321, File no. 104/1.
37. Gauba, *Inside Pakistan*, pp. 178–80.
38. IOR/L/1/1/321, File no. 104/1.
39. Gauba, *Inside Pakistan*, p. 178; 1948, IOR/L/1/1/321 File no. 104/1, microfilm, NMML.
40. IOR/L/1/1321, File no. 104/1, microfilm, NMML.
41. IOR /L/1/1321, File no. 104/1, microfilm, NMML.
42. D.M. Malik, *The Tragedy of Delhi*, December, 1947, p. 4. The booklet is accessible in the I.M. Stephens Papers, Box 19, Centre for South Asian Studies, Cambridge University, Cambridge (CSAS), IOR/L/1/1/321 File no. 104/1, NMML.
43. IOR/L/1/1/321, File no. 104/1, microfilm at the NMML.
44. I.M. Stephens Papers, Box 36, CSAS.
45. IOR/L/1/1/321, File no. 104/1.
46. Walter Rosenberger & Herbert C. Tobin (eds.), *Keesings Contemporary Archives: Weekly Diary of Important World Events*, vol. 6, 1946–8.

47. IOR Mss. Eur. D 1003, Police Papers Jack Mortan.
48. IOR Mss. Eur. D 1065/1, Police Papers,WHA Rich.
49. A.J.V. Arthur Papers, CSAS.
50. P. Brenden Papers, CSAS.
51. IOR/L/MIL/17/5/4319, Report by Maj. Gen. T.W. Rees.
52. Spate Papers, CSAS.
53. Lt. Col. John Peddie 'The Steady Drummer' unpublished memoir, no. 96/17/1 Imperial War Museum Reading Room, Kennington, London.
54. Lt. Col. R.N.P. Reynolds Papers, CSAS.
55. D.E. Lloyd Jones Papers, Box IV, CSAS.
56. I.M. Stephens Papers, Box 20, CSAS.
57. Jawaharlal Nehru Lecture delivered by I.M. Stephens at the Centre for South Asian Studies, Cambridge, 24 February 1969; I.M. Stephen's Papers, Box 1, CSAS.
58. IOR Mss. Eur. F 164/47, Muddie Collection.
59. IOR Mss. Eur. F 200/165.
60. Mridula Sarabhai Papers, Microfilm, NMML.
61. These transcripts have been acquired by NMML from the Imperial War Museum's Department of Sound Records.
62. Bhimsen Sachar, Memoir, Oral History Transcript, recorded by H.D. Sharma, 15 March 1974, Acc. no. 182, NMML.
63. Ishar Singh Majhel, Oral History Transcript, Recorded by Satya M. Rai and S.L. Manchandra, 27 June 1973, Acc. no. 454, NMML.
64. Prabodh Chandra, Oral History Transcripts Recorded by H.D. Sharma, 18 Sept. 1973, Acc. no. 465, NMML.
65. Tek Chand, Oral History Transcripts Recorded by S.L. Manchandra, 11 July 1985, Acc. no. 643, NMML.
66. IOR Mountbatten Papers, File 161A, Microfilm.
67. IOR L/1/1/665 Information Department Fortnightly Appreciation, 23 April 1947, no. 3163.
68. V.N. Datta, 'Towards Freedom: Inside Story', *Symposia Papers: 26, Indian History Congress*, 62nd Session, 2001, pp. 2–3.
69. Byron Farwell, *The Gurkhas*, London 1984.
70. Charles Chevinix Trench, *The Indian Army 1900–47*, Thames & Hudson, 1988, p. 293.
71. AICC Papers, Microfilm, NMML.
72. Shelly Bookspan, 'History Historian and Visual Entertainment Media: Towards a Rapproachment', *The Public Historian*, vol. 25, no. 3, Summer 2004, p. 9.

Abbreviations

AICC	:	All India Congress Committee
AIR	:	All India Radio
BBC	:	British Broadcasting Corporation
CMG	:	*Civil & Military Gazette* (daily newspaper, Lahore)
CSAS	:	Centre for South Asian Studies, Laundress Lane, Cambridge (UK)
DAV	:	Dayanand Anglo-Vedic—a Hindu organization committed to providing modern education along with traditional Indian.
DC	:	Deputy Commissioner
DIG	:	Deputy Inspector General of Police
ECM	:	Emergency Committee Meeting
ET	:	*Eastern Times* (daily newspaper, Lahore)
GOC	:	General Officer Commanding
HT	:	*Hindustan Times* (daily newspaper, Delhi)
IAR	:	*Indian Annual Register* (a comprehensive digest of important events)
ICS	:	Indian Civil Service
IOR	:	India Office Records—now in the British Library, London.
JDC	:	Joint Defence Council
MEO	:	Military Evacuation Organization
MLA	:	Member of Legislative Assembly
MLNG	:	Muslim League National Guard
MP	:	Mountbatten Papers
NAI	:	National Archives of India, New Delhi
NMML	:	Nehru Memorial Museum & Library, Teen Murti, New Delhi
NWFP	:	North West Frontier Province
PBC	:	Punjab Boundary Commission
PBF	:	Punjab Boundary Force
PSV	:	Private Secretary to Viceroy

PT	:	*Pakistan Times* (daily newspaper, Lahore)
RSS	:	Rashtriya Swayamsevak Sangh
SP	:	Superintendent of Police
SPC	:	*Sardar Patel's Correspondence*
SGPC	:	Shiromani Gurudwara Prabandhak Committee
SW	:	*Selected Works of Jawaharlal Nehru*
TP	:	*Constitutional Relations Between Britain & India: The Transfer of Power 1942–7*, vols. 6–12.
UP	:	United Provinces

1

Punjab's Partition: Background

We have completed our first year of independence. A year of indescribable misery and heart breaking agony. During this period we have passed through an ordeal which no people in the world had ever witnessed before. It has ruined us, it has crushed us, but it has not been able to break us. Punjab today lies prostrate and bleeding.[1]

. . . These unfortunate people (of Punjab) are ruing the day when Indian leaders compromised with aggressive communalism . . .who ever might be responsible the fact remains that India stands divided.[2]

It would be difficult to find a Punjabi who would have disagreed with the views of Gopichand Bhargava in *The Tribune*. Bhargava, as the Premier had been in the centre of it all and there was no way he and his colleagues and their counterparts in Lahore could have absolved themselves of the responsibility for the complete anarchy that prevailed across most parts of Punjab in the weeks that followed the actual implementation of the partition of Punjab. It was only natural for fingers to be pointed not only at those who managed affairs from Simla and Lahore but also at those who sat in power in Delhi and Karachi.

The list of charges with which newspapers were flooded after August 1947 ranged from more general ones to those that held leaders personally responsible for the tragic sequence of events: 'we accuse' said *The Tribune,* 'those whom providence has made the architect of our destiny of being horribly unfair and unjust to Punjabi Hindus and Sikhs . . . of accepting the satanic two nation theory and sacrificing them to it, of describing this unprecedented suffering as the price of freedom. . . .'[3]

'I blame you', wrote Abdul Rashid in an open letter in *CMG* to leaders of both of India and Pakistan, 'for inflicting untold miseries on inhabitants of both India and Pakistan . . . the consequences of which you did not realize. . . I blame you of getting intensely suspicious of each other . . . I blame you for talking of peace but heading towards war. . . .'[4] 'See what was happened' said another letter, 'in the face of the mighty assurance given by our leaders. While the big guns have found new abodes elsewhere without much difficulty the poor and helpless who were advised (by leaders) to stick to their homes have suffered.'[5]

Others were more personal, obviously reactions of people who had suffered possibly more than their share. One such person was Amir Chand Mehta: 'It is said in history books that when Rome was burning Nero was fiddling. I do not know whether this is a fact or not. But it is a fact that when Hindus were being butchered and their houses burnt Nehru, Patel and Baldev Singh were feasting.'[6] I have drawn attention to this letter by Mehta not because I believe there was merit in his statement but essentially to stress on the consistency of accusations and fingers that were raised towards the political leadership, both of the Congress and of the Muslim League, as well as on the nature of charges.

MOUNTBATTEN—3 JUNE PLAN: PREPONING THE TRANSFER OF POWER

There is no important reason on the face of it to question the last Viceroy's earnestness to hand over power to representatives of India and Pakistan as smoothly and quickly as possibly. But having said this one cannot but help wonder how the Viceroy had come to believe that acceptance of the 3 June Plan by leaders of different political parties was all it required for dividing India or rather ensuring a peaceful division.[7] Mountbatten was obviously swayed by the fact that senior Congress leaders like Jawaharlal Nehru and Sardar Vallabhbhai Patel and the League supremo Mohammed Ali Jinnah had all agreed to the 3 June Plan (whatever their reasons), but by allowing himself to be over influenced by the representative character of the leadership he committed the gross error of ignoring the simmering disapproval of the plan. Indeed what is surprising is that he overlooked the massive propaganda blitz launched in the press, saying that much of the regions that should be in Pakistan were being manipulated away from it. Even a cursory study of the *Pakistan Times*, the *Dawn* and even *Eastern Times*, all of which were established mouthpieces of the Muslim League, would have made it clear how unhappy the Muslim League cadres were with the fact that many contentuous districts were likely to be awarded to Eastern Punjab. As we shall see all methods—appeals mixed and laced with threats—were used up to the last day, that is, until the Boundary Award was announced by both the major contenders in Punjab, the Muslim League and the Akalis.

As for the Akalis, their acceptance of the Plan, if looked at more carefully, would have been seen as amounting to a rejection. Baldev Singh's position in the whole story was comical—he was made the mouthpiece in the forums of Delhi and Simla but obviously he was aware as much as anyone else that the power controlling the Panth's political destiny lay somewhere else. But even Baldev Singh was reported to have written to Mountbatten on 2 June, saying that the Akalis had serious reservations with the Plan.

Thus with both the major players—the Muslim League's middle- and lower-rung cadres as well as the 'actual' Akali leaders—having expressed their apprehension, what else was it but lack of political foresight for Mountbatten to have believed that the assent of a few select leaders was all that mattered before starting the plan to rush through the partition of Punjab? Apart from the fact that by the time that Punjab was actually partitioned both the major players had taken stands against the lines on which the division was planned, another very crucial and weak link of the process was that the person who was expected to guide Punjab through the partition had not only questioned the merit of the whole exercise but even expressed serious reservations about the possibility of its being implemented peacefully.

Sometime in mid-February 1947, Sir Evan Jenkins, the Governor of Punjab,[8] was asked by the Viceroy to record his opinion to a statement that was to made by the British prime minister in London, which later came to be known as the all-important 20 February (1947) statement, which announced to the world that Britain had after all decided to quit India by June 1948. What Jenkins recorded is one of the most important and insightful early indications of the tragedy that was coming Punjab's way and, more importantly, the note also indicated how poor was the understanding of some of the important quarters in New Delhi and London of the brewing crisis in Punjab: 'The first thing that strikes me about the document is its astonishing vagueness . . . in the Punjab. . . . The statement will be regarded as the prelude to the final communal show down and the disturbances from it might be of the gravest description.'[9]

In the light of this note and Jenkins' conviction that handing over of power even in 1948 required immediate and urgent work, one can imagine his state of mind when a decision (3 June Plan) was taken to prepone the transfer of power from the British to representatives in India by almost a year. The issue has been discussed in greater detail in the following chapter, however, it needs to be pointed out that Jenkins was absolutely clear on the futility of enforcing a scheme of partition which no community was willing to accept,[10] and sadly for Punjab, Mountbatten thought Jenkins was wrong.[11]

That Jenkins was not alone in believing things were being dangerously hurried was well known at the time. The second most important Englishman on the subcontinent in 1947, Field Marshal Sir Claude Auchinleck, while retrospecting many years later in a talk on the British Broadcasting Corporation (BBC), said that no doubt grave mistakes had been made but that blame could not rest on Mountbatten alone. Commenting on the 3 June Plan he noted: 'independence in 30 days when it really ought to have been spread over three years . . . it was quite absurd'.[12]

The list of those who condemned the hurry with which Mountbatten planned the transfer of power as proposed in the 3 June Plan is long and includes among others the most important journalist in India in 1947, I.M. Stephens (editor of the *Statesman*), but here I would like to draw attention to what the acting editor of *The Tribune*, Jung Bahadur Singh, said of the Plan in an article titled 'Rape of Our Beloved Punjab':

> The June 3 Plan was clearly a death warrant for Indian nationalism. But the Congress jumped at it. In view of the mad impatience prevailing in the country at the time, this was not surprising. But what was surprising was that no warnings were heeded and no precaution[s] were taken to avert what followed. The Pakistan volcano was seething and rumbling and I hurried to Delhi and urged Jawaharlal Nehru to have a two or three year agreement with the Pakistan Government (leaders) which might ensure the safe and free movement of men with their property between the two dominions. But with a flourish of his hand and shrug of his shoulder he dismissed my suggestion, prophesizing that Pakistan would melt and merge with Hindustan within two or three years. While I returned to Lahore fervently praying that Panditji's (Nehru's) predictions might come true. . . I could not forget that the rape of our beloved province had already begun and was going on without the slightest sign of abatement . . . what annoyed and pained me was that our leaders at New Delhi were callously indifferent not only to the great suffering we were undergoing with fortitude but also of the great suffering which we were waiting in awe.[13]

Mountbatten defended his decisions in an incisive 'conclusion' appended to his report submitted to his Majesty's Government in September 1948. In para 9 he said:

I do not consider that further political action could have been taken if power had been transferred at a later date. It had proved impossible to get out of Section 93 Government in the Punjab except by the transfer of power. . . . But not one of us, and indeed, so far as I know, no one in India, Pakistan or the United Kingdom anticipated the exact form and magnitude of what was to follow.[14]

A day after announcing the 3 June Plan, Mountbatten addressed a press conference conducted personally by Sardar Patel at the Constitution Club, New Delhi. When asked by a reporter of he foresaw any transfer of population. Mountbatten replied:

Personally I don't see it. There are many practical difficulties involved. Some measure of transfer will come about in a natural way. That is to say that people who have just crossed the boundary will transfer themselves.[15]

This statement of Mountbatten deserves far more attention than it has usually been given. I see three main reasons for this. For one, it shows how little the Viceroy and his close friends in the Congress understood ground realities in Punjab; two, the statement was taken seriously by thousands of families who were planning to move from West to East and East to West Punjab but changed their minds on the assurance of the Viceroy that the exchange of population 'was not on the cards'. This proved in due course a fatal decision for many thousands of families. And then, what the Viceroy stated in June does not fall in line with the final assessment report that he filed to his superiors in London. Whereas in June 1947 he was clear that no exchange of population was anticipated, in September 1948 he noted:

It may be said that one step which could have been taken in the Punjab, had the transfer of power been at a later date, and which might have precluded communal disturbances, was a properly organized wholesale transfer of population from each half of the Province. Pandit Nehru and Mr. Jinnah turned down the suggestion that even a start should be made on planning for this.[16]

The contents of this report have been around for many years now and yet they never fail to surprise. Rightly or wrongly not only did Mountbatten wash his hands of the single biggest failure in the execution of Punjab's partition--the failure to plan the exchange of population—but he also put the responsibility on the shoulders of Nehru and Jinnah and their other colleagues.

But coming back to the weeks that lay between the announcement of the 3 June Plan and the actual partition of Punjab, while there are scores of statements and opinions in newspapers that were saying just about the same thing it is to a note by Abell, the Viceroy's very able private secretary, to which I wish to draw attention also because this note carried with it as an annexure, a minute by Governor Jenkins. This note is dated 12 July 1947: 'The Governor is convinced the Commission (Boundary) will not be able to produce an award which will solve the problem.' The note further adds, '. . . the Sikhs are in a dangerous mood . . . delivered an ultimatum . . . would not accept the notional boundary and would go in for guerilla war fare after 15 August'.[17]

This note also carried Jenkins's assessment of the situation:

> Meetings of the Partition Committee resemble a place . . . conference with a new war in sight. In the time available it will be quite impossible to make a clean job of partition . . . after 15 August there will be appalling confusion. In civil administration certain things cannot be done in a matter of days . . . but we can only go ahead and see what happens.

'See what happens' are words that ring with irony when one realizes that the largest ethnic cleansing ever recorded in times of peace anywhere in the world was about to emerge on the horizon of India and those at the very helm of affairs had not an inkling of it.

REALITY IS IMPOSSIBLE TO COMPREHEND

There are really no exact figures of the number of people who crossed borders to acquire new nationalities in 1947. The scale of the crisis at about the time that the exchange of populations had peaked (first week of October) was reflected in a report filed by an Associated Press of India correspondent, who was part of a group of senior press reporters who were flown in a military Dakota over Punjab:

> two massive columns of humanity one stretching over 40 miles comprising of non-Muslims moving from West to East and another stretching over 8 miles and moving from East to West . . . even one who has not seen actual killings . . . gets an idea of the terrible tale of human woe and misery that lies behind the two words 'Punjab Disturbances'.[18]

O.H.K. Spate is perhaps the most widely quoted for his figure of about 17 million people who may have crossed sides both in Punjab and in Bengal in 1947.[19] For Punjab, however, Penderel Moon gives figures of about 4.5 million Hindus and Sikhs and about 6 million Muslims having crossed borders in less than three months in 1947.[20] While Moon's figures have generally been accepted, I am inclined however to depend more on the figures provided by the very eminent economist C.N. Vakil.[21] He has said that while about 6.5 million Muslims migrated from East Punjab, PEPSU, Delhi, Matsya Union and parts of Himachal, about 6 million non-Muslims appear to have moved into India. Whatever the numbers there is no doubt in that it was 'the biggest population movement in recorded history'.[22]

The number of people that were killed in the Punjab in 1947 also varies greatly—so greatly that they start from the incredibly low figure of between 30,000 and 50,000 to as high as over 500,000.[23] Taya Zinkin, the young bride of an ICS officer (Maurice Zinkin), recorded an insightful assessment of the exchange of population as well as the killings.

> The riots which followed partition were responsible for the world's greatest exodus . . . in less than two months 13 million people changed homes . . . as many as 300,000 were killed or died of cholera and pestilence . . . as a result there were virtually no minorities (meaning Hindu-Sikh-Muslim) on either side of the border (Punjab).[24]

With regard to the economic dimensions of the partition of Punjab, once again the estimates vary greatly. Moon, for example, says Hindus and Sikhs left behind (in West Punjab) property and assets in excess of Rs. 500 crore whereas what the Muslims left behind in East Punjab could be valued at about Rs. 100 crore. These figures we shall see later have all along been disputed. Moon also suggests a figure for the cultivable lands vacated by the Muslims in East Punjab and by the Hindu and Sikh population in the West. For the Muslims he gives an estimate of about 4.7 million acres, and for the lands vacated by the Hindus and Sikhs in the West, he suggests around 6.7 million acres.[25] Gauba gives figures of about Rs. 2,000 crore worth of property having been lost by Sikhs and Hindus and about Rs. 300 crore for the Muslims.[26] But once again it is upon Prof. Vakil that we can fall upon. He says no estimate of the value of properties lost can be worked out because no figures are reliably available. He refuses to accept the figure of Rs. 3,929 crore that was based on claims filed by families who had moved out of Pakistan—mainly Punjab—calling it 'exaggerated'. But while doing so he draws attention to the figure of Rs. 1,400 crore that was put up as a claim by the Government of India to the Government of Pakistan.[27] Incidentally, this is also the figure that was calculated by the Shiromani Gurudwara Prabandhak Committee.[28]

Put together, these figures, notwithstanding their differences, give to the partition of Punjab a staggering dimension and yet it is the brutality and sadism of a kind that had never been seen earlier what pushed into irrelevance everything else. 'For most it was an inferno of horror and death,' as Hansen puts it, 'impossible to comprehend.'[29] Hansen goes further: 'The character of the violence had changed . . . the main target became the private sphere . . . making it impossible for people to continue living together . . . no earlier riots had caused people to permanently leave their homes on a massive scale.'[30]

> Sexual molestation was deliberately used in order to emphasize both the vulnerability of the community and the incapability of men as protectors . . . while destroying people's living places and places of worship the violence followed an altogether new rationale. . . . The perpetrators wanted not only to remove physical presence but cultural as well.[31]

'Not only', Pandey points out, 'were millions of people torn from ancestral homes, fields and fortunes, life long friends and childhood memories,' there was in fact 'a loss of sanity'.[32] A loss of sanity it was, for what else can we call it when a people who had lived together for centuries in conditions where differences in socio-cultural norms were only peripheral and that too only in spheres where religion infringed in daily life, began suddenly and freely to violate the norms and taboos that had been respected for ages?

THE PUNJAB WAS NOT MADE FOR DIVISION: BACKGROUND

By sheer chance, perhaps, the distribution of the population on the basis of religious following in the Punjab was so conveniently placed that if an occasion ever arose, the province could, with minor strains be easily divisible.[33] Assuming Amrtisar to be the notional centre of the province, as one moved East the percentage of Muslims as components of the population decreased from 34.53 per cent in Jullundur division to 28.07 per cent in Ambala. In the south-eastern district of Rohtak, for example, the Hindu population exceeded 80 per cent, whereas on the other hand, in the western districts of Dera Ghazi Khan, for example, the Hindu population was less than 12 per cent and in Attock a mere 5 per cent. As one moved west from Amrtisar, in Jhelum district the Muslims comprised 89.42 per cent, in Muzaffargarh 86.42, in Attock about 90.42 per cent.[34]

Interestingly, In Octoer 1947, when the exchange of population had peaked, Pakistan's Minister for Refugees and Rehabilitation released to the press his government's version of the community-wise number of people in specific regions (Table 1.1).

The Sikh segment of Punjab's population was concentrated mainly in the fertile central districts. The Sikhs were not in a majority in any single district of the province, a fact which partly reflects on the community's dynamic and progressive character, following and prospering from opportunity irrespective of where it was available.

On the face of it, therefore, there should have been no reason why Sir Radcliffe when given the unpleasant task of dividing Punjab should not have chosen to base the entire plan of dividing Punjab on the line that was there all along. And yet there is an element of irony in this because so closely knit and interwoven were the Punjabis that a line drawn anywhere would have appeared artificial. More probably, there was not a single village in the whole province that could be claimed exclusively by a single community as its very own. Yes, villages were often called as Hindu/Sikh/Muslim villages, but if looked at more carefully, such villages were more recognizable by the majority caste that inhabited the village rather than their religious components. Within villages no doubt houses were often clustered along community lines, but then that was not merely the case between Hindus and Muslims but even among castes within the non-Muslim

TABLE 1.1: PAKISTAN MINISTRY OF REHABILITATION AND REFUGEES: COMMUNITY FIGURES

i. Muslims in East Punjab excluding Ambala Division	31.24 lakh
ii. Muslims in Ambala Division	13.17 lakh
iii. Muslims in Punjab states excluding Bahawalpur	9.44 lakh
Total	53.85 lakh
iv. Hindus in West Punjab	19.93 lakh
v. Sikhs in West Punjab	14.06 lakh
Total	33.99 lakh

Source: *PT*, 15 October 1947.

communities as well. This fact also needs more emphasis because most of the major castes were usually common to all the religious communities.[35]

As Talbot points out: 'the overriding characteristic of the colonial Punjab were its rural nature and co-existence of vigorous Muslim, Hindu and Sikh communities.'[36] The uniqueness of Punjab's social system was that while religion may have played a divisive role, tribal and caste ties created on undercurrent of affinity and affiliation.[37] While common cultural legacies were probably the more significant binding force, those belonging to similar castes usually also had the same type of profession, thereby binding the cultural ties with economic interests as well. The cross-cultural commonness is easily recognizable in proverbs, folklore and the like.

To Moon, there was yet another binding factor—the fact that a vast majority of Punjabi people were 'drawn from the same racial stock, spoke a common language and was "very conscious of being a Punjabi".[38] As Governor Glancy once said of Punjab, 'No Punjabi however uninformed would contemplate with equanimity so shattering a dismemberment of the province involving in effect the disappearance of the word Punjab which has been held in honour for the last two thousand years.'[39]

In addition there were a large number of other factors that gave to Punjab a unique kind of unity—the network of canals, hydro projects, the railways. All these were laid out with the whole province in mind—division could never have been perceived. Punjab was simply not planned for division.

> The other provinces of India had a two fold communal problem, in the Punjab the problem was three fold. . . . It was the province where Hindu landlords had Muslim tenants, Muslim landlords had Hindu and Sikh tenants and Sikh landlords had all Hindu, Muslim and Sikh tenants . . . tenants generally belonging to the same castes looked upon the landlords as their kith and kin.[40]

It is not surprising therefore that even as folk traditions and literature talked of invasions, conversions and even retaliation, there is scarcely any reference to the lives of ordinary people being disrupted due to religious differences. With the vast majority of Muslims and Sikhs having common pre-conversion roots with Hindus, notwithstanding sporadic tension and strife between the Muslims and the Hindus and Sikhs, the broader acceptance was of coexistence.

Much of Punjab's population (see Table 1.3) was comprised of petty landholders struggling to stay alive by working unviable holdings. These people had lived together for long periods of time, confronting the problems of shared poverty, superstition, fatalism, ignorance, and above all, exploitation by the feudal lords. The divisive lines of faith were far less assertive than the conditions that put the ordinary Punjabi together. As Mushirul Hasan has also put it: 'for neither then nor now does the clash of civilizations carry conviction'.[41]

It is hardly surprising that even the two-nation theory that began appearing in the 1920s, or a few years earlier to, say, 1906, failed initially to seed in Punjab, all the efforts of Jinnah notwithstanding—his Muslim League winning two seats in a house of 175 of which 86 were demarcated Muslim seats (1937). In 1946, the League went on to win 73 of the 86 seats. The important issue therefore is: what was it that prompted the people who had lived together for generations to take to violence in such a personalized and brutal manner?

Yes, in Punjab, just as in other parts of India, there had been the conventional sporadic clashes of groups of Muslims usually with the Hindus or Sikh as in Punjab, or both together on the other, the initiating problems always being some petty localized issue—the kind that takes up almost the whole time of India's petty crime and civil disputes subordinate courts. But whatever the nature of these petty disputes, rarely did they ever lead to widespread unrest or infringe in the broader social attitudes of coexistence. Suspicion and bitterness among communities was certainly not a routine matter in Punjab. Rarely if ever did communal strife build to a level that life became unliveable for the common man to the extent that one or the other had to leave an area because the dominant group would not allow them to live there.

I am inclined to even suggest that till about a decade preceding the partition of Punjab, if the province, was dividable at all, it was less on the lines of faith and more between the vast majority of ordinary people, irrespective of communities, on one side and the wielders of governmental authority, the feudal lords, the administrative intermediaries, the influential socio-religious leaders the wealthy barristers of Lahore and Amritsar, the state-level politicians on the other side. The division within Punjab appears more marked in terms of wealth, power and status than on faith.

It is the emphasis on the word culture that needs more attention.

Even as Punjab raced towards disaster newspapers continued to carry appeals in the form of letters and articles emphasizing on Punjab's unique cross-cultural commonness.[42] Some like J.N. Nanda[43] even pointed out how the problem of Punjab was not in fact a problem of religious or social divisions and differences but essentially traced itself to the political ambitions of the Muslim League and the Congress leaders.[44]

MUSLIMS: WAY BEHIND IN LITERACY

The other factor that requires attention (in the relative context) here is the marked backwardness of the Muslims in the field of education in Punjab (see Table 1.2). This fact was singularly responsible for the sidelining of the majority community from various kinds of commercial and other employment avenues—banks, railways, government jobs, particularly in engineering, medicine, teaching, law and the like. This drawback had far-reaching implications, a burden the community was destined to carry and which possibly made the seeding of separatist tendencies somewhat easier.

This natural handicap of the majority community influenced the course of Muslim politics in Punjab in the years preceding partition. It also greatly facilitated the continuance of the old exploitative feudal character among the Muslims in Punjab—something that was personified in the political and socio-economic significance of large landowners, socio-religious leaders like *pirs, sajjada nashins* and *biradari* leaders, the administrative intermediaries like *zaildars, lambardars, safed poshes* and the like.

LAHORE: 1947

Even as Lahore reflected in economic terms the near complete monopoly of industry and commerce by the Hindus, in another way it also showed how far behind the Muslims were in the field. For example, of the 218 major registered industries in Lahore ranging from engineering, hosiery, printing to chemicals in 1943–4, 154 were owned by Hindus, 10 by Sikhs and only 45 by Muslims. Likewise, of the 5,332 registered shops in Lahore, the Muslims owned 1,831 and the non-Muslims 3,501. The fixed investment in the industries was about Rs. 240.29 lakh, of which the Hindus and Sikhs accounted for Rs. 168.33 lakh and the Muslims for Rs. 58.91 lakh. The Hindus alone accounted for Rs. 4,171 lacs of the floating and fixed capital that

TABLE 1.2: LITERACY LEVEL OF MAJOR RELIGIOUS COMMUNITIES, 1921
(NUMBER OF LITERATES PER THOUSAND)

	Hindu		Muslim		Sikh		Christian		Jain	
	M	F	M	F	M	F	M	F	M	F
Punjab	113	11	37	4	93	13	140	93	506	47
Hisar	64	3	27	2	51	3	236	226	170	35
Rohtak	59	3	50	4	347	75	31	14	505	28
Gurgaon	71	3	33	2	177	23	266	187	529	46
Karnal	50	3	36	4	72	9	60	51	424	17
Jullundur	133	19	59	10	74	7	312	154	593	130
Ludhiana	194	24	60	13	103	16	415	433	521	39
Ferozpur	125	15	32	5	65	7	382	161	517	102
Lahore	215	56	74	15	89	13	171	126	536	78
Amritsar	144	12	43	4	82	11	103	95	461	63
Gujaranwala	207	39	33	7	136	30	22	15	339	48
Sheikhupura	127	9	28	2	80	8	27	31	605	605
Simla	441	15	259	87	498	216	795	941	881	316
Kangra	86	5	54	8	283	11	573	515	38	83
Ambala	91	9	69	10	112	12	703	796	640	117
Hoshiarpur	106	9	55	5	118	10	84	59	561	78
Gurdaspur	108	12	48	7	56	8	32	31	–	–
Sialkot	105	12	41	5	89	15	76	21	544	59
Gujarat	269	32	34	3	323	41	102	98	1,000	1,000
Jhelum	413	62	54	2	449	79	596	486	432	22
Rawalpindi	359	77	62	3	438	119	757	675	568	58
Attock	103	64	30	1	413	54	828	616	1,000	–
Montgomery	194	25	22	2	118	14	45	30	600	–
Shahpur	269	50	28	2	279	100	28	18	1000	–
Mianwali	273	11	22	–	344	23	690	700	–	–
Lyallpur	137	19	31	3	54	9	18	7	669	48
Jhang	412	39	24	2	404	68	165	65	1,000	333
Multan	279	22	24	3	262	38	431	182	462	250
Muzaffargarh	312	17	22	2	122	28	779	127	500	–
Dera Ghazi Khan	378	30	25	1	188	41	600	438	496	95

Source: *The Census of India, 1921, Punjab*, Part 1, p. 299

operated Lahore's industry and commerce, whereas the Muslims accounted for a mere Rs. 117.24 lakh.[45]

The significance of Lahore in the commercial life of Punjab can be seen from the fact that 26 banks had their head offices in the city. In 1918 Lahore had 12 bank branches, in 1947 it had 90. Of the Indian banks, only three were owned by Muslims. Similarly, of the 80 insurance companies in Lahore only two were Muslim-owned. There were two Stock Exchanges but there was only one Muslim active member/trader. Lahore also had 17 investment trusts, all owned by non-Muslims.

Lahore was also the educational heart of Punjab. The city in 1947 boasted 270 educational institutional recognized by the Education Department and Punjab University. Of these about 100 were devoted to women's education. Male students enlisted in these institutions were 64,902, the number of female students was 23,477. Surprisingly, of the 12 arts and science colleges with an enrolment strength of 10,647 only one was run by a Muslim organization, and one by the government. Of the 15 colleges devoted to technical and professional education with a strength of 2,620 students all but 3 were run by non-Muslim organizations. Lahore had 36 high schools with a strength of 26,647 students only four of these were run by Muslim organizations and one by the government.

Not surprisingly, therefore, a good number of Hindus and Sikhs were enrolled in Muslim institutions just as there were many Muslims who had enrolled in Hindu and Sikh institutions. The Muslims, however, preferred enrolment in government institutions—almost half of all enrolments in government-run institutions was from among the Muslims. Lahore had 4 important libraries, of these the Punjab library was maintained by the government and the other 3—the Dayal Singh Library, the Dwarka Dass Library and the Sir Ganga Ram Library—were all managed by non-Muslims. In 1947, Lahore had 23 newspapers, of these 5 were in English, 15 in Urdu, one in Gurmukhi and 2 in Hindi.[46]

SEPARATISM: SOME OPINIONS

So extensive are the available writings on the origin of separatist ideas—the causes that drew the line between a section of the Muslims and the others—that it would be well beyond the limited scope of this chapter to touch even the fringes of the writings.

While attempting to trace the first divisionist tendencies among communities in Punjab and India in general G.D. Khosla goes back to the first half of the nineteenth century and talks of how Western ideas, etc., contributed to the awakening of dormant political aspirations and of how the 'awakened' mind was confronted and overshadowed by the towering influence of the imperial and the 'white man's world', leading to the search for solace in the glory of ancient Hindu and Muslim civilizations.[47] Developing his thesis Khosla draws a link between Raja Rammohun Roy's Brahmo Samaj (1828), and Swami Dayanand's Arya Samaj (1875) and goes on to project that the revival of the cult of the iconic Maratha chief Shivaji and the campaign against cow slaughter that became popular under Bal Gangadhar Tilak were all essentially, though loosely knit, strands representing a Hindu revivalist trend.

It was this trend that encouraged the search for 'glory' by escaping into the past, a glory that would fortify Indian society against the imperial onslaught. But the unfortunate part in the unfolding of this search for glory, something that Khosla too has overlooked, was that it had little or no place for the Muslims or for Islam. It overlooked not only the profound contribution of Islam and the Muslim society to the broader ethos and character of the nation but also ignored the fact that by the nineteenth century, Muslims had been a part of India, its traditions and values for over a thousand years. Since Hindus talked of a glorious past in which Muslims had no contribution, it was only natural for Muslims, Khosla says, 'by a psychological process' to take 'their minds back to the glory of the Prophet',[48] the countless successful military campaigns and conquests.

Khosla refers to the Khilafat agitation as an example, though limited, of the increasing enthusiasm among Muslims in India—the emerging of a distinct identity. He adds that whether it was the Wahhabi or the movements inspired by Sir Syed Ahmad Khan, the fact is the two major players of the subcontinent were seeking different identities, different icons.

Differences that may have always existed but were understated or downplayed like, for example, in matters of dress, mannerisms, language, frontages of homes, Khosla says, began to assert themselves as natural sequels. As a result, for the last about five decades of British rule in India the use of terms like Hindu culture and Muslim culture were established and entrenched. With distinct cultural identities being asserted, the search for political power and identity was the next step. For politically ambitious people, such opportunities—those of accentuating differences—were a godsend.

I wish to add to Khosla's view here that for those who were seeking to forcefully propagate the view that the Muslims had been greatly exploited and were way behind the Hindus and Sikhs in Punjab in matters of commerce, trade, industry, banking, government jobs, etc., things became much easier mainly because these were all facts.[49] Table 1.2 gives a clear picture of the extreme backwardness of the Muslims in education at about the time that the search for identities was picking up pace. The disparity in favour of the non-Muslims in government departments was something that attracted extensive attention in later years among newspapers. Both the *Eastern Times* and *Dawn* which were strong and vocal supporters of the Muslim League almost regularly began highlighting how the Muslims had been discriminated in employment, a trend that picked up in the 1940s.[50]

But coming back to Khosla, he notes that as the separatist tendency gained force the Morley Minto Reforms (1909) and the introduction of separate electorates made it all the much easier:—The introduction of separate electorates in 1909 by Lord Minto realy sowed the seeds of bitterness. . . . Responsible government on the parliamentary model with segregated electorate can never work.[51] To Khosla the Lucknow Pact and the acceptance by the—Congress of the separate electorates was a disaster. The Congress, in its eagerness to win over Muslim opinion at whatever cost, merely acted shortsightedly. A few years later, by espousing the Khilafat cause the Congress once again, according to Khosla, sacrificed its secular ideals, 'borrowing religious emotions for gaining political ends'. Finally, Khosla charges the Congress with completely alienating the Muslims by remaining neutral towards the Communal Award (1932).

But what is significant here is that even though Muslim opinion may gradually have crystallized, it had until 1937 yet to consolidate into a formidable political force. Far from being the uncrowned king of India's Muslims that Jinnah would claim to be by the mid-1940s, a decade earlier his Muslim League had managed to poll only 4.4 per cent of the votes cast by Muslims in the 1937 elections (see Table 1.3). The total number of votes cast by Muslims was 7,319,445, of which the Muslim League secured only 321,772 votes. Importantly, 376 Assembly seats were won by Muslim candidates who did not owe allegiance to the Muslim League, while the number of those aligned to the League was only 109.

In many ways, the 1937 elections were a turning point on the road to the separate nation theory. The Congress's performance in the elections, as also of the Unionists in Punjab, had sidelined the Muslim League. A belittled Jinnah was further hurt by the arrogance with

TABLE 1.3 MUSLIM SEATS WON BY THE LEAGUE IN 1937

	Seats alloted to Muslims in Legislative Assemblies	Seat won by the Muslim League in 1937 elections
Asam	34	9
Bengal	117	39
Bihar	39	–
Bombay	29	20
CP	14	–
Madras	28	10
NWFP	36	–
Orissa	4	–
Punjab	84	1
Sindh	33	3
United Provinces	64	27

Source: S.R. Mehrotra, *Towards India's Freedom & Partition*, p. 182.

which the Congress handled the League's demand for representation of League nominees in the ministries. There was all-round distrust. As Moon, another of Khosla's distinguished contemporaries has put it:

> There is no doubt that the leaders of the Congress were responsible though quite unwittingly for this critical change in Muslim sentiment. In retrospect it seems as though a curse was laid on them . . . which compelled them invariably to act in such a way as to bring about exactly the opposite result to that which they intended. They passionately desired to preserve the unity of India. They consistently acted so as to make its partition certain.[52]

Both Moon and Khosla are of the view that the League was not wrong in expecting to be accommodated in the ministries. But the insistence of the Congress that the 'League must cease to function as a separate group' if its nominees were to find a place in the ministries was a serious, almost 'fatal', error as Moon calls it. Moon believes that the Congress offer of 'absorption' rather than 'partnership' was 'the prime cause of the creation of Pakistan, and that the League leaders were "outraged" at the suggestion that they should dissolve their organization'.[53]

Mehrotra, however, dismisses these charges saying the price demanded by the League was too high because the Congress could not have compromised its national character and that too much had been attributed to the 'ministry' incident.[54]

V.N. Datta, on the other hand, feels that by refusing to share power with the Muslims the Congress missed a great opportunity of settling the communal question.[55]

It is in this context that the October 1937 Muslim League session needs to be viewed. It is important because practically every important Muslim in the country outside the Congress influence attended the session. The list included the premiers of the important Muslim majority provinces, Sikander Hayat (Punjab), Saadulah Khan (Assam) and Fazhul Haq (Bengal). Jinnah could now, and quite unexpectedly, talk of a single Muslim voice.

Once the die was cast, reasons of why the Muslim League needed to organize in a separate mould were easier to come by and any number of such causes could be added. The Congress to begin with was easily dubbed a Hindu body. So much so, *Vande Matram* was cited as an example of the Congress's anti-Muslim mindset because the story from which the song was drawn was of struggle against Muslim power in Bengal.

The Congress ministries resigned on 22 December 1939 to protest against the pushing of India into Second World War. The Muslim League went on to celebrate the day as a 'Day of Deliverance'. But even at this stage, Khosla believes the Muslim League did not entertain the idea of partition seriously. The announcement by Viceroy Linlithgow (8 August 1940) that the Muslim League would henceforth form part of any political discussion along with the Congress was a major step forward for the League. Khosla says that Jinnah gave to the League here onwards: 'The creed of Muslim superiority implicit in the idea of Pakistan . . . and a prevailing sentiment that Islam stood in danger of perishing under Congress rules.'

The subsequent rapid growth in League cadres is partly explained by Khosla in terms of the well-known view of W.C. Smith, of how the Muslim middle class became strong supporters of the two-nation theory because they stood to benefit from it personally. Smith had said: 'They have said the Muslims and Hindus are so different that they cannot live together in one state. What they have meant [is] that these Muslim bourgeois and the Hindu bourgeois are competitive that they cannot both own the books and industries, run the commerce do the professional and other jobs.'[56]

Mehrotra while agreeing with the view has, however, put it in a slightly different perspective: 'The Muslim desire for a separate homeland of their own could not have found fulfilment. . . . It was the alliance of Muslim separatism with the Muslim will to power which proved decisive.'[57]

Kirpal Singh has written extensively on the partition of Punjab and represents a school of scholars who have presented things the way they happened—minus the ideologies, the duel of words.[58] He endorses Mehrotra's view that the idea of Pakistan was nourishable only because the region's distribution of the Muslim population was such that it almost quite naturally provided division on a platter.

David Page's *Prelude to Partition* has been fairly celebrated for its scholarship and widely quoted in most writings on theories related to the coursing of different roads by the Muslims and the Hindus along with the Sikhs. Like Khosla, Page too points out how the Chelmsford Reforms initiated in India a new political agenda. Explaining how and why Muslims increasingly jumped on to the separate nation bandwagon, he said that,

> for both majority and minority province Muslims the political future lay in co-operation at the all India level . . . Muslim politics had assumed a distinct centrifugal tendency. As the Congress began to undermine the foundations of the Raj the Muslims began to leave by the back door.[59]

Page's assessment is precise: 'the Montague Chemlsford Constitution produced two main trends in all India politics—a centrifugal trend and a communal trend'.[60] He also importantly suggests that 'until 1947 Jinnah visualized Pakistan in terms of greater autonomy . . . rather than a strict redrawing of boundaries according to religion'. He strengthens his argument by pointing out how Jinnah was, as late as 1947, still investing in shares and property in India and was even possibly planning to lead a retired life in Bombay.[61]

Another work almost as celebrated as that of Page is Anita Inder Singh's *Origins of the Partition of India*. This fine scholarship draws a notional line around 1935–6. Jinnah, she points out, as late as 1935 was talking essentially only of 'safeguards', and was willing even to forget the Communal Awards and to apply his mind to the larger questions effecting India. Pointing out the almost defunct nature of the Muslim League till the eve of the 1937 elections, she adds that between 1931–3 the Muslim League's 'annual expenditure did not exceed Rs. 3000 . . . decisions were taken . . . with only 10 out of its 310 members forming a quorum'.[62] Dwelling in detail on Congress and Muslim League relations in the years 1936–9, she suggests that even by the end of 1939 the alienation of the Muslims from the Congress . . . had . . . made them into supporters of the League.[63]

The popular subaltern school of Delhi's historians generally believes that the roots of communalism and division are more easily traceable to the to socio-economic changes brought about in Indian society by the impact of colonialism over a much longer period of time.[64]

In his brief survey of some important contributions on the separatist theme, Page, also refers to the work of Farzana Sheikh, *Community and Consensus in Islam.*[65] Sheikh argues that the Muslim elite were influenced by the Mughal ruling class culture, keen to stress on status and distinction. This class of influential Muslims was wary of democracy and individual rights. But what is even more interesting, in the view of Sheikh, is that the Muslim elite spread the notion that only Muslims could rule over Muslims. Sheikh also develops the idea that the Indo-Muslim tradition in India was inspired by a common sense of belonging, inheritance and faith, all of which were traceable to the profound impact of Mughal rule in India. She also points out that British influence and polity greatly facilitated the distinctive political organizations of the Muslims. For Farzana Sheikh the only aberration in this continuously operating Mughal impact was the Unionist period in Punjab, where provincialism and ruralism slightly obstructed the theory and agenda of separatism. It was only when the Unionist influence began to weaken that the possibility of Pakistan emerged on the horizon.[66]

David Gilmartin has contributed an interesting perception of the separatist theory in the role of a particular and influential section of Muslim society. He traces the origin of the more assertive separatist demand from about the time that the Unionist control over Punjab's politics had begun to wane—the late 1930s. 'Most (historians) have assumed in fact a direct line of development from Muslim "communalism" to Muslim "separatism" to Pakistan's creation'. He goes on to suggest that attempts to stretch Jinnah's two-nation theory backward in time is in fact little more than searching for a historical justification for what is essentially a twentieth-century nationhood case. 'Most historians have seen the emergence of a sense of nationality among twentieth-century Muslims as rooted deeply in the communal political style that was part of the colonial era.'[67]

Gilmartin gives Sir Mohammad Iqbal the credit for the Muslim League's change of fortune in Punjab after having been routed by the

Unionists in the 1936–7 elections. 'The Muslim community itself and the ideal Muslim state served for Iqbal as a symbolic cultural expression of the common striving of Muslims for Islamic fulfilment—a political manifestation of a common heritage and a common mission.'[68]

Gilmartin interestingly draws a link between the Punjab of the 1940s and the Punjab of the eleventh century, a time when the profound Sufi influence began striking roots in the region, and goes on to say that the formation of Pakistan was only to be the culmination of the process started in the eleventh century. He also argues that: 'The movement for the creation of Pakistan was the first and perhaps the most successful of those twentieth-century Islamic movements that sought to bring about an Islamic transformation of the post-colonial state.'[69] Importantly, he points out that religion shaped many aspects of Punjab's political life in the colonial period and was very much part of the imperial edifice and that the development of separate electorates and communal recruiting to government services were part and an example of this policy.

For Iqbal, Gilmartin suggests, the key to the political definition of the Muslims did not lie in competing with others but lay in expressing the positive heritage shared by all Muslims. Essentially, for Iqbal political options for the Muslims lay in political unity—a unity that was grounded in Islamic self-awareness and could be an alternate to colonial authority. Indeed it is in this context that much needs to be seen in Iqbal's address at the 1930 session of the Muslim League at Allahabad when he said that to stay 'culturally alive, Islamic followers will have to settle down in specific areas'.[70]

Gilmartin has also made an important reference to the writings of Abdus Sattar Khan Niazi and Muhammad Shafi (*Pakistan Kya He Aur Kaise Bannega*). Both, he, suggests, believed that the illiterate masses could easily be initiated into the Pakistan concept, the concept of *mard-i-khuda*. He argues that Niazi and Shafi linked through the ages the coming of Islam to India and finally the birth of Pakistan: 'Hazrat Data Ganj Baksh planted in Lahore in the 11th century . . . to Khawaja Munniuddin Chisti, to Hazarat Nizamudin Auliya, Khawaja Nasirudin Mahmud Chirag-i-Dilli.' It was their standard, they said, 'that awaited a standard bearer'.[71]

A very interesting argument that Gilmartin also puts forth is that while the early separatist trends may indeed have been concerned as urban phenomena in the events we term as the Pakistan movement, but the broader idea was bound by the power of its appeal to encompass the rural masses as well. The significance of the *pirs*, for example, in the process that followed the weakening and sidelining of the Unionists was essentially in the context that Pakistan required the linking of individuals to the concept of the new Muslim nation.

Ayesha Jalal in her well-acknowledged work suggests that for Jinnah Pakistan was in fact only a bargaining counter, so much so that even the Direct Action (1946) call was only an attempt to go along with the Muslim League tide, lest he be swept aside. She argues that there were complex issues involved and that clashes of interests were all important and that if Pakistan did become a reality a great deal of the credit for it must go to Jinnah's remarkable political and negotiating acumen.[72]

Perhaps the most brief and comprehensive yet fascinating handling of the issue comes from Jawaharlal Nehru in the chapter 'Communalism and Reaction' in his *An Autobiography:* 'Hindu and Muslim communalism . . . was political and social reaction hiding behind the communal mask'. Nehru traces events from 1857 onwards—the British policy of preventing Hindus and Muslims from acting in unity; Hindus taking to English education and Muslims falling back; new nationalism originating from the English-speaking intelligentsia thus the initial phase of nationalism being limited to Hindus; Syed Ahmad Khan and his efforts to introduce Muslims to Western education.

> The Indian Muslims had not wholly recovered from the cramping efforts of Sir Syed Ahmad Khan's political message when the events of the early years of the 20th century helped the British government to widen the breach between them and the nationalist movement.[73]

Summing up Nehru says, 'The outstanding fact seems to me how on both sides the communal leaders represent a small upper class reactionary group and how these people avoid and take advantage of the religious passions of the masses for their own ends . . . to suppress and avoid economic consideration of economic issues.' Almost a decade after Nehru had penned his views on the issue,[74] W.C. Smith developed a thesis with regard to the Hindu and Muslim bourgeoisies in search of jobs and avenues of profit.

Nehru has very perceptively discussed how little the difference really was between the vast masses that constituted the real India's Muslims and Hindus. Many years after W.C. Smith, Anil Seal went on to argue that there were as many differences between Muslims within themselves as there were between Muslims and Hindus. The factors that prompted the differences were usually unequal economic development.[75]

Mushirul Hasan has made important and extensive contributions on themes related to the partition of India. He believes that attempts to trace the genesis of Pakistan to the late nineteenth century or the times of Syed Ahmad Khan are a 'mistake'. Importantly, he points out that 'Inter community relations too were not greatly strained until the post Khilafat and non-cooperation days. If anything the lines of cleavage in north India were more sharply drawn between the Sunnis and Shias than between Hindus and Muslims.'[76] He goes on to argue that, 'the initiative towards the creation of a separate Muslim homeland . . . was the outcome of a particular scenario on the eve of and during the Second World War which . . . created much to Jinnah's relief the space for his maneuverings.'

Terming Rehmat Ali an 'illustration of obscurantist political eccentricity', Hasan goes on to say how there was no case for Pakistan till the very last years: 'There was after all no blueprint of a future Pakistan in the 1930s, no Islamic flag, no visible symbol, no common platform, no shared goals and objectives.'[77]

We have already seen Mohammad Iqbal's views as discussed by David Gilmartin, but Hasan adds:

> Iqbal's blueprint did not envisage a separate Muslim state . . . Iqbal whose vibrant patriotic poems continued to be sung in schools and colleges all over India, referred to autonomous states being formed obviously not all Muslim, based on the unity of languages, race, history, religion and identity of common interests.[78]

The separatist trend appears to have, in Hasan's scheme, gained momentum after the 'ill advised Congress decision in the summer of 1937 created the space for the revival of the Muslim League'.[79] There are numerous versions that support the manner in which the Congress handled the situation—the fact however remains that the Muslim League was certainly slighted and belittled, an injury that was aggravated by the handsome electoral gains of the Congress.

But more importantly, 'the truculence of the Congress over the coalition ministry', as Hasan puts, it served to refocus on the charges that had until now been made by scattered elements, mostly the self-seeking elite, that there were little chances and hopes of justice from the Congress for the Muslims. Newly coined terms were a natural sequel: 'Hindu Congress Cabinets', 'Coming of the Hindu Raj'. Views on differences what were earlier seen more as emotional reactions now emerged crystallized—language and the denial of equal economic opportunity now found re-emphasis, to which was added cow protection. If answers were not found, the Muslims would be victims on a much wider scale.

After the Lahore Resolution on Pakistan (1940) and Jinnah's celebrated exposition of 'two different civilizations which are based on conflicting ideas and competition', there was really no looking back, even though Hasan makes a reference to a note by James Penny and his reference to Mirza Ismail, Dewan of Mysore, as having said that as late as in the spring of 1946, Jinnah was in fact not serious about Pakistan and was treating it merely as a political ploy.[80]

Others too, Page, for example, have argued on similar lines. Yet these were answers to the fears and doubts that had begun to consolidate from 1937 onwards. Hasan forcefully dismisses the separatist theory:

> [T]he two-nation theory is grounded in the mistaken belief that Hindu-Muslims constitute exclusive autonomous entities and that religious loyalty takes precedence over ties and bonds of relationship based on tangible inter-social connections . . . communalisam and separationsm . . . did not always embrace large segments of society—they only touched limited groups in certain areas.[81]

While working out this thesis, Hasan also points out the misplaced importance given to the verdict of the 1946 elections, which were in any case highly restricted in terms of those who were eligible to vote. Thus, there was this peculiar situation that not only had the future of India been decided by less than a fifth of those who had the right to franchise, but even fewer—in fact—a handful, went on to work out the modalities of the actual and hurried transfer of power.

For Ian Talbot, an important writer on colonial Punjab and Pakistan, the separatist trends are traceable to a web of complex social and economic issues. It was the ability of the Muslim League to convince people that it had the answers, or supposed answers, to their problems that paid off and was a kind of key to the separatist road. The Muslim League masterly guised its separatist political agenda in socio-religious terms—this went down well with the masses, particularly when it was projected by the people whom the ordinary peasantry tended to trust, the *pirs* and the *ulema*.[82]

The Muslim League made a concerted effort to woo away from

the Unionist Party the important *pirs* and *sajjada nashins*, an effort in which it succeeded handsomely. Their (the *pirs*') extensive following enabled them to start a massive propaganda on behalf of the Muslim League, that the idea was a sort of 'heaven', *bahista,* on earth. Pakistan, it was said, would provide a panacea for the ills that engulfed the Punjab Muslims. There would be no poverty, no harassment, no exploitation by the Hindu moneylenders in the 'pure land'.[83]

Gyanendra Pandey, in one of his numerous important contributions on the theme, states that the trend of perceiving the separatist movement among Muslims to the times and career of Sir Syed Ahmad Khan (1817–98) is certainly 'a historical'.[84]

Elsewhere, Pandey argues that communication, vernacular press, and recording of customs prompted the search among people for their roots.[85] Pandey rejects the 1931 findings of the Indian National Congress regarding the Hindu-Muslim riots of Kanpur, which said that the prevailing impression of the Hindu–Muslim problem was 'an extremely wrong impression created by interested parties through deliberate misrepresentations about the propagation of Islam in India.[86] Pandey argues that the report's suggestion that Hindu Muslim differences 'are all products of the British period and of British policy' are questionable because they tend to sweep under the carpet of British policy the dust of many stirrings in India during the colonial period. Pandey suggests that the political control of the state is an integral part in the construction of national and community identities. Significantly, he also points out that the nationalist perspectives usually tend to homogenize and senitize, often suppressing internal differences within 'claimed communities'.[87]

LANGUAGE AND CULTURE DIFFERENCE 1947

The emphasis on drawing a line which highlighted the differences between the Muslims and non-Muslims had picked up considerable pace in the months leading to the partition of Punjab. Newspapers aligned with the League played a leading role. The *Eastern Times* published in February 1947 a lengthy two-part article by Jamila Samad titled 'Pioneers of Pakistan'. Samad argued that Lala Lajpat Rai was in fact the first Indian to accept the two-nation theory.[88] 'Lajpat Rai was convinced of the vast differences and gave up support for a united India. He thought "United India" was only a British creation. Lajpat Rai was convinced Hindu-Muslim unity was no less than a dream.'[89]

The widely circulated charges that a concerted effort was being made to diminish the significance of Urdu attracted much attention in a section of the print media in the beginning of 1947. *Dawn* carried a front-page headline attack on the new language policy of All India Radio: 'The new policy is a blow to Indian culture struck by Patel. it may be recalled that on assumption of the Broadcasting portfolio Patel received a large number of letters of Hindu communalists who asked him to crush Urdu.'[90] Interestingly, the *Hindu Outlook* the mouthpiece of the Hindu Mahasabha charged All India Radio for being anti-Hindi.[91] Patel meanwhile appears to have issued a statement in which he tried to undo the apprehension. But the very next day the *Eastern Times* carried an editorial titled 'Thief of culture':

> Patel considers himself a very clever man. Congress has made no secret of its plan to force upon all people a *Rashtrabhasa* (national language) which is to be the common language of everybody. In this Ram Rajya . . . if there has been a common language based on the usage by the largest number it has been Urdu. The better the Muslims cherish a thing the deeper shall it suffer his (Patel's) dagger's thrust . . . and still there are simpletons . . . who keep on hoping that between the Congress and the Muslim League there can be a [*sic*] honourable understanding.[92]

Congress President Acharya Kriplani was ridiculed when he suggested that Muslims need have no fears:[93] Liaqat Ali, the senior Muslim League leader and Finance Minister (Interim Government), summed up the Muslim League's stand of why Pakistan was necessary. Addressing the Convocation at the Aligarh Muslim University he pointed to the distance the Hindus and Muslims were believed to have travelled away from each other and asked: 'What happens on the departure of the British? Are we to live as a free and independent nation living our own life in accordance with Islam or are we to submit to new masters?'[94]

The essence of the argument, therefore, comes down to the view that the separatists had come to insist that Muslims were a separate nation—all the features that indicated otherwise were brushed aside. To quote one such advocate, Ziauddin Ahmad Sulerl:

> Pakistan is the outcome of an ideological conflict between Hinduism and Islam. No two sets of social concepts and beliefs could be so dissimilar in every respect. While a caste system characterised the life and institutions of the Hindus, the Quranic insistence on the unity of human origin shaped the

thoughts and actions of the Muslims. These two viewpoints so completely cancelled each other, that there was no meeting ground for the two people.[95]

Shaukatullah Ansari's fascinating little book, *Pakistan: The Problem of India* was published in 1944, well before the Muslim League had swept the Punjab Legislative election's (1946) and indeed at a time when the Unionists still had some sway in the Punjab. Ansari dwells on a case for Pakistan and with equal conviction on a case against Pakistan. While the list of arguments for both views is far too long and beyond the limited scope of this chapter, it is to one specific issue discussed by Ansari that I wish to draw attention—the question of economic interests and the control of trade, etc.

The economic interests of the Muslims of the North-West Muslim Bloc are different from the Hindus of the Southern and South-Eastern Hindu provinces. . . . Certain occupations such as shopkeeping and grain and cloth markets are almost entirely controlled by Hindus. . . . If India remains united Muslims will never gain economic parity with the Hindus because. . . . The Muslims cannot trust that very community which is at present responsible for their economic enslavement.[96]

Having made a formidable case in favour of Pakistan with regard to the economic exploitation and deprivation of Muslims, Ansari then made a case against the very points that stood in favour of the separate nation.

It is often alleged by supporters of Pakistan that the economic interests of Muslims and Hindus are different, that Hindus are capitalists and Muslim wage earners. . . . This facile classification is unwarranted because the vast masses of both communities are the exploited workers, whether industrial or agricultural, and both communities have a small section of capitalists, landlords, industrialists, etc. . . . All that can be said is that Hindu capitalist would like to have the whole of India as his field for exploitation while the Muslim capitalist would like to carve out the North-West and the North-East as his special preserves for his adventures. There is no doubt that in order to acquire power both would do exactly the same under the cloak of religion.[97]

But it is with the views of the inimitable and brilliant Dr Ram Manohar Lohia that I wish to end this part of the discussion. Lohia hit out at both the extreme views—the Right and the Left—for their role in creating conditions that ultimately led to the country's partition. He also referred to how he himself had in 1947 been greatly mistaken in his belief that a reunion of the two—India and Pakistan—was possible. About the Right—the Hindu Mahasabha, the RSS and such others he said:

Let there be no mistake about it . . . they did nothing to bring the Muslim close to the Hindu within a single nation. They did almost everything to estrange them from each other. Such estrangement is the root cause of partition. To espouse the philosophy of estrangement and at the same time the concept of undivided India is an act of grievous self-deception.

Commenting on the role of the Left he said:

Indian Communists supported partition presumably in the hope that they would thereby gain hold on the new-born state of Pakistan, obtain influence among Indian Muslims and run no big risk of alienating the unformed or effete Hindu mind. Their calculations have been proved to be wrong except in the small measure that they have acquired some pockets of influence among India's Muslims and have roused no strong indignation among the Hindus. They have therefore done no mischief to themselves, but have brought no benefit to the country.[98]

Lohia summed up the causes of partition under eight major heads: British chicanery; declining years of Congress leadership; Hindu-Muslim estrangement; lack of grit and determination among the Indian people; Gandhi's non-violence; Muslim League separatism; inability to grab opportunities as they came and finally Hindu hauteur and disdain for Muslims:

The force that separates most is a particular view of history. Groups and communities are formed principally through the view they hold of what has happened. Hindus and Muslims of India hold separate views of their common history. . . . There would be no Hindu-Muslim problem today or when partition was effected if Hindu and Muslims had been able to interpret their history unitedly and learnt to live in peace.[99]

INDIA IN 1946: POLITICS

The world that emerged from Second World War was in many ways a profoundly altered one. Across the colonized world there was a resurgence of nationalism and anti-colonialism. The Labour Party's victory in the General Elections in Britain (1945) brought with it a new hope in India—as time proved the hope was not misplaced.

In India, elections to the legislative assemblies were announced in August 1945. While we shall focus on the Punjab in the context of these elections later, on the all-India scene these elections stood out in many ways. For one, never in India's past had communal passions been charged in such a manner. The results were stunningly good for the Muslim League, particularly when compared to 1937.[100] Importantly, however, even with all the increased seats the Muslim League candidates were able to poll only a fifth of the votes of the Muslims who were eligible to vote.[101] Polling was completed by February 1946. In the Punjab, for example, the process of polling was effected between 1 and 15 February.[102]

On 15 March 1946, in line with the widespread expectations in India, Prime Minister Attlee as a follow-up to an earlier statement announced that a delegation of Cabinet Ministers would leave for India to enable India 'to attain freedom as speedily and as fully as possible'. The delegation reached Karachi on 14 March 1946 to be engrossed in extensive political dialogue with the principal actors, the Indian National Congress and the All India Muslim League. But again in line with expectations, no consensus could be worked out. On 16 May 1946, the Cabinet Delegation made, in the form of an Award, a statement which would keep the leaders of the Muslim League and the Congress locked in debate and trading of charges and countercharges till about the third week of October (1946). Not that things cooled down thereafter, but the nature of acrimony shifted to a new centre.[103]

But coming back to the Award of 16 May, to begin with, the statement was divided into two distinct parts. The short-term or the first part dealt with the formation of an Interim Government comprising only Indians and implying thereby an immediate handing over of power to the Interim Government. It was the interpretation and the implementation of the terms of this Award that delayed the formation of the Interim Government by almost five months.

The second part of the Award dealt with the framing of the Constitution. The provinces of India were divided into three groups. Group 'A', of the Hindu majority provinces of Madras, Bombay, United Provinces, Bihar, Central Provinces and Orissa. Group 'B' comprised the Muslim majority provinces of Punjab, NWFP and Sind; and Group 'C' comprised of Bengal and Assam. Each of the states was given the freedom to opt out of one group and enter another in line with laid-down norms. They were given autonomy in all subjects, save communication, defence and foreign affairs, which were to be controlled by the centre.

The Congress resolved on 24 May 1946 to seek some clarification and appeared 'hesitantly' willing to accept the second part of the scheme if some doubts could be clarified regarding the provisions for opting out of the specified groups. The Muslim League, however, accepted the scheme in 'complete' with an announcement to the effect on 5 June (1946). It was here, that is, with one of the players having agreed to the Award and the other being not quite sure, that lay the root of the initial dispute. Clause 8 of the Award provided that if either one of the two was unwilling to join the Interim Government the Viceroy could still go ahead to form the government, making it as representative as possible. With the Congress having shown reluctance, the Muslim League leaders believed it was their right to form the government without the Congress.

There was yet more to it. Originally the scheme had provided for twelve members of the Interim Government, i.e. five from the Congress, and five from the Muslim League, one from among the Sikhs and the twelfth from the Indian Christians or the Anglo-Indians. For some reason Jinnah and the senior League leadership had come to believe that even if the Congress did come into the government the League would still be in a commanding position. This 'optimism' however was short lived as on 16 June, Viceroy Wavell announced that instead of the earlier twelve-member Interim Cabinet a thirteenth member was proposed to be added, i.e. from the Scheduled Castes. Jinnah took this proposal not only as a personal affront, having already announced his approval for the original Award, but also perhaps as an attempt on the part of the Viceroy to create a situation where he (Jinnah) would not be able to outvote the Congress within the Cabinet if the need arose.

Jinnah, the master player that he was, appears even till this stage to have kept his cards close to his chest, hoping perhaps that the increasing hurdles with regard to the composition to the Interim Cabinet would prove to be inconsequential because, in any case, he was convinced the Congress was unlikely to join the government.

On 13 June, Gandhi wrote an interesting letter to Wavell, asking the soldier in Wavell to do the right thing (make a choice between the League and Congress: 'you must make your choice of one horse or the other . . . you will never succeed in riding two at the same time. For Gods sake do not make an incompatible mixture and in trying to do so produce a fearful explosion'.[104] But the Congress had other ideas. On 25 June it informed the Viceroy that it was accepting the long-term part of the Award with some modification but was unable to accept the Interim Government scheme as stated in the latest statement of 16 June. When Jinnah was informed by the Viceroy that possibly the formation of the Interim Government was being postponed and that in any case the Congress too was bound to have a share, Jinnah felt cheated.

All along Jinnah had proceeded on the assumption that by not accepting the Award announced by the Cabinet Delegation in its entirety, the Congress in view of the provisions of the Award had closed the door for its entry into the Interim Government. An indignant Jinnah therefore wanted the Viceroy to proceed as provided in the Award—form the government without the Congress. The Viceroy understandably was disinclined to do so: 'what meaning would a government have without the representatives of 75 per cent of the people of India—the Congress'.

Without going into the details of why the two sides took the respective stands they did, there is the need, however, to point out that both the Muslim League and Congress knew that the procedures provided for the scheme were 'pregnant with mischief'. The Congress was concerned and apprehensive regarding the future of the NWFP and Assam. The concern of the Congress became a cause of joy for the Muslim League. Jinnah saw in the procedure laid out in the Award for opting out by a province from one group to another the possibility, or probability if you like, of getting the NWFP and Assam into the regions that would virtually comprise Pakistan. Jinnah had all along believed that to determine whether a certain province wished to join Pakistan a plebiscite of Muslims alone should be conducted rather than a referendum of all the communities. He believed the provisions of the Award made it easy for him to achieve this goal.

Interestingly, Secretary of State Pethick-Lawerence was reported to have been of the view that the Cabinet Mission would not have failed in its objective had it not been for some reports in a newspaper which, he believed, led the Congress to harden its stand.[105] In fact, on 28 June, a day before the Cabinet Mission left India, the *Statesman* had carried a hard-hitting editorial, 'Descent'. Basically it said the whole plan of the Cabinet Mission was flawed because it provided that whichever of the two accepted the plan would form the government, and once the Muslim League accepted the Viceroy was left with no choice. The editorial questioned the feasibility of a government led by the Muslim League in Delhi with most of the provincial governments under Congress rule.[106]

An indignant Jinnah felt betrayed: 'A series of statements by Congress leaders against grouping and this assertion that they were not bound by anything except their decision to join the Constituent Assembly combined with the silence of the British heightened the apprehension of the League.'[107] Whatever be the elements, the fact remains that the Muslim League accused the British of appeasing the Congress and betraying the League.

On 22 July Wavell wrote to Nehru giving details of the proposed composition of the Interim Government, especially requesting Nehru to keep the present negotiations secret: 'on a strictly personal and secret basis between myself and the two Presidents . . . it will be best to try and reach some agreement between ourselves as a first step'.[108]

Nehru wrote back the next day (23 July), insisting that the powers of the Interim Government for one needed to be clarified in 'unambiguous language', and until then 'I am wholly unable to cooperate in the foundation of a government as suggested by you . . . the Congress . . . want the political independence issue settled before they enter the government.'[109] Nehru's reply to Wavell was considered by the latter 'more challenging': 'we cannot go on being perpetually subject to these squeezes. . . . Congress are convinced that they have got us on the run and we ought to correct that impression at once'.[110]

The Council of the All India Muslim League met in Bombay on 29 July 1946. It announced its resolve to reject the 16 May Award and said it was calling Direct Action to forestall the attempts by the caste Hindu Congress to set up in connivance with the British a Hindu Raj in India.[111] Direct Action was called for to achieve Pakistan. The Resolution talked of injustice, of breach of faith, of the time having come to get rid of the present slavery under the British and the caste Hindus. 'We have bid good bye to constitutional methods.'[112] Calling upon Muslims of India to 'stand to a man behind their sole representative organization' the Resolution had also said: 'It has become abundantly clear that the Muslims of India would not rest content with anything less than the immediate establishment of an independent and full sovereign state of Pakistan.'[113]

The die was truly cast and, as Anita Inder Singh puts it, the situation was 'novel and serious'.[114] On 30 July Wavell met Nehru for an hour and fifteen minutes, and told him that he believed that after the Muslim League's Resolution the situation had changed and that the Muslim League's step was only a sequel to some of the statements made by Congress leaders in the past weeks. Wavell records that he even told Nehru that the Congress now had a chance to show real statesmanship and give the Muslim League assurances that would bring it into the constituent assembly. Nehru, the note says, agreed with Wavell that it would be unfortunate if the League did not join. Wavell told Nehru that the main grievance of the Muslim League was the impression given by Congress leaders that the group system (contained in the 16 May Award) was not going to be given a fair chance of succeeding. Nehru, Wavell noted, understood that if it was made clear (to Jinnah by Wavell) that things would go ahead, the Muslim League was bound to come in, that in any case it would be 'fatal . . . if they (the Muslim League) were given to believe that they could hold matters up indefinitely by intransigence'.[115]

A 'top secret' telegram from Wavell to Pethick-Lawrence on 5 August 1946 was a part of the extensive exchange of notes between New Delhi and London discussing the pros and cons of inviting or not inviting the Congress to form the Interim Government. Wavell noted in this telegram that he had information from an 'unimpeachable source', of Patel's poor assessment of Nehru's working. Patel, he said, thought Nehru was 'frightened of the Muslim League on the one side and the Congress Socialists on the other'. He also said that Patel was convinced that Congress 'must enter the government to prevent chaos spreading in the country. . . . He would be prepared to resign from the working committee if his view was not accepted'. The same note also mentions that if places were left vacant for the Muslim League in the Interim Government, Patel was not in favour of joining it.[116]

On 8 August Wavell chaired a conference of Governors. The observations of the Governors of Punjab and Bengal in the meeting need to be noted. The latter had 'thought that nothing serious would happen in Bengal (referring to Direct Action) without a directive from Jinnah. If there was direct action there would be a serious food crisis in East Bengal'. The Governor did not in fact anticipate much problem.[117] But Jenkins was as usual far more apprehensive, and quite correctly so: '. . . an attempt to proceed with the Constituent Assembly with the Muslims absent in regard to the framing of the Constitutions of the Muslim provinces would have more serious effects even than [the] formation of a Congress ministry at the Centre'. In the same note Jenkins is cited as having said: 'The League felt deeply aggrieved but were disorganised and some of their leaders would not be ready to go to jail.'

This important meeting also appears to have concluded that the 'trouble was likely to be communal and not anti British except in East Bengal. . . . There would be more trouble in towns . . . reliability of dealing with the Muslim movement was somewhat doubtful'. It is also interesting to note that Jenkins had said that the police in Punjab were 70 per cent Muslim and were sympathetic to the Muslim League and until then these efficiency had only been tested on the Congress and had never had to tackle the Muslims. Nehru wrote to Wavell from Wardha on 10 August, conveying his acceptance of the offer to form the Interim Government.[118]

Even as senior functionaries including Claude Auchinleck, the Commander-in-Chief, believed that the Muslim League would not cause a serious crisis, large advertisements appeared on 16 August in the newspapers controlled by the Muslim League—the *Eastern Times* from Lahore and the *Dawn* from Delhi—calling upon Muslims in the name of Allah to dedicate their lives and possessions to the cause of freedom.[119] Provocative pamphlets were also widely distributed in Calcutta, the city whose people would not only pay a heavy price in the subsequent days, but would also set the ball rolling in a bloody war that would overrun great parts of the north and some parts of eastern India. Frederick Burrows, the Governor of Bengal, noted in a report at 8.20 p.m., 16 August: 'Fairly complete Hartal . . . in Calcutta . . . communal trouble started as early as 7 a.m. in Manikotla . . . continued to spread.'[120]

Horace Alexander of the Friends Ambulance in India, in a letter to Pethick-Lawerence, said: 'I have yet to meet any citizen of Calcutta who can understand why there was such a long delay in calling them [meaning the army].' He went on to say that the police were possibly hand-in-glove and even appeared to have forewarned the *goondas*. Charging the Governor and his adviser with negligence, he wrote: 'Perhaps they wanted the world to see how unfit we (Indians) are for self-government.'[121]

Calcutta was left with the official figure of 3,173 killed.[122] But this was only the beginning. Noakhali would overshadow Calcutta and Bihar would overshadow them all, with 5,334 Muslims and 224 Hindus being killed. But there was still a silver lining in that only 750 villages of Bihar's 18,869 were affected.[123] 'Calcutta', said Nehru, 'has been a terrible lesson. . . . This has ceased to be merely communal or political. It is a challenge to every decent instinct of humanity.'[124]

INTERIM GOVERNMENT: NEHRU TAKES CHARGE—LEAGUE STAYS OUT

The Interim Government under Nehru took charge on 2 September. 'The door to Purna Swaraj has at last been opened', Gandhi remarked at a prayer meeting on the same day.[125] He also expressed concern over the Muslim League not joining the government. Gandhi appealed to Hindus not to react with anger. He also said, 'Whatever our past quarrels with the British, we must thank them now.'[126]

The main opponents of the Congress, the Hindu Mahasabha, however, thought differently of the Congress decision of forming the Interim Government. The Sabha's mouthpiece, the *Hindu Outlook*, said in an editorial: 'our leaders have succumbed to ordinary temptations and it was easy for the Viceroy to play with these men with ordinary impulses and human frailties. . . . The speech by Sardar Patel in which he said that they entered the Interim Government to help the British to pack up and quit will only excite the smile of the British.'[127] The editorial also quoted Acharya Kriplani: 'I hope our leaders will guard themselves and the country against being coerced or cajoled into making undemocratic compromises.'[128]

The Tribune insightfully predicted a difficult future for the new government and said that 'today memorable as it was and as it would be in the annals of Indian history . . . [it] could not be celebrated with fasting and illuminations' because 'the Muslim League has not joined. . . . The Muslim League says the Hindus have deceived them.'[129]

The League felt outraged: 'it had first been deceived in Punjab now in Delhi'. It called for the observance of a 'Black Day' to protest against the Hindu Congress Government.[130] Reports also said that Muslim league cadres had vowed to make the Interim Government's functioning impossible. As a vast majority of Muslim homes and shops flew black flags in Delhi and a large number of other towns across India on 3 September, a Muslim League activist even hoisted a black flag on top of India Gate.[131] At the Aligarh Muslim University the Vice-Chancellor led a number of teachers and students in the protest by wearing black badges. Similar reports came in even from Lucknow University, and towns like Dalhousie, Meerut, Gurgaon, Ferozepur. It also said that 'the art of gentle persuasion having failed the hard road of resistance alone remains'.

On the eve of joining the Interim Government Nehru issued a statement to the press: 'I regret deeply that the Muslim League has for the moment chosen a different path. I shall continue to hope for their co-operation and the door for it will always be open.'[132] It was however not long before Nehru realized that the road chosen was a difficult one. A bare twenty days after taking charge Nehru wrote to Wavell: 'It is becoming increasingly clear that the policies and objectives pursued by the Governor-General and Governor-General in Council are in conflict.'[133] Nehru was not too happy with the manner in which Wavell was making extra efforts to bring the Muslim League into the Interim Government and prevent the Congress from appointing a nationalist Muslim as a member of the government.[134]

Nehru's apprehensions and even irritation with Wavell's inclination to go that extra inch to bring the Muslim League into the government appear in retrospect to have been well founded. In fact, Wavell's soft corner for the League is something that repeatedly stands out in his notings. For example, in a top secret note of his interview with Jinnah on 2 October 1946, he recorded: 'Jinnah was friendly and reasonable throughout, I got the impression that the League are anxious to come in if their armour [*sic*] proper can in some way be satisfied.[135] In the same note Wavell almost sympathetically records: 'Jinnah's main line was that he must have something with which to convince his Working Committee that he had not been defeated on every issue and he was coming into the government as a subordinate to the Congress.'[136] The counterpoint to the view that Wavell was being too soft towards the League could be that if he was at all soft, it was only to bring them, closer to the Congress.

Ten days later, following another meeting with Jinnah, Wavell stressed the point that even as the Muslim League appeared inclined to enter the government: 'Nehru as the Congress President has done nothing to smooth the path for them'.[137] Therefore, even as the chances of the Muslim League entering the government increased, there was still little sign of a decrease in the suspicion and rhetoric against each other. In a confidential letter to Wavell on 15 October, Nehru wrote: 'We have not raised any objection to the names proposed on behalf of the Muslim League. But . . . to tell you privately and personally . . . I regret deeply the choice the Muslim League has made. That choice itself indicates a desire to have conflict rather than to work in co-operation.'[138]

On 20 October Patel wrote to Wavell pointing out the unwarranted and provocative contents of a speech made by Ghazanfar Ali Khan after his name had been announced as a League nominee for the Interim Government.[139] The speech was delivered at Islamia College Lahore on 19 October: 'we are going into the Interim Government to get a foothold to fight for our cherished goal of Pakistan. . . . The Interim Government is one of the fronts of the direct action campaign'.[140]

As if things were not already complicated enough, Wavell demanded from Nehru on behalf of the Muslim League nominees who were likely to join the government one of the three portfolios—External Affairs (held by Nehru), Home (by Patel) and Defence.[141] Nehru replied to this letter the next day (October 23) saying the three portfolios mentioned could not be surrendered by the Congress. Nehru, while somewhat sidestepping the portfolio issue, took up the issue of the Ghazanfar Ali speech mentioned by Patel and added to it a reference to another objectionable speech made by Liaqat Ali at Karachi on 20 October. In the speech Liaqat had said that the Muslim League was entering the government only because 'Congress in its heart was averse to the League's entry'.[142]

Wavell wrote back to Nehru the same day insisting for the surender of the portfolios but this time he also mentioned an assurance given to Wavell by Jinnah that: 'the Muslim League will come into the government with the intention of cooperating'.[143] On the same day Wavell also reported by telegram to Pethick-Lawerence the problem over the portfolios: 'I am afraid this shows the Congress will still do all they can to prevent the League from coming in.'[144]

Things reached a flashpoint the following day (October 24), when Nehru informed Wavell that if the Home portfolio was taken away from Patel, as Wavell was said to have suggested or planned to do, 'Sardar Patel told you personally and has told us that he would in that event resign from the government. I take it that it is with full knowledge of this that you have taken you decision . . . we cannot continue in government without him.'[145]

Wavell telegrammed the problem to Pethick-Lawerence immediately after receving Nehru's letter. Referring to Nehru's threat, 'This may be a bluff', he also noted that he would try to break the deadlock by persuading the Muslim League to accept the finance portfolio (which the Congress was willing to part with).[146] The deal went through with the Muslim League accepting the portfolios of Finance, Commerce, Post and Air, Health and Legislative.[147]

MUSLIM LEAGUE JOINS INTERIM GOVERNMENT

The spirit with which the coalition was formed should have served as an early pointer to the problems that were to follow. Indeed for Nehru they had only just begun. Writing to Wavell, Nehru shared as head of the government not only his problems but also his bitterness: 'new difficulties have arisen, and our new colleagues in the government have openly stated that they do not subscribe to this [Cabinet and team work] approach of ours'.[148] He pointed out how the Muslim League members in the government were refusing to even meet as part of a Cabinet. He even warned that it may be difficult for the Congress to continue in the government if things did not improve.

From about the time that the Muslim League joined the Interim Government on 26 October, till the resignation of Khizr Hayat from the Premiership of Punjab, Jinnah's agenda was clearly defined. The Unionist-led ministry in Punjab had necessarily to be removed and whatever possible hurdles that could be created in convening the Constituent Assembly, had to be created, because the League was to have nothing to do with it.

Sudhir Ghosh, a close associate of Gandhi, in a 'situation summarising letter' to Cripps, wrote, 'old Vallabhbhai [Patel] says that ever since the Cabinet Mission left India, the Congress have not had a day of peace'.[149] Nehru was even more unhappy. In a letter to V.K. Krishna Menon, written about a fortnight after the Muslim League had joined the Interim Government, Nehru said: 'the Muslim League . . . are bent on mischief and . . . their capacity for giving trouble is largely conditioned by the sympathy and help they receive from other sources.'[150] Nehru echoed the same sentiments, perhaps with a greater sense of desperation, some days later to Vijayalakshmi Pandit.[151]

CONSTITUENT ASSEMBLY: THE DEADLOCK

The functioning and internal strife of the Interim Government was only a kind of sideshow because the main scene of conflict was the Constituent Assembly. The Congress was keen for the Assembly to be convened on 9 December, which Nehru conveyed to Wavell in a letter.[152] However, it was not only the Muslim League but some other prominent Muslim leaders also who had come out against the convening of the Assembly. Khizr Hayat, the Unionist Premier of the Punjab, holding in a way the key to the door of Pakistan, met Governor Jenkins on 8 November 1946 and pleaded with him to stress upon the government the need to postpone convening the Constituent Assembly. Khizr believed that the Assembly would only rake up unpleasant issues which would serve to complicate the situation and make the maintenance of law and order in Punjab even more difficult than it already was, particularly in view of what had happened in East Bengal and Bihar.[153]

Thus, both the Muslim League and its main Muslim opponent, Khizr Hayat, were equally opposed to the convening of the Constituent Assembly. Nehru, in line with Congress policy, continued putting pressure on Wavell to convene the Constituent Assembly. In a note to Abell on 16 November, for example, he said, 'it is urgently necessary to issue invitations to members immediately. I am surprised to find that instructions have been issued on your behalf to stop or delay the issue of such invitations.'[154]

When Nehru was asked by Cripps in the London conference[155] of his opinion on why the Muslim League was opposing the Constituent Assembly, he said the League had never intended cooperation, it wanted a veto on every issue, but the Congress was keen on their cooperation. But interestingly, Nehru also added that he believed that the Muslim League would ultimately come in, sooner or later, provided they felt that the Constituent Assembly was going ahead in any case.[156]

Lord Wavell of course believed differently. In a telegram to Pethick-Lawerence on 20 November 1946, he said that Jinnah was of the view that 'to call the Constituent Assembly would be the greatest possible mistake and would lead to terrible disaster'. Wavell also said that Jinnah 'no more wants civil war than anyone else, but he is probably not entirely in control of events in the League',[157] and that he (Wavell) had also warned Nehru that calling of the Assembly might accentuate the communal trouble.[158]

In a top secret note of the meeting between Jinnah, Liaqat and Alexander (5 December) in London (as part of the London Conference), Jinnah says that for the Constituent Assembly to have any legality it was necessary for both the Congress and the Muslim League to accept without qualifications the statement of 16 May.[159] Jinnah is also reported to have said in the same meeting that the Muslim League could not agree to come into the Constituent Assembly because it was convinced that the Congress did not intend to work the scheme as proposed by the Cabinet Mission.

All the great effort, therefore of flying leaders of the Muslim League, Nehru and his team from the Congress to attend the conference in London at very short notice in a state of extreme urgency, did not produce from either side even an 'inch of the rope'.[160] All tricks were tried in London including Alexander's suggestion to Nehru that perhaps the Assembly could be adjourned as soon as it met, to which Nehru replied. 'Having waited for months, how could they do so without transacting business.'[161]

Covered in diplomatic jargon, the official statement of the British government that followed the London Conference stressed on the obvious and something which the Congress may have known all along —the Constituent Assembly could not possibly force a Constitution on 'unwilling parts of the country'. By accepting the gist of the 'statement' of 6 December 1946 (that followed the London Conference),[162] namely, that the Constituent Assembly would not formulate a Constitution for unwilling parts of the country, the Congress had definitely climbed down from its earlier stand. But all the same, the Constituent Assembly opened on 9 December without the Muslim League. Gandhiji was opposed to it,[163] because, as Anita Inder Singh puts it, it was being 'held without agreement among Indians themselves'.[164]

To put it briefly Nehru and Patel persuaded the apex Congress body, the AICC, to accept the 6 December statement on the grounds that if the Congress rejected the Constituent Assembly, the British might withdraw the Cabinet Mission scheme and subsequently find it easier to hand over to the Muslim League what it had been demanding all along—Pakistan.[165] It did not thereafter take too long for Jinnah to declare the Constituent Assembly illegal and thereby the need to dissolve it (31 January 1947).[166]

THE PUNJAB 1946: MUSLIMS FEEL BETRAYED

The killings of Calcutta, Noakhali and Bihar that followed the Direct Action call of the Muslim League had surprisingly left the peace of Punjab undisturbed. In fact, 16 August saw many demonstrations, street-side meetings, but there was no major incident of violence in Punjab. Both Moon and Khosla are of the view that the disturbances in Bengal and Bihar did not have any serious impact in Punjab.

Khosla has noted: 'These [Bihar-Bengal] convulsions left the tranquillity of Punjab undisturbed. News of the events in Calcutta, Noakhali and Bihar horrified the people and gave rise to feeling of insecurity but produced no repercussion'.[167] But the relative quite, as Jenkins noted, was misleading. As things were smoothed out in Delhi for the Congress-led Interim Government to take office, rumblings of discontent had begun. Jenkins' report to Wavell written on 31 August (1946) painted a frightening picture:

> The Muslims are frightened and angry. They believe Jinnah has been outwitted and that they have been betrayed. They think that our refusal to put the Muslim League into power when the Congress was not cooperating and our apparent eagerness to bring the Congress in as soon as the party positions were reversed, can be explained only by a deep-laid plot between the British and the Congress. They regard the formation of the Interim Government as an unconditional surrender of power to the Hindus.[168]

In the same note Jenkins went on to explain the bitterness being reflected in the press and hate in the speeches that followed Friday prayers. But what is exceptional about this note is that the Governor pointed out how even old-time loyalists among the educated were turning anti-British because of the recent developments. He pointed out how Muslims in Punjab had expressed anger at some of the non-Muslim press versions, particularly the nature and content of cartoons showing 'Muslim League leaders washing in blood', in the context of the Calcutta killings, and how Muslims in Punjab believe that Muslims alone were not responsible for the Calcutta killings.

Jenkins also took up in this extremely important assessment the issue of Hindus taunting the Muslims following the retaliatory killings in Bihar, but more in a manner of victory for having a Congress government in Delhi: 'The Hindus are jubilant—they are bad winners and will do anything to taunt and humiliate the Muslims.' Of the Sikhs he said: 'The tone of the Sikh press and Sikh speakers is anti-British and anti-Muslim, and the Sikh speakers are the most violent in Punjab.'

But it is these lines that set Jenkins apart in his ability to call a spade and retain in his predictions, perhaps foresight, a level of remarkable accuracy which would in the course of time prove correct to the word:

> We have here the material for a vast communal upheaval. The hard core of the Muslim case—that the stage is set for the suppression of the Muslim community—is so nearly true that it cannot be answered with sincerity or

conviction. The Muslims are ill organized but they will fight sooner than submit to dictation from the Congress High Command.

The level of anxiety and apprehension in the minds of the Muslims of Punjab stands best reflected in an observation made by none other than Khizr Hayat, the young, handsome and earnest premier of Punjab and also at the same time enemy number one of the Muslim League. Khizr had no common interest with the League, yet even he believed that the formation of the Interim Government was bound to lead to disaster.[169] But before we proceed further it would be of some help to go back a few months and note how Khizr had come to lead the coalition government in Punjab.

THE PUNJAB ELECTIONS 1946

Soon after it became clear that the Simla Conference (July 1945) had been an exercise in fulility, the government announced on 21 August 1945 its plan for the conduct of elections to the Assemblies, which it hoped to complete by the end of the year. But in the Punjab, however, the Simla conference had produced an important change in political perceptions. For one, the Muslim League had now come increasingly to be viewed as representative of Muslim opinion. For Khizr Hayat, the Unionist Premier, this was cause for great dismay.

Talbot, the only important and competent biographer of Khizr, says: 'Khizr to his dying day regarded Wavell's capitulation to Jinnah at Simla a major British betrayal.'[170] But was there something that Khizr had overlooked? The Punjab, he had probably forgotten, was no longer the Punjab of 1937, when his party under the leadership of his predecessor Sikander Hayat, and Chhotu Ram and company, had swept away to irrelevance from Punjab the Muslim League.[171] By the middle of 1945, the Unionists had been reduced to 'a party of the past and the Muslim League as a party of the future'.[172]

A week before the elections were formally announced, Governor Glancy (Jenkins' predecessor in Punjab) reported to Wavell:

> Jinnah and his supporters are loudly clamouring for elections . . . Congress appears to be lukewarm. . . . Since Jinnah succeeded in wrecking the Simla Conference, his stock has been standing very high with his followers. . . . He has openly [said] the elections will show an overwhelming verdict in favour of Pakistan. . . . There is a serious danger of the elections being fought [by Muslims] on a entirely false issue.[173]

The note further pointed out how potently the issue of Pakistan and Islam was likely to be linked and how profoundly it would influence the uninformed ordinary Muslim. As electioneering picked up, the Viceroy made a tour of Punjab. In a private and secret report based on his impression he noted to Pethick-Lawerence: 'the League speakers are saying that these elections will decide whether there is to be Pakistan or not and if the League wins in the Pakistan provinces no further vote or plebiscite will be needed'.[174]

The ruling Unionist Party released its election manifesto in November 1945. The document was a painfully contrived attempt to stress the party's relevance. Even as the whole of India was in political ferment the Unionists were talking in terms of attaining independence by constitutional means.[175] When the situation demanded an all-India perspective, Khizr and his party were talking of the benefits to 'Punjab and Punjabis'.[176] The party's emphasis on provincial prosperity had no significance or even relevance in Muslim minds when compared to the Muslim League's demand for a new state—Pakistan.

As the Unionist party rapidly fell out of favour, losing its once formidable goodwill in rural areas, its dependence on the 'rusting imperial structure' only increased in proportion. The Unionist stalwarts represented an 'aloof body seasonally resident in Lahore or Simla remote and for all purposes out of touch with the people'.[177]

In sharp contrast, the Muslim League in Punjab was now charged with a mission. Conscious of how much advantage the Unionists had derived in 1936–7 from the support of socio-religious leaders like *pirs* and *sajjada nashins*, the League's leadership took upon itself the task of manipulating the transfer to it of the support of the vital section of Punjab Muslims. The Unionist Party's relatively non-communal approach to politics only served to make things easier for the League.[178] It was these people, the *pirs* and the like, supported extensively by Muslim student groups, who launched a propaganda blitz in Punjab. Pakistan was sold as a heaven (*bahista*) on earth. There would be no poverty, and, even more importantly, no harassment, no exploitation by the Hindu moneylender in the 'pure land'. The League in sum promised much more in an 'Islamic' idiom than the Unionists had given in a 'secular' idiom.[179] By the beginning of 1946, or the eve of the elections, the Unionist Party had lost the support of almost all important *pirs* and *sajjada nashins*, and had been sidelined almost completely from rural Punjab.

The growing irrelevance of the Unionists was also facilitated by the decreasing interest of the British in their welfare. For the rural peasantry in Punjab, the significance of their landlord patrons began to decline the moment there ability to disburse patronage became suspect. The patronage disbursed by the 'intermediary' *safed poshes* and *zaildars* was only as relevant and important as the colonial bureaucracy would allow it to be. It did not take long for influential Muslim landowners and power brokers to realize that access to positions of importance were now linked or likely to be linked to the Muslim League. It was this belief that speeded the entry of the rural elite into the Muslim League fold. In sum, when the political significance of the Unionist leaders declined on the colonial scales, they failed to receive 'petty' district-level patronage and in turn were unable to distribute it lower down the ladder. With its future itself in doubt, people left its fold rapidly.

The *biradari* network had, in better times, been well used by the Unionist Party. But since most of the important *biradari* leaders were also large landowners, they could not possibly stay away from the prospective centres of power and patronage. The League topped this with committed support from various student organizations, particularly the Punjab Muslim Students Federation. Across the villages and towns of Punjab, the Friday prayer was converted into a powerful political medium in favour of the League by dedicated and motivated student workers.

In a note assessing the probable outcome of the election, written perhaps in the first week of January 1946, Penderel Moon noted that almost without exception the Muslims in Punjab, for all practical purposes, were with the Muslim League on the question of Pakistan. In the same note but in a different context, Moon said that most of the Congress leaders in the province were not affected by the call for Pakistan because not even one important leader had property of significant value in the areas that were notionally being considered for Pakistan. On the other hand, the Congress leaders, he pointed out, were hungry for power and keen to remove all hurdles as quickly as possible. Any deadlock only meant their chance of grasping power would only be further delayed.[180]

By February 1946 when Punjab went to the polls, the Muslim League had for all practical purposes replaced the Unionist Party in Muslim minds. Of the 86 seats designated for Muslim candidates, the Muslim League won 73 (see Table 1.4). The Unionists were able to poll a mere 26.7 per cent of the Muslim votes whereas the Muslim League polled 66.4 per cent.[181]

A delighted Jinnah later remarked that the results were all the more significant because the Congress had been able to win only one Muslim seat. Punjab stood divided on communal lines like never before—a wedge had now been forced, which would go only deeper in the days that followed.

H.B. Richardson who had worked as education minister in the state of Indore noted to Prime Minister Attlee in a letter 'The Punjab elections were a bit of a chaos . . . in spite of government pressure the Muslim League won by bringing out the cry of Islam is in danger . . . in many villages speakers held the Koran in one hand and some Hindu scriptures in the other and asked Muslim voters which they would choose . . . all very cheap and vulgar reminiscent of elections in Britain 100 years ago.'[182]

The Election Commissioner of Punjab noted in his report: 'A feature of the election was that generally speaking it was run on communal issues. The Muslim League took its stand on the plank of Pakistan and Islam in danger and its appeal went home to the Muslim masses.' Interestingly the report also said that 'the elections unlike previous elections were fought on party lines and not on personal, tribal or caste considerations. Party labels . . . went a long way to ensuring the success of candidates. There was a falling away of personal influence in swaying the votes.'[183]

TABLE 1.4 RESULTS OF PUNJAB LEGISLATIVE ASSEMBLY ELECTIONS 1946

Party	Seats
Muslim League	73
Congress	51
Unionist Party	19
Akali Dal	21
Independents	11
Total	175

Source: N.N. Mitra, *Indian Annual Register*; Tanwar, *Unionists.*[184]

COALITION GOVERNMENT: CARDINAL ERROR

Even though the Muslim League had done remarkably well in Punjab, it still fell short by ten seats to form the ministry on its own. In this minor hitch lay the roots of what was to follow in the subsequent month. A more detailed reference to the events that led to the formation of the Congress, Akalis and Unionists government in Punjab led by Khizr Hayat on 7 March 1946 is therefore required.

The Transfer of Power volumes six and seven surprisingly have no significant reference to the role played by the British in the formation of the government in Punjab and how it really came about. A brief reference by Wavell in a note to Pethick-Lawerence however says: 'The Sikhs hold the balance and are trying to secure maximum advantage. . . I can hardly believe that they will join the Muslim League with its Pakistan policy, even though they might get an absurdly generous weightage in the council of ministers.'[185]

Another brief reference to the election results and the formation of the ministry in Punjab appears in a letter from Pethick-Lawerence to Wavell: 'It is a great pity that the results of the Punjab elections offer such slender prospects of stable government . . . it was no doubt inevitable that a record based on a non-communal policy [referring to the Unionist failure] should prove a poor recommendation to electors in the present communally charged atmosphere.'[186]

Moon, has had strong words against Governor Glancy's decision to permit a Khizr (Unionist) led coalition government form in Punjab, calling it a 'cardinal mistake'. 'From the public point of view', calling Khizr to head a coalition government minus the Muslim League, 'was a disaster and for Khizr personally it was political suicide'.[187]

Moon, who understood Punjab in the best British traditions of the ICS with perhaps few to rival his grasp, explained that it was a serious mistake to form a ministry in a province like Punjab where the Muslims, in line with their demographic status, had predominantly influenced the formation of every ministry since the reforms process had started in 1920. To have pushed the Muslim League to the sidelines, at a time when Muslim political opinion had been crystallized and consolidated like never before, when the Muslim League had its tail in the air, has remained unexplained.

It was an action that affronted the Muslim community and was viewed as a design to simply keep the Muslim League away from its right—power and ministry formation. It greatly swelled the rank and file of the Muslim League enabling even undecided liberal Muslims, of whom there were a large number, to make up their minds. But most importantly perhaps, the formation of the coalition ministry underlined what the Muslim League had been propagating all along—Muslims could not trust the 'Hindu Congress'.

Ishar Singh Majhel, who later became Civil Supplies, Relief and Rehabilitation Minister, East Punjab (1947–50), however, completely dismisses the point made by Moon and says that if the Muslim League had been allowed to form government the situation may have proved worse. He said that in the first place, if the Sikhs were angry it was only because of the oppressive mentality of the Muslims towards the Sikhs, a situation that would have been further aggravated had the Muslim League formed the government. As Majhel puts it, the basic issue was that the League wanted to capture the government to make it easier to capture Punjab.[188]

We need therefore to look even if briefly at the circumstances that led to the emergence of the coalition between people who had till only a few days earlier been sworn enemies and were still licking their wounds from an unusually ugly election campaign. Ideally, as the *Leader* put it, 'In one sense the Congress Muslim League and Akali Coalition could have been better.'[189] The Congress, regardless of what the Muslim League leaders of Punjab said, did make an effort for such a coalition but, as Maulana Azad said, the deal fell through because of the League's old stand that the Congress could nominate only non-Muslims, meaning thereby that all Muslims to be nominated for the ministry could only be League nominees—a repeat in this sense of 1937.[190]

Azad said:

> I am glad the Punjab has been saved Section 93 . . . but I admit the best solution would have been one in which Muslim League too had joined . . . the Punjab leaders of the Muslim League if left to themselves would have joined but when a trunk call was made to Jinnah [then in Shillong], he refused . . . so long as the Muslim League did not reject the Congress offer I did not make any commitment to the Unionists and the Akalis.[191]

The League's version for the failure of the talks was given by Iftikhar Husain. He said the main issue was the Congress insistence on nominating the Muslims that fell to its share: on this the Muslim League could not compromise: 'It is significant the Congress gave this stand up when it came to nominating from other communities [meaning Akalis] and in doing so has virtually accepted the position that Congress in Punjab represents only the Hindus.'[192]

Surprisingly Jinnah, extremely angry no doubt, was reported to have said that the Muslim League had already won the Punjab for Pakistan by winning 90 per cent of the Muslim seats (1946 elections) and as such ministry formation was not important. In this sense the talks with the League were also only a formality—because there had been no change in the League's stand on the issue, where then was the hope that the League would make an exception in Punjab.

But it is the Congress's negotiations with the Akalis that require a more detailed examination. As we know, the Akalis had won most of their seats in 1946 against the Congress, which too had nominated Sikh candidates. The margins of victory had been very low. The Congress naturally wished to retain with itself the right to nominate the Sikh nominees that fell to its share in the proportion of seats actually won.

Lahore witnessed intense politicking and negotiations which continued through the night in the week that preceded the formation of the ministry, not just between the Congress and the Akalis but even between the Muslim League and the Sikhs. *Dawn* reported a long meeting between Baldev Singh and the League leader Iftikhar Husain and Noon.[193] In fact, a report (later refuted by the Akalis) even said that the Akalis were '50:50' with regard to the party they wished to support—the Congress or the League.[194] In any case, there was little doubt that the Akalis held the key to the crisis. At the same time it is clear that there was never a chance of the Akalis siding with the Muslim League, all the persuasive efforts and generous offers of the Punjab League leaders notwithstanding. This comes out clearly from the statements of not only Baldev Singh but also Giani Kartar Singh, 'the Akali brain trust'.[195] As Baldev Singh put it, the main problem with the possibility of an understanding with the Muslim League on the issue was the basic issue of Pakistan, something on which the Akalis were in line with the Congress.

Unlike the more suave, sophisticated—let's call them clever Congressmen—the loud Akalis hardly understood the complex game, they were just not made for it, something which they would learn at great personal price in the later months of 1947. They tried to make the best of it with Baldev Singh even telling the Maulana (Azad) that the Sikhs had been mistreated by the Congress in the past. He sought an assurance from the Congress president that the Sikhs would not be mistreated in future.[196]

The talks between the Congress President and the Akalis lingered unduly even though both had no other option, mainly because, as Baldev Singh said, the Congress was hesitant to give the Akalis their due share in the cabinet, based on the seats the Akalis had won.[197] The other issue that troubled the Akalis was the non-committal approach of the Congress to the question of the status of non-Akali Sikh MLAs. The Akalis claimed from the Congress the right to nominate all Sikhs to the ministry, an issue on which the Congress had immense reservations, but to which it ultimately yielded, something that annoyed the League even more.[198] Interestingly, Kartar Singh even went on record saying that the whole process took long because some Punjab Congressmen did not want the talks with the Akalis to succeed.[199] Maulana Azad had to extend his stay in Lahore to see the deal through. Finally it was only on 5 March at 7.30 in the evening that the Maulana announced to the press that the coalition talks had succeeded.

While Bhimsen Sachar had done much of the running around on behalf of the Congress, having visited the Governor many times to put forth the claim of majority, it was only natural for the coalition to seek a Muslim 'show boy' to lead the coalition.[200] On 6 March 1946, Khizr Hayat, the outgoing Premier, was invited to form a coalition government. An outraged Muslim League declared a mass *hartal* on 7 March and Traitors' Day on 9 March. The new ministry took oath of office on 11 March. The ministry included Bhimsen Sachar (Congress) with Finance; Ch. Lehri Singh (Congress) Public Works; Sardar Baldev Singh (Akali) Development; and two Unionists, Nawab Muzzafar Ali Khan Qizilbash and Mohammad Ibrahim Barq with Revenue.

'Tooth for a tooth', screamed a huge headline of *Dawn* just as Liaqat Ali warned 'Hindu and Sikh brethren that they would be committing a serious mistake if they formed a ministry that does not command confidence of the Muslims'. On the same day, *Dawn's* editorial called Khizr Hayat 'Enemy No. 1' and dubbed him the 'most notorious henchman of British imperialism in the whole of India'. The editorial also said: 'Naked and unashamed the Congress stands allied with the prize toddies of the British empire proving that Congress can lay aside all other considerations if that will achieve the first and foremost object—hitting the Muslim below the belt.'[201]

A day later, *Dawn* depicted Khizr in a cartoon as a dog holding a bone in his mouth with 'Premiership' printed on the bone and Congress President Maulana Azad holding the leash.[202]

Jinnah was enraged with the developments in Lahore. He reminded his party cadres that this was the third time that Congress had cheated the Muslims. On the same day, *Dawn* attributed the massive outbreak of violence in Delhi, Lahore and many other places to Khizr's treachery.[203] But it was *Dawn's* editorial of 13 March that gave the first indication of where the Punjab was heading: 'Can there be peace when the overwhelming verdict of Muslims in a democratic election is circumvented? The Muslim is not bred on goats milk—he does not sit down to nurture the injured spot but goes and finds where the blow came from.'[204]

On 8 March the *Statesman* published abridged versions from a cross-section of lesser known mainly Urdu newspapers of West Punjab *Ehsan* said: 'In the Punjab Hindus have never been fair to Muslims'. Likewise the *Nawa-e-Waqt* said 'it [the Congress] defied the general will of the people'.[205]

Khizr Hayat issued a long statement on 7 March, explaining why he had agreed to lead the coalition. He said he had thought over the decision very deeply and anxiously and, 'on a balance . . . I am convinced that for a leader of any party to take up a position which would result in the breakdown of the working of an elected government,' was undesirable. Khizr also said that the success of the Muslim League in Punjab was something that could not be ignored, which was why he had wanted the Muslim League to be given the first chance to form the ministry and that he said was also the reason why he had waited. Interestingly, he also made a reference to how the constituent partners of the coalition were free to make their own decisions with regard to the future constitution.[206]

All the party politics and experiments apart, Governor Glancy's experiment fell flat on its face from day one. There was total lack of understanding between the partners, who had been staunch enemies till just the other day. Glancy's successor Jenkins observed: 'It was a weak ministry . . . [it] put forward no legislation even of non-controversial kind. . . . Muslim members of the ministry were under constant attack from the League and the Congress High Command to obey its orders—to which the Unionists strongly objected.'[207] Jenkins had earlier noted: 'Political and communal [activity] is increasing throughout the Punjab . . . all communities are said to be preparing for widespread rioting.'[208] The swearing-in of the ministry had greatly aggravated the situation on the ground—even in the lanes and streets. On 27 July, a Sikh shopkeeper was alleged to have raped a Muslim girl in Abbottabad. The following day a large crowd of Muslims got together and burnt down the Gurudwara. In retaliation some Sikhs opened fire killing three Muslims in the crowd.[209] This was the kind of situation that was rapidly developing across the province. Non-political issues were freely being given a political and communal tone.

Moon, who was then in the 'thickest of things' with a very close view, noted that if Governor Glancy had acted with more foresight and discouraged Khizr Hayat from the coalition, Khizr, who was himself not enthusiastic, would have stayed away. Khizr and Glancy knew each other extremely well, they trusted each other. But Glancy failed to see the future, and left a load of problems for his successor.

Moon also refers to some of Khizr's friends who were anxious that he should get out of the coalition at the earliest. There were some with other views as well and Moon had had the chance to advise some of them: 'The Muslim community would never forgive him (Khizr) if he appeared to cling to power in defiance of Muslim interests and wishes. His (Khizr's) party had been decisively defeated in the elections.' One of the two to whom Moon made this suggestion was also a minister in the new government. He replied to Moon: 'The reins of power should not be voluntarily surrendered . . . we have a danda in our hand and mustn't give it up.'[210] Not only was the 'danda', as Moon put it, a broken reed but the 'danda' soon went on to change hands.

Khizr Hayat was without doubt a positive-thinking, well-meaning person, for only such a person could have believed 'that the religious fanaticism of the last few months was probably a passing phase and that many of the Punjab Muslims would within a year or so be content to settle down and take a much more moderate line'.[211]

As if the formation of the coalition ministry had not already caused enough problems for Punjab, the 16 May Cabinet Mission's statement had set rolling another ball of equally complex problems. Jenkins specially deputed Punjab's Home Secretary and the Deputy Director-General CID to form an estimate of the reactions to the Cabinet Mission's Statement. He then reported his summary of the inputs to Wavell: 'The Muslims are on the whole pleased, they think the proposals give them most of what they want . . . the Hindu opinion originally not unfavourable is changing and may before long become hostile. . . . The Sikhs are intensely bitter, so much so that Tara Singh would not come to see Macdonald [Home Secretary].'

There is an interesting angle to Jenkins' assessment. He said that the Sikhs felt that if they had known what the Mission's intentions were they would have on their own worked out satisfactory terms with Jinnah, but now since their (the League's) demand and even they (the Sikhs) had been handed over to Jinnah it would not be possible to negotiate a reasonable deal. 'We may have', Jenkins noted, 'serious trouble with the Sikhs, who are intensely obstinate and formidable when aroused to common action.'[212] A few days later Tara Singh wrote to Pethick-Lawerence:

> The Sikhs have been entirely thrown at the mercy of the Muslims. . . . If the British government is not aware of the Sikh feelings, the Sikhs will have to resort to some measures in order to convince everybody of the Sikh anxiety.[213]

Jenkins appeared even more alarmed when he reported to Wavell on 29 May:

> If Sikhs are not repeat not conciliated by June 9 (date of next Panthic Party meet), I cannot say what will happen but disturbances requiring military intervention on a considerable scale might well occur by the end of the month.[214]

But as had happened so many times with Jenkins, his clear and precise understanding was outweighed and sidetracked by people who appear not to have understood the brewing crisis in Punjab or had a different focus.[215] While commenting, for example, on how Baldev Singh appears to have been over-optimistic and that the real power of controlling the Sikhs lay not in the hands of 'educated' members of the community but elsewhere (meaning Master Tara Singh, Giani Kartar Singh, etc.).[216] Jenkins once again revealed a deeper understanding of the all-important Sikh psyche. Of course, on the face of it, his comments about 'professional agitators' may not reflect too well on important Akali leaders, but Jenkins greatly 'respected' these professional agitators and remained ever conscious of their immense importance in the crisis towards which Punjab was rapidly racing.[217]

Before we move on to the crisis that immediately preceded the resignation of Khizr from the premiership of Punjab—the event that blew the chilling whistle that started the violence in early March 1947—a typical and fairly common perception among the Muslims of why Pakistan was 'essential' merits attention.

Hossain Imam, President of the Council of States was also a member of the 'Pakistan Mission' to the Cabinet Delegation even though he belonged to Bihar, but what he reportedly conveyed to Wavell is a view that can be applied quite justifiably even to Punjab. The position was that 'the entire Muslim public felt that they would not get a fair deal without Pakistan. Two and a half years of Congress rule . . . had convinced them of this. . . . They were excluded from industry and stood no chance in the future of being allowed to play their part in the economic reconstruction of the country.' The Imam further said that the 25 million Muslims who would be left behind as minorities in India would be happy to sacrifice their interest for the benefit of the rest of the community 'If the Hindus obtained power at the centre, they would behave in a most unreasonable fashion and every safeguard that might be incorporated in the Constitution would be useless because the Hindus would always been in majority. The Muslims in the minority provinces would rather face whatever was in store for them than allow the whole Muslim population to be maltreated.' Wavell quoted the Imam as saying: 'the Congress Hindus wished to step into the shoes of the British and take to themselves the powers that the British had exercised in the country. This tendency the Muslims had to resist.'[218]

JAT SIKH PEASANT AND MUSLIM RULE

Sikander Hayat, the first Unionist Premier of Punjab, had told Penderel Moon (posted as Deputy Commissioner of Amritsar in 1941) that Pakistan would mean a massacre. The massacre, Sikander had said, would be a massacre not only of the Hindus and Sikhs by the Muslims but probably the other way round as well. Sikander Hayat, as we know, understood Punjab and its people in a profoundly earthy manner. For him the crux of the Pakistan problem rested on some very basic issues.[219] It is in view of these basic realities that I wish to suggest that no amount of political wizardry and 'statesmanship' could possibly alter this situation. If Pakistan was to come, it was bound to bring violence in its wake.

We have already seen some broad demographic outlines of Punjab in terms of the actual distribution of population. But the point that is crucial is the distribution of the Jat Sikh and partly the non-Sikh Jat peasantry as well—a tough peasantry with martial traditions and racially akin to the Sikhs. For any scheme of Pakistan to materialize peacefully, it was therefore imperative to find a method which would be acceptable to the Sikhs. As Moon also points out, the Sikhs became a militant community essentially because of the militant nature of Muslim rule in Punjab: 'The typical Sikh is a sturdy Jat peasant. It was through his toughness that under the stimulus of Muslim oppression the Sikhs developed into a distinct community.'[220]

In sum, therefore, while the communal strife had varying reasons across India, in the Punjab there were added factors which were specific to Punjab and which had clearly grown out of history. As may have been noticed, considerable emphasis has been given to the cross-cultural nature of Punjab's society, the coexistence and interdependence, and yet, paradoxical as it may appear, the fact remains that there were reasons in history—very recent indeed for the Muslims and Sikhs—to be suspicious of each other. Robin Jeffrey notes that, 'In the Punjab, the virus of the disease could be traced back as far as the last years of the seventeenth century when the Sikh military tradition was founded in conflict with the intolerant Mughal Empire of Aurangzeb.'[221]

Dr Ansari very perceptively summed up the problem of the Sikhs *vis-à-vis* Pakistan:

> Mr. Jinnah still maintains that an understanding can be reached provided that the problem is treated as a local problem for Muslims and Sikhs and not complicated by the intervention of all India influence from outside. On what lines he hopes to base such an understanding is not known. It seems at present as if the attitude of the Sikhs is a major obstacle to the realisation of Pakistan. That they could be coerced into it seems unthinkable. To attempt coercion would mean a civil war, and a war which, once it had broken out, could certainly not be confined to North-West India.[222]

NOTES

1. Gopichand Bhargava, and N.V. Raj Kumar, *One Year of Freedom*, New Delhi, Indian National Congress, 1948.
2. Editorial, *Tribune*, 1 January, 1948.
3. Ibid., 1 October 1947.
4. *CMG*, 11 December 1947.
5. Ibid., 13 September 1947.
6. Ibid., 11 September 1947.

7. The 3 June Plan has been discussed at some length in Chapter 3.
8. Sir Evan Jenkins has drawn extensive and repeated references in this work. For one—because he was Governor of Punjab but essentially because he saw it all coming and never spared an occasion to make a note of it to his superiors. He was intensely disliked by the Muslim League, Nehru too was not fond of him—both have been discussed in later pages. He had a deep understanding of the Punjab—had worked as D.C. Hoshiarpur, also had experience of Amritsar and Gurdaspur. He was said to have personally visited over 1000 villages in his 'field days'. He understood and spoke both Urdu and Punjabi and was a frequent user of the term *tau* a form of addressing elders in rural Punjab, see IOR MSS Eur D 1065/1 WHA Rich papers.
9. N. Mansergh et al., *Constitutional Relations Between Britain & India: The Transfer of Power 1942–7*, vol. IX (408), hereafter the volumes are referred to as *TP*. The number within brackets is the serial number of the document as listed in the volumes.
10. *TP*, vol. X (298), Secret Note, Jenkins to Mountbatten 3 May 1947, p. 593.
11. *TP*, vol. X (321), 5 May 1947 Mountbatten to Ismay, Chief of Viceroy's Staff, p. 628.
12. The transcript is part of a compilation, *Plain Tales from The Raj*, Deptt. of Sound Records, Imperial War Museum, acquired by NMML, New Delhi.
13. *The Tribune* 22 October 1947.
14. H.V. Hodson, *The Great Divide: Britain India and Pakistan*, London, 1969, Appendix II, p. 549.
15. *The Tribune*, 5 June 1947. Interestingly almost to the day, six months earlier Gandhiji too had completely ruled out the exchange of population. 'The question of exchange of population has never crossed my mind. It is unthinkable and impracticable. . . . For me any such thing will spell bankruptcy in India, wisdom or statesmanship or both. The logical consequence of any such step is too dreadful to contemplate.' See M.K. Gandhi, *To The Protagonists of Pakistan*, Karachi, 1947, p. 214.
16. Hodson, *Great Divide*, p. 550.
17. *TP*, vol. XII (81), Note by Abell 12 July 1947.
18. *Dawn*, 7 October 1947.
19. Tapan Ray Chaudhry, 'Rereading Divide and Quit', *The Partition Omnibus*, p. 303.
20. Moon, *Divide and Quit*, p. 268.
21. C.N. Vakil, *Economic Consequences of Divide India*, Bombay, 1950; *The Leader*, 5 March 1946.
22. Rosenberger, *Keesings Contemporary Archives: Weekly Diary of Important World Events*, vol. 6, 1946–8, pp. A9049–52.

23. Moon, *Divide and Quit*, p. 269; Khosla, *Stern Reckoning*, p. 299; Gauba, *Inside Pakistan*, Delhi, 1948, p. 257; R.J. Moore, *Escape From Empire: The Attlee Government & The Indian Problem*, Oxford, 1983, p. 327; Rosenbeger, *Keesings Contemporary Archives*, p. A9050.
24. Taya Zinkin, *Reporting India*, London, 1962, p. 20. I.M. Stephens Papers, Box 21, CSAS, *Sikhs in Action*, Lahore, and *Muslim League Attack on Sikhs and Hindus in Punjab in 1947*, Amritsar.
25. Moon, *Divide and Quit*, p. 268.
26. Gauba, *Inside Pakistan*, p. 258.
27. Vakil, *Economic Consequences of Divided India*, p. 106.
28. *Muslim League Attack on Sikhs and Hindus in Punjab 1947*, p. 218.
29. Hansen, *Partition & Genocide*, p. 2.
30. Rosenbeger, *Keesings Contemporary Archives*, pp. A-9049-52
31. Hansen, *Partition & Genocide*, p. 115.
32. Pandey, *Remembering Partition*, p. 14.
33. *The Census of India, Punjab*, 1941 (the last conducted prior to the Partition of India). The population of Punjab was listed at 28.4 million of whom 16.2 million were Muslims, 7.5 million were Hindus and 3.7 millions were Sikhs. The 1931 Census had shown the Muslim population at 14.9 million.
34. *The Census 1941, Punjab*; *India Year Book Who's Who 1945–6*, p. 901, NMML.
35. Raghuvendra Tanwar, *Politics of Sharing Power: The Punjab Unionist Party 1923–47*, New Delhi, 1999, p. 33.
36. Ian Talbot, *Khizr Tiwana: The Punjab Unionist Party and the Partition of India*, Richmond, 1996, p. 4.
37. Tanwar, *Sharing Power*, pp. 30–1.
38. Moon, p. 34.
39. *TP*, vol. VI (29), *Glancy to Wavell*, 16 August 1945, p. 72.
40. A.N. Bali, *Now It Can Be Told*, Jullundur, 1949, p. 1.
41. Hasan, *The Partition Omnibus*, New Delhi, 2002, pp. xi–xii.
42. *PT*, 18 October 1947.
43. B.R. Nanda who went on in later years to make valuable contributions to modern Indian history and also became the founding Director of the NMML, New Delhi.
44. *The Tribune*, Lahore, 16 March 1947.
45. Bali, *Now It Can Be Told*, p. 9.
46. Ibid., p. 12.
47. Khosla, *Stern Reckoning*, pp. 3–6.
48. Ibid., p. 6.
49. *Eastern Times*, 19 January 1947; *Dawn*, 3 March 1947; *Dawn*, 30 May 1947; *Dawn*, 17 May 1947.
50. *Dawn*, 3 March 1947; *Eastern Times*, 19 January 1947; *Dawn* 30 May 1947; *Dawn*, 21 May 1947; *Dawn*, 17 May 1947; *Dawn*,

20 May 1947; *Dawn*, 30 May 1947.

51. Subbarayan to Prime Minister Attlee, 24 July 1947, Attlee Papers, Ac. no. 2146, Microfilm, NAI, New Delhi.
52. Moon, *Divide and Quit*, p. 14.
53. Ibid.
54. Mehrotra, *Freedom & Partition*, p. 187.
55. V.N. Datta, 'Interpreting Partition', in Amrik Singh, *The Partition in Retrospect*, New Delhi, 2000, p. 285.
56. Smith, *Modern Islam of India*, p. 331.
57. Mehrotra, *Freedom & Partition*, p. 198.
58. Kirpal Singh, *Select Documents: Partition of Punjab 1947*, Delhi, 1991; *The Partition of Punjab*, Patiala, 1972.
59. David Page, *Prelude to Partition*, p. 262.
60. Ibid., p. 141.
61. Ibid., p. xx.
62. Anita Inder Singh, *The Origins of the Partition of India*, Oxford Omnibus Edition, 2002, p. 1.
63. Ibid., p. 44.
64. Gyanendra Pandey, 'Review of writings on Communalism', *Economic and Political Weekly*, 15 October 1983.
65. Page, *Prelude*, p. xiii.
66. Raghuvendra Tanwar, *Sharing Power*, pp. 31, 51–3, 168–95.
67. David Gilmartin, *Empire and Islam: Punjab and The Making of Pakistan*, New Delhi, 1988, p. 3.
68. Ibid., p. 189.
69. Ibid., p. 1.
70. S.S. Pirzada (ed.), *Foundations of Pakistan: All India Muslim League Documents 1906–47*, Karachi 1970, p. 159; Gilmartin, *Empire & Islam*, p. 181.
71. Gilmartin, *Empire & Islam*, p. 210.
72. Ayesha Jalal, *The Sole Spokesman Jinnah: The Muslim League and the Demand for Pakistan*, Cambridge, 1985, p. 122.
73. Jawharlal Nehru, *An Autobiography*, New Delhi, 1962 edn., p. 464.
74. Ibid., p. 466.
75. Anil Seal, *The Emergence of Indian Nationalism: Competition and Collaboration in the Late 19th century*, Cambridge, 1968; Mushirul Hasan (ed.), *India's Partition Process: Strategy and Mobilisation*, New Delhi, 1993, p. 36.
76. Hasan, *India's Partition Process*, p. 5.
77. Ibid., p. 6.
78. Ibid., pp. 7 and 15; Rajendra Prasad, *Autobiography*, Delhi, 1957, p. 446.
79. Hasan, *India's Partition Process*, p. 14.

80. Ibid., p. 28.
81. Ibid., p. 34.
82. Ian Talbot, *Punjab & The Raj: Provincial Politics and the Pakistan Movement*, New Delhi, 1988, p. 211.
83. Tanwar, *Unionist Party*, pp. 175–82.
84. Gyanendra Pandey, 'Hindus and Others: The Militant Hindu Construction', *Economic and Political Weekly*, 28 December 1991, pp. 2997–3008.
85. Pandey, *Construction of Communalism in Colonial North India*, p. 113.
86. Ibid., p. 251.
87. Pandey, 'Hindus and Others', p. 3008.
88. Jamila Samad, *Eastern Times*, 12 and 13 February 1947.
89. Ibid.
90. *Dawn*, 2 March 1947.
91. *Hindu Outlook*, 5 November 1946.
92. *Eastern Times*, 3 March 1947.
93. Ibid., 3 January 1947.
94. Ibid., 29 January 1947.
95. Ziauddin Ahmad Sulerl, *Whither Pakistan*, London, possibly 1946–7 or 1948, p. 11.
96. Shakatullah Ansari, *Pakistan: The Problem of India*, Lahore, 1944, pp. 41–3.
97. Ibid., pp. 94–5.
98. Rammanohar Lohia, 'Nullification of Partition', *Mankind*, May 1971, pp. 34, 36, 38–9.
99. Ibid.
100. Khosla, *Stern Reckoning*, p. 31, N.N. Mitra, *Indian Annual Register*, vol. 1, January to June 1946, Microfilm, NMML, New Delhi.
101. Khosla, *Stern Reckoning*, p. 31.
102. K.C. Yadav, *Elections in Punjab*, New Delhi, 1987, p. 106.
103. Singh, *Origins of Partition*, pp. 142–202.
104. *TP*, vol. VII (513), Gandhi to Wavell, 13 June 1946, p. 910.
105. Letter from B.J.K. Kirchner to I.M. Stephens, Editor, *Statesman*, I.M. Stephens Papers, Box 36, CSAS.
106. Ibid.
107. Singh, *Origins of the Partition*, pp. 174–5; *TP*, vol. VIII (317), pp. 517–18.
108. *TP*, vol. VIII (63), Wavell to Nehru/Jinnah, 22 July 1946, p. 98.
109. Ibid., vol. VIII (71), Nehru to Wavell, 23 July 1947, p. 112
110. Ibid., vol. VIII (81), Wavell to Pethick-Lawerence, Telegram, 28 July 1946.
111. Singh, *Origins of Partition*, p. 175.
112. Khosla, *Stern Reckoning*, p. 43.

113. *TP*, vol. VIII (86), pp. 134–39.
114. Singh, *Origins of Partition*, p. 179.
115. *TP*, vol. VIII (91), pp. 144–5.
116. Ibid., vol. VIII (121), p. 190.
117. Ibid., vol. VIII (132), p. 204.
118. Ibid., vol. VIII (138), Nehru to Wavell 10 August 1946, p. 218.
119. *Dawn*, 16 August 1946, *Eastern Times*, 16 August 1946.
120. *TP*, vol. VIII (154), Burrows to Pethick-Lawrence, Telegram, 16 August 1946, p. 239.
121. Ibid., vol. VIII (194), pp. 287–9.
122. Khosla, *Stern Reckoning*, p. 65; *The Statesman*, 10 September 1946; IM, Stephens Papers CSAS
123. Khosla, *Stern Reckoning*, p. 86.
124. *National Herald*, 27 August 1946; *Selected Works of Jawaharlal Nehru*, vol. 15 (Second Series) (hereafter *SW)*, p. 315.
125. *TP*, vol. VIII (241), p. 386.
126. Ibid; *Tribune*, 3 September 1946.
127. *Hindu Outlook*, 3–10 December 1946. Also see Editorial, 10 September 1946, titled 'New Government'.
128. Ibid.; *The Tribune*, 3 September 1946.
129. *The Tribune*, 3 September 1946.
130. *Dawn*, 3 September 1946.
131. Ibid. 4 September 1946.
132. *HT*, 2 September 1946, also *SW*, vol. 15, p. 327.
133. *TP*, vol. VIII (353), 23 Sept. 46, p. 569.
134. *SW* (Second Series), Vol. I, p. 161.
135. *TP*, vol. VIII (395), 2 Oct. 46, p. 644.
136. Ibid.
137. Ibid., vol. VIII (435), p. 705; Moon, *Wavell: The Viceroy's Journal*, pp. 424, 429.
138. *TP*, vol. VIII (465), p. 735.
139. *TP*, vol. VIII (483), p. 755.
140. Ibid., p. 756.
141. Ibid., vol. VIII (489), p. 762.
142. Ibid., vol. VIII (469), pp. 777, 779. Also see editor's note at p. 779.
143. Ibid. (495), p. 780.
144. Ibid. (497), p. 785.
145. Ibid. (504), p. 801.
146. Ibid. (506), p. 803.
147. Ibid. (513), p. 806.
148. Ibid. (528), p. 835.
149. *TP*, vol. IX (14), 31 October 1946, p. 25.

150. *SW*, vol. I (Second Series), p. 207.
151. Ibid., p. 132.
152. Ibid., p. 117
153. *TP*, vol. IX (13), Jenkins to Wavell, 8 November 1946, p. 24.
154. Ibid., vol. IX (44), pp. 46, 83.
155. The conference was summoned in a great hurry and attended by Wavell and, after initial hesitation, some Muslim League leaders.
156. *SW*, vol. I (Second Series), Minutes of London Conference, p. 280.
157. *TP*, vol. IX (63), Top Secret Telegram, 20 November 1946, p. 118.
158. Ibid., p. 119.
159. Ibid. (158), 5 December 1946, p. 280.
160. See the Revised Draft Statement, *TP*, vol. IX (163), p. 290; (166), p. 295.
161. *SW*, vol. I (Second Series), Minutes of the London Conference, p. 137.
162. *TP*, vol. IX (166), p. 295.
163. Ibid.
164. Singh, *Origins of Partition*, p. 206.
165. Ibid., p. 207; *Statesman* 7 January 1947.
166. Ibid., p. 209.
167. Khosla, *Stern Reckoning*, p. 89.
168. *TP*, vol. VIII (233), p. 371.
169. *TP*, vol. IX (135), p. 229.
170. Talbot, *Khizr Tiwana*, p. 137.
171. Yadav, *Elections in Punjab*, p. 84.
172. Tanwar, *Unionist Party*, p. 175.
173. *TP*, vol. VI (29), p. 71.
174. Ibid., vol. VI (157), pp. 374, 377.
175. *CMG*, 29 November 1945.
176. Tanwar, *Unionist Party*, p. 176.
177. *CMG*, 29 November 1945.
178. *TP*, vol. VI (177), Tara Singh to Attlee, p. 424.
179. Tanwar, *Unionist Party*, p. 177; *HT*, 26 February 1946.
180. *TP*, vol. VI (350), pp. 771–4; *The Tribune*, 1 March 1946.
181. Mitra, *Indian Annual Register*, vol. 1, 1946, pp. 229–30.
182. Attlee Papers Ac. no. 2146, letter of H.B. Richardson, 25 March 1946, Public Relations Directorate, New Delhi, Microfilm, NAI.
183. *TP*, vol. VI (544), p. 1231.
184. Mitra, *Indian Annual Register*, vol. 1, 1946, pp. 229–30, Tanwar, *Unionist Party*, p. 183.
185. *TP*, vol. VI (499), p. 1112. Anita Inder Singh, *Origins of Partition*, p. 40; *Statesman*, 10 March 1947.
186. *TP*, vol. VI (510), p. 1130.
187. Moon, *Divide & Quit*, p. 71.

188. Majhel, 27 June 1973, Oral History Transcript, NMML, pp. 54–5.
189. *Statesman*, 6 March 1946.
190. *Dawn*, 7 March 1946; *HT*, 7 March 1946.
191. *Statesman*, 9 March 1946.
192. Ibid.
193. *Dawn*, 5 March 1946.
194. *Statesman*, 4 March 1946.
195. *Leader*, 4 and 5 March 1946 for Baldev Singh's statement. Also see *HT*, 5 March 1946 for Kartar Singh's statement that there was no chance of an understanding with the Muslim League. At one stage it was also reported that the Muslim League was willing to give the Akalis even 25 per cent of positions in the ministry, see *Statesman*, 4 March 1946.
196. *Leader*, 2 March 1946. Incidentally Baldev Singh had come into the forefront of these negotiations because both Master Tara Singh and Giani Kartar Singh had said they did not have time for such talks, and Baldev Singh would do so on their behalf, *Statesman*, 4 March 1946.
197. *HT*, 5 March 1946.
198. *Statesman*, 6 March 1946.
199. *The Leader*, 4 March 1946.
200. *The Leader*, 2 March 1946; *Tribune*, 2 March 1946.
201. *Dawn*, 7 March 1946; *HT*, 7 March 1946.
202. *Dawn*, 9 March 1946.
203. Ibid., 10 March 1946.
204. Ibid., 13 March 1946.
205. *Statesman*, 8 March 1946.
206. *The Leader*, 8 March 1946.
207. *TP*, vol. VIII, Minutes of Governor's Conference, p. 206.
208. Ibid., vol. VII (181), 2 May 1946.
209. Ibid., vol. VIII (132), Minutes of Governor's Conference, 8 August 1946, p. 207.
210. Moon, *Divide & Quit*, p. 73.
211. *TP*, vol. VII (311), p. 604.
212. Ibid., vol. VII (345), p. 644.
213. Ibid., vol. VII (380), pp. 696–7.
214. Ibid., vol. VII (401), 29 May 1946, p. 724.
215. *TP*, vol. VII (411), 30 May 1946, p. 740.
216. Ibid., vol. VII (640), p. 1083, Yusuf Meherally, *A Trip to Pakistan*, Bombay 1944, pp. 60–1.
217. Ibid.
218. Ibid., vol. VII (99), p. 244.
219. Moon, *Divide & Quit*, p. 29.
220. Ibid., p. 30.

221. Jeffrey, 'The Punjab Boundary Force and the Problem of Order: August 1947', *Modern Asian Studies*, 8.4 (1970), p. 493. Jeffrey's thesis is built mainly on a lecture delivered by the well known authority W.H. Mcleod, 'The Evolution of the Sikh Community', delivered at the University of Sussex in 1970.
222. Shaukatullah Ansari, *Pakistan: The Problem of India*, p. 77; Information Department's Fortnightly Appreciation, IOR L/1/1665, 19 May 1947, no. 3830.

2

Pointers to Disaster: Punjab in Early 1947

It was Christmas eve 1946. The crowded road, the thronged restaurant, the rippling laughter of pretty women in prettier clothes—this was the customary life of the gay town of Lahore. A Muslim friend, a journalist sat next to me. Our conversation inevitably rambled into politics. As we recalled the great Calcutta killings, the Noakhali tragedy and the Bihar frenzy we could not hide our satisfaction at the continued peace in our Province. . . . 'How long will this peace last' he asked, 'as long as Sir Khizr remains in office' I replied. My friend burst into derisive laughter.[1]

There was an element of irony in this, for since the day Khizr had taken the oath of office as the Premier of Punjab for a second term (11 March 1946), not a day had passed when demonstrations had not been organized by the Muslim League demanding his resignation, and yet there were those in equal number perhaps who thought that his continuance in office alone was the surest way to peace—an insurance against communal anarchy.

Even as Khizr Hayat now headed a coalition which comprised his diehard former opponents (the Congress), the ministry that had taken on itself the difficult task of assisting the British in governing Punjab was almost of the same colour as the previous Unionist ones.

The 'Punjab Oxen' was the title of an article by A.N. Bali, a popular commentator and contributor to newspapers in 1947. Writing in *The Tribune*, he discussed, just as Nanda and his journalist friend had noted, how the Punjab had continued walking its own pace and how the tragedies of Calcutta, Noakhali and Bihar had failed to raise tempers in Punjab however hard groups of political activists may have tried to provoke reactions:

One section would like the Punjabi oxen to turn to its neighbours to avenge Calcutta and Noakhali another would like others to do the same but avenge

Bihar and Bombay. . . . But thanks to the Punjabi ox, it has remained an ox. The hard instincts of the Punjabis and their ingrained habits are standing them well in resisting such pleadings. The name of the province was not tarnished by the occurrence of ghastly events that had disfigured the banner of others.[2]

The significance of these lines is that they were describing the ordinary Punjabi in the months that lay between the killings of Bihar and the outbreak of violence in Punjab in March 1947. The point argued by Bali is not that there were no disturbances or killings in the Punjab prior to March 1947, but that the fanaticism reflected in the killings was what the Punjabis had not easily adopted and never indulged in earlier.[3] To Bali the process of personal hate appears sudden: 'The sturdy Punjab peasant with his broad common sense was being assailed from all sides day in and day out with the result that he lost his bearings. The Punjabi oxen became an infuriated bull. The transformation was sudden.'

PUNJAB I AND PUNJAB II

But before we proceed further, I am inclined to draw attention to something that has repeatedly occurred to me through the course of this study. I have come to feel that it would be quite incorrect to believe or even to imagine that the word Punjab was good and broad enough to encompass within it the two vastly differing categories of people who differed in every conceivable manner but mostly as a result of economic disparity. Indeed at times it seems the Punjab of the 1940s was really two worlds—more aptly it should have been Punjab I and Punjab II—so vastly different were the problems confronted by the people belonging to these two worlds, so vastly different were their hopes, aspirations and reactions. While one was able, being equipped with resource and education to foresee the clouds of doom and act swiftly, grabbing prime opportunities on both sides, the other, ignorant, superstition-ridden and fatalistic did little more than allow themselves to be pushed around, pawns, by all counts, who allowed their hearts to prevail over their mind. While the mind said they should leave their age-old homes to be safe, the heart, however, compelled them to stay back, hoping perhaps that it was all a bad dream. To this hope was added more hope by wily politicians and officials, who protected there own futures in time but continued to pretend otherwise. How else can we understand the extensive advertisements relating to prime properties that began to appear in important newspapers from mid-1946 itself? A large number of prime properties had been sold and purchased by influential, well-connected people belonging to all the three major communities in Lahore, Amritsar and mainly Delhi well before June 1947.[4]

As early as January 1947, Firoz Khan Noon, the senior Punjab Muslim League leader, had warned that the manner in which Muslims in Punjab were being discriminated against in the supply of essential items like food grain and cloth might lead to riots.[5] During the months preceding the partition of Punjab, widespread shortages of wheat, sugar, rice, kerosene, matchboxes, cloth and coal were regularly reported by most newspapers.[6] Prices of wheat, a staple food in the Punjab, were reported to be manipulated by syndicates.[7] Even rice which was not a major part of the Punjabi's diet was being rationed in 24 towns of Punjab.[8] General Messervy, G.O.C.-in-C. Northern Command, noted that: 'The government controls were mostly in the hands of Sikh or Hindu agents or clerks. The Muslim peasant or labourer was only to ready to get some of his own when he got a chance.'[9]

There were of course Muslim officials too who were doing the same as well. The Ration and Food Inspector Sadat Malik of Gujranwala, for example, was arrested for embezzlement. He was caught removing 28 bags of rice, where he had a permit for only 8 bags. He was denied bail.[10]

Shortages of mill-made cloth were widely reported across Punjab in the first few months of 1947. *The Tribune* reported how homes and shops were raided by officials of the supply department to recover cloth held in excess of the prescribed norms in the small towns of Lyallpur and Kasur. In Lyallpur, for example, 180 yards of mill-made cloth concealed in soap boxes was recovered with much fanfare. In Multan, the ration of cloth per person was reduced from 14 yards to 12 yards.[11] In Dasuya, kerosene it was reported had not been supplied for three months.[12] The supply per family of matchboxes was reportedly increased from 2 to 4 in Muzaffargarh, but only after a prolonged agitation.[13] A deputy commissioner has very aptly recorded the true nature of the problem of cloth distribution 'distribution of cloth was a real problem . . . elaborate instructions would come from above . . . fine and coarse cloth to be issued . . . it was impossible to carry out these instructions as the cloth never arrived'.[14]

A serious problem which confronted the ordinary people of Punjab in the early months of 1947 was the widespread and deep-rooted corruption among (mainly junior) officials of the supplies department.[15] A large number of letters to the editor were appearing in newspapers, complaining how essential supplies were being pilfered from controlled price shops by private traders in connivance with government officials.[16] Two persons posing as food inspectors and attempting to extort money from shop owners were arrested at Ambala.[17] The Lahore Washermen's Union had threatened to strike work if officials of the supplies department did not stop selling the quota of washing soda into the black market.[18]

The shortage of ordinary cloth was also reported to be leading to accidents. The end of Second World War had led to the selling of discarded parachute material in the markets in Punjab. Women were commonly known to use the material because of its texture and for want of better cloth as a garment material. While there were many reports of such clothing catching fire, a woman in Ferozepur was burnt to death when one such garment caught fire.[19] So acute was the problem that Munshi Ahmad Din, an activist of the Congress Socialist Party, said that the Congress could easily have won the support of a vast majority of Muslims provided it had been able to solve just two problems, that of cloth and food grain.[20]

THE PRIVILEGED FEW—PUNJAB I

Even as the vast majority of ordinary people were faced with severe shortages of essential supplies, life for the select and fortunate few in Punjab in the months preceding its partition continued undisturbed. This was the world of which Nanda had written; the markets, restaurants and clubs of Lahore. Advertisement columns regularly offered a flood of luxury items. *The Tribune* reported that 13,00,000 *tolas* of gold had been smuggled into Punjab from Belgium, France and Iran.[21] The price of gold was then about Rs. 75 per *tola*; in comparison, the price of wheat at the time was about Rs. 10 per maund (approximately 40 kg). Items like cigarettes and imported cloth were regularly advertised.

Following constant pressure the Punjab government had lifted the control on the sale and purchase of motor vehicles with effect from

15 April 1947. At the same time, it had also requested the government of India for permission to import 200 American and 150 British cars per month because of the extensive demand. Till April 1947 Punjab had been receiving an average of 70 American and 50 British cars. Reports quoted dealers as saying that there was a waiting list of over two years, and as a result there existed a booming 'black market' for cars. While 33 per cent of all car quotas were reserved for the private use of government officers, an officer went on record admitting that he had been offered a sum of Rs. 16,000 for a Chevorlet which had cost him only Rs. 10,000.[22]

Dance lessons, stage plays, spring flower shows continued undisturbed as did sports events. *The Tribune* reported the Punjab Boxing results on 4 March. On the same day it also covered the visit of the Afghan hockey team to Lahore.[23] And this, as we shall see later, was the eve of the outbreak of widespread violence in Lahore. The Punjab Tennis Championship was announced for 23–30 March. On 16 March *The Tribune* carried a long report of the Aitchinson College Sports Meet and also of an important horse-racing event in Lahore on 15 March.[24] The same day mobsters burnt down 50 villages in Attock.

NEWS AND NEWS REPORTING: EARLY 1947

Lahore as we have seen was the centre of newspaper offices in Punjab, with *The Tribune* and the *Civil Military Gazette* usually setting the trend of debate and the Urdu, Punjabi and Hindi press following close behind. With communication and transport greatly limited, newspaper reporters were also at times known to base reports on word of mouth, as a result news reports were often a readable mixture of fact and rumour. But what more frequently flawed the credibility of newspapers was the open secret of editors and important contributors taking sides. This it seems was also necessary to boost circulation. Charges and countercharges of partisan reporting were commonplace. The *Hindu Outlook*, for example, charged the *Hindustan Times* and the *Dawn* with being mouthpieces of the Congress and the Muslim League, even though it was itself a spokesman for the *Hindu Mahasabha*.[25] A reader, Sharif Hussain, charged the *CMG* for ridiculing the Muslim League in its cartoons and saying nothing against the Congress.[26] When Liaqat Ali the senior League leader warned and called upon the Muslim press to remain uncommercialized and free from capitalist control, he was in fact

We have noted how black market forces had greatly added to the woes of ordinary people. There was hardly a day when reports did not appear complaining of the nexus between influential essential supplies traders and government officials (*Shankar's Weekly*, [illegible] August 1947).

having a dig at the *Hindustan Times* (Delhi) which was then under the management of an important business house.[27]

But having said this, newspapers also provided the only opportunity, or rather platform, for the 'little people', the makers and representatives of common public opinion, to speak their minds. Letters to editors, for example, often told stories very different from other accounts. 'The letter writer', as Jolly has also suggested 'actively exhorts and tugs in a much more urgent form of education . . . (creating) thus national and by implication class consensus.'[28] Letters to editors and similar editorial page contributions in Punjab acted as a medium which knitted smaller issues and events into broader ones. In this sense small events in Punjab were noticed to have actually led to bigger ones with greater and multiple implications.

Day after day headlines announced massacres, arson, rape and abduction. Punjab, however, appeared unmoved and the drift simply continued. Possibly the people of Punjab had fallen into what Susan Moeller calls, the 'My eyes glaze over' or MEGO syndrome. Explaining the possible reasons of why violence and arson committed on large scales often fails to touch the hearts of those not affected by it or those placed at safe distances, Moeller has argued that it 'may be Joseph Stalin was right when he said, one death is a tragedy one million deaths is a statistic'.[29]

One does develop an impression that even as reports of violence began to occupy more and more space from the first week of March 1947, horrific events quite easily became yesterday's news. Desperation turned to reconciliation when ordinary people began to realize that the effort required to restore civil sense and human behaviour was far beyond their personal means. A kind of 'let's move on—its somebody else's problem', attitude was commonplace, and even as newspapers carried hair-raising reports and photos of arson and bloodshed, in adjoining columns, on the same page were reports, photos and advertisements of flower shows, gymkhana meets and dance parties.

The nature of newspaper reporting was also somewhat stereotyped, almost formulaic. *The Tribune* and the *CMG* alone were able to supplement most of their important stories with photographs. Other papers did carry photographs but the cost possibly restricted their use. On 16 March, *The Tribune* published eight photographs of burning buildings in Amritsar.[30] Just as these photographs personified the violence, photographs like the one showing the two captains, Prem and Zaffar, deciding the toss in the final of the Punjab University Cricket Championship,[31] or the photographs that covered the Atchinson College Annual Sports Meet (17 March),[32] even as in large parts of Punjab the fires were still raging, are icons of the Punjab within the Punjab.

The early months of 1947 saw leading newspapers give extensive space to letters and articles, debating events, issues, and providing alternate versions to official reports. In this sense, such letters were a parallel venue for the theories that were being propounded for and against the partition of Punjab, the political chaos, the problems confronting ordinary people. Most importantly, the early signs and indications of the impending doom are in fact first noticeable in the letters' columns of various newspapers.

STUDENTS AND POLITICS

The more disturbing feature of the hatred and tension that had begun to brew from about the beginning of 1946 and which climaxed in the first week of March 1947 was the extent to which divisionist leaders were using and prompting the youth towards taking matters into their own hands. The dramatic fall in the examination pass percentages of students studying in the higher classes for the years 1944, 1945 and 1946 is an important indication of the level to which the youth had been pulled into political activity. *The Tribune* reported a statement of Mian Ibrahim Burq, Education Minister of Punjab, who gave the figures (see Table 2.1).[33]

Muslim League leaders in Punjab had made extensive and special efforts to pull the Muslim youth into active politics. An organized advertisement campaign was launched with leads like, 'What have I done for my nation?' Students of the Aligarh Muslim University played a very important role, a group of whom even attempted to persuade the legendary Khan Abdul Ghaffar Khan to join the Muslim League.[34]

TABLE 2.1: PASS PERCENTAGE—PUNJAB UNIVERSITY LAHORE

	1944	1945	1946
FA	70%	60%	35%
BA	65%	55%	30%
MA	75%	65%	45%

The deep involvement of the youth, particularly at the prompting of the Muslim League, is reflected in the concerted campaign launched by Ahmad Saeed Kirmani, Organizing Secretary of the Punjab Muslim Students Federation, to put pressure on the Vice-Chancellor of Punjab University to select a Muslim candidate to the post of Reader in the Chemical Engineering Department. The Punjab University in general and the Department of Chemical Engineering in particular, said Kirmani, were 'too Hindu ridden'.[35] The Aligarh Economic Writers Association even organized an All India Muslim League Essay Competition. The topics were thoughtfully chosen; 'Economic justification for Pakistan' and 'Methods to lift Muslims Economically'.[36]

When the Sind University Bill was being debated in the Assembly in Karachi, newspapers sympathetic to the Muslim League started their own debate. An editorial in *Dawn*, for example said: 'Hindu chauvinism has become synonymous with communalism . . . Congress opposition to the Bill is only to gain an influential hold in the Senate . . . this is a Muslim province and I think the Muslims should have a potent voice in the administration of the University.'[37]

The Muslim League even led its youth wing leaders in Punjab to target those Muslims in particular who were holding important positions but refusing to toe the League's line. The difficulties for such Muslims were manifold if they happened to be holding important positions in education. One such person who attracted the League's wrath in Punjab was Abdur Rehman, the distinguished Vice-Chancellor of Punjab University. The *Eastern Times* had launched a vicious attack against him: 'Abdur Rehman's tenure has been a period of unmitigated loss for the Muslims. What of the future? Can we break away from the shackles that have made the present University (Punjab) a Hindu body with Muslims tied to its apron? Bertand Glancy (former Governor Punjab) did Muslamans two ugly turns, he made Khizr Hayat Premier and Rehman Vice-Chancellor.'[38]

Among the non-Muslim institutions the DAV College Lahore was not only a leading institution but it also encouraged non-Muslim youth confront the Muslim Students Federation. Of course, it was way behind and could hardly have matched the influence and resources of the Federation. Not many details are actually available on the manner in which students were mobilized in the DAV College, there are, however, some references to students being organized soon after Khizr Hayat resigned. Principal G.L. Dutta was reported to have encouraged students of the college to demonstrate. In fact, the immediate incident that provoked the outbreak of violence in Lahore was the police firing on a student procession most of whom belonged to the DAV College.[39]

KHIZR HAYAT BANS THE RSS & MLNG

We have already seen in the previous chapter how Khizr Hayat came to lead a coalition ministry by outflanking the Muslim League. The League, as we know, had taken this as a challenge and had vowed to teach Khizr and party a lesson.[40] Thus, each day that followed the installation of the coalition ministry headed by Khizr Hayat throughout 1946 was like a step closer to disaster. It was a tough year for Punjab and even tougher for the beleaguered premier Khizr Hayat. A relentless campaign had, as we have already noted, been launched by the Muslim League in Punjab to bring down the coalition government. Far from being able to unitedly face the onslaught of the Muslim League, the coalition government from the very beginning had, because of internal differences begun, to fall apart.

The communal situation had gradually deteriorated particularly, as we have also seen, after the Dussehra week in October 1946. It was in view of the rapidly deteriorating communal situation that, on 29 November 1946, Governor Jenkins promulgated under section 89 of the Act of 1935, the Punjab Public Safety Ordinance. Rather than instil an element of fear among the political activists, the Ordinance further intensified the demand for Khizr Hayat's removal. On 24 January 1947, the Government of Punjab banned the Muslim League National Guard (MLNG) and the Rashtriya Swayamsevak Sangh (RSS), both of which then also represented the organized militant face of the Muslims and Hindus respectively. As Moon puts it: 'The fat was in the fire. The Punjab government had inadvertently offered a challenge to the League without the strength to go through with it.'[41] Viceroy Wavell noted in his journal on 27 January: 'the action taken in the Punjab against the Muslim Guards seems to have raised a storm. . . . The Muslim League leaders in the Punjab seized the opportunity to stir up agitation.'[42]

The ban quite obviously was hardly enforced. Quite in line with the times, decisions were taken but they remained enclosed in office chambers. Those who were expected to implement them on the ground were usually indifferent, already having taken sides on communal lines. The *Eastern Times*, while reporting these events prominently, carried a long letter by Faz-ul-Haq, the Premier of Bengal addressed to Hayat: If each political organisation has a well drilled disciplined militia in its ranks communal and sectional fights will come to an end. In my opinion the central government should compel each political organisation to have one of its own . . . we have no confidence in the military and police of the government. . . . I request you to apologize . . . for what has been done in your name, announcing boldly that you have joined the League.[43]

On the day following the ban on the MLNG the pro Muslim League papers presented it as a challenge to the League: 'Muslim India will not take it lying down'.[44] An editorial based on a statement by Firoz Khan Noon said the MLNG could not be compared with the RSS: 'it is a distortion to say that RSS and MLNG are rival corps . . . RSS activities are based on intense hatred of the Muslims'.[45]

The ban followed routine searches of the offices of the two organizations. Though nothing really objectionable was found, workers who tried to protest and obstruct the raiding parties were arrested. The situation however took a serious turn when 15 Muslim League MLAs were arrested on 25 January when they defied a ban on processions and meetings.[46] Even as newspapers gave much space to the protests and arrests, a somewhat annoyed Secretary of State sent a secret telegram to Wavell: expressing his suspicions that this action was deliberately designed to inflame Muslim feelings and thus ensure that the League did not join the Constituent Assembly.[47] It is difficult to say whether the 'suspicions' of the Secretary of State had some merit or not, the fact, however, is the Muslim League Working Committee met in Bombay on 31 January 1947 and decided to remain outside the Constituent Assembly.

Governor Jenkins' reply to the apprehensions of Secretary of State Pethick-Lawerence merits a detailed mention because it provides perhaps the best view of the important incident. Jenkins reported to Pethick-Lawerence that the matter had been in discussion since the summer of 1946, and that he (Jenkins) had told Khizr that action would have to be taken against both because they were like private communal armies. Interestingly, Jenkins says they would have been banned earlier but for the preoccupation of the police in other matters. Jenkins also drew the Secretary of State's attention to what he thought was the difference between the Muslim League on the one hand and the MLNG on the other: 'Action taken was against MLNG and not against Muslim League. National Guards have a written constitution of their own and an established commander with military titles.'

Jenkins also stated that the action was taken in concurrence with Khizr, even though he pointed out that Khizr had no idea of how seriously the League would view it. He went on to rule out any political angle in the decision, something which the Secretary of State had earlier inferred. On 26 January, Jenkins penned a long note to Wavell, that discussed the political scene following the arrest of the MLNG cadres. In the same note, Jenkins also added an interesting assessment: 'I am convinced that Muslim League are not as strong as they believe . . . Khizr's best hope is probably to win a victory on the law and order side and then to be very conciliatory, but he is undoubtedly in for unpleasant times.'[48]

A day later, Jenkins once again stressed to the Viceroy that the RSS was in fact a 'Hindu private army' and also explained that he had not initiated action against the Akali *jathas* because Sikhs had 'responded very well to request not to intervene in Hazara'.[49]

Even as Jenkins had refused to see a link between the banning of the MLNG and the League's refusal to join the Constituent Assembly, Viceroy Wavell informed the Secretary of State that not only had Khizr miscalculated the whole situation but also that 'events in the Punjab may have a fatal effect on the decision', i.e. of the League not joining the Assembly, and using the banning of the MLNG as an excuse for the same.[50]

Pethick-Lawerence's reply to Wavell sums up the blunder, or so they thought: 'after hesitating so long Khizr should have taken it into his head to ban the two organizations just in the week before the Muslim League was due to meet, the rise in temperatures this may have caused will destroy any possibility of the League coming into the Constituent Assembly'.[51]

It is also interesting to note that even though Jenkins had claimed joint responsibility for the decision, the British centres of power, both in Delhi and in London, had put the entire responsibility for banning the MLNG and the RSS and the serious political reactions that followed on the shoulders of Khizr. The fact remains, however, that Khizr could not possibly have taken the decision on his own, and that if Governor Jenkins was a party—which he admitted he was—there was no way the Viceroy and the Secretary of State could have remained unaware of it.

That Khizr could have decided to ban the MLNG and the RSS at the bidding of 'sources' in the Muslim League so as to give them an excuse to stay out of the Constituent Assembly cannot really be ruled out notwithstanding the great humiliation and insult he faced at the hands of League supporters in the subsequent days. It is the timing of the decision to ban the RSS and the MLNG that creates this suspicion. On the face of it there was no other or immediate cause.

Among those who came out in support of Khizr and Jenkins—for banning the RSS and MLNG in Punjab—was Sardar Baldev Singh. He strongly supported the banning of the two organizations and declared he 'was completely satisfied with the way things had been handled'.[52]

The banning of both the RSS and the MLNG had been projected by the Government of Punjab as an assertive, no nonsense action of people who now meant business. The withdrawal of the ban on 29 January, sadly sent exactly the opposite signal—the government was helpless and even more so its Premier.

For newspapers committed to the League's cause the withdrawal of the ban was a natural victory for the League.[53] On the same day, four prominent League supporting newspapers announced that they were suspending publication being unable to work under the restrictions imposed on them by the provisions of the Punjab Public Safety Ordinance. The papers were specifically protesting against provisions that debarred newspapers from discussing the provisions of the Ordinance.[54]

On 30 January, the *Eastern Times* published an appeal, 'Smash the Ministry'. The decision to withdraw the ban on the RSS and the MLNG did not, however, go down well with Wavell. Once again Khizr was held responsible for the muddle: 'Khizr was clearly wrong to take action against the private armies if he did not propose to see it through . . . but one effect of his resiling . . . is that the Muslim League are now on the wrong foot . . . they have rejected the proper democratic course of prosecuting the case in the legislature'. There was another important line in this note: 'Khizr will find himself under tremendous pressure it seems more than likely that his days as Premier are numbered.'[55]

There was little doubt that Khizr was heading for troubled times. Tension rapidly grew from the first week of February and widespread demonstrations were organized and reported from all districts. What was however an increasingly new phenomenon was, as Jenkins noted, that the agitation had the sympathy of almost all Muslim officials and non-officials.[56] Jenkins did, however, absolve the police of partiality, a charge that was being made vociferously by newspapers sympathetic to the Hindus and Sikhs.[57] He noted: 'Police have been staunch and good humoured. Participants are mainly politicians and their women folks and Muslims of poorer classes.'[58]

ATTLEE ANNOUNCES PLANS TO TRANSFER POWER: 20 FEBRUARY 1947

On 20 February, Prime Minister Attlee announced in the House of Commons that his government had decided to transfer power not later than 30 June 1948, and that power would be transferred to a form of central government and even if required to existing provincial governments. The most significant point made was that this would be done irrespective of whether or not an understanding had been reached between the Congress and the Muslim League. Attlee also told the House of Commons that Wavell was being replaced by Earl Mountbatten because the 'opening of this new and final phase in India is the appropriate time to terminate the war time appointment.'[59]

Before we take up the wide-ranging and far-reaching impact the announcement came to have in Punjab, a passing reference needs to be made to the replacement of Lord Wavell, an issue which attracted much attention. Sir Winston Churchill in fact had pressed the Prime Minister to give details of why Wavell was being removed, the Prime Minister however had made no comment.[60]

> In Delhi it was said that Wavell had been recalled at the demand of the Congress which felt Wavell was pro-Muslim . . . but Wavell was neither pro-Muslim nor pro-Congress; he was pro-India; he saw the dangers ahead . . . Wavell was full of goodwill but he had the wrong personality; he could not make people relax nor could he manipulate them . . . Mountbatten was quite different; he was born with the gift of ease . . . and his wife was an immense asset to him; she took India by storm and enslaved Nehru at first sight.[61]

Nehru had met Mountbatten only once before, this was in March 1946 in Singapore. Mountbatten was Supreme Commander of the Allied Force in South-East Asia and Nehru was on a private visit to Singapore. Mountbatten touched down in Delhi on 22 March 1947. Authorities in London were said to have asked Mountbatten to 'down play' the visit, Mountbatten on the contrary did the opposite, saying, 'Nehru was too important to be ignored'. Hodson has also noted that both hit it off instantly.[62]

Whether the Congress or Nehru to be specific had a role in the appointment of Mountbatten is of course only conjecture the real story obviously lies wrapped up in some file, but the fact remains that Mountbatten's relations with Nehru were altogether on a different level as compared to other leaders, both of the Congress and of the Muslim League. Numerous examples of this warm friendship emerged in the days that followed, which will be discussed in the following chapter.

The official communication conveying the change in the Government House, Delhi was received by Wavell on 19 February 1947. Moon has added a note to Wavell's entry of 19 February in the *Viceroys Journal*: 'HMG has accused Wavell of inconsistency because having strongly pressed when in London that a final date should be announced for transfer of power he had later transmitted reports from Jenkins . . . opposing such a course.'[63]

In the context of Punjab and even for matters in Delhi, Penderel Moon would easily fit into the smallest list of British officials—if such a list were drawn—who understood the ground realities as they prevailed in 1947. It is therefore surprising that even Moon should have gone for the theory that Wavell was removed for 'inconsistency', more so at a time when most senior functionaries, not only among the British but even more so among the Congress and to a lesser degree among the Muslim League, were nothing if not inconsistent. The list of exceptions to this would easily include at the top people like Patel and at the lower level someone like Jenkins.

Interestingly, among the ranks of the British officers in the Indian army Wavell's removal appears not to have gone down well. 'Wavell who had been stressing to the British Government, the problems that lay ahead was replaced without warning. . . . Wavell had told Auchinleck, "I have been dismissed as if I were a crook".'[64]

But coming back to the Punjab, Jenkins could hardly be blamed, for if anyone had been foreseen this it was he. Wavell's Private Secretary had in fact shown to Jenkins (a few days before it was made public) a copy of the statement that Prime Minister Attlee was to make in the House of Commons. Jenkins not only dubbed the draft statement as 'astonishingly vague' but also noted:

the document is intended to bring the Congress and Muslim League up against reality and to force them to cooperate with one another. In my judgement it will have the diametrically opposite effect . . . the tendency will be for all parties to seize power as they can if necessary by force.[65]

It needs no emphasis to note that Jenkins had little hope of maintaining law and order in the possibility of a major outbreak. Jenkins made another very important, and crucial observation regarding the British officers serving in Punjab: 'I do not see how British officers whose original contracts are being ended can be forced to serve on as men without hope in conditions which will certainly involve great personal risks. People will take risks in a good cause but not in a faction fight which is none of our business.' He went on to make what is perhaps the boldest prediction of what was likely to happen in the Punjab: 'The statement will be regarded as the prelude to the final communal show down and the disturbances from it might be of the gravest description.'

Jenkins, as we shall see later, had been at the receiving end of both the Congress and the Muslim League leaders, but this note leaves little doubt of how well he understood the situation and how much in advance he had issued the alarm call: 'The decision of HMG to leave India by a stated date is a very dangerous decision amounting to an invitation to the parties to make real war upon one another.'[66] Jenkins found even 1948 as an impossible date to hand over power so one can imagine his state of mind when he learnt a couple of months later that the process was being but forward by almost a year.

Widespread demonstrations and counter-demonstrations were organized in the following days. Amritsar, Ambala, Jullundur saw major incidents, police firings, and deaths on both sides. A new dimension in the renewed demonstrations that had started in the beginning of 1947 on behalf of the League was the great increase in the number of women who took to the streets demanding the removal of the Khizr ministry.[67] *CMG* editorial discussed how for the first time women wearing *burqas* had taken to the streets in Punjab. The editorial also said that the activities of these Muslim women were bound to cause a stir among women in other countries.[68]

Jack Mortan who was SSP of Lahore until March 1947 has left an interesting record of how the Lahore police handled men and women VIP leaders, particularly women who belonged to elite families: 'The Muslim League's assault was directed by Khizr's cousin the opportunist Firoz Khan Noon . . . supported by his ravishingly beautiful wife (a European) who it was said was his housekeeper when he was High Commissioner for India in London.' Since she had on many occasions led processions Mortan asked Firoz Khan what the police should do with Mrs Noon. Firoz Khan, Mortan records, advised him to arrest her and take her out of the city and then make her walk back. He learnt later that Firoz Khan had arranged for a vehicle to follow the police van and pick up the ladies when they were dropped off. As for dealing with Muslim League VIP's arrested during the agitations Mortan has recorded that almost always the leaders were taken to police stations after being arrested in full view of the public, served tea and snacks and after the crowds had dispersed sent home.[69]

Nehru's reaction to the 20 February statement was released to the press on 22 February. Nehru felt it was 'obscure in some places', but its 'outstanding feature . . . is the decision of the British government to transfer power to Indian hands not later than June 1948'. He went on to call it 'wise and courageous', and hoped that the past, with all its ill-will and conflict, was over.[70] The Viceroy's entry in his journal on 21 February reads: 'In the evening I had about an hour each with Nehru and Liaquat. They were both friendly, both I think were quite impressed with the statement. Nehru described it as a courageous document.'[71] On the replacement of Wavell as Viceroy, Nehru was reported to have said, 'I have a high regard for him . . . he has carried a heavy burden, in many ways I shall be sorry to part with him'.[72]

The impact the 20 February statement left on Nehru and how concerned he was with its contents stands out in a number of letters he wrote in the following days discussing the statement and making reference to his own reaction to it. In a letter of 23 February to Krishna Menon he discussed the implications of the statement and referred to the possibility that it might 'inevitably mean a division of Punjab and Bengal, bringing the richer parts of both these provinces including the city of Calcutta into the (Indian) Union'.[73]

On 24 February, Nehru wrote to Wavell: 'You must have seen a statement I have issued giving my reaction to Mr. Attlee's statement in the House of Commons on 20 February . . . I have deliberately not referred in my statement to many matters which are by no means clear. I wanted to emphasise on the dominant features.' Importantly, Nehru also referred in the letter to how members of the central (Interim) government were encouraging 'Direct Action' and law-breaking in Punjab and how the problem had spread to NWFP. In a letter to Asaf Ali on 24 February Nehru again referred to the possible partition of Punjab.

To Gandhi Nehru wrote: 'Attlee's statement contains much that is indefinite and likely to give trouble. But I am convinced that in the final analysis a brave and definite statement. It may not be as we would have liked it. But the real thing is they have finally decided and announced that they are quitting. Whatever their motives might be they cannot go back on this'.[74] Interestingly all these letters carried references to the Asian conference which was to open in New Delhi on 23 March (discussed in detail later), and how involved Nehru was in it.

The British Prime Minister's statement drew widespread and varying reactions, but one that requires specific attention, essentially because it came from a man widely respected in Punjab, is that of Baba Kharak Singh. He said the root of the problem in Punjab was the proposal in the 20 February statement that power would be handed over to governments in position in the provinces. This he said 'was a signal for civil war . . . I am convinced that the idea to divide India was conceived by some clever British politician . . . it is a pity that Indian leaders have been duped by these tactics. . . . As long as we place reliance on foreigner's awards, our house will never be put in order.'[75] Clearly Kharak Singh disagreed completely with Nehru's perception of the 20 February announcement and its implications.

Janvani was a popular Hindi monthly from Benaras, its significance was in that Acharya Narendra Dev was on its editorial panel and gave it his guidance. Ramnandan Mishra, in an article, charged Nehru for behaving as if he were the elected Prime Minister of free India and 'all and only on the ground of his great personality'.[76]

The British Prime Minister's statement also drew extensive attention in the *Hindu Outlook*, the mouthpiece of the Hindu Mahasabha, one of the main opponents of Nehru and the Congress. On 25 February, the *Hindu Outlook* published its reaction in a lengthy editorial:

> By putting such a heavy premium on Muslim intransigence the British government is instigating civil strife and disorder. We are afraid that instead of resolving the deadlock the statement would give rise to chaos . . . even if the British part with power they will do so after partitioning the country, the departure will be followed by the worst kind of civil strife.[77]

Some days later, the *Hindu Outlook* again gave most of its space to Attlee's statement. It quoted Dr Syama Prasad Mookerjee who seems to have been inclined to accept the proposals provided power was handed over to a strong central government if chaos was to be avoided.[78] This is important because for one, while the Hindu Mahasabha was against the British Prime Minister's Plan, its most important and well-known figure had come out with views not very different from Nehru's.

A week later, the Hindu Mahasbha's official reaction to the statement was released by L.B. Bhopatkar, President of the All India Hindu Mahasabha: 'it was good that the British government had given a date for quitting India, but what was more important was that the scheme contained a threat to divide India'.[79]

In yet another strongly worded editorial, the *Hindu Outlook* charged the Indian National Congress with having betrayed the cause of a united India:

> By its resolution on Clement Attlee's statement (20 February) the Congress has given a final blow to the integrity and unity of this ancient land and has surrendered Pakistan to the Muslims.[80]

To Deshpande, Secretary All India Hindu Mahasabha, the 20 February statement was in fact a challenge to Hindu India. As tension was beginning to build in Punjab, Deshpande also delivered a surcharged address to students of the DAV College, Lahore.[81] So worked up was the Hindu Mahasabha against the proposals that were contained in the 20 February statement that its 'mouthpiece' the *Hindu Outlook*, even went to the extent of disapproving the stand taken by Veer Savarkar and Dr Mookrjee on Attlee's statement:

> It is unfortunate that the prophet of Hindu nationalism like Veer Savarkar should have blessed the ill advised move and the powerful champion of the Hindu cause like Dr S.P. Mookerjee should have come forward to advocate and popularise a plan which would pave the way for Pakistan.[82]

The *HT* in a lead article suggested that Attlee's statement indicated 'that the British government had at least seen the light and taken a historic decision which will finally end the Indo-British conflict'.[83] *Dawn* saw in Attlee's statement the early evidence of what the Muslim League had been saying all along. Interestingly, *Dawn* also saw in the statement a rebuff to the Congress (and Nehru in particular) who had been demanding the removal of the League ministers from the interim government. So supportive did *Dawn* find Attlee's statement to the League's cause that it even absolved Viceroy Wavell of all he may have done in the past to harm the Muslim League and the Muslims.[84]

The reaction of *Dawn* needs also to be seen in relation to the assessment made by Governor Jenkins of the direct impact of his Prime Minister's statement on political relations in Punjab. For one, Jenkins had noted that the statement had pushed Khizr Hayat closer to the Muslim League.[85]

The *CMG* took the debate on the pros and cons of partitioning Punjab back by almost twenty years when it published a letter which had been written by H.S.L. Polok to the *Manchester Guardian*. Polok said:

As for the Punjab where partition is now being advocated, I recall an interesting conversation I had with the Lajpat Rai some 20 years ago . . . I suggested to him for the sake of an argument as a possible solution the partition of the province. . . . To my surprise he replied that much as he disliked the idea, as it would bring about better communal relations he would support partition.[86]

Sections of the Lahore press also carried a report based on the House of Lords Debate with regard to the latest stand of the British Government. One report cited conservative leader Sir Templewood as having said that the June 1948 date by which the government had announced its intentions to withdraw was in conflict with earlier policies and that the prime consideration should be of ensuring a orderly transfer of power.[87] *Dawn* published extensive details of the debate in the House of Lords. Lord Newal called the proposed transfer of power 'a rash gamble'. while Lord Listowel said that it was 'not the evacuation of a hostile country but the transfer of political power to a people who I believe from various accounts are better disposed towards us than they have ever been'.[88]

True possibly, but soon after the statement the Viceroy painted a rather bleak picture from the British point of view:

Our power in India has always depended on prestige rather than numbers, and it is the decline in our prestige than the lack of numbers that has reduced our control in India to its present state of something approaching impotence . . . the longer we stay the more risk we run of being involved in a civil war and being eventually forced to scuttle ignominiously.[89]

On Punjab, Wavell noted:

The position of the government has been unstable ever since the last election. . . . A month ago Premier Khizr decided to ban two institutions which are really 'political armies, the RSS and the MLNG. . . . He expected no trouble but the League reacted so strongly to the suppression of the Guards that he withdrew the ban. The situation is dangerous . . . rival communities are not balanced. . . . Hindus and Sikhs are getting restive and trouble in Punjab is likely to take a violent form.

A few days after the new plan had been announced and everyone who mattered was expressing his view on the policy, Governor Jenkins made an important communication to Secretary of State Pethick-Lawerence, sounding a serious word of caution

Importantly, Jenkins gave an early hint of how Khizr had softened towards the League and had become inclined to settle problems with the League leadership. What is even more important in the letter is Jenkin's view that 'in new conditions present ministry cannot carry on for long and that if chaos amounting to civil war is to be avoided there must be a ministry representing bulk of Muslims and Sikhs'.[90]

There were many other senior British civil servants who believed like Jenkins that Attlee's statement 'was unlikely to have the intended effect' (i.e. to shock Indians into accepting).[91]

The most apparent result of the statement in Punjab was that starting early spring the print media was forcefully debating and predicting the almost certain disaster towards which Punjab was heading. The *Eastern Times* carried a report stating that some people who were following the events of Punjab in the USA had predicted a civil war.[92] The next day *Dawn*, as just noted, in its long report on the House of Lords Debate (25 February 1947) on the Transfer of Power in India, said that many members who participated in the debate expressed the fear of widespread violence in India.[93]

It appears that a story carried by the *Eastern Times* predicting civil war in Punjab was actually carried some days earlier by the *New York Times*, which had published an interview with Master Tara Singh. Tara Singh had given this interview on 28 February, obviously as a reaction to the 20 February statement of Prime Minister Attlee. This same version was also reported by *The Tribune*: 'I do not see how we can avoid civil war . . . although of course we should try.' The report also cited, perhaps for the first time, Tara Singh saying that the Sikhs were organizing their own army in response to the Muslim League National Guard.[94]

This statement of Tara Singh drew attention across the country. *Abhyudaya* devoted a special editorial to it. It did not refer to Tara Singh by name but said that Akali leaders had warned that they would not compromise with the Muslims until there was dramatic improvement in the situation and the League changed its attitude. The editorial also appreciated the manner in which the Akalis were committed to standing side by side with the Hindus and had even declared that they would not betray the Hindus however hard the Muslim League may try to pull the Sikhs away from them.[95]

KHIZR HAYAT STEPS DOWN: PUNJAB RACES TO DISASTER

As expected and perhaps planned by Jenkins and his team, Khizr stepped down from the premiership of Punjab on the evening of 2 March (1947). Nanda, a witness to the times, recorded: 'From the purely personal point of view Sir Khizr secured in the eyes of the Muslim League following a somewhat honourable exit from an unpopular position. From the political point of view his resignation opened the sluice gates of anarchy.'[96] Various anti-Muslim League sections of the press had also come out with stories of how the elements of the government were used to facilitate the resignation of Khizr.

While Khizr said he had resigned because he could not possibly lead a coalition ministry in Punjab in which the Muslim League was not represented,[97] Wavell, however, believed that he had resigned because of the 20 February statement.[98] *The Tribune* said Khizr's resignation was forced by a section of the Muslim elements in the bureaucracy, particularly the police who had joined hands with the Muslim League.[99] *The Tribune*'s assessment was in line with what many leaders belonging to parties other than the Muslim League had been repeatedly emphasizing at the time. Mota Singh and Sardul Singh Caveeshar, for example, had said that the riots were the making of the employees of the government.[100]

It is of course difficult to categorically state whether Khizr's resignation was spontaneous or had been planned. Jenkins in a letter to Wavell informed the Viceroy that Khizr had mentioned to him his desire of spending May (1947) in Europe, an indication that Khizr had been toying with the idea of resigning for some time. But at the same time there are also important indications that even Jenkins was surprised because at the time of the resignation he had in fact been working on the details for the budget session of the Punjab Legislative Assembly.[101] The SSP of Lahore, W.H.A. Rich, who had been working extended hours preparing for the Assembly's session had no indication of the impending resignation.[102] Bhimsen Sachar, the senior Congress leader of Punjab, met Jenkins at 11 a.m. on 3 March. Jenkins has recorded that Sachar looked tired and appeared to have been awake the whole night, i.e. the night of 2–3 March, giving an indication of the political heat of Lahore in which Khizr had resigned.[103]

On 10 March the *HT's* special correspondent in New Delhi wrote 'The Congress Working Committee resolution passed on Saturday says the Khizr ministry was torpedoed by high authorities who aligned with the Muslim League. Presumably these included the Viceroy, the Governor of Punjab, a Judge and certain League ministers of the Interim Government in Delhi.'[104]

Khizr's resignation was widely welcomed by the Muslim League. A massive procession, unprecedented in enthusiasm was organized by Muslim women in Lahore to celebrate the Muslim League's victory in having forced Khizr Hayat to resign.[105] The next day (4 March), most newspapers carried reports that the Punjab Muslim League leader Iftikhar Hussain Khan Mamdot had been invited to form the ministry.[106] *The Tribune* even reported Mamdot seeking Hindu and Sikh cooperation to build a prosperous Punjab and especially the cooperation of the Sikhs to uplift the economy.[107] Mamdot's offer had no meaning and the response of the Akalis that they would oppose the establishment a government by the League was not surprising.[108]

The important issue after Khizr's stepping down was naturally who would form the ministry. And this is what the politicians of all colours in Punjab in the days that followed were essentially concerned about. As the Sikhs and Hindus joined hands to prevent a League-led ministry, the League's leaders understood fully that a ministry under their control would only make the sailing to the dream of Pakistan many times smoother.

As Lahore witnessed its largest ever political rally on 4 March, Master Tara Singh's famous 'Live or Die' statement was carried by newspapers on the same day. Also on the same day, *The Tribune* reported the Congress party's resolve to oppose the formation of any Muslim League-led ministry in Punjab.[109]

WAVELL RULES OUT MUSLIM LEAGUE MINISTRY IN PUNJAB

As expected, Khizr Hayat's resignation from the premiership threw up a whole bundle of questions and problems. While Jenkins and party came up with a list of reasons of why a League ministry was not possible, the main reason really was simple. Nehru in a letter to Viceroy Wavell shared his apprehensions that the League was adamant on forming a ministry in Punjab only to make it easy for itself to take the whole of Punjab into Pakistan.[110] The week that followed Khizr's resignation saw extensive exchanges of notes between Governor Jenkins and his superiors in New Delhi and London. That the British were in doubt both ways—that is, whether to allow Mamdot to form a League-led ministry or not, stands out in some of these communications.

Just as Punjab was rapidly being overrun by violence, Jenkins noted the specific reasons of why a League ministry was not possible at that point: 'Private information suggests that Mamdot commands only 3 votes outside the League including 1 Muslim and 2 Scheduled Castes. Risk of installing a League Ministry of this kind with parliamentary majority is enormous . . . [and would] be a fraud on the constitution.'[111] Jenkins then pointed out how the installation of a League ministry was bound to be opposed by the Sikhs and Hindus and how 'Police, troops and myself (the British) would immediately be involved on the Muslim side in what would in fact be a civil war for possession of Punjab.[112]

The very next day Wavell too informed the Secretary of State on why the League could not be invited to form government. Wavell's telegram was quite in line with Jenkins' views, and he categorically stated that the League could not be invited to form the government, and section 93 (Governor's rule) would have to continue.[113]

The Muslim League continued its pressure on the Governor to invite the League to form the government. This continued throughout March, April and till about the middle of May. In a long reply to a letter from Mamdot, Jenkins repeated the main reasons for why a Muslim League government was not possible at that stage in Punjab. In sum, Jenkins told Mamdot that the League by forcing Khizr Hayat to resign had surrendered the right to talk of constitutional means. He reminded Mamdot that the coalition ministry headed by Khizr Hayat had a larger majority in the Assembly, larger even than Mamdot was claiming for himself after Khizr had resigned, and that any communal ministry led by the Muslim League would never have the support of a large section of the Hindus and Sikhs.[114]

PUSHING PEOPLE TO THE EDGE

In the days that preceded and followed the outbreak of the disturbances, many leaders vied with each other in issuing threatening statements. The tenor and content of these statements in a way set the agenda for the rest of 1947. In an article titled 'Anatomy of Aggression', *Dawn* published a series of attributed statements.[115] Giani Kartar Singh is reported to have said 'This day the crusade starts'. Even the relatively milder Punjab Congress leader Gopi Chand Bhargava was quoted as saying: 'During these days stage such demonstrations that the renegades amongst us may find it impossible to reach a settlement with the Muslim League.' The article also carried a statement made by Master Tara Singh on 4 March: 'Our motherland is calling for blood . . . we crushed Mughalism and we shall trample Pakistan . . . the Sikhs ruled the Muslims with their might and even now shall rule.[116] G.D. Khosla, the eminent jurist who was later entrusted with reporting on partition-related violence, termed these actions of Tara Singh as antics and childish pranks.[117] J.N. Mandal, Law Member of the Interim Government of India came out in support of the Muslim League and was reported in the same article to have said: 'Muslims will establish Pakistan in Punjab, what will Stone Gods do? Mr Gandhi is our enemy No.1. I have joined hands with League because Muslims and Scheduled Castes are both poor and backward—they are mostly labourers at least in Bengal . . . Jinnah is a leader not only of Muslims.'[118]

This flood of provocative statements brought Lahore to a frenzy. with the ban on processions still in force, Bhimsen Sachar, Congress leader and finance minister in the outgoing Khizr Hayat ministry, led a procession to the Legislative Assembly and proclaimed to the collected crowd: 'I as member of the government hereby declare that you have every right to take out processions.'[119] On 25 February, *Hindu Outlook* had published a report based on a speech made by Ghazanfar Ali Khan in Lahore, in which he talked of the manner in which Mohammad Bin Kasim and Mahmud Ghazni had conquered parts of India with just a few thousand soldiers. This report while quoting Ghazanfar Ali had also said the Hindus were capable of doing the same—meaning the Muslims needed to be ready.[120]

The rally organized by the Muslim League in Lahore (4 March) to celebrate the resignation of the Khizr Ministry was attended by over 300,000 people.[121] Among others, the rally was addressed by Bhai Hari Singh, a prominent leader of the Mazbhi Sikhs: 'we 20 lac Mazbhi Sikhs have been and are maltreated by caste Sikhs/Akalis and . . . we will fight along with . . . the Musalmans . . . for the achievement of Pakistan . . . people.'[122]

A worried Jenkins noted: 'Yesterday March 3 Muslims in Lahore were jubilant and noisy. Non-Muslims especially Sikhs were correspondingly exasperated and at night a very large non-Muslim meeting was held at which violent speeches were made by Congress and Sikh leaders.'[123]

LAHORE BURSTS INTO FLAMES

It all started on 4 March with police firing on a not very large procession, mainly of Hindus and Sikhs, led, it appears, by students of whom. 125 were seriously injured and 10, all students of the DAV college, were killed. Later reports indicated that Principal G.L. Dutta had encouraged the students of his college to counter the League supporting youth.[124] Some sections of the press, sympathetic to the League, prominently displayed appeals by Mamdot to League activists not to organize counter demonstrations.[125] But the spark had been lit—there was now no stopping.

Jenkins' report of the incident said:

Today there has been much communal tension. During the morning student procession mostly Hindus clashed with the police and later raided Police office damaging property and injuring about 30 policemen of whom two have succumbed. This afternoon communal rioting has broken out in Lahore . . . Congress and Sikhs are determined to resist Muslim rule . . . situation is grave without coalition trouble on large scale seems inevitable.[126]

Jenkins had met Wavell on 13 March, and told the Viceroy that there was no doubt in that the trouble in Amritsar was started by non-Muslims.[127]

. . . non-Muslim students of Lahore were to hold a meeting at Gol Bagh. The meeting was banned and did not take place. Some of the students however, collected in a square in front of the Government College and tried to organise a *hartal*. Principal Bhukhari called the police and the peaceful crowd was subjected to indiscriminate firing. A number of persons were killed. . . . Another procession of non-Muslim students was attacked in the afternoon by Muslim League National Guards. This was a prelude.[128]

The *Dawn*'s version of the incident was in line with that of the *Eastern Times*, that Hindu and Sikh students had torn down a Muslim League flag, but it added that the students had also raised 'Pakistan *Murdabad*' slogans.[129] On 5 March, *The Tribune* came out with a strongly worded editorial that questioned the brutal use of force on young students. The *Hindu Outlook* also gave its version of the disturbances that rocked Punjab on its foundations in the first week of March:

By his resignation Khizr paved the way for Pakistan. All the anti-Pakistan elements were given a challenge and the battle in Punjab had begun. The Hindu students Federation in Lahore organised a massive demonstration on 4 March. . . . The Sikh students Federation joined the procession and . . . the Muslim Police took offensive. . . . The procession was passing through Hindu localities peacefully . . . [when it] was fired upon—up to now it was only a clash between the processionists and the police, but the Muslims jumped in and the riots began.[130]

The *Hindustan Times* which had in the first week of March spared most of its space for opposing the increase on profit taxes on business carried a report on 9 March saying the 'conflict in Punjab was not a religious conflict . . . essentially a struggle for power'. To *Dawn* it was war as indicated in a fearsome editorial on 6 March titled 'Should Storm Clouds Break over Punjab':

massive riots are coming . . . the Sikhs will join the Hindus, the RSS will support the Sikhs when rival claims are submitted to the arbitration of force . . . if Muslim patience is mistaken for weakness it is a grave miscalculation . . . the sword in Punjab is a free weapon, the Muslim hand is not unaccustomed to it.

By the morning of 6 March the major towns across Punjab including Amritsar, Jullundur, Rawalpindi, Multan and Sialkot were up in flames.[131] Most north- and west-bound trains out of Lahore were cancelled.[132] The sale of petrol and diesel was banned in many cities of Punjab.[133] Outgoing phone calls and telegrams from Lahore too were banned.[134]

A.J.V. Arthur, the Deputy Commissioner of Multan, has left a detailed record of the outbreak of violence in Multan on 5 March. He said the disturbances started around midday and were generally under control by about 3 p.m., and that the 'communal riot scheme could not be put into force because the situation was far worse than had been envisaged in the scheme'. He recorded 'undescribable scenes of brutality and bestality'. But what is important in his version of the report he filed on 6 March is that in his view, even as the origin was not quite certain the inflammatory speeches made by Muslim League leaders in Lahore on the previous day had led to great resentment in Multan among Hindus and Sikhs. It was against this background that the Hindu and Sikh students of Emerson College and DAV High School took out an 'unauthorized' procession at 11 a.m. in which provocative slogans were raised against the Muslim League. It was then that the procession was attacked near Behar Gate.[135]

Pitched battles were reported in Lahore on 5 March, with a DIG of police being injured with a brickbat.[136] Amritsar became an inferno with 27 deaths and over a 100 serious injuries on 6 March. 'The town (Lahore) and suburbs resounded with war cries . . . members of one community collected by beating of drums.'[137] Amritsar was taken over by the Army on 7 March.

On 8 March the *Dawn* editorialized: 'Tara Singh and his fellow members will do well to ask themselves just what are they waving kirpans for.[138] On 7 March, *The Tribune* was the only newspaper to be published in Lahore even as its hawkers were prevented from distributing it.[139] Murree and Taxila were burnt down on 9 March.[140]

At first count it was reported that Amritsar alone had suffered a loss of Rs. 8 crore in two days, this included the burning down of 5,000 houses.[141] The SGPC said that up to 22 May 1947, starting from March 174 Sikhs, 69 Hindus and 85 Muslims had been killed in Amritsar alone.[142] Jhelum was ravaged on 14 March and Attock on 16 March.[143] *The Indian Annual Register* reported that during the disturbances (March 1947) the number of deaths was about 10,538 in rural areas and 511 in the cities of Punjab.[144] Punjab's home secretary A.A. Macdonald had given a figure of 2,090 dead, but said the casualties were likely to be much higher.[145]

Champat Rai, Secretary of the Refugees Rehabilitation Committee, Lajpat Rai Bhawan, Lahore, said in letter that (since March 1947) at least 40,000 persons had been rendered homeless and that about 4,000 married men had been killed in the riots.[146]

The *Hindu Outlook* published a table of deaths and injuries (see Table 2.2) in communal riots for the period starting 18 November 1946 to May 1947. It concluded its figures from a speech made by Secretary of State Listowell, while replying to a Parliamentary question.[147]

The government in Punjab had known, as noted earlier, that the violence was coming. But surprisingly the response to the early violence lacked enthusiasm and even a sense of urgency. The government did, of course, initiate many measures, one was its old and tried method of collective fines. A fine of Rs. 10 lakh was imposed within the municipal limits of Multan. Those families that had lost

TABLE 2.2: DEATH AND INJURIES (NOVEMBER 1946–MAY 1947)

Province	Deaths	Injuries
Madras	0	13
Bombay	32	1,119
Bengal	186	965
United Provinces	17	53
Punjab	3,024	1,200
Bihar	70	135
Central Provinces	2	12
Assam	15	0
NWFP	414	150
Delhi	29	69

members as killed or injured or suffered serious damage of property were exempted. A collective fine of Rs. 1 lakh was also later imposed on the residents of Hodal for the 25 March riots.[148]

Both these decisions attracted criticism from non-Muslim activists. Bhim Sen Sachar, for example, spoke against the manner in which the fine was determined in Multan: 'To make owners of property alone to pay the fine is not necessarily [to] the punish the culprits'.[149] Likewise, the fine imposed in Hodal was opposed by the Hindus of the town on the grounds that the total loss of property was just Rs. 3,000 even though 8 people had been killed.[150]

The orders of the Deputy Commissioner, Multan were later altered by Governor Jenkins. The fine was ordered to be collected in the ratio of Rs. 6 lakh from Muslims and Rs. 4 lakh from Hindus. A number of people were exempted—a family whose member had been killed; property destroyed; serving soldiers, government servants; bank staff; women not owning immovable property.[151]

In response to the large number of reports that indicated involvement in the riots not only of pensioned soldiers and other officials but even of serving ones who may have been on leave, the government issued a statement saying cases of such involvement were being closely examined and strict action was proposed including the cancelling of pension and other benefits.[152]

An official spokesman told the press that over 8,000 arrests had been made in Multan alone.[153] Surprisingly, the ratio of actual trials and prosecutions for the March disturbances was never revealed. As we shall see later, trials and prosecutions of culprits were rare in

Punjab particularly, when compared with Bihar. In any case, no complete figures of arrests, trials, cases registered, prosecuted, etc., were officially stated in Punjab.[154] A *CMG* report of 29 April did however state that 2,781 people were arrested in Rawalpindi and Jhelum, and these included some big landlords, *zaildars* and ex-servicemen.

Among the decisions of the government that were widely appreciated was the continued deployment of army units in sensitive villages to enable farmers to harvest the crops.[155] Another decision that was welcomed was the fact-finding committee's decision to collect information based on a questionnaire to assess damage to life and property.[156]

Incidentally, the deployment of troops had also involved some British officers, a decision for which Governor Jenkins was pulled up. What really happened in this case was that as violence erupted in Amritsar, the 2/2 Punjab Regiment that was stationed in Amritsar and included British personnel was deployed. On 13 March the Secretary of State telegrammed Jenkins seeking an immediate explanation as a reply was to be filed in Parliament on 17 March. Jenkinss' handwritten note indicates that it was done only because the troops were readily available and that they had soon after been withdrawn.[157] In any case, there also appears to have been a policy among some British Deputy Commissioners to restrict the use of force. A.J.V. Arthur, the Deputy Commissioner of Multan in March 1947, has noted, for example, that 'our policy has been not to use force . . . there has been trouble in only districts where force was used'.[158]

There were some other decisions which were resented; for example, the order of the Deputy Commissioner of Lahore what prohibited the erection of gates and walls in lanes and by-lanes by citizens because they proved to be great hindrances when forces had to be rushed to places of trouble.[159] A large number of barricades had sprung up in Lahore and Amritsar, the Muslim and non-Muslim localities had defined their areas particularly at night by creating these temporary road and lane blocks. A Mohammad Ansari contributed a 'sensitive' letter, discussing how these barricades were destroying the centuries old trust and friendship.[160]

Tara Singh was also reported to have appealed to the Deputy Commissioner of Amritsar to order the removal of the barricades the government had put up in Hall Bazar. For him the problem was that non-Muslims as a result of the barricades were being forced to pass through Muslim areas, which he said could prove very dangerous.[161]

The Deputy Commissioner of Amritsar had also to issue special orders banning sound, light or other signals from house tops.[162]

LIAQAT ALI'S PRO-POOR BUDGET—1947

Liaqat Ali, the Finance Member in the Interim Government, presented the budget for the year on 28 February 1947. Liaqat's budget proposals included a 25 per cent tax on incomes exceeding Rs. 1 lakh and a small tax on capital gain. He also proposed an increase in the income tax limit from Rs. 2,000 to Rs. 2,500 and, more importantly, the removal of the tax on salt. All in all the budget was well received, some even termed it as a 'poor man's budget'.[163] Not all of course were happy—the Stock Exchange as usual was the first to panic—'all Stock Exchanges in the country close[d] down to avoid panic'.[164]

In the ensuing week, the week that saw Punjab going up in flames, a section of the press led by the *Hindustan Times* launched a full-scale attack on Liaqat and his proposals. However, surprising as it is, there was no official reaction from Nehru or other senior Congressmen. Wavell noted to Pethick-Lawerence: 'Nehru has found himself in an embarrassing position . . . he is personally sympathetic to . . . the 'poor man's' budget, but is not strong enough to stand up . . . to the pressure by big business, which provides the financial backing for the Congress.'[165]

Wavell was absolutely right about Nehru because soon after Liaqat Ali presented the budget, Nehru had addressed the Federation of Indian Chambers of Commerce and Industry in New Delhi where most of the industrialists present said it was clear from Nehru's speech that Liaqat's budget had his approval.[166] The little doubt that there was on the issue was removed some days later when Nehru was completely isolated among his party cabinet colleagues and found it very difficult to defend 'Liaqat's pro-poor budget'. The support Nehru received from his colleagues was only because they did not wish to hurt him and because of their respect for him.[167]

Reading through reports of the days that followed the resignation of Khizr Hayat and the gates of disaster that it opened, one is surprised to note the wide distance that press reporting had developed in the two capital cities of Lahore and Delhi. On the day that 10 students were shot dead by police firing in Lahore, for example, many papers in Delhi carried photographs of M.S. Randhawa, Deputy

The Socialists wee unhappy with the manner in which industrialists had begun to influence Congress policies. Jayaprakash Narayan, Ram Manohar Lohia, Acharya Narendra Dev had by the end of 1947 emerged as main opponents of such economic policies. Jayaprakash is shown pleading with the Congress to free itself of 'capitalist influence' (*Shankar's Weekly*, 4 July 1948).

Commissioner of Delhi, inaugurating the Delhi Flower Show.[168] Repeatedly one develops the impression that the problems of Punjab were being viewed in Delhi as too distant to be of concern,[169] and life in Delhi as such continued almost normally.[170]

CONGRESS RESOLVES TO ACCEPT PARTITION OF PUNJAB

We have already seen from Nehru's letters (February 1947) how the idea of Punjab's partition appears to have taken hold in the minds of important Congress leaders soon after Prime Minister Attlee made the 20 February statement in the House of Commons. But it took some more days for the Congress to officially accept what Nehru had in fact indicated almost ten days earlier.

The draft of the resolution to divide the Punjab which was taken up by the Congress Working Committee (CWC) on 8 March was prepared by Nehru. The fact that there was no major change in the resolution that was actually passed and presented by Nehru indicates essentially that there was unanimity, and possibly that it may have been rushed through.[171] The unanimity issue is clear, but for the latter, it appears to be so, particularly from the fact that outside the CWC many important Congress leaders later went on to criticise the partition proposals.

Nehru wrote two letters to Wavell on the day after the crucial CWC meeting. In one of the letters he announced the Resolution as having been passed by the CWC. He also referred to the possible division of Punjab in case the League continued to stay away from the Constituent Assembly.[172] The Resolution referred to how Punjab had till recently managed to stay away from the violence witnessed in other parts of India, but now: 'There has been an orgy of murder and arson and Amritsar and Multan have been scenes of horror and devastation.'[173] The Resolution added that the violence had demonstrated that a way out be found that would involve 'The least amount of compulsion. This would necessitate a division of Punjab into two provinces, so that the predominantly Muslim part may be separated from the predominantly non-Muslim part.'[174]

In the second letter to Wavell, Nehru informed him of how upset he was and of Baldev Singh's impression of how bad things were in Punjab.[175] Nehru's belief that the Sikhs were agreeable to the partition of Punjab (in his letter to Wavell on 9 March) needs a more cautious look because there were important sections of the Sikhs who were opposed to what the Congress had resolved. On 21 March, the 80-year old president of the Central Akali Dal, Baba Kharak Singh, a man widely respected across political lines, said the partition of Punjab was 'a betrayal—a deviation from the path of the great Sikh Gurus'.[176] A fortnight later, he again said the decision of a section of the Sikh Panth in demanding division of the Punjab was unfair—it dealt with the future of lakhs of Sikhs in West Punjab and should have been taken only after arranging a plebiscite. A day later Swarn Singh (Congress), possibly in reaction to Kharak Singh's demand for a plebiscite, dismissed the possibility of deciding the issue on the basis of an election 'in such troubled times', and said 'there can be no settlement on the basis of a United Punjab'.[177]

But surprisingly Swarn Singh, while talking of a divided Punjab continued to advise the Sikh peasantry not to migrate from their villages in West Punjab.[178] Yet, a few days later Kharak Singh again came out against the plan to divide, but this time his opposition was a bit mellowed: 'I am a staunch advocate of Akhand Hindustan and do not like the division of my motherland in any shape or form . . . should partition be thrust upon us . . . I would plead for legitimate safeguards.'[179]

But it is Kharak Singh's statement of 25 April which really shows how unhappy he was with the proposal of division and still believed a compromise could be worked out:

> if the Muslim League is anxious to win confidence of non-Muslims, let it condemn the recent disturbances. . . . The Khalsa is big enough to forgive and forget but under no circumstances will the Sikhs submit to humiliation. The Sikhs will not mind if they stand to lose a little under the principle of fair field and no favour. . . . India can only progress by unity. . . . It is a pity when all countries in the world are out for freedom and federation we in India have started a war among ourselves.[180]

The CWC resolution on the partition of Punjab naturally drew much attention in Punjab. The *CMG* carried a letter from Masud Anwer Qureshi 'The resolution of the Congress Working Committee recommending the division of Punjab . . . is sad for the national elements who have been opposing the Muslim League for its communal approach'. Dr Desh Raj Bhangi of Lahore also charged the Congress leadership for ignoring the nationalist Muslims particularly in the context of relief committees.[181] However, one of the most dramatic oppositions to the Congress Resolution of dividing Punjab was from Peshawar, where 20,000 women gathered to condemn the proposal on 30 March 1947.[182]

Surprisingly, even as the Congress officially accepted in principle the division of Punjab and Nehru, as we have seen, had no doubts on it, the *CMG* published an excerpt from a speech made by Dr Rajendra Prasad 'we want to remain united . . . we will have no status as a nation if we begin to divide . . . one thing is clear no problem can be solved by dividing the country. The problem which we now face will remain even if Pakistan is granted.'[183]

In distant Bengal another respected leader echoed similar sentiments. Sarat Chandra Bose in an interview to the Associated Press said: '[The] Congress Resolution to Partition Punjab is a serious departure—a complex division on religious lines is no solution for communal problems.'[184]

Generally speaking, the newspapers in Punjab did not approve of the resolution to divide Punjab. There were of course some who were in its favour. Jawala Prasad Singha in an article in *The Tribune* said that the reaction of some people to the Congress proposal of partition of Punjab was amazing—those opposing were being unreal.[185] Another article by B.M. Bhatia, 'Only by Division of Punjab can there be Peace', echoed similar sentiment.[186] Bhatia even called upon newspaper columnists and opinion makers not to split hairs and run away from reality.

GOVERN OR JENKINS' ASSESSMENT OF MARCH DISTURBANCES

Governor Jenkins recorded his assessment of the March disturbances to Wavell on 9 March. After noting the level of damage, Jenkins pointed out the crucially different nature of the disturbances from earlier ones. He suggested that the Sikhs had come to believe that they were especially targetted by the League and were caught unawares, meaning thereby that they would have to prepare in a big way. Jenkins also pointed out how the League had taken the Congress Resolution of seeking to divide Punjab as a challenge. The whole situation—of Muslims insisting on a Pakistan on their own terms and the Hindus and Sikhs seeking the Ravi River as the boundary—contained, Jenkins rightfully said, enough material for a major crisis.

While noting that the police department was unable to come up with any specific figures of the killings, Jenkins said the number had been very large because the administration was better tuned to handle such disturbances in only urban areas and had no experience in rural areas. He also pointed out that the lack of proper roads, etc., had only added to the problem because forces could not be rushed in time. Many villages which had witnessed major killings had still not been accessed for this reason. He added, 'We will do our best to keep the trouble out of rural areas; but if we fail, widespread massacres are inevitable.'[187]

On 14 March, *Dawn* in an editorial based on a report of the *Hindustan Times* said: 'The Sikhs are much better organised and better armed than Muslims . . . sometime, they have seen a civil war coming and have prepared . . . most Sikhs men and women are armed with Kirpans.' Some days earlier Jenkins had in fact conveyed to Viceroy Wavell a similar view based on a report submitted to him by senior police officers who had met Master Tara Singh 'he [Tara Singh] . . . asserts that civil war has already begun and threatens attacks on police stations and a mass Sikh rising.'[188]

I wish to draw brief attention to how even as the political scene changed dramatically throughout 1946, often moving from one end to the other, there was one perception of the problem and its consequences that remained consistent and that is that if Pakistan was to emerge from the partition of Punjab, bloodshed was inevitable. Almost everyone (with the exception of course of the Congress leaders) was stressing this point soon after the fall of the Khizr ministry. Interestingly, even Jenkins' predecessor in Punjab, Governor Glancy, had pointed out a similar possibility almost a year and six months earlier: 'if Pakistan becomes an imminent reality we shall be heading straight for a bloodshed on a wide scale'.[189]

But coming back to Jenkins' review of the disturbances, on 17 March he submitted a more detailed account of the Punjab disturbances, i.e. after 9 March. The report is a chronicle of barbarity, with terms like, 'extreme savagery', and 'butchery' being used to describe incidents. While pointing out that the 'triangle of Taxila, Murree and Gujar Khan' saw the worst, Jenkins noted that, 'there has been frightful brutality outside the triangle as well'. Importantly, Jenkins also recorded: 'Commander of the 7th Div. told me that attacks on non-Muslims had been led in some cases by retired army officers, some of them pensioners.'

Jenkins then went on to give his own assessment of how things in

Punjab had reached this stage—growth of the Pakistan idea since 1943; the communalized and heated election campaign of 1946; the frustration that followed in the Muslim League ranks after not being invited to form the government; the 20 February statement of Prime Minister Atlee and the struggle for power that followed; Khizr's resignation; the rumour that a large Sikh army was marching northwards. Jenkins naturally dismissed the theory/rumour of a large Sikh army as being untrue, but recorded that some Muslims had told him that the violent outbreak was the result of the black-marketing by non-Muslims in essential supplies, and the manner in which non-Muslims made their profits in trade. He went on also to record how outbreaks appeared to have been planned, for example, the raids in Murree and parts of Rawalpindi were simultaneous occurrences.[190]

Other Views on The Disturbances

We have already seen how the CWC while finalizing the draft resolution for the division of Punjab had deleted from Nehru's proposed draft of the resolution his suggestion that the 'police and military' had a hand in the killing of a large number of people. Interestingly, in the first report submitted by General Messervy to Field Marshal Auchinleck on the Punjab disturbances, the General especially noted how the Army had been 'steady and disciplined throughout'. The General did, however, cite a couple of cases where partiality was shown by the troops, particularly those of 1/2 Punjab Regiment under a Sikh officer who was said to have terrorized some villagers in Rawalpindi. Messervy suggested that in the future such partiality was likely to increase as the number of British officers began to decrease. Another important observation in this note was the involvement on the one hand of some Army pensioners and even Honorary Commissioned Officers in the killings, and on the other the good work done by some Muslim ex-servicemen in having protected minority communities in their areas. General Messervy pointed out that Nehru and Baldev were right in demanding Martial Law, but he (Messervy) felt that if the Army took over the rural police, the junior officers 'would be apt to throw in their hands even more than they had already done . . . thinking that the responsibility had now been shifted'.[191]

Nanda summed up the March disturbances or 'riots' as he called them: 'In so far as they witnessed gross brutality of the precedents set up by previous carnages, these riots were of the same order, but they were probably not a direct retaliation of the Muslims of West Punjab to avenge the Bihar riots.' But what is extremely significant in Nanda's assessment is the stress he lays on the root causes, something that has been ignored in official versions and finds no mention in any later works:

... very often, the occasion was a fancied grievance, a false rumour, an unwelcome slogan, a petty brawl. There was of course communal fanaticism but there was also a considerable admixture of the purely predatory element... but as a rule the raid on the minority was not made by the majority community of the same village, but of a different village... the communal riots did not suddenly destroy the bonds of neighbourliness between immediate neighbours... such hostilities... were perpetrated by outsiders.[192]

While dealing with the actual happenings, Nanda points out that there was certainly some kind of plan and organization in the riots, particularly by ex-soldiers. Importantly Nanda discusses the suggestion made by many leaders, particularly of the Congress, Nehru for one (as we shall see later), that the riots occurred more seriously in districts which were headed by British deputy commissioners. Nanda dismisses the view:

Such officers who could be said to have acted willfully against preservation of peace were however relatively few. . . . If the riots occurred in towns where the British Deputy Commissioner were posted, it may be remembered that these districts were traditionally difficult for the communal point of view and Britons had been selected to prevent the balance from tilting in favour of one or the other community.

Interestingly, Nanda argues that some of the British civilian officers were misled by junior police and other officials. But he sums up the overall British control rather meaningfully: 'By March 1947 the prestige of the white face was at a low ebb; the civil and police officials had been corrupted by communalism. Hence, the ineffectiveness of the British district officers.' To Nanda, the March riots 'finally broke the resistance of the Congress to the division of the country. . . . They also made the partition of Punjab a certainty.'[193]

I for one, in line with B.R. Nanda and the large number of press reports of the period, am inclined to accept the view that, by and large, British officers did all they could. W.H.A. Rich who took over as SSP, Lahore (1 April 1947) was on '999' duty in Lahore in the first week of March. The few British officers (four in the police) were on round-the-clock duty during the peak disturbances. Rich's diary, particularly the entries for 9 and 10 March 1947, leaves little doubt in that the British officers acted to the best of their ability.[194]

The March disturbances made the partition of Punjab a certainty: they could also be perceived as a turning point. Of course, this is not in any way to suggest that Punjab's partition or the course of the divisive events stood a chance of being altered in any major way by late March 1947. But it appears fairly certain that but for the provocations and violent events witnessed across Punjab in March, the bloodshed and mass destruction that later occurred in the days preceding and following the Boundary Award would have been greatly contained.

Both Moon and Khosla also have no doubt that March was the turning point. Moon writes: 'What had been seen in Punjab in March 1947 was only a curtain raiser. The main tragedy was still to come.'[195] Khosla also underlines the significance of the events: 'The burning and killings . . . that took place in the beginning of March . . . (created) a desire for revenge and towards the end of July, begun to assume the proportions of a categorical imperative.'[196]

Almost without exception most contemporary records have highlighted the difference between the kind of violence seen in Punjab in March and what had been seen earlier. The Viceroy, like so many others too, recorded his shock on what he heard on a visit to one of the major areas of disturbance: 'the unattractive part of these massacres is the sadistic violence . . . they seem to be fond of tying whole families and pouring oil on them and lighting them . . . until [I] had gone to Kahuta I had not appreciated the magnitude of the horrors'.[197]

The Tribune had all through the period been appealing for harmony and on 11 March it carried an appeal on its front page: 'Punjab is bleeding Where are the all India leaders? When will they come to its rescue.'[198] Jawaharlal Nehru came to Punjab on a flying visit on 14 March. He later observed: 'I have seen ghastly sights and have heard of human behaviour which would degrade even the brute'.[199] Of Amritsar he said: 'Amritsar looks worse than Monghr after the earthquake.' Nehru's impressions of the disturbances in Punjab were also carried by the *Indian Annual Register:* 'I think the disturbances will end completely within a few days. . . . A man who is panicky is a useless citizen and a danger to others . . . all that has happened is intimately connected with political affairs. . . . The Punjab has had a lesson, let it learn from it.'[200]

Almost a month later, while addressing an anniversary meeting of Jallianwala Bagh (13 April) in New Delhi, Nehru said: 'We have had communal riots in the past but they were not so big as today. . . . Ever since people knew that India was changing, troubles started in the country, some parties wanted to put political pressure, and partly they did no want the British to go.'[201]

Nehru's reference to 'some parties' not wanting the British to go is significant in a way because just a few days after Nehru said this Mountbatten met the Maharaja of Patiala. The minutes of this meeting make interesting reading:

His Highness took the usual line of expressing intense grief that the British were deserting their allies and friends of long standing by their departure from India . . . he thought it had been very unfair of us (the British) to weaken the states . . . instead of strengthening them so that they could stand on their own legs when we (the British) went. . . . He said that he was worried about the prospect of our departure, since, chaos, riots perhaps even civil war were certain. As usual he asked me whether we could not reconsider our decision to go.[202]

Sections of the press opposed to the Muslim League had, as seen (*The Tribune*, 11 March, for example), been calling upon all-India level leaders to come to Punjab and see for themselves how bad things were. The Punjab government however thought otherwise. So much so that Governor Jenkins even wrote to the Viceroy and said that political leaders, particularly members of the Interim government were putting a great strain on the administration by their travels in Punjab.[203]

The complaint did not mention Nehru by name, but the fact that the letter to Wavell followed almost immediately after Nehru had visited Punjab and that some journalists too had been touring Punjab at the time possibly indicates that the government was not too keen to see Nehru in this part of the country. In fact, Nehru had met Jenkins in Lahore on 14 March and even as the meeting was on, a message was received at Government House (Lahore) from the Viceroy for Nehru requesting him not to visit Peshawar. Nehru agreed not to go, but only grudgingly.[204]

COMMUNAL LINES DIVIDE POLICE AND CIVIL AUTHORITIES

On 11 March, Sardar Baldev Singh wrote a strongly worded letter to Viceroy Wavell informing him of the 'widespread feeling in Punjab that the administration and police have shown a marked discrimination against Hindu and Sikh demonstrators . . . non-Muslims have well nigh lost all faith in the administration and fear that the worst may yet happen.' The British in Punjab were well aware of this widespread feeling, in fact, Governor Jenkins himself had noted how non-Muslims 'are vehemently bitter against the civil service particularly the police'.[205]

The disturbances in March 1947 had rocked the very foundations of Punjab but it was Rawalpindi that had suffered the most.[206] The *Hindustan Times* carried a very revealing report with regard to the violence in Rawalpindi. There had been numerous complaints across Punjab against officials of the Punjab police who were said to be under the Muslim League's influence. But this report from Rawalpindi stands out: 'From various accounts a terrible picture has emerged . . . the chief culprits appear to be Muslim police officials . . . there is one cry on the lips of Hindus and Sikhs in Rawalpindi and Multan . . . remove the Punjab Police and we will be able to defend ourselves better . . . in Rawalpindi and Multan most of the damage occurred in the immediate vicinity of the Police stations. One police official in Multan even brought along camels to take away (looted) goods. Not a single temple is said to have remained standing in the vicinity of Rawalpindi and Multan.[207]

This report in the *HT* also said: 'we have got hold of sensational evidence which proves beyond doubt that the present massacres of Hindus and Sikhs in Punjab have been planned and directed by Muslim police officials from their headquarters'. Not so categorically, of course, but General Messervy hinted on similar lines: '. . . unanimous indictment is that the police took no steps to defend them (Hindus and Sikhs) and they accuse them in many cases of having directed and participated in attacks. . . . I fear the police in rural areas have shown partiality. . . . Junior officials are accused of the same partiality as the rural police . . . probably affected by the surge of fanaticism.'[208]

Seth Sudarshan, MLA and deputy leader of the Congress party in Punjab, gave his own detailed version of what he had seen and been told about the behaviour of some sections of the police. He give the examples of a Muslim sub-inspector of police in Multan directing mobs against Hindu families, and another Muslim inspector having brought along camels to cart away looted goods from non-Muslim households.[209]

The Punjab Police had, from the turn of the century, developed a peculiar character, for some reason it had never been a favoured profession among Hindus and Sikhs.[210] Khosla in trying to understand the basic causes for the unprecedented destruction pointed out that 74.1 per cent of the regular police force in Punjab was Muslim and 78.2 per cent of the additional police was also Muslim.[211] In better days this had never been a problem. The police force had been well rated by British officers for its ability to meet the rigorous demands of the colonial system. But by 1947 this was no longer the case.

The 1946 election campaign and the subsequent efforts of the Muslim League to force the resignation of the Khizr Hayat ministry had deeply divided the Punjab Police along religious lines. A vast majority of the Muslim constabulary had begun to feel that denying the Muslim League its rightful claim to form the ministry was in fact an affront to the entire community.

In Lahore Division, of 7,205 constables, 5,403 were Muslim. The percentage of Muslims among the constabulary decreased as one moved east. In Jullundur, of 3,368 constables, 2,119 were Muslims. In Ambala Division of 3,695 constables only 1861 were Muslims.[212] In the western districts the number of Muslims in the police often exceeded 90 per cent.

Even though reports of lower ranks disobeying orders openly were not very common, by and large, a number of the reports indicated that an indifferent attitude was the reason for the slow response of the police to calls for help. It was the communal-based reaction of the police that made the government often appear helplessly non-functional.[213] Lower ranks among the police on both sides behaved in an identical manner. It was hardly surprising then, that Hindu and Sikh leaders had started making appeals to the youth to join the police.[214] In fact, a delegation led by Sardar Ujjal Singh and comprising Rai Bahadur Janki Das and Capt. A.N. Bali met the Inspector General of Punjab Police and apprised him of the difficulty being faced by Hindu and Sikh youth in police recruitments.[215]

In a meeting with Mountbatten, Master Tara Singh, Giani Kartar Singh and Baldev Singh also raised the issue. The Punjab government, they was said, was planning to add 6,000 more people to the Punjab Police's existing strength of 32,000. The three Sikh leaders wanted all these 6,000 positions to be filled by non-Muslims.[216] Tara Singh in particular raised the issue of police partiality. While addressing a press conference in Delhi, for example, he said that while Hindus and Sikhs looted Muslim property only when the police was not present, the Muslims looted even in the presence of the police. He also referred the Deputy Commissioner of Rawalpindi's complaint that in one case even policeman raised 'Pakistan *zindabad*' slogans. In the same conference, Tara Singh went on to narrate how on 7 March he saw shops being looted just 100 metres from a police station. It was only when he reported the matter to a British officer that the officer intervened and ordered prompt action.[217]

The Railways was another department where deep lines of communal division had been drawn. The *Eastern Times* regularly highlighted how Muslim employees were being harassed by non-Muslim senior officials. There were also reports of employees of the Railways facilitating some attacks on the trains (the issue has been dealt with in detail later).

In the early days of 1947 divisions were apparent even within sections of the judiciary. The District and Sessions Judge, Rawalpindi, for example, was reported to have turned down the judgement of a lower court because he believed the lower judge, a Muslim, had pronounced a judgement against a Sikh far in excess of the established requirement.[218]

The extent to which government employees had been divided can also be seen from a complaint made by Sardar Swarn Singh and Bhimsen Sachar, both senior Congress leaders. They said that most of the telephone exchange operators in the Lahore exchange were Muslims and that they not only tapped their calls but usually delayed connecting the calls made by Congress leaders.[219]

CALLING FOR PEACE AND GOODWILL MARCH–APRIL 1947

Even as Punjab went up in flames there were people from different walks of life, mostly ordinary people who had nothing to do with the political power games were pleading for sanity, reasonable behaviour and harmony. Many appealed on various grounds, differing of course with the League's stand on why the partition of Punjab needed to be avoided. They came from all walks of life and all communities. The tragedy of Punjab's partition in fact becomes greater when one realizes that it was these reasonable and rational people with whom a vast majority of people from all communities were inclined to associate.[220] Col. G.S. Dhillon (of INA fame) was reported to have told this story to an API correspondent, later carried by *Dawn:*

On 5 March 1947 as riots broke out in Multan three Hindus sought refuge in the house of Sultan Mohammad. When the rioters learnt of this they demanded the three be handed over. When Sultan Mohammad was asked to swear by the Holy Koran, his 60 year old mother who had hidden the Hindu family in the *janana* (women's section of the house) came out with the Holy Koran on her head and swore the same. The rioters went away. Later the Hindus were safely evacuated. When the mobsters learnt of this they confronted the old woman, she is said to have replied 'I have learnt it from the Koran to protect anyone who seeks protection.[221]

Quasi Attanullah, Revenue Member, Government of the Frontier Province, issued a fervent appeal for peace: 'Lay down your life to protect the weak . . . it will be a blot on the fair name of Islam if even a hair of a non-Muslim is touched.'[222] *Dawn* carried a long translation of a pamphlet circulated in Amritsar and signed by about 20 Hindus and Sikhs: 'in Amritsar animal instincts have been influenced by Lahore . . . but Kucha Chatan (a *mohalla*—small residential locality) is a sterling example . . . our Muslim neighbours not only guarded our lives . . . they even guarded the temple . . . we appeal to Hindus, Muslims and Sikhs to protect each other.'[223]

Throughout February and March 1947, *The Tribune* in particular carried letters and small articles by ordinary people pleading for peace and harmony and even predicting the disastrous consequences that were bound to emerge from the policy of dividing people on religious lines. Baba Kharak Singh came out once again against the communal divide that was being consciously implanted into Punjab. On 28 March 1947, he issued a statement hitting out at those who were provoking ordinary people into taking sides.[224]

Dewan S.P. Singha, Speaker of the Punjab Legislative Assembly, said: 'man has become a brute, the present war was not a war of religion but of the have and have nots'.[225] An interesting report from Gujranwala pointed out that Sikhs, Muslims and Hindus had even got together to celebrate Guru Gobind Singh's birthday and that the Muslim League's local office had even organized a reception committee.[226]

An article by K.L. Rallia Ram, titled 'Communal Harmony Behind Swords', cited two examples of how ordinary people went out of their way to protect families belonging to communities other than their own.[227] Jaure *mohalla* was predominantly a Hindu area but in the centre of this locality there was a mosque with a few Muslim families. Rallia Ram noted that even as Muslim families staying in small numbers in non-Muslim localities were commonly targetted by mobsters, in this area complete protection was given to them by the lacality's people.

A widely held belief, cutting across communities, was also reflected by Nanda, who said the problem in Punjab had nothing to do with ideologies or religion but was essentially one of the ambitions of Congress and Muslim League leaders.[228] 'We are dealing with the symptoms of disease and cannot eradicate the disease by military action', recorded General Messervy the seniormost military commander in Punjab. The only complete cure is for them [political leaders of all parties] to come to some sort of agreement . . . (this) would result in immediate peace in the Punjab.[229]

R.K. Tuli of Sultanpur Lodhi had as early as in January 1947 pleaded that the subscription of sectional newspapers and literature in schools must not be allowed because such literature tended to sow in young minds ideas of hatred.[230] Ironically, Bihari Lal, in a letter to the editor had even suggested that other reasons apart, the partition of Punjab had to be avoided because sooner than later, on the same principle, some would demand a division between Hindus and Sikhs.[231] Prophelic words indeed in the light of the separatist movement that overran Punjab in the 1980s.

As professional politicians from different communities added fuel to increasing communal fires, life for ordinary people became increasingly difficult. The Lahore Tongawalla (horse cart riders) Union, for example, had to issue an appeal to the public to leave the *tongawallas* alone and to spare them the violence between communities.[232] A fair majority of the *tongawallas* were Muslims.

Another opinion that deserves attention in the context of March 1947 is that of Muhammad Sharif. A large number of refugees from the Rawalpindi area had been housed in camps near the railway station at Amritsar. Such camps had begun flying the Tricolour (the flag adopted as India's flag after 15 August had the same colours as the Congress flag). Sharif questioned the flying of the Tricolour at Hindu and Sikh relief camps at Amritsar railway station. In a way, Sharif personified the helplessness of the vast majority of people from both sides—people who had no links with the gruesome acts of violence or the hatred that was being spread. Sharif said that 'he was a proud nationalist and as proud as Hindus and Sikhs of the

Tricolour.[233] The number of Muslims in Punjab who thought like the anonymous Sharif in early 1947 will remain unknown, no doubt, but certainly it was no small number.

There were many others who tried to maintain communal harmony. Principal Jodha Singh of Khalsa College, Amritsar, played an important role in containing the violence in the city. He not only ensured that there was no rioting within a kilometre's radius of his college, but also that Hindu, Muslim and Sikh residents of the college continued to live in complete harmony.[234] Khalsa College, Amritsar was a leading institution and had students from all communities. The college continued to function normally till as late as 10 March and was closed only on the insistence of the district administration.

> On 5 March 1947 when our Annual Convocation was taking place we received the news that riots had broken out in the city and in the afternoon we learned of the sad death by stabbing of Manmohan Singh II year FEA student of the college. Precautions were taken . . . staff, students and Muslim boarders who lived in rented buildings outside the campus were shifted from there and lodged in the Cricket Pavillion where they lived safely until they could be sent safely to their homes. . . . Thanks to the sense of fellow being . . . the Muslim students had no cause for complaint. . . .[253]

Likewise the Dayal Singh School also played an active role in maintaining peace. As the clouds of communal hatred began to gather over Punjab, the school organized a declamation contest in which participants were expected to highlight the important features of all religions.[236] At about the same time, *The Tribune* also carried a big advertisement calling for articles on communal harmony in Urdu. Special prizes were announced for schools, colleges and the general public.[237]

One of the most remarkable stories of a Muslim going out of his and at great risk to himself to help some Hindu peasants is that of Ch. Chaman Khan. As Rawalpindi was overrun by riots, Chaman Khan went to village Arzai Brahmanan and escorted the minority community to his own *haveli*. For three subsequent days he and his family fought back the raiders with Chaman Khan refusing to compromise the security of his 'guests'. Ultimately he escorted the families to the safety of military protection.[238] Sheikh Karmat Ali, a Muslim League MLA, also narrated a story to newspapermen of how some Muslims in Cambelpur had lost their own lives while trying to save Hindu and Sikh families.[239]

League Leaders Appeal for Peace

As tempers cooled some Muslim League leaders publicly introspected on the Rawalpindi killings. Iftikhar Husain and Mumtaz Daultana were the first to offer of help to Governor Jenkins to restore normalcy. Jenkins advised them that instead of splitting hairs on who was more to blame, the Muslims must accept blame for Rawalpindi: 'They must act as it was necessary to act after a serious quarrel'. Daultana, Jenkins noted, 'seemed to agree'.[240]

Some days before Jenkins's report, Daultana had gone on record saying: 'the entire Muslim population should be mobilised for peace . . . we feel that guarding the honour, security and well being of our Hindu and Sikh minorities is our first duty before God and man'. In fact, Daultana it appears had taken his cue from the League supremo, Jinnah himself, who was quoted by *Dawn* the same day as saying 'protection of minorities is our sacred duty'.[241]

A day earlier *Dawn* had carried a report from Lahore, that many Muslim shopkeepers in important markets like Anarkali had reopened for business, but were saying that normalcy could return only after Hindus were assured of peace and opened their shops. Many *pirs* also came out to the minorities in Muslim majority areas.[242]

Even Firoz Khan Noon, who appears to have developed the tendency of blowing hot and cold at regular intervals, was by the end of March appealing for peace. In an interview given to an Associated Press reporter, he appealed to the Hindus, Sikhs and Muslims to win back each other confidence: 'one way of doing so is not to listen to rumours'.[243]

NEWSPAPERS TAKE SIDES

One of the more important problems that confronted ordinary citizens in Punjab in the months leading to its partition was the dearth of reliable news. Sensationalizing events that were of mass interest was a common practice. *The Tribune* reported an incident from Ludhiana where the shouted encouragements of spectate at a bull fight were mistaken for the outbreak of a communal clash. Word spread like 'fire' and within minutes the streets were deserted, the shops closed.[244] How tense and rumour-ridden the times were is illustrated by another incident in Gujranwala. A group of young men were running down a street to board a train, but the local police, noticing that their running through a busy street had in fact caused tension in the area, felt obliged to arrest them.[245]

But perhaps the best example of how images and incidents when misreported contributed to aggravating the situation can be seen from a photograph that was widely used by anti-Muslim Leage and anti-Muslims newspapers. During the early days of the disturbances, a photograph was taken from the air of a large number of people walking on a dusty road (said to be near Rawalpindi). From the air it was obviously impossible to see who these people were, where they were coming from or what they were carrying, leave alone the mood they were in. While the non-Muslim press used the photograph as proof of looters, arsonists and murderers returning after burning down villages, a couple of weeks later *Dawn* provided details of the region, and the people and said that they were actually people returning from the *urs* of Hazrat Piram Pir. Quite rightly, the report said it was customary for people to carry sticks on their shoulders and even said that people in the photograph had included Hindus as well. Ironically the photo was later traced to the Golara region. The *pir* of Golara had ordered his followers to protect about 500 families of Hindus and Sikhs. This protection was given round-the-clock—no harm was reported to these families. Justifiably the people of the region who had been living in peace were upset.[246] But the damage had already been done.

The trend failed to subside even as officials helplessly pleaded for people not to get carried away by rumours. More commonly, the smaller newspapers were the culprits. S.D. Mohoon, the Fire Officer of Lahore had in fact to make a public appeal to newspaper reporters and the public to verify facts before they acted.[247] The appeal cited the example of how the Lahore Fire Brigade was called to service seven times in one day to tend to fires, of which six were genuinely accidental but newspapers and rumour mills had built sensational stories around them.[248]

On 16 March *Dawn* published a hard-hitting editorial against Sardar Patel: 'The Home Minister . . . is conveniently asleep behind his recently barbed wired bungalow on Aurangzeb Road . . . has suddenly developed a passion for moderation in the press.' The editorial then went on to charge the 'Hindu Press with having thrown all restraint to the winds and . . . publishing reports . . . calculated to inflame passions'.[249] A day later, *Hindustan Times* charged *Dawn* for its unfair and unrelenting campaign against Gandhi, Nehru and Patel.[250]

The manner in which the newspapers had been operating in March and April greatly worried both the principal players in Lahore and Delhi. While Mountbatten was worried enough with the newspapers that he complained of it even to Mahatma Gandhi,[251] Jenkins showed no restraint and allowed the arrest of three editors of Hindi newspapers and one of Punjabi.[252] On the same day, Jillian Butt Khawaja called not only for the banning and confiscation of the booklet *Rape of Rawalpindi*, but also punishment for its publishers and distributors arguing that such biased literature was only adding fuel to the fire.[253]

LOOTING AND ARSON: BUSINESS: SUFFERS MARCH–APRIL 1947

The leading insurance company of Punjab, The Standard General Insurance, released a prominently placed announcement to newspapers on 20 March that with effect from 5 March 1947, it was not accepting any policies for riot protection, so much so that policies in transit or in process were to be deemed to have been cancelled.[254] This announcement was an important indicator that for Punjab there was perhaps no further hope and it was now on its own, a fact stressed by the stock market reports, usually known to be sensitive indicators of times to come. N.C. Chaddha, an investment adviser and a regular columnist of *The Tribune*, reflected the general sense of despair and anxiety when he wrote: '[the] market is going down and down, no one knows where it will stop . . . unless confidence is restored and investors take heart there can be no hope of recovery . . . the best thing is to sit tight, wait and watch the developments which are expected to be far reaching.'[255] A fortnight later, the same columnist wrote, '[the] situation is such one cannot be sure of anything, with looting and arson in the air who can think of industry?'[256]

A report from Amritsar also revealed how the cloth trade for which the city was the leading centre in the country had come to a standstill. Goods worth crores of rupees were lying at Bombay with traders unable to pick up supplies because banks were refusing advances to traders in the region.[257] The trade in cloth was also affected adversely because, as a spokesman of the Mill Owners Association said, a large number of Muslim workers had been goaded by Muslim League activists not to work for Hindu mill owners. Most mills as a result, were reportedly closed.[258] The situation in Lahore was as bad if not worse than Amritsar: 'Lahore is today like a man waking up from a nightmare . . . here were people who had nothing left.'[259]

Major cities like Lahore, Amritsar, Rawalpindi and Multan had practically no trade activity throughout March. Four thousand *halwais* (sweetmeat sellers) had been on strike in Lahore since 31 March, because the District Ration Controller had drastically reduced their quota of sugar.[260] However, there were letters from ordinary people who were happy that the quotas of the *halwais* had been reduced because the sugar saved was coming into the public distribution system.

In Amritsar most markets were closed even as late as the middle of April. Shopkeepers were scared to open and were seeking special police deployment. Another report said that about 60,000 bales of various kinds of cloth worth Rs. 60 crore was lying in Ahmedabad and Bombay because traders in Punjab were unable to lift supplies. Yarn dealers were unable to activate trade because factories were closed. In fact, for the first time ever in the history of the trade, a trade that had a remarkable history of communal harmony, it was reported that factory owners had begun recruiting workers on the lines of community rather than craftsmanship and experience.[261]

Even as most other trades had practically come to a standstill, the business of property developers and dealers was doing well. This was because people were starting to relocate their businesses and even homes to areas of their respective communities for security. The business of buying and selling of weapons too was doing well.[262]

Dr R.K. Chaudhry, a well-known surgeon of Lahore, who travelled through many villages in the last week of March summed up his impressions in a meeting with the press and mentioned the prevalence of widespread panic and tension in the villages. This, he said, was mainly because many ringleaders of the violence had not yet been arrested. He talked of widespread anger and disillusionment towards political leaders.[263]

Shanno Devi, a MLA and a popular figure in Lahore, told reporters that it was impossible to translate into words her feelings of deep anguish and extreme sadness when she saw the devastation of villages in the Rawalpindi region.[264] Practically all trade activity was paralysed. Ironically, even as items of common consumption disap-

One of the major complaints against Jawaharlal Nehru in 1947 was that he often gave precedence to international affairs often at the cost of serious internal problems (*Shankar's Weekly*, 20 June 1948).

peared from markets, newspapers continued to carry advertisements for luxury goods, particularly those that were commonly imported from England.

THE INTER-ASIAN RELATIONS CONFERENCE: POOR TIMING

But yet, life for the well-connected, the well-provided, moved along. The *CMG* carried an advertisement for the supply of the popular White Horse Scotch Whisky. While apologizing for the short supplies the advertisment promised: 'Better times will come, when there will be more'.[265] Lahore's popular restaurants like Globe, Volga, Standard, Metro, Stifflers and J. Lorangs continued their elite-based business.

Ironically, even though Punjab had not yet finished burying and

Another view of Jawaharlal Nehru's obsession with foreign relations (*Shankar's Weekly*, 19 December 1948).

cremating its dead, Delhi was hosting gala dinners and dances in honour of visiting dignitaries to the Inter-Asia Relations Conference, inaugurated in Delhi on 23 March 1947. To put it mildly, the need and timing of the conference was not only surprising but betrayed a sense of indifference if not ignorance of the events that had rocked Punjab in the first week of March 1947.

I remember the Arab delegates creating a fuss because there was an Israeli delegation and the Chinese delegate protesting because there was a Tibetan delegation and because he did not like a map which showed Tibet in a different colour. I had been roped in by Mrs. Sarojni Naidu and I was kept very busy interpreting and hostessing for numerous delegates. Looking back it seems strange that the conference passed off in the happiest euphoric mood . . . and nobody seemed to remember the terrible killings. The people of Delhi did not really understand . . . one cannot understand such things unless one has lived through them.

Organized by the Indian Council of World Affairs, the conference, it was said, had the blessings of Jawaharlal Nehru. The objective of the conference was to 'bring together leading persons on a common platform to study problems of common concern'.[267] Even as Nehru was inaugurating the conference, nearby Hodal (less than 100 km from Delhi) was witnessing a massacre of Meos.[268] On the same day, riots broke out in the Jama Masjid area of Delhi with curfew being enforced. One day before the inauguration of the conference, *The Tribune* carried a statement by Lehna Singh, General Secretary of the Punjab Congress, in which he narrated harrowing tales of devastation and brutality and sought immediate help for restoring a large number of abducted women.[269]

On 23 March, the day that Delhi witnessed much fanfare in the course of the conference's inauguration, *The Tribune* had carried a story of 4,000 Hindus and Sikhs killed in the March disturbances. *The Tribune* also reproduced (the same day) excerpts of an article published in the *Economist* (London) which had said: 'the nearer one gets to partition the more disastrous it appears'. As the Inter-Asia Conference was in progress, the Rewari region (touching the southern border of Delhi) saw 37 villages burnt down.[270]

A detailed report of the Rewari/Gurgaon killings was presented by Prestoria Grover of the APA. She said it started when a buffalo belonging to a Hindu was allegedly stolen by a Meo. The Jats soon recovered the buffalo but were attacked by the Meo supporters of the thief. The Jats then retaliated. The report also cited how ex-servicemen from the villages had given training to the villagers and that possibly preparation for such an attack had been going on for some time. Peace was restored only after British, Gurkha and Indian troops were deployed in the region.[271]

A team of Punjab Congress leaders led by Gopi Chand Bhargava, Bhim Sen Sachar and Ch. Lahri Singh had also visited the area. They reported that the violence had old roots in the enmity between the Jats, Ahirs and Gujjars on one side and the Meos on the other. Some locally influential people had also launched a peace campaign by organizing a committee of 50 people with 12 from each major community and then having this committee travel through the district of Gurgaon making appeals for peace.

While accepting the buffalo as the incident that led to the trouble on 26 March in Rewari/Gurgaon, the committee said the trouble that broke out in Hodal on 23 March actually started as a petty quarrel between a cycle owner and a cycle mechanic. Both belonged to the same community, but it turned into a communal dispute when a third person tried to intervene to resolve the matter, and as fate would have it the good Samaritan happened to be from the 'other' community.[272]

I have mentioned these two incidents in some detail only to highlight the irony of the situation—that the incidents happened over a whole week and were situated less than 100 kilometres from India's capital, which was then busy playing grand host. *The Tribune* published numerous photographs of the dinners and entertainment programme for the delegates. It also published a letter from Abdul Aziz who expressed his anguish at the events in Punjab and the indifferent manner in which they had been handled: 'it is the common man alone that suffers, the capitalists and feudalists irrespective of communities are together'.[273] It is difficult to say if Aziz was in fact commenting on the leaders who had enabled an event like the Inter-Asia Conference to be organized at a time such as March 1947.

On 3 April, *The Tribune* carried a large headlines of Hindus and Sikhs massacred in a train near Peshawar. In the same edition, it also carried a small report of the dance performance by Tara Chaudhary in honour of the Inter-Asia Conference delegates at the Regal Theatre in Connaught Place. Nehru, the report said, rushed from a cabinet meeting to attend the performance, but by the time he reached the Regal Theatre, the performance was over. Nehru called on the famous dancer in the Green Room and requested her to join the delegates for dinner.[274] And this was only a day after the Peshawar train massacre.

The *Dawn* was usually blunt and biased, for a change, however, it commented on the Inter-Asia Conference, its timing and need very perceptively: 'Delegates cannot be blamed for not knowing how colossal India's problems are or how mortal is the combat, a conflict which has (already) taken a toll of 50,000 lives.'[275]

Dawn also reported numerous stories against the conference. 'Amidst carefully dramatised scenes reminiscent of old Hindu rule . . . stage management from the purely Congress angle . . . in front of a huge tent a few Muslims were deliberately placed to give the impression of impressive Muslim participation.[276] In another report, it said the idea of the conference came from Birla's *Eastern Economist*. In yet another report it said the conference was a thinly disguised attempt by the Congress to boost itself politically in the eyes of foreign leaders.[277] The *CMG* also published a similar version, saying that by organizing the conference the Congress leadership was trying to build contacts with regional rulers.[278]

Nehru himself had stressed that the March disturbances in Punjab were, 'linked to political affairs'.[279] Ironically it was political attention that was not only inadequate, but indecisive, disorganized and delayed. In sum those who were concerned often appeared helpless, whereas those who could have helped either did not consider the violence in Punjab important enough or simply wished it would exhaust itself into peace. Vaguely no doubt, but it does appear that for some leaders the violence was a price that had to be paid—on expected lines, in a sense unavoidable.

Somewhat harshly, though, Bali writes of what people in Lahore thought of the Inter-Asian Conference:

> Pandit Jawaharlal Nehru was busy in making announcements in the Inter-Asian Conference about building up one world where freedom was universal. . . . The people of Lahore in spite of the tragedy surrounding them on all sides could not help laughing in their sleeves at the utterances of this great dreamer who could not ensure for a small corner of his own country the freedom and equality of opportunity which he wanted to establish in the whole universe.[280]

DISTURBANCES WILL END—NEHRU

The broader symptom of Punjab's tragedy in March 1947 was not just the breakdown of the law and order mechanism or an indifferent colonial bureaucracy; far more important was the role of political leaders. Almost without exception, leaders cutting across political lines, both in Punjab and in Delhi, appeared tired and exhausted, in a hurry to get on no matter what the price. Dangerously, while some added fuel to Punjab's communal fire, others issued reassuring statements without having at their command even a fraction of the resources to implement the assurance given ever so frequently and enthusiastically through the press. Even Nehru, like so many others, appeared out of touch and even somewhat distanced from the ground realities in Punjab. On his return to Delhi from Punjab he said: 'I think the disturbances will end completely within a few days . . . military are acting efficiently and with rapidity'.[281] Such statements issued by leaders safely distanced from the brewing hatred in Punjab were dutifully reported by the media.

The answer as to why such a vast majority of people waited up to the very last days to leave their ancestral homes is partly rooted in the belief that perhaps as the 'big leaders' were saying. things would settle down. In fact, as the early trickle of migrants began soon after the March violence, a host of senior leaders appealed to people not to migrate as this would create more problems.[282] Such statements and appeals became a regular feature throughout May and June. Jagat Narain, convenor of the Lahore Rakshak Samiti (Defence Committee), while appealing to the people not to run away to safer places said: 'it is the duty of every citizen to stick to his home and maintain a collective unity and safety of the *mohalla* (locality) and also to keep public moral high'.[283]

Among the important and influential people who appealed, through newspapers, to Hindus and Sikhs not to leave their homes and properties in West Punjab were Ajit Singh (29 June 1947, *Vir Bharat*); Sardar Patel and Baldev Singh (4 July 1947, *The Tribune*); Acharya Kriplani (4 July 1947, *Vir Bharat*); Pratap Singh (Kairon) MLA (10 and 14 April 1947, *The Tribune*); Baba Kharak Singh (17 April 1947, *CMG*); Nehru and Patel (through Jang Bahadur Singh officiating editor, *The Tribune*, 26 May 1947) and many more. Mahatma Gandhi, on 1 August in Rawalpindi and on 8 August in Amritsar, in *The Tribune* advised the people that they would remain citizens of both dominions and need not migrate.[284]

The reasons for such appeals were possibly, one, that things would improve and, two, that migration in small groups would cause a bigger problem for those who were left behind. In both cases, the leaders who made such appeals had failed to assess the implications of their public statements correctly. There was more than sufficient indication that things were only bound to go from bad to worse. The chances of an amicable settlement by the end of March were non-existent. Assurances given and appeals made by political leaders were obviously superficial because they had no plan to implement them on the ground. As the massive influx began to build up from both sides, the system, already overburdened, tired and half-hearted, simply collapsed.

PUNJAB DRIFTS TOWARDS CHAOS AND CIVIL WAR

There was an element of irony when Mountbatten told Mahatma Gandhi on 7 April that there was no need for him (Gandhi) to visit Punjab as things there were improving,[285] because only five days earlier Mountbatten had filed his first Personal Report as Viceroy: 'In the Punjab all parties are seriously preparing for civil war and of these by far the most business like and serious are the Sikhs, who already have a plan to seize the main irrigation works in order to exercise physical control over the whole of Punjab.'[286] A day earlier, Punjab's leading English newspaper had headlined on the front page: 'India is swiftly moving along the path of civil strife'.[287]

A kind of deceptive calm had come to prevail following the March disturbances, with leaders taking pains to make statements that were considered non-communal. And yet, as Jeffrey puts it, '. . . the suggestion of conciliation, however, was illusory'. Citing the important and authoritative work of Khushwant Singh, Jeffrey refers as an example to the incident in which Tara Sigh and 280 *jathedars* vowed to sacrifice their lives for the cause of the Panth. This vow was taken on the most important day of the Sikh calendar, 13 April (Vaisakhi) and at the most important place in Sikh lives—the Akal Takht. Khushwant Singh is clear in that the Sikhs had begun to arm themselves and to organize *jathas* from this date onwards.[288]

Two days after the Viceroy told Gandhi that things were improving in Punjab, Jenkins recorded that the Sikhs were preparing for civil war and that a war fund was being subscribed. He also referred in the note to a pamphlet on the Rawalpindi killings, pointing out how exaggerated it was. Jenkins also pointed out that a sum of Rs. 50 lakh was targetted for the war fund and that Giani Kartar Singh was the force behind the effort.[289] Jenkins has also recorded that Congress leader Swarn Singh had told him that the Sikhs were very short of money and had collected only Rs. 2,50,000.[290]

By the end of April over 50,000 refugees had reached Haridwar and every major railway station in East Punjab bore the look of a refugee township. Shoratages of food and clothing, and lack of sanitation were acute. Well before the national boundaries were drawn, Hindus and Sikhs had started leaving the areas that had witnessed the worst violence. But it was only a trickle, mainly of those who had financial assets and were in search of relocation in time for the early bird advantages.

The Shiromoni Gurudwara Prabandhak Committee had started a special relief section for refugees. In Haridwar, the Peerit Hindu Sahayak Sabha was doing a commendable job.[291] In fact, far too many such organizations appear to have sprung up, a situation that led B.A. Anand to write to *The Tribune:* that 'relief societies are too many, they should join the two leading ones—The Punjab Relief Committee or The Congress Relief Committee.[292]

Far from what the leaders in Delhi were proclaiming, the situation was only getting worse. Riots had re-erupted in Amritsar on 11 April.[293] A reporter of the *CMG* met P.C. Bhandari, Executive Officer of the Amritsar Municipal Corporation. His report mentioned how street after street had been vacated and unending streams of people loaded on carts could be seen leaving the city. Most banks had not done business for days and the usually busy court compounds wore a deserted look. On 13 April the Post Master of Amritsar, H.K. Basu, personally opened mail bags and ensured delivery of some post. On 14 April, Basu took a van to the homes of some of the postmen and persuaded them to come to the GPO to sort the mail; some did, but not even one agreed to go out on the streets to deliver the mail. Not a single school or college had functioned in Amritsar for the preceding many weeks.[294]

As spring faded into early summer, across the plains of Punjab clouds of doom were being regularly predicted. *The Tribune*, as early as 23 April; commented that

> Mr Jinnaha has predicted the bloodiest civil war as an alternate to Pakistan . . . the first thing that is to be done is to remove all minority women and children . . . to safe places, those who have no relations may be taken to *Dharamshalas* . . . the young and middle aged who remain behind should convert into defence corps . . . the minorities among whom we include nationalist Muslims must be given arms licences.

Yet, cutting across lines of faith there were still a large number of people who were concerned that ordinary people had little to do with the violence and that they were only being used by leaders as parts of larger agendas. Mehta Puran Chand wrote in *The Tribune*: 'Punjabis have been known for their sanity but somehow they have become insane . . . the fair name of Punjab has been blackened . . . we should awaken the conscience of the masses to the evil consequence of the seed that is now being sown.'[295]

But who was to give the lead in rebuilding trust in Punjab? Pointing out that the exit of Khizr had created a political place that had not yet been filled, that a cynical sense of drift was prevailing, an editorial of the *CMG* added:

> Deadlock is complete. Peace committees feel they are working on the edge of a volcano. Relief committees are doing positive damage by insisting an exclusive communalism. The present situation is pregnant with tragedy, but who among the leaders of Punjab will risk the jibes from his own community and the snubs of others to break the vicious circle?[296]

The vicious circle could of course be broken by either the official mechanism or the professional politicians, surprising as it may seem in the Punjab of April 1947, it was the political leaders against whom the people had more to complain. As Bali put it: 'what was the Punjab government doing to control the conflagration and what was the Central government now run by the Congress leaders doing in defence of minorities? Not much as judged from their actions excepting issuing of reassuring statements as to what they proposed to do'.[297]

The Congress leadership, at least Sardar Patel, was on record as having said that there were problems and that indeed the central government was not functioning to its best. He admitted that there would probably have been no riots if the government in Delhi was effective. To Patel the main reason for the ineffective handling was that 'the government had to contend with divisions and the immobile steel frame [bureaucracy]'.[298]

PEACEFUL PARTITION IMPOSSIBLE: A STRUGGLE FOR POWER

As mentioned earlier, on 9 April, Jenkins had sent a long note to Mountbatten of his impression of the early signs of the Sikhs preparing for civil war and that Sikh leaders had even floated a 'war fund'. He also informed the Viceroy that the Raja of Faridkot had informed him that Tara Singh and Kartar Singh had gone around Ferozepur telling the Sikhs that the time had come for them to settle scores with the Muslims. The same report also points out that the senior Akali leaders were not happy with the Maharaja of Patiala.[299]

According to Birdwood, 'Maharajas as such do not impress him (Tara Singh)'.[300] As we shall see later, even the Maharaja of Patiala with all his influence, wealth and power, and even the reasonable respect among the Sikh peasantry and the great clout in the imperial system, were unable to have much of an impact on the senior Akalis. The Akalis were understandably inclined to 'use' the resources of the Sikh states rather than to trust them. The manner in which the Maharaja of Faridkot 'tale tattled to Governor Jenkins' is one example of why the Akalis did not think too much of the royal houses of Punjab.

The complex tangle in which the political situation in Punjab had fallen into was explained by Jenkins in a meeting on 14 April with Lord Ismay. Jenkins noted that while the Muslim aim in Punjab was to dominate the whole province, the Sikhs were committed even more vehemently to ensuring that the Muslims did not achieve their goal. One other important point Jenkins noted was that the problem in Punjab would require outside troops as Punjab troops would not carry out the task. He also had no doubt that the Sikhs would fight at some stage. Jenkins also very importantly said that 'he doubted whether there was any possibility of an announcement of partition without it being followed by an immediate blow up'.[301]

As the Muslim-Sikh entangle got further strained, Baldev Singh wrote to Mountbatten stating why the Sikhs could have no truck with the Muslim League and that the percentage of the Muslim population had been grossly exaggerated by the Census of 1941. Also, of Punjab's total revenue of Rs. 4,38,13,977, the non-Muslims were contributing Rs. 2,18,44,913. The letter also dealt with the contribution of the Sikhs in settling the canal colonies.

Mountbatten showed this letter to Jenkins. What he minuted on this letter once again shows that Jenkins and party in Punjab were fully convinced that the problem in Punjab really had no solution, in the immediate context: 'This shows why the partition of Punjab would mean civil war. The Sikhs . . . want on religious grounds like the Muslims to take over and dominate areas in which they are in a minority. . . . This wont work.'[302]

Two days after Jenkins had minuted comments on Baldev Singh's letter to Mountbatten, he once again re-emphasized the complex and unsolvable nature of the Punjab situation. In this note he informed Mountbatten that Daultana was going around spreading the word in the Attock region that all the officers who had acted against the rioters will soon not only be transferred but given a 'hot time'. Once again Jenkins noted how he thought the Sikhs were preparing for civil war, adding that possibly they would wait for the British to leave and would act only after July 1948. Adding to the Sikh case he said: 'Hindus are still in close alliance with Sikhs, though there are signs that the Sikhs are not to anxious for too close a link with the Congress high command. . . . Partition of Punjab seems virtually impossible.'[303]

The hardened stand of the Sikhs with regard to the Muslim League also comes out repeatedly in the meetings the Akali leaders had with Jenkins and Mountbatten. Giani Kartar Singh had met Jenkins on 10 April. Jenkins told Kartar Singh that even if partition was granted, the Hindu Jats may want from the Sikhs a separate state for themselves.[304] Surprisingly, Kartar Singh replied that the 'Sikhs would have no problem in conceding the demand'. In any case, Jenkins says he told Kartar Singh that force would be needed to implement partition. To this Kartar Singh replied that the British had taken the Punjab from the Sikhs and it would be logical enough to return it to them.'[305]

Both Jenkins and Mountbatten, of course, took the Akali leaders seriously.[306] Mountbatten had a dig at the kirpans that both were carrying, and said if the Muslims too were to carry such big swords, civil war was certain.[307] The importance the Viceroy gave to the meeting can be gauged from the fact that no staff were present. This meeting appears to have left an impact on Mountbatten as some days later, when he met Jinnah, he told him 'that the Sikhs felt so bitter about the Muslim atrocities that they were only waiting for an excuse for their revenge'.[308]

Almost a year later Mountbatten noted the true significance of the March disturbances and the far-reaching impact the events went on to have for Punjab. This note was aptly titled: 'Sikh Problem Part II', and even while it dealt with the period 1 January 1948 to 24 April 1948, Mountbatten was clear in that what had transpired in Punjab through 1947 could in no way be viewed in isolation of the March 1947 events. While many would contest the view that the Sikhs may have chosen to stay on in Pakistan had it not been for the March killings, Mountbatten was convinced of it:

> The Sikhs would have been prepared to enter Pakistan had it not been for the March (1947) riots . . . they would have remained a measure of political identity . . . but as part of Hindustan they feared economic absorption by the Hindu . . . also religious absorption . . . they played their political cards before 15 August (1947) very badly . . . so badly that many people in high positions thought that they were exhausted and could be ignored.[309]

NOTES

1. J. Nanda, *Punjab Uprooted: A Survey of the Punjab Riots & Rehabilitation Programmes*, Bombay: April 1948, p. 7. I learnt only from the reprint that J. Nanda of 1948 was none other than B.R. Nanda of later years—one of India's most distinguished and accomplished historians. The references are from the original (1st edition).
2. A.N. Bali, *Now It Can Be Told*, p. 17.
3. Ibid.; Anders Bjorn Hansen, *Partition and Genocide*, pp. 98–9; P. Brenden Papers, CSAS.
4. *The Tribune*, 28 and 29 April 1947.
5. *ET*, 4 January 1947.
6. *The Tribune* 8, 10 and 18 January 1947.
7. Ibid., 8 May 1947.
8. *ET*, 12 January 1947.
9. *TP*, vol. 9 (560), p. 1005.
10. *The Tribune*, 3 May 1947.
11. Ibid., 27 January 1947
12. Ibid., 25 March 1947.
13. Ibid., 3 March 1947 and 24 February 1947.
14. P. Brenden Papers, CSAS.
15. *TP*, vol. IX (560), 22 March 1947, p. 1005.
16. *The Tribune*, 16 April, 24 February and 2 May 1947.
17. Ibid., 18 April and 24 February 1947.
18. Ibid., 3 May 1947.
19. Ibid., 5 May 1947.
20. *HT*, 3 February 1947.
21. *The Tribune*, 1 March and 29 April 1947.
22. CMG, 18 April 1947.
23. Ibid., 10, 15, 16 and 19 March 1947.
24. Ibid., 16 March 1947.
25. *Hindu Outlook*, Delhi, 1 April 1947, Microfilm, NMML, New Delhi.
26. CMG, 24 April 1947.
27. Ibid., 11 May 1947.
28. Margaretta Jolly, 'Between Ourselves: The Letter as a Propaganda', p. 252.
29. Susan D. Moeller, *Compassion Fatigue: How Media Sell, Disease Famine War*, p. 36.
30. *The Tribune*, 16 March 1947.
31. Ibid., 21 January 1947.
32. Ibid., 18 March 1947.
33. *The Tribune*, 11 February 1947.

34. *ET*, 4 January 1947.
35. *CMG*, 10 May 1947.
36. Ibid., 11 January 1947.
37. *Dawn*, 25 February 1947.
38. *ET*, 2 February 1947.
39. Ibid., 2 March 1947.
40. *Punjab Legislative Assembly Debates*, 28 March 1946, vol. 225, p. 192.
41. Moon, *Divide & Quit*, p. 75.
42. Moon (ed.), *Wavell: The Viceroys Journal*, p. 414.
43. *ET*, 29 January 1947
44. Ibid., 26 January 1947.
45. Ibid., 29 January 1947; RSS in Punjab, I.M. Stephens Papers, Box 21, CSAS. However, Jack Mortan (SSP Lahore 1946 to March 1947) had noted that one of the reasons for the popularity of the RSS and even the Khalsa *jathas* was that Hindus and Sikhs had begun to look towards them after the Ajuman-i-Khaksaram (Servants of Dust) had begun to organize militantly, IOR Mss. Eur. D 1003/1. This is an unpublished memoir by Jack Mortan, 'Indian Episode: A Personal Memoir', IOR Mss. Eur. D 1003/1.
46. *TP*, vol. IX (310), pp. 556–7.
47. Ibid., vol. IX (306), p. 551.
48. *TP*, vol. IX (30), pp. 556–7.
49. Ibid., vol. IX (321), 28 January 1947, p. 570.
50. Ibid., vol. IX (325), p. 372.
51. Ibid., p. 584.
52. Ibid., vol. IX (354), p. 626.
53. *ET*, 29 January 1947.
54. Ibid., 30 January 1947.
55. *TP*, vol. IX (345), p. 615.
56. Ibid., vol. IX (366), pp. 654–5.
57. *HT*, 15 March 1947, *Hindu Outlook*, 18 March 1947.
58. *TP*, vol. IX (366), pp. 654–5.
59. *Keesings Contemporary Archives*, vol. 6, 1946–8,.p. A8486.
60. Ibid.
61. Zinkin, *Reporting India*, pp. 16–17. Moon, *Wavell: Viceroy's Journal*, entry of 13 February, p. 417.
62. H.V. Hodson, *The Great Divide: Britain India and Pakistan*, p. 213.
63. Moon, *Wavell: Viceroys Journal*, pp. 421–2.
64. Lt. Col. John Peddie (7/14 Punjab Regiment), 'The Steady Drummer'.
65. *TP*, vol. IX (408).
66. Ibid.
67. *ET*, 21 and 29 January 1947, and 6 March 1947.

68. *CMG*, 4 May 1947.
69. Jack Mortan 'Indian Episode A Personal Memoir', IOR Mss. Eur. D 1003/1.
70. *SW*, vol. 2 (Second Series), pp. 41, 59; *National Herald*, 23 February 1947; *HT*, 23 February 1947; *Dawn*, 23 February 1947.
71. Moon (ed.), *Wavell*, p. 423.
72. Rosenberger, *Keesings Contemporary Archives*, vol. 6, 1946–8, p. A8487; *Anand Bazar Patrika* (Calcutta), 23 February 1947.
73. *SW*, vol. 2 (Second Series), pp. 44–5.
74. Ibid., pp. 47–9, 50–1, 53.
75. *CMG*, 14 May 1947.
76. *Janvani*, February 1947 (NMML, New Delhi).
77. *Hindu Outlook*, 25 February, 1947.
78. Ibid., 4 March 1947.
79. Ibid., 11 March 1947.
80. The Congress Working Committee had met on 8 March 1947 and resolved to accept the British prime minister's statement of 20 February 1947.
81. *Hindu Outlook*, 18 March 1947.
82. Ibid., 22 April 1947.
83. *HT*, 21 February 1947,
84. *Dawn*, 21 February 1947.
85. *TP*, vol. IX (433), p. 825.
86. *CMG*, 19 April 1947; *ET*, 12 and 13 February 1947.
87. *ET*, 26 February 1947.
88. *Dawn*, 27 February 1947.
89. *TP*, vol. IX (460), pp. 805–9; Moon, *Wavell: The Viceroy's Journal*, p. 421.
90. Ibid., vol. IX (463), pp. 814–15.
91. Wilfred Russel Diary, IOR. Mss. Eur. D 621/14 (entry 21 February 1947).
92. *ET*, 26 February 1947.
93. *Dawn*, 27 February 1947.
94. *The Tribune*, 2 March 1947.
95. *Abhyudaya*, Allahabad (Hindi), March 1947, Microfilm, NMML.
96. Nanda, *Punjab Uprooted*, p. 15.
97. *The Tribune*, 3 March 1947.
98. Moon, *Wavell: The Viceroy's Journal*, p. 428.
99. *Tribune*, 3 March 1947.
100. Ibid., 6 March 1947.
101. IOR Mss. Eur. R/3/1/176.
102. IOR Mss. Eur. D 1065/1.
103. IOR Mss. Eur. R/3/1/176.

104. *HT*, 10 March 1947; *TP*, vol. IX (473), p. 825.
105. *ET*, 4 March 1947, *ET*, 21 and 22 January 1947; *Dawn*, 24 February 1947.
106. *ET* and *The Tribune*, 4 March 1947.
107. *The Tribune*, 4 March 1947.
108. *ET*, 5 March 1947.
109. *The Tribune*, 4 March 1947. This incident involoving Tara Singh has been used as an example by many scholars to prove that Tara Singh greatly contributed to the crisis soon after Khizr Hayat had stepped down. Majhel, has recorded however that he (Majhel) was present on the occasion. He says Tara Singh did indeed unsheathe his *kirpan*, but it was as an action of defence rather than offence. He has said that infact an angry crowd of Muslims had surrounded Tara Singh and his colleagues, when Tara Singh made these remarks, see Ishar Singh Majhel, Oral History Transcript, Acc. no. 454, NMML.
110. *TP*, vol. IX (514), pp. 906–7.
111. Ibid., vol. IX (493), pp. 868–9.
112. Ibid., vol. IX (493), p. 869.
113. Ibid., vol. IX (498), 1947, p. 875.
114. Ibid., vol. X (334), pp. 646–8.
115. *Dawn*, 16 March 1947.
116. Ibid., Khosla, *Stern Reckoning*, p. 100.
117. Ibid., p. 101.
118. *Dawn*, 16 March 1947.
119. Moon, *Divide & Quit*, p. 77.
120. *Hindu Outlook*, 25 February 1947.
121. *ET*, 5 March 1947.
122. Ibid., *Dawn*, 3 March 1947; *The Tribune*, 3 March 1947.
123. *TP*, vol. IX (481), pp. 850–1.
124. *ET*, 2 March 1947; *The Tribune*, 5 March 1947; *Dawn*, 6 March 1947.
125. *ET*, 6 March 1947.
126. *TP*, vol. IX (481), pp. 850–1.
127. Moon, *Wavell: Viceroy's Journal*, p. 428.
128. Khosla, *Stern Reckoning,* p. 101. He developed his version on the basis of extensive personal interviews and records of the time.
129. *Dawn*, 6 March 1947.
130. *Hindu Outlook*, 18 March 1947; *Tribune*, 3 May 1947.
131. Reports of the events are available in most newspapers of the day, see *HT, Tribune* and *CMG* of 6 March 1947 for example.
132. *The Tribune*, 7 March 1947; *Dawn*, 6 March 1947.
133. *The Tribune*, 8 March 1947.
134. Ibid., 8 March 1947; *Dawn*, 8 March 1947.

135. A.J.V. Arthur Papers Box I, CSAS.
136. Dawn, 6 March 1947.
137. Ibid., 7 March 1947.
138. Ibid., 8 March 1947.
139. *The Tribune*, 8 March 1947; *Dawn*, 6 March 1947.
140. Ibid., 10 March 1947.
141. *The Tribune*, 10 March 1947; 'Bleeding Punjab', *Hindu Outlook*, 25 March 1947.
142. G.S. Talib, *Muslim League Attack on Sikhs and Hindus in Punjab in 1947*, p. 154.
143. *The Tribune*, 16 and 17 March 1947.
144. Mitra, *IAR*, vol. I, 17 March 1947, p. 233.
145. *CMG*, 4 April 1947.
146. Ibid., 13 June 1947.
147. *Hindu Outlook*, 3 June 1947.
148. *CMG*, 3 and 19 April 1947.
149. Ibid., 2 April 1947.
150. Ibid., 3 and 12 April 1947.
151. Ibid., 12 April 1947.
152. Ibid.
153. Ibid., 13 April 1947.
154. *CMG*, 12 April 1947.
155. *Dawn*, 13 March and 11 April 1947.
156. *CMG*, 2 April 1947.
157. IOR Mss. Eur. R/3/I.176.
158. A.J.V. Arthur Papers, Box I, CSAS.
159. *CMG*, 10 April 1947.
160. Ibid., 13 May 1947.
161. Ibid., 19 April 1947.
162. *The Tribune*, 26 April 1947.
163. *HT*, 1 March 1947. Wavell has made an interesting entry in his *Journal* regarding the influence of big business houses in controlling the economic policies of the Congress. He noted that initially senior Congress leaders—Patel, Nehru, Bhabha had agreed to Liaqat's proposal but 'finding that the Budget is not popular with their big business supporters' are backing out, see Moon, *Wavell: The Viceroy's Journal*, p. 425. On 17 March Wavell noted while recording a discussion he had with Patel on the Budget: 'has obviously got Birla and "Big Business", . . . very much on the raw and they are using every means to get it amended. . . .', p. 430.
164. IOR Mss. Eur. D 621/14, Wilfred Russal Diary.
165. *TP*, vol. IX (526), p. 927; also Sir Sri Ram in *HT*, 16 March 1947.
166. *Statesman*, 4 March 1947.

167. *The Pioneer*, 27 March 1947.
168. *Dawn*, 4 March 1947.
169. *HT*, 10 March 1947.
170. *HT*, 23 March 1947.
171. *SW*, vol. 2 (Second Series), p. 291.
172. *TP*, vol. IX (511), pp. 897–9.
173. *SW*, vol. 2 (Second Series), p. 291.
174. Ibid., *TP*, vol. IX (511), pp. 899–901.
175. *SW*, vol. 2 (Second Series), p. 294, also *TP*, vol. IX (514), pp. 906–7.
176. *Dawn*, 21 March 1947.
177. *CMG*, 8 and 23 April 1947.
178. Ibid., 11 April 1947.
179. Ibid., 15 April 1947.
180. Ibid., 25 April 1947.
181. Ibid., 26 April 1947.
182. Ibid., 2 April 1947.
183. Ibid., 16 April 1947.
184. *Dawn*, 17 March 1947.
185. *The Tribune*, 2 May 1947.
186. Ibid., 30 April 1947.
187. *TP*, vol. IX (513), pp. 912–16.
188. *TP*, vol. IX (519).
189. Ibid., vol. VI (29).
190. *TP*, vol. IX (540), p. 965; *CMG*, 9 March 1947.
191. Ibid., vol. IX (560), pp. 1006–7.
192. Nanda, *Punjab Uprooted*, pp. 16–21.
193. Ibid.
194. IOR Mss. Eur. D 1065/1, W.H.A. Rich Papers, A.J.V. Arthur (DC Multan) Papers, Box I, CSAS; P. Brenden (DC Gurgaon) Papers, CSAS.
195. Moon, *Divide and Quite*, pp. 83, 94.
196. Khosla, *Stern Reckoning*, p. 277.
197. IOR L/PO/6/123 Viceroy's Personal Reports, no. 5, 1 May 1947.
198. *The Tribune*, 11 and 24 March 1947.
199. Ibid., 18 March 1947.
200. Mitra, *Indian Annual Register*, vol. 1, 17 March 1947, p. 233; *HT*, 16 March 1947.
201. *CMG*, 15 April 1947.
202. *TP*, vol. X (184), p. 346; also see n. 434.
203. Ibid., vol. IX (540), p. 969; *Dawn*, 15 March, 1947.
204. Ibid., vol. IX (532), p. 953 (n. 2). On returning to New Delhi Nehru wrote to Wavell: 'In deference to your wishes I cancelled the visit to Peshawar . . . I was hurt by this . . . Am I to be prevented from

performing my duty and shouldering responsibility' see *TP*, vol. IX (549), p. 988. Wavell's entry in his journal on 19 March makes an interesting comment on the incident: 'I had one of Nehru's rather intemperate letters on my request to him not to go to Peshawar; it ended with a demand for the resignation of the Governor', Moon, *Wavell: Viceroy's Journal*, p. 430.

205. *TP*, vol. IX (521), 1947, p. 968.
206. A good illustration of this statement is that of 45,000 students who had enrolled for the Matric level examination in Punjab (which have since there inception been conducted in March every year), only 25,000 could actually take the examination in March 1947, *Dawn* 17 March 1947.
207. *HT*, 15 March 1947.
208. *TP*, vol. IX (560), p. 1006.
209. *Hindu Outlook*, 18 March 1947.
210. *CMG*, 12 April 1947.
211. Khosla, *Stern Reckoning*, p. 278.
212. W.H.A. Rich Papers, IOR Mss. Eur. II 1065/1.
213. Moon, *Divide & Quit*, pp. 79–80; Khosla, *Stern Reckoning*, pp. 105–7; Anita Inder Singh, *Origins of Partition*, pp. 219 and 223.
214. *CMG*, 15 April 1947.
215. Ibid.
216. *TP*, vol. X (173), Record of Meeting with Mountbatten, 18 April 1947, p. 320. Also see editorial of *The Tribune*, where it is argued that a more proportionate selection of Hindus to the Police would provide a greater sense of security, 7 May 1947.
217. *HT*, 22 March 1947. Also see a big report by Sri S. Prakash on how the Muslim League cadres are said to have conspired with Muslim ranks in the Punjab police, *Hindu Outlook*, 22 April 1947. Also see report of the Arya Pradeshak Sabha having honoured Gyan Chand Bali, DSP for saving a large number of Sikh & Hindu families in Dera Ismail Khan, *Tribune*, 8 May 1947.
218. *The Tribune*, 12 January 1947.
219. Ibid., 15 March 1947.
220. This is a view that formed quite clearly after going through a large number of letters to editors and other contributions made by ordinary people to newspapers during the first few months of 1947.
221. *Dawn*, 26 March 1947.
222. *The Tribune*, 25 March 1947.
223. *Dawn*, 26 March 1947.
224. *The Tribune*, 28 March 1947.
225. Ibid., 5 April 1947
226. *Eastern Times*, 1 January 1947; V.N. Datta, 'Towards Freedom: Inside Story', p. 4.

227. *The Tribune*, 17 April 1947.
228. Ibid., 16 March 1947.
229. *TP*, vol. IX (560), p. 1008.
230. *The Tribune*, 13 January 1947.
231. Ibid., 25 March 1947.
232. Ibid., 2 May 1947.
233. *Dawn*, 28 March 1947.
234. *The Tribune*, 17 March 1947.
235. *Annual Report*, 1947–8, 1948–9, Khalsa College Amritsar, Address of Principal Jodh Singh at the Annual Prize Distribution Ceremony, 16 February 1948, Khalsa College Library, Amritsar.
236. *The Tribune*, 2 February 1947.
237. Ibid., 11 February 1947.
238. *CMG*, 11 April 1947.
239. Ibid., 15 April 1947.
240. *TP*, vol. X (32), 29 March 1947, p. 45.
241. *Dawn*, 18 March 1947.
242. Ibid., 26 March 1947.
243. Ibid., 27 March 1947.
244. *The Tribune*, 28 March 1947.
245. Ibid., 15 April 1947.
246. *Dawn*, 25 March 1947.
247. *The Tribune*, 28 April 1947; D.D. Condon, Editor-in-Chief, British Information Service, IOR L/1/1321, File no. 104/1.
248. *Tribune* 28 April 1947; *CMG*, 3 April 1947; *HT*, 31 January 1947.
249. *Dawn*, 16 March 1947.
250. *HT*, 18 March 1947.
251. *CMG*, 7 May 1947.
252. Ibid., 11 April 1947
253. Ibid., *The Tribune*, 12 May 1947; Probodh Chandra, *The Rape of Rawalpindi*, NMML, New Delhi.
254. *The Tribune*, 20 March 1947.
255. Ibid., 13 April 1947.
256. Ibid., 24 April 1947.
257. Ibid., 25 April 1947.
258. Ibid., 29 April 1947.
259. *HT*, 12 March 1947.
260. *CMG*, 2 April 1947.
261. Ibid., 27 April 1947.
262. Ibid., 29 April 1947; *The Tribune*, 28 April 1947.
263. *CMG*, 2 April 1947.
264. Ibid., 8 April 1947
265. Ibid., 2 April 1947.
266. Zinkin, *Reporting India*, p. 16.

267. *HT*, 21 March 1947.
268. *The Tribune*, 25 March 1947.
269. Ibid., 22 March 1947.
270. Ibid., 25 March 1947.
271. *CMG*, 9 April 1947.
272. Ibid., 19 April 1947, P. Brenden Papers, CSAS.
273. *The Tribune*, 1 April 1947.
274. *The Tribune*, 3 April; *CMG*, 2 April 1947.
275. *Dawn*, 22 March 1947.
276. Ibid., 24 March 1947.
277. Ibid., 21 March 1947.
278. *CMG*, 1 April 1947.
279. Mitra, *IAR*, vol. 1, 17 March 1947, p. 233.
280. Bali, *Now It Can Be Told*, p. 34.
281. Mitra, *IAR*, vol. I, 17 March 1947, p. 233.
282. *The Tribune*, 10 April 1947. While the issue has also been discussed in detail later, a brief reference has also been made in the context of Mountbatten's assurances in Chapter 1, see n. 16.
283. Ibid., 27 May 1947 and 15 April 1947; Bali, *Now It Can Be Told*, p. 19.
284. *Muslim League Attack on Sikhs and Hindus in Punjab 1947*, SGPC, 1950, pp. 236–39, CSAS.
285. *TP*, vol. X (90), p.146.
286. Ibid., vol. X (59), p. 90.
287. *CMG*, 1 April 1947.
288. R. Jeffrey, 'The Punjab Boundary Force and the Problem of Order August 1947', p. 496. Khushwant Singh, *A History of The Sikhs*, vol. 2, Princeton University Press, 1966, pp. 272–3.
289. *TP*, vol. X (109), p. 172.
290. IOR, Mss. Eur. R/3/1/176.
291. *The Tribune*, 30 April 1947.
292. Ibid., 29 April 1947.
293. Amritsar had seen relative peace in the preceding about 4 weeks. The trouble started from the Lachmandas area 'where 5000 Muslims had collected in a Mosque for Friday prayers in Chowk Pragdas—brickbating suddenly started'. The trouble led to 15 killings, 37 serious injuries. 'The city wore the silence of the grave yard', see *CMG*, 13 April 1947. Curfew was imposed. Massive riots had broken out in Dera Ismail Khan on April 17, ten were killed, the Town Hall, the DB College were burnt down. Extensive killings were reported in the subsequent days, See *CMG*, 17, 18, 23 April. Even the Flag Staff House was attacked in Peshawar on 29 April, *CMG*, 30 April 1947.
294. Ibid., 17 April 1947.

295. *The Tribune*, 24 April 1947.
296. *CMG*, 2 April 1947.
297. Bali, *Now It can be Told*, p. 20.
298. *CMG*, 10 April 1947.
299. *TP*, vol. X (109); *CMG*, 18 April 1947.
300. C.B. Birdwood, *India's Freedom Struggle: Role of Muslims and Sikhs*, Delhi, 1988, p. 74. Also, *TP*, vol. X (184), 20 April 1947.
301. *TP*, vol. X (141), Record of Meeting Lord Ismay with Jenkins and others, 14 April 1947, p. 231.
302. The argument of Census being wrong was that the Census had been conducted in the winter months, when a large number of Muslim nomads who lived in the mountains outside Punjab usually come down to the plains and therefore had been wrongly counted as residents of Punjab, see *TP*, vol. X (240), Baldev to Mountbatten, 27 April 1947, p. 466.
303. Ibid., vol. X (263), p. 506.
304. In fact, Jenkins did have a point here, in the sense that the Jat Mahasabha had held a conference in Bharatpur on 15–16 March 1947 and resolved to demand a separate province, see *HT*, 21 March 1947. Also see the Jat leader Suraj Mal's statement of joining the Ambala Division to Western UP and having Delhi as its capital. He said this would greatly benefit the region, *CMG*, 23 April 1947.
305. *TP*, vol. X (115), 10 April 1947, p. 183.
306. Ibid., vol. X (173), Record of Meeting of Mountbatten with Tara Singh, Kartar Singh and Baldev Singh, 10 April 1947, p. 320. IOR L/PO/6/123, pt. I, Report 4, para 14.
307. Ibid.; Viceroy Wavell ofcourse did not think as highly of the Sikh leaders: 'The trouble in getting any settlement is that both the Congress and the Muslim League are controlled from outside, Delhi and Bombay; while the Sikhs who are in a position to negotiate on the spot are disunited and poorly led, Master Tara Singh is stupid and emotional.' See, Moon, *Wavell The Viceroy's Journal*, pp. 427–8. C.B. Birdwood had met both Tara Singh and Kartar Singh on many occasions. Of Tara Singh he writes: 'I have been impressed first by his complete freedom from all material attachments. . . . Secondly I have found him a man of obstinate courage in propagating every interest of his community to the exclusion of those of his neighbours. . . . Master Tara Singh has a twinkle in his eyes which persists even while he may simultaneously be engaged in fierce repartee.' Of Kartar Singh he writes: 'If he (Tara Singh) is to be regarded as the embodiment of militant Sikhism, he has with him a councillor in whose hands the manipulation of Sikh politics is safe . . . the two together are the complement of each other . . . like his colleague he (Kartar Singh) is a man of drastically

simple needs . . . it is mainly from these two men that one may expect future Sikh demands to be framed. . .', see his *India's Freedom Struggle: Role of Muslims and Sikhs,* p. 66.

308. *TP*, vol. X (229). Record of Interview of Mountbatten with Jinnah, 26 April 1947, p. 451.

309. IOR Mss. Eur. F 200/141, India Viceregal Official Correspondence Files—Sikhs Problem, Pt.II.

3

Partition and the 3 June Plan

The Congress has accepted the principle of Pakistan, I am not a party to it and I will oppose it.

MAHATMA GANDHI[1]

I have not lost faith in an undivided India. I believe no man can divide what God has created as one.

RAJENDRA PRASAD[2]

It is futile to hide the naked truth by saying that force of circumstances has compelled the Congress to accept partition. The circumstances were of their own creation . . . made inevitable by their own deeds.[3]

The spring of 1947 had seen Punjab rocked on its centuries-old moorings even as the onset of an unusually early summer brought with it a load of questions, the most important in May 1947 being, would Punjab be divided? If yes, when? Even more important, where would the line be drawn? While the people settled in the western districts and the Ambala Division were in this context aware of where they were likely to stand, the problem lay in the central districts, particularly the regions of Lahore and Amritsar. Without exception from owners of big stores in the fancy bazars of Lahore to the humble *tongawala* and rickshaw peddlers this was one issue that haunted everyone.

In fact, if anything, after the March violence many Punjabis had come to believe that their security lay in being protected by British officers and troops. So much so that many in Punjab had come to the point of even questioning the view of Indian leaders that the sooner the British left the better it would be for the people in Punjab.

Even as Gandhi called upon the British to leave, the enthusiasm for pushing them out immediately was missing in Punjab. Doon Campbell, Reuters' special correspondent asked Gandhi: 'if he subscribed to the view that the British were morally obliged to stay on in India if Hindu–Muslim differences had not been resolved by June 1948.' Gandhi replied:

> it would be a good thing if the British were to go today. . . . The Hindu and Muslims have said 'Let us have British troops . . . it is a humiliating spectacle. . . . The communal feuds you see today are the results of British presence. If the British were not here we would still go through the fire but the fire would purify us.[4]

Strange as it may seem, even as the struggle to free India was drawing to a close, people were increasingly questioning the role of important leaders in the early months of 1947. One issue that took up much space in many newspapers was that the top leaders seemed to be almost in connivance with the British and were taking decisions at the private and personal level and indeed a lot more was being negotiated behind the curtains than was being done on the table. One such view was conveyed by *Dawn* in a report that said that Nehru had gone to Simla in the first week of May to spend some time with the Mountbattens and that he had also taken along some detailed district level maps of Punjab.[5]

Interestingly, the otherwise usually cautious *CMG* commented almost in a similar vein, when it said that the plan to divide Punjab had already been cleared in detail by Mountbatten with Indian leaders before he flew to London in the latter half of May. The same editorial also noted:

> Only one week remains for the formulation of policies which may preserve India from the disaster which threatens her . . . there is no evidence that anything is being done by leaders to secure a mandate . . . while millions of people in India are burning with anxiety for what the future may hold for them . . . there is not the slightest sign of courage, resourcefulness or statesmanship being called into the highest councils of the land.[6]

A letter from Kunj Lal Gupta of Tarn Tarn, then at best a small sleepy town if not a large village, commented on the situation by saying how tragic it was that when the remedy was economic, people were obsessed with politics.[7] Almost a similar view was conveyed by another letter writer, P.C. Cutta 'innumerable are the ills of our leaders who . . . should have earnestly set about the solutions of economic ills . . . but have broken into communal frenzy.'[8]

THE PUNJABI EVERYONE WANTS A SHARE

For some reason an impression also appears to have grown in the early months of 1947 that the exit of the British would possibly be followed by territory grabbing. In fact, as early as 20 April, the Maharaja of Patiala, for example, informed the Viceroy that the Maharaja of Faridkot was 'developing ideas', that the departure of the British would bring back the territory grabbing tussles among the princes as had happened in the 19th century.[9] The Maharaja of Faridkot met Mountbatten and handed him a letter he had received from Tara Singh and Kartar Singh in which they invited him to take over the entire policy of organization of Ludhiana, Ferozepur and parts of Lahore.'[10]

On 7 May, *The Tribune* carried a statement of the Maharaja of Patiala where he demanded a separate province for the Jats, even though the statement did not clarify what the Maharaja actually had in mind. The Jat Sabha (Hindus) had also for some time been demanding a separate land for the Jats of eastern Punjab (a reference has already been made to the Bharatpur conference of Jats). However, there were many who came out against this demand. Sant Ram, an activist of the Jat Pat Torak Mandal of Lahore, for example, wrote to the *CMG* strongly opposing the demand of some Hindu Jat leaders for a separate state as well as an exclusive Jat university at Rohtak because, as he also said: 'In Pakistan a non-Muslim can hope to attain equality by embracing Islam, but no non-Jat can ever become a Jat by any process.'[11]

Not to be left behind, the Anjuman-e-Mewat, a popular socio-religious body of the Meos in the Mewat region, called for a separate homeland for the Meos. The resolution also stressed that the case of the Meos was as strong if not stronger than that of the Sikhs.[12]

With the Hindu Jats and Meos demanding their respective states the Muslims of Delhi followed suit. Over 50,000 Muslims gathered at the Jama Masjid at a post-Friday prayer meeting in Delhi. The meeting was presided over by Maulana Nasir Jalali. While demanding that Delhi province be included in Pakistan the meeting resolved that: 'Every inch of Delhi is sacred to Muslims and the Muslims shall see that they alone rule it as part of Pakistan.' The meeting also condemned the anti-Urdu stance of the All India Radio. Maulana Jalali was reported to have called upon the gathering to make every sacrifice to see that Delhi province was included in Pakistan and not to tolerate 'any attempt to hand over this old seat of Muslim Sultans and a Saints to non-Muslims'.[13]

Perhaps believing that there was no chance of Delhi going to Pakistan, a frequent letter writer under the pseudomym, 'Fair Play' suggested that Delhi should be a 'free city' administered by both Hindus and Muslims on a 50:50 basis. The letter stressed that Delhi was home to the largest number of Muslim shrines and even forts, but more importantly, it had been an important Muslim centre of culture and religion for over 800 years.[14] The demands for including Delhi in Pakistan were also raised in many towns in the region. A very large meeting of Muslims was organized after the Friday prayers at the Bari Masjid in Ambala, for example. A resolution moved by Naqvi Mashriq and Mohammad Islam demanded the inclusion of Delhi in Pakistan.[15]

If Delhi was going to Pakistan, Ajmer and Agra of course could not 'left behind'. At a large meeting at the Juma Masjid in Agra, as usual after the Friday prayers, it was resolved: 'Since Agra has been the oldest centre of Muslim civilization and culture and since no other city in India has so many historical buildings built by Muslims . . . [it is] essential to include Agra in Pakistan.' A similar resolution was also arranged by the Ajmer Provincial Muslim Students Federation.[16]

As if in retaliation, S.P. Sangar, who later taught history at Punjab University, wrote a long letter making out a case for the inclusion of Lahore in India:

> According to tradition it was founded by Lava the son of Lord Rama. For centuries it remained in the hands of Hindu kings and was taken over by Muslims in the 11th century. Seven centuries of Muslim is nothing compared to centuries of Hindu rule over the Punjab.[17]

The Sikh claim to the disputed districts was also supported by the Hindu Mahasabha because, of Pakistan's 700 Gurudwaras, most were situated in these districts and the Sikhs were running 400 educational institutions in addition to contributing about 40 per cent of the revenue.[18] The Sikh claim and case had been discussed in more detail in the following chapter.

HINDU PRESS DID NOT ALLOW US TO GROW

It was only natural that newspapers too should have taken sides. Papers like *The Tribune* and the *CMG* had large followings and were expected by readers to show the way. They did of course try to lead, but quite often their biases very evident. There is no doubt *The Tribune* (to a lesser degree), *Dawn* (to a great extent), and later, the *Pakistan Times* took clear sides in the English media, but there were charges of biases even against the *CMG*.[19] It was therefore hardly surprising, then, that the Punjab government ordered on 19 May that no newspaper would publish any photograph or statement relating to the communal disorders until they were officially stated or released.[20] In fact, only a few days before this order, *Dawn* had in an editorial attacked Jenkins for being anti-Muslim with regard to applying rules against newspapers: 'Muslim press is severely gagged . . . [the] local Hindus press is being allowed to publish.'[21]

The *CMG* like most other newspapers questioned the logic of the order and said that rumours were one of the main problems and that preventing the spread of factual information would only add to the problem: 'At the moment panic has displaced reason as the main spring [*sic*] of human action and panic thrives on rumours.'[22]

The level to which newspapers had been divided is evident from an address Jinnah delivered at the All India Muslim Newspapers Conference in New Delhi, which was reported by *Dawn* 'we are submerged in an ocean where the Hindus had practically the monopoly of the press and this powerful instrument which can be wielded against us by the Congress and the Hindus. . . . This ring did not allow us to grow.'[23] Terms like Hindu press and Congress press were commonplace.[24] In the same address Jinnah said: 'there was a time when it was difficult to find a Muslim with even elementary training in journalism . . . there was a ring around us . . . it did not allow us to grow . . . in any department'.[25]

A day before this conference, *Dawn* had also devoted an editorial highlighting how the Muslim press was different from the 'others': 'Muslim press is very much younger . . . resources at its disposal are very meagre . . . technical hands are scarce . . . despite its shortcomings and imperfections Muslim press is most democratic—unsullied by profit motives when modern journalism all over India is ruled by that motive.'[26]

The division naturally was not limited to newspapers. All India Radio's (AIR) significance had grown rapidly almost in step with the growth of violence in Punjab, therefore, its news programmes attracted the interest of community leaders. On 16 May, *Dawn* published an article saying that the AIR was Hindu intrigue at its worst. The article made a long list of charges. It said prior to September 1946, AIR had tried to maintain a balance between the views of the

Congress and those of the Muslim League, but after Sardar Patel took over as minister of the department, AIR had become biased in favour of the Congress. It pointed out that as of May 1947 there was not a single Muslim in the news editing section of the organization and that all key positions were in the hands of Hindus. The article also attacked the AIR's language policy: 'since Patel took over the real and natural language of India—Urdu has been butchered'.[27]

THE RICH RELOCATE—THE POOR SEEK FOOD

By the beginning of May 1947, most advertisements for the sale or purchase of property, besides the routine description of the property, also usually mentioned terms like 'pure Hindu', 'safe Hindu' or 'safe Muslim' colony, area, etc. For example, a huge house with extensive compounds was put up for exchange in Rawalpindi for property in a 'Hindu majority' town.[28] This had begun from the second half of 1946 when the more resourceful families on both sides began relocating.

However, on the other hand, for the ordinary citizen the issue of relocating to safer zones and doing so in time was hardly of little priority even as late as May. For the vast majority of Punjabis, making ends meet was the main problem. While the moneyed sections of Punjab's population were advised by stock market experts to liquidate stockholdings even at small profits,[29] for the vast majority the problem was the cartwheeling effect of the tremendous shortage in food grains.

Dr Rajendra Prasad's statement in Bangalore that the wheat crop had failed (having been greatly damaged by rust) and that times of greater difficulty were likely to come in the months of July to September made important news in most papers of the Punjab.[30] The Government of India's Secretary of the Food Department, K.L. Punjabi, was also reported to have said that the drop in food grain production was almost of 100,000 tonnes.[31] With a food deficit of over 400,000 tonnes, as stated by Dr Rajendra Prasad, the panic that spread across the country was alarming.[32] In Madras, Dr Rajendra Prasad also said that: '. . . the danger of suffering and starvation lies ahead . . . the stock of food grain in the government's hands is only half of what it should be'.[33] A few days later he was again quoted as saying that the government did not have enough money to import grain, and it had already suffered 'losses' of Rs. 25 crore in subsidizing the cost of importing food grain.[34]

Dawn not surprisingly went on to charge Dr Rajendra Prasad with not paying enough attention to his ministry, a situation which, it said had led to the mess. The truth of course was far from this: the Ministers of the Interim Government had been in office only for about six or seven months, a period far too short to be of consequence in decisions of grain import policies. In Punjab at least the blame for the mess could hardly be placed at the door of Dr Rajendra Prasad. *The Tribune*, for example, reported how syndicates had monopolized the procurement of wheat schemes. Such syndicates purchased wheat at Rs. 9/4 annas per maund and then resold at Rs. 11/7 annas per maund. In Gujrawala, for example, wheat was selling in May 1947 as high as Rs. 12/1 anna per maund.

In the NWFP, the governor had ordered that no establishment would serve more than three courses of food to a customer at a single meal. The order also said that 'bread, pastry, etc., will not be served with evening tea and that those violating the orders could be imprisoned for up to three years and also fined'. In Lahore, an order was passed replacing the distribution of rations from a monthly basis to a weekly one.[35]

NEW PAY SCALES FOR GOVERNMENT EMPLOYEES

If one were to search for an example of the 'for ever self seeking nature of India's officialdom', few would be better than the manner in which those managing the government were able to push through the implementation of the Pay Commission's recommendations even as the Partition of India was around the corner. A nation starved of resources and with starvation staring millions of ordinary souls in the face, the Government of India accepted the Pay Commission's recommendations in the middle of May 1947.[36] The total expenditure added due to the pay revision came to about Rs. 30 crore, of which Rs. 24 crore would go to the Railway and the Post and Telegraph employees, both departments which in the following months would be expected to play a crucial role in the Punjab.[37] Not surprising, then, that the employees of the Accountant General's Office in Simla organized a strike against the Pay Commission's recommendations.[38]

Dawn's editorial on the Pay Commission proposals said: 'Judging by the per capita income which in India is Rs. 100 per year . . . such high salaries for civil servants appears far too extravagant . . . bear in mind that the per capita income in Britain is £95 and the maximum salary paid is 3,500 pounds per year. In USA the per capita income is $ 165 the highest annual salary is $ 2500.'[39]

BUSINESS IN MAY 1947

We have already seen in the previous chapter the extensive shortage of essential commodities that prevailed in Punjab in the early days of 1947. Throughout May the situation had steadily deteriorated. Newspapers regularly reported stories of people caught giving bribes to government inspectors or black marketeering in goods of short supply. The *CMG* reported that *dhobis* (washermen) had suspended work in Lahore due to the shortage of washing soda and how the widespread shortage of cloth had forced the reduction in the per person quota of cloth from 12 yards to 8 yards. Officially the price of wheat during May was Rs. 7 per maund, but in the black market it was reported to be around Rs. 11 per maund.[40]

The Tribune also reported the arrest of Chiranji Lal, an ice cream vendor of Ludhiana, for selling sugar at Rs. 1 and 12 annas per *seer*, and the arrest of a tailor, Harnek Singh, for selling *latha* (coarse) cloth without a licence.[41] Two traders including Mohammad Yusuf, Secretary of the Muslim Cloth Traders Association, were also arrested when trying to bribe the anti-black marketeering inspector in Lahore.[42]

Two of the few trades that continued to flourish in May 1947, just as seen in the earlier months were the sale and purchase of arms, weapons and ammunition, and the exchange, selling and purchase of properties.[43] Another business, restricted no doubt but which appeared to do better than others, was that of an experimental fireproof paint. An advertisement advised people to paint their houses and wooden goods with a mixture in equal parts of carbide waste, washing soda, slack lime dust and Multani clay.[44] This it said was a good way to protect their property from arson. In later months, as arson increased, even the government began to advise people to paint their wooden items like doors, windows, etc., with such 'home made paints'.

Punjab's leading financial institution, the Punjab National Bank, called an extraordinary general body meeting on 10 May to decide on shifting its head office from Lahore to Delhi. A report of the meeting pointed out an assessment which said that about Rs. 250 crore was likely to move from the west Punjab arrears to Delhi and the east Punjab. Some sources were even cited as saying: 'After we leave will follow the deluge, Pakistan will be an economic desert.'[45]

TWELVE BURNT ALIVE—LAHORE REMAINS UNMOVED

Even as lines were being drawn, not only between communities but also between those who wanted Punjab's partition and those who did not, there occurred in Amritsar an incident which was perhaps the most gruesome of all that happened in 1947. Violence had broken out in Amritsar on 9 May, the following day a small group (mainly Sikhs) of 12 people returning after cremating the body of child was attacked by armed Muslims, doused with petrol, beaten up and set on fire. Seven died on the spot, the rest succumbing later.[46] Punjab Chief Secretary Akhtar Hussain reported the tragic incident as 'shocking in brutality'.

In many ways the incident should have been seen as a warning of what was to come, but even such a gruesome tragedy barely disturbed the pace of life in Lahore which saw on the following day the wedding celebrations of the son of the Chairman of the New Bank of India. Lawerence Road was grandly bedecked. All who mattered in Lahore and Amritsar were present. These included Bhimsen Sachar, Sardar Swarn Singh, the Muslim League leader Shaukat Hayat, the Speaker of the Assembly Diwan S.P. Singha, Gopichand Bhargava and almost the entire Bench of the High Court.[47] The guests were entertained by the Police Band intermittently interrupted by the sounds of gun fire and screaming arsonists. The battle for the control of Lahore, as we know, had already begun on the night of 9 May 1947.

What is striking about the Punjab of May 1947 is that even as parts of it had begun to go up in flames, life for the privileged few, both in Lahore and in Simla continued undisturbed.[48] By 10 May violence and arson had assumed alarming proportions. Fortunately, however, in the early days this happened only in pockets. The Punjab government on its part did make efforts to restore trust by distributing over 1,00,000 pictorial posters of Gandhi and Jinnah appealing for peace. But such efforts were easily neutralized by provocative material like the booklet *The Rape of Rawalpindi*.[49] Many said the booklet had greatly exaggerated the violence of Rawalpindi, others said it was all true, and still others said that even if true there was no need for its circulation. 'It cannot fail to aggravate communal passions', wrote the *CMG*, '. . . the tragedy of tragedies is that it is such documents which are settling the destinies of this country. Prabodh Chandra and his ilk are ensuring that reason and sobriety shall not venture where anger and bitterness now reign supreme.'[50] It was hardly surprising that, as a letter to the *CMG* noted, 'before the trouble started only about 20 per cent Sikhs carried *kirpans* now 95 per cent do . . . I saw a group of 3 Sikhs carrying 8 *kirpans*'.[51]

On 12 May, 18 people were killed in Amritsar, with over 20 incidents of stabbings and arson in 12 hours. The *CMG* reported that in one incident a *tonga* rider was killed and his horse pulled the *tonga* with the dead body of its owner to a police station.[52] *The Tribune* reported 12 deaths, 'communal madness returns to Lahore' on 14 May.[53] The next day it reported 8 killings in police firing alone. The government banned the popular Jor Mela which was scheduled for 24 May.[54] From the 13 to 18 May, Lahore and Amritsar saw widespread arson and killings, countrymade bombs were freely used in Amritsar.[55] On 17 May, 18 people were killed in Lahore with an unaccounted number of injuries: 'Lahore is in grip of panic', reported the *CMG*.[56]

So bad had the situation become that the *CMG* and *The Tribune* both faced problems in the distribution of their papers. The *CMG* even said: 'The issue has been produced in panic and absence of most staff . . . uncertain when next issue will appear.'[57] *The Tribune* too came out with an apology on 20 May saying that since 11 May the paper was being published under very trying circumstances.[58]

The situation had reached a stage when government troops were provided to protecting food grains and even to insure the food stocks held by traders because banks had stopped financing them for fear of arson and killing.[59] The *CMG* recorded that people had a heaved sigh of relief following the deployment of army units: 'fear has not disappeared nor has anxiety been allayed but the evidence of military activity . . . the sight of soldiers on foot has restored confidence'.[60] The situation was scarcely better in other parts of the region. Ambala was placed under curfew on 17 May,[61] widespread arson was reported from the Peshawar prison, where even the IG Prisons, Col. P.H.S. Smith was injured in the arson.[62]

The Mewat region in the south-east of Punjab was of course the worst hit. *Dawn* warned that the Meos were likely to be wiped out if timely action was not taken. The report said a large number of villages had been burnt down. Naurangpur, for example, was attacked by over 20,000 people. The report also pointed out how the arsonists were coming in from Alwar and Bharatpur and were mainly Jats, Gujjars and Ahirs. About 400 sq. miles of area was affected. The villages burnt down were listed as Naurangpur, Ghairatpurbas, Sakarpur, Kolika, Khera, Nawabghar, Kiranj, Ghunda, Ghudia,

Arjunbas, Shaikupur, Siancia, Bajraka, Qutubgarh, Bureta, Sabras, Unton, Sonari and Sundh. Officially, *Dawn* said the May 1947 riots had resulted in 15 deaths and 80 serious injuries, but the unofficial figures were stated to be much higher. In any case, the figures given by the government were only of those that were admitted in the government hospitals.[63]

Liaqat Ali reported his version of the Gurgaon and Mewat disturbances in a letter to Mountbatten on 30 May 1947. He said that a mob of up to 20,000, equipped in many cases with modern weapons including .303 rifles, had besieged village after village. He appealed in this letter for the use of paratroops and the cavalry.[64]

GURGAON/MEWAT: BRENDEN'S VIEW

P. Brenden was Deputy Commissioner of Gurgaon from January 1945 to June 1947, when he was posted out after extensive pressure had been put on Governor Jenkins by many Congress leaders including Sardar Patel. The document available at the Centre for South Asian Studies was recorded by Brenden only after he had read Tucker's (*While Memory Serves*) version wherein the Gurgaon disturbances were viewed as 'The Meo Rising'.[65] Brenden has noted that initially he was hesitant to share what he knew, but since his assessment was quite different from that of Tucker's, he felt compelled to put what he thought was the correct version on record. Briefly, Brenden's assessment with regard to the disturbances, mainly for the period of March to May 1947 was that in the Gurgaon region 'Palbandi' (or clanhood) had made people of the area different from others, once partition was certain, 'the Palbandi' weakened and religion took over; 'long before the real trouble started I knew that the RSS was the one organisation which I probably could not help control . . . unfortunately the Muslim League was never invited . . . (meaning as part of government) may be the slaughter may never have happened.' Brenden has also recorded that in the Gurgaon district the rumours of grain shortage were greatly responsible for increasing tension. Another point raised by Brenden makes him possibly the only senior British officer to have stated that the communal disturbances that had taken place outside Punjab (1946) had had repercussions in Punjab.

Most importantly, however, he negates completely the widely held belief that the disturbances in Mewat and the Meo demand for an independent Mewat were linked to or sponsored by the Muslim

League. While newspapers dwelt on this belief quite commonly, Brenden, records that he was a personal witness to Liaqat Ali having: 'deplored the Meo demand for an independent Mewat and thought that by making the demand they [the Meos] were only adding fuel to the fire'.

Possibly as an explanation to why powers in Delhi were unhappy with him, Brenden has also narrated an incident when he intercepted a jeep from Delhi which was not painted in a colour different from police and army vehicles as was required to prevent misuse of vehicles. The driver was carrying a pass which had been issued by the Deputy Commissioner of Delhi (Randhawa, a favourite of Patel). Brenden notes that as heated words were exchanged he ordered the confiscation of the vehicle. The incident was subsequently reported in Delhi. At about the same time, Brenden says, he arrested a Sikh near Tikri village, who was carrying a tin of explosive powder for making bombs. In sum, Brenden was convinced that a concerted and planned exercise was undertaken to clear the region of Muslims/ Meos, and in this plan the Jats and Ahirs of Alwar and Bharatpur were as active as those of the region.

The reference to the arrest of a Sikh in a region where there were no Sikh villages for miles together has been presented by Brenden as part of a broader Sikh conspiracy. This however, is obviously stretching things—the Sikhs had little interest in the waterless unfertile lands of Gurgaon and Mewat.[66]

CLEANSING AREAS OF MINORITIES

The significance of Brenden's report is that it clearly underlines that well before the 3 June Plan and the notional boundary were known, the majority communities in even those areas that were not contentious had begun to build pressure on the minorities to move out—the motivation of course came from religion but often it was from a desire to grab a fleeing family's cattle or other valuables—in some cases even temporary possession of the land.

The level to which the administration had been rattled both in Lahore in Delhi also stands out in a story which *The Tribune* quoted from the *Daily Telegraph* (London). The London report had quoted Lord Ismay, Chief of the Viceroys Personal Staff as saying that 'administration is likely to break down completely in [the] near future—and Indian services have neither the manpower nor the resources necessary to restore full efficiency'.[67]

As the Meos were forced out from the Gurgaon region, the same was happening to Hindus and Sikhs in Lahore, leading *The Tribune* to publish fearsome advice essentially for non-Muslims: 'don't desert Lahore like cowards . . . remove your women folk, children, valuables, consider your homes like castles, fight like soldiers to save civilization from jungle raj'.[68] Lala Jagat Narain, Convener Lahore Rakshak Samiti also appealed to people not to leave, their ancestral homes in panic.[69]

As the situation rapidly deteriorated there was a widespread demand in Lahore in particular to post if possible detachments of police which had representation from all the communities. *The Tribune* took up the issue with the governor and said that if it was not possible to post a larger number of mixed policemen in Lahore the city's control should be handed over to the military and that heavy punitive taxes be imposed on localities indulging in arson and killings.[70] A day later, it suggested to the governor that the highly regarded Gurkha military units be brought into Lahore. It also sought the Governor's intervention in ensuring the protection of the properties of peoples who had fled Lahore. The situation in Amritsar was scarcely better, with pitched battles being reported even during curfew hours.[71]

By the end of May over 3,000 Meos had taken shelter in Delhi. Many Muslim families vacated big *havelis* in the Sadar area for the Mewat refugees, a large number were housed in the Jama Masjid under the supervision of Abdur Rehman, convener of the relief committee. The Muslim League National Guard played an active role in the relief work. According to a *Dawn* report, a complaints register maintained by the relief committee clearly showed that most of the Meos said they had been attacked by people who had come from Bharatpur and Alwar.[72]

A report by the *Statesman* was cited by *The Tribune*: '[the] attack was described by an official as evidence of careful planning. Weapons used were modern arms, even defenders used modern arms, in one case a mortar was used to break into the villages defence.' Active medical missions were also sent to the Mewat region by the organizers of these relief camps.[73] The effort of these private organizations was greatly supported by the Delhi Municipality in terms of water, vaccination, food, etc.[74]

On 22 May Secretary of State Lord Listowel was quoted by various newspapers as having said that since November 1946, a total of 4,014 people had been killed in communal clashes in India, of these the Punjab alone accounted for 3,024 deaths and 3,646 seriously injured.[75] As far May and early June 1947 were concerned, the loss of Muslim and non-Muslim lives was almost equal, though the non-Muslims suffered heavier losses of property.[76]

Scattered reports drew attention to the fact that some Sikhs and Muslims had stood together to defend their villages. One report mentioned that a group of raiders comprising five Sikhs and one Muslim, attempted a raid on a village in Amritsar, were turned back by the Sikh and Muslim villagers fighting together.[77] Such incidents, however, by May 1947 were rare.

GOVERNOR JENKINS DOES HIS BEST

Governor Jenkins announced a Rs. 10 crore rehabilitation programme and various other measures for restoring peace.[78] Leaders like Baldev Singh and Bhim Sen Sachar also paid profuse compliments to Jenkins for the good work he had done, particularly to resettle and assuage the feelings of riot victims.[79]

Jenkins had the full support of Mountbatten in his efforts even though the problems being faced by the former were manifold, particularly the shortage of British officers to man senior positions, their role having become crucial in view of the growing divide on communal lines.[80] On 17 May Moubtbatten communicated to Jenkins, his and the Interim Government's approval for the use of maximum force including air bombing. 'I shall support you to the hilt . . . it is very vital that the very first attempt at communal war should be utterly and ruthlessly crushed.'[81]

To further strengthen Jenkins' hands, Patel suggested that the situation in Lahore required martial law. He said that he was aware that martial law caused great inconvenience to ordinary citizens, but in this case it was the ordinary citizen who was calling for it. Colville, to whom Patel had put forth this suggestion, however, replied to Patel on 24 May saying that additional troops were being rushed to Lahore and that martial law was not yet required.[82]

TARA SINGH'S TERMS FOR PEACE

An API report quoted a list of demands that Tara Singh had laid out for peace in the Punjab. He wanted abducted women to be restored; every forcibly converted non-Muslim to be restored; rehabilitation of all displaced people; recruitment of non-Muslims to bring the ratio in the Punjab police to 50:50 between Muslims and others; and, above all, he called upon the Muslim League to condemn the violence that had occurred in Punjab since the beginning of March.[83]

The Tribune's version of Tara Singh's interview to API also added that he (Tara Singh) had said that he did not attend the so-called peace conferences in Lahore as he believed that they had no meaning, because merely signing documents and not acting on them was of no use. He (Tara Singh), the report said, was keen on real peace.[84]

In fact, Jenkins too had wanted to meet Tara Singh on 13 May to discuss measures for peace. In reply to Abbats, Tara Singh wrote back the same day saying he could not come at once because the Muslim League was closely 'watching my movements . . . they are controlling the telephone systems of Amrtisar and Lahore and the operators immediately inform the Muslim League workers when they learn of any movement . . . I shall suddenly come to Lahore and take a chance of seeing His Excellency.' He also said 'I do not like to see a single person murdered. . . . How can I sit around a table. None of the League leaders have condemned the barbarities. . . . I hold them responsible for the butchery. . . . They are even now defending the arrested ruffians. . . . I shall not lick the hand bemired with the blood of my innocent children.' Tara Singh ended his letter by assuring Jenkins of his support for peace.[85]

Tara Singh's letter conceals or rather does not reveal how angry he was in the middle of May. In a statement a day earlier he had said: 'That Sikhs fall victims to the dagger of the assassin (in Amritsar) is extremely provocative and a matter of deep shame . . . there is a limit to everything . . . it is being assumed that you (the Sikhs) can also bear slavery . . . it is being seriously considered that districts like Lahore, Gujranwala, Lyallpur, Montgomery which bear imprint of Sikh glory, history, enterprise and industry can be safely dragged into Pakistan.'[86]

Some still Believed Partition was not Required

One could start from the very top. On 3 May, Health Minister Raj Kumari Amrit Kaur, a close associate of both Gandhi and Nehru, had met Moutbatten, and what she said is rather surprising particularly in view of the fact that the Congress as a policy had already asked for the partition of Punjab. She said that she herself was a

Punjabi and appealed to Mountbatten not to agree to the partition of Punjab.[87] Soon after meeting Amrit Kaur, Mountbatten also met on the same day another Congress stalwart, G.B. Pant, who also appealed to him not to agree to a decision for partition.[88]

Gandhi himself had met the Viceroy on 4 May. The minutes of this extremely important meeting were recorded by Mountbatten in a 'Top Secret' personal report on 8 May. 'I explained to him the broad outlines of the plan. . . . His comment was that it was quite wrong of the British to take any steps to facilitate the partition of India.'[89] In a separate record of the meeting, Mountbatten noted: 'He replied that he did not agree that we were leaving the people of India a free choice since we were practically imposing partition on them.'[90]

On 21 May, the main opponent of the Congress, the Hindu Mahasabha's slated its view's on partition through V.G. Deshpande. He said the proposed partition was bound to lead to disturbances and 'I earnestly appeal to the Congress leaders not to decide the fate of India without getting a decisive majority verdict from Indians by a referendum.'[91]

On 15 May *CMG* reported a speech by Rajendra Prasad from Madras, in which he appealed to the people not to misunderstand the Congress party's stand of having accepted the Partition of India: 'it is only a passing phase'. *The Tribune* also gave a detailed version of the statement by Rajendra Prasad under the headline: 'Terrible Conditions in India – Dark Clouds Around'. 'I have not lost faith in undivided India. I believe no man can divide what God has created as one . . . while we feel India is one . . . there is a demand for division. . . . From what is happening there is no escaping it unless we are prepared to go through the same barbarity and inhumanity.'[92]

Some days later, *Dawn* carried an editorial attacking Rajendra Prasad for this statement and charging him for 'suffering from amnesia': 'Not long ago he had said in the Constituent Assembly that the division of India was the need of the hour. Strangely enough he now forgets all that and hates the division.'[93]

Acharya Kriplani too was reported as having said that 'we still believe in United India . . . division of Punjab is the last alternative'.[94] On 13 May, the Hindu Mahasabha's mouthpiece the *Hindu Outlook* also quoted from a speech made by Sardar Patel in Bombay on 14 April. Patel was reported to have said that India should not be partitioned. The most interesting, of course, was the version of the *CMG* which published a long story of how Gandhi and Jayaprakash

Narayan were understood to have joined hands against the partition plan and had even called upon the Congress to revert to its earlier stand.[95]

If 'Pakistan was too high a price to pay for peace', to Norah Richards, avoiding the partition of Punjab was also a matter of the heart: 'If the League gets its Pakistan the poems of Iqbal will need revision or even cuts.'[96]

THE MUSLIM LEAGUE OPPOSES PARTITION OF PUNJAB

The most concerted opposition to the partition of Punjab, however, and for reasons of its own, came from the leaders and cadres of the Muslim League. Throughout Punjab a full-scale campaign—from the streets to newspapers, to large public meetings, to post-prayer gatherings, to colleges and schools, among government employees, among the party and student leaders—was launched to oppose the division of Punjab.

The *Dawn*, almost without exception throughout May gave a major part of its print space to news and writings opposing Punjab's partition. For example, on 15 May it reported a large meeting of Muslim women under the leadership of Begum Husain Malik resolved in Delhi to oppose the partition of Punjab; on 16 May it reported the resolution of another meeting in Lahore. A similar meeting of Muslims of had been organized in Jullundur, which resolved: that a division of Punjab would in fact be a division of Pakistan.

Firoz Khan Noon, the senior Muslim League leader of Punjab, in a way set the tone with a strongly worded statement against the partition of Punjab, in which he also warned the Sikhs: 'The Muslims have done enough to prevent the Sikhs from committing political suicide . . . but the more we try the more their leaders push the Panth into the Congress lap. We will guard every inch of Punjab—not surrender an inch.'[97] In the same statement Noon also argued that Tara Singh and party had failed to understand that their demand for the division of Punjab by the separation of the Amritsar, Jullundur and Ambala Divisions would bifurcate the Sikhs—20,50,000 in the east and 17,50,000 in the west.[98]

This statement by Noon was covered in detail by the *CMG*. as well. In its version it quoted Noon as having said: 'The Congress realizing that division is inevitable are now trying to make Pakistan not worth having.'[99] On 26 May, Noon issued another strongly worded statement announcing the Muslim resolve to prevent the partition of Punjab.[100]

Baldev Singh came out with the reaction of the Sikhs on 25 May, ridiculing the concern of Muslim League leaders for the welfare of the Sikhs:

Why this solitude for the Sikhs now? It is true that 12 lac Sikhs would be left in Muslim majority areas but the number of Muslims in East Punjab will be more than three times of that. . . . We know we shall suffer and are prepared to face the lesser evil.[101]

As part of the build up to prevent Punjab's partition, the League had organized meetings in various parts of Punjab throughout May, for example, in Amritsar on 17 May, and at Ambala on 19 May, where the resolution had recorded 'the sinister move of the Congress'. The Lahore meeting on 24 May was organized by Rashid Ali Khan, president of the Lahore City Muslim League, and resolved to set up a front to fight the 'sinister scheme'.[102]

Jinnah issued a statement on the 21 May saying that the demand for Punjab's partition had come from a 'section of vocal Sikhs', and went on to say that not only would it have disastrous results, but that the 'idea was thoughtless and reckless' and was bound 'to weaken Pakistan'. This statement is also important in a different context—for the first time perhaps Jinnah appears to have shared a general desire for good relations with India. On being asked what kind of future relations Pakistan would have with India, 'friendly and reciprocal', he had said.[103]

Khizr Hayat had met Mountbatten on 3 May and had told him that it would be 'disastrous . . . indeed suicidal' to divide the Punjab. Interestingly, the minutes of the meeting also state: 'His Excellency opened the conversation by saying that he was violently opposed to partition but as the leaders showed absolutely no sign of getting together it appeared . . . inevitable'. Khizr had also said that: 'the British should not be a party to a division . . . once a division was announced reunification would become impossible'. Khizr expressed his opposition even to the plan of initially announcing a 'notional line' that would partition Punjab, because he believed it would only further complicate the situation. He met the Viceroy for a second day and discussed the feasibility of a referendum on whether Punjab should join Hindustan or Pakistan. The minutes of the meeting also show Khizr's conviction that partition was bound to lead to civil war.[104]

A few days after this meeting, Daultana, an old 'Unionist Party' friend and associate—turned foe and friend again of Khizr Hayat, appealed somewhat nostalgically to the Sikhs not to insist for the partition of Punjab: 'Terrible happenings have made you bitter... in no case must we in anger and hatred despoil and disrupt our future.'[105]

The level to which the Muslim League had garnered its forces against the division of Punjab in May 1947 is evident from the resolution of a large body of Muslim students in Lahore, who formed a students' front and vowed to resist even with their lives the division of Punjab.[106] But having said that, it must be remembered that there were a fairly large number of Muslims who were against the concept of Pakistan itself, or at least so till about the end of May.

The *CMG* reported on 18 May the proceedings of a conference organized in London to discuss the economic potential of the new state of Pakistan. The list of speakers included many Muslims including a Dr Shahami who said that the very concept of Pakistan was flawed, because the prospect of dividing Hindus and Muslims who were so deeply interlinked seemed impossible.[107]

Similar sentiments were expressed at a meeting organized by a large group of Muslims of the Indian Workers Association in London under the aegis of the Muslim Committee of Great Britain and presided over by Ch. Akbar Khan. While the Muslim League had launched a big drive against the partition of Punjab for its own political ends, the Muslim workers in London condemned the Muslim League for the very idea of Pakistan: 'History scarcely provides another instance of a community having lost all reason.' A pamphlet opposing the division of India in any form, was also distributed at the meeting.[108]

The *CMG* report on 1 May stated that even among Muslim League MLAs there was disillusionment if not disagreement on the policy the Muslim League had adopted on the Pakistan issue. This report also said that these MLAs were unhappy in the manner in which the minorities had been alienated. Interestingly, this version, which was given to *CMG* by a 'Congress' insider, said that even then (i.e. in May 1947) there was still a chance of Khizr Hayat staging a come back with support of parties other than the Muslim League to form a government in Punjab. That this report was taken seriously by many people became clear a few days later when Khizr Hayat was once again forced to deny it clearly indicating his unflinching support for the Muslim League: 'A certain amount of speculation still continues about me in a section of the press.'[109]

Interestingly, there had indeed been some merit in the 'Congress insider's, version because a day after Khizr made the statement of his support to the Muslim League and to any effort it might make in the formation of a government in Punjab, Sardar Swaran Singh, the up-coming Congress leader, expressed his surprise and disappointment at Khizr's change of heart.[110]

The problem with Khizr's situation in Punjab was that most of the active and vocal leaders of the Muslim League there were his old-time associates of the Unionist Party days. Shaukat Hayat was the son of the popular Sikandar, whose untimely death in tragic circumstances had enabled Khizr to take over the premiership of Punjab. Even though second-generation leaders like Shaukat and Daultana had little or no experience of the politics of Unionism and consensus, the Unionist Party, notwithstanding a host of its other weaknesses, had maintained in Punjab a relative era of peace and communal coexistence.[111] Leaders like Shaukat, to be fair, had visualized Punjab as a region where there was space for all communities. This was one reason why it took the League so much time to strengthen its hold over Punjab. That so many sons of feudal lords deserted the Unionist Party and jumped on to the League's wagon in the early 1940s was more a case of opportunism than a genuine change of heart.[112] Some of these fresh entrants into the Muslim League proved in the course of time even more loyal than the original Leaguers in terms of their aggressiveness and activism. It was a race for power to capture the new state.

In this sense there was an element of earnestness in the statement issued by Shaukat Hayat on 11 May: 'I would . . . suggest that Hindu, Muslim and Sikh leaders put their heads together and find a solution which would benefit all instead of leading our masses to bloodshed—let us find balm to heal the body of our beloved land of the five rivers.'[113]

While Shaukat's appeal was of the emotional kind—the kind that was bothering every Punjabi—William Barton took the argument against the creation of Pakistan a step further. He argued in an article published in the *Weekly Spectator* that a state of Pakistan created on the vision of the Muslim League and totally divorced from India and dependent on the Islamic States of the Mid-East would in the course of time prove a big headache not only for free India but for Britain as well.[114]

PATIALA'S SOLUTION: SIKH ARMY IN PAKISTAN

A secret note in the *TP* volumes refers to a meeting between the Maharaja of Patiala and Jinnah to make the latter realize what the disastrous consequences of his demand for a division of India would be. The note says the Maharaja found Jinnah uncompromising and adamant.[115] The version of this meeting reported in some newspapers, added an interesting angle and suggested that the Maharaja had also made another suggestion to Jinnah of which the Maharaja had not informed the Viceroy's office. In its report, the *CMG*, for example, said that the Maharaja of Patiala had suggested to Jinnah that the only way to avoid the partition of Punjab and have the Sikhs stay on in Pakistan was to give them a separate army under their own commanders. Jinnah, the report said, though he was willing to go a long way to woo the Sikhs, he was unwilling to concede this.[116]

As schemes and theories were being debated as alternatives to the partition of Punjab there were some like Sardar Mohan Singh (INA) who believed, and said so in a press conference in Calcutta, that the coming partition was only a temporary phenomenon and the two, that is, the proposed two units of Punjab, would reunite.[117]

Incidentally the senior Punjab Muslim League leader, Iftikhar Hussain Mamdot, also believed that Governor Jenkins was the man who had in fact floated the idea of Punjab being ideally dividable. Mamdot said: 'He [Jenkins] is the author of the notorious fallacy that Ambala is a Hindu Division, Jullundur a Sikh Division and Rawalpindi and Multan are the only Muslim Divisions of Punjab'. Mamdot even charged Jenkins with being 'soft' towards the eastern districts of Punjab because he had spent much of his service years in those districts. He called upon Muslims 'to unite in their stand against the gubernatorial conspiracy'.[118]

CONGRESS VIEW OF SIKHS IN INDIAN POLITICS

Perhaps the strongest case for the Sikhs to reconsider their demand for the division of Punjab and stay by choice with the Muslims as a part of Pakistan was made by Balwant Singh Saini of the Commercial College of Delhi. In an article published prominently by *Dawn* on 14 May, Saini referred to the the 7 March 1947 issue of *The Eastern Economist*. This magazine, he said, was the official policy organ of the Congress. He quoted from an article: 'The Sikh is a strategic but unreliable element in Indian politics', and went on to appeal to Sikh leaders to understand the game the Congress was playing. 'The partition of Punjab is really a division of the Sikhs and their ultimate extinction.'

Saini said the Sikhs would be much better off with Muslims in Pakistan because (i) 95 per cent of the industry in Punjab was controlled by Hindus; and (ii) since almost 95 per cent of all business in Afghanistan was controlled by Sikhs, if they broke away from the Muslims they would suffer extensive economic losses. He went on to explain how he believed the partition of Punjab could be avoided. Among some of his suggestions to decrease tension and retain Punjab in its present form and as part of Pakistan was to have two home ministers—one for the western districts and the second for the eastern parts. Alternatively, the prime ministership could alternate between suggested could be to have a Muslim and a Sikh. He also suggested that the new state of Pakistan could have two exclusive Sikh universities and also ensure that 40 per cent of the provincial jobs in Punjab were reserved for the Sikhs. He argued that the Muslim League leadership would easily accede to these demands and there was no way the Sikhs could get such favourable terms in a divided Punjab. There were numerous other suggestions which, in sum, were that the economic primacy of the Sikhs was already established in the western districts, particularly in terms of landholdings and the quality of land, in a divided Punjab the Sikhs would not only have to compete with the Hindu majority but would also have to start from scratch to rebuild their fortunes.[119]

PROPERTY MUST BE EXCHANGED WITH POPULATION

To Tara Singh such schemes and the idea that the Sikhs would be better off with the Muslims made no sense, he was clear in his mind that the partition of Punjab was to be done not just on the basis of population but was to be accompanied by an exchange of property: 'Jinnah seems anxious to maintain the integrity of the Sikhs but not their independence . . . he wants Sikhs to remain united under his heel . . . no paper safeguards can obliterate lessons and practical experiences.' He went on to request Jinnah: 'to give up the hypocritical role of being a friend of the Sikhs.[120]

Congress leader Sachar ridiculed all talk of a united Punjab: 'division of Punjab is inevitable . . . even the champions of Pakistan realise the absurdity of the scheme and the problems that will arise [by not partitioning Punjab] but due to the fear of the leaders they will not publicly admit their doubts.'[121]

A couple of days after Tara Singh had issued the statement demanding not only the exchange of population but also of property, Sardar Buta Singh (member of the Council of States) echoed Tara Singh's views: '. . . it would be ridiculous to think of partition only on a population basis . . . how can either side make a free gift of their properties? Crown lands were sold by the British and were mostly purchased by the Sikhs . . . the Sikhs will resist any attempt to rob them.'[122] Sikh landowners had also at the same time organized a meeting in Amritsar on 6 May expressing great concern.[123]

On 1 May *The Tribune* reported Tara Singh as saying 'partition was coming sooner than we had imagined'. A couple of days later Tara Singh issued a more detailed statement saying that he had learned that Muslims would be given 65 per cent of Punjab's land even though they owned only 50 per cent. In this statement he also welcomed Jinnah's call for the exchange of population because he saw the exchange of population as 'quite different from immigration . . . exchange implies property as well'. Tara Singh, Baldev Singh and Swarn Singh in a telegram to Secretary of State Listowel pointed out that the proposal for carving a new state out of the 12 eastern districts was flawed. They said that the Sikhs were being deprived of the canal colonies which, in fact, had been developed by their labour and in any case the eastern districts did not have any similar resources with which the Sikhs could exchange their properties. The three demanded that the river Chenab be made the boundary.[124]

PUNJAB CANNOT BE PARTITIONED ON THE BASIS OF CENSUS FIGURES

Claims and counterclaims with regard to regions based on a range of theories took up considerable newspaper space throughout May, the *Dawn* and its counter *The Tribune* usually carrying two different versions. While *Dawn* strengthened the League's claim to almost the whole of Punjab by reeling off population figures, *The Tribune* chal-

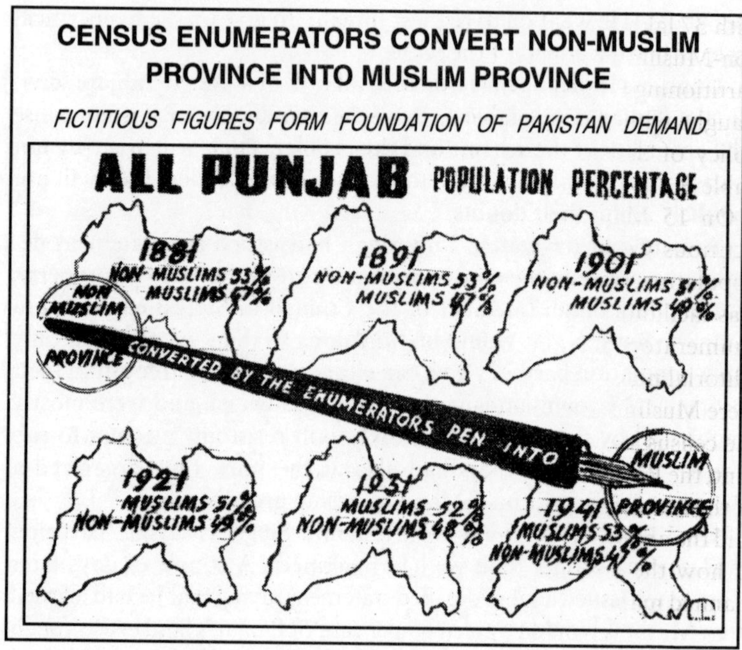
CENSUS ENUMERATORS CONVERT NON-MUSLIM PROVINCE INTO MUSLIM PROVINCE

FICTITIOUS FIGURES FORM FOUNDATION OF PAKISTAN DEMAND

Growth of Muslim Population in Punjab—1881–1941 (*The Tribune*, 19 May 1947).

lenged the very basis of such figures by suggesting that the census itself was cooked up and incorrect.

An article by Jamshed in *Dawn*, on 23 May charged the Congress with facilitating the division of Punjab by instigating the March violence so as to create a situation where it would be easy to have the division resolution approved by the apex Congress body and sidetrack opposition within the Congress to the division of Punjab. Jamshed then said it had always been the Congress policy of motivating the Sikhs to side with the Hindus in the political crisis that was in place in Punjab. Jamshed said the Congress in its partition resolution deliberately had not referred to the partition of Bengal so as to 'create an impression in Sikh minds that Congress is actually anxious to safeguard the Sikh interest'.

Jamshed provided a list of figures countering the demand for Punjab's partition and how such a partition would in fact harm both the Muslims and the Sikhs. What the Congress now wants is that 37 lakh Sikhs and Hindus in West Punjab should exchange places with 37 lakh Muslims of East Punjab, thus creating two Muslim and non-Muslim provinces. Jamshed's argument was that the policy of partitioning Punjab on the basis of district and tehsil populations was fraught with the danger of future communal friction and that the policy of division must be based on broad contiguous areas (see Table 3.1).

On 15 May, *The Tribune* cried: 'Pakistan demand is based on fictitious Census figures'. While listing detailed variations in the population, it said the abnormal growth in the number of Muslims was facilitated possibly by the fact that in some districts the census enumerators were largely Muslim. For example, in Gujarat the editorial noted that of the 3,147 census enumerators in 1941, 2,485 were Muslims. It cited Lahore as an example where it said that while the census showed the non-Muslim population to be a mere 35 per cent, the Ration Department figures however showed that 46 per cent of the ration card holders in Lahore were non-Muslim. The editorial said the abnormal variation in the population figures was a reflection of how the basic issue of population was being manipulated in a planned manner.[125]

TABLE 3.1: POPULATION IN LAKHS

	Muslim	Sikhs	Hindu	SC	Muslim %	Sikh %
Undivided Punjab	162	37	63	12	57	13.2
West Punjab 18 districts	124	17	20	3	73	10
East Punjab 11 districts	39	20	43	10	33.8	18

Source: *Dawn*, 23 May 1947.

LIAQAT ACCUSES JENKINS

Strangely, even as *The Tribune* echoed the sentiments of a large number of urban Hindus and Sikhs of Lahore and Amritsar that the law and order machinery including the police was set against them, the Muslim League's leadership believed quite the opposite, that is, the Muslims were being oppressed: 'western Punjab today groans under the heel of an oppressive tyrant (Jenkins) . . . little is known because of the iron ring of censorship. . . . This anti-Muslim censorship is typical of the province . . . Punjab's present Anglo-Hindu-Sikh regime.'[126]

Liaqat Ali in fact complained strongly to Jenkins that the Punjab administration was biased against Muslims. Naturally Master Tara

Singh thought quite the opposite. Tara Singh told Jenkins: 'The European officers are only misled by the Muslim officials who alone are near to them.'[127] Liaqat had also told Jenkins in the same meeting (25 May) that there were only two Muslim magistrates in Lahore and that British officers in particular always behaved rudely and arrogantly with Muslim non-officials.

Jenkins, however, explained to Liaqat Ali that this was not the case. He said that of about 3,600 people killed in Punjab since the outbreak of violence in early March, only 600 had been Muslims and that of about Rs. 15 crore worth of property that was destroyed in the disturbances, only about 5 per cent was owned by Muslims. In Lahore, Jenkins pointed out, for example, only a third of the casualities were Muslim. With regard to the role of the British officers, Jenkins added that 'British officers many of them gravely shocked thought the Muslim League leaders did not realise how terrible the Rawalpindi massacres appeared to be to impartial persons'. When Liaqat asked Jenkins to get tough with the Sikhs, he replied that the Sikhs were very insecure and in any case the League had not even apologized for the happening in Rawalpindi.[128]

It is against this background that I would like to draw attention to some of the notings made by Jenkins during May 1947. For example, as on 1 May he noted in a 'Top Secret' communication to the Viceroy:

> A peaceful partition of the Punjab is most improbable . . . the statement (on partition) will excite anger among all Muslims, Sikhs and Hindus who will live on the wrong side of the boundary . . . communal rioting will spread rapidly . . . we cannot impose a partition without forces, which I do not believe we possess.[129]

A couple of days later Jenkins once again showed how well he understood the problem.

> [The] Partition business seems to be getting out of control . . . it is clear that we are not going to succeed in an amicable agreement . . . we shall be manouevered into giving an award which we shall be unwilling or unable to enforce. . . . I think Your Excellency should reconsider the terms of an early announcement embodying a solution of the political problem . . . it would be futile to announce a partition of Punjab which no community would accept . . . an award which all three communities would dare us to enforce and I have no doubt that all three would begin to fight among themselves

instantly. . . . Jinnah wants the whole of Punjab, the Hindus and Sikhs insist he is not to have more than 2/5 of it.[130]

Ironically, a day after the Viceroy received this forthright and insightful note, he conveyed to Lord Ismay his own view that possibly Jenkins' assessment was wrong with regard to the Partition Plan. 'I feel that Jenkins' arguments are based on false premises. . . . Certainly in recent conversations which I have had with Jinnah he did not appear seriously to contest the need for partition but seemed even grateful for the 17 districts of the Punjab.'[131]

In yet another remarkable note to the Viceroy, this time well into the outbreak of the disturbances in the mid-May, Jenkins noted:

> we may slip very easily into what will be regarded as an award without the means or intensions of enforcing it . . . we may slip a stage further into abandonment of Punjab to chaos . . . The hope of settlement is very faint indeed since the Muslim League leaders have no sense at all [and] Tara Singh is almost hysterical.[132]

In a secret note Jenkins' office also informed the Viceroy's acting private secretary on 21 May that according to intelligence sources Sikh leaders were planning raids on Muslim villages and that even the Maharaja of Patiala was covertly supporting the move with arms and explosives, as was the Dewan of Nabha.[133]

A couple of days before this intelligence report Master Tara Singh had met Jenkins in Lahore. This was an eventful meeting in which Tara Singh admitted to Jenkins that political leaders like himself were in fact partly responsible for the widespread lack of faith and trust, a situation widely prevalent in Punjab. As usual Tara Singh once again informed Jenkins that he had no faith in the police of Punjab. Jenkins noted: 'it is lamentable that at this juncture the affairs of the Punjab should so largely be in the hands of this eccentric old man.'[134]

It must be clearly understood that right from the Governor of Punjab to the Viceroy, the Secretary of State and even Prime Minister Attlee, everyone was aware by the end of May of the tragic direction in which Punjab was moving. Attlee more than admitted the danger of a civil war in Punjab in a note to Field Marshal Smuts on 23 May.[135]

The Fortnightly Appreciation Reports compiled by the Information Department on the basis of a cross-section of newspaper reports left little doubt about the seriousness of the situation: 'In the Punjab fear of League's return to power has gathered force among Hindus and Sikhs especially after Khizr Hayat's declaration of support to the Muslim League.'[136]

BRITAIN'S DILEMMA—HOW MUCH POWER TO RELINQUISH

Even as the major British players in India, both in New Delhi and in Lahore, were clearly decided about going ahead with the partition, they seemed to be in two minds as to how much responsibility was to be transferred to the Interim Government in the immediate context. On its part, the Interim Government was keen for the transfer of maximum power and responsibility at the earliest.

To Sardar Patel the British policy of 'remaining neutral but holding on to power [was] a way of propagating civil war'. Patel was convinced that if the interim government were to be converted into a Dominion Government with the Viceroy staying out, 'there would be peace within the country in a week'.[137] He also stated that those who had committed acts of violence had done so because they felt there was no strong central government to check them. This statement by Patel at this juncture drew considerable attention in the newspapers, especially in view of the fact that Mountbatten was also believed to be keen to transfer power if it could help prevent civil war.[138]

But such were the complexities of the race for power that no sooner had Patel made this statement, than it drew strong criticism from Jinnah who called Patel's demand for the transfer of power 'monstrous . . . only his dream, the League will never agree to this'.[160] In the same statement Jinnah also ridiculed Patel for saying that the division of the army 'could take years' and said that 'it could be done in hours'.[140] *The Tribune* in fact had argued that the army, if it were decided, would soon cease to exist'.[141] A few days before *The Tribune* argued against an immediate division of the army it had also cited a news report from London which said there were considerable differences between the Viceroy and the Interim Cabinet on the issue.[142]

Liaqat Ali also came out strongly against Patel's demand for the transfer of power to a Dominion rather than an Interim Government. He said any such step would be akin to 'torpedoing the Pakistan demand'.[143] While Patel warned of civil war if the British tried to remain neutral and at the same time refused to transfer full authority, there were many others who said civil war was coming any way.

Let Civil War Decide

Acharya Jugal Kishore, a general secretary of the Congress party was reported to have said that 'Chaos and civil war in India were preferable to British rule'. When a reporter of the *CMG* asked Jugal Kishore how the boundaries were to declared, he replied that an impartial commission would finalize it and that if: 'the Muslim League disagreed a civil war would decide'.[144] These were views that unfortunately proved prophetic, the only difference being that it was not only the Muslim League that disagreed with the line of division, or rather what was expected to be the line, but so did everyone else.

Jugal Kishore was not the only one talking of civil war. *Dawn* (21 May) published excerpts from various sections of the press in Britain (the preceding day or two), most of which were timed to coincide with Mountbatten's arrival in London to discuss the last attempt or rather the issue of an early exit of the British from India. The *Liverpool Post* said: 'India was balanced on a razor's edge'; the *Western Mail* was quoted saying: 'There is implicit in the situation a threat not of one but a whole crop of civil wars.' The *Birmingham Post* recorded: 'every day that passes India is now having a forestate of the calamity of a civil war . . . Mountbatten's task is to bring Indian leaders together while there is yet time to a sense of the perils of indecision'. The *London Times* appears, in hindsight, to have been the closest to reality: 'division of Punjab', it said in a lead two-column story, 'may be theoretically practicable but will lead only to failure and destruction'. The *Evening News* commented: 'The tennous [*sic*] framework of unity imposed on India by the British Raj is breaking. . . . It is clear that immediate and vigorous decisions must be taken if a violent civil war is not to send India into pieces.'

LONDON COMMITS TO AN EARLY TRANSFER OF POWER

Throughout May (1947), there was hectic activity in London on the question of an early transfer of power. Prime Minister Attlee chaired a meeting on 5 May in which he noted that bitterness had increased after the 20 February announcement and that there were practically no chances of an amicable settlement. He also said that Field Marshal Auchinleck too had informed him that the situation in India was 'dangerous'.[145] On 8 May, Attlee chaired another meeting in which Abell, the Viceroy's private secretary, was also present.[146] In yet another meeting on 14 May, the Prime Minister noted: 'raising at this stage of the possibility of an early attainment of Dominion Status . . . seems to have produced a radical change'.[147]

A top secret coded message (15 May) from London informed the Viceroy in New Delhi that while the broad outlines of the plan would remain the same, changes were required and that Mountbatten would have to come to London. A telegram dated 12 May even suggests that Attlee was keen for the 3 June Plan to be announced by 17 May, that is, before the British Parliament went into recess. Mountbatten said it was impossible.[148]

On 19 May the certainty of Punjab's partition was boldly printed across the front pages of newspapers: 'Hope of United India abandoned', 'Division may begin in June', 'no panic withdrawal from India'. Both *Dawn* and *The Tribune* carried reports from sources in London. *The Tribune* said, 'It is no part of the present policy to execute a panic withdrawal'. *Dawn* said 'the recent wave of speculation that Britain might just pack up and clear out . . . is now generally discountenanced in informal quarters . . . the question of [the] actual date on which the British will leave India . . . depends entirely on Indian capacity to set up an authority or authorities to whom she can hand over responsibility.'[149]

The Tribune went a step further declaring that the 'British had surrendered to Jinnah', and that they were even worried 'lest India fall prey to some big power', meaning obviously the Soviet Union. The report also said that policy makers in Britain were concerned that India was moving towards civil war,[150] and that the plan of a quicker departure had only hardened the stand of political groups in Punjab rather than having a pacifying effect: 'the announcement of the date of departure far from shocking the Indian political parties into an agreement has only hardened their stands'.[151]

FREEDOM AT THE EXPENSE OF UNITY

By about the middle of May, newspapers in Punjab had also been citing reports from the newspapers in Britain that an important meeting was scheduled in the near future at the country home of the British

Prime Minister, and that the meeting was expected to take a historic decision on India.[152] Some reports even said that power was likely to be handed over sooner than June 1948.[153] On 25 May, most newspapers carried stories of the 'British cabinet having approved of a historic plan to partition India if last ditch efforts do not succeed', and that the 'final shape of Hindustan and Pakistan would emerge in 12 weeks'.[154]

As speculations and rumours vied for attention it was however fairly accepted across Punjab by the third week of May that partition was now no longer a question of June 1948 but was possibly round the corner. Against this background Gandhi's statement of 28 May was received with great excitement and a last element of hope that possibly answers to the crisis could still be found. Speaking at the post-prayer meeting on 28 May Gandhi said:

> Freedom is not worth having if it is achieved at the expense of the unity of India. . . . The British have no right to divide the country . . . even if the whole of Hindustan is burnt to ashes I will never concede an inch of India to Pakistan if it is sought to be achieved by coercion.[155]

Coming from Gandhi, these were uncharacteristic words, a clear indication that even he appeared to have no answer, and indeed things were getting out of hand. A couple of days earlier (26 May), Gandhi had once again appealed to the British to leave immediately: 'In my opinion we are unable to think coherently whilst Britain is still functioning in India . . . after it has withdrawn let me hope we shall have the wisdom to think coherently and keep India one or split it into two or more.'[156]

Gandhi's post-prayer address of 28 May in which he had said that freedom was not worth it if it was at the cost of unity had drawn attention in a wide spectrum of newspapers. Possibly a couple of days before Gandhi said this Nehru was interviewed by Norman Cliff of the *News Chronicle*. Nehru was asked if he was hopeful of persuading Mahatma Gandhi to acquiesce in any proposal that involved partition. Nehru replied, 'Gandhiji has held the opinion strongly that any arrangement for division of India or of provinces should not take place through British agency. If the people of the area desire division there will be nothing to stop them'.[157]

This interview was probably conducted in Mussoorie where both Nehru and Patel addressed meetings in the last week of May. On one such occasion Nehru said: 'we are not ignorant of the happenings . . .

I still believe in one India—Gandhi (*CMG*, 19 May 1947).

we have limitations . . . [The] time is not far when we will have real power and when our countrymen will have no worry'.[158] Nehru also made a reference to a dramatic announcement which he said was round the corner and that a new era of struggle would begin from 2 June 1947. Interestingly, he also shared his apprehensions that the transition was unlikely to be a peaceful one.[159]

On 31 May newspapers in Punjab reported in a tone of expectant excitement that Nehru had rushed to Lahore in an attempt to discuss important matters with the Akali leaders. What transpired in Nehru's meetings with the Akalis is not quite clear, but it should not be too off the mark to imagine the briefing given by Nehru to the Akalis. Newspapers had also noted that 'a serious situation had developed'.

From the point of view of the newspapers, this visit of Nehru's proved eventful. For one, Lahore's reporters had a taste of Nehru's famed temper. Someone among a fairly large group of reporters appears to have questioned Nehru as to why he always favoured foreign correspondents while responding to questions and granting interviews. Nehru did not like the observation and a heated argument followed which led ultimately to the reporters being asked to leave the conference.[160]

The Tribune greeted Nehru's arrival in Lahore (29 May) with an editorial warning him not to be misled by the temporary tranquillity. The editorial informed Nehru that people were generally happy with the manner in which Governor Jenkins and Lahore's Deputy Commissioner J.C.W. Eustance had handled the communal trouble, but also added that they were handicapped because a large part of the police was sympathetic to the League. Interestingly, the editorial discussed how the Governor's drive to increase representation of non-Muslims in the police force was being sidetracked by manipulative subordinates inclined to support the Muslim League. The editorial went on to stress the demand for Martial Law in Lahore and the division of Punjab into three interim administrative divisions in the days preceding its final division.[161]

THE 3 JUNE PLAN: A LEAP INTO THE DARK

Mountbatten flew back to Delhi from London on 1 June, bringing with him his government's plan to transfer power by 15 August 1947, a plan that had been discussed threadbare throughout May.[162] Mountbatten had a long meeting with Gandhi on 2 June. The Viceroy convened a press conference in on 4 June 1947. This historic conference was packed with expectant reporters, it had the 'Iron Man', the Sardar (Patel) himself conducting the proceedings. The Viceroy's opening remarks further charged the atmosphere: 'I mean it sincerely when I say power will be transferred completely this year as it ever would have been by June 1948. I am not bluffing.'[163] Bluffing, Mountbatten was not, because it is more than clear the British had by the end of May made up their mind to leave—in a hurry perhaps.

The conference was naturally of monumental significance on many counts, but in the context of Punjab the Viceroy placed the responsibility for partition at the door of the Sikh leadership who, he said, had put pressure on the Congress for partition and, for good or bad, what the Sikhs would ultimately get would be of their own asking and doing. Mountbatten of course shared his concern that the plan was likely to divide the Sikhs, but he asserted that the British were doing it only because they had been forced to doing it.

Clearly the decision to quit India in a hurry was greatly influenced

"You Asked For It"

Even though the 3 June Plan had been approved by leaders of all major political formations—Congress, Muslim League and the Akalis, among ordinary people the plan to partition the country was generally disapproved. Mountbatten is shown standing with a 'butcher's' knife having split a goat in two as Nehru walks away with the front, leaving the posterior for Jinnah (*CMG*, 12 June 1947).

by the conditions in Punjab. Not only was the probability of civil war looming large, as Prime Minister Attlee noted to Field Marshal Smuts,[164] but the fear of the administration collapsing was adding speed to the plans: 'Administration was getting more and more difficult; even with a stable government the loss of most of our senior British officers would be a serious blow, without a stable government the service would disintegrate.'[165]

According to M.N. Das, the plan to bring forward British exit from India by almost a year was carefully thought out and indeed possibly prompted by the Congress who too were keen to prevent Jinnah from getting more time to evaluate the division plans more carefully.[166] I am unable to buy this theory for the simple reason the Congress had little to do with the planning of 'strategies' or 'strategic decisions' in the summer of 1947. Most decisions were taken haphazardly, day-to-day some even at cross purposes, and, in any case, if Congress planners of policy were blessed with the kind of vision and foresight that Das would have us believe, surely they should also have visualized the consequences of an unplanned exchange of population on a scale such as Punjab. To credit the Viceroy for having consciously taken the decision with the intention to 'steal a victory over others' is also unacceptable. The fact is it was an error of judgement—on the part of both Mountbatten and his friends in the Congress.

The urgency to leave India at the earliest was also stressed by Prime Minister Atlee in the House of Commons when setting the 15 August 1947 deadline. He had said it was the only way out.[167] Participating in the same debate, Churchil was reported to have said: 'we must ask ourselves . . . whether any better way can be found of saving India from a blood bath that may seem so near'.[168] On 28 June *The Tribune* carried on its front page, an eleven-column report based on reports published earlier in *Time* magazine. The report said the British were keen to clear out of India before it blew up in their face.

As the realization of the departure of the British at a much earlier date dawned across the plains of Punjab, a decision that should have been received with enthusiasm saw, on the contrary, fingers being pointed at Congress leaders for the hurry with which they seemed to have accepted the June Plan. One can understand the critical comments of sections of the British press which had been following events in detail in India, but the hostility with which a fair majority of the press reacted in Punjab is surprising—the exception to this broad trend of anti-Congress, particularly anti-Nehru, sentiment were the newspapers aligned with the Muslim League.

While *Dawn* carried a huge front-page banner line, 'Pakistan *Zindabad*' on 4 June, *The Tribune* reported that 'Jinnah's hour of triumph may soon turn itself into an hour of defeat as Muslim masses will have to face growing poverty'. A couple of days later *The Tribune* reported a statement by Rafique Zakaria, President, London Majlis: 'the creation of two Indias will ruin Muslims politically, economically . . . in the near future a United India will emerge which will be beyond the power of ten Jinnahs to destroy'.[169]

India being reunited was obviously wishful thinking, but Pakistan was a reality. Bali had heard the address of Nehru and Jinnah on the radio soon after Mountbatten had announced the Partition Plan. He noted: 'In the announcement . . . one could detect a tone of muffled joy in the voice of Mr. Jinnah. He began and ended his oration by Pakistan *Zindabad*. The voice of Mr. Nehru was that of a tired man who was speaking with an uneasy conscience, while Baldev Singh who should have been the most affected of all as his home province was going to be vivisected did not show any tremors or emotions.'[170]

The significance of the new plan lay in perceptions which differed from person to person. For political leaders it was bound to mark a new beginning which would make things easier for them—with major differences having been narrowed. But for the ordinary citizen, the issue of whether partition was good or undesirable had already been decided by the leaders on their own. What remained to be decided was which town and village would go where. With the award of Rawalpindi, Multan and Ambala Divisions being clear, the most important issue of discussion throughout June was where to draw the line in the central districts.[171]

While newspapers in Punjab indulged in speculation as to what had led the British to quit in so hurried a manner, *Dawn* and the *CMG* gave the debate a new twist by publishing reports based on a *Newsweek* story titled 'Mountbatten's brilliant handling of situation: Behind the scene story'. Both newspapers said that the basic plan of Dominion Status and quick exist was suggested to Mountbatten by Nehru and Patel in about the middle of May. *CMG* added an interesting extra to the story saying that Nehru and Patel told Mountbatten that for Jinnah to accept the whole plan, it was necessary to make it appear that it was Mountbatten's idea. The report in *CMG* also said that Jinnah was in fact surprised when Mountbatten told him that the

Congress would be too willing to accept the whole plan.[172] Newspapers, both in Britain and in the Punjab, by the middle of June widely supported the view that the Congress more generally and a small group of Congressmen led by Nehru in particular were the force behind the acceptance the partition plan.

It does seem surprising that a issue which was thought to have been settled in March when Congress had resolved in favour of partition and when both the Congress and the Muslim League had accepted the partition scheme in principle, the reaction against it should have been so strong in June. This of course can be explained. The difference in June was that most people appeared to believe that what had been accepted by the leaders in March was relatively still a great distance away (1948), perhaps by then even avoidable, but what the British Prime Minister and the Viceroy announced in the first week of June was immediate—there was no escaping it.

AN ACT OF MADNESS

Soon after the historic announcement, the Viceroy learnt through Krishna Menon of how unhappy Gandhi was—so unhappy that some feared he would denounce the plan itself. The Viceroy was anxious to meet Gandhi the same day—obviously before the latter addressed the day's prayer meeting. The meeting took place at 6 p.m. Mountbatten expressed his helplessness and comforted Gandhi. The purpose of the meeting was served in that Gandhi was by the end of it reasonably pacified. In the post-prayer address, Gandhi absolved Mountbatten of the responsibility of dividing India and said the Viceroy had acted at the bidding of the Muslim League and the Congress.[173]

Talking of the Congress party and the heap of charges that were piled on it—two statements of Gandhi quoted by newspapers in the first week of June are interesting. On 5 June, Gandhi was reported by *The Tribune* as having said that 'people should not forget that Congress had been forced into this position'.[174] The following day *The Tribune* once again quoted Gandhi from the post-prayer meeting address. Reacting to a question whether he would go on a fast to prevent the partition of India, Gandhi said; 'If Congress commits an act of madness does it mean that I should die?' In its version of the same incident, *CMG* quoted Gandhi as having said that he did not believe in the two-nation theory and, 'The Congress, Sikhs and

Muslim League have accepted [partition] . . . I have nothing more to comment . . . I do not blame the British or the Viceroy'. Gandhi's disillusionment with the situation naturally received widespread attention in the Punjab press.[175]

No Way Out

The firebrand socialist Jayaprakash Narayan underlined Gandhi's unhappiness and the turn things had taken in the first week of June. While addressing a huge public meeting in Gorakhpur on 6 June, Jayaprakash said that Gandhi was unhappy with the Congress for having accepted the partition plan; and that the settlement had landed the country in a swamp from which there seemed no way out.[176]

Abhyudaya, the mouthpiece of the veteran leader Madan Mohan Malviya, was even more blunt. In a lead article titled '*Ghatnain Swayam Kahe Rahi Hain*', it said that division had destroyed the strength and vitality of India and reduced it a '*Bandar Baant*' (monkey division)'—meaning a greedy grabbing of whatever was available. It also said that leaders had accepted the partition of India thinking that it would resolve the crisis, 'but everyone knows that they are wrong'.[177] Another important media organ of Allahabad, '*Leader*' however, thought that accepting Partition was better than murder of citizens'.[178]

The Tribune in particular led the attack on a section of the Congress leadership for accepting the partition of Punjab. Extensive space was devoted in the first fortnight of June to opinions against the 3 June Plan. It started the debate by quoting a resolution adopted in a meeting at the Swaraj House in London, saying Indian leaders had simply 'yielded under duress'.[179] On 6 June *The Tribune* quoted William, Dobie, a socialist British MP and old friend of India, who in 1940 had compelled the Labour Party conference to discuss India and had even induced the British Railwaymen's Union to take up India's problems. Therefore, his views were much respected:

> Frankly I am unable to understand . . . the reasons behind the Congress acceptance of the British plan of partition . . . I am bound to support my government . . . I regret to say however that . . . we have accepted a dangerous principle namely a man changes his nationality with religion . . . whether the acceptance of this rather reactionary principle will help India to avoid civil war I do not know.'

Dr Gokul Chand Narang, the West Lahore General Rural MLA and an old and often partisan warhorse of Punjab's political arena, was more straightforward in condemning the partition plan: 'The Congress had no guts', and all the noise now was like crying over spilt milk.[180]

The Free Press Journal believed that the '3 June Plan enshrines the greatest betrayal by its own leaders that has ever been seen'.[181] *The Times of India* was more cautious and gave to the Plan a conditional acceptance: '[The] price is worth paying if it brings peace to the country'.[182]

London's *Daily Mail*, however, termed the whole plan as a leap into the dark unparalled in the long annals of political and constitutional change.[183] Quoting Harold Davies, the British socialist MP, *The Tribune's* reporter from London wrote: 'It will be dishonest to pretend that a vast majority of Indians will feel happy'.[184] *The Tribune* later devoted its lead editorial to the Plan: 'Nobody for a moment can deny that the partition of India is bound to create complications and complexities.'[185]

There were, of course, many with extensive experience of India who believed like Wavell, for example, that there would be problems, but the problems would in the course of time settle down: 'although India has dangerous and critical years ahead, [its] future is assured . . . (the) birth pangs of anything are difficult, particularly when the results are twins'.[186]

Surprisingly, even *Dawn*, which had otherwise taken a leading stand in support of partition, reported on 5 June a view of a leading Congressman who criticized the Plan 'it is our leaders, policy of grab which has brought us to this pass. India would not have been divided had our leaders played fair and accepted the Cabinet Delegation plan.'[187]

Partition a Fraud on India—Hindu Mahasabha

Not surprisingly, however, it was the *Hindu Outlook* that was the most blunt in its attack on the Congress leadership for not only having accepted but also facilitating the partition of India. It quoted in an editorial a resolution (moved by N.C. Chatterjee) of the All India Committee of the Hindu Mahasabha, saying the Congress had betrayed the nation and that the 3 June Plan was not a reward but the wreaking of vengeance. It also reported that the Sabha had decided to organize 3 July as a day of protest.[188]

In another report it also quoted a second part of the resolution. 'we refuse to accept the British plan... Hindu India shall have no tranquillity until the so-called Pakistan zones are brought back into the union'.[189] The resolution also added that the Congress had capitulated. The meeting was addressed by many of the Hindu Mahasabha leaders like L.B. Bhopatkar, who in his address said that 'What is surprising is that the Congress which was the loudest in the elections (1946) in preaching the unity and integrity of India should have quietly accepted the plea and actively engaged itself . . . it should at least have consulted the people. . . . He also said it would be a great blunder if Hindu and Sikhs accepted it voluntarily. Another speaker at the conference, Dayal Singh Bedi, said: 'it is a strange coincidence that it was Motilal Nehru who separated Sind from Bombay and now his son is separating Sind from the rest of India . . . if the Congress had to accept it why did it not do so earlier . . . why all the destruction?'[189]

Even as the speakers at the conference were unsparing in their criticism it is the texts of the two resolutions that greatly surcharged the event. The second resolution called upon Hindu provincial governments to reduce the number of Muslims in government and police service, to arm Hindus and Sikhs for offence and defence, to start a Hindu Sikh military training institute. The resolution added, 'Pakistan has been thrust on India as a direct result of Congress Commitments, follies and surrender, but still the Congress and Gandhi are telling the Hindus that they are not responsible for it. We must tell the truth.'

The same issue of the *Hindu Outlook* also carried an article, 'Partition a fraud on India', which argued that in accepting the Cabinet Mission Plan in a distorted form leading to the Interim Government, etc., Nehru had led the country into the pit: 'rather than Congress dictating the terms of transfer of power the British dictated the terms of India's freedom'. The article ridiculed Nehru for saying that 'India cannot wait and that ours must not be a moment for partition but freedom.' It charged the Congress leadership for losing the initiative and added that partition was no solution, the issue was of choosing between Pakistan and nationalism. Veer Savarkar was unable to attend the conference but he had sent a message in which he called for organizing a Black Day. Dr Syama Prasad Mookerjee had also 'condemned it unequivocally'.[190]

The relatively milder and less consequential opponents of the Congress, the Socialist Party of India, also met in New Delhi on 10 June and had resolved to reject the 3 June Plan. The resolution expressed its 'disapproval' of the plan.[191]

The Indian National Trade Union Congress which met in New Delhi on 15 June and resolved that the 'division of India though inevitable in present circumstances is detrimental to the interests of masses . . . [we hope] it will be only a temporary phase'.[192]

Many sections of the Punjab press mocked the Congress leadership for the manner in which it had accepted the partition plan. *The Tribune* columnist, 'Wayfarer', reacting to Gandhi's statement on the 3 June Plan wrote: 'How I wish Mahatma Gandhi had voiced his determination "to stake" his all for preserving unity a little earlier . . . I am afraid it has come too late. . . . When there was time, the leaders did nothing, now when it is so late they have suddenly become active.'[193]

A day after the 3 June Plan was announced, a profoundly important condemnation of the plan as well as the people who had worked for it came from none other than the great Punjabi patriot and revolutionary, Sardar Ajit Singh. In a statement issued from Dhalhousie he left no one in doubt as to the magnitude of the mistake he thought the Congress leadership had made:

> The champions of partition will not escape their condemnation in history and will be execrated by present and coming generations . . . nationalist India will certainly rise and will spare no sacrifice to see the nation reunited . . . the case must be taken to the UNO.[194]

Ajit Singh's condemnation is important not just because it came from him but also because it is a reflection of the contemporary opinion of the millions of ordinary households, the 'little' people who paid the true price. Without exception the newspapers of the time carried a vast number of letters highlighting the fact that across the plains of Punjab, partition symbolized not the freedom of India but a story of sadism, brutality, broken homes, lost loved ones and not least of all, lost fortunes and the overriding feeling that politicians had let the masses down for ends that were more meaningful and convenient to their own interests.

MUSLIM LEAGUE ACCEPTS THE 3 JUNE PLAN

If there is one thing that the Muslim League did not want, it was the partition of Punjab. Sadly for it, Pakistan as a reality had now come to be linked to this unpleasant reality of Punjab's division. When the All India Muslim League met on 9 June to discuss the 3 June Plan it really had no option other than to accept the Plan. Of the 400 members who attended the historic session, 8 voted against the proposal to accept the 3 June Plan.[195] Unlike in the Congress where opposition to the leadership's having accepted the 3 June Plan was open and loud, within the Muslim League there was as such very little opposition to the Plan, or at least openly. An important Muslim League leader who did come out against the decision was Abdul Hashim, Secretary of the Bengal Provincial Muslim League. In a statement after the press reported the League's acceptance Hashim said: 'The acceptance of the 3 June Plan by the All India Muslim League was due more to fear and helplessness rather than satisfaction and hope.'[196]

In fact, there were possibly a large number of Muslims even in the western districts who were against not just partition of Punjab but even the concept of Pakistan particularly the manner in which it was being achieved. Many such people chose to keep silent probably because the League had in a masterly stroke based the whole concept on Islamic principles. It was only natural therefore that only a few Punjabi Muslims dared to speak up against the 3 June Plan. Perhaps one of the most sensitive oppositions to the partition plan was from Sadiq Ali in an article, 'Fact and Fiction Behind Pakistan', published in *The Tribune*:

> There are good grounds for hoping that the new generation of young men brought up in a different atmosphere and Muslims living in non-Muslim regions would form a materially different estimate of the blessings of Pakistan. The Congress was aware of the reactionary character of the Muslim League. Pakistan mentality is an outrage on all that is best and noblest in Islam.[197]

The All India Majlis-e-Ahra Islam's stand against partition also drew much attention: 'Centuries old centres of Islamic culture like Deoband, Aligarh, Jamia, Nadwa will be left in Hindu India.' The resolution also added that the proposed plan would deprive Muslims of prime commercial centres like Ferozepur, Hoshiarpur, Amrtisar, and Ludhiana, where Muslims had large commercial and agricultural estates. The same report also cited A.M. Khawaja, the 'nationalist' leader, as having said that nationalist Muslims would never accept the division plan.[198]

THE SIKH RESPONSE

We have already noted that the League leadership was more than willing to roll out the red carpet for the Sikhs to remain in Pakistan because this alone could prevent the partition of Punjab. Therefore, when the working committee of the Shiromani Akali Dal, the Panthic Board and important Sikh legislators met in Lahore on 10 June, they did so to write the destiny of their people. Their decision to accept the 3 June Plan must have undoubtedly been a difficult one. Authentic versions of what actually transpired in the meeting are not available, but in the end they accepted the Plan and even sent a copy of the resolution to the Viceroy.[199]

Some days after this important Lahore resolution, Tara Singh was reported to have said that although he did not welcome or approve the 3 June Plan he could not boycott it. The report also quoted him as having said that he was impressed with the sincerity of the Viceroy, who he felt had got the best workable plan.[200]

Kharak Singh's opposition to the 3 June Plan, however, made it amply clear that the Panth was deeply divided on the issue. Kharak Singh believed the Plan was bound to cause great harm to the Sikhs and that the division of India was imminent only because senior Congress leaders had surrendered:

> Those who are saying that the division of India has become almost inevitable and in the same breath are appealing to their countrymen to get ready to receive the gift of independence are talking in contradictory terms. In my opinion the Congress leaders . . . have fallen prey to British diplomacy . . . I would appeal to the Congress not to yield to the demand for the division of India. If it does I am afraid it will be signing its own death warrant.[201]

On the day following the Lahore conference of Sikh leaders, another Sikh conference was organized in Delhi. Among those who addressed the conference were the Maharaja of Faridkot, Sardar Baldev Singh and Giani Kartar Singh. The 3 June Plan was called 'unholy' by the Maharaja of Faridkot, who also appealed to the Sikhs to unite.[202] Although what Baldev Singh said in this conference was not reported, his presence itself was significant because soon after the plan was announced he had said: 'I prefer to call it a settlement, it does not please everybody not the Sikhs anyway. But it is certainly something worthwhile'.[203] Strangely, even as Master Tara Singh and other Sikh leaders were moving towards accepting 3 June Plan (which they did on 10 June), there was hardly a day when some newspaper or the other did not carry the Master's angry response to the plan that threatened the division of the Sikhs: 'We cannot accept anything like a national division. It is not a matter of mere political power for us, our very existence is at stake.'[204]

Dawn had launched a full-scale campaign against the division plan as also a campaign to prevail upon the Sikhs to change their mind and stay on as part of Pakistan and stop insisting for the partition of Punjab. As part of this campaign it published numerous letters and articles. On 7 June it published a letter from Sardar Tarlok Singh (Simla): 'The Akali leadership is following the footsteps of the Hindu capitalists. . . . The Hindu capitalists and the so-called nationalist press have supported the division of Punjab to meet their own ends. By keeping the Sikhs on their side they have managed to secure the Ambala and Jullundur divisions.' Tarlok Singh went on to suggest that Baldev Singh and Tara Singh should reconsider their decisions. His charge that the whole problem was being prompted from behind the scenes by a small section of vested interests had many takers.

THE MUSLIM LEAGUE WOOS THE SIKHS

The Sikh leadership, of every hue—the Akalis and all the others—was truly in a difficult situation by the beginning of June. We have already noted that throughout May many senior Muslim League leaders had been putting pressure on the Sikhs to consider staying on as part of Pakistan—meaning thereby that they, the Sikh leaders, should stop insisting for Punjab's partition. After the 3 June Plan was announced this campaign by the Muslim League to woo the Sikhs picked up pace. For the Sikhs the problem was further compounded because from early indications, which the sharp minds of Tara Singh and company had understood, the provisions in the 3 June Plan and possibly the general attitude of the powers in Delhi were not moving in their (the Sikhs') favour.

Dawn commented on the Sikh position in an editorial soon after the 3 June Plan was announced: 'When a Sikh questionnaire asked Mountbatten why the Sikhs had been split into two . . . it was the Viceroy's turn to be bewildered . . . he (Viceroy) asked whether it was not true that the Sikhs themselves had not begged for partition and got the Congress to pass a resolution.' The editorial further added that what the Viceroy in fact wanted to convey was that in spite of his great love for the Sikh community, he had been unable to help them against themselves: 'the Sikhs have got the bed and now must perforce lie on it. . . . If they find it a bed of thorns, the thorns are all of their own implanting.'

The editorial then initiated a campaign advising and pleading with the Sikhs to stick on with the Muslims—by implication to stop demanding the partition of Punjab. It advised the Sikhs to turn away from the Congress and think of the unity of the Punjab. It said the Sikhs had no doubt suffered serious injury in the earlier (March) disturbances, but these disturbances had not been started by the Muslims but by the Sikhs themselves. Appealing to the heart the editorial said: 'there is nothing but sadness in Muslim hearts . . . these memories can be forgotten and wounds healed . . . friendship can emerge out of the welter of enmity. Muslims and Sikhs can together add to the glory of Pakistan.'[205]

A day prior to this important editorial, *Dawn* had based a long report on sources in Delhi stating that Sikhs were greatly disappointed by the 3 June Plan. The report dwelt on the common traditions of Sikhs and Muslims—agriculture, army, social, economic and political. The report said its sources in Delhi believed that the deterioration of Muslim–Sikh relations was a process initiated by Baldev Singh who did this because, the report said, all his financial and other interests lay in the eastern districts of Punjab. The report also added that 'a community of 40 lakh (Sikhs) if divided would be thoroughly incapacitated . . . [with] neither a homeland nor any power. In fact this would be the beginning of a Hindu–Sikh tussle for power in East Punjab.'

Dawn's editorial of 7 June clearly had the approval of senior League leaders. In any case it was rare for *Dawn* to comment on so important an issue without the approval of the League supremo—Jinnah. The timing of the editorial also appears to have been influenced by a statement of Kharak Singh, President of the Central Akali Dal:

> [T]he . . . award was most unfair and does gross injustice to the Sikhs. . . . I would appeal to the Sikhs in general in East Punjab to muster strong under the banner of the Guru and . . . get ready . . . to defend their legitimate rights . . . I would advise them not to depend on assurances of the British government.[206]

This statement of Kharak Singh opened the floodgates of comments from the League leaders. As part of its full-fledged campaign to make the Sikhs change their mind, *Dawn* also reported a statement of Iftikhar Hussain Mamdot, President of the Punjab Muslim League: 'Sikhs would have got a home land within Pakistan if they had desired an amicable settlement with the Muslim League'.[207] While Mamdot's statement was not friendly, it was the statement of Firoz Khan Noon that really rolled out the carpet for the Sikhs to retrace their steps:

> On the eve of the Sikh conference tomorrow[208] I appeal to Sikh representatives to join hands with the Muslim League. . . . The Sikh problem in Punjab is a Muslim Sikh problem and we two alone can solve it . . . with goodwill of which there is plenty on our side. . . . Sikh leaders today are unaware that Meerut Division [will be] joined with Ambala Division.[209]

On 10 June *Dawn* published yet another view that argued why the Sikhs should join the Muslims in Pakistan. In this case it was a long letter by Gurcharan Singh of Amritsar. Claiming to voice the views of the 'Khalsa Youth', and while appreciating the work of Master Tara Singh in saving many a Sikh life, it went on to charge him with falling a prey to the empty words of the Congress. The letter also said that by following the Hindu Congress blindly in demanding a separate province in East Punjab Tara Singh had signed a death warrant for the Sikhs, just like Dr Ambedkar had done for the scheduled castes by signing the Poona Pact. 'Does the Master realise that culture and wealth of the Sikhs comes from West Punjab. . . . What will be our real gain . . . while the Muslims in Punjab depended on us for the formation of any government, the Hindus in East Punjab will not have to do so.'

The League's efforts to bring the Sikhs to some kind of understanding appears to have continued even after August 1947. The Viceregal Official Correspondence Files contain an important, or let's call it an interesting report by Major Short who, as already mentioned, had access to many Akali leaders. This report was filed after Short visited Amritsar and Lahore. He noted that Mamdot had asked him to assure Master Tara Singh that all his conditions would be met with regard to the safety of the refugees and that Mamdot was very keen to meet Tara, so keen that if Tara Singh could not come to Lahore, Mamdot would himself go to the border to meet him.[210]

The Akali leadership itself appears to have been uncertain on what road to take. Satya M. Rai and S.L. Manchanda had recorded a long discussion—a kind of reflective memoir—with Ishar Singh Majhel (Relief and Rehabilitation and Civil Supplies Minister, East Punjab, 1947–50) in 1973. Interestingly, Majhel pointed out that Giani Kartar Singh had met Jinnah many times to find some way out for the Sikh future though Tara Singh did not approve of this approach. He was also asked to share his views with regard to the role of some British officers (possibly hinting at Major Short) who sought to bring the Sikhs closer to the Muslim League. Majhel made a very pertinent note: 'sometimes leaders are helpless—one has to look to the thinking and desire of the "*awam*" (masses), meaning possibly that even if the leaders had been able to work out some agreement, the people were obviously opposed to an understanding with the Muslim League and this is what weighed in the minds of the Akali leadership'.[211]

As yet another link of this sustained campaign, on 12 June, *Dawn* published a long statement by P.S. Ramdasia, General Secretary of the Punjab Achhut Federation, Lahore. He said that the majority of the Scheduled Castes population of Punjab was based in Jullundur, Ludhiana, Ferozepur, and Hoshiarpur and the Federation was clear in that these districts should be merged with Pakistan because the Scheduled Castes do not wish to live with the Hindus. He was also reported to have demanded a referendum on the issue.

CONGRESS WORKING COMMITTEE'S COMMITMENT ON 3 JUNE PLAN: A PROMISSORY NOTE

Nehru shared his views on the partition issue in many press statements and public speeches during the days that followed and preceded the announcement of the 3 June Plan. A reference has already been made to some of his statements in Mussoorie. During the same visit, he had said in Dehradun that initially the Congress was opposed to the demand for Pakistan on principle and stood for a united India. 'It now demands division on the same principle'.[212]

Gandhi too spoke his mind on the issue in a statement in the post-prayer meeting on 7 June. In his characteristic manner he said the AICC was bound to honour the decision taken by the CWC with regard to the Partition of India, because the CWC's commitment was like a promissory note written on behalf of the AICC.[213] On the following day or the day after, Gandhi went on record saying in a written statement that he believed that public opinion was in favour of the 3 June Plan.[214]

The Congress President Acharya Kriplani dealt in more detail with the issue in a long letter to Mountbatten written interestingly on the eve of the announcement of the momentous decision. 'As you know the Congress has upheld that the unity of India should be maintained. Any proposal therefore which might bring about separation of a part of India from the rest is painful to contemplate and in the opinion of the Congress harmful to all concerned.' Interestingly, in para 9 of the letter, Kriplani conveyed the CWC's belief that: 'when present passions have subsided our problems will be viewed in their proper perspective and a willing union of all parts of India will result therefrom'. Kriplani ended this important letter by telling Mountbatten that the CWC would take the plan to the AICC for its approval and would also recommend its acceptance.[215] These views of Kriplani do tend to indicate that there was in fact a major difference on the issue between Kriplani and Nehru. While for Nehru Partition was essential for the integrity of India, the Congress President however still had in the back of his mind the lingering hope that both India and Pakistan could reunite some day.[216]

CONGRESS WORKING COMMITTEE RESOLVES ON PARTITION

This meeting of the CWC was perhaps its most important one. Much has already been written on it. Dr Ram Manohar Lohia with his strong biases and often unpleasant words for Nehru notwithstanding has recorded a memorable account of the meeting. I am conscious of the fact that when it came to Nehru, Lohia was unsparing, often unreasonable, but all the same what he has recorded needs a mention:

> Barring . . . Mahatma Gandhi and Khan Abdul Gaffar Khan, none spoke a single word in opposition to partition. . . . Acharya Kripalani was a pathetic figure at this meeting. Nevertheless, the absence of serious opposition to partition even from a man like me, who had absolutely no selfish axes to grind showed the depths of weakness and fear to which our people and I, as an ordinary one among them, had fallen. I should like especially to bring out two points that Gandhiji made at this meeting. He turned to Mr. Nehru and Sardar Patel in mild complaint that they had not informed him of the scheme of partition before committing themselves to it. . . . Before Gandhiji could make out his point fully, Mr. Nehru intervened with some passion to say that he had kept him fully informed. On Mahatma Gandhi's repeating that he did not know of the scheme of partition, Mr. Nehru slightly altered his

earlier observation. . . . He said that Noakhali was so far away and that, while he may not have described the details of the scheme, he had broadly written of partition to Gandhiji.

Lohia then stated that the issue was not whether Nehru had misled Gandhi but 'whether Mahatma Gandhi knew of the scheme of partition before Mr. Nehru and Sardar Patel had committed themselves to it. 'Mr. Nehru and Sardar Patel had obviously between themselves decided that it would be best not to scare Gandhiji away before the deed was definitely resolved upon.'[217] Lohia also stated that both Nehru and Patel were unusually aggressive towards Gandhiji and that he (Lohia) had 'had a few sharp exchanges with both (Nehru and Patel)'.

AICC RESOLVES TO ACCEPT 3 JUNE PLAN

The first meeting of this historic session of the AICC took place on 14 June at the Constitution Club. Eighteen Speakers spoke on the first day and the debate could not be completed.[218] Gandhi came to the meeting first at 5.45 p.m., then went away after an hour, to return again at 8 p.m. The atmosphere was charged with excitement and even anger. Loudspeakers were installed outside the hall so that the large crowd could listen to the proceedings. Congress President Kriplani opened the proceedings by giving a detailed account of the events.

The vehement opposition to the CWC resolution on the Plan was led by Purshottam Das Tandon. Tandon was loudly cheered when he got up to speak. He said it would be unfair to believe that the prestige of the CWC would be damaged and lowered if the AICC disapproved of the proposal.[219] Arguing that the CWC resolution was only a surrender to the Muslim League and the British, he pleaded with the AICC that the CWC had failed them (the AICC) and reminded them that they had the right and strength to turn down the resolution: 'The CWC has accepted it in desperation. And at the same time they expressed the hope that they would later unite. That was dishonest.'[220]

Tandon also said the Interim Government had been intimidated. So heated had the scene become that Kriplani had to request Gandhi to intervene. Jagat Narain Lal also reminded the AICC of how they had in 1942 rejected a plan for a possible division of the country. The Punjab Congress Committee President, Dr S. Kitchlew forcefully said: that 'the resolution put up by the CWC was nothing but a surrender and the fight was between nationalism and communalism'. He said thousands like him who had worked for the Congress their whole life fighting for nationalism were disheartened. The resolution only showed that communalism had succeeded.[221]

Abdul Ghani accused the Congress leadership of betraying the Pathans and the nationalist Muslims who had fought against Pakistan. He asked why a referendum had not been held in Punjab and Bengal. A similar plea for referendum was made by Jagan Nath Rao, who said that the adult population of the regions to be divided should have been consulted.

Bihar's popular kisan leader, Swami Sahajananda also pleaded for a vote against the CWC resolution, on the grounds that the Congress had all along been against any such division and it must not now be a party to it. Another member, Ahzar Hirwani, in fact compared the acceptance of the 3 June Plan to British Prime Minister Chamberlain's surrender to Hitler in 1939.[222]

The Socialist Party had prior to the AICC session already announced its resolve to oppose the 3 June Plan. On 13 June Acharya Narender Dev said: 'Mentally we shall never accept the two nation theory but we shall not oppose the Congress resolution.'[223] Rammanohar Lohia taking his party's line said that 'while he agreed the CWC resolution needed to be rejected, he could not vote against it because the Congress leaders were themselves responsible for the 3 June Plan.[224]

However, it was in an editorial in *Janvani* that the stand of the socialists was elaborated in detail. The editorial was obviously written by Acharya Narendra Dev himself. It said that the socialists did not oppose the resolution in the sense that they knew that there were no other options in view of the fact that the Congress had itself closed all other doors. He also said that by accepting the modified version of the Cabinet Mission Plan the Congress had completely given up even the thought of any further struggle or fight. The result was that whatever the decision by the Boundary Commission the Congress had left no option for itself to oppose it or seek remedy.[225]

Interestingly, many top Congress leaders met Gandhi on the morning of 15 June, the day the AICC took up the resolution for vote. Among the leaders who took the stage in defence of the CWC proposal was Gandhi himself. Almost in line with Lohia's views, Gandhi said that 'the settlement was an evil thing but it had been accepted on behalf of the Congress. They must work it out as to make good come out of evil'.[226] He went on say that things had gone from bad to worse. 'I met some non-Muslim[s] from Rawalpindi. . . . I enquired of them whether now that Pakistan was almost a settled fact there was any difference in the behaviour of the Muslims for the better. . . . I was startled to be told that the difference was . . . for the worse.'[227] Sardar Patel made a similar observation in his address, but said that there was no alternative and that the whole of India would have become a Pakistan.[226] 'Today every Muslim be he a high official or a peon is behind the Muslim League.'[229]

In his appeal to the AICC, Gandhi had said that he was not pleading with them on behalf of the CWC but the fact remained that if the AICC rejected the CWC resolution it would amount to a no confidence and the committee would have to resign. Practically the same line was taken by Congress President Kriplani: 'if you reject it [CWC resolution] . . . you should be prepared to accept our resignation'.[230] The most articulate and focused defence of the CWC resolution in the AICC came from Jawaharlal Nehru. He spoke with his usual passion and clarity of mind: 'India's heart has been broken but her essential unity has not been destroyed . . .[231] the most urgent task is to arrest the swift drift towards anarchy and chaos.'[232]

Nehru rejected the charge that the CWC had been frightened. Referring to Punjab, he said some had said the Congress had let them down. 'What did they want me to do, should I send an army.' In a surcharged tone Nehru also told the AICC that Punjab had simply become uncontrollable and that Partition was better than the murder of innocent citizens.

This important address also included a reference to his belief that the killings and the breakdown of law and order were more critical in areas under the control of British officers. Nehru argued that while in the past the British had effectively handled bigger anti-government movements, now, particularly in Punjab which was completely under British control, there was complete chaos.

G.B. Pant moved the resolution for vote, which was seconded by Maulana Azad. Pant said that 'it was better to accept the 3 June Plan than to fritter away energies in trying to keep unwilling people in the Union'.[233] Azad said that 'division was like an attempt to divide a river by drawing a line, sure that there would be a reunion before long.[234] The whole process of voting, which started at 2.30 p.m., 15 June, was hurried and pushed so much so that members began

There was widespread anger and disillusion soon after the adoption of the plan to Partition India—political opponents of the Congress saw opportunity for growth. The Congress in turn sought to sideline and suppress all opposition (*Shankar's Weekly*, 15 August 1947).

B. Bhopatkar, President All India Hindu Mahasabha had said that the 3 June Plan had 'meant the end of India as a nation'. Prime Minister Nehru is shown consoling Bhopatkar—'the shop is still the same, even if my partner has decided to open his own firm'. In the background Pakistan's Prime Minister Liaqat Ali is shown helping Jinnah fix the new signboard 'Pakistan Stores—new venture (*HT*, 25 June 1947).

casting their votes even before Pant had finished speaking.[235] Of the AICC's total strength of 400, 218 were present in the session. While 159 voted in favour of accepting the CWC resolution, 29 were against it.[236]

Durga Das, at the time a young journalist and contributor of some of the finest news stories, wrote many years later: 'In the final analysis the Congress leaders and the party as a whole were too weary to carry on the struggle any further and were in their heart of hearts, anxious to grasp power and enjoy its fruits without further delay.' He then drew attention to what the Frontier Gandhi, Badshah Khan, had told him in 1967: 'Some colleagues in the High Command did toy with the idea of going ahead with the fight. But the majority accepted the view that they might then miss the bus.'[237]

CONGRESS OUT OF TOUCH WITH GROUND REALITY IN PUNJAB

I have repeatedly drawn attention to how Congress leaders both in Punjab but more so in Delhi continued to dwell on an optimism which had no substance and the more the country moved closer to the actual days of Partition the more pronounced this trend became. What better illustration can there be than the Congress President himself stating a few days after the AICC session of 15 June that henceforth 'minorities have nothing to fear in west Punjab, because up to now it was in the interest of the Muslim League to create strife which is no longer the case'. The very next day he said in Calcutta: 'Independence of India will not be complete until we are one again.'[238] Nehru in fact went a step further: 'Both from practical and legal point of view India as an entity continues to exist except that certain provinces and parts seek to secede.'[239] A few days later, possibly taking the lead from their central leadership, the Congress party's senior leaders in Punjab, Sachar and Swarn Singh, went on record saying, 'we hope to see a united India again drawn together by geographical and fundamental ties of common interest'.[240]

How out of touch senior leaders were with ground realities in Punjab is illustrated by the fact that Jawaharlal Nehru while defending the CWC resolution in the AICC had, as noted earlier, made a statement mentioning how law and order was worst in districts which were headed by British officers. This statement was surprising on many counts because, apart from Nehru, the only other relatively unbiased and important person who was reported to have made a similar charge in May–June 1947 was Mian Amir-ud-din the Mayor of Lahore. Amir-ud-din was reported to have said: 'never was the British officer so callous and unresolved in the discharge of his duties as he proved himself in connection with the riots in Punjab. The general impression is that peace would not have been disturbed if the British authorities had a mind to maintain it.'[241]

On the other hand, and rather interestingly, many important leaders in Punjab went on record stating their appreciation for the good work done by Jenkins and his field officers. The League leaders no doubt were bitter critics of Jenkins, but as we have noted the charges were more political in nature than administrative; they had even resolved on 21 June to seek his removal from Punjab.[242]

Jenkins himself strongly contested the charge made by Nehru in a note to Mountbatten. He said that not only was the charge 'without foundation', but that Nehru should not forget the killings in Bihar, Bombay and the NWFP where it was the Congress governments who were in control.[243] Some days later, Mountbatten wrote back to Jenkin's informing him that he was not showing Jenkins' reply to Nehru because 'he is in a rather difficult state of mind and I do not wish to add to the state of emotional attrition on which he now exists . . . only the overriding necessity of getting this political settlements though compels me to avoid anything which tends to break with principal Indian leaders.'[244]

Among the senior leaders in Punjab who had recorded their appreciation of the manner in which British officers, particularly Governor Jenkins, had handled the disturbances were Baldev Singh,[245] Bhimsen Sachar[246] and even Master Tara Singh.[247] Som Nath Kapur, in fact, profusely praised the acting Deputy Commissioner of Lahore for his earnest efforts in controlling the problem and even visiting riot-affected families to share their grief.[248] And yet, the *HT* obviously toeing the Nehru line remarked in an editorial that Governor Jenkins was like a modern Nero.[249]

But coming back to the AICC Session, in the subsequent days many newspapers commented on it, the *Dawn* taking strong exception to some of the speeches: 'These Congress leaders . . . regrettably laid emphasis on the wrong places . . . painting the Muslims as greater villains.'[250]

The Tribune came out with a powerful editorial on 24 June. On the face of it the editorial was a reaction to a statement that appears to have been made by Vijay Lakshmi Pandit, that the Congress was never keen for division, but in fact, the editorial was also *The Tribune*'s answer to the speeches made by Congress leaders at the AICC session of 15 June: 'If the Congress had stood fast on the unstable rock of nationalism and refused to compromise things would have been different and the spectacle of a divided country would not have been witnessed.'[251]

Surprisingly, the top Congress leaders had begun to believe that the Congress by accepting the plan had really solved a major part of the problem. The Congress President went on record saying that things were bound to or should improve for non-Muslims in West Punjab now that the main demand of the Muslim League had been met:

I would therefore ask the minorities in the future Pakistan not to get unduly nervous or panicky and not to be in hurry to immigrate. They should stick to their homes, lands, professions to which they have as much a right . . . it is in the obvious interest of the majority to win the confidence of the minority.[252]

Surprisingly the Viceroy, too, like many Congress leaders, thought the road to be clear once the Congress had accepted the 3 June Plan. A relaxed Mountbatten proceeded soon after to the cool climes of Srinagar, to attend civic receptions and relax on fishing picnics. At one of these grand events he invested Raja Hari Singh with the GCVO and the Maharani with the CI.[253]

To no one's surprise, it was leaders of the Hindu Mahasabha who were unsparing in their attack of the Congress after the AICC had officially resolved to accept the 3 June Plan. As usual, Bhai Parmananda led from the front: 'It is strange that Gandhi who would give the whole of India to Pakistan soon gave in and exhorted the AICC to accept the 3 June Plan.' The same issue of the *HO* carried an article by one Nathu Lal who termed the whole affair as politics of treachery. He argued in the article, saying that the AICC stand as the only cure for the ills of the time was in fact like hastening the end of the patient to cure the disease.

N.C. Chatterjee, President of the Bengal Hindu Mahasabha, while speaking in Chandni Chowk on 23 June said that the 'present situation had arisen as a result of British conspiracy with Jinnah and Congress cowardice'.[254] The Hindu Mahasabha called for a 'Day of Shame and Humiliation' on 3 July. The *Hindu Outlook* accused the Congress of pushing India back to where it was in 1750, providing 'a Muslim neighbour who will always hit at us'.[255] The Information Department's all important Fortnightly Appreciation Report made a special mention of how 'Hindu leaders' had warned the government to stop appeasing the Muslims and how some sections of the press were discussing the demand for removing Muslims from important positions in the government.[256]

VIOLENCE CONTINUES UNABATED

The month of June was relatively quieter than March had been, but there was hardly a day when reports of violence did not come in. *Dawn* in fact asked 'why the killings were continuing when all the three major parties, the Congress, the League and the Akalis, had accepted the 3 June Plan: 'The Muslims have reconciled to the partition of Punjab . . . they can no longer have any reason for violence . . . we would go so far as to say that if any Muslim still feels tempted to put his knife into a Hindu or a Sikh . . . by doing so he will be stabbing Pakistan.'[257]

Few, however seemed to have realized that Punjab had drifted unguided and uncared for by political leaders for too long, as a result of which such appeals now had little meaning. On 21 June, 46 cases of arson and stabbing were reported from Lahore alone, with 150 houses being burnt down. On the following day, *Dawn* reported the burning down of another 100 houses.[258] Lahore was paralysed, with a mob of invaders from neighbouring villages having attacked major markets. Buses were suspended, there was no supply of milk and vegetables.[259]

On 20 June, over a hundred major cases involving rival communities throwing bombs at each other were reported in Amritsar. The situation had reached such a level that policemen were contributing to the loot and arson. A report mentioned how some policemen entered a house to search for weapons and while doing so stole jewellery. An old lady who was then alone in the house came out screaming. An inquiry was conducted and a case was registered against the officials of the 'D' Division police station in Amritsar.[260] As a report from Amritsar put it: 'Just before violence broke out on 5 March Amritsar was at the zenith of its glory today [June] it is blitzed by arson and fires.'[261] On 12 June a *tonga* driver was killed. The police intervened as the crowd was trying to burn the body. One person was shot dead by the police when the crowd tried to resist.[262] In a typical case, students had to petition the High Court because the policemen who had arrested them were forcing them to name some senior Sikh leaders in a murder case.[263] Another report said Amritsar was worse than London during Second World War bombings.[264]

In distant Mewat, the situation remained as bad as it had ever been. Sheikh Abdus Salam, acting president of the Delhi Muslim League, told reporters that armed troops and Jat villagers from Bharatpur with local support were responsible for the disturbances.[265]

Dawn published an article by Mohd. Yunas Khan, a pleader of Gurgaon, in which he reported that pockets in Mewat were cut-off from the outside world by Jat villagers, and that in the preceding two weeks lorry loads of armed people were being transported into Mewat from Bharatpur and Alwar to attack Meo villages. 'On 20 June', he said 'three Meos were shot in cold blood by soldiers of the Kumaon Rifles'.[266] Two thousand men were reported to have raided 2 villages in Gurgaon, killing 60 people and injuring about 200.[267] On 15 June, the *HT* on the other hand, carried detailed reports of armed Meos and Baluchis attacking Tikri village near Gurgaon, killing 30 people and seriously injuring another 18, in addition to burning down 150 houses.

THE TWO WORLDS OF PUNJAB

Jang Bahadur Singh, *The Tribune's* fiery, unsparingly straightforward and occasionally partisan officiating editor, contributed a sensitive piece on 28 June, dwelling on how the well-provided and secure world of the fortunate then spending their summer in Simla was at a great distance from the realities of the plains, particularly cities like Amritsar and Lahore which were rapidly being drenched in blood. In many ways this piece sums up the summer of 1947—and the two worlds that constituted the Punjab:

> [T]wo days at Simla were like two years. The memory of Lahore writhing in agony made my stay an unbearable burden . . . when an empty Ambulance wheeled around Scandal Point my imagination transferred me to Lahore where Ambulances crawled with melancholy loads. . . . But in the aristocratic crowd nodding and giggling and chatting at a distance there was no consciousness of the proximity of suffering.

In sharp contrast was a letter in the *CMG* which drew attention to how ordinary people like vegetable hawkers and *tongawallas* remained completely free from the divide and continued their work up to the very end and in the most trying of conditions. The tragic tale that was beginning to unfold was really the story of the common Punjabi, who even if he had the foresight to see what was coming, had not the resources to act on the intuition. The choice for the vast majority of the Punjabi populace who comprised this unfortunate section was greatly limited. Prof. Roshan Lal Verma, in an article 'Fate of Non-Muslims in West Punjab', exhorted non-Muslims not to give up their secure professions in panic by shifting away to the eastern districts, etc.[268] Such advice was commonplace, given in earnestness. Ironically it served only to increase the confusion and certainly the fear of what was coming—no one quite knew its exact form. Instructions issued by government officers no doubt in all earnestness served only to unnerve the man on the street even further. A long list of what should and should not be done was issued by the deputy commissioner of Lahore. People were advised, for example, to keep every vessel filled with water on all floors of the house because water thrown on adjoining houses would help prevent fires from spreading. The Lahore Corporations Engineer even ordered all houses to have eight buckets filled with water and four with sand ready at all times.

J.J. Singh, President of the India America League was right when he observed in a radio broadcast that in the communal animosity and the political wranglings, the masses of India had been totally forgotten: 'Hungry people both in India and Pakistan will demand clothing. . . . And if there is any reality in India it is the poverty stricken masses of that country.'[269]

For this vast majority of the common people, June 1947 was extraordinarily difficult. 'Wheat position to be critical in July & August' ran one headline in *The Tribune*: On 28 May, the *CMG* ran a headline: 'India is confronted by four months of starvation'. On 18 June, the *CMG* reported a major failure of the wheat crop. The position of wheat stock was so bad that the Government of India appealed through its representative, N.G. Aonyankar, to the International Emergency Food Council in Washington: 'I do not recollect any period so dangerous', Aonyankar said, 'as the coming four months in India when the worst type of starvation is possible'. He called India's food problem a challenge for the world.[270]

There was strict rationing of almost all popular consumer items. The regulations that controlled the distribution of wheat were fearsome—any family caught storing more than a month's quota of wheat could be arrested, the police having been given powers to search homes. With such shortages, it was a black marketeer's world. A large number of rowdy elements had taken over trade particularly in cloth. It was widely believed that sooner or later the control of essential commodities would end, and therefore those traders who were able to withhold and hide their stocks were bound to make huge profits later in the coming days.[271] There were regulations even on the sale and purchase of the humble aerated soda water bottle, with no family being allowed to purchase more than two such bottles.[272]

For the handful who owned motor vehicles, life was more difficult because the District Rationing Authority of Lahore had also issued a notice saying that applications for the supply of petrol would be received between 25–8 June, and the supply would be made on July 10.[273] Incidentally many influential and rich families were known to have started storing petrol for their vehicles just in case the run to India had to be made in a hurry.

HINDU BUSINESSES ASSURED EQUAL TREATMENT TO PAKISTAN

All routine activity in Punjab's two major centres, Lahore and Amritsar, had come to an abrupt standstill in June. For example, a 2 June report from Amritsar said teachers had not been paid salaries for the past three months. The crisis of faith that had brought the two major cities to a complete halt also had a rolling effect on smaller towns and villages particularly in the Lahore and Amritsar regions. The depot holders of smaller towns and villages were afraid to visit Amritsar and Lahore to collect essential supplies. As the days passed the problem became acute and was even discussed in a meeting of the Civil Supplies Advisory Committee, presided over by Kanwar Bhan Nirula, ADC.[274] In the following months (as we shall see later) efforts were made by government agencies to send supplies to the depot holders by government vehicles.

Clearly it was those without financial support who had no choice, the rich were by the end of June making quick decisions in matters of selling property and moving to east or west Punjab as the situation demanded. The *CMG,* in particular, published numerous detailed reports of how big businessmen were moving out from Lahore.[275] The *HT* in its 'Punjab Newsletter' reported during the week (16–23 June) that 18 banks and insurance companies besides other commercial establishments had moved out of Lahore to the eastern districts. The report also said that no earnest effort was being made by Muslim League leaders to persuade people not to shift their businesses.[276]

Just as Muslim businessmen with adequate resources were in the race to occupy and fill the gap being created by the exit of non-Muslim capital and enterprise, similar sentiments appeared to have prevailed in the eastern districts—capturing houses, businesses and properties to be vacated by Muslim families. In fact, a story from a Soviet Union periodical *New Times* reproduced by *HT*, said that Indian business magnates were keen to push out the British in a hurry so that they could capture new avenues of profit.[277] In the early days of June, the prices of property in Lahore went down rapidly as the number of incoming Muslims from East Punjab was far less than the number moving out. The Sikhs alone were however adamantly refusing to move.[278]

Lala Kesho Ram Sehgal wrote a letter from Simla giving details of how a large number of people had suddenly opened property dealing offices. In fact, he suggested that since most of these people who were organizing the exchange of property between Hindus and Muslims were usually cheating both sides, the government should provide official facilities for such exchanges.[279] At one stage Jinnah himself had to issue a statement to the press that reports regarding his having sold his Malabar Hill bungalow in Bombay to the well-known industrialist Dalmiya were false.[280]

The *CMG* weekly stock-market report for the last week of June left little to imagination and certainly no hope: 'Stock Market lies prostrate before the disturbances . . . leading Hindu businessmen are shifting their offices from Lahore to Delhi . . . even the Stock Exchange Committee is thinking of shifting to the East Punjab.'[281]

So critical had the situation become that Professor Hasan, a leading commentator on economic affairs in Lahore and member of the Pakistan Constituent Assembly, issued an appeal to Hindu merchants not to leave the western Punjab: 'Muslim League leadership should ensure [*sic*] minorities that it will be worth their while to stay rather than emigrate in panic. . . . Hindus would be treated as sons of the soil.' He went on to say that the flight of Hindu capital must be checked, and that since Pakistan would require extensive resources Hindu investors should be given preference and favour. He wondered why, in spite of making good profits, the Hindus were keen to leave.[282]

Dawn came out with many editorials on the issue. In one it said that over Rs. 200 crore of Hindu capital had already left west Punjab, and that in the last days of June over Rs. 6 crore had been withdrawn.[283] It said there were three main reasons for the flight of Hindu capital: some were doing it to cause harm to the new state of Pakistan, others were worried that Hindu bank accounts would be frozen, and yet others believed that Hindus were bound to be discriminated against in the future Pakistan. The editorial also appealed to Hindus not to be misled by false propaganda.

Even as commercial activity had come to a standstill by June, unscrupulous land developers had started developing colonies along communal lines. In Lahore, for example, even as late as June 1947, properties were being offered in 'exclusive Hindu' areas and 'only to

Hindus'.[284] One other business that appears to have thrived, as mentioned earlier, in all the commotion was the sale and purchase of weapons and ammunition. Interestingly, even though it was the peak of summer, another item much in demand in Lahore in June was the Jinnah cap, which was being sold from Rs. 2/9 annas to Rs. 20 per cap. The Mirza Cap House was reportedly doing good business from the sale of the Jinnah cap.[285]

Typewriters and people with typing abilities were like sugar, kerosene, cloth, wheat, arms, the Jinnah cap much in demand in the Punjab in June 1947. The government of Punjab and the government of India it appears had sometime in June decided to maintain all records in typed duplicates, so that when the government was divided the actual partition records could also be conveniently divided. This placed a great premium on people with typing skills.[286]

EAST IS EAST AND WEST IS WEST

All the brewing disapproval and disillusionment with the plan for partition notwithstanding the fact remained that the leaders of the three major political formations of Punjab had accepted the 3 June Plan, and in turn, were expected to complete the formalities and stamp their acceptance in the Legislative Assembly.[287]

The Assembly was convened for a special Session on 23 June, to resolve on the issue. The official notification was made on 14 June by Governor Jenkins.[288] The Punjab government on its part made extensive security and other arrangements for the historic session. A large area around the Assembly complex was cordoned off, so much so that new traffic movement rules were enforced with all roads going towards the Assembly sealed. Entry by passes was strictly enforced.[289] Even the number of press was greatly restricted. Passes were issued only for the Joint Session and not for the separate Sessions of the East and West members, the plea being that there was not sufficient room in the Cabinet and the Tea Rooms where the two were to meet separately—the East members meeting in the Cabinet Room and the West in the Tea Room. Almost as an omnious pointer, a kind of early forecast, the air-conditioning plant of the building broke down just as the meeting got underway, raising temperatures quite in proportion with the apprehensions among the members. Pedestal fans were used for the Joint Session. To add to the comic element members were heard joking that since Lahore was receiving electric supply from Jogendernagar, which as per the notional line of division was likely to go to the East Punjab, the power failure had been caused deliberately. For the first time in the history of the Assembly foreign journalists were permitted into the press gallery to witness the Joint Session.[290]

The government on its part took no chances, but surprisingly, members from both sides appeared more relaxed than they had ever been in recent months. In fact, a number of days before the Assembly actually met newspapers in Lahore had begun publishing statements by leaders that no hard words should be used during the Session and there was to be 'no letting out of steam' in Assembly speeches. The Muslim League leaders in particular were heard saying that since matters had been resolved, the need was of cooling down tempers and restoring normalcy.[291]

Exactly at 9 a.m. on 23 June, 168 of the Punjab Legislative Assembly's 175 members were present in the Assembly. For the first time in the history of the Assembly, the speaker, S.P. Singha, who chaired the historic session also cast his vote. Three members were absent, Nawab Allah Bakhash Tiwana, Jathedar Man Singh and Ch. Harbaj. In the Joint Session, 91 votes were cast in favour of a new Constituent Assembly and 77 for the existing Constituent Assembly. The 91 votes that were cast for a new Constituent Assembly, Pakistan, included all the 88 Muslim members including Khizr Hayat, two Christian members—S.P. Singha (Speaker) and Fazl Elahi—and one Anglo-Indian C.E. Gibbon. Every Hindu, Sikh and Scheduled Caste member voted for joining the existing Constituent Assembly of India.

Once the vote for the creation of Pakistan had been cast the members of the Assembly then met separately, as mentioned earlier. In the East section, presided over by Sardar Kapur Singh, 50 voted for partition and 22 against the partition of Punjab. In the West section, presided over by S.P. Singha, 69 voted against the partition of Punjab and 27 voted for the partition of Punjab. The whole procedure of dividing Punjab was completed in less than an hour. Once the required formalities for partition were complete, the Assembly soon turned into the kind of setting that resembled the last dinner of a boarding school's graduating class's farewell. As emotions overcame almost all the members irrespective of community or region, they were heard saying 'that perhaps they would one day unite', even though a member was also heard quoting Kipling: 'East is East, West is West and never the Twain shall meet.'[292]

Bhimsen Sachar, the senior Congress leader, remarked: As a Punjabi I am distressed . . . one has now to reckon with fait accompli . . . we need one thing above all and that is mutual accommodation. Krishan Gopal Dutta said: 'The surgical operation which we underwent today in the Assembly was excrutingly painful.'[293] Diwan Chaman Lal, pleaded that even though Punjab was divided its heart must continue to beat as one.[294]

The proceedings of the Punjab Assembly were printed in newspapers across India, and some of the reactions were hard hitting. Purshottam Das Tandon said in Allahabad: 'Vande Matram which has been our national song has no meaning now . . . the map of India has been redrawn . . . our map has changed due to our weakness'.[295]

The actual formalities of the parting of ways having been completed, Punjab thereafter saw a spate of appeals for peace, harmony and understanding, all of which, as time proved, left no impact whatsoever. The most significant was a long joint Muslim League and Congress appeal. Signed among others by Sachar, Swarn Singh and Mamdot it said:

> Now that Punjab has been partitioned the time has come for we who believe in an ordered society to concert measures for the protection of the innocent . . . no reason now remains for the continuation of hostility.

On behalf of the League, Mamdot also said: 'I solemnly pledge to my Hindu and Sikh brothers complete justice and fairness of treatment in Pakistan. I call upon the Muslims to guard with their lives the words I am pledging.'[296]

TOWN HALL LAHORE: WINDOW DRESSING NOT REQUIRED

On 26 June Lahore saw unprecedented scenes in the Town Hall. Mayor Mian Amiruddin presided over a meeting which included not only every councillor of the city but also leaders from all the political parties. Mamdot in a solemn pledge said he would personally shoulder all responsibility for any harm done to the minorities. While Congress leader Sachar appealed to everyone to take up the peace initiative, Swarn Singh said the 'need was to change people's mentality which had been poisoned by the long drawn strife.'[297]

The following day, *Dawn* commented in its editorial on the proceedings of this important meeting and said that it was good that leaders like Swarn Singh had joined the appeal but what mattered was the likes of Master Tara Singh 'who undoubtedly have greater weight within their communities'. On 25 June, Gandhi too issued an appeal in his post-prayer meeting to the Punjab leaders to arrest the impending destruction 'and win appreciation of posterity'.[298]

The Town Hall meeting was important and eventful also for the manner in which many lesser known people stated their views, that the present problems were in fact the creation of the leaders themselves, and that people wanted actual peace not just 'window dressing'. Some insisted that appeals for peace could be meaningful only if Tara Singh was also a party to them.[299] Shaukat Hayat made an appeal on AIR, Lahore: 'Fraternity is the greatest heritage of Islam . . . the safety of the life and property of non-Muslims is the responsibility of the Musalmans. If they do not pay any attention to this it will bring discredit to Pakistan and to Islam.'[300] Mian Amiruddin, the Mayor of Lahore, wondered what the fight had been about and, in any case; 'Now that the political struggle which apparently led to all this turmoil and carnage has come to an end with three major parties accepting the British Award the continuation of violence and lawlessness can only be attributed to mischief.'[301]

MOUNTBATTEN'S UNWARRANTED OPTIMISM

Even as the Punjab leaders were treading down memory lane, in distant New Delhi, Mountbatten had begun pushing things at greater speed—an approach that reflected either a complete lack of awareness of what was breeding on the ground in Punjab or on optimism that things were indeed on track. Since there was hardly any other reason for optimism, Mountbatten possibly believed that a massive redeployment of the armed forces from other parts of India into Punjab would facilitate the implementation of the Plan. In fact, Lahore had witnessed extensive and hurried activity in the days preceding the announcement of the 3 June Plan. On 31 May, the Deputy Commissioner of Amritsar had, for example, boldly declared to press reporters that 'there was no chance of any future violence and that the government was prepared to meet any situation'.[302] The following day (1 June) a press conference was addressed by Major General Bruce, the General Officer Commanding, Lahore. The GOC talking to the press was certainly not a routine affair, especially when the Viceroy himself would comment on the same issue only a day later. General Bruce said that three divisional headquarters and eight brigade headquarters were now in Punjab. Three regiments of armoured corps, six of Artillery and twenty-seven battalions of Infantry, besides transport and medical units, had been deployed with immediate effect in important towns of Punjab. The army, he said, would support the civil administration and 'army commanders had been placed along side Commissioners and Deputy Commissioners'.

Bruce also said that Punjab had been divided for military purposes into three zones. Rawalpindi was put under Major General Lovett; Lahore, Multan, areas of Ferozepur, Kangra were under Major General Bruce; Jullundur zone comprising all other areas minus Gurgaon was placed under the Delhi Area Commander.[303] Mountbatten later explained the new army deployment: 'Up to now the distribution of armed forces was on a normal basis throughout India. At the moment we know where disturbances are going to break out and so we are taking the risk of denuding the other parts of India of armed forces to concentrate them in particular areas.'[304]

By the middle of June, the redeployment of troops in Punjab had to a large extent been completed. The number of redeployed troops was never considered safely sufficient, yet the movement of troops did make a difference—a better sense, a feeling of greater safety among the people. In a way troop deployment seems also to have further enhanced Mountbatten's optimism. His unfounded optimism was also it appears based on the belief that the partition of Punjab was little more than a formality on paper, a view that may have been strengthened by the smooth manner in which the MLAs had parted ways in the Assembly complex and even issued moving appeals for peace. So convinced was Mountbatten that nothing was likely to go wrong, and that all known hurdles had been crossed, that he even ordered a special calendar to be prepared which would fix day-to-day targets for the ultimate transfer of power by 15 August. For example, the calendar would remind officials that on '27 June—49 days were left'.[305] This is one of the countless examples of the hurry, the frivolities and the 'distanced', almost insensitive approach with which this momentous task was undertaken.

CONGRESS—THE NEW TICKET TO POWER

As the legislative struggle for Punjab's partition came to a rather sudden and unsung end, another race had begun within the Assembly itself. All along there had developed an impression that when the time arrived, the premiership of East Punjab would be offered to a Sikh.[306] As events began to unfold and it became clear that this was unlikely, an element of resentment crept in. The ink had barely dried on the joint appeals for peace when the *CMG* commented that the Congress had let down the Sikhs and in any case the latter had gained little.[307]

Within the Congress, in Punjab itself a race for power had clearly developed by the end of June (1947). The East Punjab Congress Legislative Party met on 29 June to elect a leader, but even after great effort it failed to arrive at a consensus on any one of the three who were in the race for the premiership. It was decided to leave the matter to be resolved by the Congress High Command.[308] On 3 July, *Dawn* carried a long report on the selection of Bhargava as leader of the East Punjab Congress Legislative Party, a position that would ensure for him the Premier's chair. The report also said that the Congress High Command had turned down the idea of having a Sikh as premier as this would lead to a bad precedent and that the Maharaja of Patiala was likely to be the first Governor of East Punjab, something that was unlikely to go down well with Baldev Singh who himself was keen on the position.[309]

Even as disaster waited round the corner Congressmen appeared hardly concerned. Bhimsen Sachar has recorded a view that Bhargava was made Premier only because he enjoyed the 'solid support' of Sardar Patel and while he (himself) was Nehru's man. Sachar has also noted that Bhargava did not enjoy even the support of Maulana Azad (Congress president). He said that one reason why he was denied the leadership of the Congress was because he had retained his membership of the Pakistan Constituent Assembly.[310]

The other view is that there were too many complaints against Sachar—possibly a fallout of the factionalism. All the same, Seth Sudarshan, Chief Whip of the Congress Legislative Party in Punjab, had written some time earlier to Maulana Azad complaining that Sachar was inaccessible, that he had used his position as finance minister in the coalition government to promote his own business interests, like the Sun Light Insurance; that he had enabled a relative

Call to Duty!

Just as the bureaucracy was widely charged of corruption and nepotism, Congressmen aspired for positions of influence. In the East Punjab this race among Congressmen had reached absured levels. A note has been made in particular of the complaints and counter complaints against each other as also of the manner in which Congress legislators fought with each other in the first session of the East Punjab Legislative Assembly (November 1947). Even as Punjab reeled in disaster legislators spent most of the Assembly's time enhancing their pays and perks (*Shankar's Weekly*, 10 October 1947).

to establish a cloth and *ghee* plant; had shown special favours to his father-in-law Rai Bahadur Mukund Lal Puri; etc. Sudarshan Lal had also made some complaints against Lehri Singh and told Maulana Azad that 34 MLAs were in favour of Diwan Chaman Lal as leader, whereas Sachar did not have comparable support.[311] These changes are suprising because Sachar's commitment to and involvement in the struggle for freedom and his personal integrity were beyond doubt. The charges were obviously a part of factional politics.

As the long and arduous journey of the British neared its end it was only natural for people to seek the fruits of office. The best colour to wear in the new race was naturally that of the Congress. It appeared the only alternative for a career in politics or, more pointedly, the surest way to grasp a little piece of the 'cake'. Not surprisingly the first to redefine their political loyalties were leaders from the Ambala Division. Hardly had the proceedings of the Assembly concluded in Lahore when a joint statement was issued by Suraj Mal, Mohar Singh and Prem Singh: 'Khizr has supported the Muslim League . . . we feel the Unionist Party has ceased to exist from today . . . we consider it necessary to say that now there is no need left for having any other party in Ambala Division'.[312] The life of the Unionist Party had no doubt been short, yet it had been eventful, and therefore the manner in which a handful of legislators decided to write it off into history is a sad reflection on the political culture that had begun to breed even before the British had actually exited from India.

P. Brenden, as noted earlier, had, one of the 'hottest' posts, Deputy Commissioner, that of Gurgaon, from January 1945 to June 1947. Just before Brenden left India, he had lunch with Rao Mohar Singh (ex-MLA) at the Imperial Hotel in New Delhi. Of this meeting Brenden said that: 'Rao Mohar Singh thanked me for saving his career as a "moderate" by having sent him to prison and making him a martyr.'[313]

THE MAIN CASUALTY

Till the day he stepped down from the premiership of Punjab Khizr Hayat had personified the spirit of Unionism, keeping the Punjab and India united and facing the onslaught of the League with grit and determination. We have seen in Chapter 2 how he capitulated to the sustained campaign of the League. In many ways he was the last resort, the old face of Punjab, where communal differences had always been in existence and yet Punjab had rolled along never quite reaching the point of no return where restoring old ties would have been impossible.

Of all the emotional and nostalgia-ridden statements made by the members of the Legislative Assembly, many with moist eyes as they came out of the Assembly building on the evening of 23 June, Khizr's needs emphasis:

> No Punjabi can be happy over it. Associations, centuries old common martial traditions in adversity and victory, comradeship in arms across the globe are torn asunder. . . . The economic structure is too interdependent. The past history of Punjab and its success and glory in every sphere of life was built on sure foundations of mutual good relations. Differences were solved by mutual give and take. The Punjab was in the vanguard of India's economic and constitutional progress . . . but today in the last leap of freedom it has become the main casualty.[314]

Silence of the Graveyard: Some Thought the Worst was Over

Sadly for Punjab, its leaders in particular and a good majority of the people, because of the statements of the leaders, had begun to believe the worst was over. On 23 June, when the partition of Punjab had been formalized by the Assembly, no one (with the exception of a few like Governor Jenkins) seemed to understand that deep down, hidden away from the eyes, a volcano of disquiet was brewing.

In a letter of 22 June to Mountbatten, Nehru shared his pain and concern over events in Punjab. Surprisingly Nehru pointed out how he was concerned with the situation in Amritsar, Lahore and Gurgaon, and in fact believed that elsewhere things were under control:

> [T]he statement of 3 June has had a sobering and calming effect in most places. Whether people like the decision or not they accept them and have a general feeling that a settlement has been arrived at. The old tension is gone or is much less. There is no more talk, as there used to be of civil war and the like.[315]

How then did senior, well-informed and well-meaning leaders like Nehru form an opinion that things in Punjab were on the way to improvement? One possible answer is that since senior Congress leaders in Delhi had been putting pressure on the provincial Congress activists to restore normalcy, the latter, and quite naturally so, had begun presenting a picture that was far from the realities on the ground—a misrepresentation that would cost the ordinary Punjabi very dearly. It was not only the leaders of the Congress who launched a blitz of optimistic statements. There were many others too. As the word spread in Lahore during June that the city was likely to go to Pakistan, reassuring statements from leaders like Baldev Singh, said there was no chance of such an eventuality.[316]

Till about 10 June, Kharak Singh appeared to stand alone in his call to the Sikhs 'to muster strong under the banner of the Guru and organise themselves and get ready for the fight to defend their legitimate rights'.[317] Master Tara Singh appears almost confused at the time. On the one hand, he was guiding the 10 June conference in which the main Sikh parties accepted the 3 June Plan, at the same time he hardly missed an opportunity to vent his anger and apprehension with regard to the 3 June Plan's potentially anti-Sikh content.

On 19 June the Master issued a press statement in Delhi: 'The Sikhs face extinction . . . they have been thrown bound and foot at the mercy of the others'. In the same statement he appealed to the Sikhs living in the western districts to begin their shifting to the eastern districts, so as to 'consolidate' the community.[318] This statement came as quite a shock to the Sikhs in the Rawalpindi region, where an all-party Sikh committee met to discuss the issue. Generally most of those who attended the meeting disapproved of Tara Singh's statement.[319] The incident, among other things, was an early indicator that important leaders like Tara Singh possibly misjudged the minds of their people.

Principal Teja Singh of the Khalsa College Bombay, contributed a long article to the *HT*, in which he demanded the line of division on the river Chenab and not the Ravi:

> Punjab is being divided admittedly for the Sikhs . . . the division should therefore satisfy their genuine demand . . . to deprive the Sikhs of Lahore and Gujranwala would be to wipe out all traces of their political and historical traditions. . . . Can the Sikhs give away Shahidganj the symbol of Sikh Martyrdom, Dera Sahib where guru Arjun was burnt alive on heated plates . . . the birth place of Ranjit Singh. . . . No the Sikhs cannot live without them. They will not rest until they have won them back.[320]

On 28 June, the Shromani Akali Dal called for a countrywide strike by Sikhs on 8 July. Details of how the strike was to be observed

One of the issue that drew repeated attention throughout 1947 was the manner in which Indian leaders and bureaucrats rapidly filled the space vacated by the British—the ostentatious lifestyle, extravagance, big social events even as India was confronted by one of the severest shortages of food grain in 1947–8 (*Shankar's Weekly*, 27 June 1947).

appear, in retrospect, to be early and ominous signs of how betrayed the community felt: no peasant was to plough the fields; no shop was to opened; no Sikh was to sleep on a bed (a sign of mourning death in the family); prayers were to be conducted, etc.[321]

SUMMING UP MAY AND JUNE 1947

More than fifty years later, when one studies the photographs of the grand dinner hosted by Sardar Baldev Singh, Defence Member of the Interim Government in honour of Field Marshal Montgomery on 24 June 1947, in New Delhi, a feeling tends to persist that at the time the corridors of power in New Delhi had somehow lost touch with the hot and dusty plains of Punjab where there was a brewing mixture of fear, hatred and apprehension.[322] It was surprising against such a backdrop for the Viceroy to have believed that his 3 June Plan was bound to bring peace to Punjab.

NOTES

1. *CMG*, 11 May 1947.
2. *CMG*, 3 June 1947.
3. Chimanlal Setalvad, *India Divided Who is to Blame For It*, Bombay, p. 6.
4. *CMG*, 7 May 1947; This view of Gandhi drew extensive attention in British official circles, see IOR L/1/I/665 Information Deptt. Fortnightly Appreciation, 3 June 1947, no. 4259. The 3 June reference was to a similar statement made by Gandhiji on 26 May, see *TP*, vol. X (560), p. 1037.
5. *Dawn*, 10 May 1947. The *Dawn* report was based on 'informed' sources in Delhi. Even Hodson does make a reference to how Mountbatten acted on 'his hunch' of trusting Nehru and showed to him (in Simla) the first plan for the transfer of power, see his, *The Great Divide*, p. 214. Durga Das too has referred to Mountbatten's having 'informally consulted Nehru, who gave his consent to it', see his *India: From Curzon to Nehru and After*, London, 1969, p. 254.
6. *CMG*, 25 May 1947.
7. Ibid., 7 May 1947.
8. Ibid.
9. *TP*, vol. X (184), Viceroy's Meeting 78, record of Maharaja Patiala's meeting 20 April 1947, pp. 346–7.
10. IOR L/P0/6/123 Pt. I, Viceroy's Personal Reports, no. 424, April 1947.
11. *CMG*, 24 May 1947.
12. *Dawn*, 17 May 1947; Brenden Papers, CSAS.
13. *Dawn*, 24 May 1947. Sections of the press sympathetic to the Muslim League charged All India Radio for replacing Hindustani with Sanskritized Hindi in its news bulletins, saying this was done intentionally to harm Urdu and make things difficult for Muslims, see *Dawn*, 13 June 1947.
14. Ibid., 22 May 1947.
15. Ibid., 2 June 1947.
16. Ibid., 3 June 1947.
17. *CMG*, 2 May 1947.
18. *Hindu Outlook*, 20 May 1947.
19. *CMG*, 18 May 1947.
20. Ibid., 20 May 1947.
21. *Dawn*, 14 May 1947.
22. *CMG*, 20 May 1947.
23. *Dawn*, 11 May 1947.
24. Ibid., 6 June 1947; 'Surveys of Policies of newspapers in India since Introduction of Provincial Autonomy', IORl/1/1332.

25. *Dawn*, 11 May 1947.
26. Ibid., 10 May 1947.
27. *The Tribune*, 5 and 30 May 1947; *Dawn*, 16 May 1947; in article by Balwant Singh Saini, see *Dawn*, 14 May 1947.
28. *The Tribune*, 5, 15 and 30 May 1947.
29. *CMG*, 4 May 1947.
30. *Dawn*, 11 and 12 May 1947.
31. *CMG*, 9 May 1947.
32. *Dawn*, 11 May 1947.
33. *The Tribune*, 16 May 1947.
34. *Dawn*, 20 and 22 May 1947.
35. *The Tribune*, 8, 22 and 23 May 1947.
36. *Dawn*, 16 May 1947; *CMG*, 16 May 1947.
37. *CMG*, 16 and 11 May 1947.
38. *The Tribune*, 27 May 1947.
39. *Dawn*, 17 May 1947.
40. *CMG*, 3 May 1947.
41. *The Tribune*, 18 May 1947.
42. Ibid., 15 May 1947.
43. *CMG*, 10 May 1947.
44. *The Tribune*, 23 May 1947.
45. Ibid., 7 May 1947.
46. *CMG*, 11 May 1947; *The Tribune*, 11 May 1947; *Dawn*, 11 May 1947.
47. *CMG*, 14 May 1947.
48. *The Tribune*, 26 May and 1, 2, 9 June 1947.
49. The booklet is accessible at the NMML, New Delhi.
50. *CMG* 7, May 1947. In Delhi the booklet was banned and forfeited on 28 May, see *Dawn*, 29 May 1947. On 17 May *CMG* published a letter from S.P. Sangar (Lahore) Sangar criticized the editorial of the *CMG* on 'Rape of Rawalpindi' and said the culprit and offender was not Prabodh Chandra but the so-called leaders who started the trouble. He called upon the international community to come forward and lawfully try those who caused the killings. Sangar also charged the central and state government for their inept handling, *CMG*, 17 May 1947.
51. Ibid., 10 May 1947.
52. Ibid., 13 May 1947; *Dawn*, 12 May 1947.
53. *The Tribune*, 15 and 16 May 1947.
54. Ibid., 16 May 1947; *CMG*, 17 May 1947.
55. *CMG*, 14 May 1947.
56. Ibid., 18 May 1947.
57. Ibid., 15 May 1947.
58. *The Tribune*, 20 May 1947.
59. *CMG*, 15 May 1947.
60. Ibid., 4 June 1947.

61. Ibid., 18 May 1947.
62. Ibid., 22 May 1947.
63. *Dawn*, 30 May and 1 June 1947.
64. *TP*, vol. X (558), 1947.
65. P. Brenden Papers, CSAS.
66. AICC Papers, File G-26 1947–8, Part II, Microfilm, NMML.
67. *The Tribune*, 20 May 1947.
68. Ibid., 22 and 23 May 1947.
69. Ibid., 27 May 1947; *Muslim League Attack on Sikhs and Hindus in Punjab 1947*, SGPC, 1950, pp. 236–9, CSAS.
70. *The Tribune*, 20 and 23 May 1947.
71. Ibid., 21 and 29 May 1947.
72. *Dawn*, 8 June 1947.
73. *The Tribune*, 1 June 1947.
74. *Dawn*, 10 June 1947.
75. *CMG*, 22 May 1947; *The Tribune*, 22 May 1947.
76. Khosla, *Stern Reckoning*, p. 222.
77. *CMG*, 29 May 1947.
78. Ibid., 19 May 1947.
79. Ibid., 4 and 28 May 1947.
80. Note of Abbot to Capt. Brockman, Acting P.S. to Viceroy, *TP*, vol. X (335), 7 May 1947.
81. Ibid., vol. X (468).
82. Ibid., vol. X (531), Colville to Patel, 24 May 1947.
83. *Dawn*, 31 May 1947; IOR L/1/1/665, Information Deptt., Fortnightly Appreciation, 3 June 1947, no. 4259.
84. *The Tribune*, 29 May 1947.
85. *TP*, vol. X (425–6).
86. M.N. Das, *Fateful Events of 1947: The Secret British Game of Divide and Quit*, New Delhi, 2004, p. 279.
87. *TP*, vol. X (294), 1947, p. 588.
88. Ibid., vol. X (296), p. 590.
89. *TP*, vol. X (354), Viceroy's Personal Report, no. 6, 8 May 1947, p. 681.
90. Ibid. (309) Record of Interview between Mountbatten and Gandhi, 4 May 1947.
91. *CMG*, 21 May 1947. Interestingly the Sialkot wing of the Hindu Mahasabha had earlier demanded partition and the River Chenab as the boundary, *The Tribune* , 2 May 1947.
92. *The Tribune*, 15 May 1947.
93. *Dawn*, 25 May 1947.
94. *The Tribune*, 17 May 1947.
95. *CMG*, 25 May 1947.
96. Ibid., 7 and 11 May 1947.
97. *The Tribune*, 6 May 1947.

98. Ibid.; *Dawn*, 12 and 15 May 1947.
99. *CMG*, 7 May 1947.
100. Ibid., 27 May 1947.
101. *Dawn*, 26 May 1947.
102. Ibid., 18, 20 and 25 May 1947; *CMG*, 13 May 1947.
103. *Dawn*, 22 May 1947.
104. *TP*, vol. X (295), p. 589.
105. *CMG*, 8 May 1947
106. Ibid., 13 May 1947.
107. Ibid., 18 May 1947.
108. Ibid., 6 May 1947.
109. Ibid., 12 May 1947.
110. Ibid., 14 May 1947.
111. Henry Craik, *CMG*, 18 May 1947.
112. Tanwar, *Unionist Party*, the chapter on the 1946 elections.
113. *Dawn*, 12 May 1947.
114. *CMG*, 17 May 1947.
115. *TP*, vol. X (492), p. 915.
116. *CMG*, 21 May 1947. If there is merit in this, what could the Maharaja of Patiala have had in mind. It is obvious that he was visualizing himself as some kind of buffer between India and Pakistan.
117. Ibid., 25 May 1947.
118. *Dawn*, 11 May 1947.
119. Ibid., 14 May 1947; IOR Mss. Eur. F 164/16-17, Muddie Collection.
120. *CMG*, 6 May 1947; *HT*, 14 June 1947; Rosenberger and Tobin, *Keesings Contemporary Archives*, vol. 6, 1946–8, p. A8634.
121. Ibid., 7 May 1947
122. Ibid., 10 May 1947.
123. *The Tribune*, 7 May 1947.
124. *TP*, vol. X (340), 7 May 1947, p. 660. Similar telegrams were sent to Prime Minister Attlee and S. Cripps.
125. *The Tribune*, 15 May 1947.
126. 'Sorrows of Muslim Punjab', *Dawn*, 14 May 1947.
127. *TP*, vol. X (426), 13 May 1947, p. 803.
128. Ibid., vol. X (537), Abbot to Brockman, p. 985.
129. *TP*, vol. X (274), Jenkins to Mountbatten, 1 May 1947, p. 528.
130. Ibid., vol. X (298), 3 May 1947, p. 593.
131. Ibid., vol. X (321), Mountbatten to Ismay, 5 May 1947, p. 628.
132. Ibid., vol. X (450), Jenkins to Mountbatten, 15 May 1947, p. 834.
133. Ibid., vol. X (510), Abbot to Capt. Brockman, 21 May 1947, p. 942. Another report from Jenkins to Colville said widespread riots were expected in Jullundur, Amritsar, Lahore, Sheikhpura, Lyallpur, Montgomery, see *TP*, vol. X (549), 27 May 1947, p. 109.
134. *TP*, vol. X (483), p. 893.

135. Ibid., vol. X (528). p. 975.
136. IOR L/1/665, 19 May 1947, no. 3830, Information Department.
137. *TP*, vol. X (506), the Note by Abell, 21 May 1947, p. 935.
138. *CMG*, 11 May 1947; Das, *Fateful Events*, p. 105.
139. *CMG*, 13 May 1947.
140. Ibid., *Dawn*, 12 May 1947.
141. *The Tribune*, 28 May 1947.
142. Ibid., 22 May 1947.
143. *CMG*, 13 May 1947.
144. *CMG*, 31 May 1947.
145. IOR L/PO/6/120 (ii) *Transfer of Power*, Viceroy's Plan, Proceedings IB 21, Meeting 5 May 1947.
146. Ibid., Proceedings 23, Meeting 8 May.
147. Ibid., Proceedings 24, Meeting 14 May.
148. IOR L/PO/6/120 (i).
149. *The Tribune* 19 and 20 May 1947; *Dawn*, 19 and 20 May 1947.
150. *The Tribune*, 27 May 1947.
151. *Daily Telegraph* cited in *Dawn*, 20 May 1947.
152. *CMG*, 19 May 1947.
153. Ibid., 9 June 1947.
154. Ibid., 25 May 1947; *Dawn*, 25 May 1947; Hugh Tinker, 'Jawaharlal Nehru at Simla, May 1947: A Moment of Truth', *Modern Asian Studies* 4, 4 (1970), pp. 349–52 and 357. Tinker says Nehru was aware of the contents of the Plan that was taken to London by Ismay, after it was thrashed out on 10–11 May in Simla and that Nehru's famous outburst in Simla was only temporary, he was soon convinced by Menon and Mountbatten and in any case Nehru's initial problem was not with the plan but the notion that it had been changed by authorities in London.
155. *CMG*, 31 May 1947.
156. *TP*, vol. X (560), p. 1037; IOR L/1/1/665, Information Deptt. Fortnightly Appreciation, 3 June 1947, no. 4257.
157. *TP*, vol. X (560), Enclosure (iii).
158. *Bombay Chronicle*, 26 May 1947, Nehru Clippings, Microfilm, NMML.
159. *Anand Bazar Patrika*, 26 May 1947, Nehru Clippings, Microfilm, NMML.
160. *CMG*, 31 May 1947.
161. Ibid., 30 May 1947.
162. IOR L/PO/6 120 (i) and (ii), *Transfer of Power*, Viceroy's Plans, Proceedings of Meetings, nos. IB 21, 23, 24 of 5, 8 and 14 May 1947.
163. *The Tribune*, 5 June 1947.
164. *TP*, vol. X (528), p. 975; ibid. (386); ibid (450), 10 May 1947.
165. Ibid. (335), p. 648.

166. Das, *Fateful Events*, pp. 55–7.
167. *CMG*, 5 June 1947; *Dawn*, 5 June 1947.
168. *Dawn*, 5 June 1947.
169. *The Tribune*, 7 June 1947.
170. Bali, *Now It Can be Told*, p. 23.
171. *HT*, 24 June 1947.
172. *Dawn*, 14 June 1947; *CMG* 14 June 1947; *HT*, 14 June 1947.
173. Das, *Fateful Events*, p. 75; *The Tribune*, 7 August 1947.
174. *The Tribune*, 5 June 1947.
175. Ibid., 6 June 1947; *The Pioneer*, 6 June 1947; *CMG*, 6 June 1947; *Dawn*, 6 June 1947.
176. *The Tribune*, 8 and 9 June 1947; *HT*, 8 June 1947.
177. *Abhyudaya*, June 1947.
178. *Leader*, 17 June 1947, Nehru Clippings, Microfilm, NMML.
179. Ibid., 5 June 1947.
180. *The Tribune*, 9 June 1947.
181. Ibid., 7 June 1947.
182. Ibid.
183. *Dawn*, 7 June 1947.
184. *The Tribune*, 5 June 1947.
185. Ibid., 7 June 1947.
186. *HT*, 13 June 1947.
187. *Dawn*, 5 June 1947.
188. *Hind Outlook*, 10–17 June 1947; *HT*, 8 June 1947; *The Pioneer*; 8 June 1947.
189. *Hindu Outlook*, 10 June 1947. The Resolution was seconded by Dr Narang who called the plan 'unwise', *HT*, 9 June 1947.
190. *HT*, 9 June 1947.
191. Ibid., 11 June 1947.
192. Ibid., 16 June 1947.
193. *The Tribune*, 7 June 1947.
194. Ibid., 9 June 1947; *HT*, 18 June 1947.
195. *HT*, 10 June 1947.
196. Ibid., 13 June 1947.
197. *The Tribune*, 22 June 1947.
198. *HT*, 13 June 1947.
199. Ibid., 11 June 1947. The resolution did contain qualifying riders 'solidarity', etc. Interestingly a day earlier *HT* had carried a report on the basis of 'highly placed Sikh sources' that the Sikhs had been given an assurance of a homeland in the Eastern Punjab once India was free. For the reference to the rider of solidarity see *CMG*, 13 June 1947.
200. *HT*, 12 and 13 June 1947.
201. *The Tribune*, 25 June 1947; *The Pioneer*, 2 June 1947.

202. *CMG*, 14 June 1947, *HT*, 14 June 1947.
203. *Dawn*, 4 June 1947.
204. Ibid., 6 June 1947.
205. *Dawn*, 7 June 1947.
206. Ibid., 6 June 1947.
207. Ibid., 9 June 1947; *HT*, 9 June 1947.
208. This conference of Sikhs resolved to accept the 3 June Plan.
209. *Dawn*, 9 June 1947; *HT*, 9 June 1947. The joining of Meerut Division to Ambala Division (Haryana) has ever since been on the agenda of many politicians in Haryana—mainly because the Meerut Division has a large number of Jat peasantry.
210. IOR Mss. Eur. F 200/129, no. 284, Viceregal Official Correspondence Files.
211. Ishar Singh Majhel, Memoir, Oral History Transcript, Acc. no. 454, NMML.
212. *HT*, 27 May 1947. A detailed understanding of Nehru's views can be had from the draft resolution of the Congress Working Committee—1 May 1947.
213. Ibid., 8 June 1947.
214. Ibid., 10 June 1947.
215. *SW*, vol. 3 (Second Series), p. 91.
216. *The Tribune*, 16 June 1947, *CMG*, 17 June 1947, *Dawn* 16 June 1947; *National Herald*, 16 June; *SW*, vol. 3 (Second Series), p. 110.
217. Ram Manohar Lohia, *Guilty Men of India's Partition*, Allahabad, 1960, pp. 8–10.
218. *HT*, 13, 14 and 15 June 1947; *Dawn*, 16 June 1947. On 13 June the Viceroy had convened a meeting of senior Congress and League leaders. The meeting lasted for three hours.
219. *HT*, 15 June 1947.
220. *Dawn*, 16 June 1947.
221. *HT*, 15 June 1947.
222. *CMG*, 17 June 1947; *Dawn* 16 June 1947.
223. *HT*, 14 June 1947.
224. *Dawn*, 16 June 1947.
225. Editorial, '*AICC Ka Prastav*', *Janvani*, June 1947.
226. *HT*, 15 June 1947.
227. *The Tribune*, 16 June 1947.
228. *HT*, 16 June 1947.
229. *Dawn*, 16 June 1947.
230. *HT*, 15 June 1947; *The Pioneer*, 15 June 1947.
231. *HT*, 25 June 1947. The paper published a cartoon in response to All India Hindu Mahasabha President B. Bhopatkar's statement that the '3 June Plan means end of India as a nation'.

232. *SW*, vol. III (Second Series), pp. 110–13; *National Herald*, 16 June 1947; *The Tribune*, 16 June 1947; *CMG*, 17 June 1947; *Dawn*, 16 June 1947.
233. *Dawn*, 16 June 1947.
234. *HT*, 15 June 1947.
235. *Dawn*, 16 June 1947.
236. *CMG*, 17 June 1947; *Dawn*, 16 June 1947; *HT*, 16 June 1947.
237. Durga Das, *India From Curzon to Nehru*, p. 255.
238. *HT*, 19 and 20 June 1947.
239. IOR L/1/1/665 Information Deptt. Fortnightly Appreciation, 18 June 1947, no. 4717.
240. Ibid., 24 June 1947.
241. *CMG*, 25 June.
242. *HT*, 22 June 1947.
243. *TP*, vol. XI (370).
244. Ibid.
245. *CMG*, 28 May, 1947.
246. Ibid., 4 May, 1947.
247. *HT*, 22 March 1947.
248. *CMG*, 28 June 1947.
249. *HT*, 24 June 1947.
250. *Dawn*, 17 June 1947.
251. *The Tribune*, 24 June 1947.
252. *CMG*, 19 June 1947.
253. *The Tribune*, 18 June 1947.
254. *Hindu Outlook*, 18 June 1947.
255. Ibid., 1 July 1947.
256. IOR L/1/1/665, Fortnightly Appreciation, 4 July 1947, no. 5140, Information Deptt.
257. *Dawn*, 16 June 1947.
258. Ibid., 23 June 1947.
259. Ibid., *HT*, 23 June 1947.
260. *The Tribune*, 21 June 1947; *HT*, 13 June 1947.
261. *HT*, 21 June 1947.
262. *Dawn*, 13 June 1947.
263. Ibid., 1 June 1947.
264. *CMG*, 4 June 1947.
265. *Dawn*, 8, 10, 15, 19, 30 June and 1 July 1947.
266. *Dawn*, 28 June 1947. The Viceroy accompanied by Governor Jenkins had already visited 5 villages on June 1 and addressed Sikh & Gurkha troops in Gurgaon, *Dawn*, 2 June 1947.
267. *The Tribune*, 18 June 1947; *Dawn*, 2 July 1947.
268. *The Tribune*, 22 June 1947.
269. Ibid., 8 June 1947.

270. *Dawn*, 28 May 1947.
271. *The Tribune,* 16 and 30 June 1947.
272. Ibid., 2 June 1947.
273. Ibid., 24 June 1947.
274. Ibid., 10 June 1947.
275. *CMG*, 15 June 1947. As the rich of Lahore moved out, prices of properties in Delhi began to rise. On 13 June, for example, *HT* published an advertisement of a person wanting to purchase a shop in Connaught Place at 'any cost'.
276. *HT*, 24 June 1947.
277. *HT*, 19 June 1947.
278. *CMG*, 15 June 1947; *HT*, 17 June 1947.
279. *CMG*, 15 June 1947.
280. *The Tribune*, 11 June 1947; *HT*, 29 June 1947.
281. *CMG*, 29 June 1947.
282. *Dawn*, 14 June 1947; *HT*, 13 June 1947; *HT*, 24 June 1947. *The Tribune*, 8 and 20 June 1947.
283. Long queues were common in banks of Lahore—withdrawings, *HT* 25 June 1947.
284. *The Tribune*, 6 June 1947.
285. *Dawn*, 15 June 1947.
286. *The Tribune*, 29 June 1947.
287. *TP*, vol. XI (209), 15 June 1947.
288. *HT*, 15 June 1947.
289. *CMG*, 19 June 1947.
290. *The Tribune*, 24 June 1947.
291. *CMG*, 18 June 1947.
292. *Dawn*, 24 June 1947; *The Tribune*, 24 June 1947; *CMG*, 24 June 1947; *HT*, 24 June 1947.
293. Ibid.
294. *CMG*, 25 June 1947.
295. *The Tribune*, 25 June 1947.
296. Ibid.; *HT*, 25 and 26 June 1947. Gandhiji also commended the Punjab leaders for the appeal, *HT*, 26 June 1947.
297. *Dawn*, 27 June 1947.
298. *The Tribune*, 26 June 1947.
299. Ibid., 27 June 1947.
300. *Dawn*, 29 June 1947; *HT*, 30 June 1947.
301. *CMG*, 25 June 1947.
302. *The Tribune*, 1 June 1947.
303. *Dawn*, 4 June 1947.
304. *The Tribune*, 5 June 1947.
305. *Dawn*, 27 June 1947.
306. Ibid., 11 June 1947.

307. *CMG*, 28 June 1947, Editorial.
308. *The Tribune*, 30 June 1947.
309. *Dawn* 3 July 1947.
310. Bhimsen Sachar Memoirs (Oral History Transcript), NMML, Acc. no. 182, pp. 107–14.
311. *Dawn*, 4 February 1947.
312. *The Tribune*, 24 June 1947.
313. P. Brenden Papers, CSAS.
314. *CMG*, 25 June 1947; *HT*, 25 June 1947.
315. *SW*, vol. 3 (Second Series), Nehru to Mountbatten, 22 June, pp. 180–1.
316. Bali, *Now It Can Be Told*, p. 24.
317. *Dawn*, 6 June 1947.
318. *HT*, 20 June 1947.
319. Ibid., 24 June 1947.
320. Ibid., 22 June 1947.
321. Ibid., 29 June 1947.
322. Ibid.

4

The Boundary Commission: Punjabis Reject the Award

During the period 1945–7 Nehru was at odds with himself and with others. When writers can free themselves from the 'Heroic' image of the man, we shall see that Nehru's contradictions were a sizeable factor in the run-down of that period. To state this is not to deny Nehru's greatness . . . a recent study of Churchill reminds us that great men can be erratic, wrong, even ridiculous, and yet at other times rise to greatness.[1]

THE NOTIONAL BOUNDARY: SEEDS OF CONFLICT

In many ways the 3 June Plan marked the end of the deadlock, or so it seems, that had dominated politics in India for many years.[2] On the face of it both the leading political players, the Indian National Congress and the Muslim League, had ample reason to be happy. For the Congress it marked the end of a long-drawn struggle, the prospect of freedom which would also bring even if only as a bonus the reins and right to rule India. For the League it meant the achievement of the cherished goal of Pakistan. In fact, all this added to the building up of an impression that along with India's even Punjab's problems were now in the past, the future was only bright. This feeling of cheer was widely prevalent in most political circles in Punjab in July 1947. Indeed the desire to bury the past and part as friends was the general feeling in the corridors of power after years of bitter fighting and slandering. But the point that was possibly missed was that all this cordiality was limited only to the highest level, it had not percolated downwards—to the streets and tea shops where public opinion was and is moulded.

Gandhi understood the 'pulse' of India like no one else. In his post-prayer address on 6 July, he observed that the lack of enthusiasm even when freedom was now beckoning among the masses was possibly because the country was being divided: 'my mind was full of questions . . . was the fight for freedom acclaimed as noble approaching an inglorious end.'[3] Gandhi's apprehensions were not out of place because, ironically for India and more so for Punjab, the very plan that was viewed by politicians and their active supporters as the signal of good times to come contained in it the inherent seeds of a conflict that would for years make every Punjabi hang his head in shame.

A sense of unclear doom, of unclear expectancy hung across Punjab; everyone knew there was no hope and yet only the few and resourceful, mostly the well provided, prepared for the worst, the rest just waited. The notional line which Mountbatten announced as part of the 3 June Plan became in due course a major root of the crisis. While it was projected as only a 'notional line of division', as time proved it became, with only marginal differences, the final line.[4] The Plan itself came on to the Punjab, accepted so readily by the leaders who had all along ridiculed such a possibility and rejected by almost everyone else. Many aspersions were cast on the people who had negotiated the settlement soon after the announcement was made, charges that continued to fly in the years that followed.

Sri Prakash, a member of the Constituent Assembly of India, criticized the manner in which the agreement had been worked out with the British by a handful of leaders completely bypassing the Constituent Assembly. Speaking in the Assembly he said:

> I would like to lodge a strong protest against all that has happened. . . . These negotiations have resulted in cutting up of the country. . . . Things happened in an overwhelming manner in which we poor fellows had nothing to do.

As the debate proceeded Sri Prakash suggested that the irregularity be now regularized. Jawaharlal Nehru reacted to the suggestion by saying that propriety had been followed but he was in agreement with Sri Prakash that a committee draft a resolution to formalize the decisions taken without the House's consent.[5]

JENKINS PREDICTS APPALLING CONFUSION AFTER 15 AUGUST

The *TP* volumes contain a note written by Abell, the Viceroy's Private Secretary, which precisely sums up the Punjab scene in early July 1947: 'I have no doubt that the Sikhs are in a dangerous mood.

Kartar Singh who met the Governor on 10 July practically delivered an ultimatum that the Sikhs . . . would go in for Guerilla warfare after 15 August. . . Hindus and Sikhs are unwilling to set up government at all except in Lahore on 15 August. They consider that to move from Lahore would prejudice their claim to the city and they absolutely refuse to accept the notional boundaries.'[6] This note was put up by Abell to the Viceroy with the comments that Jenkins was correct in maintaining the view that the Sikhs in fact did have a point in stressing their claim on the fertile colony lands of Montgomery and the new canal colony lands of Lyallpur. Abell also pointed out to the Viceroy Jenkins' view that there was no way a peaceful solution could be worked out and, more interestingly, Jenkins' belief that there was little chance of the Boundary Award being out before 15 August.

The more significant part of this important note was a brief assessment of the situation made by Jenkins and annexed by Abell with his own note. 'The communal feeling is now unbelievably bad. In Ambala Division outside Gurgaon the Muslims seem resigned to their fate, the same is possibly true of non-Muslims in Rawalpindi Division, the districts of Dera Ghazi Khan, Muzzafargarh, Multan, Jhang. In Lahore and Jullundur Divisions tension is very high. The Sikhs threaten a violent uprising immediately after the transfer of power unless.' Jenkins went on to say (para 3): 'The higher services have virtually disintegrated. In the ICS not one non-Muslim is prepared to serve in West Punjab.' Referring to the working of the Partition Committee, Jenkins said: 'Meetings of the Partition Committee resemble a Peace Conference with a new war in sight. In the time available it will be quite impossible to make a clean job of partition . . . after 15 August there will be appalling confusion. In civil administration certain things cannot be done in a matter of days or weeks . . . From mid July many new officers will be posted to key appointments and the new government will face the critical time in August with district (administration) even weaker than we have had in the past couple of years. There will be much wrangling for (key) postings. . . The prospect is far from encouraging but we can only go ahead and see what happens.'

On 13 July Jenkins noted yet again to Mountbatten: 'The Muslims seem quite happy about the notional boundary because it gives them Lahore . . . the Hindus are very unhappy. They believe they are entitled to Lahore . . . the total number of districts disputed is 14 out of 29.' Jenkins explained that the Hindus and Sikhs felt that once they accepted the notional boundary, it would be impossible to undo it later as the Muslims would then develop control over Lahore and that in view of this they would like to keep the East Punjab government in Lahore until the actual announcement of the Award. Ideally Jenkins wanted both claimants to shift their East and West Punjab governments out of Lahore until the announcement of the Award.[7]

Both sides were naturally adamant on Lahore. The newspapers too played an active role in the debate. Interestingly, a letter by a Muslim challenged the general assumption that the Muslims of Lahore were as a class unanimous in the view that Lahore would go to Pakistan. The writer said: 'I am positive that if a referendum were held in Lahore its majority vote would be for it to be a part of Hindustan . . . remember every Muslim is not a follower of Jinnah . . . all Muslims do not want to be a part of Pakistan.'[8] As the tension mounted, the *CMG* reported on 24 July that the West Punjab government also secretly planned to move its new capital of divided West Punjab either to Gujranwala or to Rawalpindi in the eventuality of Lahore being awarded to East Punjab. The report added that senior officials had in fact even started a secret survey of available accommodation in the two cities.

THE PANTH CALLS FOR *HARTAL*

Essentially the problem in Punjab in early July, as a sequel to the June Plan and notional line of division, boiled down to the fact that almost 14 or 15 of its 29 districts were claimed and counterclaimed by both sides, in the process making a mockery of the Plan and the notional line of division.[9] The Sikh leaders, called for a mass *hartal* to be organized on 8 July. While explaining the objectives of the *hartal*, Master Tara Singh said on 4 July: 'we should accept the 3 June Plan only if the government accepts the river Chenab as boundary, thereby maintaining solidarity of the Sikhs'.[10] On the same day, Baba Kharak Singh issued a similar statement: 'The only effective protest against partition is its boycott. Therefore, those who consider it unjust should disassociate themselves from its schemes.'[11] Kharak Singh also appealed to the Panth for its full support to the *hartal*.

Whereas the Sikh leadership was talking in terms of the river Chenab as a natural boundary, the Muslim League had other plans. Sufi Abdul Hamid, the League MLA from Karnal, went as far as demanding Panipat's inclusion in Pakistan.[12] Firoz Khan Noon who

LOST SHEEP: Found two stray sheep on Chah Miran Road. Owner can claim on identification. A reference to Master Tara Singh and Giani Kartar Singh (*Pakistan Times*, 24 July 1947).

Counting the Shrines (*Pakistan Times*, 19 July 1947).

was more important in the League hierarchy in Punjab than Abdul Hamid issued a statement demanding that the river Sutlej should be the rightful boundary.[13] This demand was rejected outright by *Dawn* in a powerful editorial which obviously had the approval of the League supremo himself. It argued that Noon was wrong in demanding the river Sutlej as the line of demarcation because this would leave out large Muslim-populated areas—Ludhiana, Hisar, even Kangra which controlled the irrigation and hydro head works of Punjab: 'How can Amritsar be given away to the Sikhs just because it contains a shrine of the Sikhs? With the exception of Tarn Tarn tehsil, Amritsar is a Muslim majority region.' *Dawn* as part of its policy of sparing no opportunity to hit at Governor Jenkins added: 'we have reason to believe that Jenkins the notorious Englishman who still clings to the Governorship of Punjab is using the influence to persuade the higher authorities to recognise the demands of the Sikhs.' It even suggested that 'underhand' deals were in fact 'being struck'.[14]

A day later, and not surprisingly, Shaukat Hayat spoke up on behalf of his party in response to the Sikh demand for the boundary of the river Chenab: 'By agreeing to the river Sutlej as the boundary the Muslims had evinced a desire to accommodate the Sikhs even at the cost of their own brethren. . . . But now the Muslims shall not rest content until the boundary line is drawn at the river Yamuna.'[15]

As the date of the *hartal* called by the Sikhs in protest against the 3 June Plan and supported by a large number of Hindu organizations drew near, Congress leaders like Bhargava and Swarn Singh and Muslim League leaders like Noon tried to sidetrack the issue. Bhargava speaking at the Rotary Club in Lahore when he shared the stage with Swarn Singh and Noon said: 'I hope the void created in [the] lives of Punjabis by the division will not last long. It would be realised soon that the two had to live together, the demarcation would not keep them apart for too long . . . the need was to remove the mistrust . . . it was for the majority to heal the gaping wound.' While Swarn Singh said partition was inevitable, Noon said that now that contentious issues were more or less resolved, peace should be restored.[16] The irony was that far from being resolved, the real issues had not even been touched. Where could a line be drawn to meet Giani Kartar Singh's demand of ensuring that at least 85 per cent of the Sikhs were consolidated in East Punjab.[17]

The *hartal* was a resounding success. On the preceding day (7 July), a joint appeal by leading Sikh figures for a peaceful *hartal* had been made. Across the province including Delhi the call received stupendous support not only from the Sikhs but the Hindus as well. Lala Bihari Lal, MLA, had also appealed to all Hindu families to fully support the Panth's call.[18] Markets were closed in most parts of Delhi, almost completely in Lahore, Amritsar, Rawalpindi, Solan, Ambala, Ferozepur, Patiala, partly in Srinagar, Kanpur, and completely in Lyallpur, Jullundur and Ludhiana. Resolutions were passed across the Punjab demanding the integrity and solidarity of the Sikhs, adequate share in canal waters and protection of Sikh shrines. The sentiment that prevailed and the tenor of the speeches at the massive meeting in Lahore as well as in many other meetings, were early pointers to the seriousness of the discontent among the Sikhs.[19]

In Delhi Sardar Baldev Singh addressed the large gathering at Gurudwara Sisganj. He said the Sikhs had accepted the 3 June Plan only in principle and the proposed division was not acceptable. Significantly, he pointed out how the Sikhs had in fact sought a Sikh province, even in 1942, but then the 'Congress and the Lahore newspapers had opposed it'. If they had not opposed the Sikh demand, 'there would have been no Pakistan today'. Sardar Jogender Singh Mann renounced his MBE on the grounds that 'when the entire Panth is in mourning, I am morally bound to protest', because the British had not honoured their word.[20] Baldev Singh's speech at Gurudwara Sisganj appears to have attracted attention in the high quarters of New Delhi from where he was probably asked to make some clarifications. On 11 July he issued a statement saying that he had not said the Sikhs should fight for their rights or resist if the Award was not in their favour.[21]

Even as there was not a single report of any violent incident related to the *hartal* of 8 July, it was the huge *Diwan* at the Golden Temple that set the tone of action for the Panth in the days that followed. Tara Singh was naturally the star speaker. He said he anticipated a big struggle for their (Sikh) rights. Incidentally, while the report did not elaborate on the details, Tara Singh was reported to have also said in the *Diwan* that Sardar Baldev Singh had asked them (the Sikh leaders) to ensure peace but if the award went against them, they were to be prepared to vindicate their honour with all sacrifice.[22]

The historic *Diwan* also drew attention for another very significant observation by Tara Singh. He referred to how there had been much discussion on his refusal to sign a peace pledge with the leaders of other parties like the Muslim League and the Congress. He said that while he stood for peace it could not be at the cost of the Panth: '[The] present peace moves were designed to deceive the Sikhs'.[23]

Reuters Indian Service said of the 8 July *hartal*. 'India's 5,70,000 Sikhs most of whom live in Punjab wore black arm bands as they prayed in their Gurudwaras today in protest against the threat to split their community under the British plan. The report also that 'Gurudwara congregations approved a resolution declaring that "any partition that did not secure the integrity and solidarity of the Sikhs would be unacceptable and create a difficult situation".' Interestingly this report too cited Baldev Singh as having said that Sikhs should be prepared for sacrifices if the verdict of the award went against them.[24]

The *HT's* version of the *hartal* was that in some meetings, Sikh, speakers had expressed extreme views regarding a separate state. The editorial advised the Sikhs to plan an organized exchange of population and not to make their claim on the basis of religious shrines because the Muslims too were losing many of their sacred shrines. With regard to the Sikh leadership's demand for the exchange of population along with property, the editorial said, 'property is for people not people for property', and that 'where welfare of men, women and children is concerned property has to be subordinated'.[25]

MINORITIES CONVENTION—RAWALPINDI 7 JULY

The West Punjab Minorities Convention which met in Rawalpindi on 7 July was attended by about a hundred select representatives from all the western districts of Punjab.[26] While the newspapers did not make any such indication, it does seem, particularly by the timing of the convention, that its organizers' possible intention was to minimize or decrease the impact of the Panth's *hartal* of 8 July. Pindidas Sabharwal while inaugurating the convention asked the minorities to cooperate with Pakistan. Sardar Uttam Singh Duggal said that even as of 'now' (July), the killers of Rawalpindi had not been condemned by the League leaders, and on the contrary, those among the killers who had themselves been killed by the minorities in self-defence had been termed as martyrs. Uttam Singh, however, also added that the partition plan could do nothing to resolve the problem of the minorities on both sides. Sant Singh argued that if the Sikhs stayed back in West Punjab they would still constitute about 27 per cent of the population and that their numbers would be such that no state could afford to ignore them.[27]

The Tribune said the main resolution at the convention was moved by Krishan Gopal Dutt (MLA). Among other things the resolution demanded security of life and property of minorities, equal rights as citizens of the new state, freedom of worship and no forced religious conversions, guarantee that no legislation or legal measure affecting Hindu–Sikh religious cultural life would be made without the consent of the minorities, and finally, reservation of elected seats for minorities in legislative bodies.[28] Bhimsen Sachar had also moved a resolution appealing to the minorities in towns and villages not to migrate. He relayed a message from Mamdot assuring the minorities that, 'those who have left must come back, we will do everything to rehabilitate them . . . let us make determined efforts to restore goodwill.

PEACE UNLIKELY

Jang Bahadur Singh, officiating editor of *The Tribune* was also present at the Rawalpindi convention. Sadly for the organizers he refused to give false assurance and in his rather blunt manner said that 'peace was unlikely, and he could only advise people to face with fortitude and courage the times that were to come. Another report of *The Tribune* said that when asked by the ordinary people at the convention what they should do;—the leaders' stock reply was, 'don't lose heart'.[29]

It was not just the leaders and opinion makers in communities like those that passed resolutions at the Minorities Convention at Rawalpindi who were making an effort to convince Hindus and Sikhs not to leave west Punjab, there were many others as well. Avtar Narain, a Congress leader of Rawalpindi, called upon the minorities to join the Pakistan mainstream. He added that if minorities 'behaved', it would induce the majority to accept them as equal members of the new state.[30] *Dawn* quoted him as saying, 'My idea is that we should not panic and face reality with patience and courage.'[31]

A more pointed appeal to the minorities not to migrate from the West Punjab was made by Dev Raj Sethi (MLA), who on returning to Lahore said that he had met important Congress leaders in Delhi who had all said that the minorities should rest assured and avoid panicking and certainly not leave their homes, lands, businesses, etc. Sethi went on to appeal to the rich and influential to set an example by not migrating.[32]

With uncanny foresight, M.M. Saeed, in an effort to persuade minorities not to leave West Punjab in favour of East Punjab, said in a letter: 'When the state of East Punjab actually takes shape and they find an alien culture along with its illegitimate child of languages—the 'Hindustani' language thrust on them and economic ruin staring them in the face, they will I am sure try to resume their former ties if not now may be in ten years.'[33]

NO EXCHANGE OF POPULATION, SAYS PRESS

Even as late as 11 July, *The Tribune*, widely accepted to be the best-informed newspaper in Punjab, noted that the transfer of population was ruled out and therefore the Muslim League leadership should give assurances to the minorities regarding the safety and security of life and property in the West Punjab. In fact, there was really no need for *The Tribune* to seek assurances on behalf of the minorities from Muslim League leaders because such assurances were being given more than willingly throughout early July. Among the early appeals, a reference could be made, for an example, to Daultana's statement (10 July): 'Pakistan is on test and the first fulfilment of the test must be the security and well-being of the minorities . . . I advise my Hindu and Sikh friends make Pakistan your home . . . share with us the building of a new world . . . the Muslims are determined to do justice.'[34]

The problem for ordinary citizens particularly the minorities in Punjab in the months June, July and August was what to believe—Mamdot and Daultana whose views were similar or Firoz Khan Noon who had issued a statement on 12 July refuting the Sikh basis for redrawing the notional line, arguing that land in 'Punjab was owned by the state and revenue was paid half by the owner [allottee] and half by the tenant'. He then added that since most of the tenants were Muslim the Sikh claim meant nothing.[35]

GANDHI ADVISES SIKHS NOT TO DOUBT JINNAH

The editor of the popular *Ajit* who met Gandhi sometimes in the first week of July asked him that if the Sikhs and Hindus accepted his (Gandhi's) advice to remain in West Punjab, 'will you give them the solemn assurance that if they were once again made victims of communal frenzy that you and the Congress would not sit idle—will the Congress retaliate?' Gandhi reply was quite characteristic: 'I advise Hindus and Sikhs not to rely on me or the Congress but on God's help. They should not suspect that they will have less than justice in the new state.'[36]

However, things on the ground were far more complex and certainly not as simple as Gandhi made them seem. Surjan Das Kumar editor *National Industry and Finance* wrote to *CMG* that there was complete chaos and confusion and that no one was clear as to what would be the status of those who stayed behind. He said that they were worried not only of the status of the political rights but also of the bank accounts and economic rights of the non-Muslims who might stay on in West Punjab.

SIKH LEADERS WARN GOVERNOR JENKINS

Even as some leaders like Gopichand Bhargava continued talking of the two states 'living like good neighbours in the future', differences were far more acute than wily politicians were letting on.[37] On 11 July Jathedar Mohan Singh and Sardar Harnam Singh had a meeting with Governor Jenkins. Even though the minutes prepared by Jenkins of the meeting seem almost hurried and overstressed, the point remains the Sikh leadership minus those Sikhs who were aligned with the Congress were mentally reconciled to fighting it out. Jenkins notes that Mohan Singh's argument was the same as Giani Kartar Singh's (who had met Jenkins the previous day) and that Mohan Singh felt the only solution to the difficulties being faced by the Sikhs said: 'was a substantial exchange of population. If this did not occur the Sikhs would be drawn to facilitate it by a massacre of Muslims in the Eastern Punjab'.[38]

Jenkins also noted that the two had even said that Sikhs were being ridiculed as cowards by Hindus, but they would act only after the transfer of power. Interestingly, Jenkins' view was that Mohan Singh appeared to understand that there would be little gain from violence yet he (Mohan Singh) also felt that it was inevitable.

LEADERS AVOID BASIC ISSUES

The Punjab Partition Committee held an informal meeting in Lahore on 10 July. The proceedings were alarming in the sense that while it had earlier been assumed that only 2 or 3 districts were disputed, as it transpired in the meeting, both sides were laying claim to at least 12 of the 29 districts. The second problem that the *HT* reporter learned from 'informed quarters' was that neither of the two sides was even remotely willing to discuss the possibility of a new capital city as this would make it appear that they had surrendered their claim to Lahore. So acute were the differences in this informal meeting that the routine practice of issuing a press statement was done away with—because there was practically nothing to which the two sides had agreed.[39] And yet, important leaders from both sides were issuing, high-sounding statements—of trust and goodwill and that there was 'nothing to fear'.

JINNAH MEETS THE PRESS

On 13 July Jinnah held an important press conference at his residence in New Delhi. Much of what Jinnah said at the conference was also a kind of reaction to some of the issues that had been raised at the Minorities Convention in Rawalpindi. It was a hot and sultry Sunday morning and as the press corps leisurely trooped in they were surprised to find that the governor general designate of Pakistan had already started the proceedings—well before the scheduled time. The crowd of reporters appeared to have taken the organizers by surprise, the early birds managed chairs while others were left standing with the small room being stuffy and hot, the single table fan in the room was naturally 'fixed' on Jinnah Sahib. The heat as a report said appeared to have drained Jinnah of energy as most reporters were heard complaining that he was barely audible and tended to avoid questions. But all the physical discomfort of the reporters notwithstanding, the conference was momentous on all other counts. Jinnah issued perhaps his most categorical assurance regarding the guarantee of protection to minorities in the new state—to their life, property, culture, religion and belief. In return he said he wanted only loyalty to the new state. Jinnah said it was unfair to make an issue out of single statements. After all, there were crooks, cranks and mad men all over the world. This was probably aimed at some junior League functionaries who had made provocative statements in west Punjab. When a reporter asked him whether he would like the minorities to stay or would like to see the population being exchanged, he replied: 'As far as I can speak I can say there is no reason for apprehension . . . it is for the minority to decide . . . I cannot order them.'[40]

I DO NOT KNOW WHAT A THEOCRATIC STATE IS

When a reporter wished to know—'will Pakistan be a secular state', Jinnah replied: 'you are asking me a question that is absurd. I do not know what a theocratic state means'. The reporter insisted on a more detailed answer and tried to explain to Jinnah what a theocratic state meant: 'where only people of a particular faith are full citizens and others are not'. Jinnah was visibly irritated: 'For God's sake get this non-sense out of your head—I do not know what is a theocratic state.' When a reporter sought to know whether his interest in 'India's citizens would continue as of today', Jinnah replied: 'My interest in India's citizens will continue, particularly the Muslims.'

The following day *HT*, however, published its conclusions of this conference by suggesting that Jinnah had not committed himself to a secular, modern democratic state.[41] It is difficult to comment of what Jinnah said came from the heart or was influenced by the 'secular winds of Delhi', but there are also no reasons to doubt the sincerity of his statements. But either way, such statements naturally meant little to those who had already made up their minds to leave; for others who were inclined to stay on in the West Punjab, Jinnah's assurances brought great relief. This also meant peace of mind for the millions of Muslim families who were in a similar position in East Punjab as were the Sikhs and Hindus were in the West.

In Rawalpindi Jinnah's statement was very well received. For example, Tilak Raj Bhasin said: 'The statement of Mr. Jinnah clinches the issue . . . fulfils the demands of the Minority Convention to a considerable degree . . . however some explanation is required (in the context of Sind) regarding the differences between assurance and actions.'[42]

But even as the Quaid-i-Azam himself was issuing statements of assurances to the minorities, there were many who questioned their significance. Rajendra Magoo of Gujarat, in a letter questioned the sincerity of the Muslim League's assurance regarding equal rights and their statement that 'Pakistan is the common heritage of Hindus and Muslims', by pointing out that in spite of all such assurances the fact remained that the proposed flag of Pakistan did not symbolize the common heritage of Hindus and Muslims.[43] Sant Ram Sanyal questioned the relevance of such assurances on the grounds that they were meaningless because the leaders making such appeals actually had little control over ordinary League workers who were the source of the problem in the first place.[44]

There were naturally others who said the same about the leaders guiding the Sikhs and Hindus. Charanjit Lal, President of the Hindu Defence Committee of Peshawar noted that the Muslim population was being guided in a timely and organized manner whereas the Hindus were in complete confusion, and that widespread confusion was the predominant feature of the Hindus in West Punjab and the NWFP: 'in the Punjab kingdoms have changed hands a hundred times and a thousand times battles have been fought but the state of the people was never such as seems of the Hindus today'.[45] At the local level, small organizations continued to meet and find answers but there was obviously no stand of significance at the provincial level.[46]

ANTI-CONGRESS SENTIMENT

There was considerable reportage in July of the widespread anti-Congress sentiment in Punjab. G.S. Gideon of Nainital, in a letter to the *CMG*, advised Christians not to associate with the Congress because it had accepted the Partition of India by bowing to the Muslim League and in the process had ceased to be a nationalist party: 'the era of power politics has begun in India'.[47] Thakur Dutt Sharma, a pronounced Amritdhari, traced the crisis to the work of some political ringleaders: 'Hindustan is shorn of its glory and bereft of its greatness. Free only in name . . . Hindustan is gone . . . only platitude remains.'[48]

On 2 July about a dozen Municipal Councillors of Amritsar had tried to bring together people of different communities to decrease the growing tension in the city, but no sooner had the meeting started than the tone was changed by the audience who vented their anger against the Congress leadership for having not done enough during the disturbances.[49]

Possibly as a result of Jinnah's press conference many in Punjab continued to believe that there was really no need for the minorities to plan an exchange of population. One such person was the widely popular and respected Sardar Ajit Singh. He appealed to the minorities to stay where they were and 'give full support to the new state', and that if they are brave and fearless they could not be ignored. 'No state however, can tolerate a fifth column within its boundaries. We must be true citizens in every sense of the term. This applies with equal force to Muslims of Hindustan.'[50] Even as prominent figures like Ajit Singh were advising the minorities not to worry some like Haji Maula Bux, brother of the better known late Allah Bux, believed that the people of the two countries had so much in common that they were bound to reunite.[51]

THE PUNJAB BOUNDARY COMMISSION

The composition of the Punjab Boundary Commission (PBC) had been announced on 30 June. Essentially it was a judicial commission, the four members being Justice Teja Singh, Justice Mehar Chand

Mahajan, Justice Din Mohammad, and Justice Mohammad Munir.[52] Khawaja Abdur Rehman and Nawab Singh, both of the ICS, were made Secretaries to the Commission. Sir Cyril John Radcliffe was appointed Chairman, for both Punjab and Bengal Commissions.[53] In the context of Radcliffe's appointment *Dawn*, quoting its sources in London said that his assignment was more like that of an umpire, the decisions were to be taken by the four judges.[54] On 17 July formal procedures for the conduct of the Commission were announced in Lahore by the Secretaries of the Commission. It was to meet for nine days starting 21 July in the room of the Chief Justice of the Punjab High Court. Hearings were to be conducted in public but since space was limited entry was to be regulated by passes, a specific number for members of the Bar and the Press. It was also announced that both the Muslim and the non-Muslim sides would be given four and half days each, with arguments being opened by the non-Muslim side.[55]

The Viceroy's Personal Report, no. 13, 18 July contains an interesting observation by him on the relations betwen the members of the PBC. Mountbatten noted that the four judges got on very well to the extent that they even agreed to have in the absence of Sir Radcliffe, Justice Munir as chairman. At Radcliffe's suggestion that they rotate the chairmanship, the other three refused saying that 'they all trusted Justice Munir'. Mountbatten found this 'atmosphere of common sense and tolerance . . . promising'.[56]

Even as leaders in Delhi were heaving sighs of relief, in Punjab apprehensions that the transfer of power deadline was appearing to be greatly hurried were growing because, as *The Tribune* while discussing Sir Radcliffe's statement that the Award would be ready in two months said, there could be serious problems if the Boundary Award announcement was delayed or that the transfer of power was to precede it.[57] Jenkins had already noted on July 11 that 'it is difficult to see how the PBC can report by 15 Aug.'[58] Even staunch Congressman and Nehru loyalist Swarn Singh went on record saying: 'Sikhs feel that a transfer of power before settlement of boundaries would prejudice the issue against the Sikhs—they are determined to resist it.'[59]

Surprisingly sections in the press, mainly those that were sympathetic to the League, had launched a covert campaign questioning the credibility of the Commission itself. The *PT* in an editorial called it a hoax, an eyewash.[60] But at the same time, there were those like Firoz Khan Noon who not only trusted the Commission but even advised it to complete its work outside Punjab 'because if he [Radcliffe] came to Punjab and shook hands with the Sikhs and was seen doing so by a Muslim they would think he was with the Sikhs or if he had a cup of tea with a Muslim, Sikhs would think he was with the Muslims'.[61]

While Governor Jenkins had confidence in the abilities and working of Sir Radcliffe,[62] Spate, who was contracted by an Ahmaddiya association to plead their case with the Boundary Commission, has recorded that the functional process of the Commission itself was flawed. To Spate the issue was that while the hearings would be conducted by the Indian judges in the absence of Sir Radcliffe, the final judgement was to be pronounced by him. Spate has also made a rather intriguing entry—that he had heard Mrs Firoz Khan Noon saying that Justice Din Mohammad had been offered a bribe of Rs. 25,00,000 (obviously by India).[63]

Much of course has already been written for and against the conduct of the PBC. Charges of various kind have been made that Mountbatten used his 'magnetic charms' to influence Radcliffe; that the British government issued secret instructions. Hugh Tinker, while raising these issues conclusively suggests that Mountbatten did not influence Redcliffe or the Award. This is exactly in line with what Jenkins, as we shall see later, had come to believe as also many other senior officials.

It is however another point Tinker has raised that requires more attention. It is well known that the major cause of suspicion of the PBC and its functioning was the fact that everyone believed that no honest and judicious award could possibly be worked out in so short a time. Tinker says that when Radcliffe was first approached to act as Chairman of the PBC, independence was expected to be granted in June 1948 or at the most a few of months earlier. By the time Radcliffe arrived in India, however, he had little over three weeks in hand. Tinker of course has argued that if Radcliffe had wanted he could have taken more time, as provided in the Independence Act and that he did not take this time because he was under pressure to release the details not before or not too long after 15 August.[64] This issue has been taken up in greater detail towards the end of this chapter.

THE KING WISHES IT: THE INDIA BILL

Sir Radcliffe's arival followed by the announcement of other details related to the PBC had greatly electrified the scene in Lahore and Amritsar, and then came the news that the King had given his assent to the India Bill at 10.40 a.m., GMT, 4.10 p.m. IST, on 18 July. The ceremonious ritual of granting approval to the Bill was reported by newspapers in detail. 'Le Roy le veult' (The King Wishes It)', were the fateful words that created the two nations.[65] Britain's empire in India had thus come to an end.

Commenting on the content of the speeches made during the course of the debate in the British Parliament, the *HT* said most speakers complimented Mountbatten 'for a job well done', and for avoiding a possible bloodbath. Flowing against the tide of assessments being telegraphed to London by Jenkins among others, members of the British parliament had surprisingly begun feeling that the worst was over.[66] In London itself, of course, old Punjab hands of the Indian Civil Service knew things were not as simple as they seemed. Malcolm Hailey, the not very popular former Governor of Punjab while, addressing the Annual Conference of Indian Civil Service in London had voiced his apprehensions a few days before the Bill was voted in the House of Commons: 'Britain seems to have been caught in a tidal wave carrying her rapidly to a destination we do not know . . . we do not know whether there will be chaos or peace in the country.'[67]

The House of Commons had voted the Bill as passed on 15 July and as a rare exception there was no division—the main debate had taken less than three hours.[68] The great urgency with which the Bill was drafted and cleared with the opposition comes out repeatedly in the files relating to the Transfer of Power Plans.[69] On 13 June, for example, the British cabinet discussed whether the India Bill needed to be shown to Indian leaders, which Mountbatten was keen to do. The cabinet was hesitant fearing an obstruction and delay, but finally the Prime Minister resolved that it would be safer to have Mountbatten tell the Indian leaders the main points rather than nothing at all.[70]

In fact, even in the House of Commons, when Prime Minister Attlee introduced the Bill for the second reading on 11 July, he commented on the urgency: '[The] House is being asked to pass this Bill in a very short time—a time not commensurate with its great importance . . . the continuance for any long period of a government containing leaders

The Miracle

During the debate on the India Bill Mr. Attlee expressed the hope that the Dominions might again merge into one. (*CMG*, 22 July 1947).

of two parties that wished to separate was impossible . . . the House will realise that it has been an arduous and exacting task to prepare this Bill.'[71]

Clause 4 of the Bill dealt with the division of Punjab. Many members expressed sadness. Mr Butler (Conservative): 'Punjab had one of the greatest tradition of any country or any part of the world', and that the decision had broken the heart of many Englishmen, who had served there.'[72] Godfrey Nicholson (Conservative) described the division of Punjab as nothing less than tragic: 'I believe the Punjab will within five years be reunited. Commenting on the difficulties of the Sikhs, Nicholson added: 'As for the Sikhs I suspect they can look after themselves and will certainly do so.' The *CMG* reported from the speeches of John Hope, Dr Guest and Prime Minister Attlee. While Hope believed that the division of India was bound to weaken it, Dr Guest thought otherwise: 'India would undoubtedly be leader of the eastern world',[73] he said.

Prime Minister Attlee spoke with nostalgia of good friends in India: 'now that this big idea of domination is being removed we must work as friends'. But the speech also made a comment, the merit of which was rather suspect: 'In India unity was brought about when it was superimposed—when that was taken away old rivalries have appeared again.'

Lord Sellborne (Conservative), one of the two major opponents of the Bill, was not only unsparing in his criticism but painted a depressing picture, which, in July 1947 must have appeared out of place but as time would show, proved exceedingly prophatic. He drew attention to the extensive disturbances that followed the 'withdrawal of British troops' and how he believed a slaughter was bound to follow. 'Racial and religious fires,' he said 'had burnt fiercely and it would be impossible to believe that peace will be maintained.' Lord Wavell said that he 'had always had faith in the people of India'. Lord Pethick-Lawerence was quoted as saying. 'For the coming of this day I have hoped and striven and I am happy to think it has come in my life.' These and other views were repeated by the press.[74]

BRITISH TROOPS WILL NOT INTERVENE

Before we go back to the Punjab, the days following the passage of the India Bill, it is interesting to see what took up an important part of the attention of British decision makers both in New Delhi and in

London in mid-July. A *TP* volume contains some interesting entries which show, and for obvious reasons that a great part of British attention in July was focused not on preparing for the civil war that was being predicted from every house top in Punjab but on the intricate and complex matters of the defence interests of the British as can be seen from the minutes of a 9 July meeting in London chaired by Admiral Sir John H.D. Cunningham and attended by several of the top brass of the British military administration. The unanimous view was that no more defence-related concessions were to be made to India and that sensitive defence-related negotiations should be completed before 15 August because after that date, it was felt the British may not be in a position to exert enough pressure on Indian leaders who, in the view of some members, already had too much on their hands. Nehru's request for British officers to continue even after 15 August was cited during the course of the discussion as an example of the existing goodwill which needed to be protected.[75]

The issue of when to withdraw British troops was uppermost in the minds of British authorities in New Delhi and London. Lord Ismay was categorical that after 15 August the entire responsibility for internal security was to rest on the new governments. He also wanted enough British forces to be kept available in India to protect British lives.

Jenkins raised the issue of the withdrawal of British troops with Mountbatten first, having discussed the matter with the Army Commander and the Lahore Area Commander. He was of the view that if the British forces had to be withdrawn it was best to do it at the earliest because, as he put it; 'it would be awkward if trouble on a large scale started while relief [meaning withdrawal] was in progress. My own advice would therefore be to make the change before the end of July, if it can be made so soon.'[76]

The minutes of the meeting between Mountbatten and Field Marshal Auchinleck on 15 July once again reveal that even as late as mid-July there were numerous doubts about how the army was to be handled, the command intricacies, etc. For example, Mountbatten told Auchinleck that he had pulled up Sardar Baldev Singh (Defence Minister) for having doubted the integrity of some senior British Commanders. Both expressed concern on the possibility of British officers having to command troops which may have to face each other—India and Pakistan.[77] They also gave much attention to arranging the farewell ceremonies of the first contingent of British troops that was scheduled to depart from Bombay on 17 August.[78] On 15 July, Mountbatten sought by an immediate telegram the Secretary of State's permission to formally announce that British troops would not be available for deployment in internal disorders after 15 August.[79]

TENSION WITHIN THE PANTH

As the date of the PBC's first scheduled meeting drew near things began to heat up in Punjab, more so as the Sikhs began to increasingly realize the direction in which things were moving. The Minutes of the Partition Council meeting of 17 July clearly show that the follow-up action on the notional boundary announcement demanded that the East Punjab government shift from Lahore to Simla.[80] Some of the other decisions were: the disturbed area districts should preferably correspond to civil districts; troops were to be deployed in disturbed districts by 7/8 August; troops were to be Indian but commanded by both Indian and British officers; and Maj. Gen. T.W. Rees was to be appointed as Joint Commander on behalf of both India and Pakistan to control the forces in a defined area. It was also decided that officers were to be posted on the basis of the notional boundary and that the administrative mechanism should be in place at the latest by 1 August.[81] This meant that Muslims were to be appointed in districts which were falling in Pakistan as per the notional line and non-Muslims in the districts likely to come into East Punjab.

On 19 July, at a convention in New Delhi of 50 prominent Sikhs from various parts of Punjab, Nihal Singh, the convener of the Reception Committee, said the proposed work of the PBC was like raising a structure on foundations of sand because 'decisions have already been taken . . . the PBC is a mere show to satisfy the Sikhs and other aggrieved parties'. Speakers like Mota Singh accused the Congress of letting the Sikhs down.[82] The Convention resolved to reject the notional line and demanded important Sikh shrines and a fair exchange of property and population. Nihal Singh even demanded that a representative body of Sikhs be asked to draw the line of division. Most importantly, it called upon the Shrimoni Akali Dal to launch a *morcha* against the unjust 3 June Plan.[83]

Sikh members of the Punjab Legislative Assembly also met in Lahore on 17 July, and while they finally announced that they would at no stage participate in the Constituent Assembly of Pakistan they also said that they would not accept any line of division that ignored the solidarity of the Sikhs, their shrines and their lands.[84]

Sardar Jodh Singh, Principal Khalsa College, Amritsar the widely popular and respected intellectual figure of the region, in a letter to the *CMG* said, among other things, that the inclusion of Sikhs areas in the West Punjab on the basis of the notional line of division would in fact put at stake the most favoured profession of the Sikhs—the armed forces. Since the army in Pakistan was most likely to prefer only Muslims, what were the 17 lakh Sikhs who would remain in the western districts to do? Jodh Singh wanted the Muslim League to accept a line of division that would enable the Sikhs to migrate with minimum bitterness.[85]

Even as the Sikh stand began to gradually harden, there were still some last-ditch efforts to get the Sikh leadership to change its mind. Amjad Ali from Ambala Cantonment, wrote to the *CMG*: 'The best cause for the Sikhs to maintain solidarity would have been to keep the Punjab united. . . . The Sikhs could secure a honourable place in the Pakistan government. Nature has cast the fate of the Sikhs among Muslims. The prominent Muslim League leader Ghazanfar Ali Khan also issued a statement on the 19 July: 'there is only one way that they can keep the bulk of the Sikh population in one state . . . inclusion in Pakistan of the entire Punjab minus parts of the Ambala Division'.[86]

Reacting to charges in sections of the press that the Sikh leadership—mainly the Akalis—were now backing out from their acceptance of the 3 June Plan, Giani Kartar Singh issued a statement in Lahore on the eve of the first meeting of the PBC: 'It is wrong and against facts,' he said, 'that the Sikhs have accepted the 3 June Plan in an unquestionable manner such have not accepted.' 'Our stand' had been conveyed to the Viceroy in a letter on 2 June, which, to remove any doubts on this, was being released to the press.

> They (the British) committed the worst treachery in world history when they took Punjab as guardians of the minor Maharaja. They let down the Sikhs in the 1919 (Montague Chemlsford Reforms) and repeated the same in 1935. Again they treated the Sikhs badly in the Cabinet Mission Plan in 1946. Yet again they have left the Sikhs in the lurch in the 3 June Plan. The Sikhs now ask only their integrity be maintained and their shrines be saved from Pakistan. This will be the last time the British will have a role in Anglo-Sikh relations . . . I appeal to Sir Radcliffe for justice.[87]

A cross-section of senior Sikh leaders met on 20 July in Lahore to put the Sikh case before the PBC in a united manner. This important meeting was attended by Master Tara Singh as well as Sardar Swarn Singh. They decided to demand the boundary on the River Chenab and the inclusion of Lahore in East Punjab. They also decided to plead the Sikh case on the basis of history, culture and religion.[88] The Arya Samaj of Lahore also met on the eve of the first PBC meeting in Lahore. Its resolution gave to the Sikh cause some backing—it said that it was in Lahore that Swami Dayananda had founded the Samaj in Punjab and also that it was on the banks of the river Ravi that the Vedas were recited.[89]

MUSLIM LEAGUE WILL FIGHT TO THE 'LAST DROP OF BLOOD'

Just as newspapers like *The Tribune* and partly the *HT* were building up a case for the Sikhs and Hindus in the hope that the PBC would be influenced, others like the *PT* and *Dawn* were, on the eve of the PBC's meetings, fully committed to the Pakistan cause and the Muslim League's vision of it. On 17 July, the *PT* carried abstracts from about 40 letters, all speaking the same language—that Muslims would not tolerate injustice and if that happened civil war was certain. The story of claims and counterclaims was unending. The Anjuman-i-Jats, a smalltime organization in Ludhiana, said, for example: 'Ludhiana Muslims expect full justice regarding boundary. [Be] ready facing all eventualities if decision otherwise.' Most letters used terms like 'will resist tooth and nail', 'last drop of blood'.[90]

As the Sikhs were building a case for their claims through the newspapers, those writing for the League were countering them point for point. Malik Mohammad Amin refuted the Sikh claim for the line of division merely on the basis of property ownership and taxes. Just as leaders representing Sikh organizations and even ordinary people were aggressively putting forth the Sikh and Hindu claim, others like Baji Rabia, a Muslim League worker of Jullundur, warned that Muslim women would resist an unjust award.[91]

On the eve of the PBC's first meeting in Lahore, seven prominent leaders of the Punjab Muslim League issued a joint statement warning the PBC against injustice to the Muslims who 'will fight to bitterest end if a single man or a single acre of land which rightfully belongs to us is kept away from us . . . we are as well prepared, as determined, wholly resolved as any one else to protect to guard and if need be to snatch what rightfully is ours.' The statement was signed by Mumtaz Daultana, Firoze Khan Noon, Begum Shah Nawaj, Sheikh Karmat Ali, Mian Iftikharuddin, and others.[92]

The Muslim League's campaign to build pressure on the PBC was far better organized and forceful than that of the Sikhs. In a telegram to the Viceroy, the general secretary of the Amritsar unit of the League said: 'we convey to you the unflinching demand of all Muslims for every inch of contiguous area where Muslims are in a majority . . . we claim all areas extending East 30–50 miles across the River Sutlej'.[93] A concerted campaign was also launched with telegrams flooding newspaper offices. In a single day *Dawn* received telegrams from Gurgaon, Ferozepur, Lahore, Gujrat, Lyallpur, Sargodha, Jhelum, Jhang, Attock, Rawalpindi and Cambellpur, almost all saying the same thing that they would fight till the 'Last drop of blood'.

On 17 July, the telegrams published by *Dawn* included one from Anjuman Islamia Lahore: 'any division except on population basis will be unjust'. The Secretary of the Muslim League's Kartarpur unit said: 'Muslims will resist to the last for every inch of Muslim majority area. . . . The PBC must take this grim resolve of the Muslims before embarking on an haphazard, arbitrary demarcation.' The Akhari Tehsil (Jullundur) League said: 'The Muslims who fought for Britain in two wars can also fight for their own rights.' The Kasur unit added: 'will leave no stone unturned . . . we want the PBC to know this before hand'. Similar warnings came in from Chinot, Hansi, Wazirabad, Batala.

The campaign to building pressure through telegrams was also the result of a statement that was reported to have been made in the course of the India Bill debate in the House of Commons. Arthur Henderson (Under Secretary), while explaining how the PBC was likely to draw its verdict was reported to have said: 'the primary basis was to be whether the majority was Muslim or non-Muslim but in certain cases there might be special factors which would justify departure from the principles . . . so that location of Sikh shrines could be taken account of.' *Dawn* which in fact was the first to draw attention to Henderson's statement then went on to call it 'double cross' and warned that 'all concerned be told that if [they]attempt to do so (as suggested by Henderson) they shall do so at the peril of Asia's perhaps the world's peace.' Anwar Saeed, General Secretary of the Amritsar Muslim League, in yet another telegram to Prime Minister

Attlee said: 'shocked at Henderson's unjust interpretation. . . . Muslims warn the government that they will strongly resist any favourable treatment to Sikhs and this will mean the beginning of an unending serious trouble.'[94]

Dawn continued the campaign with a large number of telegrams from practically every town in Punjab, even from undisputed areas like Ambala. The paper went on to warn: 'it will be the height of folly either for the British or for political elements in the country to try to treat lightly the widespread resentment which has been aroused over the Award'.[95] But it was in its editorial of 21 July that *Dawn* issued the ultimate warning to the Boundary Commission:

> We formally declare with the fullest sense of responsibility that every man woman and child in Muslim Punjab will fight to the bitterest end if a single person or a single acre of land which belongs to Pakistan . . . is kept away.

When the PBC was meeting in Lahore *PT* published an article titled 'Eastern Boundary of Punjab' by Lahore advocate Joshna Fazl-ud-din appealing to the PBC to ignore the recent riots, etc., while deciding the boundary, because, as he put it: such riots are not a common feature of the communal relations of Punjab and have appeared in their present form for the first time in a hundred years . . . the provincial leaders were inspired by central high commands and thus people of the Punjab cannot be held responsible for the situation.

So far so good, but surprisingly, the otherwise balanced article then went on to charge the Congress: 'the Congress leaders who visited Punjab soon after the riots (March) prescribed the remedy of partition with such haste that it gives the suspicion that these leaders had this plan up their sleeves and were waiting just for an excuse which the riots supplied.' Interestingly, Fazl-ul-din also charged the Congress for creating the problem in the first place by denying to the Muslim League an opportunity to form the government after it had emerged the largest party in Punjab. Fazl-ud-din also raised the issue of the 'Brahmin and his hatred for the Punjab and the Punjabis. He has not been able to establish his superiority over the Hindus of Punjab'. The article ended with the argument that the whole object of some industrialists (in the Congress) who prompted the Congress was to delay the start of Punjabi industrialists so that they could develop their own monopolies.[96]

The Tribune once again showed remarkable foresight when as early as 11 July it came out with a strongly worded editorial which advised urgency in the demarcation of the boundary.[97] It pleaded for the transfer of power to the people of the East and West Punjab only after the PBC verdict had been delivered and accepted and the line of demarcation fixed finally. The following day, while discussing a statement by Sir Radcliffe that the Award would be ready in two months, the editorial warned of serious problems if the award was not 'ready and declared', by the date of the transfer of power.[98]

It is important to understand that the Sikhs at this juncture were equally if not more disturbed and angry as the Muslim League. Even more important is the fact that authorities in Delhi and Lahore were well aware of it. Exactly a week before the PBC started its work in Lahore, Jenkins had observed in a note to the Viceroy: 'The Sikhs are unlikely to approve of any boundary and now seem almost as suspicious of the Congress as they are of the Muslims.'[99] In staff meeting (59th) with Mountbatten, Rao Bahadur Menon said that the Sikhs would cause great problems and would even destroy canal banks.[100]

A day before the PBC started the formal proceedings, Mountbatten was in Lahore to preside over a meeting which included Governor Jenkins, Lt. Gen. Messervy, and Maj. Gen. Rees. Among other decisions taken at the meeting it was also decided on the recommendation of Rees to clear the districts of Sialkot, Gujranwala, Sheikhupura, Lyallpur, Montgomery, Lahore, Amrtisar, Gurdaspur, Hoshiarpur, Jullundur and Ferozepur for 'special military measures'. Rees would have under his control five brigades and an armoured regiment and two advisers, Brig. Brar, a Muslim from Pakistan, and Brig. Tiwana, a Sikh from India. The minutes of this meeting also show that even by 20 July the British Commanders were still not certain of how many British officers would actually be available to them for duty.[101]

The formation of the Punjab Boundary Force was announced in a joint declaration on 24 July. The announcement also said that with effect from 1 August 1947, twelve districts—seven of West and five of the East Punjab—would be placed under the overall command of Rees, who was to report directly to the Joint Defence Council.[102]

VICEROY PRESSES RADCLIFFE FOR EARLY AWARD

The speed with which the 'time-table' of 15 August—transfer of power—and the associated hurry with which the PBC was expected to complete its hearings led many to doubt its credibility. The main reason for this was because it had come to be widely believed that no meaningful work could possibly be done with fairness in so short a time. It was also well known that Sir Radcliffe had actually committed very little time to the PBC.[103]

The question of the Commission having been given so little time to decide a matter of such significance does indeed come out to be surprising. In fact, throughout July, Jenkins, repeatedly requested Mountbatten for a copy of the final Award as early as possible and before it actually came into effect on 15 August.[104] On his part, Mountbatten, understood and appreciated the urgency. In a note to Radcliffe on 22 July he said: 'we should all be grateful for every extra day earlier that you could manage to get the Award announced'. In the same note Mountbatten also emphasized that 'the risk of disorder would be greatly increased if the Award had to be announced at the very last moment before the 15th'[105] Sir Radcliffe replied to the Viceroy's note the following day: 'The time schedule as you know has to be a fine one owing to the necessity of giving adequate time first for public hearings and then for full discussions of their differences with the Judges. Unless the Punjab Judges agree with each more than I have reason to expect I do not think that I can manage the 10th: but I think I can promise the 12th and I will do the earlier date if I possibly can.'[106]

DISTRUST AND SUSPICION ARE WIDESPREAD

While the Viceroy and leaders in Delhi, Simla, Lahore and Karachi worried about the 15 August timetable, what no one seemed to be concerned about was the suspicion and hatred that was rapidly spreading from the dusty lanes of small towns in south-east Punjab to the developed and modern roads of Karachi. Two examples will substantiate this point. For years the transport of commuters between Panipat and Rohtak (the Gohana Road) had been in the hands of Muslims, but as the line of divide went deeper, non-Muslims of the area suddenly realized that the Muslims who had been earning their livelihood thus for years were violating the law—by overcrowding, the vehicles—and began demanding that this be stopped and the old railway route be relaid and reopened.[107] The second example is that of Muslim sweepers and washermen who had for years been employed by Hindu households in Karachi and who suddenly decided that they would boycott Hindu shops and homes. Both these incidents are only small examples, thousands of similar incidents must certainly have occurred across the plains of Punjab. Confidence and mutual trust had suddenly disappeared.

The overriding and widespread sense of suspicion and hatred needs attention because what it did was to completely derail the plan of the 'notional boundary' or 'provisional partition', and also greatly added to the problems of the PBC judges. The plan of notional division was actually supposed to restrict the area of conflict, but the suspicion and distrust, fanned by vested interests both financial and communal, ended up creating the very situation that the plan was expected to avoid.

If it had been clearly announced that the final verdict of the Radcliffe Commission (PBC) would make only nominal or inconsequential changes in those that had already been announced in the 'notional boundary', it is possible the situation might have in fact been less disastrous than it finally turned out to be. This is because, and as I tend to believe, that in such a situation by the time that the boundary became finally effective a major part of the 'dust'—the chaos and confusion—would have settled down, no doubt the haze would have remained but that too would have in the course of time blown away.

Thus, throughout June and July, the Punjab saw an unprecedented effort to compile various kinds of statistics—land revenue, property, population, schools, colleges, factories, temples. These facts were handled by able lawyers, and were generously supported by the newspapers in the belief that the Radcliffe Commission would be influenced by their arguments in the final decision. But this great battle of words served only to whip up excitement and increase tension, and in all probability the massive amount of documentation was not even read properly. Where was the time? The four learned and senior judges were after all only human.

AMBEDKAR ON THE PBC

The credibility of the PBC was further eroded when Dr B.R. Ambedkar issued a press statement in New Delhi on the eve of the first meeting of the PBC (in Lahore). The time and the content of the statement are important because Dr Ambedkar was known to be a careful chooser of both. He said it was wrong to assume that the respective partition of Bengal and Punjab were merely local problems. He believed the primary concern of both commissions should be to determine the natural border for the two countries. Dr Ambedkar pointed out that no matter where the line was drawn, the problems of people left on the wrong side were bound to remain and in any case the problem was essentially of having a sound border in the military sense for both sides. He also stressed that if the commissions ignored the natural frontier concept, both India and Pakistan were bound in the future to have problems. He called upon the Ministry of Defence to act promptly and intervene in the matter before it was too late.[108] Dr Ambedkar's advice was not taken seriously, and as time has proved, it was well founded.

THE PBC

In all the Punjab Boundary Commission received 51 memorandums on behalf of major and minor political parties and organizations. Of these 18 were from the Muslim League, 10 from Hindu bodies and parties including the Congress, 9 from Sikh parties including the Akali Dal and 7 from Scheduled Caste federations.[109]

THE SIKH'S CASE

The Joint Memorandum of the Sikhs to the PBC was argued by Harnam Singh and ran into 75 pages.[110] It was argued that from 1881 to 1901 the Sikhs had been in a majority in the Punjab and it was only after 1911 that the Muslims were shown as a larger segment. The memorandum said that the census figures were flawed.[111] For one, it argued that they unduly took into account and recorded the floating Muslim population which always increased in the Punjab in the winter months when nomadic families moved to the plains from the hills. Interestingly, it was argued that the number of Muslims was exaggerated also because the Congress had boycotted the last census, as a result of which most of the census staff was Muslim. The memorandum pleaded for a contiguous tract in the Punjab for the Sikhs.[112]

The memorandum pointed out that in Ambala Division Muslims formed only 28.7 per cent of the population, and of the total land revenue of Rs. 66,40,971, they were paying only Rs. 15,94,082. Likewise, in Jullundur, while Muslims formed 34.54 per cent of the population their share in the land revenue out of a total of Rs. 74,68,945 was only Rs. 2,18,060. While making a claim for Lahore the plea was that in Lahore even as per the census figures there were 85,714 non-Muslims and 75,481 Muslims. The strongest argument by the Sikhs was naturally for the old and new canal colonies. Apart from the fact that these lands had been made fertile almost without exception by the Sikh peasantry, the memorandum pointed out that most of those who worked the colony lands had left their families in the central districts, and, therefore a large number of Sikh families were likely to be divided by the 3 June Plan. It was also argued that the Plan would deprive East Punjab not only of the major food-growing areas but also of most of the water for irrigation.

The Shrimoni Akali Dal had even sent a delegation under Sardar Ganga Singh to London, where at a press conference it demanded the river Chenab as the boundary. On 1 August, about 300 Sikhs even gathered at a public meeting in London where Sardar Ganga Singh again delivered a fiery address.[113]

THE MUSLIM LEAGUE'S CASE

The Muslim League's case was argued by Sir Muhammad Zafarullah Khan. Essentially his argument was based on the grounds of contiguity with regard to population, to be determined not below the tehsil level because that would lead to overlapping and more problems. Major emphasis was laid on ignoring religious sentiments, land ownership banking and factories as the question of partition was related to different issues. He wanted the Sutlej as the border—to meet the geographical and natural frontier concept. He said the main reason for the partition demand by the Muslim League was the economic disparity and inequality prevailing between the Muslims on the one hand and the rich Hindus and Sikhs on the other, and this alone dismissed all the claims of owning banks and factories and urban properties made to the commission on behalf of the Hindus and Sikhs.[114]

Countering two important reasons put forward by the Sikhs to better their case for the division and inclusion of certain areas in East Punjab, Zafrullah Khan stressed that Muslim rulers in the past had helped the Sikhs and even made endowments to Sikh shrines, and that Muslims were not historically against Sikhs. The most recent example, Zafrullah said, was that even as Bihar and Bengal were overrun by violence, the Muslims in Punjab had remained peaceful.

Also, in his opinion the March disturbances were started not by Muslims but by Hindu and Sikhs agitators who provoked clashes in Lahore, Gujranwala and Rawalpindi.

The Sikhs' claim to the canal colonies was easily the most convincing, yet Zafrullah made out a formidable case against it: 'Commenting on the canal colonies, the Muslim League's counsel asserted that the land was originally the homeland of Muslim nomadic and pastoral peoples. More importantly, the area allotted by the Crown in the canal colonies also showed that Muslims constituted a majority.' He then went on to quote figures to support his argument.[115]

THE CONGRESS—HINDU MAHASABHA'S CASE

The Congress case was argued by the renowned legal luminary of Bombay, M.C. Setalwad.[116] Interestingly the Congress's stand was perceived less as a representation of a major political party and more as one representing the Hindus of Punjab. In fact, the secretary of the Punjab Hindu Mahasabha even issued a statement saying that it was in agreement with the contents of the arguments proposed to be represented in the Congress memorandum to the Boundary Commission.[117] As the *CMG* put it: 'So far the Congress has rarely had its policies questioned by the Hindu Mahasabha. Indeed there has been so close a resemblance between the policies advocated by both that it led observers to believe that Hindu Mahasabha was only a mirror of the Congress so far as decisions effecting the Congress were concerned.'[118]

The line of argument taken up by the Congress at the outset was that even the notional division was flawed because it was based on the 1941 Census which was not completely dependable, and in any case, even if they were taken as correct a host of economic and cultural factors required an extension in the line of division. The representation also argued that the incidents in Rawalpindi (March) had made it clear that the Sikhs could not possibly stay on in Pakistan and, therefore, it was important the division did does not drastically disrupt the integrity of the Sikhs, particularly in the context of the Sikh shrines.[119]

Setalwad pointed out that the notional division was not only of all Crown lands but practically all the assured irrigated land. Taking up the case of Lahore, Setalwad said that the Muslims owned only 32 per cent of the land in Lahore and non-Muslims the remaining, and that non-Muslims had been paying more than double the urban property tax having more than 186 large factories with Muslims owing just 78. In Lyallpur it said non-Muslims owned 84 large factories and the Muslims only 23. In Lahore the banking capital in operation owned by the non-Muslims was about Rs. 100 crore against the 50 lakh owned, and that two-third of all houses and shops in Lahore were owned by non-Muslims and added that of 80 insurance offices in Lahore only 2 were being managed by Muslims.[120] In terms of the area claimed for India Setalwad pleaded for the whole of Ambala, Jullundur and Lahore Divisions, and the districts of Lyallpur and Montgomery. Such a division he said would consolidate about 34 lakh Sikhs from their total population of about 37,57401 in East Punjab. The memorandum then took up the case of education. It said of 16 non-government colleges in Lahore only 3 were run by Muslims and likewise of 40 non-government schools only 13 were being run by Muslims and also that of all the candidates who had appeared in the Punjab university examinations a mere 28 per cent of were Muslims.

These facts and figures were presented in a masterly manner to the PBC by the able Setalwad, who was widely applauded for his brilliance in the 'club' circles of Lahore. On the day he left Lahore for Bombay he was given a large farewell, and his reputation and stature grew manifold when it was reported that he had refused to accept the then huge amount of Rs. 50,000 offered to him as his counsel fees.[121] Spate who, as noted earlier, had been especially brought in from England to plead the Ahmaddiya case to the Commission, however, did not think too highly of Setalwad and thought of him to be a not very impressive speaker—'though lucid, [he] spoke for three hours without saying anything which was not either old, obvious or very dubious.'[122]

But just like almost everything else in the Punjab of the time, the essence of the facts raised by Setalwad and widely reported in the press was ignored. In hindsight, the points raised by Setalwad to make out a case for bringing in Lahore to the eastern side of Punjab also inadvertently perhaps told a different story. The manner in which trade, commerce, industry and education had been dominated by the Hindus in Lahore, Lyallpur and Sialkot came out clearly in the arguments and facts which had been labourously collated by non-Muslim organizations. What the Congress memorandum presented as points in favour of the non-Muslims in Punjab were in fact among the important issues the Muslim League had been highlighting for some time—as examples of the exploitation of Muslims by the Hindus. This was in fact one of the basis for the demand for Pakistan in the first place. The PBC ended its sittings and hearings in Lahore as planned on 1 August to reconvene at Simla on 7 August.[123]

Spate, who was in Lahore on 30 July, noted in his diary: 'there will certainly be trouble and I don't suppose Baldev Singh's signature to the joint India Pakistan statement that both sides will effect and enforce . . . the decision means nothing to him let alone the Sikhs generally.'[124]

DEPARTURE OF RICH AND RESOURCEFUL LEADS TO PANIC AND CHAOS

As rumours overran the Punjab, economic activity by the end of July was almost completely disrupted. It was quite commonly believed that the chaos in trade, commerce and other related activities was created in a major way by influential and rich Hindu business families, who started in the first place the race to sell their properties in the towns of West Punjab and purchase new ones in Delhi and Uttar Pradesh.[125] The leaders were accused of making appeals only to ordinary and less resourceful families to stay back in West Punjab and doing nothing about the rich and important families who greatly benefited by selling their properties well before the glut of selling and the rush of buying had started. The vast majority of the minorities on both sides had limited means and naturally were hesitant to put their scarce resources at risk.[126]

I.S. Johar, who in due course went on to become a popular figure in the Bombay film industry, had been occasionally contributing a column to *The Tribune*—'Mumbo-Jumbo'. On 6 July he said: 'Punjab evacuees are complaining against Delhi landlords who are claiming huge *pagrees* (black money) . . . black marketeers are not only after our *pagrees* but also our pants.'[127]

The Tribune's weekly share market report for the week ending 3 July said: 'The market wears a grim and sullen appearance. The decision to divide the province has created a panic of the worst type. . . . All sorts of rumours are afloat . . . some say the people's holdings will be freezed [*sic*]. Others talk of discriminatory legislation which will tell heavily on economic conditions of non-Muslims. Who can think of investing in industry?'[128]

So insecure and unsure was the situation in major towns that traders as mentioned earlier, were refusing to lift their goods from railway godowns and were happy to pay demurrage, believing the goods were safer in railway custody. The North-West Railway issued a statement that a large number of railway wagons were out of movement because they were unable to unload their goods as there was no space in Railway godowns and platforms were overflowing with people. The authorities had to increase the working hours of railway goods clerks from 6 a.m. to 8 p.m. and had even waived demurrage charges for a week—11–19 August—to encourage traders to take delivery of their goods.[129]

PUNJAB NATIONAL BANK LEADS THE PANIC

Capital resources, mainly in the form of silver and gold but also currency, had begun exiting the small and larger towns of West Punjab in a major way soon after the March disturbances, but it was the announcement of the Punjab National Bank on 1 July that it was shifting its head office out of Lahore that started the 'great Bank rush'. The fact that the move took place with retrospective effect from 26 June, only added to the problems of smaller traders greatly contributing to the panic in trade and commerce.[130] Indeed it was a formulate decision for the bank because just as they had feared, after 15 August, smaller banks were presented from moving out of were Punjab. But from the view of ordinary citizens, the small traders, the salaried, the pensioners, it was a 'signal of flight'. If the Punjab National Bank was so unsure—what were lesser mortals to do? But more importantly it was widely believed that the bank's decision was taken by informed people who knew that Lahore was going to West Punjab. The subsequent flood of capital from the West to the East that followed justifiably caused much concern among Muslim League leaders and more so among the handful of economists who were actually available to the Pakistan authorities.

Property prices fell in West Punjab, including in Lahore, by over 50 per cent in six months.[131] A report quoting a property adviser (who refused to be named) said he knew of a big landlord (non-Muslim) in West Punjab who had deposited in the bank vaults of Bombay and Delhi jewels and gold worth over Rs. 10 million. The same report said that prices of diamonds had doubled in the six months—January 1947 to June 1947.[132]

The Punjab Newsletter of the *HT* was a fairly dependable source for events in Punjab. On 2 July, it reported that gold and silver worth Rs. 250 crore had left West Punjab in the recent days. By the third week of July, gold was selling for Rs. 108 per 10 grams.[133] On 2 July, a *CMG* caricature report highlighted that gold worth Rs. 20 crore had left Karachi for Bombay in the preceding week and that huge amounts of currency was daily leaving Pakistan for India. Khwaja Bashir Bakshi, managing director of the Australian Bank Ltd., Lahore, wrote to *CMG*: 'Yes, Hindu capitalists took away Rs. 300 crore from Punjab . . . we are responsible as our leaders were busy with petty squabbles rather than watching capital going out of the province whole sale.'[134]

ANARCHY IN THE MARKET—PRICES OUT OF CONTROL

With goods being locked up in railway godowns and railway wagons and traders converting their existing stocks into silver and gold for the convenience of easy handling and securing their wealth in sound custody, not knowing when a bunch of goons would simply break into a shop and happily cart away the contents, there was only one way that prices of essential commodities could possibly go. With this and the massive flight of capital and the non-availability of petrol, the scene for anarchical market prices and trading attitudes was set.[135]

The extreme shortage of petrol was also reportedly a sequel to the strike by about 1,500 dock workers at the Karachi port. It was also believed that the strike had been willfully organized by Muslim League workers to retain stocks in Pakistan.[136] In any case, all efforts to end it had failed. The shortage of petrol was not only a problem for small traders but also for the rich, who were unable to drive to the hills of East Punjab or to Delhi. *The Tribune* had warned those planning journeys to Simla that no petrol was available at Kalka.[137]

As the situation worsened there was widespread resentment against shortages, cheating, high prices, black marketeering, etc.[138] The *CMG* reported on 22 August that prices of essential commodities had increased by three times in one week—15–22 August. In Lahore things were simply not available.

A letter from S. Sannllah (Peshawar) complained that traders in Lahore (Muslims who had taken over) increased prices by up to

Problem Solved!

The shortage of food grain greatly added to the problems that confronted ordinary people in the months leading to and following partition. It was commonly said that the government does too much of talking and propaganda and takes little action (*Shankar's Weekly*, 18 July 1947).

400 per cent after their Hindu competitors had left Lahore. He said: 'A Muslim ink merchant was charging Rs. 6 and 8 annas for a pound of roller ink as compared to Rs. 2 and 4 annas charged by non-Muslim traders a year ago. . . I trust the Muslim League workers will make the shylocks realise the harm they are doing to Pakistan's economy.'[139]

The food crisis in Punjab of course was not a recent phenomenon nor was it a local one. For the past many months, India had been reeling under a serious shortage.[140] Even in Delhi where the food situation was far better than other parts of India the crisis was ever present. The *HT* reported an incident when a *tonga chalak* (horse-cart driver) was fined Rs. 100 for trying to bribe a police constable to let him cross with a few bags of rice from a ration-controlled area of Delhi to a non-ration controlled area.[141]

In Punjab, however, as compared to the central and western districts, the shortage of food grain was far more acute in the eastern districts. Famine like conditions prevailed in the districts of Hisar where a large number of cattle were perishing daily. The monsoon having failed completely in the region, village ponds had dried up and people were having to walk miles for water.[142] The *CMG* said that 'if rains failed for another 10 days the Kharif crops would be wiped out' and that fodder was already selling for Rs. 4 and 8 annas, nearly four times the normal price. The situation had reached a stage where authorities allowed villagers to cut leaves from the trees along the canals and roads to feed cattle. Animal carcasses were a common sight.[143]

The *PT* carried a report on 18 July saying that about 100,000 maunds of wheat had been smuggled out of Lyallpur to the eastern districts. The term 'smuggled' was at this stage not quite appropriate but it did reveal the growing feeling among influential Muslim League leaders that even though the final division had yet to be announced the western districts must begin to conserve their stocks of food grains.

In the high quarters of the government decisions, however, were still being taken on a needs basis. The Partition Committee decided to send 75,000 tonnes of wheat from the western districts to the east in return for 25,000 tonnes of gram. *The Tribune* said the decision also included 21,000 tonnes of rice.[144] These were important decisions but as time was to show they were only partly honoured. Rumours supported by a section of the newspapers added to the confusion that, in turn, increased the speculation in prices at the street level. All in all, it was once again the ordinary citizen who bore the brunt.

Some time around the first week of July, it was reported that the government of India had stopped the export of 1,200 tonnes of sugar to Sind. Without verification and with great promptness the authorities in Karachi announced that Pakistan was stopping the supply of wheat to India. The government of India officially denied the 'Sugar report', in fact, Dr Rajendra Prasad himself issued the denial.[145] Authorities in Karachi took another 20 days to reconfirm that they would honour their commitment made with regard to food grains even after the creation of Pakistan.[146] However, the very next day, the Pakistan government announced that the Sind government had been ordered not to export wheat or wheat products to India.[147] With such pressure on food grains there was naturally much black money to be made. Not surprisingly, a report from Karachi said a minister in the Sind government had made a tidy some of Rs. 80,000 by selling permits for food grain handling to 'Hindu' traders.[148]

Those with money and influence converted the shortage crisis into an opportunity. As a result the gloomy predictions of the stock market in the beginning of July (week ending 3 July) had by the end of the month changed dramatically: 'in view of the scarcity of goods and the transfer of power, prospects for Indian industrialists (read capitalists) were very bright.'[149]

DIVISION: ASSETS AND MANPOWER

On 11 August *The Tribune* carried a small report which reflected the sad times on which the lively and beautiful city of Lahore had fallen: 'thirsty and deserted Lahore had its first shower of rain this (10 August) morning . . . the usual joy of children playing and asking "God" for more rain so that homes could have more grains and food were missing. . . . *'Rabba Rabba Meinh Warsa Sadi Kothi Dane pa"*.'[150]

The plight of Lahore and how life had ebbed out of it was also reflected in a statement issued by a spokesman of the Lahore film producers' association. It said the industry had fallen on 'unimaginable bad times'. Cinema halls which were always full had now been almost empty for days together. Major film producers were yet to decide where they should shift to because 'Lahore was unlikely to be the same again'.[151]

For a city that was once reputed for the impeccable character of its public utility services it was a reflection of the times that even services such as telephones were now being maintained on communal lines. A report said that 95 per cent of all telephones that had not been functioning for many days were actually those of Hindu and Sikh families.[152] But what really reflected the tragedy of Lahore was the initiation of the process that was expected to divide the soul of Lahore—the Punjab University.

On 2 July, it was announced that a committee had been formed comprising Justice Mohammad Sharif and Justice G.D. Khosla to advise Punjab University on how it should be divided.[153] On 18 July the Senate of the University met to discuss and vote on the division—the proposal was to give 60 per cent of the assets to West Punjab and 40 per cent to East Punjab. Of the 48 members who voted, 35 were in favour of division and 13 were against it. All Muslim members were naturally opposed to the division. The atmosphere in the meeting was tense but cordial. Din Mohmmad speaking on behalf of the Muslim members said, 'we shall part as friends, it is a division between two brothers'. Rai Bahadur Durga Das spoke on behalf of the non-Muslims.[154] *The Tribune* said the debate lasted for two hours, there was confusion but warmth, it also quoted Din Mohammad: 'we may never meet again as fellows of Punjab University, we worked like brothers all these years and we cherish happy memories of the days spent together.'[155]

Fortunately, however, the University Senate's decision was undone by the Central Partition Committee, which ordered that the university would go undivided to the side that was awarded Lahore.[156] This decision made Punjab University one of the very few institutions in Lahore to be saved the agony of the division of assets, which, in many cases, went down to the absurdity of counting chairs, almirahs and ceiling fans.

A *Dawn* report from New Delhi said that although the Archaeological Survey of India was headed by an Englishman 90 per cent of its staff was Hindu, as a result of which, in the preceding months, these Hindu employees had shifted rare antique artefacts from the Mohenjodaro Museum at Larkana (Sind) and also some rare pieces from the Taxila Museum to New Delhi. The Muslim League also complained that in the six committees that had been formed to distribute the assets of the North-West Railway under the supervision of A.G. Hall (General Manager), there was not a single Muslim.[157]

Under such widespread suspicion and distrust the division of assets at the governmental level naturally proved to be exceedingly difficult.

The Punjab Partition Committee met in Lahore on 29 July. It drew up a set of norms to assist and guide officials in dividing the assets of the Punjab government. It decided that at the outset that a financial evaluation be done of all the assets that were to be divided and that physical division of only those assets that were movable was to be done and to ensure that actual structures were not damaged.

Regarding the division of officers and other employees it said that All India Service and Gazetted officers were to be given a choice and that if such officers were not shifted to their state of choice by 15 August they would be treated as on deputation, but the government would be bound to repatriate such officers within three months. The Punjab Partition Committee also decided that non-gazetted officers were to be given six months to choose the state they wished to join.[158] It was, however, not clear whether this decision superseded earlier ones because some reports mentioned 14 July as the last date for non-Gazetted officers to inform the government of their choice of state.[159]

It appears that the senior officials who had taken over the reins of authority on behalf of Pakistan were moving well ahead of schedule compared to the authorities in East Punjab. For example, as early as 10 July *Dawn* published a detailed report based on official sources which included a long list of guidelines for employees who had opted for Pakistan and were to travel from Delhi to Karachi. This report said that all such employees were to begin movement on 1 August and the process was planned to be completed by 10 August. It said that no joining time was being allowed and that leave would be given only in exceptional cases. The report also advised such employees to keep their belongings packed and ready to move at short notice.[160]

While government of India employees based in Delhi, who had asked for Pakistan by choice did not face many difficulties in moving to Karachi or other centres in Pakistan, for those in Lahore and under the purview of the government of Punjab the problems were far too many. A peculiar problem which confronted the authorities in the East Punjab was that the number of Punjab government employees opting for East Punjab were far more than required. An issue of the Punjab Newsletter of the *HT* said that in the North-West Railway for example, of the total of 252 in the officers cadre 100 were Hindu,

60 Muslim and the rest European. Of the 151 permanent subordinate judges, 65 were Hindu, 26 Sikh and 52 Muslim. The Civil Secretariat had positions for 120 peons, but over 130 out of the total strength of 281 had opted for the East.[161]

The problem was even more serious in the lower positions in the North-West Railway, with about 25,000 non-Muslim employees opting for India. With major parts of the railway network including the famous rail workshop at Lahore going to Pakistan, the authorities had a difficult time, adjusting the staff accordingly.[162] The two transfer officers appointed especially for the purpose, A.K. Dhull and Muhammad Ibrahim, had a difficult time in convincing people to join duty in distant and unfamiliar places. Incidentally, while the number of Muslims working in various railway networks of India who chose to stay on in India is not clear, certainly it was very large; on the other hand, the number of non-Muslims in the Railways who opted for Pakistan was less than 1 per cent of the total non-Muslims working for the Railways.[163]

With most of the canal systems having gone to Pakistan, the government of East Punjab found on its hand a big problem with regard to the number of Irrigation Department officers who opted for East Punjab. As the Table 4.1 shows, almost 56 per cent of the officers were Hindus and Sikhs.

Similarly, the scene with regard to senior and key positions in the civil secretariat was chaotic. Most of the important positions were held either by non-Muslims or by British officers.[164] The problem for the East Punjab was of how to handle surplus staff, for the West it

TABLE 4.1: OFFICER GRADE COMMUNITY-WISE—IRRIGATION DEPARTMENT

Post	Muslim	Hindu	Sikh	Other	Total
Chief Engineer	–	3	–	3	6
S.E.	6	15	2	15	38
XEN	19	43	7	23	92
Asstt. Engineer	37	56	18	6	117
Sub-Engineer	–	3	1	–	4
Temporary Engineers	75	45	32	3	155
Deputy Collector	24	12	19	–	45
Total percentage	34	38	18	9.5	–

Source: *PT*, 24 July 1947.

was a problem of being understaffed. Likewise another report said that of 202 officers of the Indian Service of Engineers, 72 were from Punjab alone, and of these 37 had opted for India, 11 for Pakistan and 24 were to retire.[165]

Mountbatten as, we have already seen, had visited Lahore on 20 July. In the following days there had been numerous reports in the newspapers that the Viceroy had passed orders that the East Punjab Secretariat was to be shifted to Simla by 10 August and that if the need arose, that is, on the chance of Lahore going to the East, the West Punjab secretariat should be ready to move to some other site at short notice.[166]

The Viceroy's Personal Report referring to this decision carried more detail. Paragraphs 6 and 7 make interesting reading. In para 6, the Viceroy expressed the desire that 'unessential' people of East Punjab government in Lahore must necessarily shift to Simla by 10 August, but surprisingly, in the next paragraph it appears the Viceroy still did not know to whom Lahore would be awarded or that it had already been awarded to the West: 'if Lahore was placed in East Punjab the Government of West Punjab should leave Lahore by midnight Aug. 14/15 and detail plans be made for this contingency.' The point is that while the orders to the East Punjab government were categorical, 'move by 10 August', those to the West Punjab government were based on an 'if'.[167]

A committee headed by Dr Jehangir Khan, Principal, Government College Ludhiana and including Mohmaddad Said Ullah, Secretary to Records Keeper, K.S. Thapar, Lecturer in History and Prof. G.L. Chopra, Government College Lahore, was set up to divide the records of Punjab. All members appear to have agreed that with the time being so short there was no way a judicious division could be done without destroying the sanctity and value of the records. This is probably the main reason why the exercise never really took off. [168]

A report described the scene in Karachi and Delhi in the first week of August: 'Karachi is humming with activity . . . with pioneers . . . picknicking improvising with an air of excitement . . . cabinet ministers of Pakistan are using packing cases as desks and are seen cracking jokes with white-washers who are seen working in the same room often casting drops on the ministers . . . even the Governor-General designate does not as yet have a direct telephone.' Delhi on the other hand presented a picture of frustration, with Hindus and Sikhs feeling cheated by the British.[169] Possibly exaggerated, or at least somewhat, all the same the report does tell a story of how the two cities were reacting to the crisis.

On 1 August the government of East Punjab made the much 'dreaded' announcement that its offices records and staff would begin leaving Lahore on 5 August, the process of relocating, it was said, would be completed by 15 August.[170] It was in fact completed ahead of schedule. The offices of the East Punjab government were finally and for ever closed in Lahore on 9 August, to reopen in Simla on 14 August.[171] As newspapers announced the closure of the offices it was also officially stated that the Punjab Partition Committee would transform into a Council composed of two ministers from each side and the finance secretaries of both the East and West Punjab to function as a Joint Steering Committee.[172]

ADMINISTRATIVE CHAOS

The basic reasons for the anarchy and chaos that overtook Punjab for about 45 days starting with the actual handing over of power are far less complex than they have usually been made out to be. The most important reason remains the fact that power was handed over to the governments at a time when they were in a state of non-function. While a vast majority of lower staff at the district and sub-division level were actually in transit or, more importantly in a transit frame of mind, those who had joined duties in new postings were yet to get a 'hang of things', others who were yet to be shifted to their new places of postings in the states for which they had opted understandably had only an indifferent interest in their work. In any case, a general sense of commitment was completely missing. As Charles Trench put it 'the whole of the civil administration of Punjab including the police was on its way some where else'.[173]

With all that had transpired in the preceding days and months—the violence and particularly its fanatical nature—how were petty government officials—the ones on the road—expected to function at their optimum levels? With most of them ridden with fear and even anger, expecting officials, both civil and police, to enforce law and order, keep the system moving, was being unwarrantedly optimistic.

A major problem which followed the 10 August deadline ordered by Mountbatten for the East Punjab government to vacate Lahore was also of space—where were people to go? Mountbatten was aware of the shortage of space in Simla and yet orders were passed that the whole government move there on a fortnight's notice.[174] At a time that the government machinery should have been fine tuned to face the oncoming catastrophe, employees who were the acting hands of the government were going around complaining about not being able to find a place to put even their luggage.[175] There were similar scenes not only in Simla but also in Amritsar and Jullundur where officers of the East Punjab government were shifted for short durations.

In sharp contrast to the handling of the 'space' problem by the East Punjab government, the Pakistan government acted with great purpose. On 23 July the government of Sind ordered all schools and colleges in Karachi to be closed for a month to accommodate 20,000 employees and records that were to be transferred from India.[176] On 27 July, the Sind government announced the acquisition of 5,350 acres of land to provide buildings for the new offices—a capital complex. The value of this land was placed at Rs. 2 crore.[177] In the East Punjab, accommodation was so scarce that at one stage even Ambala was considered as a possible place for a new capital only because a large number of dilapated army barracks were lying vacant.[178]

It also needs to be understood that almost every single official who could not be shifted to his state of choice before 15 August remained in his position of posting against his wishes. In any case, there was little any one could do about it, with the Punjab Partition Committee itself, saying: 'that it would not be possible to transfer all officers to the country of their choice without seriously affecting the administration'.[179] While there are no statements of how officials were chosen—meaning those who would shift to the country of option to begin with and those that would follow—contacts and financial resources must have played a major role in who was moved earlier and who later. Thus those on whom the government came to depend to keep its wheels moving were unhappy people—unhappy people do not make good workers.

In the last days of July a considerable number of smaller details had been agreed upon even as the more crucial and dangerous ones were undecided. There was to be, it was announced on 1 August, a common currency for both the countries up to 31 March 1948; the Reserve Bank would manage the work for both; passports initially would not be required; for trade a free passage would be allowed.[180]

JINNAH LEAVES DELHI

Even as the last days of July were days of high drama and tension in Lahore, with the arguments being put forth by leading legal brains to the PBC, appeals to bury the past, protect minorities and assurances continued to pour into newspapers. These continued into August until they were finally reduced to irrelevance by the tide of violence which followed.

Jinnah personally admonished Muslim League leaders and workers in Punjab for frightening the minorities and not treating them well.[181] Some days later (on the eve his departure from New Delhi for Karachi) he called upon the people of both countries to bury the past: 'let us start afresh as two states . . . I wish Hindustan prosperity and peace'.[182] Incidentally, Jinnah's departure from New Delhi was a secretive a quiet affair, for security reasons, but his reception at Karachi more than made up for it. His plane circled Karachi airport to give a view to the unprecedented crowds. He landed at Karachi at 5.30 p.m. (on 7 August). A three-mile-long procession of hundreds of vehicles followed him into Karachi.[183]

Dawn reported that Jinnah's house at 10 Aurangzeb Road had been purchased by the Indian industrialist Dalmiya. The *CMG* gave a more detailed report, saying the house had been purchased for Rs. 300,000 and that Dalmiya had converted it into the headquarters of the Anti-Cow Slaughter League, which would celebrate 10 August as Cow Day.[184] For a prominent Indian (Hindu) industrialist to have announced that the residence of the founding father of Pakistan was to be converted into the headquarters of the Anti-Cow Slaughter movement, which already had the support of important leaders, naturally contained in it an element of drama which gave the new owner, countrywide publicity. Whatever the objective, the government of India was impressed enough to declare that 15 August would be a meatless day in India.[185]

LEADERS APPEAL: BURY THE PAST

Liaqat Ali made a passionate appeal to the people of both countries: 'bury the past and with it all unpleasant memories'.[186] But perhaps the most powerful appeal to bury the past came once again from Jinnah in his first and historic address in the Constituent Assembly of Pakistan. Appealing to the minorities in Pakistan, Jinnah said: 'If

DELHI, FRIDAY, AUGUST 8, 1947. 20 RAMAZAN-UL-MUBARAK, 1366 A.H

JINNAH WISHES HINDUSTAN PEACE AND PROSPERITY

'Past Must Be Buried and Let Us Start Afresh'

MESSAGE TO DELHI CITIZENS

Departure For Karachi In Viceroy's Plane

NEW DELHI, Thursday.

"I WISH Hindustan prosperity and peace," declared Qaed-e-Azam Jinnah on the eve of his departure to Karachi this afternoon in a statement to the Press.

"I bid farewell to the citizens of Delhi, amongst whom I had many friends of all communities and I earnestly appeal to every one to live in this great and historic city with peace. The past must be buried and let us start afresh as two independent sovereign S...

Holiday In Sind To Mark Jinnah's Arrival

KARACHI, Thursday.—The Sind Government have declared today a public holiday throughout the province to mark the arrival this evening of Mr. M. A. Jinnah, Governor-General-designate of Pakistan.

The arrival will be private.

The Sind Government have provisionally sanctioned Rs. 200,000 for Pakistan celebrations. It is proposed to commute the death sentences of convictors and also to release old and infirm prisoners. The jail delivery will take place on the morning of August 15.

About 2,000 poor will fed on the day, and sweets distributed to 1,000 prisoners in the Karachi Prison.—API.

Dawn, 8 August 1947.

you work in a spirit of co-operation forgetting the past and burying the hatchet . . . everyone of you no matter what your community, caste, creed, is first, second and last a citizen of the state with equal rights, privileges and obligations.'[187]

In the Congress camp at the provincial level, Bhimsen Sachar issued frequent appeals to both sides to forget the past: 'beware of the people preaching distrust and suspicion of the other state . . . let us not dwell in our past.'[188] But surprisingly, for Acharya Kriplani, the Congress President, there still appeared some hope of the two states reuniting. While speaking to newspaper reporters in Karachi, Kriplani said: 'there can be no peace and prosperity in the two parts of India until they come together'.[189]

Mahatma Gandhi was in Lahore on 6 August. From the residence of Rameshwari Nehru, he issued a statement appealing to the people not to flee Lahore. He said that he would spend the rest of his life in Pakistan, West or East, and that he was 'grieved to hear that people are running away from West Punjab, Lahore is being evacuated by non-Muslims . . . it should not be . . . if you think Lahore is dying do not run away . . . die with what you think is the dying Lahore'. Referring to the Sikhs, he said: 'my conception of a Sikh is of a brave person who did not fear death and would not do any harm to any innocent person'. When a woman said that Sikh women were not afraid to die, but what were they to do to save their honour, Gandhi replied 'if a woman were prepared to die no one would dare touch her honour'.

Gandhi's statement that he would live in Pakistan came as a surprise to many in Delhi; some said it was his way of reminding the people of what he had said earlier, that 'division was a sin'.[190] *Dawn*, quite obviously with the approval of the highest quarters in the League commented in an editorial on the statement: 'Strange are the ways of Mr. Gandhi . . . beyond the comprehension of the average man'. Giving a characteristic twist to Gandhi's statement, it added: 'Gandhi wants to do this so as to comfort the minorities . . . this in fact reflects his doubt in Pakistan's fair play . . . we would have liked Gandhi to wait and see whether those assurances are honoured or not.' The following day Kriplani, possibly as a sequel to Gandhi's statement and the unfortunate twist given to it by the Muslim League's mouthpiece said: 'To me there can be no division of a country which is one by nature, civilization and culture.' Kriplani even warned that he would take to Satyagraha if passport restrictions were imposed for travel between India and Pakistan.

But strangely, even as the Congress President was insisting that India's division was against 'nature', 'civilization' and 'culture', Jawaharlal Nehru at about the same time was explaining why Congress had accepted the Partition of India: 'Firstly the demand very urgent in nature had come from Bengal and Punjab. . . . Secondly certain sections did not want to remain with the rest of India . . . division was better than union of unwilling parts.'[191]

Sardar Patel while addressing a gathering in New Delhi on 11 August also dwelt in detail on why the Congress accepted Partition: 'we took these extreme steps after great deliberation . . . I agreed to it because I was convinced that in order to keep India united in future it must be divided now'. Patel also appealed to all to forget the past and 'deem it a terrible nightmare it'. He wished Pakistan well, success and strength saying 'there could be no friendship between a strong unit and a weakling. India harboured no ill-will towards Pakistan, [and] would do all in her power to help the new state.'[192]

Such goodwill was not merely one-sided: Liaqat Ali, while intervening in a debate in the Constituent Assembly of Pakistan which was debating the new flag of Pakistan, considered it important enough to give a clarification to a resolution moved by Bhimsen Sachar to the effect that the new flag of Pakistan should have been chosen by taking even non-Muslims into confidence. Liaqat said the flag of Pakistan was not the flag of the League, nor was it a religious flag. He said it represented all the Hindus, Sikhs and Muslims of Pakistan and that even senior Muslim League leaders had seen the flag only for the first time in the Assembly itself.[193] This exchange of views between a non-Muslim leader of the provincial level and a leader as senior as Liaqat Ali on an issue as important as the new flag of Pakistan has not somehow received the attention it deserves it.

TALK OF PEACE AND GOODWILL IRRELEVANT

With such goodwill flowing from both sides it must have seemed, even if only momentarily, that the clouds of doom would probably blow away. But as Punjab waited with bated breath there were important signals, early warnings that serious trouble was brewing and that all the statements of the leaders were now hardly relevant.

The *HT* noted that the Sikhs were confused and even though both Pakistan and India had pledged to accept whatever the PBC may award and even though Baldev Singh had signed on behalf of the Akalis, by and large, the Akalis remained unmoved in their opposition to any line of division that would ignore the solidarity of the Sikhs. The *HT* newsletter of the following week also reported that among important Sikh circles it was being widely discussed that either the governor or the premier of Punjab must be a Sikh, and since Chandu Lal Trivedi had taken over as the former, the Sikhs were keen that the premier should be a Sikh.[194]

A sure indication of the forthcoming crisis was the spate of calls in the first half of August for the boycott of the 15 August celebrations. A Sikh *Diwan* organized on 7 August resolved that the Sikhs would not participate in the celebrations. Giani Kartar Singh also appealed to the Sikhs to boycott the 15 August programmes.[195]

L.B. Bhopatkar, President of the All India Hindu Mahasabha, also appealed for a boycott of the celebrations: 'August 15 will go down in history as a day of mourning . . . any talk of India having achieved freedom is a myth and a vain attempt to conceal realities. . . . The Congress consent to vivisect India had killed both itself as a political party and India as a nation.'

V.D. Savarkar, while addressing a large convention of the Hindu Mahasabha in Delhi on 9 August said there was certainly no reason for rejoicing when the country had been torn apart. While calling upon Hindus to unite, Savarkar also said: 'Congress had stated that it accepted partition to avoid bloodshed. It was wrong. So long as Pakistan remained there was danger of further bloodshed.'

Following the convention, the Working Committee of the Hindu Mahasabha called for a boycott of the 15 August celebrations and asked its cadres to work towards reuniting Hindustan.[196] Interestingly even as prominent national leaders of both the Congress and the Muslim League had been trying, as we have seen, to clear the road for each other, the *PT* published an editorial on 2 August that charged the Congress and the Hindu Mahasabha with being hand in glove.

The growing significance of the *PT* in these days needs to be understood in the context of the fact that as leading League leaders began to leave Delhi for Karachi and Lahore, the principal platform for the League's point of view, *Dawn* (Delhi), came under increased pressure from non-Muslim official and non-official elements. *PT* became the mouthpiece for the Leagues' views from Lahore.

The *PT* editorial of 2 August could not possibly have been published without approval of important League leaders in Lahore:

There have been occasions when the Congress has opposed the Mahasabha (Hindu) in a mild way to bolster its position as a non-communal organisation. . . . But the Muslims have found Congress policy and action in the last resort have seldom been far removed for what the Mahasabha advocated . . . the last elections (1946) showed how accommodating the Congress could be to Hindu communalism. This fraternal attitude of the Congress towards the fire eating Savarkar has been responsible for the Muslim repulsion towards the Congress.

The editorial went on to dub the Hindu Mahasabha as the younger brother of the Congress. On 2 August *Dawn* published the demands that the Hindu Mahasabha had put forward to G.B. Pant, Premier of the United Provinces. Demand number 4 said: 'Only Hindus be appointed to important positions and present Muslim officers be removed from posts'. In point number 7; it demanded that the Home Minister must also be a Hindu. Some days earlier about 10,000 'Hindus' had signed a memorandum given to Dr Rajendra Prasad which called for India to be named 'Bharatvarsha' and for the flag of India to be only of deep orange and also that India's official language should be free from any Persian influence.[197]

In fact, the language issue had also been much of in the news in the second half of July. On 17 July, for example, Congress members of the Constituent Assembly had met to resolve a policy on the language problem. What transpired was a heated debate and high tempers, ultimately it was decided by a vote—63 were in favour of Hindi and 32 were against it.[198] It was against this background that Frank Anthony, the prominent Anglo Indian leader, while addressing a youth meeting of the Congress in New Delhi warned the people who were talking of a resurgent Hinduism that: 'actions and utterances of Hindu Mahasabha leaders were doing great disservice to the cause of India's nationalism and unity. Such actions represented a menace which if allowed to grow would disrupt and destroy India'.[199]

THE RACE FOR POLITICAL POWER AND OFFICE

The first half of August also saw numerous articles and letters discussing how the political leadership had let the people of both the countries down and how many of the leaders were working to derive personal advantage from the chaos.[200] Well before the actual line of demarcation had been announced the race to capture positions of influence in both the East and West Punjab had started in earnest. As early as 6 July the *CMG* had felt the need to comment on the bitter rivalry that had developed between Noon and Mamdot, the two main leaders of the Muslim League in Punjab. While dedicating an editorial to the race for power it said the whole issue was little more than a question of personal ambition. However, the Muslim League was able to resolve the crisis in the days that followed. In the eastern Punjab the question of leadership—power—was far too serious and complex, mainly because most of the Congress leaders were in the race for berths in the cabinet and even for premiership. The race for power created lobbies within the Assembly, which stood out embarrassingly when it met for the first time after partition in November. But more of this is in due course.

With leaders scrambling for offices and power even as clouds of doom were rapidly gathering over Punjab, the *PT* in an editorial 'The Scramble', said that the race for power had begun among the Muslim League and Congress workers the very day that the Punjab Legislative Assembly had voted for partition: 'The methods that are being employed to ensure election might have been envied by the worst exponent of Unionist Opportunism . . . public offices or promises of offices are being bartered away.'[201] The editorial then referred to the political games being enacted in West Punjab circles: 'all the fetishes of clan and kindered that we hoped Pakistan would rid us of are being invoked'. Commenting on the bleak future of Pakistan it said: 'Shall we not again be plagued by family cliques and monopolies.'

Governor Jenkins very perceptively noted:

> The average Leaguer in the Punjab is an old Unionist and thought Pakistan would give him some political influence and pickings. Thus even before the birth of Pakistan, the solid unity of Muslim League [had] suddenly begun developing some cracks as various contenders scrambled for power. As the jockeying for power intensified the future of politics in an independent Pakistan appeared to some as full of foreboding. One of the first to read the signs of things to come was Khizr Hayat. He told the Governor that with free elections the League would split within four or five months as there were too many personal animosities and economic differences within it.[202]

The race for political office was not limited to the corridors of power in Lahore or Simla where the main offices of East Punjab had begun to relocate. The situation was only marginally better even in New Delhi. Mountbatten had made some interesting observations in his Personal Report of 1 August on the problems being faced by Jawaharlal Nehru in selecting his cabinet colleagues. There appears to have been great pressure on Nehru from senior Congressmen for inclusion in the Cabinet. But Mountbatten stressed on Nehru the need to bring in people like 'Bhabha and Mathai . . . since they were extremely able and fearless,' and to get rid 'of a lot of top weight like Rajagopalachari and Maulana Azad.' Subsequently (after this meeting with Mountbatten), Nehru convened a meeting of some Congress leaders where the list that had earlier been prepared was torn up and many hours were spent in trying to prepare a new list.[203]

In para 40 of the Report Mountbatten noted:

> Jai Prakash Narain's price for bringing the Socialist Party in (the Cabinet, in support of Nehru) was the Finance, Home, and State Department portfolios and 25 seats in the new Legislative Assembly. Much as they need the Socialists in, Congress cannot afford to pay such a price. They (the Congress) are now trying to get the Hindu Mahasabha in.

MAHATMA GANDHI IN PUNJAB

The widely prevalent anti-politician and anti-bureaucrats sentiment possibly contributed to the unfortunate incident that took place at the Amritsar railway station on 31 July. None of the reports have named the people who organized the agitation. Gandhi was on his way to Kashmir by the Frontier Mail, which had reached Amritsar at 8 a.m. A crowd of about 1,000 people mainly young Hindus raised anti-Gandhi and anti-Congress slogans. The demonstrators entered into a verbal conflict with some Congress workers, which later led to a physical fight. The chaos continued for 15 minutes. Gandhi's niece was reported to have been sitting beside Gandhi and silently weeping. Some youths were reportedly carrying 'garlands made of shoes' for Gandhi. As the train moved out of Amritsar, messages were flashed to Lahore and a heavy deployment of troops was made at the station. A large noisy crowd had gathered, there were, however, no slogans. Gandhi asked the people to go back to their homes 'I cannot address you . . . I do not have the strong voice with which I used to address you'.[204]

At Rawalpindi in a post-prayer meeting Gandhi was asked by *The Tribune*'s reporter why he was going to Kashmir and not spending a week in Rawalpindi to see for himself the suffering of the Hindus and Sikhs. Gandhi answered that 'it was all in God's hand and that he had not forgotten Punjab'.[205]

JENKINS REVIEWS JULY

Before discussing the PBC verdict and the monumental consequences it went on to have, a look at the reports of the violence, the measures initiated by the government, and above all, the factors that added to the building up of tension in July and early August would not be out of place.

On 30 July Jenkins wrote to the Viceroy what is possibly the best assessment of the situation that prevailed in Punjab in July 1947. He started by noting that the law and order situation was particularly bad in the rural areas of Amritsar, Jullundur, Gurdaspur and Hoshiarpur; '[and] aggressors in all these areas seem to be Sikhs . . . I have the impression that they have made certain preparations, some of which are now being disclosed prematurely'. He went on to note:

> Partition work is going very slowly and I am now clear that a considerable muddle on 15 August cannot be avoided . . . the Muslims are naturally pleased at the establishment of Pakistan but as Punjabis they want the whole of Punjab, the Hindus and Sikhs on the other hand are apprehensive and most reluctant to leave Lahore. It would be difficult enough to partition within six weeks a country of 30 million people which has been governed as a unit for 93 years even if all concerned were friendly and anxious to make progress . . . there is a background of fear and suspicion and much time is wasted in trivialities. We have so far been unable to reach an agreement on the principles on which assets should be divided.

Jenkins ended this remarkable note by informing the Viceroy that he would expect to relinguish charge on 14 August afternoon and leave for Karachi on 15 August.[206]

SIKHS FEEL CHEATID

With his note Jenkins enclosed the minutes of his meeting with Giani Kartar Singh which revealed not only how upset Kartar Singh was but the almost hopeless position the Sikh community found itself in and the great misconception that had come to prevail with regard to the Sikhs having accepted the 3 June Plan. 'The Giani said that what the Sikhs had originally agreed to was a report by a Boundary Commission which they believed was only to be considered by the Governor General. The report was suddenly turned into an Award which would be final. This was contrary to what the Sikhs had accepted.'

When Jenkins observed to Kartar Singh that he did not expect any change in the notional boundary, Kartar Singh, Jenkins recorded, wondered, where then was the need for the PBC if no significant change was intended. The Giani also told Jenkins that if the government had simply announced the notional line as the final one the Sikhs would at least have known where they stood. He also pointed out that the future of the Sikhs had been placed in the hands of the Chairman of the PBC who knew nothing about them or about the Punjab.

The last para of these crucial minutes also conveys the rather surprising impression that Jenkin appears to have developed—that the two Sikh leaders Kartar Singh and Tara Singh had messed up the Sikh position. The best thing for them to have done was to have got rid of the non-Punjabi speaking districts and kept the rest of the Punjab in Pakistan. 'I think the Sikhs appreciate this now; but it is [too] late to do anything about it.'

In retrospect it is clear that the Giani was dead right when he pointed out that if no changes were likely in the notional line of division where then was the need for the PBC. In fact, it does now appear that apart from putting a stamp of approval on the notional boundary that had come into being on 3 June, the PBC meetings, hearings and the tremendous tension that built up as it began to meet—the arguments, and counter arguments—may only have created the very situation that it was supposed to prevent.

FEAR AND UNCERTAINTY DRIVE PEOPLE AWAY

The tenor and content of the statements and telegrams that had flooded the newspapers to put pressure on the PBC, as we have seen, was unprecedented. The slow-paced, easygoing Punjab had never seen anything like it. Never had Punjab seen such provocative and hostile warnings. The communal frenzy and organized madness that had built up by the end of July and the first week of August was largely rooted in the campaign to browbeat the PBC.

The level to which Lahore in particular had fallen stands reflected in the tragic killing of Prof. Brij Narain. Reference has already been made of his articles and letters in the English press, mainly *The Tribune* and the *CMG*. In many of his writings he had critically exposed the mishandling of Punjab by the Congress as a result of which he had widespread support even among the Muslims in Lahore. Against the background of the views expressed by him in his writings, he obviously believed no harm would come to him, but such was the madness that had gripped Lahore that even he was brutally speared in front of his own house, and his valuable library was reduced to ashes.[207]

SOME REPORTS ON THE DISTURBANCES

The exodus from Lahore had begun in the first week of July itself, more specifically after the burning down of Shahalini Gate. About 1,50,000 people were reported to have left Lahore.[208] In the second week, as soon as the curfew was lifted unending streams of carts and *tongas* were seen moving towards the railway station, 'fear and uncertainty driving the baffled people away'. The first week of July had also witnessed a call for an anti-Pakistan Day by the Hindu Mahasabha. The call had an impact all over the country with incidents of violence being reported from Bombay, Madras, Hyderabad, Poona, Dacca. In the Punjab, the call yielded a fairly good response.[209]

Dawn in an article which was in fact addressed to the Viceroy, reported that the state of Faridkot had distributed over 1,000 firearms to the Sikhs in the state and that every Sikh household had been adequately fortified. The report said that the ruler had done this in the belief that the exit of the British would be followed by chaos in the region, during the course of which the lands of weaker neighbours could be grabbed as had happened in the nineteenth century.[210]

Amritsar, Rawalpindi, and Lahore saw extensive violence on 8 July, leading to the imposition of curfews in the first two. From the other end of Punjab numerous incidents of violence were reported from Ballabhgarh where Jats were reported to have invaded 13 villages. The report also said that in a meeting held at Nigaon on 30 June, Jats from 300 villages had gathered in a village which was well known for its large number of ex-servicemen.[211] In neighbouring Gurgaon, even though Jats of the region as well from Bharatpur and Alwar were the main rioters, the Muslims of the area still relied on the Jat troops for their security, having made a special request for protection.[212]

A joint committee comprising Mamdot, Iftikharudin, Bhim Sen Sachar, Gopichand Bhargava, Lehri Singh and Jaswant Singh Duggal travelled to Gujranwala on 12 July to appeal for peace. Another such committee had already been formed with Governor Jenkins as Chairman. At the local level many smaller organizations were trying to restore normalcy. Gurdaspur, for example, organized a communal harmony week in the beginning of July,[213] just as many *mohallas* in Amritsar had also organized their own local peace committees.[214]

The government on its part did try to get tough by imposing collective fines and recovering the fines as land revenue, as was done in Multan.[215] However, there was no apparent improvement in the situation. A major flare-up of violence occurred in Lahore on 13 July with 15 cases of serious arson and looting, and 22 cases of serious fires being reported in a single day.[216] Garhshankar in Hoshiarpur saw a major communal clash on 19 July leading to 20 deaths. It started when a woman of one community was abducted, leading to retaliation from the other side.[217]

The first major incident of trains being held up and the slaughter of passengers in the July sequence of violence occurred in Mughalpura on 23 July. Eight people were killed, but what could have been a far greater tragedy was averted by the presence of mind of the driver who managed to pull the train to Harbanspura by getting down at great personal risk rule and removing the boulders that had been used to stop the train.[218] Such incidents went on to soon become almost a routine feature. The subsequent days saw many stories of brave engine drivers and their helpers saving trains from mad crowds. But even the engine drivers soon became suspect. Passengers refused to let a train move from Karachi when they learnt that the driver was a Hindu, not even allowing a Christian to drive. They demanded that a Muslim driver be provided. Such incidents were greatly demoralizing. But the stories of heroic engine drivers did not end. Some days later a brave fireman saved a train load of passengers from being massacred by feeding the coal as well as driving the engine after his driver had been injured in a hold up between Batala and Qadian.[219]

Gandhi, as noted earlier, had travelled by the Frontier Mail on his way to Kashmir. A miscreant mistaking the Delhi Express for the Mail threw a bomb at it near Phillaur on 1 August. Fortunately the bomb failed to explode.[220] The target obviously had been Gandhi. The person who threw the bomb was soon arrested. On 30 July another train was attacked near Tangra in Jullundur, once again a major incident was averted though some killings did take place.[221]

THE BRITISH DECIDE NOT TO DEPLOY

As the situation rapidly began to slide out of control, there was an increasing demand for troop deployment, with numerous letters demanding that British troops be deployed or at least troops commanded by British officers. One such letter was from B.W.S. Dhillon. While advising the Congress leaders to invite British troops to help in the eventuality of riots he said: 'no where was their partiality questioned by any common man. Special mention was made of them even in vernacular papers and the news (of their possible deployment) was always welcomed every where.'[222]

Quite naturally the common people had little or no idea that the British had no intention of deploying their own troops in the communal disturbances. On 29 July, Lt. Gen. A. Smith had issued a top secret directive that British troops could not be deployed in communal disturbances and were to be used only to save British lives. Even when British lives could be saved only after suppressing a communal disturbance, permission was to be sought from the Commander-in-Chief for any such deployment. The order also said that constitutionally British troops could not serve under Indian officers.[223]

Mountbatten of course remained convinced that the best way to ensure that army units were not subverted by communal and other interests from within was to have British officers associated with them.[224] It was on the basis of the decisions taken in one such meeting that most of the units commanded by General Rees as Commander of the Punjab Boundary Force had British commanders.

THE PUNJAB BOUNDARY FORCE

As earlier discussed, the Punjab Boundary Force had come into being through a joint declaration subsequent to a meeting chaired by Mountbatten in Lahore on 20 July. The force was deployed with effect from 1 August in 12 districts.[225] On 4 August, Rees addressed his first press conference in Lahore. He said the troops that formed the PBF were Indian and of mixed classes with senior commanders being British. The PBF would assist the civil and judicial administration and he would vouch for its impartiality.[226] While seeking the co-operation of the public, he said, 'we will back up the police . . . we have considerable force . . . we will do our utmost.'[227] In a subsequent press conference, Rees, accompanied by Mamdot, Shaukat Hayat, Gopichand Bhargava, Bhim Sen Sachar and Sardar Swarn Singh, once again promised fairness and impartiality.[228]

DIWAN AT NANKANA SAHIB

Meanwhile, even as the PBC was conducting its hearings in Lahore, a Sikh *Diwan* was announced at Nankana Sahib. For some reason Jenkins decided to ban the gathering of people at Nankana Sahib.[229] So much so that orders were issued to railway stations falling on the route to Nankana Sahib not to issue any tickets for the shrine town.[230] One hundred and three people were arrested at Amritsar while trying to proceed to Nankana Sahib.[231] This was one of the rare occasions when at first it appeared that Jenkins had 'proceeded on the wrong road'. The Viceroy too thought it incorrect.[232] However, Abell, his Private Secretary, differed and believed that Jenkins, by declaring the *Diwan* illegal had restricted the size of the gathering and since the police had later to open fire, the decision of Jenkins may indeed have averted a great tragedy.[233] Even though the administration had gone to great lengths to ensure that a gathering could not take place at Nankana Sahib, about 10,000 people still managed to reach the meeting place. The scene was further electrified by the dramatic appearance of Sardar Dalip Singh MLA.

More important, however, was, and as had come to be believed in the Viceroy's office, that if the Sikhs were denied Nankana Sahib there was bound to be serious trouble and that the Muslims were aware of this and had made appropriate preparations. This note also made a reference to people from both sides making efforts to subvert troops.[234]

TARA SINGH ASKS THE PANTH TO WAIT FOR THE AWARD

Even as the Nankana Sahib Convention was thought to have fizzled out, British sources in Lahore were convinced that serious disturbances were likely—initiated by the Sikhs even before the Boundary

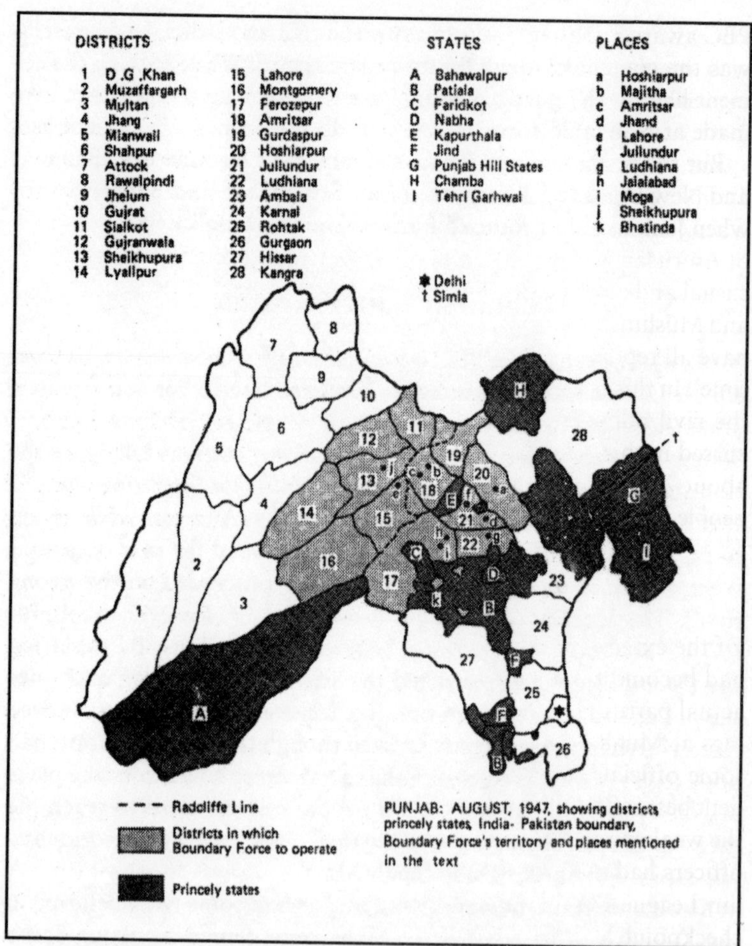

Source: Jeffrey, 'The Punjab Boundary Force and the Problems of Order August 1947', *Modern Asian Studies* 8, 4, 1947, p. 499.

Award was out. Jenkins' office informed Government House in New Delhi that raids on Muslim villages had begun in the regions of Amritsar, Lahore, Hoshiarpur, and Jullundur.[235] For some reason, however, the Viceroy's staff was inclined to believe that the Sikhs would wait for the PBC award.[236] This impression was created by a statement by Master Tara Singh that the Nankana Sahib *Diwan* had achieved its objective and that the Sikhs now needed to wait for the

PBC award.[237] What really transpired at Nanakana Sahib and what was the content of speeches made is not clear because the government had by an order banned reference in the press to the speeches made at Nankana Sahib.[238]

But the point remains that yet again Governor Jenkins was right and New Delhi was wrong. The PBC award was still ten days away when Jenkins noted: 'Situation is now most serious. . . . In rural areas of Amritsar, Hoshiarpur, Jullundur we have had for some days both casual and organised raids in most of which Sikhs are the aggressors and Muslims the victims. Rural areas of Lahore, Ferozepur, Ludhiana have all reported similar outrages. . . . Gurdaspur may blow up any time'. In this crucial and early warning, Jenkins also pointed out that the civil administration was beginning to fall apart. He also discussed in this note the difficulty of controlling 12 districts with just about 7,500 'Rifles', including 1,500 of the PBF, for over 12 million people.[239]

LIBERAL JUSTICE AND A CORRUPTED POLICE

Of the extensive reports of how the civil and police administration had become very partisan, two stand out in the days preceding the actual partition of Punjab. Soon after the first incident of train killings at Mughalpura, residents of Harbanspura had openly charged some officials of having facilitated the killings.[240] The second incident best reflects how high-handed the police had become because of the weakening of the chain of command, something to which senior officers had made repeated references. Maj. Ashiq Hussain, a Muslim League MLA, was travelling in his car in Lahore. At a police checkpoint his car was asked to stop. The driver appears to have stopped at some distance away from where the checking policemen were standing. After a heated exchange the car was allowed to proceed. Returning by the same route, Hussain was again waved down and this time the policemen were more high-handed. As words were once again exchanged, the constable on duty shot the MLA dead.[241] A *PT* editorial reporting on the incident said: 'For a long time now the police have represented all the evils . . . a lawless tyrant who had to be avoided like the plague.'[242]

If this is how the police dealt even with MLAs, one can imagine the plight of ordinary people. There were numerous reports detailing incidents of high-handedness. In fact, a sub-registrar, a pleader and a *zaildar* were arrested for their role in the Garhshankar (Hoshiarpur) killings.[243] The situation with regard to the behaviour of the police was bad enough for Governor Jenkins to have reported to Mountbatten that the police, particularly in Lahore, and Amritsar, had become unreliable and even the railways were not safe until the army could take over.[244]

On the face of it, jail statistics appear to indicate that the police had been doing a good job. The number of people in the jails of joint Punjab, it was reported, in normal times was usually around 2,800, but in the months of March to July 1947 the number had averaged around 8,000.[245] Even so, with the kind of situation that prevailed at the time 8,000 is far too low a figure. This view can be supported by numerous reports which clearly indicate that the courts in Punjab were being liberal and not giving punishment in line with the nature of the offences. The overall trend and administrative attitude of the courts of handing down light punishments and liberally granting bail even in cases of heinous crimes may in fact have contributed to the general situation of anarchy that Punjab went on to experience.

From the columns of court proceedings in the lower and High Courts of Lahore, it is abundantly clear that judges were short cutting the system. In one case, two people—Humayun and Raju—were handed down a punishment of two years and six months for a clear role in riot killings. The judge while handling the case shifted his focus from Section 302 to Section 304 of the Indian Penal Code. In another case, Subedar Major Dost Mohammad of Rawalpindi was clearly charged with killings, but was allowed bail against an amount (large no doubt) of Rs. 10,000. In fact, the number of bail applications in cases of riot and murder increased with the days with large numbers being disposed every day.[246]

But the blame for this too lay with the police force. With a thoroughly partisan and corrupted policeforce, cases put up to the courts naturally contained loopholes, leaving no option for the judges but to grant bail. When those charged with murder and rioting were back in their *mohallas* in a couple of days, they became instant heroes and went on to act with greater frenzy. Justice A.M. Jan of the Punjab High Court, possibly because his court was listed for the bail applications, stands out for the liberal manner in which bail applications were handled. In a single day he granted bail in several cases of murder and rioting.[247]

There was of course another angle to the low rate of criminal convictions. A note by the Criminal Investigation Department (CID) East Punjab stated: 'Life is now cheap . . . there is not quite the same indignation when communal stabbings occur . . . few men will give evidence against persons of their own community. . . . It is not difficult . . . to settle scores and so carry out the crime as to create the impression that the motive was communal'.[248]

NEW MEASURES HAVE NO IMPACT

As the violence increased rapidly both in terms of the number of incidents and the nature of the brutality the Punjab government initiated a series of measures. Sant Prakash Singh was appointed the first Inspector General of Police for East Punjab on 27 July. In his first press conference he appealed to the people to begin trusting the police and said the force would undergo a complete change. He also appealed to the youth to no longer treat Police jobs as undesirable and come forward to join up.[249]

On 29 July, the government announced that military pickets would be set up in Lahore and that with effect from 1 August law and order in Lahore would be looked after by the army.[250] This was still short of bringing Lahore under martial law, as was being demanded by many leaders of the Congress. Gopichand Bhargava asked for the deployment of more troops in Lahore,[251] even as the number of fires and stabbings multiplied.[252] With effect from 1 August, the District Magistrate Lahore ordered that up to 15 August no public meetings would be allowed. The order also prohibited the use of any private vehicle—jeep or truck—painted in a military colour.[253]

Even though the district magistrate believed that things were improving in Lahore,[254] other sources said Lahore was only getting worse, particularly with the increase in the number of cases involving explosives.[255] On 4 August the Punjab Government Gazette Extraordinary announced under Section 93 of the Government of India Act four new Acts which it was believed would adequately empower it to deal with the situation. The Punjab Disturbed Areas (Amendment) Act contained among others a provision for capital punishment for possessing or manufacturing illegally any form of explosives.

The Punjab Land Trespasses (Emergency Provisions) Act provided for stringent punishment for unlawful cultivation of land and was enacted mainly to control the extreme situation that had arisen in Gurgaon where villages were burnt to make people flee so that their lands and crops could be controlled.[256] Existing provisions were lengthy and punishments were inadequate. The Act even provided for compensation. Similarly, the Punjab Requisition of Immovable Property (Temporary Powers) Act and the Punjab Special Tribunals Act were expected to strengthen the government's hands.

To encourage its officials to function fearlessly, the government of Punjab even issued an order which said that in the case of the death of an employee while on duty a member of the family would be given employment in the government.[257] Preventive measures however failed to have any significant impact on the violence or checking the outflow of refugees.[258] By the first days of August, the *HT* reported that Delhi alone had received over 80,000 refugees most of whom were without food and shelter.[259] What was even more worrisome for the authorities was the manner in which the violence was spreading in rural areas—an early example being the raid on Jand village near Phillaur which had left 18 dead.[260]

In Amritsar when a daring crowd refused to be controlled, the police had to open fire, killing five on the spot.[261] PBF troops did for a day or two restore some confidence in Lahore by night patrolling, even through narrow lanes, but the action soon lost its impact.[262] On 11 August 48 cases of serious stabbing with 14 dead were reported from Lahore alone.[263]

Anarchy in Lahore

By all accounts Lahore was taken over by anarchy by 10 or maybe 11 August. The *HT* Punjab Newsletter of 7 August had earlier reported various incidents of attacks on trains, bomb blasts, platform attacks.[264] To add to the feeling of fear highly provocative and threatening posters mysteriously appeared in many parts of Lahore during the night of 9 August. One such poster said: 'If factors of stones and shrines were taken into consideration the Muslims will not rest until what is there [*sic*] by right'. The poster was in the name of 'The Greater Pakistan Youth League'.[265]

The madness was reflected in incidents like the one in which a truck loaded with household goods leaving Lahore was reduced to ashes by arsonists.[266] On 12 August, the violence in Lahore left 33 dead, 25 seriously injured and 35 major fires were reported. Reports also said the death figure of the 11 August stabbings had risen to 40. On 13 August, as a result of uncounted stabbings, 111 people were killed and 4 places of worship were burnt down.[267]

All the violence in Lahore, the vast amounts of property that had been destroyed, however, seemed to have failed to impress Mountbatten who while addressing the Pakistan Constituent Assembly on 14 August was reported to have said: 'I had received reports of madness in Lahore . . . the devastation is far less than I expected, it amounts to not more than 18 houses per thousand.'[268]

Jenkins, however, viewed the situation as 'very serious'. He said the explosive situation in Lahore and Amritsar was the result of the derailment of a Pakistan special near Bhatinda, the Sikh outrages in Amritsar district, and the disarming of Muslim policemen by a Hindu acting superintendent of police in Amritsar.[269] The train in question ran over a mine about 15 miles from Bhatinda on 9 August at 9 p.m. The few deaths that occurred did so from accidental injuries, the train was not otherwise raided.

Importantly, Jenkins had already telegrammed to the Viceroy as early as 12 August that 'Strength of PBF is not adequate to present and future tasks'. Describing Lahore, he said, 'Feeling in Lahore is now unbelievably bad'. In another telegram to Mountbatten the same day, Jenkins said: 'Police in Lahore and Amritsar now unreliable . . . there was [sic] serious disturbances in the Recruit Training Centre at Lahore today . . . railways will not be safe unless army can take over on war department lines. Muslim League National Guard are now very active in Lahore and exceedingly truculent to non-Muslims.'

PUNJAB CID INDICTS TARA SÌNGH

After the Partition Council meeting on 5 August, Mountbatten asked Jinnah, Patel and Liaqat Ali to stay and hear what Captain Savage of the Punjab CID had to say with regard to Master Tara Singh and some others.[270]

According to Savage, Pritam Singh an INA soldier who had been arrested had given a statement indicting Master Tara Singh for producing explosives and also for planning to blow up some river headworks. Likewise, a clerk of the Lahore Secretariat, Gopi Rai Khosla, too, had charged Tara Singh with making plans to blow up Pakistan special trains which would carry Pakistan officials from New Delhi to Karachi. Khosla, Savage stated, had even said that arrangements had been made to keep Tara Singh informed by wireless of the movement of the trains. Khosla was also reported to have quoted Tara Singh as having said that small groups of Sikhs were planning to blow up trains with remote control devices.

While the others expressed great concern, Sardar Patel, however, dismissed Captain Savage's report on the grounds that statements made by arrested people could not be relied upon. Savage insisted that though no evidence could be produced the statements were quite true. He also reported the view of the Punjab CID that Sikh leaders appeared to have lost control over the peasantry and that many of the former were convinced that sooner than later India and Pakistan were bound to clash in conflict. He also informed the leaders that Tara Singh had started collecting arms through Sikh army officers and also with the help of the Raja of Faridkot.

It is interesting to note that even though it was Jenkins who deputed Captain Savage to brief the Viceroy, his own views with regard to the role of Master Tara Singh were somewhat different. In a note of 9 August Jenkins told the Viceroy that any attempt to arrest Tara Singh would only serve to worsen the situation, and that it was clear that the village raids and other violence initiated by Sikhs were not specifically directed by Master Tara Singh, though they may have been the result of his propaganda. Jenkins noted: 'I believe the report[s] submitted to your Excellency on Tara Singh's personal activities are substantially true but I doubt if in fact his alleged plans will come to anything.'[271]

Jenkins also told the Viceroy in this note that Tara Singh's arrest was not advisable at any stage: 'their arrests now or simultaneously with the Boundary Award would almost certainly lead to a sharp reaction among the Sikhs and would jeopardise what hopes there are that the Sikhs in West Punjab will accept the award and settle down quietly.' Jenkins also added that his opinion on the Tara Singh's role was also backed by Chandulal Trivedi (Governor Designate East Punjab) and Francis Muddie Governor (Governor Designate West Punjab).

On 14 August, the *PT* (quite surprisingly) printed in the centre of its front page an appeal by Master Tara Singh for peace: 'Communal situation in Central Punjab is assuming menacing proportion . . . I appeal to Sikhs to desist from violence . . . forbearance and restraint are the qualifications of a brave man.' Tara Singh's statement was immediately welcomed by Mamdot, the League leader in the Punjab:

'I am pleased that Master Tara Singh has spoken for peace, I welcome his statement.'[272] In the same statement Mamdot strongly appealed to Muslims in West Punjab for peace.

GOVERNOR JENKINS' LAST REPORT

The last detailed letter by Jenkins (a situation report normally written by governors to the Viceroy) is an interesting document in view of his excellent summing up of the last few days of British rule in Punjab: 'The communal disturbances have naturally overshadowed everything else during the first half of August . . . raids and murders are now so frequent that it is impossible to keep track of them all. . . . During the past week Amritsar district including the main roads has become unsafe. . . . Most of the rural casualities . . . have been caused by Sikhs working in large bands and raiding Muslim villages or Muslim pockets in mixed villages. The Muslims in Amritsar district have occasionally hit back. . . . The Sikhs as was expected behaved with extreme brutality. . . . Yesterday [an unarmed] party of Pathan labourers . . . was set upon—30 Pathans were killed.'[273]

This note also explains the immediate background of the outbreak of violence in Amritsar, which went on to have a snowball effect in Lahore. Jenkins said an ASP (Kaul) asked Muslim policemen of Amritsar who had opted for West Punjab to report at the Police Lines for their written orders. This was an oral order, but when it was cyclostyled for distribution, someone (probably ASP Kaul), Jenkins says, added some unauthorized lines which said that Muslim policemen who wished to go to the West would have to hand in their arms before they assembled at the Police Lines. Thus when these policemen arrived at the Police Lines for their order, they were in a very bad mood and demanded immediate transfer, several went off to Lahore creating trouble on the way and spreading all kinds of stories. The report also said Muslim policemen were withdrawn from rural stations as well.[274]

Talking of the future Jenkins noted: 'The Sikhs . . . wish to take revenge for the Rawalpindi massacres and they wish to assert themselves on the boundary question. . . . It is impossible to defend their conduct in any way but the Muslims have failed to understand the horror caused by the Rawalpindi affair and seem to think that by reprisals they can bring the Sikhs to a less violent frame of mind. . . . I believe reprisals in Lahore will only lead to further outrages by the

Sikhs and so on.' The Hindus, Jenkins noted, 'are thoroughly terrified and the Muslim movement from the East is balanced by the Hindu movement from the West.'[275] Jenkins went on to say, 'I wish I could have made a cleaner job of partition but the Committee really agreed about very little.' The report ended on a sentimental note: 'This I suppose [is] the last letter to be sent by a British Governor of the Punjab to a British Viceroy.'

JENKINS DEPARTS FROM PUNJAB

Jenkins' depature went almost completely unnoticed. A small report in the *CMG* stated that 'six British officers arrived in Karachi by air from New Delhi and spent the night at the airport to catch an early morning flight to London.'[276] The six included Jenkins and Sir George Abell, the Viceroy's Private Secretary. Chandu Lal Trivedi, ICS, who succeeded Jenkins as Governor of East Punjab arrived in Lahore almost ten days before he actually took charge.[277]

FIELD MARSHAL AUCHINLECK ON THE PUNJAB SITUATION

Field Marshal Sir C. Auchinleck while returning from Karchi, where he had gone to attend the inaugural ceremonies, stopped at Lahore on 14 August. While in Lahore he appears to have reviewed the situation and prepared a note of his impressions. It is not clear whether this note was prepared on the instructions of Mountbatten, but all the same it formed an important part of the agenda in the first post-15 August meeting of the Joint Defence Councils of India and Pakistan. Of Amritsar he noted: 'The strife was started by the Sikhs who have formed armed bands of considerable strength which carry out raids on Muslim or predominantly Muslim villages . . . one such band is reliably reported to have killed 200 Muslims in one village some days ago.' He went on: 'There are Muslims bands organised for the same purpose but these are fewer in number, smaller in size and less well organised apparently.'[278]

Interestingly, in contrast to what Mountbatten had said in his address in Karachi on 14 August, Auchinleck said that close to a tenth of all houses had been destroyed by fire in Lahore, many were still in flames, the roads and streets were deserted. He also pointed out that ex-INA personnel were known to have been involved in the killings in the East Punjab. While reviewing the communication position, Auchinleck noted: 'police arrangements for the protection of railways had completely broken down . . . railway personnel are afraid to leave their homes to go to work'. As a result the North-West Railway had been compelled to stop a large number of its train services.

Auchinleck's note clearly states that the delay in the PBC award had greatly added to the problem: 'the delay is having a most disturbing and harmful effect . . . it is realised of course that the announcement may add fresh fuel to the fire but lacking an announcement the wildest rumours are current and are being spread by mischief makers of whom there is no lack.' Auchinleck's views stand out also because his conclusions differ in a significant context not only from those of Moutbatten regarding the destruction in Lahore but also from those of Governor Jenkins on the role of the police: 'The most disturbing feature here is the defection of the police, particularly the special police who are predominantly Muslim. There is a very strong evidence that the police are taking little notice of the orders of their officers (all the remaining European officers left yesterday) and that they actually joined hands with the rioters in certain cases.'

Field Marshal Auchinleck also came down heavily on those who were accusing the PBF of not being impartial. He said, 'people in responsible positions', were only adding to the problem by expressing doubts on the impartial credibility of PBF commanders, who were doing their very best. He ended the note by saying that there was practically no possibility of more troops being deployed in Punjab.

DELHI TRADERS HOARD THE TRICOLOUR: AUGUST 15—NOT A DAY FOR REJOICING

As we have noted, during the first fortnight of August the exchange of notes between Government House, Lahore and New Delhi was not only extensive but most of the communications clearly indicated that Punjab was heading for disaster. For some reason the political leaders still continued to believe and behave as if all was well and the worst was over, all that remained was to celebrate the day of deliverance—15 August.

In Delhi, notwithstanding the calls for boycott by many people including the Hindu Mahasabha, the tempo for the celebrations had begun to speed up from the beginning of August itself, so much so that it was reported that some people were even hoarding (in true Delhi style) and selling the Tricolour, which was in short supply, in the black market.[279] Over 300 flag-hoisting ceremonies were reportedly planned for Delhi alone.[280] The celebrations in Karachi were unprecedentedly elaborate, grand and colourful, as *Dawn* put it. One thousand people were invited to a grand banquet given by Jinnah in honour of Mountbatten on 13 August.[281]

In the East Punjab, however, the situation was quite different. There prevailed almost a complete lack of enthusiasm among the common people in most parts. Officially, the government of East Punjab issued instructions to all the 12 deputy commissioners on how celebrations were to be organized. Every district was to organize a main function which was to be attended by all officials, where the new flag of the Republic was to be saluted. Arrangements were to be made for illuminating important government buildings. It was also said that funds had been sanctioned for the programmes.[282]

In Simla, special arrangements were being made to decorate places of worship, organize prayers, *prabhat pheris*, feed the poor, distribute sweets to schoolchildren, organize *charkha* competitions, etc. The elite of Simla talked of the day as a 'special occasion for the rich and poor alike'.[283] The Simla Municipal Corporation even announced that a sum of Rs. 10,000 had been earmarked for the 15 August celebrations.[284] In Rohtak the Congress Sewa Dal was reported to have planned an ambitious celebration which included a march-past.[285]

Interestingly, many reports discussed how the new cabinet of India was to be sworn in at one minute past midnight (14 August) as the confluence of stars on 15 August was not auspicious. This decision was taken because the same astrologer who had predicted this had earlier also predicted the failure of the Simla talks.[286]

The complete lack of enthusiasm among common Punjabis also stands out repeatedly in the appeals made by Congress leaders to also celebrate 15 August.[287] In an appeal to the minorities of West Punjab, Sachar said: 'I have been beset by inquiries from minorities in West Punjab, as to the attitude they should adopt towards 15 August . . . it is the day of rejoicing, the British are leaving . . . but at the same time I cannot forget the prevailing mood and temper of bewildered minorities . . . they have suffered terribly . . . ; no wonder they lack the urge to join the celebrations.'[288] Gopichand Bhargava, the leading Congress figure in the East Punjab was also worried by the lack of enthusiasm and had to make special appeals.[289]

Mahatma Gandhi took up the issue of the disenchantment of the non-Muslim masses in West Punjab in his post-prayer meeting address on 21 July, by reading out a letter from a non-Muslim in West Punjab: 'you people are talking about celebrating 15 August as Independence Day. Have you thought how we non-Muslims of Pakistan are to celebrate the Day? . . . when you will be celebrating we will be afraid of our safety . . . can it be a day of anything but mourning?[290] Gandhi said in response to the letter: 'All I can say is Jinnah Sahib has become Governor-General of Pakistan and says non-Muslims will not be harmed. . . . My advice is trust [his] word.'[291]

Durlab Singh, while commenting on the appeals being made by Congress leaders to celebrate 15 August, said in a letter: 'No doubt it is a great day but leaders fail to realise that thousands of families of west Punjab will be mourning the loss of their relatives or are still in camps . . . it would be appreciated that all money proposed for lighting, fireworks, etc., be spared for providing food and clothing. This would be a good move for the lasting memory of 15 August.'[292]

Not surprisingly the widespread gloom and sadness that prevailed across Punjab appears to have in no way interfared with the pomp and pageantry in Delhi and Karachi and even Lahore where Muddie was sworn in as Governor of Punjab at 10.45 a.m. on 15 August 1947. Even as Lahore was being overrun by violence a great part of the attention and effort of senior functionaries of the government was being devoted to arranging a grand event in the Ballroom of Government House. The invitation card carried details of dresses to be worn and elaborate protocol that was to be followed.[293] As Muddie took oath of office with bands and salutes, sounds of gun fire, looting and screaming and dark clouds of smoke from burning buildings formed the backdrop.

At some stage Mountbatten appears to have been of the impression that both Nehru and Gandhi had agreed to have on the Indian Union's flag, even if in a symbolic manner, the Union Jack. Mountbatten was reasonably sure that the Congress would accept the idea and in believing so had ready on his table a design of the proposed flag when Nehru came to meet him on 24 June. As Das also notes, it is difficult to know what Nehru thought or how he reacted mentally to the proposal, but certainly the gentleman that Nehru was, he did not say anything to Mountbatten. Nehru even took the design with him on the grounds that he would discuss the matter with other leaders. Mountbatten even appears to have thought that a similar proposal might carry conviction with Jinnah as well.[294]

Jinnah of course was blunt and straightforward when a similar proposal was put up to him. In a note appended to the proceedings of this meeting, Mountbatten recorded that while Nehru said that 'extremists in the Congress would not agree', Jinnah said that 'it would be repugnant to the feelings of Muslims to have a Christian cross alongside the crescent'.[295]

The same document also shows that at some earlier stage Mountbatten had also reached a decision with senior Indian leaders that even after 15 August (1947) the Union Jack would be flown in India on special occasions which included the Foundation/Dominion Days of Australia (26 January); New Zealand (24 September); Canada (1 July); King's Birthday (12 June); Empire Day (24 May); and the Independence Days of India and Pakistan.[296]

PUNJAB BOUNDARY COMMISSION: THE RADCLIFFE AWARD

On 12 August 1947, at about midnight a top priority secret telegram was dispatched from Moutbatten to Jenkins: 'It is now clear that awards for Punjab and Bengal will not be ready for publication till 15th evening or 16th morning . . . Governments of East and West Punjab must take charge according to the notional boundaries.'[297]

After having completed the hearings in Lahore, the PBC members reconvened in Simla on 7 August. Sir Radcliffe had arrived in Simla a few of days earlier—3 August.[298] The PBC Award was earlier expected to be released on 13 August. The *HT* said the delay of a day was also (probably) because Mountbatten was to attend the inaugural ceremonies in Karachi on 14 August.[299]

In Simla, as the rumour mills worked overtime, the PBC officially closed office on 8 August and Sir Radcliffe left for New Delhi.[300] In Lahore, however, it was widely reported that 'reliable sources had confirmed that Lahore was going to the West'.[301] All the earlier talk of good relations and cordiality notwithstanding all four members of the Commission—two Muslim, one Sikh and one Hindu—submitted separate reports, as they failed to agree on major issues, leaving Sir Radcliffe to take the final decision.

Considering that all that the PBC did was to put its seal of approval on the notional line of division in Punjab that had been around for over two months, the suspense and mystery of where the line would come even among those at the highest level like Mountbatten, Jinnah and Nehru, appear today to have been pretensions Mountbatten even wrote to Nehru: 'Sir Radcliffe is sending me the Award of the Boundary Commission in the course of today (14 August) but it cannot arrive before I leave for Karachi. At present therefore, I have no idea of its contents.'[302] Liaqat Ali, and naturally Jinnah too, certainly had access to inside information as is testified by the former's angry oral representation to Ismay through Mohammad Ali where he said he was shocked to learn that a large part of Gurdaspur was being given to India.[303] Many years later Jenkins in a personal letter to a friend observed: 'I certainly didn't think M. (Mountbatten) tinkered personally with the Award'.[304]

It is certain, as Tinker suggests, that a select circle of the Viceroy's personal staff had advance information, which is how Muhammad Ali learnt of Gurdaspur coming to India and Sardar Patel learnt of Chittagong Hill Tracts going to Pakistan. But what is interesting is that even though the Award on Punjab had reached the Viceroy—all complete—on 13 August, he continued to pretend that he still had no idea. One answer to this of course is that, having been informed of the contents by the able Menon (V.P.), he knew that both the Congress and the League would be angry and therefore decided to look at it only after returning from Karachi on the night of 14 August. Tinker even suggests that Jenkins may have heard of crucial details as early as 10 or 11 August, because that is when he was asked through a 'secrephone' scrambled message to make a change in the original communication.[305]

The suspense finally ended on 18 August when the newspapers carried stories of the details. The *HT* put it simply: 'Punjab divided on notional line'. Sir Radcliffe while prefacing the award details said: 'The task of defining a boundary in Punjab was a difficult one. Claims of the respective parties ranged over a wide territory . . . the truly debatable ground in the end was the area between the Sutlej and Beas and river Ravi. He said that he had 'pondered much over the areas around the Sutlej and Beas where Muslims had good concentration'. The *PT* also cited Sir Radcliffee as saying: 'in the course of the Commission's discussions the divergence of opinion among my colleagues was so wide that an agreed solution to the Boundary problem was not to be obtained.'[306]

Dawn reported the Award in its characteristic manner, with a second headline on the front page 'Parting Kick of the British', and 'Pakistan may not remain a member of the Commonwealth'. The words 'parting kick' were in fact credited to Abdur Rab Nishar, Pakistan's Communication Minister, who had said the Award was 'extremely unfair and unjust and not based on any facts . . . we believe it is a parting kick'.[307]

As if anticipating the extensive criticism from all sides Radcliffe also said: 'There are bound to be criticisms on the line drawn, but they would have been all the same even if the line was drawn elsewhere.' He also explained how there was no way to avoid disrupting the canal, road and electric transmission systems: 'The award can not satisfy hopes aspirations held by either side . . . only political understanding can meet such aspirations . . . with political arrangements, I am not concerned.'[308]

REACTIONS TO THE PUNJAB BOUNDARY AWARD

Interestingly the Government of Punjab had passed an order that disallowed any discussion, comments, even in letters to the editor, on the Boundary Award, until it was announced.[309]

The Agriculture Minister of Pakistan, Ghazanfar Ali Khan, was the first to 'bombast' the award: he called it 'disgusting—unjust not based on any principle', and said that Pakistan may now not remain in Commonwealth.' Begum Shaj Nawaj said 'it was unjust and the British had gone back on their word'.[310] I.M. Chundrigar, Pakistan's Commerce Minister, while saying it was unjust also warned that Pakistan would not now remain in the Commonwealth. S.P. Singha, Speaker of the West Punjab Assembly and a prominent Christian leader said: 'it was unfair . . . the principle of contiguity of majority areas has been overlooked'.[311] Shaukat Hayat, while charging the British with unfairness, said: 'the Award shows whose real friends the British were'.[312]

The first strong reaction from among the Sikhs came from Baba Kharak Singh: 'award is arbitrary and unfair, injudicious. . . I am deeply hurt by the injustice. The last act of the British will go down in history as the most ungrateful done to the Sikhs who had laid down their lives for the defence of the British Empire . . . we shall fight to the last to vindicate the glory and the prestige of the Khalsa.'[313] Master Tara Singh reacted by saying: 'I am today a most miserable man . . . but still have hope.'[314]

Justice Tek Chand, a former judge of the Punjab High Court, said in a long statement to *CMG*: 'The Award has broken the solidarity of the Sikhs by dividing [them] into little over 23 lakh in East and 14 lakh in the West Punjab . . . it has taken away the nerve centre of the Hindus (Lahore) and wrenched off the canal colonies which the

Sikhs had developed by their 50 years of blood sweat and tears.'[315] Sardar Ujjal Singh said the Sikhs had been deprived of everything that they had been concentrating on, Canal colonies, shrines, Nankana Sahib. Sunder Singh Majithia said the Sikhs had been greatly weakened.[316]

Almost without exception, newspapers that were of some standing in the region condemned the Award. Their reasons, of coursc, differed. The *HT* also criticized the Award on many points: it was based on population alone; it deprived the Hindus of Lahore and; the Sikhs of their shrines and their 'colony' lands. But its editorial comments were far milder, more probably because of the association of the owners of the *HT* with the top leadership of the Congress. More generally, it took the view that no demarcation could have satisfied all parties.[317]

The *CMG* came out with what was perhaps the best assessment: 'the Award creates as many problems as it solves. . . Sikhs have been neglected . . . the delay (in announcement) for which no explanation is forthcoming has led to speculation and which aggravated an acute communal situation . . . [an] announcement prior to August would have given the leaders an opportunity to reaffirm their decision of acceptance which urgently needs such endorsement to make it acceptable to the Punjabis.'[318]

Some days later the *CMG* came out with another editorial on the issue: 'Reactions to the award continue to be condemnatory, the only favourable commentary so far being . . . that since all communities are displeased the award must be fair to all.' The editorial then countered the charge made by some Congress leaders that the *CMG* and other papers had highlighted only the violence in Punjab as well as only the critical views on the award: 'The area of the arson [and] loot is admittedly small on the map of India and the population living in it might be very small in comparison with India's 400 million but the area is like a cancer, if not treated [it] will cause the death of the body.'[319]

The *PT* in an exhaustive comment reminded readers that it had warned many days earlier that the PBC proceedings were only a hoax. 'Our most exaggerated fears of British efforts to placate the Sikhs and the land grabbing Hindu Mahasabha leaders have proved to be true.' Interestingly, it pointed out that while the award had taken much of what should have come to Pakistan it was still unable to solve the Sikh problem.[320]

As usual, and as expected, the *Dawn* editorial was the most hard-hitting. Titled 'Territorial Murder', it said: 'The Muslim nation has been betrayed . . . Pakistan has been cheated . . . drafted in a caviliar [*sic*] fashion [the award] does not possess the essential characteristics of a legal judgement. Let us make it perfectly clear even if the government may accept it the people will not.'[321] A few days later, *Dawn* gave the population figures on the basis of tehsils and communities (see Table 4.2).

But it was Ghazanfar Ali Khan who sounded the most serious note of warning: 'Although leaders have given their word previously to accept the Award, Muslims generally will not accept it.'[322] An unsigned letter truly summed up the feelings of ordinary Punjabis. The person who wrote the letter quite aptly called himself the 'average man': 'it will not be surprising if in [the] course of time ordinary people begin to feel that they have been cheated . . . the problem of minorities is unsolved . . . freedom which has been received with open arms is of no use'.[323] Riaz Hussain Jan, resident of a small village, also felt cheated but for other reasons: 'Muslim League leaders claim they have won Pakistan on the plea to safeguard the rights of the poor and backward Muslim masses from Hindu capitalists and monopolists. . . . The Muslim League who have come to power and their parasites who are scurrying to share the loot are mostly autocrats (feudalists) and capitalists.'[324]

The problem with the PBC Award was not merely the placement of the line of demarcation, because as Sir Radcliffe said the problem would have remained whereever the line was drawn, so closely knit had the Punjab been. In this sense, therefore, the real issue that

TABLE 4.2: POPULATION: HINDUS/SIKHS, MUSLIMS—SELECT DISPUTED TAHSILS

Tahsil	Muslims	Hindu/Sikhs
Gurdaspur	1,71,488	1,33,674
Batala	2,07,277	1,49,846
Pathankot	1,49,600	86,800
Chunian	2,37,829	1,40,110
Ferozepur	1,60,371	1,23,331
Zira	1,37,586	69,072
Ajnala	1,30,939	83,401
Nakodar	1,35,918	91,803

Source: *Dawn*, 22 Augsut 1947.

confronted the millions of ordinary souls on both sides was the hurried and urgent manner in which the wedge was planted. Ever since the notional boundary was announced (3 June), every leader at the provincial and the national level—including Gandhi, Jinnah, Nehru, Liaqat Ali, Bhargava, Swarn Singh, Mamdot, Noon, Shaukat Hayat and the panic leaders—had been telling people to stay where they were, that no harm would come to them. Millions of Hindus, Sikhs and Muslims who were not even remotely connected with the decisions being taken in New Delhi and Simla with regard to their future waited till the last days, believing that things would be resolved. And then, suddenly, they were expected to leave. 'What was the hurry? Why was a smoother exchange of population not worked out?' What were the compulsions that made the decision makers in Delhi put at stake millions of lives? How would things have been different if, say, a couple of months' time was given to plan the exchange of population?

Newspapers in Lahore were flooded with letters and reports of people appealing to the leaders to seek out a resolution of the problem without compromising the safety and security of people on both sides. For ordinary families time was hardly a factor and quite rightfully so. Darbara Singh (probably a lecturer) of Khalsa College, Amritsar, had commented with great foresight on this issue a day before the PBC started its hearings in Lahore. He said that exchange of population on a large scale had been organized with limited loss of life and property between Bulgaria and Turkey and Turkey and Greece. Why, he argued, could it also not be done in Punjab? He appealed to the Viceroy to give a guarantee that families would be allowed to take their belongings and would also be given enough time to decide which side of the border they wished to live.[325] Darbara Singh also said that for the smooth exchange of population it was necessary to ensure that the PBC Award was not announced till adequate arrangements had been made to handle the exercise in a manner in which the safety and security of the people was paramount.

Mountbatten had obviously foreseen criticism on the issue of the enforcing of a transfer of power at such short notice followed naturally by the exchange of population. Not surprisingly, he noted in a Top Secret Personal Report on 1 August: 'I am more than convinced that if the date of transfer had been 1 October there would have been a serious risk of a complete breakdown before that date.'[326] This note leaves me wondering what would Mountbatten have written if he had dictated this note on 1 October 1947? Could things have been worse?

I.M. Stephens who was probably the most influential journalist in India in 1947, delivered the second Jawaharlal Nehru lecture on 24 February 1969 at the Centre for South Asian Studies, Cambridge, the first having been delivered by Mountbatten. Stephens gave an unsparing, almost embarassing, assessment of Mountbatten and his transfer of power plan, and highlighted a very crucial point—that while the Attlee Government was keen for a transfer of power only in June 1948, some time in May 1948, Mountbatten had 'suddenly' decided on acceleration and 'persuaded a reluctant and bewildered Attlee government to agree'. As a result, 'Inevitably, therefore, the operation would become a subtle (affair). All sorts of big important things which might have been arranged in a more orderly manner under the previous programme would now need to be done less tidily . . . appalling things . . . happened after his mid-August stopping point . . . things which indisputably were the fruitation; the practical outcome of the particular course of action he had decided on while Viceroy in May (1947). . . . Nothing during my life has appalled me so much . . . possibly events would not have been so bad—had time been taken . . . Mountbatten possibly served the need of Britain rather than India and Pakistan . . . India was too big for war torn Britain.'[327]

NOTES

1. H.R. Tinker, 'Jawaharlal Nehru at Simla May 1947', *Modern Asian Studies*, 4, 4, 1970, pp. 357–8. Rhodes, *Churchill a study in Failure 1900–39*, London, 1970.
2. *Kessings Contemporary Archives*, vol. 6, pp. A8631–8634.
3. *HT*, 7 July 1947.
4. IOR L/PO/6/120 (i), the first reference to the line is traceable to two maps in a file—Transfer of Power Viceroy's Plan—a clear indication that authorities in London knew months in advance where the line would be drawn.
5. *PT*, 27 July 1947.
6. *TP*, vol. XII (81), Note by Abell, 12 July 1947, pp. 117–21.
7. *TP* , vol. XII (90), p. 134.
8. *CMG*, 9 July 1947.
9. *PT*, 15 July 1947.
10. *CMG*, 5 July 1947.

11. *HT*, 5 July 1947.
12. *PT*, 15 July 1947.
13. *Dawn*, 13 July 1947.
14. Ibid., 16 July 1947; *TP*, vol. XII (337), 1947.
15. Ibid., 18 July 1947; *CMG*, 18 July 1947.
16. *HT*, 7 July 1947.
17. *CMG*, 16 July 1947; *The Tribune*, 16 July 1947.
18. *The Tribune*, 3 and 9 July 1947. The reference to Hindus here must be seen in the broader sense. Of course the Hindu Mahasabha had for sometime been very keen to strengthen bonds with the Panth as C.B. Birdwood puts it: 'There is a constant mild flirtation in progress with the onus of seduction on the Mahasabha.' He has also cited Dr. Syama Prasad Mookerjee who had said: 'I have always felt the need for complete understanding between Sikhs and Hindus in Punjab', see his *India's Freedom Struggle: Role of Muslims and Sikhs*, p. 73. Also see IOR L/1/1/665, Information Deptt., Fortnightly Appreciation, 19 May 1947, no. 3830.
19. *HT*, 10 July 1947; also *CMG*, 10 July 1947.
20. *HT*, 9 July 1947.
21. Ibid., 12 July 1947.
22. *CMG*, 10 July 1947. Possibly it was this reference to Baldev Singh that led him to issue a clarification a day later, naturally under pressure from New Delhi.
23. *Tribune*, 10 July 1947.
24. *TP*, vol. XII (17), p. 17.
25. *HT*, 10 July 1947.
26. Ibid., 8 July 1947; *The Tribune*, 9 July 1947, *CMG*, 8 July 1947.
27. *HT*, 8 July 1947; *CMG*, 8 July.
28. *The Tribune*, 9 July 1947.
29. Ibid.
30. *CMG*, 9 June 1947; Satya Pal Vismani, *CMG*, 3 July 1947.
31. *Dawn*, 10 July 1947.
32. *The Tribune*, 5 July 1947.
33. *PT*, 11 July 1947.
34. *CMG*, 10 July 1947, also *The Tribune*, 10 July 1947.
35. *Dawn*, 13 July.
36. *The Tribune*, 9 July 1947; *CMG*, 10 July 1947.
37. *CMG*, 8 July.
38. *TP*, vol. XII (67), pp. 103–4.
39. *HT*, 11 July 1947.
40. *Dawn*, 14 July 1947; *PT*, 15 July 1947; *CMG*, 15 July 1947; *The Tribune* 14 July 1947; *HT*, 14 July 1947.
41. *Dawn*, 14 July; see also *CMG*, 20 July 1947 for an article which had appeared in a current issue of the *Economist* (London). 'Mohd. Ali Jinnah's assumption of Governor-Generalship of Pakistan was a

development all the more serious because his rule gave promise of being a very thinly veiled dictatorship.' It went on to question an active party politician become a Governor General—this has altered the nature of the dominions bonds.

42. *The Tribune*, 16 July 1947.
43. *CMG*, 12 July 1947.
44. *The Tribune*, 16 July 1947.
45. *CMG*, 18 July 1947.
46. Report on the Arya Samaj meeting at Lyallpur, *The Tribune*, 6 July 1947.
47. *CMG*, 6 July 1947.
48. *The Tribune*, 2 July 1947.
49. Ibid., 3 July 1947.
50. *CMG*, 18 July 1947.
51. Ibid., 16 July 1947.
52. *HT*, 1 July 1947.
53. *The Tribune*, 16 July 1947. Mountbatten, while delivering the Jawaharlal Nehru lecture at Cambridge (1968), referred to how all the parties—meaning naturally the Congress and the Muslim League—had agreed to have a British to head the Commission. A copy of the lecture is accessible in the I.M. Stephens Papers (Box 21), CSAS; V.N. Datta 'Interpreting Partition', in Amrik Singh (ed.), *The Partition in Retrospect*, New Delhi, 2000, p. 277.
54. *Dawn*, 13 July.
55. *The Tribune*, 18 July 1947; and *CMG*, 18 July 1947.
56. *TP*, vol. XII (162), p. 225.
57. *The Tribune*, 12 July 1947.
58. *TP*, vol. 12 (81), p. 121.
59. *CMG*, 8 July 1947; *HT*, 7 July 1947.
60. *PT*, 19 July 1947.
61. *CMG*, 8 July 1947. Also *HT*, 7 July 1947.
62. IOR, Mss. Eur. C.645.
63. Spate Papers, Diary Entry, 19 July 1947, CSAS.
64. Hugh Tinker, 'Pressure, Persuasion, Decision: Factors in The Partition of Punjab, August 1947; *Journal of Asian Studies*, vol. 34, no. 4, August 1977, p. 695.
65. *CMG*, 20 July 1947; *HT*, 19 July 1947. Although the assent was originally planned for 17 July, Mountbatten suggested 18 July for the assent to the India Bill, IOR L/PO/431 (i).
66. *HT*, 12 July 1947.
67. *CMG*, 6 July 1947.
68. *HT*, 16 July 1947.
69. IOR L/PO/6/122 (ii) *Transfer of Power*, Viceroy's Plan, n. 24, June 1947, Secretary of State, no. 96/47 to Prime Minister, File 262.
70. IOR L/PO/6/122 (ii) Proceedings IB Meeting 102, 13 June 1947.

71. Attlee Papers, Microfilm, Acc. no. 2146 (NAI). Extracts from Indian Constitutional Files—Independence India Bill.
72. *Dawn*, 16 July 1947.
73. *CMG*, 17 July 1947.
74. Ibid., 18 and 20 July 1947.
75. *TP*, vol. XII (41), Chief of Staff Committee Meeting Minute 2, Confidential Annex, 9 July 1947, pp. 43, 45; *The Tribune*, 6 July 1947 (Magazine Section).
76. Ibid. (46), pp. 58–9.
77. Ibid. (113), p. 165.
78. Ibid., p.166; Mss. Eur. R/3/I/176.
79. Ibid. Also see ibid (50) and (124), p. 182.
80. Ibid. (148), pp. 206–10.
81. Ibid.
82. *HT*, 20 July 1947, also *PT*, 22 July 1947.
83. *HT*, 20 July 1947.
84. *HT*, 17 and 18 July 1947.
85. *CMG*, 19 July 1947.
86. Ibid. 20 July 1947.
87. *HT*, 21 July 1947; IOR L/I/I/665, Information Deptt., Fortnightly Appreciation, 3 June 1947, no. 4259.
88. *HT*, 21 July 1947.
89. *The Tribune*, 21 July 1947.
90. *PT*, 17, 18, 19 and 20 July 1947.
91. Ibid., 13 July 1947.
92. Ibid.
93. *Dawn*, 16 July 1947.
94. Ibid., 19 July 1947.
95. Editorial, *Dawn*, 20 July 1947.
96. *PT*, 26 July 1947.
97. *The Tribune*, 11 July 1947.
98. Ibid., 12 July 1947.
99. *TP*, vol. XII (103), 14 July 1947, p. 147.
100. Ibid. (108), Item 3, Minutes of the Viceroy's Staff Meeting, 14 July 1947, p. 158.
101. *TP*, vol. XII (184), Minutes of Meeting held in Government House Lahore, 20 July 1947, pp. 272–4.
102. *HT*, 25 July 1947; *The Tribune*, 26 July 1947; *CMG*, 26 July 1947.
103. *CMG*, 19 July 1947.
104. *TP*, vol. XII (131), Abbott to Abell, 6 July 1947, p. 191.
105. Ibid. (200), 22 July 1947, pp. 290–1.
106. *TP*, vol. XII (209), Radcliffe to Mountbatten, 23 July 1947, p. 305. The word 'think' was underlined as pointed out by the volume editors.
107. *The Tribune*, 9 August 1947.
108. *HT*, 21 July 1947.

109. *HT*, 20 July 1947; *PT*, 20 July 1947.
110. *PT*, 26 July 1947.
111. Ibid., 16 July 1947.
112. *HT*, 25 July 1947.
113. Ibid., 4 August 1947.
114. Ishtiaq Ahmad, '1947 Partition . . . Arguments Put Forth', in Ian Talbot and Gurharpal Singh (eds.), *Region and Partition: Bengal Punjab and the Partition of the Sub-Continent*, Oxford, 1999. pp. 138–9.
115. Ibid., pp. 140–1.
116. *PT*, 16 July 1947.
117. Ibid., 20 July 1947.
118. *CMG*, 20 July 1947.
119. *HT*, 5 August 1947.
120. Ibid. A report possibly inspired by the memorandum that was submitted to the PBC had appeared in *CMG* on 17 July 1947. It said the non-Muslims also owned—all the 17 investment trusts; 4 of the five chambers of commerce; both the stock exchanges. It also said that if the workers of the North-West Railway Workshop majority of whom did not belong to Lahore and 18,000 of the total of 20,000 were Muslims were excluded from the count, the percentage of Muslims in Lahore would further decline. The report also made out a case of how the increase in the Lahore municipal limits from the earlier 39.39 sq. miles to the present 128.95 sq. miles had altered the actual scene by including villages in the Municipal area. On 24 July *CMG* also carried a report that pointed out that of 805 main industries situated in West Punjab Lahore alone accounted for 314. Between them Lahore and Amritsar accounted for about 40 per cent of Punjab's total industrial set up.
121. *The Tribune*, 2 August 1947.
122. Spate Papers, Diary Entry, 21 July 1947, CSAS.
123. *PT*, 1 August 1947.
124. Spate Papers, Diary Entry, 30 July 1947, CSAS.
125. Dwarka Nath Duggal, *CMG*, 24 July 1947.
126. *The Tribune*, 6 July 1947.
127. Ibid.
128. Ibid., 3 July 1947.
129. *PT*, 24 August 1947.
130. *CMG*, 1 July 1947.
131. *The Tribune*, 14 July 1947.
132. Ibid.
133. *HT*, 23 July 1947.
134. *CMG*, 12 August 1947.
135. For petrol shortage see letter of Krishan Mohan, *The Tribune*, 12 July; The District Magistrate Lahore ordered on 18 August that

no petrol would be issued to private persons without a permit from the office of the DM or SDM, *CMG*, 19 August; also *PT*, 19 August By the end of August Petrol was selling in Punjab for Rs. 8 per gallon, see *HT*, 30 August By comparing the price of gold and petrol (1947) the price of petrol in todays terms would be about Rs. 480 per litre and that too on permits.

136. *The Tribune*, 26 July 1947.
137. Ibid., 3 August 1947.
138. *The Tribune* 5 July, 1947; Din Mohammad of Kot Abdullah Shah Mozang, *PT*, 30 and 31 July 1947; *The Tribune*, 14 July 1947.
139. *CMG*, 30 August 1947.
140. *HT*, 11 July, 1947.
141. *HT*, 24 July 1947.
142. *Dawn*, 9 August 1947.
143. CMG, 9 August 1947; *The Tribune*, 29 July 1947.
144. *PT*, 24 July 1947; *Dawn*, 24 July 1947, *The Tribune*, 25 July 1947.
145. *The Tribune*, 14 July 1947.
146. Ibid., 5 August 1947.
147. Ibid., 7 August 1947.
148. Ibid., 2 August 1947.
149. *CMG*, 27 July 1947.
150. *The Tribune*, 11 August 1947.
151. *CMG*, 17 July 1947.
152. *The Tribune*, 19 July 1947.
153. *CMG*, 3 July 1947.
154. Ibid., 20 July 1947; *The Tribune*, 20 July 1947; *HT*, 21 July 1947.
155. *The Tribune*, 20 July 1947.
156. *HT*, 24 July 1947; CMG, 24 July 1947.
157. *Dawn*, 17 July 1947.
158. *CMG*, 30 July 1947.
159. *Dawn*, 13 July 1947 for example.
160. *Dawn* 11 and 19 July 1947.
161. *HT*, 2 July 1947.
162. *The Tribune*, 3 August 1947; *HT*, 3 August 1947; *PT*, 3 August 1947.
163. *HT*, 3 August 1947; *The Tribune*, 3 August 1947.
164. *HT*, 21 July 1947.
165. *Dawn*, 12 August 1947.
166. *PT*, 22 July; *The Tribune*, 23 July 1947.
167. *TP*, XII (258), Viceroy's Personal Report, 25 July 1947, p. 334.
168. *PT*, 26 July 1947.
169. *Dawn*, 11 August 1947.
170. *CMG*, 1 August 1947.
171. *Dawn*, 10 August 1947; also *PT*, 10 August 1947.
172. *PT*, 10 August 1947.

173. Charles C. Trench, *The Indian Army 1900–47*, Hudson 1988, p. 293; R. Jeffrey, 'The Punjab Boundary Force and the Problem of Order August 1947', pp. 511–12.
174. *TP*, vol. XII (228), Viceroy's Personal Report No. 14, 25 July 1947, p. 334.
175. *HT*, 31 July 1947.
176. *PT*, 24 July 1947.
177. *The Tribune*, 27 July 1947.
178. Ibid., 2 July 1947; S. Kapoor (Patiala), *The Tribune*, 16 July 1947.
179. *Dawn*, 24 July 1947.
180. Ibid., 2 August 1947.
181. *The Tribune*, 25 July 1947.
182. *CMG*, 8 August 1947; *Dawn*, 8 August 1947, *The Tribune*, 8 August 1947, *HT*, 8 August 1947.
183. *PT*, 8 August 1947; *Dawn*, 8 August 1947.
184. *CMG*, 10 August 1947.
185. Ibid., 12 August 1947.
186. *Dawn*, 2 August 1947.
187. *CMG*, 13 August 1947; *The Tribune*, 13 August 1947.
188. *CMG*, 20 July 1947.
189. *HT*, 4 August 1947; *The Tribune*, 13 August 1947.
190. *The Tribune*, 8 August 1947; *CMG*, 8 August 1947; *HT*, 8 August 1947.
191. *PT*, 10 August 1947. Also see *HT*, 10 August 1947.
192. *Dawn*, 12 August 1947.
193. *HT*, 12 August 1947.
194. Ibid., 7 August 1947.
195. *PT*, 8 August 1947; *HT*, 9 August 1947.
196. *CMG*, 24 July 1947.
197. *PT*, 24 July 1947.
198. *HT*, 18 July 1947.
199. *CMG*, 9 August 1947.
200. Ibid., 5 August; Ahmad Shafi, ibid., 8 August 1947.
201. *PT*, 3 August 1947.
202. Das, *Fateful Events*, p. 283; *PT*, 10 August 1947.
203. *TP*, vol. XII (302),1 August 1947, pp. 451–2.
204. *PT*, 1 August 1947; *The Tribune*, 1 and 3 August 1947.
205. *The Tribune*, 3 August 1947.
206. *TP*, vol. XII (292), Jenkins to Mountbatten, 30 July 1947, pp. 426, 427.
207. Bali, *Now It Can Be Told*, p. 35.
208. *HT*, 2 July 1947.
209. Ibid., 8 July 1947.
210. As already noted, the Maharaja of Patiala had conveyed to Mountbatten a similar view about the Maharaja of Faridkot, see *TP*,

vol. X (184), Record of Interview Mountbatten with Patiala, 20 April 1947.

211. *HT*, 9 July 1947; *Dawn*, 9 July 1947.
212. *Dawn*, 13 July 1947.
213. *The Tribune*, 1 July 1947.
214. Ibid., 7 July 1947.
215. *Dawn*, 27 July 1947.
216. *HT*, 14 July 1947; *Dawn*, 14 July 1947.
217. *HT*, 20 July 1947.
218. *HT*, 24 July 1947; *The Tribune*, 24 July 1947; *PT*, 24 July 1947, *CMG*, 24 July 1947.
219. *HT*, 27 July 1947.
220. Ibid., 2 August 1947.
221. *CMG*, 31 July 1947.
222. *CMG*, 25 July 1947.
223. *TP*, vol. XII (267) Enclosure to 267, 29 July 1947, p. 395; IOR Mss. Eur. R/3/1/176, p. 81; *PT*, 8 August 1947.
224. *TP*, vol. XII (276), Minutes of the Provisional Joint Defence Council, 29 July 1947, p. 403.
225. Also see *HT*, 25 July 1947; *Tribune*, 26 July 1947; and *CMG*, 26 July 1947.
226. See *Tribune*, 5 August 1947; *PT*, 5 August 1947; *Dawn*, 5 August 1947.
227. *Dawn*, 5 August 1947.
228. *HT*, 10 August 1947; *PT*, 10 August 1947; *Dawn*, 10 August 1947; John Masters, *The Road Past Mandlay*, p. 285, cited in Robin Jeffrey, 'The Punjab Boundary Force and the Problem of Order August 1947', p. 498, Alan Campbell Johnson, *Mission with Mountbatten* (Bombay, 1951), p. 148.
229. *HT*, 25 July 1947.
230. *The Tribune*, 27 July 1947; *CMG*, 27 July 1947.
231. *Dawn*, 28 July 1947.
232. *TP*, vol. XII (256), Minutes of Viceroy's Sixty-Fifth Meeting, 28 July 1947, p. 373.
233. *Statesman*, 28 July 1947; *The Tribune*, 28 July 1947; *Dawn*, 28 July 1947.
234. *TP*, vol. XII (250), Viceroy's Conference, 27 July 1947, p. 369.
235. Ibid. (306), 1 August 1947, p. 459.
236. Ibid. (305).
237. The statement was credited to *Statesman*, 28 July 1947, see *TP*, vol. XII (298), Lord Ismay to Mountbatten, 31 July 1947, p. 439, n. 4.
238. *Tribune*, 30 July 1947; *PT*, 31 July 1947.
239. *TP*, vol. XII (382), Jenkins to Mountbatten, 8 August 1947, pp. 583, 584.
240. *The Tribune*, 29 July 1947.

241. *PT*, 1 August 1947.
242. Ibid., 5 August 1947; *PT*, 14 August 1947.
243. *HT*, 5 August 1947.
244. *TP*, vol. XII (448), 12 August 1947, p. 688.
245. *CMG*, 24 July 1947.
246. *PT*, 8 August 1947.
247. Ibid., 10 August 1947.
248. G.D. Khosla Papers, File no. 15, NMML, CID Note, East Punjab, March to June 1947.
249. *The Tribune*, 28 July 1947.
250. Ibid., 30 July 1947.
251. Ibid., 3 August 1947.
252. Ibid., 30 July 1947.
253. *Dawn*, 2 August 1947.
254. *The Tribune*, 4 August 1947.
255. *PT*, 2 August 1947.
256. *The Tribune*, 5 August 1947; *CMG*, 5 August 1947; *Dawn*, 5 August 1947.
257. *CMG*, 25 July 1947.
258. *HT*, 3 August; *The Tribune*, 2 and 4 August 1947; *PT*, 2 August 1947.
259. *HT*, 5 August 1947.
260. *The Tribune*, 4 August 1947; *CMG*, 5 August 1947; *Dawn*, 2 August 1947.
261. Ibid., 8 August 1947.
262. Ibid., 9 August 1947.
263. *CMG*, 5 and 12 August 1947.
264. *HT*, 7 August 1947.
265. Ibid., 11 August 1947.
266. Ibid., 12 August 1947.
267. *CMG*, 14 August 1947.
268. *HT*, 15 August 1947.
269. *TP*, vol. XII (437), pp. 674–5.
270. Ibid., pp. 537–8.
271. *TP*, vol. XII (403), p. 636.
272. *PT*, 14 August 1947.
273. *TP*, vol. XII (459), pp. 700–1; W.H.A. Rich, IOR Mss., Eur. D. 1065, Misc. Police Material (Secret).
274. Ibid., p. 701; *TP*, vol. XII (432), Note by Maj. Gen. D.C. Hawthorn, 11 August 1947, p. 667.
275. Ibid., XII (459), p. 701.
276. *CMG*, 19 August 1947. A small classified announced Jenkins' death on 3 November 1985 at the age of 90. He was cremated at the Putney Vale Crematorium. In his last days he was looked after by his devoted Italian housekeeper, W.H.A. Rich Papers, IOR Mss. Eur. D 1065/1, file relating to Jenkins' letters to Rich.

277. *The Tribune*, 6 August 1947.
278. *TP*, vol. XII (468), Note by Auchinleck, 15 August 1949, p. 734.
279. *The Tribune*, 6 August 1947.
280. *HT*, 14 August 1947.
281. *Dawn*, 14 and 15 August 1947. Das has given some very interesting details on the protocol requirements of ceremonies, particularly the seating arrangements in Karachi, see *Fateful Events*, pp. 448–9. Mountbatten too has recorded some interesting details of the events in Karachi: 'I sat between Miss Jinnah and Begum Liaqat Ali. They pulled my leg about the mid night ceremonies in Delhi saying it was astounding that a responsible government could be guided by astrologers. . . . ' Mountbatten also noted that he barely managed to refrain from retorting and reminding the ladies that: 'the whole Karachi programme had to be changed from lunch to dinner because Jinnah while finalising the bauquet programme had forgotten it was Ramzan . . . ', IORL/PO/6 123, Pt. 3, Viceroys Personal Report, no. 17, 16 August 1947. Initially the lunch in Karachi had been planned to enable guests to fly back to Delhi from Karachi on the same day.
282. *The Tribune*, 3 August 1947.
283. Ibid., 4 August 1947.
284. *Dawn*, 2 August 1947.
285. *The Tribune*, 9 August 1947.
286. Ibid., 2 August 1947; *Dawn*, 1 August 1947.
287. *CMG*, 12 August 1947.
288. *Tribune*, 9 August 1947; also see his appeal of 6 August 1947; *The Tribune*, 7 August 1947.
289. *The Tribune*, 12 August 1947.
290. *HT*, 22 July 1947.
291. Ibid.; *Dawn*, 14 August 1947.
292. *CMG*, 6 August 1947.
293. IOR Mss. Eur. F/164/16–17, Muddie Collection.
294. IOR MP File no. 161-A, Microfilm, Reel no. 15557; ibid, Various Conference Papers, no. 132; Das, *Fateful Events*, pp. 440–1; *PT*, 23 July 1947.
295. IOR MP File no. 161-A, Viceroy's Conference Papers, no. 132.
296. IOR 161/B, Viceregal Official Correspondence—Transfer of Power Ceremonies, Reel no. 15557.
297. *TP* (446), vol. XII, *HT*, 15 August 1947.
298. *The Tribune*, 7 August 1947.
299. *HT*, 15 August 1947.
300. *The Tribune*, 9 August 1947.
301. *CMG*, 13 August 1947.
302. This appears to have been written in response to a query of Nehru, or so it seems from the tone of the letter, see *TP*, vol. XII (454), Mountbatten to Nehru, 14 August 1947; pp. 693–4. Tinker has

made an interesting observation in this context: 'It appears that the Viceroy did not wish the Award to be published before independence; indeed he took steps to ensure that the Award was not released until after the actual transfer was formally effected . . .', see his 'Pressure, Persuasion . . . Factors in the Partition of Punjab', p. 698.

303. *TP*, vol. XII (428), Ismay to Liaqat Ali, 11 August 1947, p. 662.
304. IOR Mss. Eur. C. 645. Also see V.N. Datta's 'Interpreting Partition.' Datta notes that the Radcliffe Award almost corresponded with the detailed demarcation of the boundary made by Wavell on 7 February 1946, which he communicated to Pethick-Lawerence, p. 278. Also Datta's reference to *TP*, vol. VII (410). Reference has earlier been made to a file known as Transfer of Power Viceroy's Plan, which includes two rough maps that clearly indicate that senior functionaries in London had a clear idea of where the final line of demarcation was to be drawn, see IOR L/PO/120(i).
305. Tinker, 'Factors in the Partition of Punjab', p. 700.
306. *PT*, 19 August 1947. For complete details/statement of the PBC Award see *PT*, 19 August 1947.
307. *Dawn*, 18 August 1947.
308. Ibid. While extensive coverage was given to the flaws in the Award, Radcliffe's version of the problems was also well covered. See for example, Roserberger and Tobin, *Keesings Contemporary Archives*, p. A8813.
309. *CMG*, 20, 22 and 23 July 1947.
310. *HT*, 18 August 1947; also *CMG*, 19 August 1947.
311. *Dawn*, 18 August 1947; also *CMG*, 19 August 1947.
312. Ibid., 21 August 1947; Spate Papers, Diary entry, August 1947—date not clear, p. 67, CSAS.
313. *HT*, 19 August 1947.
314. Ibid., 20 August 1947.
315. *CMG*, 20 August 1947; also *HT*, 19 August 1947.
316. Ibid., *PT*, 21 August 1947.
317. *HT*, 19 August 1947.
318. *CMG*, 19 August 1947.
319. Ibid., 21 August 1947.
320. *PT*, 19 August 1947.
321. *Dawn*, 19 August 1947.
322. Ibid., 22 August 1947.
323. *CMG*, 22 August 1947.
324. Ibid., 24 August 1947.
325. Ibid., 20 July 1947.
326. *TP*, vol. XII (302), Viceroy's Personal Report, 1 August 1947, p. 444.
327. I.M. Stephens Papers, Box I, CSAS.

5

Taken Unawares: Punjab Pays the Price

August 15: Lahore

In lesser [sic] time than it takes to partition a small family property among real brothers, the partition of two big provinces of India and of the assets and liabilities of such a big continent as India was attempted to be done. The fateful day arrived. . . . In obedience to the orders of the High Command the Congress rulers of East Punjab also issued an order for illuminations, flag hoisting and feasting while the Punjab was profusely bleeding. . . . But no sooner was the order given than it was countermanded. The East Punjab government . . . realised the enormity of the crime they would be committing against their own people by adhering to this programme.[1]

On 15 August 1947, the front page of the *HT* carried a photograph of Jawaharlal Nehru delivering the 'Tryst with Destiny' address, just below it was another small headline reporting that 50 people had been killed in Lahore on the preceding day.[2] The following day the paper reported that 200 Hindu and Sikh bodies were lying in the verandah of Mayo Hospital in Lahore because there was no one to cremate them.[3]

The *CMG* reported that by 19 August, of Lahore's normal population of 300,000 Hindus and Sikhs less than 10,000 remained.[4] By a queer chance of fate or coincidence perhaps, Sardar Ajit Singh who had all along opposed the partition of Punjab and India died in Dalhousie at about the same time that Gopichand Bhargava and his collegues were being sworn in as ministers in Independent India's East Punjab government.[5] The death of Ajit Singh having come almost as an ironic pointer towards the disaster that Punjab was soon to meet.

In the days that followed many questioned whether in the context of Punjab independence and its dimensions had any significance. One such view was published by the *PT* on 6 September:

When prestige has been shattered and faith in justice destroyed no authority can survive. This is what has happened in Punjab. The initial mistake was to concentrate Muslim officers in West Punjab and non Muslims in the East Punjab . . . after the Award (PBC) town upon town was purged. . . . Even the beast of belsen will turn in his grave at what has happened . . . what self determination—what independence—what freedom?[6]

From both sides there were appeals for peace as well as announcements that the government was determined to firmly handle the situation. Master Tara Singh's appeal for peace was widely welcomed by the League. Mamdot reciprocated and Jinnah too issued a passionate appeal through Radio Pakistan: 'Let us impress the minorities with words, deeds and thoughts.'[7] On his part Nehru also sought to 'put an end to all internal strife'.[8]

NEHRU MEETS LIAQAT ALI IN AMBALA

On 17 August, a high-powered meeting between India and Pakistan took place at the Circuit House in Ambala. Among the many leader present were Nehru, Liaqat Ali, Baldev Singh, Trivedi and Francis Muddie, the Governors of East and West Punjab respectively, the premiers of the two Punjabs, Bhargava and Mamdot and many senior police and other officials including T.W. Rees, Commander of the Punjab Boundary Force.[9]

Following the meeting, on 18 August 1947 a joint statement was released to the press from Lahore by Nehru and Liaqat Ali saying that, 'arrangements have been made to put down firmly all elements of disorder,' and that, 'if disorders continue in an area it will be considered a failure of the area's officers'. The leaders assured the field officers that their actions of firm handling would be fully supported. They also appealed to the public to forget the past and that 'we are confident that the measures which have now been initiated will succeed indeed a marked change for the better is already noticeable.'[10]

A joint statement by ministers of the East and West Punjab, signed by Mamdot, Bhargava, Karmat Ali and Swarn Singh was also carried prominently by most newspapers on 19 and 20 August: 'we have set up a machinery for the closest co-operation . . . we appeal to all to let old wounds heal . . . help in the establishment of peace and security. Peace in one part of the province is linked with peace in the other'.[11] The statement went on to say: 'we are determined to put down disorder and to this end we shall adopt every step open to us . . . no government worthy of the name can tolerate such lawlessness . . . whatever the cost peace and order will be restored'.[12]

On the night of 19 August, Nehru delivered an address over All India Radio. In this broadcast he discussed the decisions that had been taken in the Ambala conference and gave assurances that the orgy of violence would be brought under control. Interestingly, he also said that while the government would assist those who wished to migrate, it would not encourage people to come to East Punjab.[13]

The most significant appeal, one which was expected to have a greater impact in Punjab came as a response to a request made by Rees to Giani Kartar Singh and Master Tara Singh. Rees asked the two to tour the region and appeal for peace, something which both of them did earnestly.[14] In fact, Kartar Singh not only toured Kasur but also met Premier Mamdot and Quarban Ali, Inspector General of Police, West Punjab, and urged them to avoid the bloodshed.[15] In a press report, Kartar Singh was said to have asked Sikh organizations to send telegrams to leaders in Delhi to urge them to reserve 33.5 per cent of Legislative Assembly seats and 6 per cent of Central Assembly seats in East Punjab for them. On the following day, newspapers also reported an appeal for peace signed by 11 leading Akalis.[16] The government's determination to control the Punjab was further stressed by East Punjab Governor, Trivedi, who told an API reporter in Simla on 21 August that he would 'not return to Simla until normal conditions are restored . . . I am shifting to Jullundur with a skeleton staff.'[17]

In Delhi, the Union Cabinet met in an emergency meeting on 21 August. The official statement that followed mentioned various measures, but more importantly, it said: 'the situation though grave in certain areas is improving and being brought under control'.[18] But for reasons that have not been adequately explained the Cabinet decided on changing the command of troops from British officers to Indian officers, literally in midstream.[19] This decision had far-reaching implications and served only to further demoralize the people on both sides in the disturbed districts because the issue was not of competence but of faith, which, in the Punjab of 1947 was deeply on community basis.

ADMINISTRATION HAS DISAPPEARED—16 AND 17 AUGUST: LAHORE

Two staff reporters of the *HT* were in the Lahore and Amritsar region on 15 and 16 August. One of the reporters noted that he was warned by a policemen not to stop his car even if a lone, harmless-looking man waved for help. This correspondent reported that the early trouble started in rural areas mainly in a village near Hoshiarpur, where a group of people had forced a person from another community to part with a religious symbol. The same report also gave another version—that refugees from the Rawalpindi area had spread stories of destruction in the villages around Hoshiarpur.

The second report filed from Lahore quoted officers that the trouble in Lahore was mainly due to the dual control of the army and the police. In fact, the reporter said that in Lahore there had been a series of clashes between the troops and the police and in some cases the police had even led the rioting mobs. The report went on to say that senior officers were of the view that if the army was given a free hand, order could be restored in 48 hours. Describing the situation in Lahore on 15 and 16 August, the report said that the administration had disappeared and fully armed gangs had taken over the streets. More than 100 people were killed on 15 August.[20]

Incidents of holding up trains looting, killing and the abduction of passengers had occurred intemitently earlier, but after 17 of August, they had become almost routine all over the region. Arson and killings were widely reported to have occurred on 16 and 17 August from places like Harnal near Rawalpindi, in a village near Ambala 30 were killed; and another village near Ludhiana was eliminated.[21]

The swearing in of Francis Muddie as Governor of West Punjab on 16 August was almost a symbol of the times. Even as the swearing in was in progress, in the background were heard loud noises of firing, and screaming, and fires were visible with the sky over Lahore black with smoke.[22] By 18 August Lahore had been overrun by an orgy of violence. Shops had been looted in broad daylight, the looted goods in many cases being buried in specially dug holes to evade detection by the police.[23] A helpless Zaffarul Hasan, the Deputy Commissioner, admitted to the new trend of daylight looting and appealed to owners of houses and shops to return, saying he would ensure that possession was returned to them.[24] The great panic that spread over Lahore, particularly on 17 and 18 August, was also

This cartoon explains to a considerable extent the grounds for the anarchical conditions that prevailed in the days leading to and following the transfer of power (*Shankar's Weekly*, 1 August 1947).

reportedly the result of accounts given by uprooted families from both sides—the Muslims from the East Punjab flaring up things in Lahore and the Hindus and Sikhs from the western districts doing the same in Amritsar.[25]

COMPLETE ANARCHY PREVAILS

By the beginning of the third week of August there was complete anarchy in Punjab. It did not take much to incite mobs to put whole towns to flame. In Quetta, for example, some Muslims, possibly League workers, wanted to hoist a flag (Pakistan) on the mosque. Some Pathan youths appear to have objected. The quarrel soon engulfed the whole town—over 30 people were killed within an hour and about 40 were seriously injured. H.A. Oliver, the Superintendent of Police (Multan), was in Quetta on short leave. While trying to help the local officers he too was seriously injured.[26] There was extensive violence in Ambala, Lahore, Ferozepur, Gurgaon and Amritsar.[27] On 21 and 22 August, *PT* carried headlines describing the savagery in rural areas. On 21 August a spokesman of the East Punjab government in a statement from Simla said that most towns of West Punjab had witnessed serious riots and that Muslim police officers were widely involved.[28] 'Not a day passes when the outrages of yesterday are outdone . . . the bloodbath in the western side of the border rivals in fierceness and intensity that on the east. In rural areas it is limited only by the availability of victims.'[29]

The *HT* Punjab Newsletter reported that in the preceding ten days over 3,000 people had been killed in Lahore alone. This *HT* report is important because it is perhaps the only known 'immediately contemporary' account which has tried to discuss answers to questions that were asked in 1947, and continue to be raised even today—why did people who stayed back, particularly, in Lahore not leave when there was still time? The impression gathered by the correspondent was that most of those who stayed back in Lahore and its neighbouring areas did so in the hope that once the PBF troops were deployed they would be safe. But as time proved there were simply not enough troops for such deployment.[30]

Heavy loss of life and property was reported from Jullundur, Gujranwala, Quetta, and Moga. The *HT* gave details of how the violence had started in Sialkot, peaking on 14 and 15 August. People of the minority communities (Hindus/Sikhs) had initially shown resistance, but soon gave up, with every single *dharamshala* and religious place being burnt down. This report also cited how some police officers had openly celebrated the violence with League workers.[31]

RAJKUMARI AMRIT KAUR ON SIALKOT

Rajkumari Amrit Kaur also described an incident in the larger tragedy that engulfed the beautiful and moneyed town of Sialkot. On 26 August a convoy of 60 vehicles escorted by Brigadier Coolier left the town. Ironically this escort which was comprised totally of Muslim troops was under the command of a British officer. For some reason the British officer was under orders to return to Sialkot after a particular stretch of the journey had been completed. When this convoy reached the river Ravi, most of the drivers disappeared on and when they returned after two hours they were accompanied by a mob of over 1,000 armed people. A lathatthatrge number of people of the convoy were killed. Amrit Kaur said that she and Lady Moutbatten had seen the battered convoy entering Amritsar and Lady Mountbatten herself counted 13 dead bodies which the families were still carrying, most of the other bodies had earlier been thrown into the Ravi.[32]

A NARROW ESCAPE

The anarchy that had come to prevail in most of East Punjab and the whole of West Punjab came very near to securing an ironical symbol. It so happened that Sardar Baldev Singh (Defence Minister) and two Brigadiers Thorat and Thimayya were touring some highly disturbed rural areas of Amritsar. A patrol of the East Punjab Additional Police mistook them for raiders and opened fire on the them.[33]

REFUGEES RUSH TO DELHI

As Muslim refugees reaching Lahore from the eastern districts had begun forcibly occupying houses and shops in cities like Lahore, so were the Hindus and Sikhs displaced from the western districts in Delhi. The situation resulting from the inflow of refugees into Delhi had reached such a critical stage that by 27 August authorities in Delhi had to announce that no more refugees would be allowed into Delhi the city had already taken in 120,000 people.[34] The Deputy

Commissioner of Delhi even issued a stern warning to refugees from the western districts 'not to misuse the hospitality of the Delhi people by spreading their harrowing tales and provoking people'.[35] Another report gave details of how Delhi was choked with refugees, with the cafes and restaurants all full, the postal system in collapse and food prices shooting up by a hundred per cent in a week.[36]

By the end of August there were six major camps in Delhi, which, it was reported, were being run on strictly communal lines,[37] as the city also had a large number of Muslim refugees from the Gurgaon area. *Dawn* reported that the Id prayer at Jama Masjid was attended by over 300,000 people.[38] In comparison about 300,000 refugees had reached Lahore from the eastern districts by the same date.[39]

SIMLA UNDER REFUGEE PRESSURE

The *HT* newsletter of 31 August reported that about 10,000, mostly well-to-do refugees had reached Simla in the fortnight following 15 August. These families rented whatever little space was available and at whatever price. Since their resources were far in excess of what the local residents had at their disposal they were reported to have stocked up supplies of edible items, sending price up within a week. The report went on to say that 'after 2 p.m. provided the weather was clear, these well heeled, colourfully dressed people could be seen on the Mall killing time discussing what they had left behind'.

MUSLIM OFFICIALS DESERT EAST PUNJAB

Many reports gave details of how Muslim officials posted in various eastern districts had deserted and left for West Punjab. Their sudden departure particularly from police positions only added to the plight of the Muslims who were left behind. The Dalhousie massacre for one would certainly have been avoided if even a handful of Muslim constables had been around.

Jalil Kharir wrote that the administration was simply non-existent and jungle raj was all that prevailed. He pointed out how Muslim officials had left in search of more important postings in the West. The ordinary Muslims, he added, 'had been turned into a minority by a sheer freak of history'.[40]

There were extensive reports of violence from rural areas in the central districts. The *PT* had started a special column, called 'Refugee Corner' to highlight problems and situations encountered by people who came into the West from East Punjab and the Delhi areas. On 30 August, for example, it reported that a village in Batala had been surrounded by raiders and when some villagers managed to flee and approach a police station, four policemen on guard at the station possibly mistaking them for raiders opened fire killing a large number of Muslims in the process.

The situation was as bad in the towns and villages of Ambala District. A 20-hour curfew was imposed in Ambala after major riots in the Sadar Bazar area on 30 August. Troops had also to open fire to control rioting mobs in Jagadhri. In Dehradun, curfew was imposed to check riots on 30 August.[41]

CARNAGE ON TRAINS

The governments on both sides could do little but admit, as an official statement put it that 'there have been increasingly dastardly attacks on trains'. The PBF wanted the railways on both sides to cut down the number of trains as most of the casualities in the moving trains were people travelling from east to west or west to east.[42] But of course, the governments could not possibly reduce the number of trains, on the contrary, there was an effort to put in as many new trains as possible. The West Punjab government in fact restricted the movement of goods trains to put the available bogies into passenger use. A system was even drawn to exchange crews of trains as they entered each other's territories. This was necessitated because the crews refused to drive trains across the border.[43]

On 31 August, *CMG* gave brief details of some of the train hold ups, while discussing the tragedy that had befallen Sialkot: 'There was complete chaos in Sialkot on the 13, 14, 15 August. A train coming from Wazirabad was slaughtered all Hindus and Sikhs except 50 people who were seriously injured [*sic*] were killed . . . two more trains were targetted on 15 and 18 August and yet again another two trains were attacked on 25 August.'

The attach on the Sind Express started a new trend as attackers now not only killed for blood, but also to get rich. When the train reached Karachi, rioters were seen breaking open the luggage of the people who were lying dead in the bogies and on the platforms. The number of deaths in the attack would have been much more had it not been for the presence of mind of the driver of the express.[44]

While many engine drivers had performed heroic deeds charges of complicity were also made frequently. For example, in an editorial dedicated to the 'unsafety of rail travel', particularly on the Delhi–Bathinda route, the *PT* said that the Jaito train hold up was possible only because the driver and the guard, both being non-Muslims, intentionally held up the train for 45 minutes. The editorial advised the East Punjab authorities in whose area most of the hold ups it said were taking place to provide pilot engines.[45]

The charge that a large number of train attacks had taken place because of the complicity of railway staff was a serious one, made repeatedly at various levels, even in the highest body, the Emergency Committee Meetings. In fact, Swarn Singh, Home Minister East Punjab made a note of this in one such meeting on 29 September, saying that time schedules of trains were conveyed in advance to raiding parties.[46] The issue was also taken up, as we shall see later, by East Punjab Governor, Trivedi.

Trains were the only convenient mode of transport, therefore newspapers continued to advise people that: 'no railway passenger is safe . . . special risk to Muslims', particularly on the Lahore–Delhi route.[47] *Dawn* suggested in an editorial that to make trains safe villages in the areas where trains carnages too place should be held collectively responsible.[48]

After the initial savagery services between Lahore and Delhi were suspended for a few days, but so great was the pressure on both sides that they were resumed on 26 August, with five refugee specials being organized on the same day.[49] As train tracks got overcrowded, goods movement was restricted, adding to the problem of the shortage of supplies, which was further compounded by the severe shortage of coal to drive the trains.[50]

The extreme shortage of coal in the West Punjab greatly added to the problem not only in the movement of passenger trains but also of goods. The crisis had begun to develop from the moment partition was enforced. As most of the Pakistan area's coal came from the Bengal fields, the supply was completely disrupted. A.G. Hall, Director General of Railways in Pakistan, had to personally visit Delhi[51] to sort out the problems. The visit does not appear to have helped. The daily requirement of coal in Pakistan, mainly for the railways, was estimated at 2,100 tonnes, whereas the available supply was only of around 400 tonnes.[52] The problem was so serious that a large number of trains had to be cancelled.[53]

NEHRU'S SINCERITY NOT IN DOUBT

In an interesting editorial in its 28 August issue, *Dawn* said that the holocaust was limited only to East Punjab:

> Today is the 15th day of the East Punjab holocaust and still it goes on. . . . The Boundary Force have failed to control it . . . the Government of India have not effectively intervened, the East Punjab Government have failed to discharge duties . . . it is a grave situation . . . there is no abiding profit to any side in this business of butchery . . . we do not doubt Nehru's personal sincerity . . . (but he) must rise above political antipathy. . . . These possible horrors can be averted by stern action today . . . any Muslim who thinks he will be avenging his compatriots in East Punjab by counter violence will be really stabbing Pakistan.

Nehru landed at Adampur air base in pouring rain on 24 August. There was so much water on the air strip that he had to walk through knee deep water to reach the motor transport that had been arranged for him.[54] While speaking to reporters at Jullundur he said the only way to stop killings of Hindus and Sikhs in the West was to protect minorities in the East Punjab.[55] But it is the other point that he raised both at Jullundur and in the evening on the same day in Amritsar that left people surprised: 'I am not in favour of whole scale migration . . . it is not in the interest of most people to be uprooted from the soil.'[56] For one, the statement revealed how little the powers in Delhi appeared to have understood or foreseen the road Punjab was taking.

What was surprising, however was that while senior leaders were saying that they did not wish to 'uproot' people, at the same time in Delhi great haste was being shown in arranging for the transport 20,000 Meos from Delhi to Bhawalpur (Pakistan). These Meos had moved into Delhi following the disturbances in the Mewat region. In fact, it was decided to arrange seven trains and also to request the Nawab of Bhawalpur to make arrangements to receive the Meos. The decision followed a statement by Health Minister Rajkumari Amrit Kaur that the Meos were in fact subjects of the princely states of Bharatpur and Alwar and as such their health could not be guaranteed.[57] The keenness to rid Delhi of the Meos was also influenced by reports that some Meo youths were causing law and order problems in Delhi.

But coming back to Nehru's visit to Amritsar, as a result of a meeting between him, Giani Kartar Singh and Master Tara Singh (what transpired at the meeting is not clear), an appeal for peace was issued on 27 August by eight prominent Sikh leaders including the Giani and the Master as well as Udham Singh Nagoke.[58] Another result of Nehru's visit to Amritsar appears to have been the tough warning issued by the East Punjab government to field officers that failure to curtail the disturbances would be a reflection of their professional competence,[59] and possibly also the decision of the Joint Defence Council to reduce the area under the control of the PBF to make it more effective.[60]

LEADERS APPEAL FOR PEACE

The last week of August saw a flood of appeals and statements from leaders of both the sides. Shaukat Hayat said that since Pakistan had been achieved it was the duty of all, particularly Muslims living in Pakistan, to restore peace.[61] The Quaid-i-Azam himself went on record saying: 'Pakistan should be kept free from disorders. . . . I have watched with increasing grief the orgies of violence in East Punjab. . . I appeal to Muslims to temper sentiment with reason and not retaliate.'[62]

The once highly provocative Firoze Khan Noon also issued a statement on the 30 August: 'If you want to preserve the freedom you have won I want you to make a solemn promise that today you will stop fighting against Hindus. . . . We are at peace with the Hindus all over India.'[63]

A statement for peace was also issued in the third week by Gandhi who was then in Calcutta.[64] The problem in Punjab was that while leaders with all their good intentions were appealing for peace, measures to enforce it were hardly evident. The *CMG* in an editorial asked important leaders to forget about giving statements and instead initiate action on the 'ground'.[65]

The 'ground' situation was portrayed in a letter by the manager of the Gurudwara Sri Panja Sahib (Hasanabad) Cambellpur, to Master Tara Singh. In fact, the letter was sent through the office of the Commander-in-Chief of the Pakistan Army. It said: 'The disturbances in East Punjab have seriously perturbed the Muslims on this side . . . it was natural for them to have thought of reprisals . . . if this happens you can imagine the plight of over 100,000 Hindus and Sikhs in the region.'[66]

MUCH TALK BUT LITTLE ACTION

Somewhat harsh no doubt, but one G.W. Barrett (Lahore) conveyed the anguish and pain of ordinary people: 'The leaders glibly talk of birth pangs . . . none of them has had a prick from a dagger nor anything other than the finest material against their abdomen . . . the moneyed have left long ago, only the ordinary remain, it is they who are being slaughtered.'[67]

There were others too, who felt that there was indeed too much talking, assurances and the like but little action. Nazir Ahmad wrote to *CMG*, that Nehru must stop saying 'we must do this', 'we must do that', and just try to restore peace in East Punjab, this would immediately be reciprocated by peace in the West, making the resettlement effort much easier.[68]

Even in New Delhi there was concern that people might begin to believe that the tragedy unfolding in Punjab was being largely ignored. Algurai Sastri even raised the issue in the Constituent Assembly, when it met to observe a minute's silence in memory of those who had died in Punjab: 'It should not be said', he commented in the Assembly, 'that we were fiddling when Rome was burning.'[69]

There were reports that many Hindus were inclined to stay on in the western Punjab if things could be made safer. Karmat Ali, a minister in the West Punjab government, in fact, quoted some people in the Sialkot camp who wished to remain provided people in the East Punjab stopped attacking the Muslims.[70]

NEHRU'S FIRST MAJOR PRESS CONFERENCE

Nehru addressed a large press conference in New Delhi on 28 August. He started with the usual appeal—not to retaliate as retaliation was making things impossible. He then appealed to the press to show restraint: 'A great deal depends on how the press says and what it says.'[71] He then took up the touchy issue of who was to blame: 'it is easy to go into past history and trace the cause of what has happened and is happening . . . that (this) history will not be complimentary to those who are condemning the East Punjab. That (this) history began in any case six months ago in Rawalpindi and Multan it never really stopped . . . throughout the period there has been a ceaseless campaign of hatred and violence we saw the fruits of that six months ago and we are seeing the bitter fruits now'.[72]

Nehru also explained how retaliation was adding to the problems: 'retaliation is not the method; I am not talking of the moral aspect but the practical aspect, if there is to be retaliation it must be government retaliation and punishment which means war'. While briefly reviewing the situation up to 28 August, he said: 'The East Punjab had to start from scratch . . . the whole communication system—railway, telephone, telegraph, postal services everything was connected to Lahore . . . suddenly in the amidst of crisis the communication system broke down . . . Lahore did not help . . . every message had to go through Lahore. The West Punjab government had practically everything working.

He touched on the law and order situation: 'I can not speak much on the situation in the West Punjab, there is a complete black out of news. . . . At present the situation in the East Punjab is more under control than the West.'[73] He also dwelt on the problems being faced on a government-to-government level: 'we are not getting concurrence from Pakistan for many of our schemes'.[74]

When Nehru had visited Punjab on 24 August he had categorically stated that the government did not wish to encourage a mass exchange of population. With a mass exodus already having begun, the statement caused much amusement. By the time Nehru met the press in New Delhi on 28 August, he appears to have received some feedback of his Punjab visit. Therefore, in New Delhi he appeared more open to the problem: 'we have not been inclined to encourage mass migration . . . but things being what they are, a large exchange of population will take place'.[75] Nehru also dismissed reports that there was some friction between the central and the East Punjab government.[76]

The *PT* version also added the significant mention that Nehru had made of the violence in East Punjab being linked to people coming in from the princely states: 'Much of this railway business is probably due to bands coming out of the states . . . we are unable to get hold of them.'[77] This was happening because the princely states did not have proper control.[78]

On the loss of property Nehru said, 'the largest sufferers have been

Hindus and Sikhs. . . . In Lahore people are forcibly occupying houses owned by Hindus and Sikhs'. Interestingly Nehru distanced the present set-up of government from the problem and put the blame on the past—the British: 'We have not a shadow of doubt that what we are having today is the result of the past years activity.'[79] Nehru then went on to say that if there had to be an effort to put blame for the crisis 'let there be an analysis of what led to these happenings'.[80]

In this all-important press conference, Nehru also expressed unhappiness with the manner in which the foreign correspondents were exaggerating and mixing fact and fiction in their reports.[81]

The *Statesman* reported that 'Nehru looked tired and fatigued', and that his face was 'flushed with anger' when he talked of undue emphasis on accounts of the killings in East Punjab being given in the Pakistan press.[82]

Search Light, while appreciating Nehru's appeal to the press to be moderate, added that most newspapers did not need to add colour, the colour was already there, 'so ghastly were the tales from Punjab, the 'truth is so appalling'.[83] The *Free Press Journal* said that the PBF had been abolished because it had not been able to do the job expected of it and also because public opinion had wanted the disturbed areas to be handed over to other authorities.[84]

The Pioneer was less charitable to the Prime Minister. In a special editorial on the press conference it said that while Nehru discussed issues that were already known, 'when all is said and little is done, there still remain the minorities'.[85]

PAKISTAN TIMES REACTS TO NEHRU'S VIEWS

The *PT's* reaction to Nehru's statement that the July–August violence in Punjab was traceable to the March disturbances in Rawalpindi and Multan was sharp: 'Does he forget the sword brandishing ceremony and do or die orders that inaugurated the bloodiest chapter in the history of the Punjab? Never in the history of the sub-continent have millions owed their misery to so few individuals.' The editorial also questioned Nehru's views that a great part of the attack on trains was by 'gangs' 'from the princely states, and said that this was only a cover up for the failure of his own party.[86]

There were some others too who believed Nehru was incorrect in tracing the crisis to the Rawalpindi and Multan disturbances. Salamdin Khawaja (Lahore), wrote to the *CMG* saying that things had settled down after the Muslim League agitations of 1946 and early 1947. But the provocative demonstrations of Sikhs and Hindus in Lahore (Chowk Moti) and of Amritsar (Chowk Pragdas) were the immediate reasons for the killings of Rawalpindi and Multan.[87]

THE *TIMES* (LONDON) REPORTS

Although the objective of this narrative is not to dwell on the violence that rocked Punjab in August and September, an idea of what occurred would not be out of place. The *Times* (London), significantly biased against the Sikhs, no doubt, carried two reports within a few days, one dealing with how Sikhs *jathas* had mercilessly killed Muslims in the Eastern Punjab,[88] and the other relating to the massacre of Sikhs in the Sheikhupura region.[89]

The report, filed from Jullundur on 24 August, carried a bold banner: 'Muslims butchered by Armed Sikhs—Breakdown of Civil Administration'. It went on that as a reminder 'that this communal war is not one-sided, a train loaded with Sikhs refugees from West Punjab was attacked by a Muslim mob west of Ferozepur yesterday and arrived with 25 dead bodies on board and more than 100 passengers with stabbing wounds of varying degrees of seriousness'. The report described how, 'When the Punjab Mail train was derailed and attacked on Tuesday night by Sikh mobs east of Ferozepur, a valiant and successful defence was organized by two British passengers. They were Harington Hawes, secretary to the Agent for the Punjab States, and Maj. Rob Mayor, late of the Indian Political Service, who was on his way to Kashmir with his wife and daughter. After a long description of the defence, the *Times* said: 'There is no doubt that but for the presence of these two Britons the entire train load of passengers would have been massacred, as had occurred in several instances.'

The same report went on to narrate how the Sikh *jathas* operated:

> 'A thousand times more horrible than anything we saw during the war,' is the universal comment of experienced officers, British and Indian, on the present slaughter in East Punjab.[90] . . . The Sikhs *jathas*, armed mobs . . . assemble usually in the Gurdwaras . . . before making a series of raids. . . . The armament of a typical *jatha* consists of one or two firearms, army and home-made grenades, spears, axes, and *kirpans*—the Sikh sabres, which are also religious emblems. The Muslims are usually armed only with staves. . . . The Sikhs attack scientifically. A first wave armed with firearms fires to bring the Muslims off their roofs. A second wave lobs grenades over

the walls. In the ensuing confusion a third wave goes in with *kirpans* and spears, and the serious killing begins. A last wave consists of older men . . . who carry torches and specialise in arson. Mounted outriders with *kirpans* cut down those trying to flee.[91]

Mountbatten too made a similar note many months later while talking of the Sikh role in the violence: 'their long connection with the Army has served them well'.[92]

Major Clifford Williams, 11 Infantry Brigade, 4th Division, has also recorded how they saw bodies of women (along the G.T. Road) whose breasts had been cut: 'I gazed at the gruesome sight . . . a woman still alive with both breasts chopped off D.D. Wells of 7th Gurkha recorded gruesome sights near Dera Baba Nanak: 'women and children with intestines hanging out'.[93] No doubt some of the early brutal incidents in East Punjab, particularly the central districts, have been attributed by most contemporary sources to violent Sikh *jathas*, but, then, as Jeffrey has put it:

[I]t would be wrong indeed to suggest that the 'blame' for the horrors of partition rested solely on the Sikhs. Abandoned by the British, tolerated by the Congress, taunted by the Muslim League, and, above all, frustrated by the failures of their own political leadership, the Sikhs, until the month of August, were more sinned against than sinning. Towards the end of August, and in September and October, they were to suffer dreadfully from Muslim attacks in West Punjab, But for the first three weeks of August, the Sikhs led the Boundary Force on a grim chase through the rural areas of central and east Punjab, and imposed upon it a strain which became, both physically and morally unbearable.[94]

Interestingly, many years after he had left India Field Marshal Auchinleck in an interview by the BBC, made an observation which has not received adequate attention in the context of the early killings of Muslims in the border districts, a crisis allegedly started by Sikh *jathas*. Auchinleck said: 'The Sikhs may have started on the Muslims, but may be, it was some hill tribes,' who started the initial attacks.[95] In fact, the *Times* carried a report with a 4 September Lahore dateline which also said that some Baluch tribes had begun to invade the plains in the Dera Ismail Khan area with the sole objective of looting and plundering.[96]

But coming back to the balance in the killings, the same *Times* reporter was in Sheikhupura a couple of days later, and filed another report this time dealing with the manner of Muslim madness. The headlines of this report read, 'Sikhs slaughtered at Sheikhupura'. The report said that the small town of Sheikhupura 'with a population of half Muslim, half Sikh and Hindu had been regarded as one of the quietest in West Punjab. When the arrival of Muslim refugees caused tension to rise, the Deputy Commissioner persuaded the army to station a platoon of troops in the town. How the trouble started is not clear. However, an orgy of killing and burning suddenly began. Within 24 hours at least 800 people, nearly all Sikhs and Hindus, were brutally killed. Several hundred had been wounded and whole areas, Muslim as well as Sikh and Hindu, had been reduced to ashes.

One hundred and fity Sikhs were murdered in cold blood. 'Whatever the origins of the flare-up, the main aggression here was undoubtedly Muslim. Nearly all the troops were out in the country on patrol, and the Muslim police, far from trying to stop the trouble, actively helped the rioters'. The report also stated that

> [A]t a civil hospital there were no nurses, few drugs, and only two aged dispensers, with whom a Sikh doctor was trying to minister to 86 patients, some of them grievously wounded. Altogether 360 persons had passed through the hospital, but most had refused to stay, fearing that the Muslims might attack again. The stench was revolting, and flies swarmed thick upon the blood-clotted bandages and dirty rags that served as bandages. One four-year-old girl had two spear wounds in the stomach. Driving through the town we came to a *gurdwara* (Sikh temple) where several hundred Sikhs had shut themselves up in a state of complete panic, and were refusing to come out. They were afraid (probably with justification) of being shot down by the Muslim police who stood at either end of the street. Gradually as they realised that there were British officers and unarmed correspondents outside, they gained confidence, and before the afternoon was out, a beginning had been made with evacuating them to Lahore. I can say with truth that during this week in the Punjab I have supped full of horrors.[97]

Almost a month later, the *Times* summed up August and September in the Punjab:

> The magnitude of the crisis is unfortunately not open to doubt. The dire consequences resulting from this transfer of whole communities are not limited to the sufferings endured by the migrating millions . . . and to the economic dislocation which now threatens to invest the food shortage already menacing the whole Indian peninsula. . . . Wherever the refugees arrive they infect the inhabitants of the areas receiving them with a thirst for reprisals against the opposite community; and the resulting panic among the local minority in its turn sets a further stream of refugees in motion. As

these fugitives . . . painfully make their way by road and rail to the areas where they hope to find safety, they are often fiercely attacked and sometimes ruthlessly butchered by mobs whose communal passions blind them to every impulse except a vindictive lust for blood.[98]

COMMUNAL VIRUS IN THE ARMY: RAJKUMARI AMRIT KAUR

A day after Nehru's important meeting with the press in New Delhi, Rajkumari Amrit Kaur, India's Health Minister also held a press conference. This press conference is important because for the first time perhaps a senior functionary of the government of India went on record with the view that the 'Communal virus has entered the army—Muslim, Hindu and Sikh troops will not fire on people of their own communities.'[99] Amrit Kaur demanded that henceforth, for the safety of convoys, the community of the escorting troops be kept in mind. 'Armed units,' she said, 'were no doubt of mixed composition but still the fact remained that there were more Muslim troops in West Punjab than there were Sikhs and Hindu troops in East Punjab.' Interestingly, she also pointed out how all the medical supplies and equipment were available only in Lahore with practically none being available for the East Punjab.[100]

Predictably the Pakistan authorities disagreed with Amrit Kaur. Fazlur Rehman, the Interior and Information Minister said the problem was not necessarily communal, the problem was that the 'East Punjab Government was unable to exert pressure on the Sikhs: 'repressive measures are possible only when a government has full public support—but the government of India does not have the support on the Sikhs.'[101]

General Frank Messervy, Commander-in-Chief of the Pakistan Army noted in a letter to Field Marshal Auchinleck (see Chapter 4), that the police on both sides was a hundred per cent communalized and there was an omnipotently prevalent bitterness everywhere.[102] The General also noted that one of the DIGs in West Pakistan had lost all his property in Amritsar and that a deputy commissioner in West Punjab had learnt that his house in Jullundur had been reduced to ashes and that his mother was missing. This letter by Messervy is important on another count it makes the exceptionally rare reference to two British officers being shot dead by a 'Jat piquet of the Raj. Rif. (Rajputana Rifles)', and of the widespread complaints he had received from Muslims in Amritsar that they would have protected themselves much better without the troops.

Auchinleck himself seems to have agreed that there was an increasing tendency of troops to take sides. In a memo which was to be considered by the Joint Defence Council in its meeting on 29 August, Auchinleck referred to the view of Maj. Gen. Rees who had said that beyond mid-September the impartiality of the troops could not be assured—'This is an extremely serious statement for a Commander to make.'[103]

It must of course be also remembered that the intervention of the army to assist the civil police involved a whole set of procedures and rules that had to be followed. A four-page handy list of instructions printed on thick paper gave orders for all kinds of situations and the procedures that were to be adopted by officers commanding army troops. Officers were to be personally responsible for the extent of force used and officers could not take cover in the excuse that a Magistrate had ordered the use of a particular extent of force. Instructions were clear that under no circumstances were troops to involve in hand to hand combat; enough warning was always to be given before opening fire; and so on and so forth. The instructions highlighted the fact that 'military are not civil police'.[104]

CAPITAL PUNISHMENT FOR THOSE WHO FAIL IN DUTY

Indeed Mountbatten too appears to have arrived at the view that a major reason for the violence was the fact that troops, particularly when guarding trains and convoys were not opening fire when the raiders were of people of their own community. While presiding over the first Emergency Committee Meeting Mountbatten noted:

> There was only one way in which the (troops not firing on their own communities) could be stopped—it was brutal, but the object was to save lives. If a train was attacked successfully the guards would be arrested, those who were wounded would be released, and the rest shot within half an hour. Could that be done under any law but Martial Law? Sardar Patel, who was present in this meeting said that a summary trial was, in any case, necessary, and that even if India was to take this extreme step, he (Patel) was sure that Pakistan would not give capital punishment to policemen and soldiers who failed to perform their duty.[105]

There were of course a large number of incidents in which troops accompanying convoys and trains had saved thousands of lives by sheer grit and determination in extremely adverse conditions. One such case was that of a Gurkha Subedar who ensured that not a single casuality occurred on the train carrying Muslim refugees under his charge when it was attacked near Bahadurgarh (Rohtak). Brigadier Thimayya gave the Subedar a reward of Rs. 800.[106] Another such report was revealed in an official statement of the East Punjab Government, which said that a British officer entrusted to guard a Muslim refugee train taking refugees from Paharganj (Delhi) gave his life protecting the train. This was one of the very serious incidents in which only 600 people of a full trainload survived.[107]

ARMY HAS REMAINED STEADY

There are two reasons why Mountbatten's suggestion of capital punishment for erring troops appears out of place. For one, there were not too many incidents of troops or policemen shirking their duty while escorting trains. But more importantly as Field Marshal Auchinleck said: 'this massacring that went on was very difficult for the army because the soldier knew his own folk might be killed any day, yet it amazed me that the army remained steady'.[108]

Lt. Col. Lewis Collinson, 2nd Battalion, Assam Regiment, has recorded his impressions of troops under his charge in the Punjab in September 1947. His Battalion was moved from Malakand (Peshawar) to Madak near Otacmund (south India). The Muslim driver of the train that was bringing the Battalion to Amritsar refused to take it across the Ravi bridge, out of fear. The Battalion waited for almost 24 hours for a non-Muslim engine driver to take the train to Ambala. At Ambala they were suddenly ordered to be ready for duty—protecting trains and Muslim refugee camps. Even though the troops were fed up of being pushed around, they took the task in all earnestness: 'they didn't give a damn or understand what the quarreling was about'. Collinson also noted that one of the reasons why the Battalion became very popular among the Muslims in East Punjab was that most thought they were Gurkhas.[109]

Like so many British soldiers who described the event of 1947 in letters home, a 19-year-old Lt. Col. R.N.P. Reynolds, 2/9 Gurkhas Rifles wrote money letters to his mother of his experiences. For example, on 3 September 1947, while returing to Ropar from Ambala with reinforcements, he noted that there were bodies of Muslims all along the road and railway track, 22 in one small corner alone. On 3 November he escorted a train to Attari, packed with almost 9,500 people: 'the train was so slow that three of the passengers actually died of thirst'. Reynolds went on to give a graphic account of the Muslim convoys they encountered while returning by road. His impression was that Muslims moving to the West were better organized than the Hindus and Sikhs coming into East Punjab who were in a pathetic state.[110]

HARDY'S ACCOUNT

Hardayal Hardy, an advocate of Karachi travelled by the Lahore Mail to Montgomery on 26 August. He recorded his experiences in an article for the *HT*. When the train reached Montgomery, the platform was packed with scared people because the station itself was surrounded by hundreds of armed Muslims who were trying to break the police cordon to attack the station. On seeing the scene Hardy decided not to detrain at Montgomery and to continue to Lahore. Similar scenes were being enacted at Okara, Patoki, Mian Chanwan and Raiwind. The Lahore Mail itself was saved only by the timely firing ordered by the Muslim officer commanding the train escort. Hardy describes how almost every village en route to Lahore was in flames. At Lahore the scene at the station he says was indescribable. Hardy managed to get off at Lahore, and with the help of a Muslim railway official who had travelled with him from Karachi, he managed to reach the house of a friend. But finding that all his Hindu and Sikh acquaintances had left, he contacted a Muslim friend who was also a senior officer. The officer took him to his own house. Under his protection Hardy had a chance to travel through Lahore. The refugee camp at DAV College had over 30,000 people, the condition was pathetic. Interestingly, Hardy said that he also saw prominent businessmen in the camp.[111]

Hardy then gave details of a discussion that took place over dinner at his friend's house where they were joined by a magistrate and a police officer. The magistrate who was blatantly communal and wanted the PBF removed immediately. The Muslim police officer on the other hand was all praise for it. The magistrate was quoted by Hardy as having said that the Muslims had more than made up for the killings of Muslims in East Punjab.

The issue of the complete breakdown in the chain of command has been discussed later, but, as an article in the *HT* pointed out, the uncertainty of where the line of partition would be drawn only added to the problem. The article said that the violence was in fact also related to the need of making space for the Sikh population that was to be exchanged—to facilitate or rather ensure the exchange it was necessary to push out the Muslims from the prime lands of the central districts.

Interestingly, the article then said that many Hindus and Sikh officers who had come into East Punjab had seen family members and friends being killed and properties looted. They had also seen at first hand the partisan behaviour of the Muslim police, particularly the lower ranks as also of the judicial officers, which is why in their new places of postings, let things take their course and in some cases even took sides against the Muslims. The article also pointed out that the policy of dividing the army and police immediately and in such a quick manner actually divided not only the communal officers but the good ones as well.[112]

AMRITSAR AT END OF AUGUST

P.C. Bhandari was the Executive Officer of the Amritsar Municipal Committee. On 2 September, Bhandari and another official, Mehta, issued a statement describing the condition of Amritsar: '50 per cent of the walled city is completely destroyed—this area was believed to have the densest population in the world.' Seventy Five per cent of the Municipal staff were Muslims. Bhandari said they had all left, he also said that of the 24 tube well attendants only 4 remained and that there was not a single person to do sweeping duty and also that people from outside were unwilling to come to the city for work, not only because they were afraid but also because there was no transport to bring them from the villages.[113]

SHORTAGE OF POLICEMEN

The decision to divide law-enforcing agencies without adequate replacement suddenly left the East Punjab authorities short by 17,000 police, their share coming to only 3,000. The rest were either already in the western districts or had left for the west. The report also mentioned the view of people who thought that the East Punjab Government should after 15 August have retained Muslim policemen for some more time, but the government of East Punjab, under guidance from New Delhi, proceeded on the assumption that all Muslims were communalized and therefore allowed them to desert their postings and move to the West Punjab.[114]

In this sense, by allowing the Muslim policemen posted in the central and east Punjab districts to leave for the west at a time when the force was most required the government itself created a crisis, the result was that with no Muslim policemen in the central and eastern districts the Muslim population was left completely at the mercy of non-Muslim policemen, just as the minorities in the western districts had been left at the mercy of Muslim policemen. It is almost certain that if the government of India had as a policy encouraged Muslim policemen to stay on in East Punjab, the killings would have been less both in numbers and in the level of brutality. The retaliation in the western districts would also have been far less horrific than it was.

JOINT DEFENCE COUNCIL MEETS IN LAHORE

Meanwhile, the supreme executive body of the time, the Joint Defence Council, met in Lahore on 29 August. Initially it was to meet at Ambala. From the Indian side the meeting was attended by Mountbatten, Nehru and Baldev Singh and from Pakistan by Premier Liaqat Ali and the Pakistan Minister for Communication Abdur Rab Nishtar. A large number of senior officials from both sides were also present. The most important decision taken at the meeting was to abolish the PBF with effect from 31 August. The reason given was that the problem had outgrown the specific region making the PBF redundant. The meeting also decided that Nehru and Liaqat would jointly tour the major disturbed areas, a decision welcomed by Jinnah.[115] Two teams were formed, one comprising Nehru, Liaqat Ali, Swarn Singh and Shaukat Hayat to tour Amritsar, Gurdaspur, Lyallpur, Sheikhupura, Hoshiarpur, Montgomery, etc., and the other comprising Baldev Singh, Abdur Rab Nishtar to tour the Ferozepur and neighbouring areas. For Nehru this was to prove an eventful tour, which moved him like nothing else had done.

TOURS FOR PEACE

The Nehru and Liaqat team left Lahore on 30 August.[116] During this tour the senior leaders came face to face with the true nature of the tragedy and suffering of the ordinary. It was also during this tour that they encountered the largest foot convoy of refugees recorded in history, stretching over 60 miles long, and comprising almost 300,000 people, mostly distraught, suffering, injured and angry Sikhs.

It so happened that Nehru's party stopped on the road from Okara to Montgommery to watch a three-mile-long convoy of battered people, mostly Sikhs who had survived the Sheikhpura massacre. An *HT* staff reporter who was with Nehru's team reported that Nehru was deeply moved by the plight of these people. The report said that the people in the convoy were attracted by the vehicles and armed escort of the team but showed little interest in Nehru himself, to the extent that it appeared they may not even have recognized him.[117]

When Nehru wanting to show his concern, asked a family where they were from, an old 'rustic' woman counter questioned 'if you wanted to partition Punjab why did you not arrange for the exchange of population earlier—see what misery has come on us'. The report noted that Nehru did not answer. The huge convoy was escorted by Gurkha and Dogra troops and ablebodied Sikhs most of whom were carrying *kirpans* and spears.[118]

While touring Hoshiarpur, Nehru addressed a meeting at village Kouper. While going to the village he noticed a group of frightened Muslims who told him that the Sikhs had warned them that if they did not vacate the village by nightfall they would be killed. An angry Nehru jumped on to a *charpoy* and warned the Sikhs that if any harm came to those Muslims, he would take extreme measure and that the nonsense had to stop.[119]

For some reason, papers associated with the Muslim League, mainly the *PT*, boycotted the reports coming in from the eventful and unprecedented tour on the basis that they were biased.[120] In an editorial, *PT* asked 'why have they (Nehru and the reporters) forgotten to mention that not a single Muslim from about 200,000 is left today in Amritsar?'

Interestingly, some reporters who were on this tour, took the rather unconventional step of filing a joint report, which said that the leaders had made sincere peace appeals and asked people not to panic and not to leave their homes, at least not permanently. Some of these stories also gave details of numerous incidents. When a group of non-Muslims, for example, asked Nehru to help evacuate them, Liaqat Ali intervened and asked the minorities not to think of leaving.[121]

In Lyallpur Nehru also told a gathering that Punjab was engaged in an act of suicide. West Punjab was the heart of Pakistan and if this province was ruined Pakistan would be ruined. Nehru's words were practically dittoed by Jinnah himself in an address on Radio Pakistan.[122]

The appeals for peace came from all sides. A reference has already been made to Master Tara Singh's earnest appeal on 5 September. On 7 September the working committee of the Hindu Mahasabha appealed for peace in Delhi. It was necessary, the statement said, to restore peace in Delhi because otherwise the evacuation work would be hampered.[123] Prakash Dutt Bhargava, Secretary of the RSS, Delhi, also issued a statement appealing for peace. The riots in Delhi, he said, were essentially a backlash of the West Punjab disturbances.[124]

On 9 September Nehru spoke on All India Radio, of the 'horrors' of Punjab, and how Delhi was now 'none too pleasant a place to stay in'. On 10 September, newspapers reported a joint statement by Liaqat Ali and Nehru, which said that rioters would be shot. Fleeing families were assured that henceforth refugee camps would be protected by troops in whom the inmates of such camps had faith—Muslim troops for Muslims, Hindu and Sikhs troops for Hindu and Sikh camps.[125]

Two large meetings were arranged at Mandi Bahaudin in Gujarat on 6 September and Jhang a couple of days later.[126] Ghazanfar Ali Khan, the Food Minister of Pakistan, had after playing a leading role in building the hype of hatred in the pre June 3 Plan days, had come in later days, particularly after the creation of Pakistan, to play a leading role in trying to restore confidence among the minorities.

The meeting at Mandi Bahaudin attended by an unprecedented number of Sikhs and Hindus who had turned up to listen to Ghazanfar Ali: 'I have come to you with deep sorrow and keen regret . . . the nefarious activities of loose elements in the East and West Punjab are a shame to mankind. . . . Don't blame Pakistan for all that has happened. . . I assure you that when the present upheaval subsidies, it (Pakistan) will be a heaven . . . we want each one of you to stay . . . this phase of history will soon pass.' There followed a thunderous cheer. Ghazanfar went on: 'Today I stand before you steeped in shame and mortification. . . I could never believe that some of us were so desperate . . . acts which could not be justified under any circumstances and arguments—-moral, religious, or political expediency, . . . we have been held up before the entire world in shame.' Later Ghazanfar Ali addressed similar meetings at Jhelum and Jalalpur Jattan, which were attended by Muslims and non-Muslims.

The *CMG* added in its report said that Ghazanfar Ali had addressed the meeting from an improvised stage, and was repeatedly cheered through his speech. It quoted him as saying that 'loot, arson, murder are against the tenet of Islam . . . every Muslim should hang his head in shame over what is happening amidst us . . . there shall be no differentiation . . . if you insist on evacuation we shall provide all security. I stand before you steeped in shame . . . we have been held guilty by the entire world and must hang our head in humiliation.'[127]

At Jhang, where the gathering had an equal share of Muslims, Ghazanfar said: 'there is a danger of Muslims themselves weakening the foundations of Pakistan by indulging in lawlessness'. At Lyallpur Ghazanfar Ali was even more forthright when he had a heart-to-heart talk with Muslim League cadres: 'I am here as the Quaid-i-Azam's representative, he wants perfect peace at all costs', and while reminding the Muslim League National Guards of their pledges, he said, 'the greatest duty you can do is to restore peace . . . wealth whether it belongs to Muslims or Hindus and Sikhs is Pakistan's, any attempt at usurping it is a hostile act on the state'.[128]

Unfortunately no such meetings could be organized in the eastern districts of Punjab, particularly in the more disturbed central districts and the Mewat area. However, appeals for peace were more numerous and possibly more earnest in Delhi. Addressing a post prayer gathering in Delhi, Gandhi said: 'Let not future generations say you lost the bread of freedom because you could not digest it, stop this madness . . . the name of India will become like mud/dust in the eyes of the world.'[129] Sardar Patel, as usual more blunt and straightforward, appealed to the refugees in particular to stop retaliation as it was only hampering the peace process and the evacuation of people.[130]

Such appeals for peace appear to have had only a marginal impact. There were of course stories of families going out of their way and at great personal risk to help people of other communities. These acts could possibly have been an outcome of such statements.[131]

HT Special Representative Travels with Nehru and Liaqat

The best or rather what appears to be the most authentic impression of the ground situation at the end of August and in the first days of September is available in two long reports filed by a special representative of the *HT*. This senior staffer who chose not to give his name had accompanied the tour of Nehru and Liaqat Ali and travelled over 2,000 miles in the highly disturbed areas with the Nehru and Liaqat team. Even though the reports merit a complete reproduction, they are being too long and a smaller version of extracts seems more appropriate: 'Murder in the eyes of men, violence in the eyes of officials, misery and starvation on the face of the refugees and a feeling of despair among politicians . . . this is what I saw in Punjab.' The two Prime Ministers, the reporter noted, were doing what was humanly possible, assuring refugees of safety, food, pulling up officials and pointing out how the Punjabis in their fury had themselves destroyed the prosperous province.[132]

He then reported his impression of how military officials in Pakistan were dreaming of conquering India and of how he thought some officials in East Punjab too had come to believe that a military showdown with Pakistan was imminent (see Chapter 7). The report said that already, i.e. by the end of August, about 100,000 had already been killed and over 3 million had been disrupted and ruined.[133]

An important point raised in the report is that even as senior functionaries were striving to maintain a sense of balance and fairness, the officials who mattered at the lower level and the ones upon whom the administrative burden actually fell were doing exactly as they liked. To substantiate the view the report cited an example. The National Sikh College in Lahore had been converted into a camp for Hindus and Sikhs. But when the Chief Liaison Officer of the Government of India went to take actual possession of the building the Sub-Inspector of Police under whose jurisdiction the building was refused to let him. After much argument and delay, and only after the Sub-Inspector received orders from the highest authority in Lahore did he relent. When this was the case even in cities like Lahore, where a chain of command was still operating, one can imagine the state of affairs in the remote areas.

The report also referred to how throughout West Punjab even petty officials were stripping people of everything that was of worth: 'no evacuee has any right to property movable or immovable'. 'It was a fatal step the Muslim League took (over the preceding about two years) in dividing the army, police and civil authorities on communal lines . . . they let loose a frankestine.' seventy per cent of the casualities in the West, in the preceding three weeks, the report said were inflicted by the lower officials of the police. 'Throughout September there was' as another contempo-rary put it, 'a complete lack of government in West Punjab'.[134]

Talking of the violence in the East Punjab the *HT* report said Hoshiarpur was the worst.

> Pandit Nehru . . . a saddened man . . . probably wondered whether it was wise to yield to the logic of events and agree to partition. Certainly in doing so the politicians took little count of the inevitable consequences considering the emotions of the people. Lord Mountbatten hurried with the partition without making sure the PBF would be able to maintain peace. Commander-in-Chief Auchinleck . . . did not send enough troops. Gen. Rees (PBF) . . . sensed danger only in the East Punjab and accordingly deployed most of his force leaving the minorities in the West Punjab at the mercy of Muslim troops.

The second part of this report (Punjab Situation II) was published the following day titled 'Origin of Riots'. It was in the form of an introspection. It started by saying the March killings were viewed by sections of Muslims in Punjab as vengeance for the Bihar killings (1946), and that the Sikh leaders had begun after March to talk of the Sikhs being safe only in the central districts. The report went on to say that the violance in the central districts was initiated by the families of the Canal Colony landowners in retaliation for the killings of their people in March.[135]

The Punjab Situation Report II also sought out that while the West Punjab had inherited a well-organized administrative system that was still operational, it was a system in which a vast majority of the Muslim officers had come to believe as a result of the past few years of Muslim League propaganda that in the new state Muslim officers could have a free hand. That Pakistan meant a place where Muslim officials could act at will was a belief that greatly contributed to the chaos of August and September.

The report also discussed in some detail the pattern of killings in some of the major incidents, like Sheikhupura, for example. It said that at first a false alarm, that a gang of armed Sikhs was coming in a particular direction, was raised, followed quickly by the imposition of curfew by the local police, followed thereupon by National Muslim Guard youths setting houses on fire, forcing people to come out, and as they came out on the streets the police fired upon them for violating curfew. Interestingly, this report also pointed out how most of the refugees the reporter had met in the camps were of the view that the peak violence was yet to come.

THE PBF IS DISMANTLED

The JDC which had met in Lahore on 29 August had also resolved that both India and Pakistan would set up separate military headquarters for controlling the area previously looked after by the PBF, and that PBF units would be relocated on both sides.

The decision to abolish the PBF at such short notice went on to have far-reaching consequences. Major General T.W. Rees, the PBF Commander, after the dismantling of the PBF, was once again given Command of the 4th Indian Division following the creation of a new Army Area that was called the East Punjab Area comprising Gurdaspur, Jullundur, Hosharipur, Ludhiana, Ferozepur and Amritsar. The Pakistan Government appointed Major General Gane as Commander of its Lahore Area.[136] A third Army Area was also formed with the Delhi Cantonment as its headquarters, and comprising Delhi, Ambala, Gurgaon, Rohtak, Hisar, Simla, Ajmer and Marwara. Major General Rajender Singhji was appointed Commander.[137]

The PBF had received much criticism in Pakistan newspapers, much so that the *PT* even devoted an editorial justifying the JDC decision: 'judging from its performance it was badly commanded, badly officered and badly advised.[138] During the last three weeks it has been out manoevered, out intelligenced, out done not by regular troops but by bands of blood thirsty marauders.'[139]

The editorial also said that while it failed to understand how the PBF could have failed to protect even main roads and small strips of land between Amritsar and Lahore, where just positioning a few tanks could have saved thousands of lives. The editorial went on to suggest that the PBF failed because possibly it did not receive enough support from the East Punjab Government. There was also however a small news item in the *PT* the same day which also said that it was abolished because 70 per cent of all attacks on trains or on road convoys had taken place in areas which were not under its purview.

Interestingly there were also complaints against some units of the PBF for bad and unreasonable behaviour.[140]

While no reason was officially stated for the disbanding of the PBF, the fact remains that it was unable to meet the objectives for which it was set up. Robin Jeffrey, perhaps the most authoritative and authentic source for an assessment of the PBF, says that not only were General Lockhart and General Messervy, the Commanders of the Indian and Pakistan armies after independence, not consulted in the process of setting it up, but even Francis Muddie, Governor (Designate) West Punjab was not consulted. Muddie noted on 31 August, that is, a day before the force was disbanded: 'Any support I may have given to the proposal to abolish the PBF has not been in the view of failure of performance but merely because I considered the setting up of your force was constitutionally and politically wrong. The decision to create the force was, however, taken at a high level and I can express my opinion only in private.'[141]

With this being the attitude of even the Governor, the chances of the PBF being able to do anything worthwhile were obviously limited. The task assigned to the Force was almost an impossible one. Initially it started with about 15,000 men, by 24 August the number was pushed up with great difficulty to 23000.[142] With this small number, 'the Force was unable to cope with the twelve districts it had . . . within its jurisdiction . . . the Sikh princely states stood like islands and peninsulas within the Force's twelve districts.'[143]

But on the whole, Jeffrey goes on to suggest the role of the Sikh princely states could not have been too much. The organizational part of the Sikh *jathas* was managed by ex-INA Sikh officers, mainly Lt. Col. Niranjan Singh Gill, because the traditional leaders like Tara Singh and Kartar Singh appear to have lost control or at least the ability to disband the *jathas*.[144] For the PBF this only added to its impossible task.

Jeffrey has discussed many other issues that contributed to the failure of the PBF, there is one other point he raises which requires a detailed look. He suggests that relations between officers—British, Indian and Pakistani as well as between troops—were not what they should have been:

> One characteristic case involved a battalion of 2 Punjab Regiment (50 per cent Muslim, 25 per cent Dogra, 25 per cent Sikh) stationed in Montgommery under the command of a Sikh Lieutenant-Colonel. On 20 August Sikh soldiers shot and killed a Muslim municipal commissioner who, they claimed,

was leading a mob of curfew-breakers. This enraged the Muslim civil authorities, and the Battalion's Commanding Officer wrote a two-page letter to Rees to defend 'my Sikhs' and ask for the Battalion to be moved.

In this instance, the troops were moved in time to avoid further trouble. However, little could be done to lessen the mistrust and ill will that existed between communities and between civil and military authorities. An additional reason for such feelings may well have been that British officers found it distasteful to work under, or in cooperation with, Indians and Pakistanis. One account records that Rees told Thimayya, one of his four advisers, that '. . . if you think I intend to listen to your advice you are mistaken.'[145]

A very crucial factor which possibly influenced the relationship aspect within the Force and something that Rees had to contend with was that everyone knew that 'British Officers within the army were counting their days to departure and that Regiments would soon be divided.'[146] To be fair therefore the heaps of criticism piled on the functioning of British army officers including those assigned to special tasks like the PBF appear to have ignored the fact that from the beginning of 1947: 'British servicemen were extremely restive as they watched friends depart.'[147] Lt. Col. John Peddie said: 'it came as a shock in early 1947 therefore when an order pronounced that all British regular officers attached to the Indian army from British regiments were to be posted home . . . a cruel blow to the hopes of those who were working hard for a efficient successful hand-over . . . viewed in the light of the communal disturbances . . . this can only be described in the kindest of terms as an extraordinary decision.' Peddie has recorded that most of the troops, both Indian and British, were shocked with the decision to divide the Indian army and how this was serving to destablize moral among troops.

Therefore, what Rees was commanding as the PBF was really a mixture of officers—many homesick—of troops who no longer trusted their friends, a situation which months earlier had been unthinkable in the circles of the distinguished Indian army, a situation so bad that troops had to be reminded of Regimental honour. As Jeffrey has put it: 'Finally, it was the morale of the Force which began to crack, and it was this which led to the Force's disbandment.'[148]

Jeffrey suggests that it was the brutal killing of over 200 Sikhs, many of whom were burnt to death after they had clashed with Muslims of the 3 Baluch Regiment, which led to the disbanding decision. In this incident it was said that Hindu troops of the Regiment had challenged the Muslim troops. Finally both Rees and Auchinleck appear to have agreed that neutrality of the Force could no longer be assured.[149]

On 15 November 1947 Rees minuted an extremely important note with regard to the situation in Punjab from 1 August 1947 to about the middle of September 1947. He made no attempt to absolve himself or his command of the charges that politicians had made, but assessed the situation, causes and possible answers that could have produced better results.

Rees has also noted in this report that the problem was started in the first week of August with the attacks on Muslim villages by Sikh *jathas*. He noted that they were supported by ex-INA soldiers with whom the villages of the central districts abounded and that these *jathas* numbered from about 20 to (in some cases) even 600 and that local non-Muslim villages did all they could to support these *jathas* with food and lodging.

Rees has a very critical word for the police, particularly in the districts of Jullundur, Ferozepur and Hoshiarpur, where he notes that non-Muslim policemen did not cooperate with the PBF. With regard to Amritsar he says, the city should have had 800 policemen when the trouble started but actually it had only 200. Even though he noted that 'both communities were temporarily maddened' the problem of refugee movement could have been more securely handled, only if a high-powered properly staffed organization had been set up in a timely manner. This he adds could not or was not done because both sides insisted on having their own people to occupy important positions.[150]

While summing up Rees noted that part of the problem was also that 'during July when the mechanics of partition were being discussed trouble of such degree was not anticipated by the Government of India or Government of Punjab', and this may have been because the 'people to be divided had lived together . . . for centuries using the same language and many common customs'.

Indeed, as Rees and many other senior British and Indian officers believed a major part of the problem was rooted in the failure on the part of the Government of India and Pakistan to assess the true dimensions of the crisis that waited round the corner. One consequence of this was that the governments were more concerned about getting 'hold' of actual power and posting its own people in prime positions. As a result officers who had manned, for better or worse, sensitive positions at the district level were replaced at random, by people who were not only new but also lacked experience. For example, Brenden who had managed the troubled district of Gurgaon as Deputy Commissioner since 1945 was suddenly posted out in June 1947.[151] West Punjab Governor Muddie cited the inexperience of Deputy Commissioners and Superintendents of Police as a major reason for the chaos: 'what could govt. do itself in disorganisation . . . Most SPs and DCs were new. . .'[152]

The story of Rich, the SSP of Lahore is a good illustration of how difficult it must have been for officers sitting on hot seats to function effectively and that no excuse would have been necessary for not being committed to their assignments. Like most other officers Rich too had been busy planning his journey home throughout July. With all arrangements having been confirmed by 29 July for his departure from Bombay on 21 August, he was to learn on 2 August that the government had decided not to relieve him until the Punjab Boundary Commission had announced the Award.[153] Such was the case with many other officers.

Almost a month after the PBF had been demobilized, the *Times* briefly reviewed the charges against the role of the British officers and troops in general, making specific reference to an article by H.N. Kunzru.

> Although it is certain that 'the man in the fields' does not share the Indian politicians' resentment against alleged gloating by Britons over India's misfortunes, there has also been criticism of British officers serving in the Indian Army for their alleged failure to take effective steps to stop disturbance. An instance of such criticism is a statement issued yesterday by the veteran Liberal leader from the United Provinces, Pandit H.N. Kunzru, on the Punjab troubles, which included the following passage: 'The officer commanding the Punjab Boundary Force was British; every brigade commander was British; and 90 per cent, or more of the unit commanders were British. Had the force acted impartially, the situation would very probably have been brought under control and the British officers would rightly have been given the credit for this achievement. They must therefore equally legitimately bear discredit for its failure and the resulting catastrophe.'[154]

Kunzru's criticism of the PBF in particular and of the British officers in general drew an immediate reaction from Auchinleck, who sent a handwritten letter to Mountbatten. He said such criticism was an unfair attempt to discredit the PBF and the British officers: 'in view of the great problem my officers do not ask for praise but at least fair play'. He also added that the position of the British troops and officers was being made 'more and more difficult in India,' and that 'I may even consider representing (to the Government in London) that we may have to leave if this were the attitude. Such reports were baseless.'[155] Interestingly, even Gen. Frank Messervy, Commander-in-Chief of the Pakistan Army, while accepting the fact that troops may have taken sides in the Amritsar region, complemented the PBF.[156] Auchinleck, also recorded that the PBF could not be held responsible for the killings as over 70 per cent of the attacks on the trains had occurred in areas which were beyond its control and that the position of the PBF was almost impossible.[157]

Unlike many other Congress leaders, including senior ones, Nehru was always large-hearted in such matters. As the British troop withdrawal from India began and the first contingent was ready to sail, Nehru sent a special message: 'Few things are more significant of this change than the withdrawal of British troops . . . they are essentially armies of occupation . . . I know the good qualities of the British soldiers . . . I should like our own armies to develop them . . . it is rare in history that such a parting takes place not only peacefully but with goodwill.'[158]

COMMUNICATION BREAKDOWN

Another decision taken by the JDC of 29 August, was to air drop a large number of leaflets in Punjabi and Urdu appealing jointly for peace. But like almost everything else such measures were only a reflection of faith and trust that was little more than skin deep. While on the one hand both the governments had decided on this measure, on the other both felt the need of an information mechanism which was their own, so deep was the level of distrust. For example, the Government of India announced on 30 August that 10,000 copies of newspapers of English, Hindi and Urdu published only in Delhi would be distributed daily in the relief camps at Lahore, Amritsar and Jullundur.[159] A few days later the Pakistan government in a counter move started a special radio channel for refugees.[160] As the days passed charges against each other of spreading disinformation became increasingly common.

East Punjab Governor Trivedi was reported to have stated as an example of the state of communications in Punjab that, 'he as Governor had been unable to arrange a telephone for his official use in Jullundur'.[161] Trivedi had even reported in the Emergency Committee on 18 September the problems he was having with regard to communications. He said of the two transmitters installed at Jullundur one had a range of 14 kilometres the other of 40 kilometres. He also pointed out that the practice of sending messages to distantly placed officers via conventional radio announcements had not proved very useful, as he for one had received only one message through radio and, in a lighter vein, he added that he had of course managed to listen to a lot of music on the radio while waiting for messages.[162] The situation was no better in Simla where the Post and Telegraph Department had in fact to disconnect 200 private telephone connections to provide connections to important offices.[163]

The Post Master General of Lahore believed, however, that officials on the Indian side had greatly aggravated the problem. In an official statement on 30 August, he said: 'The Government of India has made no attempt to send Mail from Amritsar to Lahore for last ten days . . . telephone operators in Amritsar have been abusing operators in Lahore and never put through trunk calls for Muslims.' The situation was no better in Lahore as the *CMG* found out to its cost. It complained about the Post Master General of Lahore, whose response was: 'if the lines are down—they are down there is nothing we can do about it'. He did however add that the repeated breakdowns were the result of telegraph offices being manned by unskilled people.[164]

SITUATION WORSENS

Two trains were attacked between Delhi and Panipat on 1 September. In one of the attacks six Muslims were killed near Narela.[165] On 4 September 30 Muslims were killed in a train attack between Ghaziabad and Khurja. On the same day yet another train attack took place near Moradabad.[166] On 1 September a special train carrying the goods of employees of the Pakistan government was looted at Bahadurgarh. This train had earlier been delayed at Delhi station for two days—waiting for a Muslim engine driver and guard. There were no casualities since the train was heavily guarded, but 30 of the 50 bogies were looted and burnt down.[167]

A staff reporter of the *HT* was in Bhiwani on 30 August. He reported how a minor quarrel between a shopkeeper and a customer (28 August) turned the whole region into a battlefield. The report said Muslims from neighbouring villages fought a pitched battle for eight hours with the police, with bombs and heavy ammunition. Over 3,000 people were involved. Ultimately when things settled down, over 100 people had been killed and about 180 seriously injured. The people of Hansi, Hisar and Rewari, the report said, were demanding that either arms be made easily available to them or those owned by the Muslims be confiscated.[168]

Restrictions on Sikh movement in UP

As discussed earlier, in the central districts, the *CMG* reported that most of the trouble was being caused by armed *jathas* of Sikhs, many of which were operating in military uniforms and in military style.[169] Another report said that groups of Sikhs from among those who were vacating districts of Sialkot, Montgomery, Sheikhupura and even Gujranwala, while moving eastwards were operating in *jathas*. In many areas such groups were burning down the crops of the regions they were vacating.[170] The Muslims vacating East Punjab were following a similar scorched earth policy.[171]

This fearsome reputation of the Sikhs had preceded them, so much so the authorities in Sismau Cantonment passed orders which restricted the free movement of Sikhs and they had to seek special permits from the deputy commissioner.[172] The decision to restrict the entry of refugees from West Punjab into UP was in fact taken in New Delhi only on 7 September, and therefore the local administrations order of putting restrictions on movements of Sikhs in particular was possibly at the behest of the provincial leadership—in this case mainly G.B. Pant.[173]

As expected, the reaction of the Sikhs was one of disbelief and anger. The Mountbatten Papers contain a 'top secret' note which deals with the issue. The note points out that a large number were already unhappy as they began to realize that the lands they were to receive in lieu of what they had left behind were of inferior quality besides the fact that they were not receiving acre for acre. The note then adds that the Sikhs were also questioning why they should be banned from Delhi and UP: 'Are we outcastes—does the Indian Union not owe us a place in the Sun?'[174]

THE REFUGEE FALLOUT IN DELHI

The first few days of September witnessed continued widespread violence not only in Punjab but also in Delhi. Widespread violence broke out in Delhi on 5 September. There was little doubt that it was prompted by distressed refugees who had flooded the city. Over 50 people were killed, most parts of the city were placed under curfew including New Delhi which saw curfew for the first time.[175] Over 700 people were arrested and no train left Delhi on the Karnal or Gurgaon routes on 5 September. Karol Bagh, Lodhi Colony, Rohtak Road saw serious disturbances. The prestigious Kalka Mail was also suspended for onward journey to Kalka as sufficient escort for the train was not available.[176]

Karmat Hussain Shah, an advocate of Lahore informed the *PT* that Akhtar Hussain, a naib tehsildar, was shot dead in Dabwali (Haryana) by acquaintances. Similarly, Saghir Husain, a sub-inspector of police, and Afzal Hussain a head constable, were shot dead in Hissar. This report also detailed how nine girls had been kidnapped from a Muslim convoy near Hissar.[177] The killing of junior officials by personal staff had become fairly common. In Gurdaspur, a Sikh magistrate was reported to have been killed by his own driver.[178]

The level to which things had fallen can be understood from an incident which occurred on 10 September. Delhi had been declared a dangerously disturbed area on 9 September with no trains leaving the city.[179] The Delhi Area Commander had also issued an Order of the Day on 9 September which read: 'Shoot to Kill Lawbreakers.'[180] As luck would have it, Mountbatten's personal staff driver was going to visit a hospital when an army patrol failing to identify the vehicle even though it carried the Viceroy's Crown insignia, fired on it killing the driver, who happened to be a Sikh. Two British officers in the car, including Wing Commander Johnson, the Governor General's Press Attache, were however unhurt.[181]

Monday 8 September happened to be Janamashtami, but posterity will record it as one of the blackest days in Delhi's history. Over one lakh people of one community were rendered homeless. The city was paralysed. There are no figures of the numbers killed but a report said that more people were killed by the military and police firing than by the rioters.[182] Police and army detachments in Delhi were, in many cases, overactive, so much so that an army patrol even waved the Governor-General's car to a stop, even as the Governor-General was himself in the car.[183]

On 12 September, Gandhi visited the Jama Masjid area where he was received by thousands of Muslims. Many complained of the shortage of rations. A Muslim woman who had recently lost her husband was reported to have told Gandhi that no Muslim had wanted this kind of Pakistan.[184]

Delhi was again in flames on 13 September. A report said some Muslims had fired from a mosque on some passerby in Faiz Bazar—the area was soon in flames. A massive riot broke out in Daryaganj. The same day the police was reported to have also recovered from Nizamuddin a box of guns which had come by train from Bombay. In nearby Kahr village (12 miles from Bahadurgarh, Haryana), a massive mob of 25,000 attacked a Muslim village. Fortunately a disaster was averted by a courageous unit of troops who had been assigned to protect the village.[185]

Delhi disturbances: The Muslim League's version

Contrary to the charges made in Pakistan, that the newspapers in Delhi had understated the dimension and nature of the disturbances in Delhi, most newspapers had given the tragic happenings the space they deserved.[186] Even so, the West Punjab authorities published their own version of the Delhi disturbances in an Appendix to the booklet titled *The Sikhs in Action* (Govt. Press Lahore, 1948).[187] Appendix VII was titled 'Delhi Disturbances', and was based on a report compiled and submitted by an army officer on 21 September 1947. The report said that the riots had started on 3 September near Palam Airport. It said many Muslim students going to Karol Bagh were killed and that there were a large number of killings in the Lodhi Road area. It also said that every single shop owned by a Muslim in Connaught Place was looted and burnt on 8 September.[188] The most astounding allegation in the report is that about 10,000 bodies of Muslims were cremated near the Purana Quila Camp and some 'official sources' in fact started a rumour that the huge column of smoke that came up was from the burning of condemned rubber.

Another report on the disturbances was prepared by D.M. Malik, Chairman, Ad Hoc Committee, Provincial Muslim League, Delhi. The report gave extensive details and photographs. It quoted several newspapers like the *Times* (London) which had carried stories of how police and troops had taken sides against the Muslims in Delhi, and the *Daily Mail* which said that a great part of the looting of Muslim property in Delhi had been organized with support from the police. The report particularly emphasized an incident in Subzi Mandi where soldiers had opened fire on unarmed Muslims on 8–9 September.

The most shocking reference in the report was to the manner in which it said efforts were made to close and clean up Muslim refugee camps in Delhi so that international delegates who were expected for the International Labour Organisation's Conference (27 October to 8 November) would not see them. The figures of Muslims killed in the disturbances were certainly and greatly exaggerated, but all the same, it said 25,000 Muslims had been killed in Delhi alone and 350,000 Muslims of Delhi had in some way or the other been affected by the disturbances. Most importantly it said 137 mosques in Delhi alone had been desecrated.[189]

ANARCHY IN LAHORE

Mohammad Iqbal, Secretary of the Young Muslims Defence Association of Lahore, said that many Muslim refugees had been robbed in Lahore by Muslim gangsters who were doing this by luring the refugees with assurances of getting houses and shops allotted to them.[190] This could naturally not have happened without the connivance of the area's police and other officials. An editorial of the *CMG* in fact discussed how the law enforcement agencies themselves were in connivance with local hooligans and anti-social elements. The editorial said so serious had the situation become on both sides of the border—not just in big cities like Lahore—that the very foundations of the new states could be threatened.[191] Even in a time of such crisis air tickets for travel from Rawalpindi and Lahore to Delhi were being sold at huge premiums.[192] The same thing was happening in Quetta where, a letter said, agents had booked seats in black and then sold them at double the rate.[193]

The mediums and modes of corruption and the connivance of anti-social elements with authorities assigned the task of regulating evacuation were numerous. While the ordinary, less fortunate, who moved on foot or in trains packed to maddening levels were harassed and searched at every step, even the well to do with greater resources had more than their share of harassment. Reports said that when people arrived at airports to catch flights they were often searched and valuables were seized, very often by the military and police in connivance with each other.[194]

The East Punjab Premier, Gopichand Bhargava, went to the extent of saying that every refugee he had met had complained of being looted.[195] The robbing of migrating families under the petence of ensuring that they did not carry out of Pakistan any item on the gazetted list continued throughout September even as the Government of India kept protesting.[196] The *HT* published an editorial, detailing how refugees were not allowed to carry even personal belongings and that the so-called agreements between the two countries which had recorded that this would not happen were limited only to the paper they were written on—they were not followed on the ground.[197]

MIGRATION WAS UNEXPECTED

One of the biggest ironies of the partition of Punjab was that those who were for the division of the country had for some reason come to believe that permanent migration from the western to the eastern districts and vice versa would be to the bare minimum if at all. Therefore, even as they were racing to meet the 15 August deadline they pushed along the whole administrative system to meet the impossible cut-off line, and in doing so they failed to prepare for a situation which would dominate everything else—the refugee problem.

The Partition Council had met in New Delhi on 6 August. The meeting was presided over by Mountbatten and attended among others by Jinnah, Liaqat Ali, Sardar Patel and Dr Rajendra Prasad. *Dawn* reported that the Council had decided to restrict the exodus of people from one side to the other. It was also decided that the Refugee Camps would be for the safety of people who came in on a temporary basis only to return to their homes when things had quietened down, and also that property temporarily vacated by such families would be looked after by officers designated for the purpose.[198] Thus these early camps were not expected to function as transit camps for immigrants but as temporary safe homes from which people were expected to return to their houses.

The possibility of mass displacement was on no one's mind. The prosperous town of Kasur is an example. Dr Bodh Raj, a municipal commissioner of Kasur wrote a long letter giving details of how the peace and communal harmony that had prevailed in Kasur was shattered overnight. Kasur, a major commercial centre, had a population of 45,000 Muslims and 15,000 non-Muslims. 'On 16 August, the

Radio announced that Kasur had gone to Pakistan. The non-Muslims being over confident of the protection promised by the Muslims had no intention of migrating. On 16 and 17 August about 2,000 to 3,000 refugees arrived from Ludhiana. On 18 August a teacher, his wife and child were killed near the High School where the refugees had camped. On the same day some refugees with protection of Balauch troops broke open shops of Hindus and Sikhs and looted them. As some Hindus and Sikhs tried to leave Kasur they were killed and their bodies were thrown into the Sutlej.'[199]

So completely unprepared was the Government of India by the massive tide of refugees that it was compelled to hand over the evacuation process to the army on 30 August.[200] The Pakistan government had already done the same a day earlier.[201] By the first week of September, over 150,000 people from the western districts had reached UP,[202] about 10,000, mainly the well-to-do had reached Simla,[203] about 1,25,000 in the Kashmir valley.[204] Apart from the refugees from West Punjab, Delhi had also to house 50,000 Meos who fled their homes in the Mewat and Gurgaon areas.[205] About 8,000 Kashmiri labourers who were based in and around Simla were also reported to have appealed to the Maharaja of Kashmir to have them evacuated.[206]

Incidentally, and quite importantly the flow of refugees was greater in the initial days from the east to the west. A statement issued by the Public Relations Department West Punjab said on 8 September that 8 special trains and about 350 lorries were arriving in West Punjab daily, thus approximately 50,000 people were entering West Punjab from the Indian side everyday. The camp at Kasur was flooded with 2,50,000 people by the first week of September. Rahmat Ullah Chaudhry, Vice-President of the Lahore District Muslim League, however, said the camp at Kasur had by 8 September handled over 600,000 refugees who had come in from East Punjab. 'Kasur', he said, 'was a tale of the bleeding of the Muslims of East Punjab.'

The problems at the Kasur camp, which was the largest in those early days were numerous—only 30 hospital beds, the outbreak of cholera, etc. A cholera epidemic was averted only by a massive effort launched in the West Punjab to forcibly innoculate the refugees.[207] By 3 September over 1,000 people had died of cholera in the Kasur camp alone. A large number of medical students were also reportedly working round the clock in the camp.[208]

On the Indian side, refugees from West Punjab were reported to have reached as far as Madras, where the government was making special arrangements to receive and look after them.[209] By the first week of September Delhi too was receiving about 600 well-to-do refugees everyday—these were people who were coming in by air.[210]

More generally, between the two sides it appears that the Pakistan authorities were doing a better and cleaner job of the evacuation process than the Indian and East Punjab governments. While there was chaos on both sides, it was generally believed that the Indian side did more talking while the Pakistanis were more motivated.[211]

Fuelled by the zeal and enthusiasm of having created their new home the Pakistan authorities put up a far better show of managing the crisis if not for the ordinary people then at least for government employees.[212] By 22 August, 13 special and 10 baggage trains had left Delhi for Karachi, where there were special reception offices which provided directions for accommodation, food, medicine, etc. Buses and trucks were kept waiting, ration cards were issued at the station itself, so much so even P&T facilities were provided on the station.[213]

Of course such arrangements were greatly limited and mainly for officials of the government. For example, on 4 September the Pakistan government said that it had arranged for 20 aircraft to fly officials from Delhi to Karachi, the first batch of these flights landing at Karachi on 1 September.[214] But even otherwise, many reports said that the trains that were ferrying people from the west to the east were returning to the west carrying far fewer people than their capacity. Pakistan authorities said that this was because authorities in East Punjab were not making enough effort to collect Muslims together or give them security up to the stations, from where the security was usually taken over by the train escort.[215] In fact, a group of newspaper editors based in Lahore complained to Jinnah that Hindu and Sikh officers who were entrusted with the task of arranging the evacuation of Muslims from East Punjab were not taking their work seriously.[216]

MILITARY EVACUATION ORGANIZATION

Lahore witnessed two important conferences in the first week of September. The conference on 3 September was attended by Nehru and Liaqat Ali, and all the top civil, police, military and railway officials. Among other things, it was decided to improve the coordination between the two governments, appoint district-level coordinating officers, and make a more concerted effort to check the illegal and forced occupation of properties on both sides.[217] It was also decided to put Brigadier Chimni in charge of the Indian Military Evacuation Organization (MEO). Brigadier Chimni was to report to Rees. The meeting also decided to place 500 army and 500 civilian vehicles at the disposal of the MEO.[218]

On the following day a second conference met to work out more details. This was attended by Sardar Patel, Ghazanfar Ali, the Commander-in-Chief of the Indian Army. General Rob Lochart, General Gani of Pakistan, the Governors and all the provincial ministers of the East and West Punjab.[219] It was decided that henceforth the entire responsibility of the refugee camps would be of the government in whose territory they were situated. The meeting also resolved that both the governments would not recognize illegally occupied property under any circumstances.

The conference for the first time perhaps acknowledged the seriousness of forced conversions, forced marriages and above ail the inhuman manner in which girls and young women were being abducted on both sides. While resolving that forced conversions would have governmental sanctity and approval it was also decided to make every possible effort to recover and restore abducted women.[220]

PUNISH NEWSPAPERS FOR WRONG REPORTING

In view of the menace of the rumours and unfounded reports being circulated both governments decided to issue on a daily basis an official press release dealing with issues that were likely to interest the common people. In this context it was also resolved to take strict action against newspapers that were publishing stories without basis.

This decision of the conference was rather surprising, because not only were the leading newspapers of Lahore and Delhi clearly taking sides under the patronage of the respective governments, but the little information that was actually available was being disseminated only through the newspapers. The resolution of tough action, however, saw no further action, the government did little more than request newspapers to check their facts before going to press.[221] *The Tribune*, the region's leading English anti-Partition, anti-Muslim League paper had been virtually pushed out of Lahore under dangerously dramatic circumstances on 15 and 16 August. It shifted to Simla with extremely limited resources and remained out of print for several weeks. With the *CMG* alone taking a fairly objective role, this left the Delhi-based *HT* to counter the *Dawn* and the *PT* which were also supported by the *Eastern Times*—all three had no problem in associating fully with the Muslim League or the Pakistan perspective, which in early September was little more than that the killings were triggered by the Sikhs and the Muslims were only reacting into this.

The problem of course was far more serious in the large section of the Urdu press, reason enough for India to be more disturbed about biases and exaggeration in the press than Pakistan. Incidentally, Lord Mountbatten who in his initial days in India had been somewhat apprehensive of the press, had become by the middle of August one of its great admirers. In a letter to some editors he wrote: 'tribute to the constructive attitude of the Press. . . I have seen the valuable contribution the Press has made to the great events we are now celebrating.'[222]

Dawn was among the first to complain about a Hindu bias in the administrative circles in Delhi. It had been served a notice by the District Magistrate of Delhi, directing it not publish anything that would directly or indirectly promote feelings of enmity or hatred between communities. The paper charged the administration for having singled it out.[223] But by September charges of partisan reporting flew from both sides. While Nazir Ahmad accused the *CMG* and All India Radio of being grossly biased towards India,[224] Satyanand Mehta of Lyallpur complimented the *CMG* for its impartiality: 'I pray to editors of Urdu newspapers to follow the *CMG* and ignore for the sake of humanity even if they think that Muslims have suffered more in East Punjab.'[225]

Both Radio Pakistan and All India Radio charged each other of being biased and for exaggerating the killings on the 'other side'.[226] To counter the influence of Pakistan Radio, particularly in the greatly surcharged atmosphere of the Hindu and Sikh relief camps in the western districts, the Government of India even arranged for the supply of 12 radio sets so that people could listen to All India Radio.[227]

While Delhi and Lahore, even in the worst of days, saw only a temporary closure of newspaper offices, in Amritsar the situation was different. The Akalis were keen to tell their side of the story but were unable to arrange for printing paper, so much so that, Master Tara Singh even asked Major Short to request the Deputy Commissioner of Amritsar to provide some newsprint. This could not be arranged.[228]

THE TRIBUNE PUSHED OUT OF LAHORE

The Tribune as discussed (in the Preface) was possibly the most influential newspaper in Punjab, and among its many admirers was Gandhi, who had referred to it as the 'best views paper in India'.[229] The circumstances of its exit from Lahore were not just dramatic but more importantly indicate the fate that must have fallen the less important institutions—if 'This could happen to *The Tribune* what of lesser beings?' Its losses were colossal—paper, machines and property estimated at Rs. 25 lakh. Six of its typewriters were even taken over by the *Pakistan Times*.[230]

D.R. Sud chronicled the last days of *The Tribune* in an article, '*The Tribune* Leaves Lahore'. In better days, and with sufficient printing paper, *The Tribune* could have easily adjusted the long article in a single edition, but *The Tribune* of Simla was a pale and impoverished 'country cousin' of *The Tribune* of Lahore and so spread the article over three editions—25 and 28 December 1947 and 5 January 1948:

> As the 15 August drew near the temper of fire raising and knife plunging grew no member of the (*Tribune*'s) staff was safe . . . it was felt that *The Tribune* had special responsibility . . . and if the paper stopped publication it would mean the collapse of Hindu and Sikh morale . . . the crash that we had all feared came on 15 August. On 14 August two clerks Jagan Nath and Vidya Sagar while trying to leave Lahore were shot on the way to the station. . . . The night of 14 August . . . Muslim officials and masses alike went wild . . . shouting and gesticulating 'death to the *Kafirs*' . . . the editorial staff stood guard. . . . But leaving Lahore was not so easy . . . unless one has lived in Lahore one cannot understand the almost personal love that it inspires in the hearts of its admirers . . . the point was how to go—trains were ruled out as Lahore station was crawling with Muslim League National Guard cadres and policemen in plain clothes. . . . At 4 p.m. on the fateful day (15 August) 80 people were packed like Sardines in one small truck and . . . with mixed feelings *The Tribune* convoy moved slowly out.

MINISTRY OF REFUGEES (INDIA)

Having toured the highly disturbed areas—travelling over 2,000 miles by air and road with his Pakistan counterpart Liaqat Ali—Nehru returned to Delhi and the first thing he did was to create an Emergency Committee on Partition and a separate Ministry of Refugees.[231] He 'informed' his colleagues in the cabinet that he had invited K.C. Neogy to take charge of the new ministry.[232] At this same meeting it was decided to provide the death penalty in grave offences and to give magistrates and police officers even below the rank of sub-inspectors the authority to use force to disperse violent crowds without having to wait for prior permission.[233]

PROTECTING DELHI

By the third week of September over 6,000 troops had been assigned the work of law and order in Delhi alone.[234] This left the whole of East Punjab with a mere 3,000 policemen, a shortage of about 17,000 men to policing norms.[235]

The Muslim population of Delhi had suffered greatly in the preceding days. Jinnah's reaction to the tough and timely measures initiated in Delhi was naturally one of relief: 'I am informed that the Government of India are taking all possible measures to suppress the lawlessness that has raised its head in Delhi.'[236]

The ECM that met on 10 September spent considerable time on discussing the security of refugee convoys which were greatly handicapped by the shortage of escort troops. Mountbatten, who presided at the meeting, said that reinforcements were not to be made available to East Punjab authorities at the cost of Delhi: 'Delhi should remain overriding first priority.' Nehru, the minutes said, agreed with the Governor-General's view.[237]

The shortage of convoy-escorting guards was once again the main agenda in the very next ECM (11 September). Rees, now East Punjab Area Commander, said that at least one company of troops was required to protect 35,000 people moving in a foot convoy. Arguing the point he told the ECM that in one case 400 Muslim refugees moving in a foot convoy from Faridkot had been slaughtered in less than ten minutes.[238]

WEST PUNJAB GOVERNMENT MORE PURPOSEFUL

In Lahore the police had started in the beginning of September a drive to recover looted property. In just the first couple of days goods worth Rs. 332,000 were recovered, and incidentally of the two women arrested initially for theft and loot, one was a Muslim the other a Hindu—Shanti Devi and Khursid Begum.[239] The West Punjab authorities, particularly those in Lahore, appear to have been more enthusiastic in such matters, at least in early September. For example, as early as 2 September, the West Punjab authorities had announced that no house or other vacated property was to be taken possession of without the presence and assent of a prescribed magistrate. These magistrates had been directed to make inventories of household goods in vacated houses and were expected to lock these goods in separate rooms.[240] There was naturally a great rush of refugees from East Punjab and Delhi. The Deputy Commissioner (Lahore) stated on 2 September that they had already allotted 12,000 vacated houses to refugees and that the remaining about 4,000 houses were being kept for government officials who were expected to shift to Lahore from various parts of East Punjab.[241] The Deputy Commissioner in fact advised people seeking accommodation in Lahore to go to places like Sialkot, Gujranwala, Sargodha, Montgommery and Sheikhupura.

The pressure of refugees on Delhi was even greater than on Lahore. The Indian Government stated on 3 September that plans had been made to expand New Delhi by about 900 acres, at a cost of Rs. 600,00,000 to provide accommodation to about 2 lakh people.[242]

The East Punjab authorities followed the lead of the West Punjab authorities who had announced a general policy of resettling rural families. On 1 September the Pakistan government announced that about 400 families, or about 3,000 people, would be settled on 2,500 acres of land. The provincial government, the announcement said, would be custodians of vacated lands. It was also announced that some families would be resettled as tenants of big landlords and that *taccavi* loans for seed cattle, etc., would be distributed immediately. Importantly, district officials were required to report the progress made on these fronts on a weekly basis.[243] By as early as the 12 September, the West Punjab government had been able to work out a plan for rehabilitating skilled workers: 'Durrie weavers at Gakhar, Woollen Handlooms at Jhang, Cotton at Gujarat and Multan'. *Charkhas* were being mass produced and distributed by the government and people who had the resources to repair workshops and factories were being selected to lease the vacated factories.[244]

But as happens so often, and more so when the stakes were so high, on paper things appeared normal but in practice there were a large number of complaints of corruption, pick and choose, unmerited use of discretion, the lack of norms, etc. Fazal Hussain of Lahore narrated how the allotment of houses in Lahore was being controlled by *mohalla* Chaudhris and no rules being followed. There was not even a list of vacated houses in a given colony. Hussain also said that the rules for applying for accommodation were far too tedious and, in any case, the favourites or the resourceful were given immediate possessions and others were kept waiting.[245]

The West Punjab government was also the first in appointing squads to recover abducted women. Deputy Superintendent of Police, Mohammad Abdullah, was given the charge of this cell which was to operate in coordination with the East Punjab authorities.[246] On 18 September, for example, a Government of India press release said 750 non-Muslim women had been recovered from Jandiala Kalan in West Punjab.[247] The Military Evacuation Organization statement, however, put this figure at 1,000.[248] There were similar reports from the Pakistan side where, the number of women recovered was of course much smaller.

ECONOMIC CRISIS IN EAST PUNJAB

The first 30 days of independence, both in Pakistan and East Punjab witnessed a complete dislocation of economic activity—distribution of food, banking, retailing and there was naturally no question of commercial production. Before we look at some of the problems that came up in this regard in the early days that followed the partition of Punjab, an overview of the basic facts would be in order.

The partition of Punjab gave to the East 48 per cent of the area and about 42 per cent of the population, but significantly only 39 per cent of the land that had irrigation and of this the share of canal irrigated land which came to the East was only 21 per cent of the total of undivided Punjab.[249] This fact had far-reaching implications in terms of grain availability, particularly in the regions that later came to form Haryana.

In respect of industrial activity, too, the East found itself way behind West Punjab after 15 August (see Table 5.1). Out of the total number of factories in Punjab, the East got 415 employing 43,000 people and the West 602 employing 110,000 people.[250]

Problems for East Punjab were further complicated by the fact that while industries in the East Punjab—flour milling, cotton textile, chemicals, etc., depended for raw material on the West, but there was also the fact that over 70 per cent of the labour employed in these industries was Muslim.[251] The industries of the border districts, which before 15 August were known as the central districts, bore the brunt of the crisis.

A survey by the Board of Economic Inquiry showed that following the migration of Muslim labour the wage rate in these districts rose

TABLE 5.1: NUMBER OF FACTORIES IN EAST AND WEST PUNJAB

Industry	East Punjab		West Punjab	
	No. of factories	No. of workers	No. of factories	No. of workers
Textiles	106	14,071	16	20,074
Engineering	79	6,437	154	24,135
Minerals and Metals	67	3,691	75	7,666
Food, Drink & Tobacco	40	3,562	39	4,295
Chemicals, Dyes, etc.	18	1,548	36	2,816
Paper and Printing	08	1,733	42	3,899
Wood, Stone & Glass	14	1,067	38	7,789
Tanneries	2	106	3	1,954
Gins and Presses	72	4,155	178	14,842
Miscellaneous	9	6,654	21	22,000
Total	415	43,024	602	109,471

Source: Vakil, *Economic Consequences*, p. 151.

from Rs. 48 p.m. in 1946–7 to Rs. 63 p.m. in 1947–8. The survey also pointed out that the total gross value of industrial output in the central districts of Amritsar, Jullundur, Gurdaspur, Ferozepur and Ludhiana fell in one year (1946–7) from Rs. 12.5 crore to less than Rs. 10 crore (1947-48).[252]

Pakistan Backs Out of Wheat Commitment

The other important problem that confronted administrators on both sides of Sir Radcliffe's line was of feeding hungry people. A large number of reports and letters appeared, detailing the sad plight of people in transit and in the camps.[253] One Ghulam Rasul of village Nadala in Kapurthala gave details of a camp in Subhanpore (Kapurthala) which had over 3,50,000 Muslim refugees, lacking clean drinking water and food.[254]

Initially, that is, within the first few days following partition, Pakistan had said it would honour its food commitment to India,[255] but a few days later it backtracked, saying that it was not in a position to send food grain to India because of crop failure in parts of Pakistan mainly, the Sind area.[256] In the second statement Ghazanfar Ali, Pakistani's Food Minister, said that this was also because vast stretches of fertile land were lying unsown because of panic in the rural areas (see Table 5.2)·

TABLE 5.2: AREA SOWN AND GRAIN PRODUCED: EAST & WEST PUNJAB, 1947

Crop		East Punjab	West Punjab
Wheat	Area in thousand acres	3,343	7,259
	Production in tonnes	1,055	2,300
Rice	Area in thousand acres	436	395
	Production in tonnes	115	327
Gram	Area in thousand acres	4,117	2,037
	Production in tonnes	730	456
Cotton	Area in thousand acres	386	1,047
	Production in bales	148	805

Source: Vakil, *Economic Consequences*, p. 149; *CMG*, 27 August 1947.

Dawn reported that whatever grain was left with the western wing of Pakistan, would, after meeting its own requirements, be shipped to East Pakistan. It said that in normal years the Pakistan region's average surplus had been about 240,000 tonnes of which about 70,000 tonnes was taken up by the NWFP and Baluchistan, whereas the East Pakistan had always been in deficit.[257]

Peasants Burn Standing Crops as they Leave

But there was another problem which added to the shortage of food grain—as angry and scared families began fleeing age-old homes and fields, in many cases they ensured that those who had forced their migration got nothing of value on their departure. There were numerous reports of standing crops being burnt or destroyed and the stocks of grain could not be carried also destroyed, for example, Sikh peasants were burning standing crops or even destroying them by flooding the fields in Gujranwala, Montgomery, Sheikhupura and, Sialkot.[258] The Muslims migrating from the eastern districts were doing the same.[259] The damage in the eastern districts was relatively less because the wheat crop had already been harvested. But in the western districts assured irrigation had led to a third crop being sown (summer), which the migrating peasantry destroyed.

The complete failure of the rains in south-east Punjab greatly added to the problem. The *HT* Punjab, Newsletter reported on the crisis in parts of Ambala Division, and even said that if timely action was not taken the 'region would become a burden on India like the NWFP was on British India'.[260]

The *CMG* gave a detailed report on the food and water crisis in the Hissar region and said the government was doing all it could—supplying water by train and selling *bhusa* at subsidized rates. The report also said that relief measures had been put under the charge of non-officials.[261] Ironically, as the southern districts reeled under drought conditions, as if nature was hitting back at Punjab with all its vengeance for the blood that had flown, the central fertile districts and major rice-producing areas saw extensive damage by floods. So extensive was the damage that the production of rice was expected to fall by half.[262]

As mentioned earlier, there was an acute shortage of coal. To this was added, as Mohd. Amin-ud-din (Lahore) pointed out, the part played by a nexus of unscrupulous elements and railway employees who were stealing large amounts of railway coal and selling it to coal dealers.[263] While the shortage of coal had an overall effect on the movement of food grain by rail, the extreme shortage of petrol adversely affected not only the availability of road transport for refugees but also the distribution of food grain at the retail level.[264] The petrol crisis was important enough to be debated repeatedly at the highest level.[265]

Prime Minister's Household Lines Up for Rations

The food grain crises was widespread, from Delhi to the remotest village in East Punjab. *HT* quoted an interesting report filed by the news agency API on 10 September. Prime Minister Nehru's domestic help had stood in line at the Hastings Road commodities ration supply booth to procure the ration allotted to the Prime Minister's house. But the shopkeeper, as was the usual practice, closed the shop after a while on the grounds that supplies had run out. The servant went back and complained to Nehru, who personally went to the ration shop and gave the 'fellow' an example of the famed Nehru temper—the Prime Minister's domestic help and all others in the queue got their ration.[266]

Although prices were officially regulated, the regulations were more commonly violated.[267] The shortage of wheat had reached such a level the government had to pass an order that all ration-card holders would have to take a part of their wheat ration in the form of rice as well.[268] Reports indicated that the shortage, apart from the disturbance-related problems was also due to the fact that the overall production of important food grains and pulses in Punjab had shown

THE EXPENSIVE DYE: ' You see the extra charge is for the special black dye'.

The Partition of India brought along a hoard of problems in the Punjab and Delhi, one important being the manipulation of prices in essential commodities—food grain, match boxes, sugar, ghee, soap. The illustation shows a man, obviously a displaced person being talked into by 'black marketeer' (*HT*, 10 October 1947).

a five-year low in 1946–7.[269] The requirement of wheat in East Punjab was estimated at about 50,000 tonnes, whereas the government of India was in a position to supply a mere 3,000 tonnes.[270]

FLOODS COMPOUND FOOD SHORTAGE

The floods (1947) in the Lahore and the central districts which were also the major rice-producing areas broke a record which had stood since 1900. Because of the flood damage, in the Punjab the net value of rice was expected to fall from Rs. 20 crore to less than Rs. 10 crore in 1947.[271]

The *Times* reported that although flood waters had begun to recede by the first week of October, vast area were still under water. The report also said that a large number of refugees had lost their bullock carts and cattle in the floods, as also their only stocks of food grain.[272] As the Sutlej went on a rampage, over 100,000 people in the Lahore region were rendered homeless in the last week of September. The water supply system was completely out of gear in Lahore, so much so there were reports that while restaurants were serving food they often were unable to provide water.[273] Four to six feet of water flowed through Ferozepur town, with almost every road and bridge in the region suffering damage.[274] Seven miles of the crucial Grand Trunk Road was washed away near Kartarpur.[275]

CHOLERA MAKES MATTERS WORSE

The outbreak of cholera epidemic was therefore only a natural sequel. Even troops were affected—the Dogra Regiment for example lost four soldiers to cholera.[276] On its part the government did not spare any effort to tackle the crisis. A New Delhi report said a million doses of cholera vaccine were being produced weekly at facilities in Calcutta, Bombay and Shillong. In the western districts cholera was widespread in towns like Kasur, Jhang and Okara. In Kasur alone over 1,000 people were reported to have died by 3 September. In the central districts Amritsar was also among the cities seriously effected by cholera.[277]

THE WHOLESALER–RETAILER ADMINISTRATOR NEXUS

It is also important to understand that the food problem was not merely that of shortage—it was also of distribution. While we have seen that there was rampant corruption among the chain of lower officials that supervised the distribution of essential supplies in normal times, one should also examine the reasons for the sustained existence and prospering of this corrupt chain.

Many years after Penderel Moon had left India, the BBC recorded some of his impressions of the Raj. The observations of Moon in the context of corruption are interesting. While what Moon said was obviously a generalized view and certainly not specific to 1947, it did show how the rich traders of Punjab were able to benefit from the situation, which was possible only with the patronage of the senior bureaucracy. Moon was asked to comment on the extent of corruption among British officers in India. He said that while corruption among the lower levels (Indian officials), particularly at the sub-inspector of police, tehsildar and patwari levels was rampant, among senior officers, particularly the British, it was limited. It was well known that rich traders usually ensured a regular supply of essential commodities and groceries to the households of some British and senior Indian officials. He also said that some British officers mainly of the political department were known to accept the generosity of Indian princes particularly for occupying prime residential properties in Simla.[278] As Moon put it, the humble patwari with a monthly salary of Rs. 25 was assigned the onerous task of maintaining about 5,000 land records. Thus when the small peasant/landowner was confronted with the patwari, a deal was bound to be struck. The same applied at every level—doctors, lower judiciary, and the worst of them all the ration controlling officers.

ECONOMIC CRISIS IN WEST PUNJAB

Virtually every trade and commercial activity had come to a standstill within a few days of the enforcement of partition. An anonymos letter from Lahore said it all: 'These silly and shortsighted statements (by Muslim League leaders) have intensified panic among the minorities, who are leaving in increasing numbers . . . shops, offices are deserted . . . after this universal exodus who will pay the taxes and fill the coffers of the government' . . . geese laying golden eggs are being killed by the silly and suicidal policy of the government. Reason and sanity are at discount.'[279]

The collections of the Lahore octroi had fallen from an average of Rs. 12,000 per day to less than Rs. 1,200.[280] In fact, the *CMG* (22 August) even commented on the issue:

[U]nconfirmed reports state that in Lahore only 10000 Hindus remain from the earlier about 300000 . . . the rest have learnt through their cost that the knife and torch speak louder than words . . . one consequence of the panic exodus has been the strangulation of all business in which Hindus played an important part . . . the Hindus were now it is being realised the cog that kept all the business running. . . . Many will soon realise if they have not already done so how great is the dependence on the few who are no longer their [*sic*].

The exit of Hindu traders from the western districts was likely to affect not only the tax collection of the government, but there were Muslim farmers who believed the panic movement would be detrimental to peasant interests as well. This is what an influential landowner of Multan, Niaz Ahmad Qureshi, had to say in a letter: 'peace is essential to Muslim farmers because proper prices for the agricultural products can be paid only by Hindu traders who will return to their business only if there is peace'.[281]

Banking Collapses

The collapse of the banking system in the initial few weeks personified the anarchy. On 5 September, the West Punjab government enacted an ordinance—the Punjab Public Safety Act (Amendment 8, 1947) which banned the removal of bank assets to East Punjab.[282] The ordinance also empowered designated officials to enter the premises of those who were not traceable to prepare inventories of assets. The Government of India took up the matter the very next day obviously because the assets of influential people who had shifted to Simla and Delhi were involved. However, the Finance Minister of Pakistan was evasive in his response—that it was only an ordinance and not yet been implemented and that depositors were free to withdraw their assets and also that the order was only to restrict bank managements to ensure that the interests of the depositors were protected.[283] Speaking of the safety of valuables and the credibility of banks, a report interestingly also discussed how most people with money felt it was safer to bury it in the ground than keep it in the bank vaults.[284]

The collapse of the banking system in West Punjab was not merely (as earlier believed) a result of Hindu bank clerks having run away, it was also because even Muslim bank officials, in Lahore in particular, had deserted their posts. About 500 clerks, mostly Muslim, had deserted from mid-August to the beginning of September in Lahore alone.[285] To restore some element of normalcy, the West Punjab government announced special protection facilities for non-Muslim bank staff who wished to return to duty. The announcement even added that the protection would in fact be provided by Gurkha troops. The collapse of the banking system was also not really due to a shortage of currency or the depletion of resources, but that cheques were not being cleared because there was no one to clear them.[286]

The Punjab National Bank, the premier bank of Punjab, unfortunately, as we have already seen, was among the first to shift its head office from Lahore, business wise a good decision but on a more profound level a decision which perscribed the business community and brought Punjab's commercial activity to a grinding halt. As time showed, the staff it left behind in Lahore too deserted their posts, leading the bank management to issue an advertisement calling on its employees to report for duty by 10 September, failing which their services would be terminated.

One of the multinationals of the time, the Bata Shoe Company, too, was encountering the problem of employees having fled: 'employees who have left are informed that [the] situation in the locality is now calm and they are earnestly requested to return not later than Monday 8 September. Up to this date positions will be kept open and also their accommodation in the colony . . . military protection is continuing.' Another multinational, Grandlays Bank, made a similar appeal. For smaller concerns like the Rex Hampton Civil & Military Tailors, the popular tailors of Lahore, the problem was not of deserting employees but of customers who had failed to turn up to collect their orders, leaving the company with no choice but to warn its customers that after 10 September the company would not be responsible for the clothes.[287]

EDUCATION IN CHAOS

On 9 September newspapers carried reports that the Khalsa College for Women, Lahore had closed permanently.[288] This of course was only the beginning. Dayal Singh College announced that it was terminating the services of its employees but added an assurance that if and when the college reopend in East Punjab, as many former employees as was possible would be re-employed.

The fallout of the sudden closure of institutions was naturally wide ranging. The worst affected were science, and medical students. Bakshi Tek Chand was assigned the task of contacting students of Balak Ram Medical College, Lahore so as to help them get admissions in other medical colleges of India. Likewise, students of King Edward Medical College, Lahore, were asked to contact the Principal of Glancy Medical College, Amritsar.

The problem was further complicated by the fact that established institutions had not only to leave at short notice but also had no appropriate places to relocate—be it in the eastern or the western side. Zia-ud-din, a student of Mayo College, Amritsar, suggested in a letter that since college buildings run by Muslims in Amritsar had been burnt those being vacated by Hindus and Sikhs in Lahore should be allotted to institutions that had reloated from Amritsar.[289]

CIVIL ADMINISTRATION IN EAST PUNJAB

The level to which the civil administration had collapsed in East Punjab stands underlined by none other than the Governor-General himself. Mountbatten asked Governor Trivedi if the East Punjab government was still in a position to maintain law and order, to which the Governor said rather plainly, it could not be done without military help because East Punjab was short of at least 7,000 policemen.[290] A few days earlier (29 August), Field Marshal Auchinleck as Supreme Commander, while giving his views on a note that was to be discussed by the Joint Defence Council, went to the extent of saying that 'civil administration had ceased to exist in East Punjab'.[291]

The Indian High Commissioner to Pakistan had telegraphed authorities in New Delhi from his camp office in Lahore as early as 27 August conveying the views of Rees the PBF Commander that if things did not immediately improve in the East Punjab, we (India) should be prepared for a whole scale massacre of Sikhs in the western districts.[292]

GOVERNOR TRIVEDI PULLS UP HOME MINISTER SWARN SINGH

It was against this background and the rather embarrassing position in which Governor Trivedi appears to have found himself (in view of the observations of the Governor-General and the Supreme Commander) that occurred the most amazing exchange of views between the two people who were directly heading the civil administration in East Punjab—Governor Trivedi and Home Minister Swarn Singh. On 4 September, Trivedi wrote to Swarn Singh: 'you know that I have made no secret of the fact that the problem of restoring law and order in East Punjab is largely one of putting a stop to the activities of the Sikhs—there is undoubtedly an organization behind these activities'. Trivedi then said that the appeals for peace by senior Sikh leaders like Giani Kartar Singh and Master Tara Singh had obviously not gone down to 'what we might describe as low level leaders at tehsil and village level—my information is that the *jathas* are getting bigger'.[293]

Again on 11 September, Trivedi wrote to Swarn Singh wanting to know if the appeals of the senior Akali leaders were having an impact at the ground level. Trivedi told Swarn Singh that he had also been informed that some Sikhs gangs had even started attacking non-Muslims.[294] Swarn Singh did not reply, so Trivedi shot off another letter the following day, giving a list of incidents in which some *jathas* were involved.[295]

Swarn Singh finally replied on 17 September. He categorically stated that there was no organization behind the Sikh attacks and that they were only sporadic: 'we (the Punjab Govt.) have not been able to detect an organized effort'. He said there could not be an organized effort in view of the fact that the senior Akali leaders were working towards restoring peace and there was little chance of any parallel organization being in existence. Swarn Singh also suggested that since communications had broken down, it was possible that the appeals of the senior leaders were not reaching the village level.

SWARN SINGH ACCUSES RSS AND COMMUNISTS

Swarn Singh's reply to Governor Trivedi's letter also carried two other significant statements. Swarn Singh said that the Sikhs alone were not the ones breaking the law in East Punjab: 'I have in possession facts showing that large scale looting was resorted to by Hindu and Sikhs alike with respect to abandoned property.'[296]

The other important point raised by Swarn Singh in the letter was:

> Along with the propaganda from the west is the subtle propaganda of the RSS and Communists, both of whom want to utilise the present conditions for building up goodwill of the people in order to build up power for the

future . . . whatever service they do, but one thing they certainly do and that is to excite the Hindus and Sikhs against each other and to spread a feeling of bitterness against the Provincial and Central Government.[297]

Trivedi in a curt note on 26 September, said he did not agree with Swarn Singh's view that there was no organizational effort supporting the killings in East Punjab. He pointed out it was not possible for hundreds of people to gather at a place to conduct an attack without an organization's support.[298] Trivedi said he had been informed that on many occasions even the arrival time of trains had been publicly announced. He expressed to Swarn Singh his anguish that in many districts the district superintendents of police and the district magistrates were doing nothing to control the situation.[299]

This letter of Trivedi also contained an interesting revelation relating to the differences of opinion between him and his home minister about the *kirpan*. It appears that Governor Trivedi was keen to ban the carrying of *kirpans* more than 9 inch in length, but 'on seeing your reaction to the proposal in the Cabinet meeting I dropped the idea'.[300]

THREE WEEKS LATER

A special correspondent of the *Times* based in Lahore reported on the problems being encountered in ensuring the safety of trains and refugee convoys.

It is too early yet to say whether the abolition of the Punjab Boundary Force and the transfer of responsibility to the Dominion armies and administrations are effecting a radical improvement. Policy henceforth is that, whenever the evacuees of one community have to be protected and escorted through hostile territory, the guards and escorts will be of the same community as the evacuees. On the Indian side of the frontier (but not in Pakistan) all Brigade and Battalion Commands are being placed in Indian hands.[301]

The same reporter also made an interesting observation: 'What made these sturdy Sikh settlers many of them ex-soldiers leave their rich agricultural lands? Here it was less fear from Muslim neighbours than fear from the police.' Writing a kind of report card for the first about three weeks the *Times* reporter also said: 'The slaughter in East Punjab was worse than in the West because the Sikhs were better armed and better organized, but there have been massacres in West Punjab, like that in East Punjab and the brutalities have been just as bad on both sides.'[302]

The report then touched upon a broad general picture of the three weeks—15 August to 4 September:

The crisis in the Punjab is changing in character. The main slaughter is over. . . . The chief problems now are large-scale looting on both sides of the frontier and sporadic attacks on the minority communities as they are evacuated on foot, in trucks, and by railway. There are several reasons for this drop in the curve of violence. First, satiety, secondly, the evacuation has already been on such a large scale that there are few villages left to burn and few minority communities left to kill. Thirdly, the determined efforts made by the leaders on both sides, among whom there has been complete agreement in desiring to check this calamity, show signs of at last percolating to the lower administrative levels.

STICKING ON IN LAHORE

Like the *Times* reporter who believed that the killings and the killers had exhausted themselves, there were others too who thought normalcy was returning. An unnamed 'Hindu' wrote to the *CMG* from Lahore: 'I decided to stick to Lahore because I am one of those who believes that Hindus and Muslims cannot do without each other' and that 'conditions are now improving'. He also said that Muslims too had fled Lahore and even though people were returning, travelling was still unsafe. The letter went on to say that Hindus were wanted back in Lahore and could easily be convinced to return if, among other things, the police and magistrates were more courteous towards minorities.[303]

Authorities in Lahore issued a statement saying that the looting and arson had been controlled and only stray incidents were now occurring. In fact, there were many others who were keen to return to Lahore from Amritsar. *CMG* received many queries with regard to the situation in Lahore. A letter from Rai Bahadur, said: 'a large number of people had left the Model Town of Lahore because of looting by Jats from neighbouring villagers they now want to return'. As the *CMG* had been doing in other cases, it informed the writer of the letter, that things had returned to normal in the Model Town area of Lahore.[304]

NEHRU SUMS UP THE FIRST MONTH

Nehru addressed a major press conference in New Delhi on 13 September. Mountbatten was also present as was Rajkumari Amrit Kaur.[305]

As he had done on 28 August, Nehru briefed the large number of reporters with his assessment of the situation and started by admitting that the government had indeed underestimated the crisis in mid-August. He then very emphatically stated: 'it is totally untrue that Sikhs are responsible for it'. Characteristically, he said that: 'we were taken unaware . . . and if a government is taken unaware it must suffer for it', and that 'sitting in Delhi allows local events to overwhelm us'.[306] Nehru blamed the foreign press for holding the Sikhs responsible and asserted that the Sikhs no doubt had 'misbehaved' but so had others. Indians, Nehru, said were peace-loving people: 'something must have happened that completely deranged them and upset the mental machinery'.[307]

Once again Nehru linked the crisis to the March disturbances and even to the Calcutta killings of 16 August 1946, as well as the subsequent disturbances. He explained that the fallout of the March killings in Rawalpindi was that a large number of people migrated from the region, 'may be up to 400,000', and these people, he said, brought terrible stories. Secondly, Nehru, explained, that the forced migration that followed the March killings disturbed the balance of the population between communities which had for ages enjoyed peace. Once the balance was upset, the one-sided killings became easier. What followed Rawalpindi was the killings of some Muslims in Amritsar, followed thereafter by the targetting of Sikhs in Lahore.

Nehru also for the first time gave his estimate of the number that may have been killed in the first month—15 August to 15 September. He first ridiculed the reports in the foreign press and even the Pakistan press that over 500,000 people had already been killed. He said, 'the official view was that about 1,000 had been killed in Delhi, and about 15,000 in West and East Punjab . . . but my estimate is about 30,000 killed'.[308] The *Statesman* added that Nehru had given a figure of 15,000 killed, which he himself said appeared low and could easily be trebled.[309] These figures came as surprise and were not generally acceptable to observers then or even years later. In any case, even India's High Commissioner in Karachi, Sri Prakash, had quoted a couple of days before this press conference that 150,000 had already been killed in Pakistan alone.[310] The Pakistan government in early 1948 listed its own estimates of the killings in a small publication titled *Note on Sikh Plan*. In this highly controversial note it said that between 500,000 to one million Muslims had been killed by Hindus and Sikhs, mainly the Akal Fauj and the RSS, in

Punjab and Kashmir in the first few weeks following the partition of Punjab.[311]

THREE WEEKS—AN IMPOSSIBLE TASK

Nehru, true to himself, had been bold enough to admit that indeed the government may have failed in its duty of anticipating the monumental crisis, but who could possibly have foreseen the scale of the problem. Shaukat Hayat, the son of the late Sikander Hayat, the first Premier of Punjab, himself now the Revenue Minister of West Punjab, also summed up in a statement on 10 September the monumental dimensions of the crisis that Punjab was undergoing and was to undergo in the days that followed. Shaukat said: 'the magnitude of the refugee problem is without precedent, the only one that can be thought of is the exchange of population between Turkey and Greece after the First World War. But that was done with the support of the League of Nations, with immense resources, took one year to complete and involved just a million people. As against this we have been given 3 weeks and with no resources.'[312]

HOW COULD THE GOVERNMENTS HAVE UNDERESTIMATED

It is abundantly clear that everyone from Lord Mountbatten, Nehru and Jinnah down to the lowest functionary in the government of Punjab, both East and West, was taken by surprise both by the dimension of the crisis and even more by the nature of the hatred and viciousness that had got hold of the people. If the inept manner in which they tried to handle the situation is discounted in view of the surprise, one could easily come away believing that the best that could be done was indeed done.

But the counterview seems far more comfortable to support. That the system of government should have been taken by surprise becomes inacceptable when one looks even casually at the weeks that preceded the violence. What happened in Punjab in the first month—15 August to 15 September—was something that was being predicted by everyone, in letters and articles in newspapers, in street gossip. But even if this were ignored, how could the government have remained unprepared after the large number of reports filed by Governor Jenkins who had repeatedly warned that if the partition plan was pushed through there was just no way the Punjab could be prevented from blowing up?

But then this too is only one aspect. The main charge that was made by newspapers particularly against the Government of India was that there was just no general plan of how to handle the crisis—the government was left to merely react to situations rather than to prevent them.[313] An interesting report has detailed how things had simply collapsed in Amritsar and of why and how this happened and also of how the leaders, the police, the civil authority, had failed to discharge their duties. I am inclined to believe that the case of the collapse of Amritsar can with some minor modifications, be applied to the whole of Punjab: 'Despite [the] dawn of freedom Amritsar's administrative machinery has reached breaking point . . . [it is] hopeless in efficiency . . . [there is] no coordination, aimless running around by officers.' The report then said that far too many politicians were coming and going, they were doing nothing but just talking and taxing a hopelessly overburdened administration.[314] Mridula Sarabhai, the report said, was one exception to this, she stood out for the good work she was doing in Amritsar.[315] The report also drew attention to the extensive complains of loot and complete lack of discipline in the police: 'While one senior officer said the seniors were helpless because of the indiscipline at the lower level, the juniors said the senior officers were helpless only because they too had a share in the loot'.[316]

In fact, even Nehru acknowledged the charges against the police and even sections of the army. In a radio broadcast (9 September) he had said: 'I have heard complaints against the army and the police that they were not impartial and had not acted when required remaining just onlookers . . . during the last few days I have supped my fill of horror. My mind is full of the horror of things I have seen and heard.'[317]

The scenes of horror to which the Prime Minister referred were partly the result of the misplaced optimism and enthusiasm with which political figures had made loud promises. As the head of the Ahmediya Community, Mirza Bashirudin Mahmood said in a conference in Lahore on 8 September—Muslims in East Punjab suffered because of overconfidence and ignorance, because all along they had been made to believe that Gurdaspur and Ferozepur would go to West Punjab and, therefore, they had made no arrangements to leave in time or leave safely.[318] This was exactly the case with a large number of

Hindus and Sikhs who were in the border districts and who had all along been told that even Lahore, for example, was coming to East Punjab.

Part or a major part of the problem was that no sooner had both the countries stepped into freedom than, a large number of people began to view the new-found freedom as a ticket to personal growth—of self, family, friends and acquaintances. Thus, people who should really have been striving to restore order were in fact striving for personal aggrandisement. Zakir Mashadi of Lahore said that the new government that was formed after 15 August in West Punjab started from the first day to give important positions and postings to the favoured few the 'sons, sons-in-law, brothers of a few people'. He went on to urge the government to put a stop to nepotism and intrigue and replace the old time bureaucrats with good officers.[319] Mubarak Ali of Lyallpur wrote: 'with the advent of Pakistan favouritism has become rife . . . key posts are going to favourites'. He cited an example of the junior-most person being appointed Principal of the Government Veterinary College Lahore.[320]

East Punjab Premier Bhargava Reviews the First Month

On 16 September, East Punjab Premier Gopichand Bhargava issued a statement to the press. He said that over 17,00,000 non-Muslims had so far crossed over into East Punjab from Pakistan and about the same number of non-Muslims still remained to be evacuated. There were daily reports of Muslim police and troops attacking the non-Muslim refugees in West Punjab, and that there were also reports in East Punjab of government officials rioting. The government, he said, had decided to impose punitive fines on such government employees.[321]

MEO's First Report

The Military Evacuation Organization (MEO) which had been set up under Brigadier S.B.S. Chimni with headquarters at Amritsar, and which had become functional by about 1 September also issued a press statement on 16 September saying that in the preceding nine days the MEO had moved about one million people, 300,000 of them by train, 100,000 by motor transport and about 600,000 by foot convoys.[322] The statement also said that 750 abducted women had been recovered in Jandiala Kalan (East Punjab).

The task obviously was far greater than anyone had imagined, newspapers in the middle of September were filled with appeals from people stuck in various parts of Punjab seeking help from evacuation authorities. On 17 September, for example, there were appeals for help from Multan, Sargodha, Mianwali, Jhang, Dera Ghazi Khan, and Mandi Bahauddin. The villagers of Bilwapur, Jodhpur and Kabirwala (all in the Khanewal Mandi region) reported that they were surrounded by hostile people. Dera Ghazi Khan was cut-off by the river Indus, and over 50,000 people were collected in pockets.[323]

Strange and ironic as it is, even as hundreds of thousands of people waited for evacuation from both sides, there were reports that six special refugee trains that had taken Muslim refugees from the East Punjab to Pakistan had come back empty.[324] Dr Mathai, Transport Minister, India, who was present in the ECM (meeting) where the issue was raised said he had in fact heard of similar complaints from the West Punjab authorities, who were saying that refugee specials carrying non-Muslims into East Punjab were returning empty.

As charges and countercharges flew from both sides, and the two prime ministers entered into a war of words[325] as to which side, the East or the West, was responsible for more killings, Mohan Lal, Vice-President of the Servants of People Society (Lahore), said that while he did not wish to criticize either of the two governments, it was clear that the West Punjab government was doing a better and more planned job of the evacuation of its people. He said the West Punjab authorities were evacuating Muslims from East Punjab not only from railheads and big towns but even from remote places—Dharamshala being one such place. As of the first week of September he said the Government of India appeared to have no effective plan for the minorities in the West Punjab. Interestingly he noted that only two non-official agencies of the non-Muslims in Punjab, the RSS and the Akali sewadars, were playing a frontal role in the refugee evacuation and relief work.[326]

NEHRU TIRED AND FATIGUED

Price Day was a reporter with *The Baltimore Sun* and had reported Second World War and various other events in the post-War period.

He had been assigned to cover the impending independence of India. He wrote:

In his moment of triumphs, Nehru was compelled by circumstances to consider first not the program of long-range reforms on which he had built his career, nor even the urgent daily administrative and diplomatic problems, but an outbreak of communal killing on a tremendous scale. . . . Deaths ran into the tens of thousands, and then into the hundreds of thousands. . . . Millions of refugees took to the roads. Disease, including cholera, spread over the northern plains. Government administration limped almost to a halt. Communications were in chaos. No food moved on the railways, which were packed with refugees.

. . . Denied so much as an hour of pause and reflection, Nehru shuttled constantly between Delhi and the Punjab. . . . The Prime Minister, already fatigued by the innumerable decisions that had to be made before the transfer of power, grew wearier. . . . The two extremes of his temperament, gentleness and quick impatience, became more pronounced, the one in regret at the toll of death and suffering and the blot on India's victory, the other in sharp anger at those Indians who encouraged murder and those foreigners who insisted on taking a patronizing attitude toward India in its time of distress.[327]

The *HT* summed up the first month of the crisis with a cartoon which showed a tiger locked in a cage, the word lawlessness written in bold letters on the cage. Outside the cage was shown Nehru standing with a gun—'you wont catch me napping again',[328] went the line. The *HT*, as time would prove, was obviously doing some wishful thinking. The 'Tiger' was yet to be caged, and thousands of lives were yet to be lost.

NOTES

1. Bali, *Now It Can Be Told*, pp. 37–9.
2. The photograph also showed the ambassadors of USA and China in the Constituent Assembly.
3. *HT*, 16 August 1947.
4. *CMG*, 20 August 1947; The exodus was sudden, a small example of the desperation with which families fled being that even the Librarian of the Punjab Public Library (a Hindu) left Lahore without a trace. The keeper of the main keys could not be traced for days together, *PT*, 30 August 1947.

5. *CMG*, 19 August 1947.
6. *PT*, 6 September 1947.
7. *CMG*, 14 August 1947.
8. Ibid., 17 August, 1947.
9. Ibid., 19 August 1947.
10. *Dawn*, 19 August 1947; *HT*, 19 August 1947.
11. *HT*, 19 August 1947.
12. *CMG*, 20 August 1947; *PT*, 21 August 1947.
13. Ibid., 21 August 1947 also *HT*, 20 August 1947.
14. *CMG*, 22 August 1947; *PT*, 22 August 1947, *HT*, 22 August 1947.
15. *Dawn*, 22 August 1947.
16. *CMG*, 23 August 1947.
17. *Dawn*, 22 August 1947.
18. *HT*, 22 August 1947.
19. Ibid.
20. Ibid., 17 August 1947.
21. *HT*, 18 August 1947. The West Punjab Government officially announced that trains were unsafe and people should avoid travelling particularly between Lahore and Delhi, *CMG*, 26 August 1947.
22. Ibid., 17 August 1947.
23. Ibid., 19 August 1947.
24. *CMG*, 26 August 1947.
25. Ibid., 22 August 1947.
26. Ibid., 22 and 23 August 1947.
27. *HT*, 20 August 1947.
28. *HT*, 22 August 1947.
29. *CMG*, 26 August 1947.
30. *HT*, 24 August 1947.
31. Ibid., 25 August 1947.
32. Ibid., 30 August 1947.
33. *HT*, 26 August 1947 and *CMG*, 26 August 1947.
34. Ibid., 28 August 1947; *CMG*, 29 August 1947; *PT*, 29 August 1947.
35. *CMG*, 27 August, also *PT*, 27 August 1947.
36. *CMG*, 28 August 1947.
37. *PT*, 28 August 1947; *Dawn*, 27 August 1947.
38. *Dawn*, 21 August 1947.
39. Ibid., 27 August 1947.
40. *PT*, 22 August 1947; *PT*, 3 September 1947.
41. *HT*, 31 August 1947.
42. *CMG*, 30 August 1947.
43. *PT*, 28 August 1947; *Dawn*, 28 August 1947.
44. Ibid., 26 and 27 August 1947.
45. *PT*, 28 August 1947.

46. Extracts of Emergency Committee Meeting (hereafter ECM), 18th Meeting, 29 September 1947, Mountbatten Papers (hereafter MP), File 131-B, Microfilm, NMML, New Delhi.
47. *Dawn*, 25 August 1947.
48. Ibid., 27 August 1947.
49. Ibid., 26 August 1947.
50. Ibid., 28 August 1947, *CMG*, 9 September 1947.
51. *PT*, 28 August 1947.
52. *HT*, 5 September 1947.
53. *CMG*, 9 September 1947; Over 13,000 railway wagons were of the track, *CMG*, 29 August 1947. So severe was the coal crisis that the fund starved government of Pakistan was trying from the very first days to arrange supplies from South Africa, see *CMG* 18 September 1947.
54. *CMG*, 26 August 1947.
55. *Dawn*, 25 August 1947.
56. Ibid.; see *HT*, 23 August 1947.
57. ECM, 5th Meeting, 9 September, MP, File 131-A.
58. *PT*, 28 August 1947; *HT*, 31 August 1947.
59. *CMG*, 26 August 1947.
60. *HT*, 26 August 1947.
61. *Dawn*, 23 August 1947; *CMG*, 24 August 1947.
62. Ibid., 26 August 1947; also *Dawn*, 25 August 1947.
63. *CMG*, 31 August 1947; also *PT*, 31 August 1947.
64. *HT*, 24 August 1947.
65. *CMG*, 24 August 1947.
66. Ibid., 29 August 1947.
67. Ibid., August 1947, ibid. 27 September 1947. Yet another letter by Ahmad Qureshi said that Hindu traders alone were capable of paying a good price for the farmers produce, 28 September 1947.
68. Ibid., 14 September 1947.
69. *HT*, 26 August 1947.
70. *CMG*, 26 August 1947.
71. Ibid., 30 August 1947; *HT*, 29 August 1947; *PT*, 30 August 1947.
72. Ibid., *Times* (London), 29 August 1947 (Cuttings compiled by Intelligence Deptt.); published by University Microfilms Buchinghamshire, NMML.
73. *CMG*, 30 August 1947 *HT*, 29 August 1947; *PT*, 30 August 1947.
74. *PT*, 30 August 1947; *CMG*, 30 August 1947.
75. *CMG*, 30 August 1947; and Press Information Bureau, New Delhi, 29 August 1947, Nehru Clippings.
76. *CMG*, 30 August 1947; also *HT*, 29 August 1947.
77. *PT*, 30 August 1947 The issue that Sikh raiding *jathas* were un-

controllable because they were operating from the Princely state territories was raised repeatedly in August and September. See for example Extracts ECM, 8th Meeting, 22 September, MP, File 129, where such *jathas* were reported to be causing problems in the Simla territory, and Nehru orders Simla DC to seal borders at Kalka and Tara Devi. Also *Free Press Journal*, 29 August 1947, Nehru Clippings, 1947, Microfilm, NMML

78. The G.D. Khosla Papers (File 16) contain numerous letters (original) exchanged between the Maharaja of Kapurthala Jagjit Singh who had shifted his family to Srinagar during the disturbances and his Prime Minister Lakhpat Rai Sikund. On 14 September Lakhpat Rai reported to the Maharaja: 'Sikh bands of hooligans and marauders have started hovering every-where. Their aim is to loot and murder Muslims and abduct their women.' The letters also include detail of some Muslim killings and the fact that Muslims and fled even from the state services. The situation obviously could not have been any better in the other Sikh states of East Punjab.
79. *PT*, 30 August 1947.
80. *CMG*, 30 August 1947; Press Information Bureau Note, Nehru Clippings, 29 August 1947.
81. *HT*, 29 August 1947; *HT*, 14 September 1947; *CMG*, 14 September 1947.
82. *Statesman*, 29 August 1947.
83. *Search Light* (Patna), 31 August 1947, Nehru Clippings, 1947.
84. *Free Press Journal*, 30 August 1947, Nehru Clippings, 1947.
85. *The Pioneer* (Lucknow), 30 August 1947, Nehru Clippings, 1947.
86. 'Vanished Truth' *PT*, 31 August 1947. Tara Singh's famous and inciting speech made in front of the Punjab Assembly building in March—a reference has already been made to this. Isher Singh, Majhel's Memoirs (Oral History Transcript), NMML.
87. *CMG*, 5 September 1947.
88. *Times* (London), 25 August 1947.
89. Ibid., 29 August 1947.
90. Ibid., 25 August 1947; This report has also been cited by Lt. Col. John Peddie (7/14 Punjab Regiment) in his unpublished memoir titled 'A Steady Drummer', accessible at the Imperial War Museum, London. Peddie has also recorded how a Bishop who had worked in Lahore had told him of the Church having started three special hospitals in Lahore, to treat women whose breasts had been amputated and for those whose limbs had been cut and a third for those whose nostrils had been torn, p. 44.
91. I have deleted a few lines at the end of the report—which are clearly one sided and are not printable in present times, see Ibid. Commenting on the role of these *jathas* the Defence Minister of Pakistan had sent a tele-

gram to the Joint Defence Council of India and Pakistan saying that the *jathas* were having a free hand in Hoshiarpur, Jullundur, Gurdaspur, Ludhiana and Ferozepur. He pleaded with the JDC to be ruthless and use even planes—see Telegram 28 August, MP Reel 15.

92. Mss. Eur. F 200/141 India Viceregal Correspondence Files, 'Sikh Problem Pt. II', draft in the form of an Aide-Memoir by Governor-General Mountbatten, 1 January 1948 to 24 April 1948.
93. Byron Farwell, *The Gurkhas*, London, 1984, pp. 244–6.
94. Jeffrey, 'The Punjab Boundary Force', pp. 505–7.
95. Interview with Field Marshall Claude Auchinleck Playback, 19 December 1972, BBC Tape Transcript, Imperial War Museum, Deptt. of Sound Records, NMML, p. 56.
96. *Times*, 5 September 1947.
97. Ibid., 29 August 1947.
98. Ibid., 30 September 1947.
99. *CMG*, 31 August 1947; *PT*, 31 August 1947.
100. *PT*, 31 August 1947.
101. *CMG*, 31 August 1947.
102. Extract from letter Messervy to Auchinleck, 25 August 1947, MP, Reel 15.
103. Note by Supreme Commander for JDC, 29 August 1948, MP, File 128, Reel 15.
104. Misc., 185/Item 2781, Imperial War Museum, London, Reading Room Document Section.
105. Extracts from ECM 1st Meeting, 6 September 1947, Item no. 4, MP, File 128, Reel 15; *HT*, 18 September 1947.
106. *HT*, 16 September 1947.
107. *CMG*, 26 September 1947.
108. Interview of Field Marshall Claude Auchinleck, Playback, 19 December 1972, BBC Tape Transcript, p. 56.
109. Lloyd Jones Papers, Box IV, CSAS.
110. Lt. Col. R.N.P. Reynolds Papers, CSAS.
111. *HT*, 2 September 1947.
112. 'Migration in Punjab', IOR Mss. EUR. F/64/47/Muddie Collection; Lord Ismay 'India Situation', IOR Mss. F/200/165, 5 October 1947.
113. *CMG*, 3 September 1947.
114. Ibid., SOS message by Simla Deputy Commissioner, Extracts from ECM, 11 September 1947, MP, File 128, Reel 15.
115. *PT*, 30 August 1947; *HT*, 30 August 1947.
116. See *PT*, 2 September 1947.
117. *HT*, 4 September 1947.
118. Ibid.; Madan Lal Khurana, 'The Bloodshed could have been avoided', in Ahmed Salim (ed.), *Lahore in 1947*, New Delhi, 2001, p. 223.
119. *PT*, 3 September 1947.

120. Ibid., September This was possibly because Nehru's charisma easily overshadowed the Pakistan Prime Minister and the tour's proceedings were reduced to nothing but the presence and views of Nehru.
121. *CMG*, 3 September 1947.
122. Ibid. Also *HT*, 2 and 3 September 1947.
123. *HT*, 8 September 1947.
124. Ibid., 14 September 1947.
125. *CMG*, 10 September 1947.
126. *PT* and *CMG,* 9 and 10 September 1947.
127. *CMG*, 9 September 1947.
128. Ibid., 10 September 1947.
129. Ibid., 14 September 1947.
130. Ibid., 5 September 1947, and *PT*, 5 September 1947.
131. Mela Ram Mohan (Lahore), *CMG*, 14 September 1947.
132. *HT*, 6 September 1947.
133. Ibid.
134. IOR Mss. Eur., D 621/14, Wilfred Russel Diary Entry, 24 September 1947.
135. Magazine Section, *HT*, 7 September 1947.
136. *HT*, 31 August 1947.
137. *HT*, 2 September 1947; *CMG,* 3 September 1947.
138. *PT*, 30 August 1947.
139. PT, 31 August 1947.
140. *HT*, 2 September 1947.
141. Jeffrey, 'The Punjab Boundary Force', p. 497, Rees Papers, 31 August 1947.
142. Jeffrey, 'The Punjab Boundary Force', p. 498; also see Charles C. Trench, *The Indian Army 1900–47*, p. 294.
143. Ibid., 'The Punjab Boundary Force', pp. 504–5; Andrew Roth, 'On the Sikh Muslim Frontier', *The Nation*, 20 September 1947.
144. Ibid., 'The Punjab Boundary Force'; Khushwant Singh, *History of the Sikhs*, vol. II, p. 273; Pyarelal, *Mahatma Gandhi*, p. 385.
145. Ibid., pp. 510–11.
146. Trench, *The Indian Army*, p. 294.
147. Lt. Col. John Peddie (7/14 Punjab Regiment), 'The Steady Drummer', unpublished memoir, no. 96/17/1, p. 17, Imperial War Museum, Reading Room, London.
148. Jeffrey, 'The Punjab Boundry Force', p. 514.
149. Ibid.; *The Times* (London), 29 August 1947.
150. IOR L/MIL/17/5/4319, Report on the PBF by T.W. Rees—15 November 1947, p. 16.
151. P. Brenden Papers, CSAS.
152. IOR Mss. Eur. F/64/47, Muddie Collection, draft of an article by Muddie, 'Migration in Punjab'.

153. IOR Mss. Eur. D 1065/1, Police Papers, W.H.A. Rich.
154. *Times* (London), 26 September 1947.
155. Auchinleck to Mountbatten, 27 August 1947, MP, File 128, Reel 15.
156. Messervy to Auchinleck, 25 August 1947, MP, File 128, Reel 15.
157. Note by Supreme Commander, 29 August 1947, MP, File 128, Reel 15.
158. *HT*, 18 August 1947.
159. Ibid., 31 August 1947.
160. *CMG,* 4 September 1947.
161. ECM, File 128, MP Reel 15.
162. Extracts from ECM, 13th Meeting, 18 September 1947, MP, File 129.
163. *HT*, 14 September 1947.
164. *PT*, 31 August 1947.
165. Ibid., 2 September 1947.
166. Ibid., 5 September 1947.
167. Ibid., 2 September 1947.
168. *HT*, 3 September 1947.
169. See government statement (official) which said that there were many reports of Sikhs wearing military uniform, in one clash with police four such Sikhs were killed, these included a prominent INA figure, *CMG,* 6 September 1947. As also discussed earlier, the reports of these *jathas* were numerous, Nehru raised the issue many times as did Trivedi, Governor East Punjab, see for example Extracts, ECM 8th Meeting, 22 September 1947, MP, File 129. This note discusses how these *jathas* were invading the Simla region, committing crimes and going back into Patiala. Nehru ordered the Deputy Commissioner Simla to put check points at Kalka and Tara Devi. Trivedi raised the issue in a curt note with East Punjab Home Minister Swarn Singh, see, Trivedi to Swarn Singh, 4 September 1947, MP, File 129. Also see n. 187—the reference to G.D. Khosla Papers, and the *jatha* activities in Kapurthala.
170. *CMG*, 4 September 1947.
171. *HT*, 11 September 1947.
172. *CMG*, 6 September 1947.
173. Extracts ECM, 3rd Meeting, 7 September, MP, File 131-A.
174. 'Sikh Problem', Part II (9) 18 April 1947 to 17 September 1947, Indian Viceregal Correspondence, MP, File 140.
175. *HT*, 6 September 1047.
176. *CMG*, 7 September 1947.
177. *PT*, 5 September 1947.
178. Ibid., 6 September 1947.
179. *HT*, 10 September 1947; *CMG*, 10 September 1947.
180. *HT*, 10 September 1947.
181. *HT*, 12 September 1947.
182. *CMG*, 11 September 1947.

183. *HT*, 13 September 1947. The incident occurred in Connaught Place. There were many more similar stories—for example the car of Sucheta Kriplani too was similarly stopped. Ibid. The Commander-in-Chief of the Indian Army General Rob Lockhart also had a similar experience, see *CMG*, 14 September 1947.
184. *CMG*, 11 September 1947.
185. Ibid., 14 September 1947.
186. D.M. Malik, *The Tragedy of Delhi*, 1947.
187. For the counterview that is of the atrocities committed by Muslims on Hindus and Sikhs see *Muslim League Attacks on Sikhs and Hindus in Punjab 1947* (published by SGPC, 1950). The Sikh and Hindu version of the massacres is placed here in table form—place—district—date—attackers—titled—injured. The list covers 592 major incidents.
188. IOR Mss. Eur. F 164/47, *The Sikhs in Action*, Appendix VII, 'Delhi Disturbances'.
189. Malik, *Tragedy of Delhi*, pp. 1, 4, 22.
190. *CMG*, 10 September 1947.
191. Ibid., 9 September 1947.
192. *HT*, 2 September 1947.
193. *CMG*, 14 September 1947.
194. *HT*, 5 September 1947.
195. *PT*, 30 August 1947.
196. *HT*, 25 September 1947.
197. Ibid., 30 September 1947.
198. *Dawn*, 7 August 1947. *TP*, vol. XII (353), 6 August 1947, pp. 547–8.
199. *CMG*, 14 September 1947.
200. *HT*, 31 August 1947.
201. *CMG*, 29 August 1947.
202. Ibid., 2 September 1947; *HT*, 31 August 1947.
203. *HT*, 31 August 1947.
204. Ibid., 6 September 1947.
205. Ibid., 5 September 1947.
206. *HT*, 11 September 1947.
207. *CMG*, 9 September 1947; Also *PT*, 9 September 1947.
208. *CMG*, 24 September 1947.
209. Ibid., 10 September 1947.
210. *HT*, 6 September 1947.
211. *CMG*, 24 September 1947.
212. *CMG*, 4 September 1947.
213. *Dawn*, 23 August 1947.
214. *PT*, 5 September 1947.
215. Ibid., 7 September 1947.
216. Ibid., 5 September 1947.
217. *HT*, 3 September 1947.

218. Ibid., 5 September 1947.
219. *CMG*, 5 September 1947; *PT*, 5 September 1947.
220. *PT*, 5 September 1947.
221. *CMG*, 3 September 1947.
222. *Dawn*, 15 August 1947.
223. Ibid., 27 July 1948.
224. *CMG*, 16 September 1947.
225. Ibid., 20 September 1947.
226. Ibid., 6 September 1947; *PT*, 27 August 1947.
227. *PT*, 5 September 1947.
228. Major Short's Report of visit to Lahore, 24/25 September 1947, MP, File 129.
229. Rangaswami Parthasarthi, *Journalism in India*, p. 277.
230. Prakash Nanda, *History of the Tribune*, New Delhi, 1986; *PT*, 14 October 1947.
231. *HT*, 7 September 1947; *PT*, 9 September 1947.
232. *PT*, 9 September 1947. Mountbatten took extra interest in the setting up of the new Ministry and even ordered that L and M Blocks in the Secretariat which were vacant be allotted to the Ministry. See, Extracts for ECM, 1st Meeting, 6 September, MP, File 131-A.
233. *CMG*, 9 September 1947.
234. Ibid., 23 September 1947.
235. Proceedings, ECM, 11 September 1947, MP, File 128, Reel 15.
236. *CMG*, 10 September 1947.
237. Extracts from ECM, 6th Meeting, 10 September MP, File 131-A.
238. Extracts from ECM, 7th Meeting, 11 September MP, File 131-A.
239. *PT*, 7 September 1947.
240. Ibid., 2 September 1947.
241. Ibid. 3 September 1947.
242. *CMG*, 5 August 1947.
243. Ibid., 2 September 1947; also *PT*, 2 September 1947.
244. *PT*, 14 September 1947.
245. *CMG*, 6 September 1947.
246. Ibid. 7 September 1947.
247. Ibid. 18 September 1947.
248. *HT*, 20 September 1947.
249. Vakil, *Economic Consequences*, p. 146.
250. Ibid., p. 146.
251. Ibid.
252. Ibid.
253. *HT*, 14 September 1947.
254. *CMG*, 10 September 1947.
255. *HT*, 22 August 1947.
256. Ibid., 27 August 1947.

257. *Dawn*, 27 August 1947.
258. *PT*, 3, 4 and 9 September 1947.
259. *HT*, 11 and 27 September 1947.
260. *HT*, 19 August 1947.
261. *CMG*, 3 August 1947.
262. Ibid., 1 October 1947.
263. Ibid., 17 September 1947.
264. *PT*, 19 August 1947; *CMG*, 28 August 1947; *HT*, 30 August 1947, *PT*, 3 September 1947; *CMG*, 5 September 1947.
265. 7th Meeting of ECM, 11 September 1947, MP, File 128, Reel no. 15.
266. *HT*, 10 September 1947.
267. *CMG*, 14 September 1947.
268. Ibid., 23 September 1947.
269. Ibid., 19 September 1947.
270. ECM, 22 September 1947; MP, File 129.
271. *CMG*, 1 October 1947; *Times*, 9 October 1947.
272. See *Times*, 7 October 1947.
273. Ibid., 30 September 1947.
274. Mountbatten Papers, Daily Notes, Part II, 1 October to 31 October 1947, File 188, Reel 23, Microfilm, NMML, New Delhi.
275. Ibid., Daily Notes, 2 October 1947.
276. ECM, 13 September 1947, MP, File 128, Reel 15, Item 2.
277. Ibid., 19, 24 and 27 September 1947.
278. 'Plain Tales From the Raj', Imperial War Museum, Deptt. of Sound Records, BBC Transcript—Penderel Moon, NMML, New Delhi.
279. *CMG*, 24 August 1947.
280. Ibid., 27 August 1947.
281. Ibid., 28 September 1947.
282. *HT*, 6 September 1947.
283. Ibid., 7 September 1947; Vakil, *Economic Consequences*, p. 58.
284. *CMG*, 27 September 1947.
285. Ibid., 30 August 1947.
286. Ibid., 13 September 1947.
287. *PT*, 7 September 1947.
288. *CMG*, 9 September 1947.
289. *PT*, 7 October 1947.
290. Extracts from ECM, 2nd Meeting, 4 September 1947, Item 9, MP , File 128, Reel 15.
291. Supreme Commander's Note for JDC, 29 August 1947, Extracts from ECM, MP, File 128, Reel 15.
292. Indian High Commissioner's telegram 27 August 1947, MP, File 128, Reel 15.
293. Trivedi to Swarn Singh, 4 September 1947, MP, File 129, Reel 15.
294. Ibid., 11 September 1947.

295. Ibid., 12 September 1947.
296. Swarn Singh to Governor East Punjab Trivedi, 17 September 1947, MP, File 129, Reel 15.
297. Ibid.
298. Ibid., 26 September 1947.
299. Ibid. For the version that the Sikh *jathas* were operating to plans in an organized manner, also see a note by Mridula Sarabhai where she notes that many political groups were organizing the killings and that 'Gurudwaras were being used for weapons production', Mridula Sarabhai papers, Reel I, note of 10 November 1947 (NMML, New Delhi) Microfilm. For reference to complains that Sikh *jathas* were operating in an organised manner and were operating from the state territories mainly Patiala see Mamdot's letter to Mahatma Gandhi, 21 September 1947, MP, File 129, Reel 15; and the reference to the G.D. Khosla Papers, File 16.
300. Ibid. Also see a note by Rob Lochart, Commander-in-Chief Indian Army, which said the problem in East Punjab was that the Government was unable to control the carrying of weapons, Extract from ECM, 15th Meeting, 22 September 1947, MP, File 129, Reel 15.
301. *Times*, 5 September 1947.
302. Ibid.
303. *CMG*, 16 September 1947.
304. Ibid., 14 September 1947.
305. *Statesman*, 14 September 1947.
306. *HT*, 14 September 1947.
307. Ibid., ECM of 13 September, see MP, File 131-A.
308. Ibid., *CMG*, 6 September 1947.
309. *Statesman*, 14 September 1947; Press Information Bureau, 29 September 1947, New Delhi, Nehru Clippings, NMML.
310. *HT*, 10 September 1947.
311. *Note on Sikh Plans*, Suptd. Govt. Press, Lahore, 1948, MP, File 128, Reel 15.
312. *CMG*, 11 September 1947; Vakil, *Economic Consequences*, p. 77.
313. *HT*, 5 September 1947, Isher Singh Majhel, Memoirs (Oral History Transcript), NMML.
314. *CMG*, 7 September 1947.
315. Ibid., *HT*, 14 September 1947.
316. *CMG*, 7 September 1947.
317. Ibid. 10 September 1947.
318. *PT*, 9 September 1947.
319. Ibid., 2 September 1947.
320. Ibid., 23 August 1947.
321. *HT*, 17 September 1947; *CMG*, 16 September 1947.
322. ECM Extracts, 6th Meeting, 10 September 1947, MP, File 131-A.

323. *HT*, 17 September 1947.
324. ECM Extracts, 5th Meeting, 9 September 1947, MP, File 131-A.
325. *HT*, 19 September 1947.
326. Ibid., 17 September 1947.
327. Price Day, 'Experiment in Freedom' part of a compilation of articles compiled and published by *The Baltimore Sun*, 1948, p.15, NMML.
328. *HT*, 17 September 1947.

6

Early Dimensions of the Disaster

The Muslim League had always criticised the Congress because it was supported by Birlas, Dalmias and other capitalists. But . . . in your (Jinnah's) regime people on the pulpit are Nawabs, big landlords and money bags. . . We the poor masses . . . want complete extinction of the Rais factor in Pakistan . . . what knowledge of the hardships and misery of life they can possibly have?[1]

According to a modest estimate the loss suffered by Hindus and Sikhs has come to about Rs. 2000 crore . . . the poor have been stripped naked . . . Sikhs and Hindus (Muslim also) are lying with naked bodies on roadsides as a result of paying the price of liberty.[2]

EXCHANGE OF POPULATION

On 8 October newspapers in Delhi and Lahore reported that the largest foot convoy had crossed into India: 'small shopkeepers, landlords, artisans, doctors, labourers, even dogs, starved cattle', so vast was the size that it took eight days for it to cross a given point.[3] The convoy had left Lyallpur on 11 September to slowly trudge the 150 kilometre route into India.[4] 'These Sikhs marching out of Lyallpur were on amazing sight . . . many were robbed on the way. . .[and] reached the promised land penniless and in rags.'[5]

The irony was that even as these unfortunate people were walking along half naked, ill-fed, sick and broken with memories that were filled only with the brutality that they had seen towards a future that was filled it seemed only with doom, the Congress Working Committee (CWC) was holding a meeting (23 September) in Gandhi's room at the Birla House in New Delhi, and after much debate the main decision arrived at was that the exchange of population needed to be discouraged because neither of the two countries could bear the financial burden that it would entail.[6] What is surprising therefore is that even after all that had transpired in the preceding month, there were still people in the Congress who believed that the millions who were leaving their ancestral homes and hearths were doing so out of choice and therefore could still be dissuaded from moving or persuaded to go back to their homes.

If leading Congressmen were talking along these lines it was mainly because Gandhi himself belived that an exchange of population was undesirable. In fact, two days before the CWC meeting, he had raised the issue in his post-prayer address, saying that the demand for the exchange of population was 'shocking'.[7] The day Gandhi made the observation he appears to have received a letter from West Punjab Premier Mamdot, which pointed out that even at this (21 September) stage there were a large number of Muslims in the districts of Ambala, Karnal, Rohtak and Hisar who were, if given protection, inclined to stay in East Punjab. Francis Muddie, Governor of West Punjab, has also recorded a similar view.[8]

Mamdot had also sought Gandhi's help in preventing the East Punjab government from disarming Muslims, something that was being done on a large scale.[9] In fact, Congress leaders of Simla had even passed a resolution to disarm the few Muslim policemen who had chosen to stay on in India.[10] There was a similar report that the Karnal Deputy Commissioner was exerting pressure on Muslim residents of Panipat to leave at the earliest.[11]

Mamdot's letter to Gandhi was also in line with the wider belief among Muslim League leaders that ideally the exchange of population should not have involved the Muslims of Ambala Division. Fazlur Rehman, Pakistan's Minister for Refugees and Rehabilitation, in an important statement on 14 October shared the view: 'We had hoped that Ambala Division would remain unaffected but the Sikhs made it impossible in the states and the Ambala Division.'[12]

Gandhi did not conduct the prayer meeting on 22 September because some people in the audience had objected to his citing lines/references from the Koran. The incident naturally upset him because he often cited from various religious scriptures. On 3 October, for example, he read out a verse from Guru Gobind Singh. In this particular post-prayer meeting address he even quoted Guru Arjan Dev, saying that the *kirpan* was meant to fight only tyranny. Gandhi emphatically told the gathering that the *kirpan*, the Gurus believed, was only for the defence of the innocent, never to kill the innocent.[13]

GANDHI ADDRESSES RSS

Gandhi was naturally pained that his statements with regard to the Muslims being an integral part of India should be repeatedly misunderstood. On 16 September, he addressed an RSS meeting attended by about 500 RSS workers at the Valmiki Temple, New Delhi. Gandhi complimented the RSS for its discipline and organizational ability what was seen in its work in the relief operations, and asked it to use this to strengthen India. He told the workers that 'any organization that was inspired by sacrifice was bound to grow'.[14]

Gandhi did not waver in his belief that the exchange of population had ever been desirable or a solution. Even as late as mid-November he still promised to do whatever was in his power to enable refugees from both sides to go back to their homes.[15] *Dawn* quoted Pandit Sunder Lal, whom Gandhi had deputed to try and restore peace in the disturbed areas, as saying that if both governments immediately stopped the evacuation effort and concentrated on restoring law and order and punishing the rioters, a lot of people may decide not to evacuate.[16]

The stand Mahatma Gandhi had taken, that is, the hope that people would still, after all the bloodshed, reconcile and go back to their homes had both opponents and supporters. But it was H.S. Suhrawardy (ex-Premier Bengal) who put things in perspective 'Gandhi had staked his very existence in combating the theory of a Hindu India'.[17] Naturally there were bound to be people, and certainly a large number, who believed on the other hand that leaders like Gandhi and Nehru were wrong in expecting or asking people to go back to their homes. Krishan Chander of Ferozepur, for example, questioned the logic of such appeals and wanted instead Gandhi and Nehru to spend their 'energies' on safely evacuating people.[18]

But there were of course people who felt reassured by the efforts of senior leaders like Gandhi. Many Muslim employees of the East India Railway, for example, had earlier opted in writing for Pakistan, only to change their minds some time later. These people managed to 'lose' their earlier written requests, leaving the Railway authorities wondering how the records had disappeared—and all this to stay on in India.[19]

Gandhi's views need also to be seen in the context of the campaign that had been initiated in various quarters to increase the outflow of Muslims not only from East Punjab but also from Delhi. On

18 September *Organiser* announced a survey based on four questions: (i) should only Muslims of East Punjab be exchanged with non-Muslims of West Punjab or also Muslims of Delhi; (ii) after partition (and the incidents that had taken place) would Muslims who remained be expected to be loyal to India; (iii) was it advisable for Muslims to be retained in high and important positions; and (iv) should Muslims be recruited into the army and the police.[20] The questions were repeated on 25 September.[21]

On 25 September the *Organiser* published a report that 100,000 people had signed a representation asking Gandhi, Patel and Nehru to evacuate Muslims from Delhi, because Delhi, had always been a part of Punjab, therefore why should they be allowed to remain. This demand did not weaken and again on 23 October, in an article titled 'Exchange of Population', the *Organiser* questioned the Congress leadership as to why partition had not been taken to its logical conclusion.[22]

Nehru blunt as ever replied: 'As long as I am head of government, India cannot become a Hindu State . . . the Muslim as a community has not betrayed India.'[23] A couple of days later *Dawn* quoted Nehru as saying that the demand for a Hindu State was 'medieval, stupid and fascist'. The real danger to India, Nehru was reported to have said, was not from Pakistan but from a section of Indians themselves.[24]

Nehru addressed students of Ramjas College (University of Delhi) on 3 October 1947. The gathering also included a large number of ordinary citizens. Once again at his remarkable best on the point, Nehru interestingly traced the growth of fascist tendencies in a section of Hindus (implying the RSS, naturally) to the hatred spread by the Muslim League and added that the Muslim League was itself greatly influenced by Nazi fascism. He said he had noticed this when he returned from Europe in 1938. He also called the demand to send the Muslims out a menace: 'if the Muslims proved traitors to India we could punish them, but how can we force them to migrate? . . . there were Hindus too who had acted treacherously, to which country could they be asked to migrate?'[25]

Gandhi once again spoke on the issue on 8 October. While referring in his post-prayer address to the murder of Rafi Ahmad Kidwai's brother in Mussoorie/Dehradun, he said, 'his only fault was that he was a Muslim. Am I to tell all the Muslim to leave India? Where are they to go?' Gandhi also complimented both Nehru and Patel for the stand they had been taking on the call by some people to forcefully vacate Muslims from the region: 'they could not act against their conscience and regard that India belonged only to the Hindus'.[26]

The situation was complicated enough as a result of the call from various leaders in Punjab to evacuate the Muslims from Delhi and the neighbouring areas, when the UP government proposed some time in the middle of October to make Hindi the official language in the province. Yet again Gandhi took up the issue and said that such a policy was against the Muslims '¼ of India's Muslims live in UP are they to forget Urdu?'[27]

Muslims must Vacate Delhi and Neighbouring Areas—Tara Singh

Even though the *Organiser* had been raising the issue of evicting Muslims to make place for Hindus and Sikhs coming in from the West, the RSS in general did not press the point. The credit, or rather discredit, for making this demand goes mainly to Master Tara Singh. The fiery Akali leader had no doubt greatly mellowed by the end of September and was in fact frequently in touch with Nehru, yet on this issue he continued to believe that both Nehru and Gandhi were wrong in asking the Muslims to stay on in Delhi.[28]

To be fair, Tara Singh did not view the issue in line with the RSS—Hinduism, Hindu culture, heritage, etc., for him it was simply a question of the estimated 2.5 million acres in excess that the Sikhs and Hindus had already or were in the process of vacating in the West Punjab districts, as compared to the land vacated in the East Punjab districts.[29] 'Mahatma Gandhi and other leaders must pay attention to this side of the question and not ask Muslims to stay . . . all along I have been asking for an exchange of population along with property.' He also said if Muslims were not made to vacate lands in West UP and Delhi the Sikhs were likely to perish.[30]

The Muslim League naturally launched a full-scale attack on the Master. *Dawn* countered Tara Singh by pointing out that his calculations were incorrect because he had not calculated the properties being left behind by fleeing Muslims in Patiala, Alwar and Bharatpur: 'there is no way the government can compute any such figures'.[31] H.S. Suharwardy released a strongly worded statement against Tara Singh's stand on 8 October: 'I think the time has come when forces of peace order and toleration should assert against forces of disorder and bigotry. I wonder if Tara Singh realizes that by his statement he was laying himself open to the charge that an attack on Muslims of Delhi and UP was deliberate and in pursuance of a policy to eliminate them from these areas.' Suharwardy also appealed to Muslims if the area to stick on and not move.[32]

Possibly to indicate that Hindus and Muslims were one on demanding the removal of Muslims from Delhi and its neighbouring areas, Tara Singh had also issued a statement ridiculing reports in a section of the press supporting the Muslim League, that the Sikhs were demanding a Sikh land in the East Punjab.[33] He said such rumours were being spread to divide the Hindus and Sikhs: 'I repeat once again that Hindus and Sikhs will rise and fall together. Their fates are linked. If Hindus die Sikhs will not be able to survive and if Sikhs die Hindus will also die.' Tara Singh added that for two years the Muslim League had been trying to divide the Sikhs and Hindus by telling the Sikhs not to participate in the communal quarrel since it was only between the Muslims and Hindus. In this long statement Tara Singh went on to point out that more Hindus had died simply because their population was more and in any case the Muslims had made no distinction while selecting their victims.

Hindu Sangathans Ideology to Fight Islamic Offensive—Savarkar

For Savarkar, unlike for Tara Singh, the Muslim question had dimensions which were far more important than a mere couple of hundred thousand acres of land. On 7 October Savarkar issued an important statement in defence of Hindu Sangathans and as an obvious sequel to the statements of Nehru and Gandhi: 'In the nature of things neither the Gandhian ideals nor the pseudo-nationalist ideology of the Congress can ever cope with the Islamic offensive and the Hindu Sangathanist ideology alone will be able to fight out this danger. Vital interests of Hindus and Sikhs demand that some arguments put forward by Congress ministers should be promptly refuted.' Savarkar then referred to a statement made by Nehru:

> Nehru has of late been stating that right of retaliation belongs only to the state, but he forgets the practical aspects of his policy. What are people to do if the state proves unwilling or pusillanimous to defend its own people? What are thousands of people in danger of being murdered in cold blood to do? . . . Hindu Sangathanists kept shouting from house tops of dangers ahead. But they were declared traitors, communalists and hunted out. . . . If

Pandit Nehru and his colleagues are still safe they owe [it] to the brave bands of Hindus and Sikhs.[34]

Surprisingly it was Dr Ram Manohar Lohia who in a strong statement countered the call for a Hindu Raj. Lohia while speaking at a meeting in Daryaganj, said that calls for Hindu Raj and Muslim Raj (obviously referring to Savarkar's statement) will only create difficulties for the government in resolving the problems it had on hand. India, he said, could never have a Hitler type of government.[35]

Even as the war of words built up in Delhi, the fiery Kashmiri leader Sheikh Abdullah put the blame for the crisis at the door of the Muslim League, for it was they, he said, who had preached the two-nation theory. While addressing a meeting of over 100,000 people, the Sheikh assured Hindus and Sikhs: 'As long as I am alive their life and property will be safe . . . my head hangs in shame that people are being killed in the name of religion.' 'What have', he asked, 'the crores of Muslims of India gained from Pakistan.'[36] These were bold and earnest sentiments, but things had gone way beyond control.

BLOODSHED ACROSS PUNJAB

Daily pitched battles between troops escorting convoys and raiding parties were almost routine throughout September. On 18 September, a reporter of the *CMG* gave an eyewitness account of an attack on a Hindu and Sikh convoy near Mughalpura a couple of days earlier. The area, as we know, had developed for itself a formidable reputation for its thirst for blood. The report said that about 500 people had planned to attack a train, the train, however, left ahead of schedule which led the mob to the foot convoy. It was a horrifying sight, with vast amounts of blood flowing and women and children screaming. On 19 September, *CMG* gave details of an attack on the village of Sham Chorasi (Jullundur). Fortunately the timely action of the troops saved the Muslims of the village.

Around the middle of September, the *HT* had started a special column the 'SOS' which began giving detailed accounts of incidents which had taken place earlier and were reported by its chain of correspondents from various relief camps. Most of these reports, in fact all of them, were of incidents in the western districts. The first of these reports appeared on 18 September and dealt with villages around Mianwali. A revenue assistant who was given magisterial powers ordered all the Hindus of village Harnoli on 9 September to surrender their arms. As soon as this was done, the village was attacked. Similarly, the mainly Hindu villagers of Alluvali and Karakot were brought to a railway station on the pretext of being evacuated, but no sooner were they near the station than they were attacked.

On 22 September a long report described events in Akbargarh (Wazirabad tahsil), an area famous for the quality of its rice. The report said that Dogra troops, which were considered the safest by the Hindus and Sikhs had been protecting Akbargarh which was surrounded by hostile villages since the outbreak of the violence. But suddenly on the basis of a false report that Hindus and Sikhs of the village were collecting arms for an attack with the help of the Dogra unit, the Dogra troops were withdrawn from the scene on 30 August and in their place were posted troops of the Frontier Force. The report noted that no sooner was the force changed than the soldiers started threatening and harassing and extracting bribes. On 7 September, the Jamedar of the unit asked the residents to deposit all weapons, including licensed ones, even small knives. The villagers were then assembled in a camp where the women and children were separated and taken to a school building, where according to the report 60 young women and girls were handed over to the rioters. In the camp where the men were housed around 200 people were injured in random firing by people from the roofs of neighbouring buildings. Akbargarh was looted house to house. The report said over 80 kg. of gold and heaps of silver coins and ornaments were forcibly taken away.

Most issues of the *HT* gave these area-specific reports in the subsequent days. On 23 September, for example, there were reports of similar incidents from Gujranwala and Multan. On 25 September the column detailed events at Jhang as narrated by a victim who said that Mubarak Shah, a prominent landlord, had started as early as 10 August to spread the word that Jhang would be attacked by 25 August. The matter was reported to the Deputy Commissioner and the Superintendent of Police. The attack took place on the 21 August itself and a large number of people were killed. The remaining people collected in the house of Chaman Lal Sahgal. The local police assured them that they would be safe if they parted with their valuables. Many people were reported to have handed over their valuables, but even after this there was extensive violence leading to over 2,000 deaths. On 27 August over 30,000 people of the area were collected in the Mandi ground.

The report also gave details of the Mandi ground camp—eight

hand pumps for 30,000 people, cholera, no rations, etc. Finally a train carrying Muslim refugees was reported to have reached Jhang on 7 September, this train was expected to take its load of non-Muslims away from Jhang—30,000 people trying to enter a single train. This train when it did leave Jhang, suffered repeated attacks and was held up at the Badami Bagh station for over eight hours.

On 26 September the SOS column reported gruesome incidents from villages in Mianwali, Piplan and Panj Garhia. This report also gave details of extreme brutality in Multan, mainly the village of Ranpur where many leading families like those of Ch. Chaman Das, Ch. Ram Chand, Ch. Uttam Chand, Dr Raghunath Rao suffered extensive loss of life.

Sital Prakash Jain of Ambala Cantonment, but originally from Pasur, in a letter to the *CMG* narrated how most families had initially decided to remain in Pasur because of the promises made by the local Muslims so much so that on 15 August they had not only publicly accepted the Pakistan flag but even celebrated with Muslims. He noted that the first incident of violence occurred on 28 August when three Hindus were killed in a bus going towards Sialkot. The letter says that when the mob that had surrounded the bus, asked the passengers whether there were any more *kafirs* left in the bus, Sulkar Nain a civil supplies inspector, pointed out another Hindu, who was pulled out of the bus and speared. The mob leaving him for dead and moved on. The injured man recovered and wanted to file a report because he had learnt the names of the assailants, but no one was willing to write the report. By 4 September, Jain said, the town of Pasur was vacated with not one Hindu family staying behind, only because, as he put it, 'Muslims had been wronged elsewhere'.[37]

On 16 September *CMG* gave the details of a 28 hour struggle by the residents of Bhaller village (Sheikhupura). The village had a mixed population, the Hindus and Sikhs slightly out numbering the Muslims. A few days before the attack, the Muslim families had suddenly left the village. About 8,000 Muslim villagers of the neighbouring villages were reported to have surrounded the village openly led by Muslim League National Guard activists, some soldiers and even policemen. The tragedy of the attack was compounded by the fact that about 70 women and young girls were killed by their own men to save them from molestation. Jathedar Narendra Singh, who led the defence, himself killed his own wife and niece. Over 1,000 people on both sides were reported killed in the incident.

Another report dealt with the defence of village, Kamalia (Lyallpur), by six Hindu youths on 6 September against a large mob. The boys fought all night till the village was overrun; all six and a large number of others were killed.[38] Twelve raiders were killed by the troop escort near Attock when a large gang attacked a Sikh convoy on 17 September.[39] The *CMG* gave detailed reports of more incidents in the East Punjab on 23 September. A train of Muslim refugees was stopped by raiders near Ludhiana. Fortunately the escort was well equipped, even so three officers were injured. The casualities among the raiders were heavy but could not be established because of darkness. In other parts of south-east Punjab as well, Muslims evacuating villages were under constant attack. Muslim settlements, particularly in the area of Gannaur, Hassangarh and Bahadurgarh of the Rohtak district, saw extensive and brutal killings because they were usually surrounded by Hindu Jat villages.[40]

In Rewari, a British officer, Major Ousty, was shot dead in a Muslim *mohalla* as he led troops to maintain order. On the road between Kurukshetra and Jagadhri (at Radaur) over 50 Muslims were killed in a serious clash. In fact, the entire region around Ambala was extremely tense in the third and fourth weeks of September.

G.D. Khosla has recorded that 3,299 Muslims and 328 non-Muslims lost their lives in the district of Rohtak alone between 15 August 1947 and 15 October 1947. The figures calculated by him for other districts of East Punjab for the same period were: Hissar 1,081 Muslims, 384 non-Muslims; Gurgaon 332 Muslims and 568 non-Muslims; Karnal 515 Muslims and 273 non-Muslims; Ambala 1,000 Muslims and 200 non-Muslims.[41]

The killings of course stood evenly matched on both sides. An Indian Army Major, Ram Singh of the 2nd Battalion Rajput Regiment, was killed while escorting a non-Muslim convoy from Tandianwala. In this case the report said the attackers had used bren guns, bombs and other such equipment, even hand grenades were used.[42]

Two of the most gruesome attacks on refugee specials followed each other, the second obviously a sequel to the first. There are different versions of both tragedies but it is reasonably clear that the attack on the Muslim refugee special at Amritsar on the night of 22/23 September near the Khalsa College Amritsar, was in answer to the three attacks on the Pind Dadan Khan, non-Muslim refugee special.

The Tribune published a detailed version of the Pind Dadan Khan refugee special massacre on 2 October, based on the eyewitness account of Chanan Shah, a military contractor. *The Tribune* report said that the train left Pind Dadan Khan with about 3,000 passengers on 20 September. At Kamoke about 10,000 to 12,000 people attacked the train and abducted over 400 women. The train was again stopped at Harbanspura where over 500 people were killed and about 60 women were abducted. The report said the train did not stop at Lahore station and was taken to the Mughalpur railway shed where it was washed. A Hindu doctor was brought to attend to the injured only to have two of his sons who had come to assist him killed in yet another attack on the train.[43] One version of the incident also added that two lorry loads of policemen had searched the train at Kamoke. These policemen not only tightened the passengers but also looted them of their valuables.

The official report of the incident filed in a telegram by East Punjab Governor Trivedi more or less confirmed that abut 1,500 passengers had been killed and about 150 women had been abducted.[44] The West Punjab government on the other hand said in a press note that the casuality figures in the incident were 350 killed and 250 injured, following the attack at Kamoke on 21 September. The statement said the attack lasted 40 minutes and that 76 attackers were killed. The mob managed to enter the last four bogies of the train.[45] The West Punjab government issued another statement on 26 September saying the death toll had risen to 410.[46]

Whatever the figures of those killed at Kamoke and other stations, the fact is the attack set in motion a mad retaliation. Governor Trivedi telegrammed New Delhi and his counterpart in West Punjab, suggesting that the massacre of the trainload of Muslim refugees near Khalsa College, Amritsar, was in fact a fallout of the Dadan Khan train tragedy.[47] The West Punjab authorities on the other hand, said that the Dadan Khan (Kamoke) tragedy itself was possibly in reaction to the massacre of Muslims in a train that had come from Alwar (22 September) near Amritsar. The same reason was cited for the attack on a train near Gujranwala.[48] The attack on the Muslim refugee special near Khalsa College is also important because a British officer was killed while trying to protect the train.[49]

The sheer brutality of the Amritsar and Kamoke killings shocked the governments on both sides. The government of East Punjab imposed curfew in the vicinity of railway tracks near Amritsar and the West Punjab government banned the moment of east-going trains for the sake of safety, and said trains would restart after things had cooled down somewhat. In fact, the West Punjab authorities went a step further and even ordered the halting of a massive Sikh convoy that was moving from Lyallpur to the East.[50]

All these measures failed to have an immediate impact. Yet another train from Meerut was stopped near Amritsar on 24 September. But this time its passengers were armed Muslims troops. For 15 hours there was sniping from neighbouring fields. Two soldiers in the train were killed.[51]

On 26 September the *HT* reported that some Muslims passengers on the G.T. Express had been thrown off the moving train near a station called Dabra after a small argument had developed with other passengers. The report specifically noted that contrary to earlier versions there were no Punjab refugees on the train carrying their 'tales of poison' to other parts of the country, as some Congress leaders in Delhi had begun pointing out. Reports of attacks on trains were so many and so gruesome that copywriters did not have to exaggerate or to sensationalize. Take, for example, the straightforward report published in the trusted *CMG*: 'a train arrived from Delhi and had been attacked at Beas railway station—166 bodies including 59 children and 29 of women were removed at the station'.[52] One can imagine the scene at stations when such trains arrived and the tension and strife that must have built up when the bodies were carried through the streets for disposal.

Railway Employees Facilitated Attacks

The main issue discussed in the 18th Emergency Committee Meeting (ECM) on 29 September was the increasing number of attacks on trains. This meeting was presided as almost always by Mountbatten and attended by Nehru, Mathai (Transport Minister), and Swarn Singh (Home Minister, East Punjab). Those present were shocked to learn from Swarn Singh that there was concrete evidence that railway employees in many cases had facilitated the attacks on trains. Mathai agreed with the views of Swarn Singh who informed the Committee that in some cases when even the Deputy Commissioners and Superintendents of Police had no information with regard to the arrival of trains, such arrivals was announced over loud speakers to collect people on the stations. Swarn Singh also told the Committee that there were specific reports of trains being intentionally delayed to give time to the attackers to prepare for the attack. Nehru, while observing that the 'behaviour of railway employees had been scandalous', ordered that the movement of trains be stopped until adequate protection was made available (this decision in fact had already been taken at the provincial level).[53]

Among the many incidents reported of the connivance of railway employees with raiders was one by the D. Company of 2/9 Gurkhas. A Hindu train crew of a Muslim refugee train stopped the train on the grounds that the engine had developed a fault. But as fate would have it, among the Muslim passengers were some engineers who told the Gurkha escort that there was no problem with the engine.[54] Lt. Col. Lewis Collinson, 2nd Battalion, Assam Regiment, has also recorded an incident when Muslim railway employees clearly conspired with 'train raiders' by ensuring a delay and a change in the route of a train carrying Hindu and Sikh refugees.[55]

DELHI FIDDLED WHILE PUNJAB BURNED

Aziz Sheikh of Lahore commented that: 'The leaders on either side must admit, if they have the courage to do so that they never imagined . . . a death march of refugees . . . their tales of horror are flaring passions'. An angry Tara Singh also asked Baldev Singh, his party's nominee in the Government of India, to resign because Hindus and Sikhs were being mauled simply because there were no escorts available: 'I advise you to resign if you are unable to alter the callous attitude of your government.'[56]

Charges that people in positions of authority and power had been lax and indifferent were common in September and applied to both sides. Amin Chand Mehta, an advocate of Lahore, addressed an open letter to Gandhi on the issue: 'It is said in history books that when Rome was burning Nero was fiddling. I do not know whether this is a fact or not, but this is a fact that when Hindus were being butchered and their houses burnt, Nehru, Patel and Baldev Singh were feasting.'[57]

A more reasonable assessment of the role and responsibility of the leaders was given by Durga Das. In an article written for the *HT* and published on 25 September (1947), he said: 'India can be saved by a government that either leads the people or is led by them. The present situation is inevitably making for chaos.' He went on in his inimitable style to state that ministers in India were often saying—when criticized for wrong decisions: 'what can I do, I thought like you? go and put some life and some sense in your Panditji'.

The article by Durga Das was the first of a series he wrote on Punjab. The second appeared a day later (26 September) under the title 'Why Law and order Broke Down in Punjab'. In this review he discussed at length the background to the crisis and noted: 'the Congress agreed to partition to avoid civil war for which the Muslims had prepared and the Hindus had not.' This view has been countered earlier in this study, but it is the finger he pointed at Gandhi that needs to be discussed. Gandhi, he said, had foreseen the disaster that would come 'but did not press his objection on the Congress High Command'. While raising the issue of why the Congress High Command had not been challenged by anyone, he went on to provide an answer—that there was no alternate leadership and that the existing Congress leadership was 'irreplaceable'.

In fact, throughout September and October there was hardly a day when newspapers did not carry views that essentially said that leaders on both sides, particularly so on the Indian side, were concentrating on merely statements and appeals rather than on deeds. For example, a letter from Surender Singh (Rawalpindi) said: 'we read big statements everyday, but nothing is happening . . . the Muslims are getting restless because of the sensational stories being published in the Urdu press . . . if we are killed the blame will be on the Indian government.[58]

The *CMG* also commented that good results could be achieved if people followed Gandhi's way of getting to the root of the problem and believing in deeds rather than statements, much as he had done in Calcutta and later in Delhi.[59] A letter from one Multani (Multan) said: 'we read of innumerable statements from Congress leaders about evacuation arrangements . . . but we find that practically no arrangements have been made. . . . I wonder why the Congress is these days appointing people who know neither fair play or justice and who want to merely make more money.'[60]

Dawn, somewhat absolving the Congress leadership for the disaster, picked up an editorial from the *Yorkashire Post* to establish that it was the Sikhs to whose doors the crisis could be traced: 'No impartial observer can doubt that the tale of massacre was begun by the violence of the Sikhs whom the Indian government would not or could not restrain', and added that the fact that Bengal was relatively peaceful only strengthened the view.[61] Interestingly, Sarojni Naidu, the senior Congress leader and close associate of Nehru and Governor of UP, also went on record saying that the Congress had agreed to division only because it was overwhelmed with pressure from the Sikhs who demanded it.[62]

On 10 October the *CMG* published two long letters on the events that had transpired in the preceding couple of weeks each letter telling its horrid tale. Of the hundreds of letters persued for this study, these two are among those that stand out as they focus on some of the bitter truths that we have generally been inclined to ignore.

Maheshwari from Amritsar wrote, making a passionate appeal to rich and influential men (leaders) to stop giving advice because they were unable to understand the plight of the millions of poor, innocent families who had lived for centuries in clustered, tight and dirty lanes, merely managing a living but all the same happily co-existing and then suddenly being asked to leave at a minute's notice: 'Imagine the plight of such people and what all this political division has meant to them.' Maheshwari ended the letter with words that must have haunted millions of minds and will continue to do so: 'till recently we had thought this was all a temporary phase and things would come back to the old days . . . it is now it seems, too late'.

Mohammad Saddat Ali of Lahore described what possibly transpired in the minds of the vast majority of ordinary law-abiding citizens who on either side of the boundary had nothing to do with the violence and happened to be in the wrong place at the wrong time:

> law abiding citizens are deeply pained but helpless to check the arson and killing . . . fear of punishment which the government can inflict has been cast to the winds . . . the local police has itself stooped low to feed on the untold wealth left behind by the fleeing non-Muslims . . . official sources are silent . . . officials and local influentials have indulged in loot and plunder . . . while hundreds of thousands of poor were being driven out of ancestral homes . . . these practical elements were looting and filling their already filled homes.

On 25 September the *CMG* commented on the ground realities in the Western Punjab: 'Inexperience of ministers is proving a tragedy for the West Punjab. At the moment the province is being ruled not by Mamdot and his colleagues but by police constables and goondas. . . . The public is being ground between the upper millstones of ignorance and incompetence and the lower one of corruption and self-aggrandisement.'

The point made by the *CMG* that the chaos in Punjab was greatly related to the inexperience of ministers, however, was countered in an article by Joshna Fazl-ud-din, in which she suggested that the functioning of the ministries in both East and West Punjab was greatly handicapped because of the complete control exercised by their respective high commands based in New Delhi and Karachi.[63]

In fact, Firoze Khan Noon, the senior Muslim League leader, had a dig at the functioning of his party's government in West Punjab which he argued was drifting towards dictatorship because there were far too many ordinances being used for measures where legislative approval was required, particularly with regard to evacuee property, the canal colony lands, etc.[64]

The morale of the ordinary citizen on both side of course could be lifted only by tough and decisive action of which, sadly, the examples were too few. Damayanti Talibuddin of Lahore appealed for the destruction of the gangs because 'when the only cure for riots in a place is evacuation of refugees—some one who matters has admitted defeat . . . I do not know about high politics but I do know that fleeing frightened people are a disgrace for us all'.

There were thousands and thousands of those like Talibuddin who knew and believed that people who could have controlled the situation had obviously not done their jobs. From Amritsar an unsigned letter noted: 'riots would never have spread either in East Punjab of the West but for the treachery of the Police . . . rotten from top to the bottom'.[65]

Dhikkar Ho—meaning literally 'be cursed' was the title of a poem published by *Abhyudya*, the paper that had been edited and nurtured by Madan Mohan Malviya for almost half a century: *shanti sthapit karne ke bahane itna rakt baha diya. hazar jahaz ter sakte hai parantu shanti sthapit na hui* (so much of blood was shed all in the name of peace that a thousand ships could sail in it and yet there was no peace).[66]

NATURE TOO VENTS ITS FURY

Almost as if nature too had decided to teach the Punjabis a lesson many of the central districts as also the catchment areas of the rivers Sutlej and Beas received the heaviest rainfall in 'recent memory'.[67] An *HT* report said: 'Today the attacker and the attacked are alike in flight from the waters of the Beas, Sutlej and Ravi'. The report said over 100,000 refugees were seen waiting in miserable conditions on the eastern mudbanks of the Beas, with another about 300,000 standard on the banks of the Ravi.[68] A large number of Muslim lives were in fact saved in the area between the Bea's and the Sutluj with the help of local Sikh villagers who provided drinking water. With wells having been flooded, drinking water was more difficult to come by than even food.

The *Dawn* wrote: 'to the sorrow of Punjab have [*sic*] been added the disaster of the floods'.[69] It took two days for the west-moving foot convoys to traverse the distance between Jullundur and Amritsar.[70] Hoshiarpur had a continuous downpour for over 60 hours, as if even the gods wanted to wash away the blood that had drenched the soil.[71] In the last week of September more than half of all structures in Ferozepur collapsed.[72] The situation in Ludhiana and Jullundur was only marginally better. To add to the plight the flood waters damaged the Jogender Nagar powerhouse plunging 16 towns into darkness.[73] Amritsar, for example, went without electricity for seven days. There was a complete breakdown in the supply of potable water. Road and rail transport, overburdened beyond capacity, received some rest when sections of the railway track and the Grand Trunk Road were washed away.[74]

Around Lahore about 120 villages were completely washed away.[75] A report said that 2,000 bodies were recovered in the Jullundur area alone after the floods had receded. In Delhi the flooded Yamuna caused another unique problem: cattle from the flooded villages marched into Delhi and settled down on the vast expanse of India Gate.[76]

To the great credit of the Indian Army in particular the crisis resulting was brought under control in a fairly reasonable time. The Sappers & Miners, Madras Regiment did a commendable job in restoring the Grand Trunk Road, and by about the 15 October rail traffic between Delhi and Amritsar had resumed.[77]

THE ARMY DOES A GOOD JOB

A reference has earlier been made to a statement by Pandit Hriday Nath Kunzru that a great part of the responsibility for the killings in Punjab rested with the PBF, which failed to act in time and effectively. This unfortunate charge (later denied by Pandit Kunzru), however, drew much attention because close to 90 per cent of the officers associated with the PBF were British.[78]

The *HT* printed a strongly worded editorial on the controversy basing its opinion mainly on a statement issued by the Government of India: 'The Government of India has regretted the general charges made against British Officers. The Government of India feels that these officers have discharged their duties to the best of their abilities and the government must express appreciation for their work. We must remember British Officers have also lost their lives fighting the trouble.'[79]

A couple of days earlier the *CMG* had published a letter from a reader who obviously felt that British officers in particular were being unfairly criticized: 'British officers have looked even into individual needs of the sick and suffering besides maintaining commendable sanitary conditions along routes of the convoys . . . if epidemics have been controlled it is largely due to the . . . British officers in and not because of some 'bandobast' on the part of the civil administration'.[80]

Rallia Ram was a frequent contributor to English newspapers, writing usually on public-related issues. In a letter of 14 October, he specifically praised officers of the 4th Division, PBF: 'For Maj. C.H.G. Tyndale of the PBF I have not sufficient words of praise. I could mention dozens of others who were splendid in the prompt and willing help they gave to Muslims and non-Muslims alike.'[81]

Some leading Sikh families of Daultana village (Rawalpindi), in a letter to General F.W. Messervy, Commander-in-Chief Pakistan Army, applauded the role of the Muslim troops of the 14 Punjab Regiment, for their 'impartial treatment and behaviour' in the evacuation process.[82]

From Sargodha some Hindu and Sikh refugees especially wished to thank the Deputy Commissioner of Lyallpur, Hamid, and the Deputy Commissioner of Sargodha, Lehghari. Both these officers had taken great pains to look after the Hindu and Sikh refugees in their areas.[83]

There were others, however, like India's Chief Liaison Officer, Nathu Ram, who not only discredited themselves but also their country. He was an employee of the Dalmiya concerns and had somehow managed to have himself (temporarily) appointed as Chief Liaison Officer of India in Lahore. The complaint against him was that among the first things he did on being appointed to the 'honorary' position was to use military vehicles to move records of the Allenbury and Co. and the Bharat Bank from Lahore to East Punjab.[84]

On 17 September, Nathu Ram, the complaint went on, was

approached by a Muslim gardener for the safe transit of about 20 Hindu girls who had been under his protection for the past three weeks. The gardener, the report said, was shocked by the indifferent attitude. The hesitancy and delay on Nathu Ram's part it appears was because the vehicles assigned to him for recovery and evacuation, as in this case were in fact being deployed by him to transport the household goods of Diwan Ram Lal, the newly appointed Chief Justice of East Punjab High Court.

Among other accusation, the complaint said that on 16 September Ch. Faqir Mohammad (*zaildar*) village Marh Bhangwan (district Sheikhupura) informed Nathu Ram that he had given protection to 45 Hindus and Sikhs in his *haveli* and requested him to arrange for their safe transit. The village was about 22 km from Lahore. In this case the Chief Liaison Officer took no action, instead he sent his vehicles to Dandot to remove the records and some employees of the Dalmiya concerns.[85]

Ironically Rai Bahadur Nathu Ram even suggested that reports of killings from Multan, Dera Ghazi Khan and Muzzafargarh his office had received were exaggerated. He even recorded his appreciation of the work being done by the authorities in some of the non-Muslim camps.[86]

RECOVERY OF ABDUCTED WOMEN AND CHILDREN

The abduction and recovery of women was an issue which caused much concern among the governments as well as ordinary people on both sides. This was one issue upon which leaders had no double standards. Progress was slow and painful because of the magnitude, the dimensions, of the problem which were way beyond those that any governmental system could have handled. This was a tragedy that had no answers.[87]

It must be clearly understood that the atrocities committed on Hindu and Sikh women were by no stretch greater than those that were committed on Muslim women—indeed, if there was any balance it was in the beastly behaviour of the men on both sides who tried to outdo each other in what they did to the women of the 'other side'. To list the events of such nature in detail is well beyond the scope of this study. Besides, attempting to do so without bringing out the details would be doing an injustice to the victims of this monumental crime. Therefore, it would be more approprite to draw attention to the kinds of problems faced by those associated with the recovery of abducted women. In doing so I have deviated somewhat from the newspaper reports and focused more on the Mridula Sarabhai Papers.[88] The recovery of abducted women was an exercise which continued for almost two years, the pace beginning to pick up only towards the end of 1947.[89]

Mridula Sarabhai was deputed by Nehru to organize the relief and recovery of abducted women. Her private papers contain a document she prepared, titled 'Brief History of Recovery of Abducted Women'. She records the many difficulties she faced mainly due to the nature of the problem but more 'because of the social prejudices against the return of abducted persons'.

The process of recovery was in three stages. Of the first—up to 6 December 1947 when immediate recoveries were made and recovered women were put in camps—she says there were no exact figures. The second stage was from December 1947 to July 1948, when both the governments worked jointly. The third stage was from July 1948 to December 1948, a period when Sarabhai says, the work was practically at a standstill.[90] Unfortunately the details of the number of women abducted, the regions, the authority that organized the recovery, etc., are not available.

Mridula Sarabhai's papers also contain a very important note written by her on 1 January 1948, 'Note on Guardians of Minor Children' copies of which were sent to Gandhi, Nehru, Neogy and Swarn Singh: 'The MEO authorities . . . while clearing pockets . . . have come across cases in which whole families have been converted to Islam . . . the women members want to stick on with husbands while the brother and fathers of such women want them to be rescued . . . I personally feel that if we cannot get the husband out by force we should not insist that the wife should be asked to leave. . . If the father refuses to be rescued and the mother takes help of the rescue party what happens to minor children?'

The West Punjab authorities appear to have taken the lead in handling or at least making a beginning in providing relief to the women and children who had suffered. The *CMG* reported that the authorities were preparing to open a third home for destitute women in the Sir Ganga Ram Girls School (Lahore).[91] On 14 October the West Punjab authorities also announced the opening of industrial training homes for destitute *mohajir* (refugee) women.[92]

APPEALS FOR PEACE BEGIN TO YIELD RESULTS

On 25 September Master Tara Singh and Udham Singh Nagoke made a joint statement: 'We know that Sikhs stooped to these low depths only in retaliation . . . this has falsified tradition . . . if we do not desire friendship of Muslims . . . we may have to fight them again, but we shall fight a clean battle. . . . Killing women and children and those who seek asylum must stop at once'.[93]

In the subsequent days, newspapers published appeals for peace by East Punjab Premier Gopichand Bhargava stating that retaliation was bound to boomerang and also by Akali leaders like Ishar Singh Majhel, Jathedar Mohan Singh and Sardar Sohan Singh.[94] Some days later another appeal followed from the Akalis specifically pleading to the community to let Muslim convoys pass peacefully.[95]

The crucial appeal for peace, which clearly had a widespread impact in the Lahore and Amritsar region, was made by Sardar Patel at a mammoth public meeting in Amritsar on 30 September. Over 200,000 people turned up to listen to him. Patel spoke for almost an hour, reminding the Punjabis of their chivalry and saying that retaliation was a 'mad man's dream'. He called for an immediate cessation of hostilities for almost three months.[96] For a change *Dawn* reported the speech in more detail and without satirical overtones. The *Dawn* had never been an admirer of the Sardar; indeed if there was anyone among the senior Congress leaders who was spared the *Dawn's* hard-hitting and personal attacks it was Nehru alone.[97]

Dawn reported Patel as saying: 'All of you know how dear the Sikhs are to me.' Patel then appealed to the Sikhs to raise a volunteer force that would provide complete immunity from attack to the refugees. 'If they must fight . . . they must wait for the right time . . . to fight against the refugees was no fight at all, no laws of humanity or war permitted slaughtering of people who had sought shelter and protection.'[98] Some days later Patel was again in Amritsar and met senior Sikh leaders Tara Singh, Jathedar Sohan Singh, Jathedar Udham Singh.[99]

The other big meeting addressed by Patel in East Punjab was in Patiala on 23 October, where he once again appealed to the Sikhs 'for dispassionate calm' and not to 'besmirch the honour of their swords by spilling innocent blood'. Patel also thanked the massive gathering for the response the Sikhs had given to his appeal for peace made in Amritsar, particularly for letting the Muslim convoys pass peacefully.[100]

During the course of his visit to Patiala, Patel was also reported to have made a statement which attracted much criticism in the Pakistan press: when the right time comes you can use your sword to your hearts content. Now you have to sheath it so that you can raise the moral tone of the people which is now at such a low ebb.'[101]

The *PT* took strong exception to Patel statements and even equated the Sardar with Master Tara Singh. It said Patel had talked only of temporary truce 'so as to get non-Muslims out safely'. The editorial added that people who are wanting their minorities to leave are only making things difficult for the restoration of good relations between the two countries. Incidentally Patel later categorically denied he had talked of getting all non-Muslims out of West Punjab and all Muslims out of East Punjab. This impression he said had been created by a section of the media in Pakistan.[102]

Nehru, while addressing a public meeting in Delhi, also appealed for peace: 'If they continued to take law into their own hands the result would be absolute anarchy the type of which followed the Mughal Empire . . . we can understand our enemies placing obstacles but unfortunately our friends are also doing so. . . India will suffer the consequences . . . much could still be done if people desisted from doing evil for evil.'[103]

Gandhi too appealed to the people saying the retaliation against Muslims in India would not help non-Muslims in Pakistan.[104] There is little doubt that retaliation was by far the most prominent reason for the widespread violence. Mridula Sarabhai had in fact made a detailed statement on how refugees from Gujranwala had told her that they had suffered only because of the attacks on Muslims in the East Punjab.[105]

The appeals for peace from the Pakistan side were as if not more earnest. The Pakistan Premier Liaqat Ali in a radio broadcast on 7 October said: 'those who had even the slightest political sense know that any conflict between India and Pakistan would be suicidal for both . . . the whole world knows that it is not we who did greater wrong, but still I consider it a disgrace for Pakistan that . . . the majority has failed . . . to protect the minority'.[106] He also said those 'that disturb peace are stabbing their country in the back.'[107] Jinnah too appealed for the protection of the minorities. While speaking to a select gathering in Karachi he said: 'I have repeatedly made clear that we have to treat the minorities fairly, nothing is further from our thought than to drive them away . . . I regret to say the minorities did not give us a chance to prove our bonafides.'[108]

Fazlur Rehman, Pakistan's Minister for the Interior was reported to have said 'it is our genuine desire to promote friendly relations with India . . . we will spare no measure to root out feelings of revenge and retaliation among the Muslims of Pakistan'.[109] Ghulam Mohmmad, the Finance Minister of Pakistan, went a step further: 'protection of minorities is the cornerstone of Pakistan's state policy'.[110]

Dr S. Radhakrishnan also spoke on the issue. Praising Jinnah for his earnest desire to protect the minorities he also said it was Jinnah's followers who were finding it difficult to reconvert from their two-nation theory to the single national concept—a single Pakistan comprising several communities. Dr Radhakrishnan further said: 'if the minorities have a sense of security there will not be these large scale migrations . . . we see all round suspicion, anger, doubt, pity, grief, absence of hope which is worse than grief'.[111] A few days later, possibly in response to Dr Radhakrishnan's views on the two-nation theory and the role of Jinnah's followers, Fazlur Rehman said there was no reason why people of all communities could not live in peace in spite of the two-nation theory, and in any case, only Pakistan's enemies wanted the Hindus to leave to cripple Pakistan's economy.[112]

One of the more important gesture was an appeal from Aligarh to the All India Muslim Cattle Dealers Association, calling upon people to abstain from slaughtering cattle on Baqr Id.[113] A similar appeal was in fact reported even from Lucknow, where the Shia Muslims announced through Mohammad Wasi Naqvi, Secretary, All Party Shia Congress that they would abstain from slaughtering cows on Baqr Id. Similar sentiments were also expressed by a large number of speakers in a massive anti-Pakistan rally following the Friday prayers at Delhi's Jama Masjid. Speaker after speaker condemned the Muslim League for misguiding the Muslims. Among those who spoke were Mir Mustaq Ahmad, Sardar Ali Sabri, Aziz Hasan and Tayab Nikhabandi.[114]

NEWSPAPERS MUST SHOW RESTRAINT—GANDHI

The results of such appeals for peace became fairly apparent in the pages of newspapers, by the increase in the number of reports of how people of different communities had helped each other during the crisis. Although they had always been doing so, these stories had not received much publicity until them.

Gandhi had in fact taken up the issue of the newspapers not giving enough attention to the good deeds by people of different communities in his post-prayer address on 16 October. He said that he wished the newspapers would give publicity to such news and avoid the mention of foul deeds which excited the spirit of revenge and retaliation.[115] Gandhi had made a similar statement about a week earlier. He had appealed to editors and reporters to be careful while reporting and gave the example of a report of an attack on some Meos which had turned out to be incorrect.[116]

M.A. Khusro, the Sind Premier, was more blunt and simply warned newspapers to be careful: 'No Muslim paper in India would dare to write things that the Hindu press is writing here.'[117] Sadly there was an element of truth in this. The *PT*, in an editorial of 14 October, discussed the burning down of the *Dawn*'s Delhi office (on 12 September) and of how most of its employees were living in refugee camps. The editorial said *Dawn* had been asked to deposit a sum of Rs. 3,000 as security: 'to demand security from a newspaper after making it defunct is killing a person and then insisting that he be bound over by good behaviour'.[118]

Surprisingly even as the West Punjab authorities went on to lift controls on the press, the Indian Government at about the same time went on to adopt a new code for newspapers on the grounds that such controls were necessary to decrease strife. The Indian Newspapers Conference held in Bombay on 11 October 1947, resolved that editorials would not attack leaders, news of violence, etc., would not be displayed very prominently, casualty figures would not to be given in headlines; casuality figures would always be checked with reliable sources, and news that created harmony would be given more prominence.[119]

As already noted, Patel's public address in Amritsar (30 September) and his second visit a few days later had resulted in spontaneous commitments for peace from most Sikh leaders who were present, including Tara Singh, Jathedar Sohan Singh and Udham Singh. The result was that many Sikh villages now not only began to abstain from attacks but also began to provide food and other support to Muslim convoys that were passing through the villages. A report on 9 October said that a Muslim convoy of several thousand people walked unescorted from the village of Rakon to Bahran (about 20 km.) and Jat Sikh villages en route offered food and milk.[120] For many days the kitchens of the Golden Temple, Amritsar, provided large amounts of food to the Muslim convoys passing through Amritsar.[121]

Another report narrated how four Muslims in the Faizpur village of Sheikhupura district saved a group of 30 Hindus who were travelling unescorted. For five days these Muslim men protected them against repeated attacks.[122] In yet another report, Ram Narain, a railway employee, told press reporters in Amritsar that a refugee train of non-Muslims had been served food by Muslims in Multan, under the personal supervision of the Deputy Commissioner of Multan.[123]

Agha Riaz Mahmood, President of the Muslim Students Federation of the F.C. College Branch, issued a bold statement 'we invite our non-Muslim friends to jointly work with us for the prosperity of Pakistan . . . we offer our friendships with the firm belief that we are one in the sphere of culture and knowledge. The non-Muslim staff of the Punjab Electricity Power Corporation was also reported to have written to the Director, Jalab Khan: 'we express to you our deep gratitude for protection and other arrangements'.[124]

One of the direct fallouts of the earnest appeals by senior leaders of the Muslim League was that Muslims now began to come forward to help non-Muslims just as Jat Sikh farmers did to help Muslims.

However, it was the Sikh villagers of village Bhail in the Naorwal Police Station and of the village Rupowali in the Kathumangal Police Station of Amritsar district who set new standards of bravery and chivalry. An official statement from the East Punjab Police Headquarters said that the people of these two villages had taken it upon themselves to protect the Muslims of their area, fighting back a gang of 15 Sikh raiders and ensuring that not a single Muslim was injured in the incident.[125]

Then there was the report from Faizpur of how a truckload of unescorted Hindu men and women who had got stranded by the floods were saved from raiders by four Muslim passersby who happened to be armed. The Muslim men then took the Hindu refugees to their village and when the floods receded five days later escorted them to of a refugee camp.[126]

EFFORTS TO RETAIN AND RESETTLE HINDUS AND SIKHS IN WEST PUNJAB

Ghazanfar Ali Khan, Pakistan's Minister for Food started in October a campaign to restore confidence among the minorities. This campaign did not get much attention in Indian newspapers, possibly because it was not taken seriously. Ghazanfar addressed a huge public meeting in Sargodha on 6 October where he said: 'Unless we in Pakistan radically change our attitude towards the non-Muslims and refuse to be misled by petty communal sentiments . . . it will be difficult to consolidate the new state.' In the same address he was also critical of the police. 'Islam does not provide for distinction in law enforcement.'[127] The following day he was at Chakwal, where he addressed a meeting of about 2,000 ex-servicemen. It was a remarkable event in the troubled times not only because of the scenes of communal harmony and amity but because even the guard of honour presented to him by the residents of Chakwal included people from the minority community.[128]

Avtar Narain, a Congress leader and also a member of the Pakistan Constituent Assembly told press reporters on 9 October that 20,000 non-Muslims had decided to stay on in Chakwal and Pind Dadan Khan tehsils mainly due to the efforts of Ghazanfar Ali.[129]

Ghazanfar Ali went on record (while addressing a meeting at Cambullpur) saying that some people were trying to sabotage his efforts to retain the minorities, but at about the same time a large number of reports that talked of Hindus and Sikhs having reopened their shops in Jhelum, Chakwal, Sargodha and Gujar Khan.[130] A Quetta report even said that some Hindus and Sikhs had even returned from Delhi where the conditions in the camps were very bad. The Baluchi-stan Muslim League President Qazi Mohammad Isa was reported to have taken the lead in restoring confidence among the minorities and even appointed a Peace Committee comprising Muslims and non-Muslims members to tour the area.

But it is the other point that Ghazanfar Ali was reported by the API to have made and which requires more attention: 'Hindus in general were in a much better frame of mind as regards their allegiance to Pakistan. This unfortunately was not the case with the Sikhs. . . . This was because of the Congress and Akali attitudes. The Congress had accepted Pakistan (that is why the Hindus have done so) but the Akalis have not (explaining why the Sikhs had not done so).

Ghazanfar's efforts to retain the minorities in West Punjab were commented upon by the *PT* in an editorial on 14 October. It said that in the beginning there was all kinds of opposition to his efforts. Some said it was wrong of him to be concerned about non-Muslims when Muslims were suffering, others said his work would impede efforts to resettle the Muslim refugees who had come in from the East, but time had shown, the editorial said, that people had softened and the results of his efforts were fairly good. Interestingly the editorial also said if Ghazanfar's efforts were followed in other parts of West Punjab, it would serve 'to strengthen the hands of the Indian Prime Minister in the struggle against the forces of reaction and communal chauvinism'.[131]

But having said this in the context of Ghazanfar Ali, it has been difficult to assess the extent to which other important Pakistan leaders actually wanted the non-Muslims to stay because, on the ground, the actual concrete measures were far less in proportion to the assurances that were given by the leaders. As someone who called himself a 'Pakistan Muslim' pointed out, if the Pakistan leaders were keen for the non-Muslims to stay, they would have to do much more than merely issue appeals, like reserve places in government service for non-Muslims, compensate them adequately for loss of property, etc.[132]

On similar lines, Mrs E. Ansari in a long letter discussed how Indian history was a reflection of Hindu and Muslim coexistence—with Muslims looking after governance and Hindus trade and commerce. She argued that good commerce is essential for any state and Hindus must not be allowed or encouraged to leave.[133]

Even as all these goodwill gestures were being enacted in the Western districts, an off-the-cuff remark by G.B. Pant, Premier United Provinces, somewhat derailed the process of trust building. Pant, while addressing a meeting at Purshottam Park in Allahabad, was reported to have posed a question to Muslims who had remained in India: would they shed their blood fighting Pakistan troops if Pakistan invaded India? Pandit Pant said he hoped that this test would never happen but also asked the Muslims to search their hearts and if they had even a shadow of a doubt they should migrate to Pakistan.[134]

The Pakistan government's response to this casual remark came from Fazlur Rehman, Interior Minister. He said it was Pakistan's genuine desire to promote friendly relations with India and 'we should refuse to dub non-Muslims as disloyal to make them leave'. He also ridiculed Pant for 'testing the loyalty of Muslims to India'.[135]

Pandit Pant's remark revived the war of words, and as expected, there followed a flood of statements and charges from both sides.[136] The *CMG* too came out with an editorial appealing to both Liaqat Ali and Patel to stop the tirade of political accusations. However, it was Bhimsen Sachar, the leading Congressman of the western districts, who put it clearly and plainly as to why the efforts of Ghazanfar

Ali were bound to fail. To him the most obvious reason was that after all the minorities had undergone there was just no way their confidence in the Muslim League, particularly its junior cadres, could be restored. More importantly, Sachar added that, 'Besides one notices a sharp difference between statements of Ghazanfar and the actions of the West Punjab Government . . . I do not doubt Ghazanfar but he has thought of the plan too late—complete exchange of population is only a matter of days.' To stress his point Sachar pointed out that the shops and houses vacated by fleeing families were already being allotted to incoming Muslim refugees.[137]

Sachar was not alone in believing that Ghazanfar's efforts would yield no results. Similer views expressed by Congress leaders from the West Punjab and Sind districts in the Delhi Congress conference were widely reported by the press. *PT* wrote a strongly worded editorial against them. It accused them for talking only of violence in the West Punjab and closing their eyes to what had happened in East Punjab. It said it was these very people who flared and fanned the flames of violence following Khizr Hayat's resignation in March 1947: 'we consider that these are the maggots who have eaten away the once virile and healthy tissues of the social organization of Hindu and Muslim people . . . it is they who are trying to demolish our mosques and temples and seats of culture and learning.'[138]

That some of the Congress leaders felt that Ghazanfar's campaign to retain the minorities was only a superficial attempt was understandable, but the real surprise was the reaction of Iftikharudin, the West Punjab Refugees Affairs Minister. On his return from a tour of several towns in the East Punjab, he issued a statement in Lahore saying that he had not come across a single Muslim who supported Ghazanfar's campaign of trying to resettle non-Muslims in Rawalpindi and Muslims in Ambala Division of East Punjab.[139]

Interestingly, the Ministers statement notwithstanding, Governor Muddie has noted that, 'at first it seemed that Muslims of Ambala Division would stay'.[140]

ECONOMIC FORCES WILL BIND INDIA AND PAKISTAN—NEHRU

Two important political trends stand out throughout October. On the one hand was the belief among certain influential Indian leaders that there was still some scope for unity, in Pakistan on the other hand, most of the leaders ridiculed the talk of unity saying there was not even the slightest chance of its happening.

In a press conference in New Delhi on 13 October Nehru said: 'the business of transfer of population was not of our seeking . . . it simply took place due to various reasons . . . we had to adopt ourselves . . . none of us envisaged a major transfer of population at any time . . . perhaps it was a lack of judgement on our part. As this flow of population . . . from one side to the other proceeds it becomes difficult for small pockets to remain. So, we took the Punjab as a whole . . . for the rest of the country it was a question of individuals wanting to go or come.'[141] He also said that the problems were not being handled well because instructions given by higher authorities were not being carried out by subordinate staff.[142] And what he said towards the end of the conference created quite a flutter: 'Even if they (India and Pakistan) went further apart economic forces would bring them together.'[143]

A few days later, Rammanohar Lohia was reported to have said that the people of Pakistan would either overthrow the Muslim League government and form a secular state or would rejoin India once they realized the folly of the two-nation theory.[144]

An American delegation which included Sterling Cole had met Gandhi around the same time (possibly 20 October). During the course of the meeting, someone asked Gandhi whether he expected the two countries to reunite, Gandhi was quoted as saying: 'Of course I do hope they will unite, but it may take some time, both wish to live together.'[145] A day later Maulana Azad addressed the post-prayer gathering at the Jama Masjid in Delhi. As usual, he attacked the Muslim League for the crisis and said the tragedy that had fallen on the Muslims in India was of the making of the Muslim League, and in any case, a vast majority of Muslims had no faith in the two-nation theory.[146]

For some reason, the *CMG* was rather liberal with its column space for views of reuniting the two countries or at least of a common heritage. On 24 October, for example, it published a letter by Miss Nazir Ghafoor which said that the term India stood for the whole region, and the term Hindustan would be more appropriate because: 'we must realise that Pakistan has not ceased to be a part of India although it is distinct from the Union'.

There are two other views on the 'reuniting issue' that are important because they are of people who went on to climb the highest positions in their respective careers. Major General Cariappa (later the Chief of Staff of the Indian Army) was quoted by *CMG* as saying 'Alas today our country is divided. Speaking as a soldier I believe we soldiers of India will be able to bring the two parts together, perhaps in a year, or couple of years or may be five years.'[147] The second was the view of Karanjia, editor of the *Blitz*, who was quoted by *Dawn*: 'Constitutionally if possible, by violence if necessary we will have the whole of India under one flag.'[148]

All this talk of a possible reunion or the so-called unity moves were 'officially' dashed to the ground by none other than Jinnah himself on 23 October, when he talked exclusively with Duncan Hooper, Reuters Special Correspondent. Jinnah condemned what he called the propaganda in India on the possibility of India and Pakistan reuniting. He said: 'I want to make it quite clear that Pakistan will never agree in any shape or form to any constitutional union between the two sovereign states with one common centre.'[149] But he did talk of friendship with India: 'We shall try to bury the past despite all that has happened, we shall remain friends.'[150]

GOONDAS GIVE MORAL COVER FOR THEIR LUST FOR LOOT

But coming back to ordinary issues and ordinary people, an *HT* report described the situation in Lahore on 26 September. The city, the report said, had been dying for some weeks but the end had come suddenly—within a week. When the first wave of refugees came, the report said, people found a house and broke into it, no permission was taken, at most the local sub-inspector was taken into confidence. Since the new occupants were scared to use items left behind by owners they exchanged goods with other houses. Bribery had touched the sky, even petty officers disobeyed orders with impunity. Shops were looted from back doors in broad daylight. The report also added that no Hindus (of the few left) would dare to walk in the streets and lanes of Lahore if they were not disguised as Muslims.[151]

On the following day, the *HT* carried a report by Durga Das, who had travelled extensively in Punjab throughout September: 'The average man on the street says we are dealing with *goondas* who have given a moral cover to their lust for loot . . . Muslims in Pakistan believe that the property of Hindus and Sikhs represents the blood of Muslims who have been exploited for centuries. By murdering a Hindu or a Sikh some Muslims believe they have earned a place in heaven.'[152]

The lust to kill as also to loot was widespread on both sides. A Hindu father and son travelling in the Lahore Mail were thrown out of the fast-moving train by their co-passengers, both losing their lives as a result.[153] In Delhi Dr P.H. Mufti, a Muslim medical officer, was stabbed to death while he was trying to help some non-Muslim families, and supervising the cleaning up of Paharganj.[154] Just as gruesome was the senseless killing of another Muslim who, while working as municipal officer in Mussorie, continued his duties.[155] Dr Mufti's cold-blooded killing had led Gandhi to remark, 'The incident causes me to shudder.'[156]

In Lahore, S.R. Sawhney, a district engineer was stabbed mercilessly not by street *goondas* but by his own subordinates, only because he still dared to come to work.[157] Banwari Lal a retired engineer of the PWD and a popular figure in his locality, was shot and killed by a Muslim policeman as he was waiting on the roadside for a *tonga* near a tea shop, for no reported reason.[158]

The cold-blooded murder of Pindi Das (Khanewal) was yet another instance of a good Samaritan losing life. Pindi Das was a popular Congress leader of Khanewal. On the day he was stabbed he was in fact returning from the railway station after organizing relief work and seeing off a group of Hindus leaving Khanewal.[159]

The problem with sudden attacks whether it was against convoys, small groups of people and even individual cases was, as General Thimayya put it, the attackers came out from narrow lanes particularly in cities like Lahore, Amritsar and Delhi, and after committing the crime simply disappeared again.[160] In fact, in a meeting of the ECM (24 September), Dr Bhaba had even noted that most of such senseless killings, on whichever side they may have been, were usually the handiwork of mischievous refugees who lived at night in camps and spent their days floating around the city lanes—more so in Delhi.[161]

Throughout October newspapers continued with extensive reportage on the violence, some events were actually those that had occurred earlier but were later reported by reporters on the basis of accounts narrated by survivors—often these stories contained the inevitable exaggeration and sensationalism.[162]

One such report was published by *The Tribune* under the title, 'Story of Sheikhupura Carnage', dealt with events that had occurred in the last week of August. The report said: 'Sheikhupura one of the most flourishing rice markets of the province witnessed a carnage on 25 August On 26 August, Brig. Thimayya and Maj. Brar left Lahore for Sheikhupura. From a distance they saw the city burning.' Citing a witness, the report said: 'we saw with our own eyes the District Magistrate and the DSP in the crowd helping the rioters. Next morning a bribe was paid to the military officials to disarm the non-Muslims. People were asked to come out of houses . . . the girls were separated . . . the orgy restarted with firing from house tops and continued up to 3 p.m. (27 August) resulting in over 3,000 killings (on 27 August).' The report estimated that over 15,000 had been killed in and around Sheikhupura, with vast amounts of property being looted in an organized manner.[163]

Dawn had earlier published a report, 'Great Bharatpur Massacre'. Like the report on the Sheikhupura killings it contained sensational details, that there had been a conspiracy to eliminate the Muslims in Bharatpur and the Raja of Bharatpur was at the centre of it, and that close to 80,000 Muslims had been killed in Bharatpur alone.

This long and gruesome report also gave details of how the Ajmer Agra Mail was stopped at Bharatpur on 8 September and how many Muslim girls were abducted. On 10 September the Raja himself led 50 troops of J.H. Infantry, the clash led to the killing of about 400 Muslims after they had been disarmed. The most gruesome attack on the Bharatpur Muslims was reported to have occurred on 15 September in which about 600 Muslims were killed in the Jama Masjid at Bharatpur. Yet another massacre was reported from a place near the Nadbhai railway station on 17 September, in which about 400 people were killed.[164]

Exaggerated, no doubt, but a very detailed version of the killings of Muslims in Bharatpur and Alwar was also compiled in a booklet by Syed Azhar Husain Zaidi, an advocate of Bharatpur. He noted that the RSS supported by both the Akalis and the Hindu Mahasabha had organized the Bharatpur and Alwar killings of Muslims.[165]

On 11 October the *HT* gave abridged reports of a large number of incidents, for example, an attack on a refugee camp at the Lyallpur Khalsa College, on 1 October and a clash between the West Punjab police and an armed gang of Sikhs near Kasur in which 60 Sikhs were killed (10 October).[166] On 8 October *The Tribune* also reported the violence in Lyallpur and details of a clash between the two communities in Hisar. The Hisar incident was reported to have been handled firmly leading to the shooting of 40 people by the army.[167]

Smaller scattered details were regularly published by the *CMG* whose versions, as we have noticed, were usually less sensational than other newspapers. On 7 October *CMG* gave details of an attack on a Muslim convoy near Batala in which about 500 people were killed, another report of 22 October gave details of an attack on a Muslim refugee train near Kalka.[168] In an attack on a non-Muslim convoy near Umarkot the escort troops killed 60 of the Muslim raiders. About 30 refugees were also killed.[169]

Away from the Punjab districts, there was a major preplanned attack on the Delhi–Howrah Express near Sikanderpur. *Dawn* reported that a gang of Sikhs boarded the train and started the attack near Sikanderpur, and while the armed guards watched helplessly, more than over 200 Muslims were killed.[170]

In another incident, possibly thousands of lives were saved by the grit and determination of British officer Colonel Frye and Ghulam Mohammad, Deputy Commissioner. A.N. Gujral the Government of India's Liaison Officer said that an informer told Colonel Frye that about 1,000 Muslims were lying in wait for a non-Muslim convoy which was proceeding from Jhelum Frye promptly led his forces to the place where the raiders were hiding and shot dead 20 people, the convoy passed unharmed the following morning.[171]

INDIFFERENCE AND INSUBORDINATION OF OFFICERS

It is difficult to say whether the governments of East and West Punjab and those of India and Pakistan could have done or should have done much more than they did. When one examines the large number of complaints, reports of incidents and the complete lack of state authority for weeks together, one comes away with the impression that a great deal of what happened could have been avoided if people had done their assigned duties.

But at the same time, the scale, the nature, the extent of the crisis if viewed dispassionately, leads one to believe that even the most heroic and committed of government machines could have done only marginally better. Indeed, the mistakes made earlier, the hurried transfer of power, only added to the complexities of the communal problem. Perhaps the single most important factor that served to derail the efforts and plans of both governments—India and Pakistan—as well as the provincial ones was the widespread indifference and insubordination of the police and lower revenue staff.[172]

There was of course a failure to anticipate the breakdown of civil administration. By as late as 27 July 1947, 150 of India's 846 ICS officers had not indicated whether or not they intended to remain in service after 15 August, another 131 were due for retirement, 101 officers had sought postings in Pakistan, 84 had said they would continue only for a short period. Thus almost 55 per cent of the 'steel frame' was either retiring, uncommitted or on the move. At the lower level there was the understandable reluctance among civil servants to proceed in administrative and law-and-order decisions against people of their own communities.[173] In this sense, community compulsions forced officials into insubordination—of the quiet kind where orders which required action against people of their own religious community were handled with indifference.

This insubordination was greatly fuelled by a complete breakdown in the communications network. So bad was it that in many cases orders from state headquarters could not be conveyed even to Deputy Commissioners.[174] Ch. Lehri Singh, Food Minister of East Punjab, said that 'smooth working was impossible' because of the practical non-existence of communications, particularly the telephone network. It was only around the first week of November that telephone calls from Simla could be put through to Amritsar.[175] A transmitter of the All India Radio became operational in Jullundur from 1 November.[176] Interestingly, on many occasions the government of East Punjab began conveying orders to its field officers through the radio, with officers being instructed to keep their sets tuned for messages between regular radio programmes. Governor Trivedi even believed that one fallout of the poor communications was that peace appeals made by senior leaders did not reach the grass-roots workers in time (see Chapter 5).[177]

Even the army had to build a Tactical Military Headquarters on a train consisting of 14 bogies, with radio, signals, a motor transport unit and armed guards. This 'train headquarters' came to be used by Lt. Gen. D. Russel, Commander of the Delhi and East Punjab Areas.[178]

But coming back to the issue of insubordination, Mohmmad Bashir Ali of Jhelum wrote to *CMG* listing some of the factors that had led to the anarchical situation. For him, in order of priority were corruption, nepotism, breakdown of law and order and malaria. 'The officials are taking advantage of the disordered state of the country and are using easy means to enrich themselves. Favouritism, nepotism are seen everywhere. These are days to oblige friends and relations.'[179] A helpless Ishar Singh Majhel, East Punjab's Minister for Relief and Rehabilitation also believed that the problem was because the bureaucracy had not changed it believed it was still under British rule.[180]

The Tribune published an editorial on 19 October:

> The government of East Punjab consists of some very estimable gentlemen who even though they are new to the work are devoting themselves with zeal. But their output does not commensurate with the zeal of the demands of the moment . . . administration moves rather slowly . . . the needs of the travelling public have been suppressed for weeks postal services completely disrupted, people feel marooned . . . the telephone lines are monopolised by ministers, their relatives, friends and friends friends . . . this is a scandulous state . . . the government has lost its elasticity and seems to be living for and in itself.[181]

In another editorial some days later (8 November), *The Tribune* dealt with the bureaucratic attitude. The editorial was titled 'Sack These Officials':

> These men posted in districts still go merrily along insulated against popular current . . . their attitude easily infects their inferiors (provincial services) . . . the . . . majority of them are little Neroes who are still fiddling even though our Rome has been burning for a long time. . . . The feeling is particularly strong against the Police and Civil Supplies Departments who find it most paying to exploit the common man. . . . No human society can possibly exist without providing opportunity for graft but the scale on which it is being practised in our province leaves one amazed.

A retired North-Western Railway head clerk from Amritsar wrote to *CMG* 'I have been made an exile at 65 years of age . . . I claim British protection if it can still be given . . . there is absolutely no Indian government worth the name . . . I am at the mercy of others . . . is this Azadi or Barbadi?'[182]

Reports of looting by the police and other officers were routine. Jogendar Singh, sub-inspector of police, Beas Police Station was arrested by SP, Amritsar, Ch. Ram Singh, for possessing vast amounts of looted goods.[183] While participating in a debate in the East Punjab Legislative Assembly, Sadar Sajjan Singh remarked that 'there was hardly a policeman in entire Amritsar district, except one head constable who had not been a party to loot. It was only after the present Superintendent of Police Ch. Ram Singh [came] that things had changed.'[184]

Among the Amritsar police there was another problem which, in fact led Governor Trivedi to initiate a special drive to overhaul it.[185] The problem was that over 70 per cent of the Amritsar force had been Muslim, who to the last man had left East Punjab. These vacancies were filled by people who came from the western Punjab districts, many of whom as chance would have it had suffered personal tragedies. As a result they were filled with hatred and a desire for revenge and therefor rarely lost an opportunity to loot Muslim pro-perty or even facilitate attacks on Muslims.

Goods worth Rs. 200,000 were recovered by Ch. Ram Singh, SP, Amritsar within the first few days of the 'recovery of looted goods drive' launched by him. In fact, a large number of policemen in Amritsar voluntarily surrendered stolen goods.[186] The situation was as bad in Jullundur. A group of British officers passing by Jullundur recorded how they saw six policemen looting the bullock carts of refugees.[187] The report did not specify whether the refugees were Muslims or non-Muslims, but although Indian policemen were reported to have looted even non-Muslim refugees, such incidents were more common in the immediate border areas and not as deep as Jullundur.

The level to which insubordination had crept into the lower constabulary also comes out in an unfortunate incident which took place at Nizamuddin Railway Station in New Delhi. An API report said that, Mishra, a young IAS officer, in his capacity as Deputy Commandant of the Purana Qila Muslim Refugee Camp stopped a policeman from harassing a Muslim refugee who was trying to load three bicycles on the refugee special train. An argument appears to have followed between the officer and the constable. Soon after, the report said, the body of Mishra was found lying in a ditch near the station. Six people including a head constable were arrested.[188]

Things in Lahore were as bad if not worse. The government of West Punjab had by a special ordinance created the posts of duty magistrates to keep a check on the widespread trend of breaking into houses and shops of fleeing owners. According to a report, one such magistrate was himself suspended for breaking into the shop of a rich trader.[189] Abdul Aziz, sub-inspector of police, was arrested for looting non-Muslim property.[190] Abdul Ghara, a convoy commander was arrested along with a patwari, Abdul Ghani, for seeking bribes from refugees for seat allotment in transport vehicles.[191]

Qurban Ali Khan, the Inspector General of Police, West Punjab, as already noted, was highly reputed for his honesty and fairness. Soon after taking charge he had launched a campaign against corruption and looting by government servants. By the middle of October, 76 officials including 1 additional district magistrate, 3 tahsildars, 4 sub-inspectors of police had been suspended.[192]

The complete disappearance of governmental authority is seen in yet another field—the refusal of people to buy railway tickets. *Dawn* reported that the daily receipts of the Lahore station before the outbreak of disturbances had been about Rs. 100,000, but by the beginning of October they had fallen to Rs. 40.[193] Ticketless train travel, it was said, had caused a loss of Rs. 4 crore in two months. So serious was the situation that the West Punjab government had to issue a stern warning—any refugee found travelling in a non-refugee special (train) without a ticket would forfeit his resettlement concessions. This report said that not only had all stations been overrun by refugees but travellers who were buying tickets for routine trains were unable to enter them because the refugees had taken over the whole train. This report also said that the government had banned the settlement of refugees near railway stations in West Punjab.[194]

Whether it was check posts, major bridge heads, or entry into railway stations and convoy transport centres, there were numerous complaints of harassment and corruption against people manning these position.[195] One such example of alleged high-handedness occurred at the bridge checkpoint on the river Beas. Diwan Ram Lal, Chief Justice of the East Punjab High Court, was travelling from Amritsar to Simla. On being stopped at the checkpoint the party showed the pass that had been issued by the brigadier of the area. But the soldier on duty disallowed the pass on the ground that he took his orders not from the brigadier but from the havildar who was stationed about one furlong away. As the Chief Justice's party entered into an argument, the soldier was reported to have mounted his rifle.[196] Another version of the incident however added that this particular detachment of soldiers was of the Pakistan army and happened to be present at the checkpoint.[197]

Another incident reflecting how high handed some of the employees of the government involved in the refugee movement could be was reported by the *Tribune* on 30 October. It so happened that a refugee special coming from Mandi Bahaudin was stopped near Tanda station because the Jullundur station was overcrowded. The engine driver detached his engine from the train and simply drove off, leaving the train and about 2,000 passengers stranded for three days with no water and food.[198]

A common complaint from ordinary people was against officials who misused vehicles which were allotted to them for refugee evacuation purposes, but were actually used for the benefit of their families, friends and other influential people. In fact, Brigadier Mohate of the MEO intercepted three such lorries that should have been evacuating refugees but were actually loaded with household goods. The Brigadier was quoted by the report as saying: 'It was shameful to allow influential people to use precious lorries to carry their goods while human beings were being killed for want of transport.'[199]

In this context too West Punjab took the lead over East Punjab by passing, an order which allowed for the requisitioning of all vehicles abandoned by non-Muslims, to place them under the Provincial Transport Controller. Such vehicles were to be used for refugee movement. The public was also asked to report any vehicles that may not have been surrendered.[200]

Jinnah himself warned the people of Pakistan against those who were converting a crisis into an opportunity for personal gain. Commenting on his speech, *CMG* said:

> The tendency to deprive citizens of their rights because of their religion is assuming alarming proportions. A case has come to light of two Muslims visiting the house of a Christian and asking him to hand over to them a truck because the truck belonged to a Sikh whose house had been allotted to one of them. When the Christian asked them what authority they had they replied in any case there was no law and order in the city (Lahore).[201]

THE BLACK MARKET THRIVES

The prices of essential items like matches, salt, pulses, cloth were exorbitant in most parts of Punjab.[202] An editorial of the *PT* noted: 'blackmarket in Lahore is many times worse than the worst days of the war (Second World War). During the war the blackmarketeers were scared of the law—did business underground but now it is open.'[202] In another editorial some days later, the *PT* said a packet of cigarettes was selling at one rate in the morning and double of that in

"Do Oblige!"

Black marketing in the supply of essential commodities was a major problem in 1947 and 1948 (*Shankar's Weekly*, 6 June 1948).

the evening of the same day. Influential retailers, the editorial pointed out, had cornered large amounts of stocks.[203]

Sugar was in extreme short supply particularly in the western districts because of the breakdown in supplies from Abdullapur. The West Punjab districts had only one factory at Mardan which was not large enough to meet the extensive demand.[204] *Dawn* noted that there was no shortage of goods but only that traders had hoarded all supplies and were selling at self-determined prices. As prices sky rocketed, traders indulged in widespread smuggling. A report from Mirpurkhas, for example, said that the driver of the Bombay Mail was caught trying to smuggle 25 bags of sugar hidden under the coal dump in his engine. He was arrested along with his accomplices who included a Hindu sub-inspector of police.[205]

In Delhi, there was intense competition between local traders and the 'refugees' who had set up shops on the pavements of Chandni Chowk. A report said that most of the goods being sold on the pavements were looted.[206] Potatoes were at selling exhorbitant rates. The East Punjab government in fact passed an order banning the movement of potatoes from East Punjab. In Simla there was an extreme shortage of virtually everything in the open market.

As famine-like conditions came to prevail in East Punjab, the problem was greatly aggravated by the fleeing refugees from both sides. As mentioned earlier (see Chapter 5), people were not only burning down standing crops, but even poisoning the wells they were leaving behind. The conditions of man-made shortage, whether it was hoarding grain or burning crops, caused severe problems for the governments on both sides. The trading community came in for much criticism for using the disturbed conditions as an opportunity. Congress President Acharaya Kriplani while addressing the Merchants Chamber of Commerce in Bombay called upon businessmen to play fair: 'we took over the administration from the British in a peaceful manner . . . much of it has broken down . . . we cannot burden it with the task of regulating the entire economy. But if you play the game and ignore social aspects we may be constrained to undertake it.'[207]

GANDHI ON FOOD CONTROL

Mahatma Gandhi had been saying for some time that black marketing was in fact being encouraged by government controls.[208] Addressing a meeting on 4 November, he said that controlling the sale and purchase of food encouraged hoarding and black marketing. He said he had been receiving a large number of letters from people complaining of corruption in the food supply department. Gandhi in fact wanted the government to open its own food supply shops which would help it to control prices and check smuggling.[209]

Pratap Singh Kairon, the 'go getting' East Punjab Minister and had no doubts as to who the culprit for the food crisis was. While addressing traders in Jullundur he said: it is a shock to know that some traders who deal in essential items are charging exorbitant prices . . . imagine your countrymen who have lost everything coming to the land of their forefathers going hungry and unclothed being squeezed out for the last penny . . . black marketing must be fought . . . if it does not stop by 17 October I will take serious action.'[210] Of course ministers and members of the East Punjab Legislative Assembly did not have a problem procuring rations as the office of the Assembly had taken upon itself the task of ensuring adequate supplies for the families of the members.[211]

These shortages of even basic commodities greatly contributed to the inhuman and gruesome manner in which people had begun to react to situations—the slightest provocation and bloodshed followed—

a situation where society had virtually lost the mechanism of balance. As V.N. Sethi of Jullundur put it in a letter: 'it is an unpleasant but solid fact that people have lost faith in the government and also in each other, social inhibitions have become irksome, social structure is disturbed . . . social sanctions have vanished . . . this tendency is bound to lead to anarchy.'[212]

Shankar Deo Rao, a general secretary of the All India Congress Committee, admitted at a press conference that not only did the government have no clear plan to handle the crisis, but in fact it had failed to win the confidence of the people. He also agreed that there was widespread corruption not only among the police but even Congress leaders 'are guilty of unpardonable offences, an average man sees no change around him, corruption, bribery and nepotism are rampant'. The Socialist Party of India's call for an immediate end to the 'temporary' political character—Dominion Status and holding of elections by June 1948—was based on similar arguments: people had no faith in the provisional set up.[213]

As stated earlier, even if the governments on both sides had worked at their optimum best there was just no way the crisis could have been managed any better. The haste with which partition was enforced had left no time for the logistics to be worked out and had destroyed the little chance there was of things being less traumatic for ordinary people. The scale of the arrangement to be made for partition at short notice was way beyond anything that had ever been comprehended—there were just no precedents for such an exercise anywhere in the world.

Many years later, Ishar Singh Majhel noted: 'when you leave home even for a few days, you are worried—food, lodging, clothing—millions were leaving their homes for ever'. He also added not only did the government have no experience, 'nothing simply occurred to us—what advise could we give'.[214]

As the rich of Delhi, Lahore, Simla and Karachi converted their assets into the safety and 'confidential holdings' of diamonds,[215] the government of East Punjab was trying to arrange for a million pieces of woollen blankets for refugees who had left behind even simple clothing.[216] The Ministry of Relief and Rehabilitation, Government of India issued a statement on 6 October that it was arranging 4,00,000 shirts, 10,000 woollen coats and about 700,00 yards of other cloths for distribution among refugees in East Punjab.[217] The effort was nationwide, with people in Bombay taking taken upon themselves the duty of trying to cloth the residents of one relief camp—Kurukshetra—where the report said about 50,000 people were without basic clothing.[218] In Punjab, a large number of organizations were contributing in various ways by collecting utility items. Master Tara Singh personally led one such group along with Prof. Darbara Singh and Prof. Prem Nath.[219] K.C. Neogy, Minister for Relief and Rehabilitation, India, told press reporters that orders had been placed for 10,00,000 quilts, 10,00,000 jackets and that about 4,000 quilts were being produced daily.[220]

A.K. Banerjee of Simla wrote complaining that the Muslim *dhobis* of Simla had had to leave so suddenly they were unable even to return the clothes of their clients. These clothes were then looted by local residents and some refugees who had by then reached Simla. As Banerjee put it, 'cloth was more valuable than jewellery and money'. He demanded that those who had stolen the clothes from houses of the *dhobis* should be brought to book and special cloth permits be issued to people whose clothes had been stolen.[221]

As discussed in Chapter 5, when it came to cholera vaccine, Calcutta and Bombay were able to produce large quantities of vaccine which was sent to West Punjab via Karachi at short notice. At the Kurali camp near Ambala the number of cholera deaths averaged almost 30 a day.[222] The large number of deaths in the East Punjab non-Muslim camps led to another peculiar problem. Since most of the stalls that sold firewood had belonged to Muslims who had now left, there was a serious shortage of wood for cremation. The situation in Rohtak was so serious that it was even brought to Gandhi's attention by Justice Tek Chand. A trainload of firewood was subsequently delivered at Rohtak.[223]

REFUGEE MOVEMENT

The level to which the government of India had to strain its resources can be gauged from the fact that as early as 15 September Chimni, Commander of MEO, had pointed out that if evacuation was to be completed within, say, a month, about 1,500 lorries would be required, whereas on 15 September the MEO had at its disposal only 206 vehicles.[224] Chimni was a popular figure in the area, but for reasons that were not clear he was suddenly posted out of the MEO.[225] But before he relinquished charge he addressed a press conference. The reports of this conference are important because from the Indian point of view, this was the first official and detailed statement giving specific figures of the evacuation and exchange of population. Chimni said that in the month ending 4 October 7,57,037 non-Muslims had been evacuated, another 3,00,000 were in movement, about 20,00,000 were awaiting evacuation, of whom about 6,00,000 were in scattered and isolated pockets. He said of these, 3,50,000 had moved by train, 2,85,000 on foot, 1,38,000 by motor transport and 1,027 by air. Of the 20,00,000 awaiting evacuation, besides the 6,00,000 in scattered pockets, 7,00,000 were in rural areas and 7,00,000 in urban areas. With regard to Muslim refugee movement from East Punjab, Chimni said, in the same period 3,10,000 Muslims had been moved by train, 1,06,000 by motor transport and about 455,000 in foot convoys, and about 1,50,000 were awaiting evacuation.

Chimni also noted to press reporters that one of the big problems in this whole effort had been that despite the MEO being a predominantly military organization, had been placed under the civil authority of the Ministry of Refugees and Rehabilitation, as a result the MEO had been unable to operate along military lines. Chimni said the clubbing of the MEO with the Ministry was possibly one of the factors that had contributed to the insubordination at the lower level in the MEO.[226]

Both sides stated their own figures with regard to the exchange of population, sometimes they appeared to overlap, sometimes they were confusing. For example, Fazlur Rahman, Pakistan's Minister for Refugees told press reporters on 14 October that 34,59,000 Hindus and Sikhs had been evacuated, while of the estimated 52,75,000 Muslims in East Punjab and the Sikhs states, about 30,00,000 were yet to be evacuated. The minister also said that while it was difficult to give exact figures, but as on 14 October about 15,00,000 Muslims and 17,00,000 non-Muslims may have changed sides. He said that the problems and scale of violence were bad because: 'our initial plans did not work'. Although it had been planned to move convoys strictly on earmarked routes—the Muslims leaving East Punjab by the GT Road to Lahore and the Sikhs leaving West Punjab through Ferozepur into Ludhiana and Sikhs from Sheikhupura, and Lyallpur coming to the Baloki Headworks avoiding Lahore and going to Ferozepur—the attacks by the Sikhs on trains and convoys had not only upset the planning, but also delayed the whole movement plan by about a fortnight. It was this delay of two weeks that cost a great deal of lives, including deaths due to the floods.[227]

An official statement by the Government of India noted that the whole of the district of Lahore and most of Sialkot had been cleared of non-Muslims.The statement while dealing with problems being encountered noted that while at least 20 trains were needed to move between the two sides, at present (17 October) only four were going from India to Pakistan with Muslim refugees and only two were coming back from Pakistan with non-Muslim refugees. Both governments it, however, added had decided to double the number of such trains.[228]

PARTING OF WAYS

Left purely to itself, and certainly without the police, it is almost certain that the army would have done a far better job, an example of the army's efficiency being the evacuation of the Muslim cadets of the Indian Military Academy, Dehradun. A total of 141 Muslim cadets of whom 105 were from the IMA and 36 from the Royal Indian Military College (RIMC) were transported in complete secrecy by truck in the middle of the night from Dehradun to Saharanpur. Secrecy was so complete that even the cadets had no idea of when they were to leave. In the middle of the night of 13 October everyone at the IMA collected to bid a warm farewell to the Muslim cadets. A battalion of Gurkha troops and non-Muslim cadets of IMA guarded the entire route from Dehradun to the Saharanpur air base from where the cadets were air lifted.[229]

Indeed what is surprising in the chaos that prevailed is that not even on one occasion did the troops of the army take sides against each other on communal lines, at least openly so. No doubt commanders worried about their of troops coming out against each other on religious lines (see Chapter 5) but not once did this happen. On the contrary there were numerous reports of warmth and unity between troops of the two sides. The 8 Punjab Regimental Centre, for example, saw unprecedented moving and emotional scenes as Sikh and Gujar troops left the Centre for India, scenes of hugging and weeping were reported by witnesses.[230]

REFUGEES AIRLIFTED

K.C. Neogy, India's Minister for Relief and Rehabilitation addressed an important press conference in New Delhi on 20 October. Where he gave the figure of the numer of refugees evacuated thus far.

Neogy also said that about 50,000 people had already left Delhi for Pakistan, and that the government of India was requisitioning about 30 planes—all that were available—to assist in the evacuation of not only government employees but others as well. These planes he said would pick up people from Mianwali, Chakwal, Multan, Rawalpindi, Lyallpur, Sargodha, Peshawar and Dera Ismail Khan, and would land in Ambala.[231] The minister also informed reporters that very high priority was being given to the establishment of orphanages and homes for destitute women. These homes, he said, were to be set up at Karnal, Kalka and Jullundur. Neogy said the number of orphans under ten years of age was very large and therefore would like to appeal to families to come forward and house such children.[232]

REFUGEE CAMPS

Although the harshest of words were often used by the displaced masses to describe the state of affairs in the refugee camps, yet it was these camps that were also the symbols of the stupendous effort that was put in by the cash-starved governments of both sides, to give some solace, comfort and security. Both sides of course accused each other of not giving enough attention to the management of the camps: there were stories of corruption, of theft of medicine and supplies, of trading in women, of organized looting of refugees.[233] Yet, as reiterated earlier, no government anywhere in the world could have been prepared for the demensions and the logistics.

Let us take the example of the Walton Refugee Camp for Muslims going into West Punjab from the East. The camp was planned to house 1,30,000 people. On September 11, it had 1,42,606 inmates. It was certainly one of the better-run camps. It had 200 people managing it, every refugee on arrival was given an identity card, adequate daily rations were given to expectant mothers. The biggest problems were sanitation and disease.[234]

The East Punjab government said there was no discrimination with regard to rations and medicines between Hindus and Muslims.[235] Yet there were extensive complaints. A report in *Dawn* said the Kurali Muslim camp near Ambala was badly managed; it had opened on 1 September and was said to have almost 200 deaths a day.[236] Another report discussed how Indian authorities had stage-managed Lady Mountbatten's visit to a Muslim camp in Amritsar. Not only were adequate rations supplied, but medicines were displayed, newly painted boards were put up, lime powder was sprinkled, etc.[237] On the other hand, Hindu and Sikh refugees coming into East Punjab from Lyallpur gave accounts of how bad things were at the camp there.[238]

The shortage of food in Muslim refugee camps in East Punjab was however corroborated by Lt. Col. Lewis Collinson, 2nd Battalion, Assam Regiment. In September, the Battalion was assigned the task of protecting the Muslim refugee camp at Karnal. Collinson says the camp was not only ill-planned but 'inmates lived like animals—with no sanitation whatsoever'. He also records how Hindus and Sikhs of the area constantly preyed around the camp, sometimes to kill but mostly to sell a few 'chappatis' at exhorbitant rates.[239]

Just as the West Punjab authorities were focusing on finding fault with the Muslim camps in East Punjab, there were many people who charged the West Punjab authorities for stage-managing publicity with regard to the Hindu and Sikh camps on their side. Brij Lal, Refugee Officer, DAV College Refugee Camp, Lahore, refuted a statement by the West Punjab authorities which said that 200 tins of milk powder had been supplied to this camp. Brij Lal said that not a single tin of milk or any fresh vegetables had been supplied to the DAV camp in Lahore.[240] Most camps were full to the brim, and refugees took to the pavements. The situation was equally bad on both sides: The shortage of sweepers, the resultant problems of hygiene, the shortage of medicine--there was no difference between East and West Punjab.[241]

The camp for non-Muslims refugees at Kurukshetra was of course said to be a model one, having been visited on different occasions by leaders like Nehru and Kriplani. Mahatma Gandhi had even recorded a special message for the inmates of the Kurukshetra camp on All India Radio.[242] The camp was under the charge of Maj. Gen. Nathi Singh and had provisions for 2,00,000 people.[243] The camp was important because of the Indian governments policy that since everyone coming from the West could not immediately be resettled or absorbed in the economy would be retained at Kurukshetra in the interim.[244]

Managing such large camps was not merely a question of manpower; far more important was the financial resources that were required. Both governments were under great strain, the Pakistan government in particular with its far less and limited resources. Mumtaz Daultana, Food Minister, West Punjab, said there were in the first week of November about 3,00,000 people in West Punjab completely on the dole.[245] A report also pointed out that even though extensive opportunities of new work were available, a large number of the refugees preferred to stay on the dole.[246] When Jinnah visited the Walton camp, for example, he was surprised to see the vast amounts of food being cooked and remarked: 'Evacuees must work, they are not state guests for all time.'[247] Jinnah had even started a relief fund, which attracted generous donations—by 23 October the fund had collected Rs. 18,00,000.[248] The Sind government had in fact stopped the free feeding of refugees and had even banned the entry into Sind of even Muslim refugees from West Punjab.[249]

Pakistan with far limited resources than to India also received help from Canada and Britain. A Large quantities of blankets, shoes and other clothes were contributed by a British charity. Canada donated penicillin to both India and Pakistan.[250] The Archbishop of Canterbury and Lord Pethick-Lawerence (former Secretary of State for India) issued an appeal for relief volunteers for the Christian Council of India, and as a result seven doctors were flown to work in camps at Lahore and Delhi. The Society of Friends too contributed a team of 18 doctors, including some Indian, British and American, to work in the camps.[251]

An Anglo–American 'humanitarian' organization sent two volunteers to assess the working of the camps on both sides. G. Alexander visited camps in East Punjab and J.R. Symonds toured the camps of West Punjab. Symonds reported that the conditions in the West Punjab camps were satisfactory and treatment towards the non-Muslims was fair, but in the case of the camps in the East Punjab, Alexander reported there was widespread shortage of food and especially of clothing.[252]

The East Punjab authorities had at the peak of the crisis allowed refugees to take shelter in public buildings, mainly schools. However, with school building occupied by refugees, the government was unable to plan the reopening of schools, which it had initially proposed to do in the entire province from 27 October. To have the schools vacated meant arranging for about 30,000 tents.[253] A deputation of the East Punjab Recognized Schools Association even met the senior East Punjab ministers, Swarn Singh and Pratap Singh Kairon, to seek their help in restoring school routine which had been completely disrupted.[254] Once again it was the army that came forward and released 15,000 tents, most of which were made available at the Kurukshetra camp.[255]

WE HAVE TURNED THE CORNER

Leaders and administrators on the Indian side had begun to feel by about the first week of October that things were now under control. Even though the killings and arson continued the ferocity and scale had begun to decrease. In fact, Governor Trivedi had stated in the ECM (10 October) that 'for the first time he considered that the corner had definitely been turned as regards the Jullundur Division'. Trivedi attributed the improvement in the situation to the visits of Sardar Patel to Amritsar, where his public address had had as we have noted a great impact. Trivedi in fact said that 'the government was now functioning'.[256]

Nehru as mentioned earlier addressed a press conference in New Delhi, and possibly being influenced by what Trivedi had said in the ECM the previous day, also suggested that: 'we may have turned the corner'.[257] He repeated a few points he had been making all along but admitted: 'None of us envisaged a major transfer of population at any time—perhaps this was a lack of judgement on our part but in this as in various events that happened the problem was thrown at us.'

Indeed, what Governor Trivedi and Prime Minister Nehru said with regard to the corner having been turned was true of the situation on the ground. Trains had begun to run without incident on the seriously disturbed Delhi–Lahore route and delivery of postal mail was resumed in Gurgaon from the middle of October.[258] Even *Dawn* accepted that all the Muslims of Delhi who had fled for safety to refugee camps had now gone back to their homes and even to their villages in the neighbouring areas. The rest had left for Pakistan, leading the Government of India to close the Muslim refugee camps at Purana Quila and Humayun's Tomb.[259]

In Delhi, essentially as a result of the tough and assertive decisions enforced by the government under the personal supervision of Nehru, things returned to relative normalcy much faster than anyone could possibly have expected. By the middle of October, for example, Chandni Chowk and its markets were again doings brisk business and were crowded like old times.[260]

But the enormous problem of finding place for the vast number of displaced and angry families—to settle down, rebuild—rethink remained untouched. Tara Singh had for some time been calling for the vacation of Delhi and its neighbouring areas of all Muslims to accommodate displaced Hindu and Sikh families. But it was quite something when even Ishar Singh Majhel, the Relief and Rehabilitation Minister, East Punjab, said that the Muslim League which had originated the two-nation theory, should take away all Muslims from India.[261]

This strongly worded statement of Majhel, who otherwise had been working very hard to make some sense of the rehabilitation effort appears to have been prompted by a statement issued in a press conference in London by Yusuf Haroon, President Sind Unit of the Muslim League. Haroon while raking up old issues said the Sikhs should not have backed out of accepting the 3 June Plan once it had been accepted on their behalf by Baldev Singh. He also attacked Master Tara Singh for demanding that Muslims from Delhi and its surrounding areas be evicted.[262]

Jinnah also appears to have taken Majhel's statement seriously. In an exclusive meeting with Duncan Hooper of Reuters he charged the Indian government with having been soft on the Sikhs and in fact said it was the Sikhs who were solely responsible for the crisis.[263]

NEHRU ON THE FOREIGN PRESS

As things began to quieten down, it was only natural for people to look for somwhere to lay the blame and responsibility. The BBC, it was generally felt, had been exceedingly biased in this context. It said that the level of barbarity had been far more in East Punjab and even compared the Sikhs to the Huns and also said that it was Nehru who had messed up everything by his 'incompetence'.[264]

The *HT* came out with an uncharacteristically hard-hitting editorial which charged some important British newspapers—mainly the *Daily Mail* and the *Daily Telegraph*—one-sided coverage of the disaster in India, particularly for holding the Sikhs more responsible for the killings.[265] The *HT* said it was shocking that not a single paper aligned with either the Conservative or Labour parties in the United Kingdom had held the British responsible for what had happened in India. The editorial gave examples of how the *Daily Mail* in particular had sensationalized issues. It had converted, a casual remark by Gandhi—on the possibility of a war between India and Pakistan—into a headline 'Gandhi talks of war with Pakistan'.

In the earlier months of 1947, as already noted, some newspaper reporters in Lahore had often complained that Nehru was always more inclined to give more ear and time to foreign correspondents. But later, particularly after August, Nehru, had developed quite a dislike for foreign correspondents who, he said, were bent upon exaggerating and sensationalizing events. The *Statesman*, one of the more balanced and respected papers, while covering Nehru's press conference of 28 August wrote: '[Nehru's] face was flushed with anger when he talked of undue emphasis on accounts of East Punjab being given by the Pakistan press and foreign correspondents'. He criticized the foreign correspondents for trying to be patronizing and said: 'it is not for them to be virtuous'.[266]

CHURCHILL AND ATTLEE DEBATE RESPONSIBILITY

From the beginning Churchill had launched an attack on the Labour government, holding it squarely responsible: 'A year ago I said to you, Indian unity created by British rule will swiftly perish and no one can measure the misery and bloodshed which will overtake these enormous masses of humble helpless millions . . . you can judge how far the forecast has already been fulfilled.'[267] Gandhi reacted in a manner most uncharacteristic of him, angrily: 'If Mr. Churchill knew of the fate that would befall India after she became free from the British yoke, did he for a moment stop to think that the blame belonged to the building of the Empire.'[268] Even as the debate on the responsibility for the disaster in India raged on in London, the irrepressible Krishna Menon, India's High Commissioner in London commented that 'Pakistan was the price paid by India to get rid of the empire'.[269]

The Tribune (31 October) reported Prime Minister Attlee's answer to the charges made against him by Churchill: 'I do not know anybody who suggests that in the position in which affairs had got into in India you could have done anything else but go forward on the lines we did. The time had come when Indian affairs had to be managed by Indians.' *Dawn* (31 October), however, sided with Churchill and party on the issue and said: 'The division of India could have been accomplished much more fairly and peacefully if the Attlee—Mountbatten set up had not decided to stampede.'

THE RUSSIAN VIEW

Russian interest in India had bothered the British throughout the nineteenth century, and with the onset of the 'cold war' imperatives, India had become an important element in the Soviet Union's scheme of things. On 25 October 1947, newspapers in Punjab reproduced Radio Moscow's version of the crisis in Punjab. Quite characteristically Moscow said that: 'the recent events in India show that the seeds of national and religious strife were planted deliberately in the British political plan. . . . Hindus and Muslims have no grounds for quarrel.[270]

NO ONE KNOWS WHAT HAPPENED: LORD ISMAY

I have gone through a large number of 'situation assessment reports', recorded by people of different backgrounds. For the first couple of months that is till the end of September, it is to a report filed by Ismay, Chief of the Viceroy's Staff, that I am inclined to draw attention: . . . in the first week of August Hindu officials had given warm farewells to Muslim officials . . . difficult to believe that within three weeks the imagined mutual trust of a life time indeed of many life times would be dissipated: '. . . the last months have been so chaotic that it would be difficult to find two people who agree as to how the trouble started, why it was not checked, what actually happened . . . it must be frankly admitted that neither its character nor its extent were anticipated by anyone in authority . . . in the history of the world—has there ever been simultaneous mass migration on this scale. . . .'[271]

THE EAST PUNJAB LEGISLATIVE ASSEMBLY'S FIRST SESSION

Perhaps the most important pointer to the fact that Punjab was possibly on the road to normalcy was the convening of the first session of the East Punjab Legislative Assembly. It was announced on 12 October that the Assembly would convene at Simla on 1 November. East Punjab Premier, Bhargava said that not only would he welcome the participation of Muslim members in the proceedings but also that all possible steps had been taken for their comfort and security.

Of the 82 members only 52, however, turned up in Simla. The inaugural formalities included the hoisting of the Union flag atop the Viceregal Lodge and the Council of State building.[272] Sardar Kapur Singh, Deputy Speaker of the Punjab Legislative Assembly (combined), was sworn in as Speaker. The first session—swearing in—had its funny side. When Ch. Suraj Mal was called to take the oath,

Rai Bahadur was prefixed to his name, at which members from the south-east Punjab (Haryana), mainly Sahib Ram, had a dig at him for his Rai Bahadur title. Shanno Devi created quite a scene when taking the oath. She pointed out the grammatical errors in the oath script, for which she was pulled up by the Speaker.[273]

The Tribune reported that to everyone's surprise some of the Congress members were behaving like opposition members arguing over the Minister's Salary Bill, which was among the first items to be taken up by the House.[274] The whole day was spent discussing the Salary Bill. Some members said the House's time was being wasted, others said opposition to the Home Minister's proposal was based on personal grounds. Ch. Lehri Singh chided Suraj Mal for having gone around 'telling people that he (Suraj Mal) was a bigger Minister than the Punjab Ministers because he was drawing a bigger salary'.

The debate took quite an ugly turn when Bhargava said that 'some members who were expressing concern for the poor refugees were themselves trying to grab big evacuee houses'. During the course of the debate it appears some members had pointed out that the Congress itself had prior to 1947 suggested that the salaries of ministers should not exceed Rs. 500, but as soon as they (the Congress) were in power senior leaders had conveniently changed their stand. Nehru's name it appears had been mentioned by some of the members in this context, to which Premier Bhargava said that Nehru should not have been dragged into the debate.[275] Likewise the Speaker's Salary (Amendment) Bill too was vociferously debated, the demand was to reduce the annual salary from Rs. 30,000 to Rs. 18,000.

The Tribune came out with a strongly worded editorial on the issue of MLAs' and the Speaker's salaries: 'Life . . . is at a stand still—adulterated rations, scarcity, wretched housing, no transport and on top of that the unchanged unresponsiveness of the average government official render ineffective all the Ordinances. . . . It is strange that one should think that Rs. 1500 p.m. is an excessive salary for a minister when prices have soured 500 per cent.'

To decrease the expenditure of the government, Premier Bhargava who also held the Finance portfolio told the house that henceforth no officer in government service would draw more than Rs. 2,000 per month, even though old officers would continue to draw their earlier salaries. He also said that the Governor's salary was being reduced from Rs. 100,000 to Rs. 60,000 and that even the expenditure on the Governor's house would be reduced. Sri Ram Sharma had also demanded that the government must stop spending money on luxuries for the bureaucracy and that the Circuit Houses be disbanded—'they were relics of the past'.

Suraj Mal who could not be checked in his attack on Bhargava and party said that the Congress High Command had entrusted the Punjab to weak and incompetent hands and also accused some ministers and members, saying their family members were responsible for many of the killings and looting.[276]

Fortunately the House was also able to spare time for some of the real issues. Sri Ram Sharma, among the more articulate of members told the House that he had heard refugees in Rohtak and Hisar say that they had been much better off in West Punjab Refugee Camps where the government had made better arrangements. While reacting to the point raised by Sri Ram Sharma, Premier Bhargava said there were times when he was helpless because the Government of India did not accept some of his suggestions. To this Shanno Devi added that if this were the case Bhargava had no business to be Premier—he must resign.[277]

Sardar Udham Singh told a shocked House that 'he knew of officers who had not hesitated to kill Hindus and Sikhs for personal loot'. When he wanted ministers to end the rampant corruption in the allotment of houses, shops and lands, Shanno Devi once again intervened and asked how could minister fight corruption, when they were themselves generating it by making recommendations in the matter of house and shop allotments to refugees. Sardar Shiv Singh said that a great deal of the problem was rooted in the police and in the fact that large amounts of money being released for rehabilitation work was actually being wasted and looted by corrupt officers. Another issue that attracted much opposition was the move to establish the High Court at Simla. Sardar Udham Singh and Prabodh Chander said it would not be easy for common citizens with limited means to travel to Simla for High Court work.[278]

The list of complaints against ministers and Congressmen in particular made on the floor of the House was long, to this were added some more charges by the Akali Dal.[279] Even as the Assembly was in session, the Akali Dal issued an official statement that criticized the Government of India for banning the entry of Sikh soldiers into Pakistan to provide escort to the refugee convoys and trains coming to India.

From the government's side the main defence was put up by Swarn Singh, Ishar Singh Majhel and of course Premier Bhargava.[280] Swarn Singh explained the breakdown of law and order by pointing out that in the regions that now formed East Punjab it had all along been a British policy to post non-Hindu and non-Sikh Deputy Commissioners and Superintendents of Police. After 15 August (1947), Hindu and Sikh officers, since they had never served in these areas before, were taking time to get used conditions. He assured the House that officers who failed to improve would be removed. Swarn Singh also shared the concern of the members with regard to the bureaucracy and its wide-spread involvement in corruption and nepotism. He said it was his hope and desire 'to make the police as friendly as the police in Britain', and was happy that Harijans too had now started coming forward to join the police.[281]

Ishar Singh Majhel took the floor to defend the government against the long list of complaints regarding the resettlement and movement of refugees. He started the defence by saying that a major problems in Ambala Division had been that there were several pockets where Muslims still remained and this being so, it was not possible to resettle Hindu and Sikh refugees up to many miles of such Muslim settlements.[282] The House was also informed by the minister of the relief that had already been discussed and was also being arranged, and of the relief grants that had been provided.

Gopichand Bhargava made long statements on the economy, the budget, education, law and order but he was also unsparing of his opponents. He said he had lodged strong protests with Nehru and G.B. Pant, the Premier of UP on the issue of the banning of the movement of refugees into UP and other provinces. He said he was sorry to note that some members who were talking loudest against communalism were at the same time saying that refugees of one community should not be allowed to go and settle in some districts.

What transpired during the course of the debates was summed up in an editorial by *The Tribune*: 'A noisy House whose dignity was impaired by certain members of the Congress party who seemed determined to throw all decorum to the wind. The East Punjab Assembly presented today on many occasions the appearance of a fish market. The Speaker showed great leniency.'

EDUCATION—THE REBUILDING EFFORT

Of all the institutions that suffered the consequences of Punjab's partition Punjab University would certainly find place near the top of the list. We have already noted the dramatic manner in which its assets were divided, leaving the East Punjab wing with practically no movable assets. Scattered and broken, the East Punjab University started its 'Phoenix'-like revival by opening its first office on 1 October at the Army General Headquarters Press Building in Simla. D.N. Bhalla was appointed the first Officer on Special Duty. Pran Nath Lekhi described the sad state of the University: 'the university today has no Vice-Chancellor . . . the Registrar's office is at Simla, the Dean's office is at Solan . . . the DPI is no where and every where, the Science Faculty is at Delhi'. Lekhi then went on to suggest that the University must be gathered at one place and if nothing else is possible it must be shifted to Aligarh to compensate for the loss of the University at Lahore.'[283]

Dayal Singh College too had to leave Lahore without movable assets. Majid Paricha, Secretary of the Dayal Singh College's Muslim Students Union said in a letter to *PT* that to begin with it was a mistake to assume that Dayal Singh College was a Sikh College, because Dayal Singh Majithia was in fact a Brahmo by faith.[284] He said the college had never discriminated against any community and in any case it was managed by a trust and therefore could not be transferred to any other place.[285] Another important college, the DAV, too, left Lahore empty-handed, but was more fortunate in that it reopened in a very basic form at Jullundur towards the end of October.[286]

Leading colleges in the West Punjab were however more fortunate in that they did not have to face the more serious pangs of partition. But for the teachers who left for India, the colleges remained practically undisturbed. In fact, Islamia College for Women Lahore and the very famous Lyallpur Agriculture College had started their new admissions process in the middle of October itself. Islamia College, Peshawar had also started a unique scheme which provided that those students who joined the college for the B.T. Course (see Table 6.1) and undertook to serve in the province for a minimum of two years would be exempt from the course fee of Rs. 350.[287]

For some reason Punjab was behind other provinces in the percentage of college students who enrolled for technical and professional education (see Table 6.1).

TABLE 6.1: PROFESSIONAL/TECHNICAL EDUCATION STUDENT ENROLMENT 1947–8

	Technical education—engineering, medicine, agriculture	Professional—teacher training/commerce	General—B.A., B.Sc., M.A., etc.
Punjab	6.6%	3.1%	90.4%
U.P.	10%	17%	73%
Bombay	10.9%	14.1%	75%
West Bengal	7.8%	14.5%	77.7%

Source: Educational Statistics of the Punjab 1947–8, 1949–50, Publication No. 4, Govt. of Punjab, Punjab Civil Secretariat Library Chandigarh, 1952, p. 2.

In the case of Punjab University (Lahore), however, the problem, unlike that of the East Punjab University, was not of facilities, accommodation and the like, but of teachers. A good majority of Punjab University's faculty as we have noted earlier had been non-Muslim. The University administration had to release an advertisement asking its teachers and employees to report for duty within 14 days failing which their positions were to be declared 'resigned' and vacated.[288] Therefore, as one half of Punjab University had its teachers looking for places to reconverge and restart, the other half had class-rooms and students but no teachers.

The situation in the case of schools particularly in Sind was practically the same. With a vast majority of teachers having left, the Sind government had to temporarily close the schools till alternate arrangements could be made for the appointment of teachers.[289] The impact of the migration of the Hindus and Sikhs, particularly on education, as pointed out by Fazal Karim (Pleader, Gujarat) in a letter to *CMG*, was that the contribution of the minorities had been very significant to education and that there exit had led to gigantic problems.[290]

But coming back to the problems of the East Punjab University, even as the Assembly debated the draft of the new University Bill, the provisional authorities had announced that a camp college would begin functioning in Delhi from 17 November and that teachers of Punjab University who had opted for East Punjab were to report at Pataudi House, New Delhi by 15 November. All other permanent staff of the University were also asked to report at Solan by 10 November.[291]

Gopichand Bhargava who also held the Education portfolio made a major policy statement on education in the Assembly. He said it was planned to take over all 'school appropriate' buildings and the government would offer assistance to organizations to restart schools provided of course that such organizations were not sectarian or communal based.[292]

Bhargava told the Assembly that students who had not been able to appear for the school-leaving examination could enroll in the first year in the colleges where, it was said, the principals of the colleges would conduct promotion tests at their own level (see Table 6.2). This provision however was not to apply to Engineering and Medical students.

Bhargava also announced in the Assembly that Inspectors of Schools had been asked to prepare detailed lists of all refugee teachers, so that they could be given priority in filling the existing vacancies in the schools. He also said that the managements of private schools had been asked to follow a similar system so that refugee teachers of private institutions did not suffer. With regard to the East Punjab University, he said all efforts were being made to minimize the problems being faced by the students.

It was the early onset of winter, however, that put a spanner in Bhargava's plan of restarting schools at an early date. Faced with the impossible demand of providing livable accommodation to over 10,00,000 people, the government had no option but to close down all colleges and schools till 29 February 1948, so that these buildings could be used by refugees. This decision, however, was not to apply to the primary and middle schools which, the government, said were to open on 17 November.[293]

When Premier Bhargava made the statement on education on the floor of the Assembly (November 1947) he could not possibly have been aware of the surprising figure that came up from the Census of displaced persons who had come into India from West Pakistan. It was said that of the 4.4 million people enumerated nearly 1.4 million of them were less than 15 years of age.[294] Obviously a large majority of these children were in East Punjab. In this sense the state found itself burdened (though it realized this only later) with the added responsibility of taking care of such large number of tender minds who had witnessed the barbaric violence.

TABLE 6.2: RESULTS OF EXAMINATIONS
PUBJAB 1947–8

	Number appeared		Number passed	
	Male	Female	Male	Female
Intermediate*				
B.A.	601	99	428	72
B.Sc.	120	02	89	02
M.A.	267	42	154	36
M.Sc.	45	–	45	–
LL.B.	51	–	26	
MBBS	65	61	43	32

Note: *While 9,168 was the combined strength of those enrolled in the East Punjab for the Intermediate the number who appeared and passed is not available.

Source: *Educational Statistics*, Table 15, pp. 56–7.

TABLE 6.3: NUMBER OF SCHOOLTEACHERS
IN PUNJAB 1947–50

Trained Teachers	1947–8		1948–9		1949–50	
	Male	Female	Male	Female	Male	Female
With college degree	1,757	171	2,000	227	1,975	282
Passed Inter/Matric	1,737	236	2,064	291	2,253	289
Passed Middle	9,141	1,754	10,001	2,118	10,062	2,540
Passed Primary	99	181	104	250	–	–
Not Primary	18	11	56	–	–	–

Source: *Educational Statistics*, Table 5, p. 30.

THE RICH FLED FROM AFFECTED AREAS LEAVING THE POOR BEHIND

Reports of violence, loot, abduction had considerably decreased by about the middle of November, yet the suggestion that things were improving and that a corner may have been turned was only half true. Earlier it had been violence and loot which went hand in hand, but sadly, even as the scale of violence decreased that of loot and corruption touched new heights, the difference being that earlier both the rich and the poor had a chance to kill and get rich, but now it was only the rich, resourceful and well connected who had the rich 'pastures' to themselves. The story of the resettlement of refugees, the allotment of lands, shops and houses to the new claimants is a story of widespread corruption, nepotism, favouritism, red tapeism, harassment and exploitation. Attractive statements supported by huge statistics indicating the dimensions of the resettlement effort were routinely issued, sadly these statements concealed a whole body of corrupt decisions of injustice and unfairness. This trend increased as days and months passed for as long as the resettlement measures continued.

Reprehensive as it may seem but some were of the view that the inhuman and barbaric violence that had swept through Punjab had played a great levelling role—the swords of the killers rarely had time to distinguish between the rich and the poor and in this sense at least in death did the blood of the rich and poor mix and drench the soil together.[295] During the peak days of violence the difference between Punjab I and Punjab II had been greatly reduced, but ironically no sooner had the first signs of peace begun to emerge, than the rich and the poor went their own separate ways.

The manner in which the burden of Punjab's partition in its various dimensions fell to the share of the poor,[296] was something that even Gandhi commented. Addressing the post-prayer gathering on 1 November, he drew attention to the unhealthy gap between the rich and poor and said he had noticed even in Noakhali as also in Delhi that the rich managed to flee from affected areas, leaving the poor behind. He wondered why the rich never helped the poor and why they 'do not sink and swim together'.[297]

This issue needs emphasis because throughout October and November there were a large number of appeals to the rich to bemore considerate and come forward. There were just as as many reports about the luxury lifestyles of the rich and influential even at the peak of the crisis. Indeed these were the days when fortunes of families depended on how much silver and gold they had been able to carry across or on their links with the officials who allotted vacated properties.

A report from Lahore gave details of how once-prosperous business concerns deserted by fleeing families were auctioned and sometimes handed over by underhand means for a pittance: a chemist and drugs store on the Mall in Lahore got a new owner for Rs. 1,000, a store was sold in Anarkali for Rs. 500.[298] A double-storey house in a prime locality of Rawalpindi was bought for Rs. 20,000, less than half of the actual price.[299]

In Lahore some of the best properties fell vacant overnight with their valuable furniture and other assets. As K.L.Gauba put it: 'And so began a scramble for Hindu houses and sofa sets.' Mian Nurullah (MLA) had taken over Bakshi Tek Chand's house on Fane Road; M.S. Muttaqai was the new owner of Rai Bahadur Seth Ram Rattan's huge bunglow. Firoz Khan Noon had taken over the house of Rai Bahadur Sohan Lal, Danepur Road, Farukh Hussain (Barrister) was the new owner of A.N. Grover's house on Fane Road, Barrister Tassaduq Hussain got a new home in a large bungalow on Fane Road, the list was endless. 'And while Muslim Leaguers from Lahore were drawing their first dividends from Pakistan, thousands and thousands of their less fortunate brothers were pouring into the promised eldorado homeless, tired, hungry, and stricken with disease.'[300] It was the same on the other side as well.[301]

S.D. Khanna (Roop Mahal, Simla) wrote to *The Tribune*: 'who says the British Empire has ended? . . . I saw the British Empire walking on the Mall . . . Black, Brown, . . . latest cut of English style clothes. . . . The British Empire is a mode of thought which has been deeply imbibed through schools, colleges, careers . . . can it end? It made me particularly sad when I recollect. Proud looking Hindus and Sikhs with all their worldly goods tied up in untidy bundles . . . with their women, with no privacy, ill-covered . . . what a contrast to what I see in Simla and Delhi. . . . The state we are told is poor, but much can be accomplished through voluntary effort . . . is the freedom that has come a source of joy or of grief?'[302]

The East Punjab government's decision to declare hill stations like Simla and Solan non-refugee areas did not come as a surprise. Premier Bhargava said buildings in Simla were needed for government use, but this was also only half the truth because, in reality it was only the influential and rich who were managing access to properties be they in Lahore, Simla, Delhi or Karachi, as we shall see in the next chapter.

The rich in Delhi as well were now prospering. *CMG's* special reporter filed a story, 'Activities of Wealthy People from Lahore'.[303] The report said people of Delhi had got used to the comings and goings of refugees and the exhorbitant increase in the cost of living. A small section from Lahore 'seem but on a pleasure trip despite the large number of Punjabi Hindus in misfortune . . . a casual glance

There was extensive criticism of the manner in which political leaders grabbed early opportunities of power and patronage. In the East many MLAs were even charged with loot and theft (*Shankar's Weekly*).

at Delhi's cafes, restaurants and clubs gives the impression of this class—completely divorced from misfortune'. It was this class that had cornered vast properties and was indulging in the large-scale black marketing.[304]

The situation was just the same in towns like Karachi and Lahore. *Dawn* noted that rich Muslims coming into Karachi were buying evacuee property at exhorbitant rates, but rather than admit that a similar situation prevailed in East Punjab the paper argued that: 'the most unfortunate part is that Muslim money is going into Hindu pockets . . . who are taking it out of Pakistan'.[305]

Zafarul Hasan, the District Magistrate of Lahore appears to have done a better job than some of his counterparts in Simla and Delhi. For one, he issued orders on 3 November that all property transactions enacted after 15 August would be invalid. More importantly, he added that 20 per cent of all evacuated shops in Lahore would be given to people coming in from Delhi.[306] The government of East Punjab too tried to ensure that people vacating prime properties in Lahore were given comparable ones in Delhi or Simla. As we shall see in the following chapter, a large number of rich business concerns managed not just one similar property in Delhi or Simla but usually in both the places and naturally at the cost of those who were less influential.

SHARE THE STATE'S BURDEN—PAKISTAN

Interestingly, in West Punjab, too, there were many senior leaders who argued that a great deal of the problem of resettling the millions of uprooted families could be resolved more easily if vested interests were prevented from cornering lands and properties. In fact, Shaukat Hayat, Revenue Minister, West Punjab, even stated while addressing a public meeting at Taxila that the government was planning (first as an experiment), the acquisition of all land owned by any family in excess of 1,000 acres and one-third of all land owned by any family in access of 500 but less than 1,000 acres.[307] *PT* commented in an editorial that the proposal of Shaukat Hayat if implemented would yield a surplus of about 500,000 acres.[308]

There were also reports stating that sometime in the middle of October the West Punjab government had decided that it would not be possible for very big landowners coming into West Punjab from East Punjab to be fully compensated. By these yardsticks it was said the biggest loser would be none other than Mamdot himself.[309] The last Premier of Punjab, Khizr Hayat, too, it was said, would be losing a great part of his estate, which was to be divided into units of 100 acres and given to the eronies of ministers.[310]

The only prominent woman in the Muslim League hirarchy, Begum Shah Nawaj, possibly in response to Ghazanfar's statement, said that her family had been the largest landowner in the Thal area for three generations, yet they would not mind if lands were nationalized. But she added two riders—that lands be nationalized not only in West Punjab but all over Pakistan, and that 'we shall be glad to surrender all our lands provided all ministers do the same'. Two other leaders of the Punjab unit of the Muslim League, Abdulla Malik and Ghulam Nabi Bhullar, also demanded the nationalization of all industry and agricultural land with no family being allowed to retain more than 13 acres.[311]

Quite characteristically, leaders on both sides shied away from the actual and concrete decisions, taking the softer and easier option of mere window dressing. One such decision of the West Punjab government was to abolish the *zaildar* system, calling it a relic of the past and a stooge of the bureaucracy.[312] It was against this background and the obvious political intrigue and power grabbing that Iftikharuddin Mian resigned as Refugee Minister in the West Punjab Cabinet.[313] He said while he was for immediate nationalization of land, serious differences on the issue had developed with his colleagues. *CMG* commented in an editorial on the resignation: 'Mian Sahibs ideological leanings made it clear that his solution of the problem would borrow far more from communism than would be palatable to the firmly entrenched faith in land lordism of most of his colleagues.'[314]

THE RICH AND RESOURCEFUL GRAB THE BEST PICKINGS

On paper there were numerous schemes for rehabilitation of refugees.[315] Majhel wanted accommodation to be rationed to the extent that people who had big houses were expected to surrender a part to the refugees.[316] The East Punjab Public Works Department came up with yet another scheme—which remained only on paper. It said the government had asked deputy commissioners to provide to refugee families from the properties vacated by Muslims living areas of 50 sq. ft. per adult and 30 sq. ft. for each child. These were broad outlines prescribed by the PWD but in reality most deputy commissioners worked out their own rules. In Simla, while no applications were being accepted for residential accommodation, for business purposes applicants were expected to fill out detailed proformas and submit them by 12 October.[317]

In Amritsar the authorities were more 'straightforward'; a committee of 12 people including 4 MLAs was to allot vacated houses on nominal rent. Rules were also prescribed to categorize the towns from which people had shifted. For example, a person coming from a district headquarter town would be given accommodation in a similar town, likewise for the tehsil towns and so on.[318] For people who had been displaced from larger properties, a Central Registration of Claims Office was set up in Delhi. Decisions such as this one were obviously taken by people who were greatly distanced from ground realities. Expecting refugees to travel to Delhi, at a time when managing a railway train ticket was among the most difficult of things only showed a complete lack of vision and sensitivity.[319]

The Tribune (1 November) was more blunt: 'There is not a single West Punjab Hindu or Sikh who has not suffered grievously. . . He is indeed lucky who has lost only his belongings and abode and escaped with lives of his dear and near ones. . . . Their cry is a house for a house it is said that such people may get their losses registered in Delhi . . . the danger is such registers will be shelved and allowed to be moth eaten later.'[320]

To add to the plight of the refugee families the government in its wisdom declared many of the cleaner and better managed towns as non-refugee areas.[321] The decision to restrict as far as possible the refugee families to East Punjab and strictly debar them from entering neighbouring UP[322] was taken probably to prevent the spread of anti-Muslim sentiment that came along with most of the families that had come in from the western districts. There are no reports to indicate that this must indeed have been the reason, but it is difficult to imagine any other. In fact, in a subtle manner Nehru appears to have made an indication of this when he noted in an *ECM* that many provinces were willing to take in refugees but were hesitant to take in the kind—'the group kind' who had been spreading trouble.[323] The restriction caused widespread resentment among refugees in East Punjab. Once again the more resourceful, the financially sound, managed better opportunities in distant towns, the less privileged were left to spend a great deal of their future in the long queues that became a common sight in East Punjab. An *HT* report of 18 October gave details of 3,000 West Punjab refugees who reached Patna being housed and looked after by organizations like the Hindu Sabha, the Arya Sabha and the Punjab Relief Committee. S.K. Sinha, the Premier of Bihar, it was said had taken personal interest in settling the families, so much so the Arya Samaj had even started work to open a Punjabi Market in Patna.

Some Sikhs families who had managed to reach Bhopal were however less fortunate. While details are unavailable, a report however said that the police had humiliated and maltreated Sikh refugees in Bhopal. The incident was serious enough for a large Sikh gathering in Delhi to pass a resolution condemning the Bhopal police and expressing great resentment against the policy. This decision of the Government of India to restrict the movement of refugees was condemned by many members in the East Punjab Assembly in its first session (November). Even Gopichand Bhargava, not one to cross someone like Nehru had no option but to state on the floor of the House that he had conveyed a protest to Nehru with regard to this policy. Ironically non-Muslim refugees who had flooded Delhi 'were being encouraged', as the *HT* put it, to leave even Delhi for towns in East Punjab. This was being facilitated by running special trains to various towns in East Punjab from Delhi.[324]

A NEW CAPITAL FOR EAST PUNJAB

There are numerous other indications of the Government of India's keenness to free Delhi of the refugee burden—a burden that completely disrupted routine life, supplies and hygiene. The issue formed a major part of the 17th Meeting of the ECM (26 September). Neogy told the Committee that a large number of refugees would leave Delhi the moment a decision was taken with regard to the new capital for East Punjab. All members were unanimous in that the decision needed to be taken at the earliest—not later than a week.[325] The issue was taken up again in the next meeting (18th) by Nehru who suggested that the best idea would be to build the capital at a new site from a scratch.[326] On 12 October a report from Simla said that the new capital for East Punjab was likely to be about 20 miles from Ambala.[327] The new capital project was officially announced on 26 October, also that the offices of the East Punjab government situated at Jullundur would shift to Simla.[328] A subcommittee consisting of R. Anand, D.R. Bhambri, M.R. Sharma, U.M. Apte, R.C. Kinra and R.C. Mehta was constituted to work out the exact location and other details.[329]

Well before work on the project had actually started, newspapers had begun debating what the new city should be like. An early indication came from an editorial in the influential *HT* which said that any new plan of the new capital must necessarily keep in mind the fact that of all those Hindus and Sikhs who had vacated Lahore almost 2,00,000 were associated with government work, the Punjab University, the courts, hospitals, newspapers, banks and other government and semi-government institutions as well as established private sector companies.[330] The babudom character of Chandigarh was thus laid out well before the plan was drawn.

CORRUPTION IN RESETTLEMENT

As the process of resettlement picked-up pace so did the misuse of authority. There were even complaints that since a Sikh, Sardar Tarlok Singh, was in charge of the special assistance fund created by the Government of India to assist industry and rebuild houses, there was a bias towards the Sikhs.

A large number of complaints were about the allotment of properties in Simla. Although public opinion was in favour of the properties vacated by Muslim being disposed, of either by a draw of lots or by open public auctions, the authorities adopted complex procedures which only served to facilitate the dishonest use of decretionary power. Makhan Singh Bajaj (Jullundur), observed: 'nothing has been done to rehabilitate refugees coming from urban areas . . . all the houses owned by Muslims have been taken over for government use at Ludhiana, Ambala, Jullundur, Amritsar . . . even the humblest of government servant was being allotted good accommodation . . . only people with influence were being allotted . . . to add to the woes of the refugees greedy land lords are playing havoc with refugees. . . . *Pagree* and other satanic devices are being used to fleece the last penny that may have escaped the eyes of the Pakistan searchers . . . only a small drop but timely drop can save the thirsty, but after death a whole ocean cannot revive life.'[331]

EXCHANGE OF LAND

The exchange of agricultural land turned out to be more complex than any one had foreseen, the problem was not only in terms of the size of holdings involved but also in the context of the fertility of the soil and the availability of irrigation. As the eminent economist Vakil stated:

> The immigrants who poured into India left behind large tracts of land in West Pakistan. It is well known that areas in West Pakistan and Sind were amply provided with a network of irrigation facilities. The Muslims who migrated from East Punjab, PEPSU and surrounding areas owned less land and that too land which depended upon the vagaries of rainfall. Thus the problem of rural resettlement has been rendered very difficult.[332]

The true dimensions of the problem can be seen from the fact that following partition, East Punjab got a mere 30 per cent of the cultivable area of undivided Punjab (see Table 6.4) but more importantly, just 28 per cent of it was irrigated and of this 28 per cent only 21 per cent had canal irrigation. Vakil's estimate, perhaps the most authentic, is that non-Muslims in West Punjab abandoned about 6.7 million acres of land of which 4.3 million acres was irrigated, whereas Muslims abandoned in East Punjab and PEPSU 4.7 million acres of which 1.3 million acres was irrigated.[333]

The disparity between the West and East Punjab with regard to agricultural potential comes out further when we study the sources of irrigation of both provinces (see Table 6.5) and how the production of the two major crops, wheat and rice, was influenced by the sources of irrigation. In West Punjab, wheat with assured irrigation was sown in 43,51,000 acres as compared to 1,62,000 in the East. Rice in West Punjab had assured irrigation for 7,57,000 acres, whereas the East had a mere 2,90,000 acres under irrigation.[334]

Initially the government of East Punjab had planned to allot land to refugees on a family basis—about 6 to 8 acres—as a temporary and time-saving method so that crops could be sown for the season. This scheme provided that ownership would not be given immediately and rent would be paid by the tenants. But by September 1947,

TABLE 6.4: CULTIVABLE LAND—EAST AND WEST

	East Punjab	West Punjab	Total Punjab
Total area according to village documents	22,980 × 000	37,239 × 000	60,219 × 000
Net area sown	12,904 × 000	17,028 × 000	29,932 × 000
Area under forests	769 × 000	1,150 × 000	1,919 × 000

Source: Vakil, *Economic Consequences*, p. 148.

TABLE 6.5: EAST AND WEST PUNJAB—IRRIGATION (ACRES)

1943–4	Govt. canals	Private canals	Tanks	Wells	Other
East Punjab	2,512 × 000	92 × 000	8 × 000	2,017 × 000	27 × 000
West Punjab	9,971 × 000	402 × 000	30 × 000	2,199 × 000	123 × 000

Source: Vakil, *Economic Consequences*, p. 159.

the Department of Rehabilitation had come into being and it was decided not to implement the family holding scheme and instead allot land in groups so that it would be done quickly and would make it impossible for the refugees to claim specific pieces of land. It would also enable the refugees to stay together and pool their resources.

This scheme was discussed in detail in a note prepared by the Ministry of Relief and Rehabilitation, 'Resettlement of Refugees in East Punjab'. The Deputy Commissioners were in charge of land allotments and were to decide the size of the holding to be given to each group. The Deputy Commissioner was also to ensure that all refugees who had owned land or were tenants in West Punjab, including minors and widows, were eligible for the allocation.[335]

To ensure that refugees did not have to rush around haphazardly the scheme provided guidelines of tahsil to tahsil allocations (see Table 6.6). This scheme too, however, got bogged down in controversy because influential landlords who had not taken allotment under the scheme began to oppose it and pressed the government for individual rights and permanent settlement. The government also learnt that some allottees had joined different groups and managed more than one allotment in different regions. On 7 February 1948, the government proposed a new scheme which would take into account holdings of refugees in West Punjab but once again there emerged a problem—refugees filed greatly exaggerated claims. It was then decided to verify claims by obtaining records and an agree-

TABLE 6.6: TAHSIL ALLOCATION OF LAND

West Punjab	East Punjab
1. Land holders from colony area of Punjab	Their own former tahsils in East Punjab, i.e. from where they had migrated
2. Kasur tehsil, West Punjab	Kasur tahsil, East Punjab
3. Sialkot & Shahangarh tahsil	Gurdaspur
4. Gujranwala, Sheikhupura, Chunnian	At first in Ferozepur, then Sikh states, lastly Karnal
5. Lahore	Ajnala
6. Rawalpindi	Ambala (minus Ropar) and Ludhiana
7. Rai Sikhs	Ferozepur, Fazilka, Muktsar
8. Mianwali, Jhang, D.G. Khan Montgomery	Wherever they wish to go

Source: MP, File 131-B.

ment to this effect was signed between the West and East Punjab governments in July 1948.[336]

There was yet another problem that related to individual non-cultivating landholders, usually big landlords. The East Punjab government drew up a table where such holders received a particular amount of land (for less in comparison) for what they had held in West Punjab. This was because the lands vacated by Muslims in East Punjab and PEPSU, as discussed earlier were substantially less, almost a million and half standard acres, than the lands vacated by non-Muslims in West Punjab, etc. Fortunately, however, this policy having been more thoughtfully worked out provided that the graded cuts in the slab system were such that larger landholders lost more land than the smaller ones.

On paper these schemes appeared easily workable, but on the ground land allocation was as complex a problem as could be possible.[337] As a result, rampant corruption, favouritism and the doctoring of documents were routine. The humble patwari, the tahsildar and such officials of the Revenue Department became the most important officials in the East Punjab government. The patwari's 'pen', the saying went, was mightier than that of the Financial Commissioner. Allotment of land a few kilometres this way or that was all it took to make or mar the fortunes and future of a family.

The dominating problem in the rural resettlement in East Punjab was not just the decreased size of holdings and the rampant corruption, but also the almost complete absence of canal irrigation. The peasantry from western Punjab had been used to larger tracts of land with assured canal irrigation as well as better equipment, which they had to leave behind.

There were many reports of families who left their liquid capital buried in the ground of their ancestral villages, believing it would be safe till their return. The manner in which evacuating families were looted by police and officials at every step resulted in a vast majority reaching East Punjab empty-handed. It was the difference in the welcome for those who carried money and those who had nothing that made life difficult for a vast majority of proud Punjabi families who suddenly had to learn to live on the dole, lining up for dried chapatis and parched gram.

The census of displaced persons conducted in 1948 showed that over 50 per cent of those who vacated West Pakistan were dependent on urban professions, whereas the all-India average was only 14 per cent.[338] Cities like Rawalpindi, Sialkot, Lahore and even Karachi were largely the products of the spirit of enterprise for which the non-Muslims were famous. Naturally there was a remarkable difference in the wealth and quality of life of the people who came from West Punjab and the Muslims who migrated from East Punjab to the West. Most studies have pointed out that over 80 per cent of all industrial undertakings in West Punjab belonged to non-Muslims. Vakil has also drawn attention to a *Punjab Board of Economic Inquiry (1945–6) Report* which, noted that non-Muslims contributed close to Rs. 5 crore out of the Rs. 6 crore invested in the factories of Lahore. The entire money market, and close to 95 per cent of all deposits were with non-Muslims. Eighty per cent of the property in Karachi was owned by non-Muslims. In Lahore, the non-Muslims paid three times more tax on property than did the Muslims (see Chapter 1 for details). It is in view of such figures that one can understand the true implications of the displacement and how it affected individual families who came away with nothing.

BANKS AND POST OFFICES—TRUST BETRAYED

This brings us to the issue that drew widespread attention during October–November—the contents of bank deposits, bank lockers and postal deposits (see Chapter 7 for details).[339] Roop Narain Raina, editor of *Banking Insurance Commerce* wrote in *The Tribune* that a large number of people had acted on the advice of political leaders and deposited their valuables in the lockers of banks in West Punjab. But now, he said, the government seemed unable to help people recover their valuables.[340] A.G. Advani complained that banks in East Punjab even after being given adequate proof of deposits in bank branches in West Punjab were not allowing withdrawals of even 10 per cent of the balances maintained by account holders.[341] Surprisingly not only were banks hesitating to allow withdrawals of even small amounts but as a Dr Grower of Simla wrote, some Indian banks were violating established procedures and giving loans against fixed deposits at exhorbitantly high rates of interest.[342]

In Pakistan, for some reason there was a difference in the policies followed by banks in Sind on the one hand and by banks in West Punjab on the other. The Habib Bank permitted withdrawals in its Karachi branches by account holders of its Delhi branches.[343] On the other hand, a report from Montgomery said that the district officers were citing an order of the Pakistan government which banned the transfer of accounts of Hindus and Sikhs to India.[344]

There was so much pressure on the East Punjab government that Premier Bhargava had to seek assistance from the Government of India to resolve the issue and even sought Gandhi's personal intervention to prevent the Pakistan authorities and other 'vested interests' from depriving evacuated families of their valuables.[445] Bhargava said it was difficult to believe that even banks would fail to honour the trust placed in them. Neogy, Relief and Rehabilitation Minister of India, told Parliament during Question Hour that Prime Minister Nehru had warned Pakistan not to open safe deposit vaults in the banks and that if it did so, India would be forced to take action.[346]

There were also a large number of complaints against post offices which were not releasing payments even on production of receipts and pass books. Across East Punjab's towns, a report said it was common to see hundreds of people gathering everyday at post offices in the hope of withdrawing some money from their accounts. Fortunately the Government of India intervened in the first week of November and passed orders that permitted refugees to withdraw on a limited basis, funds from their post office accounts opened before 14 August 1947. This order also said that saving certificates of up to Rs. 500 could be cashed and that post offices were to accept the premiums of insurance policy holders.[347]

The situation in West Punjab was no better. H.D. Ahmad (Kalaske, Gujranwala) appealed to the government to help people recover money left behind in post office accounts in East Punjab.[348] Iftikhar Ali Abasi (Lahore) complained that people were facing great hardships because post office accounts of a large number of people had not been transferred from the East Punjab to the West.[349]

CONCLUSION

If there is a reason to end this chapter in the middle of November it would be Governor Trivedi's rather confident assertion in Simla on 14 November that law and order had been restored, 'I had taken a pledge not to return to Simla until law and order had been restored', Trivedi told press reporters in the beautiful Barnes court. He also said that police stations in East Punjab, even in rural areas, were now fully functional; looted property of about Rs. 50 lakh had been recovered; a large number of policemen had been suspended for corruption; and a volunteer corps of 18,000 people had been recruited.[350]

On the refugee front, he said evacuation now likely to be completed by 15 December. No more foot convoys were coming in or going out and by 17 November Jullundur Division was expected be completely free of all Muslim movement. In Ambala Division there would still remain some Muslim convoy movement which, he said, was likely to be completed by 15 December.[351]

As Trivedi was speaking to reporters in Simla, Mountbatten was unveiling Prime Minister Nehru's portrait in India House in London. Mountbatten said, only 3 per cent of India's 40,00,00,000 were involved in the trouble the rest were living in peace. . . . But that is not news . . . news is not what is going well. . . . News is what is going badly. How much do you read about those living peacefully?' Then speaking on Nehru, he said that 'he was one of the greatest men of the century, a man of integrity, who had never at any time suggested any policy or action of which he or his countrymen would ever need to be ashamed.[352]

But in India, and within the top Congress leadership, there were obvious differences of opinion on how things had been handled. Congress President Kriplani said that he no longer wished to continue in his job and more importantly, he declared that the Congress Executive was not happy with the government and its functioning.[353] Virtually censuring his party leadership for the decisions it had taken, particularly for accepting the 3 June Plan, Kriplani said: 'Looking back over the ghastly tragedy . . . I have no doubt that we would have been wise that before accepting partition we had made Mr. Jinnah face the logical consequences of his two-nation theory . . . we cannot absolve ourselves of our responsibility . . . they (the masses) suffered they believed us fervently. . . . It is not they but we who voted for the 3 June Plan. . . . They accepted our decisions in good faith.'[354]

Abhyudaya came out with a special feature following Kriplani's resignation. It said Kriplani had been unhappy with a lot of what had happened in the preceding months but had restrained himself from speaking out simply due to his commitment and respect for the Congress.[355]

While Kriplani was telling the world that the blame for the disaster lay as much at door of the Indian leadership as it did anywhere else *Dawn* was criticizing Mountbatten's statement of 14 November which, it said, 'is only an attempt to minimise the grave situation . . . Mountbatten knows that he is the 20th century's greatest bungler . . . he is anxious to prevent the world particularly his countrymen from discovering the fact'.[356]

By sheer coincidence, perhaps, or maybe not, Gandhi also chose

15 November, the very day that Kriplani had spoken 'out of line', to share, with a heavy heart, his feeling that he was no longer of any significance in Indian politics.[357]

NOTES

1. Nazir Bedi, *CMG*, 28 September 1947.
2. *The Tribune*, 22 October 1947.
3. *CMG*, 8 October 1947; also *Dawn*, 8 October 1947; *HT*, 7 October The *HT* story was based on reports filed by a special team of reporters mostly foreign journalists, that flew over the convoy in the Governor-General's Dakota—at a height of 500 to 1,000 ft. in the morning of 6 October Also see *HT*, 15 September 1947, for early reports of the convoy.
4. *Dawn*, 8 October 1947.
5. 'Migration in the Punjab', IOR Mss. Eur. F/64/47, Muddie Collection.
6. *HT*, 24 September 1947.
7. Ibid., 22 September 1947.
8. 'Migration in Punjab', IOR Mss. Eur. F/64/47, Muddie Collection.
9. Mamdot to Gandhi, 21 September 1947, MP, File 129.
10. *The Tribune*, 11 November 1947.
11. *PT*, 12 October 1947.
12. Ibid., 15 October 1947.
13. *HT*, 3 October 1947.
14. *HT*, 17 September 1947; see an 'interesting change of heart' in Lehri Singh, Public Works Minister, East Punjab, who said that earlier he was not sure of the RSS and its work, but now after seeing the good work it had done he had changed his views, and was now an admirer of the RSS. Lehri Singh made these observations while addressing a Vijaydashmi gathering in Jullundur, see *Organiser*, 30 October 1947. *The Tribune* also reported this statement: 'He (Lehri Singh) wanted the RSS to make itself known to Indian leaders so that misconceptions can be removed. Now that India was free every party had a right to organise. . . There is very little difference between the objectives of the Congress and the RSS . . . the Congress wanted to establish Hindustani Raj while the RSS wanted unity and progress.' 30 October 1947; also *Organiser*, 18 September 1947.
15. *CMG*, 13 November 1947.
16. *Dawn*, 24 October 1947.
17. *CMG*, 9 October 1947.
18. *HT*, 8 October 1947.
19. Ibid.

20. *Organiser*, 18 September 1947.
21. Ibid., 25 September 1947. The answers were to be published in a subsequent issue, which is untraceable.
22. Ibid., 23 October 1947.
23. *HT*, 1 October 1947.
24. *Dawn*, 4 October 1947.
25. *Statesman*, 4 October 1947.
26. *Dawn*, 9 October 1947.
27. *PT*, 17 October 1947.
28. *CMG*, 7 October 1947; *Dawn*, 7 October; *HT*, 6 October, *PT*, 8 October 1947.
29. His estimate was that Hindus/Sikhs would vacate 42,51,540 acres in West Punjab while Muslims would vacate 25,37,281 acres in East Punjab a shortfall for Hindus and Sikhs of about 17,14,259 acres, *CMG*, 7 October 1947; *Abhyudaya*, 20 October 1947.
30. *CMG*, 7 October 1947; *PT*, 8 October 1947; *HT*, 6 October *1947*; *CMG*, 7 October 1947.
31. *Dawn*, 7 October 1947.
32. *PT*, 8 October 1947.
33. As already discussed, there had been reports that the Sikhs had been assured that either the Governor or the Chief Minister of East Punjab would be a Sikh. Incidentally there is a query in a note to the possibility of some political negotiation between the Congress leaders and the Sikhs having taken place as a result of which the Sikhs had mellowed down. This issue is raised in a secret note under the title 'Sikh Problem'—the note does not make a mention of the author and generally discusses issues relating to the Sikhs up to the middle of September, see Indian Viceregal Office Correspondence, Sikh Problem, Part II (9) 18 April 1947 to 17 September 1947, File 140.
34. *HT*, 8 October 1947.
35. Ibid., 9 October 1947.
36. Ibid., 6 October 1947.
37. *CMG*, 3 October 1947.
38. *HT*, 1 October 1947.
39. *CMG*, 20 September 1947.
40. Tek Chand, Memoir, Oral History, Transcript, Acc. no. 643, NMML.
41. It is not clear as to how these figures were worked out, but possibly they were based on official sources and therefore are almost certainly on the far lower side, see G.D. Khosla Papers, File no. 15, 1947, NMML.
42. *HT*, 3 and 15 October 1947.
43. *The Tribune*, 2 October 1947. A brief version was carried on 1 October 1947 as well, which incidentally appears to have been less counter checked because the initial figures of the dead and injured were far from correct. Extensive details are also available in F. Tuker, *While Memory Serves*, pp. 485–88. Lt. Gen. Tuker has based his version on reports

submitted by British Officers who were on another train that crossed both the sites where the Muslim refugee and the non-Muslim refugee trains had been attacked soon after the attacks.

44. MP, File 131-B, East Punjab Governor Trivedi to Governor West Punjab, New Delhi, 25 September 1947.
45. *CMG*, 26 September 1947, *The Tribune*, 26 September 1947.
46. Ibid., 27 September 1947.
47. MP, File 131-B, 25 September 1947.
48. *HT*, 26 September 1947.
49. *CMG*, 25 September 1947.
50. *HT*, 25 September 1947.
51. *CMG*, 28 September 1947.
52. *CMG*, 23 September 1947; K.L. Rallia Ram, *CMG*, 16 September 1947; Sheikh Akbar Hussain (Ravi Road, Lahore, *CMG*, 10 October 1947.
53. Extracts from ECM, 18th Meeting, 29 September, Item 8, MP, File 131-B.
54. Byron Farwell, *The Gurkhas*, p. 248.
55. Lloyd Jones Papers, Box IV, CSAS.
56. *CMG*, 8 September 1947.
57. Ibid., 11 September 1947; Majhel Memoir, Oral History, Transcript, NMML.
58. *CMG*, 28 September 1947.
59. Ibid., 11 October 1947.
60. Ibid., 26 September 1947.
61. *Dawn*, 2 October 1947.
62. *HT*, 20 October 1947.
63. *CMG*, 12 October 1947.
64. Ibid., 11 October 1947.
65. Ibid., 20 September 1947.
66. *Abhyudaya*, 17 November 1947.
67. See *HT*, 16 September, 28 September and 1 October 1947. Even the movement of Apples from the higher reaches had to be abandoned for many days, *The Tribune*, 28 September 1947.
68. *HT*, 2 October 1947, *The Tribune*, 1 October 1947.
69. *Dawn*, 2 and 3 October 1947.
70. *The Tribune*, 1 October 1947.
71. Ibid., 3 October 1947.
72. Ibid., *PT*, 12 October 1947.
73. *The Tribune*, 4 October 1947.
74. Ibid., 3 October 1947.
75. *PT*, 9 October 1947.
76. *HT*, 9 October 1947.
77. *Dawn*, 8 October 1947.
78. *HT*, 27 September 1947; *HT*, 8 October 1947; *CMG*, 25 September 1947.

79. *HT*, 27 September 1947.
80. *CMG*, 25 September 1947.
81. Ibid., 14 October 1947.
82. Ibid., 28 and 30 September 1947.
83. Ibid., 3 October 1947.
84. *HT*, 30 September 1947.
85. Ibid., 30 September 1947; *Sind Observer*, 30 May 1947, Nehru Clippings, 8786.
86. *Dawn*, 25 October 1947.
87. *HT*, 16 September 1947; *CMG*, 18 October 1947; *CMG*, 26 and 29 October 1947; *Dawn*, 25 October 1947; *CMG*, 2 November 1947.
88. See Bibliography.
89. Weekly Summaries, 17 October 1947 to 19 December 1947, MP, File 190, Reel 23.
90. Mridula Sarabhai Papers, NMML, Microfilm, Reel 1.
91. *CMG* 10 October1947; *PT*, 8 October 1947.
92. Ibid., 15 October 1947.
93. *CMG*, 25 September 1947; ECM, MP, File 129.
94. *CMG*, 26 and 27 September 1947.
95. Ibid., 8 October 1947.
96. Ibid., 3 October 1947.
97. A good example of how *Dawn* made a choice between Nehru and Patel is available in an editorial of 4 October 1947. While praising Nehru's appeals for peace it said: 'Nehru at least ostensibly has launched a peace campaign and is attempting to recivilise the barbarous multitudes.' But of Patel's attempts to restore peace the same editorial said: '. . . (he) speaks a different voice. He has no condemnation for what the Sikhs and Hindus have done. . . . Has made much show of his love for the Sikhs (calling them the flower of manhood.'
98. *Dawn*, 2 October 1947.
99. *HT*, 9 October 1947, *The Tribune*, 7 October 1947.
100. *CMG*, 24 October 1947.
101. *Dawn*, 24 October 1947.
102. *PT*, 12 October 1947.
103. Ibid., 8 October 1947; *The Tribune*, 8 October 1947.
104. *CMG*, 9 October 1947.
105. *PT*, 14 October 1947.
106. *Dawn*, 8 October 1947.
107. *PT*, 9 October 1947.
108. *CMG*, 12 October 1947; *HT*, 12 October 1947; *The Tribune*, 13 October 1947.
109. *Dawn*, 14 October 1947; *HT*, 9 October 1947.
110. *Dawn*, 10 October 1947.
111. *CMG*, 9 October 1947.
112. *HT*, 14 October 1947.

113. *Dawn*, 2 October 1947.
114. *PT*, 17 October 1947.
115. Ibid.
116. *PT*, 10 October 1947.
117. *Dawn*, 5 October 1947.
118. *PT*, 14 October 1947.
119. *PT*, 9 October 1947.
120. Ibid., 9 October 1947.
121. *The Tribune*, 28 September 1947.
122. *PT*, 10 October 1947.
123. Ibid., 12 October 1947.
124. Ibid., 17 and 18 October 1947.
125. *CMG*, 26 September 1947.
126. Ibid., 10 October 1947.
127. *PT*, 7 October 1947.
128. Ibid., 12 October 1947.
129. *PT*, 11 October 1947; *CMG*, 11 October 1947; *CMG*, 14 and 19 October 1947.
130. *CMG*, 22 October 1947.
131. *PT*, 14 October 1947.
132. *CMG*, 19 October 1947.
133. Ibid., 22 October 1947.
134. *Dawn*, 9 October 1947; *CMG*, 9 October 1947.
135. *CMG*, 14 October 1947.
136. Ibid., 16 October. 1947.
137. Ibid., 17 October 1947.
138. *PT*, 7 October 1947; *Dawn*, 4 October 1947.
139. *Dawn*, 5 October 1947.
140. 'Migration in Punjab', IOR Mss. Eur. F/64/47, Muddie Collection.
141. *Dawn*., 14 October 1947.
142. *CMG*, 14 October 1947.
143. *Dawn*, 14 October 1947.
144. *CMG*, 19 October; also *Dawn*, 22 October 1947. Many years later (1971) Lohia in an article in *Mankind* referred to this speech and said perhaps he had been wrong in believing that India and Pakistan would some day reunite.
145. Ibid., 24 October 1947.
146. Ibid., 26 October 1947.
147. Ibid., 29 October 1947.
148. *Dawn*, 30 November 1947.
149. Ibid., 24 October 1947.
150. *CMG*, 24 October 1947.
151. The situation was bad enough in Lahore but only marginally better in Simla—*The Tribune*, 14 October 1947; *HT*, 26 September 1947.
152. *HT*, 27 September 1947.

153. *The Tribune*, 5 October 1947.
154. *HT*, 20 October 1947.
155. *PT*, 9 October 1947.
156. *Dawn*, 22 October 1947.
157. *The Tribune*, 4 October 1947.
158. Ibid., 6 October 1947.
159. *HT*, 15 October 1947.
160. ECM, 25 September 1947, MP, File 131-B.
161. Ibid., 24 September, MP, File 131-B.
162. *The Tribune*, 17 October 1947.
163. Ibid., 27 October 1947.
164. *Dawn*, 4 October 1947.
165. Syed Aghar Husain Zaidi, *New Nazis*, 1948 or 1949, I.M. Stephens Papers, Box 19, CSAS.
166. *HT*, 11 October 1947.
167. *The Tribune*, 6 and 8 October 1947.
168. *CMG*, 7 and 22 October 1947; *Dawn*, 22 October 1947.
169. Ibid., 29 October 1947.
170. *Dawn*, 9 October 1947.
171. *CMG*, 11 October 1947.
172. Ibid., 4 October 1947.
173. Jeffrey, 'The Punjab Boundary Force', pp. 511–12.
174. *The Tribune*, 16 October 1947.
175. Ibid., 7 and 17 November 1947.
176. *CMG*, 4 November 1947.
177. Trivedi to East Punjab Home Minister Swarn Singh, 4 September 1947, MP, File 129.
178. *HT*, 17 October 1947.
179. *CMG*, 26 October 1947.
180. *The Tribune*, 4 October 1947. In fact, he recorded many years later that no one had even the foggiest of ideas as to how the crisis was to be handled—Memoirs, Oral History, Transcript, NMML.
181. *The Tribune*, 7 October 1947.
182. *CMG*, 13 November 1947, G.D. Khullar, *CMG*, 25 October 1947.
183. *The Tribune*, 5 and 6 October 1947.
184. Ibid., 5 November 1947.
185. *CMG*, 12 October 1947.
186. Ibid. 7 November 1947.
187. IOR Mss. Eur. F 164/16-17, Muddie Collection.
188. Ibid., 22 October 1947.
189. *PT*, 11 October 1947.
190. Ibid., 18 October 1947.
191. *Dawn*, 11 and 14 October 1947.
192. *CMG*, 25 October 1947.

193. *Dawn* 5 October 1947, also *CMG*, 7 October 1947.
194. *CMG*, 17 October 1947; *PT*, 15 October 1947; *Dawn*, 18 October 1947; *The Tribune*, 3 November 1947.
195. *The Tribune*, 7 October 1947.
196. Ibid., 15 October 1947.
197. *HT*, 18 October 1947.
198. *The Tribune*, 30 October 1947. For high handedness of railway employees also see Extracts of 18th ECM, 29 September 1947, Item 8, MP, File 131-B. There were many reports including official railway statements that said a large number of thefts in the railway, were occurring because railway employees were involved in it, for this see *The Tribune*, 8 October 1947. One of the major losses suffered by the East Punjab government because of theft in the railways was the loss of a large number of records that were sent through the railway from Lahore to Simla—the records simply disappeared enroute see *HT*, 18 October 1947
199. *The Tribune*, 30 October 1947.
200. *CMG*, 9 October 1947; also *PT*, 8 October 1947.
201. *CMG*, 3 October 1947.
202. *The Tribune*, 12 October 1947; *The Tribune*, 4 October 1947; *CMG* 12 October 1947; *CMG*, 28 September 1947, Brenden Papers, CSAS.
203. *PT*, 18 October 1947.
204. *CMG*, 26 October 1947.
205. Ibid., 7 and 8 October 1947.
206. *Dawn*, 11 November 1947.
207. *The Tribune*, 13 October 1947.
208. *HT*, 18 October 1947.
209. *The Tribune*, 5 and 7 November 1947.
210. Ibid., 15 October 1947. There were reports that some starving Muslim refugees were forced to sell their gold at Rs. 15 per *tola* to buy food, after a camp had been closed down on 21 September 1947, *Dawn*, 12 October 1947.
211. *The Tribune*, 18 October 1947.
212. Ibid., 29 October 1947.
213. Ibid., 20 October 1947.
214. Ishar Singh Majhel, Memoir, Oral History, Transcript, NMML.
215. *The Tribune*, 7 October 1947 see the report from London that says Indians are purchasing diamonds in large quantities.
216. Ibid.; Dr P.N. Anand in an interview by the author described of how he, then a 4th year student of Medicine at Balak Ram Medical College, Lahore, and his classmates had to flee Lahore, unable even to pick up a few clothes. (Interview 2 December 2003.)
217. *HT*, 8 October 1947.
218. *The Tribune*, 29 October 1947.

219. *CMG*, 28 September 1947.
220. Ibid., 22 October 1947.
221. *The Tribune*, 6 and 14 October 1947.
222. *CMG*, 1 November and 4 October 1947.
223. Tek Chand Memoir, Oral History Transcript, NMML.
224. *CMG*, 16 September 1947.
225. *HT*, 9 October 1947.
226. Ibid., 8 October 1947; also *Dawn*, 8 October 1947.
227. *Dawn*, 15 October 1947.
228. These trains usually comprised of about 20 bogies, with three open bogies being attached—one on each end and the third in the centre for the armed escort that accompanied such trains. Soldiers were also placed in each bogie, see *HT*, 12 and 18 October 1947; *CMG*, 18 October 1947; *PT*, 18 October 1947.
229. *PT*, 15 October 1947.
230. *CMG*, 2 October 1947.
231. Ibid., 22 October The process of evacuation of refugees by air had already been in progress for many weeks. Infact *Dawn* reported on 25 October that up to 22 October, BOAC alone had flown 76,000 miles in 26 planes, mainly Dakotas, flying people from both sides. When these planes landed, there were chaotic scenes at the air strips—with people begging to board—all tricks being tried often there were moving scenes with families being separated, see a report from Multan *Tribune*, 10 October For more on this issue see a note prepared by Field Marshall Auchinleck, for use of the Joint Defence Council, in which he says that to ensure upkeep of RIAF aircraft (mainly Dakotas), their use for evacuation of refugees could be allowed only for a limited period—atmost 12 planes for 4 days, in the course of which they would be able to lift about 2,400 passengers, see Extracts of ECM, 6 September 1947, MP, File 131-A.
232. *CMG*, 22 October 1947.
233. *PT*, 12 October 1947; *Dawn*, 15 October 1947.
234. *PT*, 11 October 1947.
235. Ibid., 7 October 1947. By the end of 1947, 7,21,000 non-Muslims refugees were housed in 85 camps in East Punjab, Amritsar district with 5 camps accommodated 1,29,398 people. By November 1947 the Kurukshetra camp alone accounted for 3,00,000 non-Muslim inmates. Extensive details of the camps are available in *Millions on the Move: The Aftermath of Partition* (Ministry of Information & Broadcasting, Government of India), pp. 11–18.
236. *Dawn*, 28 October 1947.
237. *PT*, 14 October 1947; *Dawn*, 11 October 1947.
238. *The Tribune*, 15 October 1947.
239. Lloyd Jones Papers, Box IV, CSAS.

240. *CMG*, 24 October 1947.
241. *The Tribune*, 5 November 1947.
242. Ibid., 14 November 1947.
243. *HT*, 19 October 1947.
244. *CMG*, 19 October 1947. The Tata School of Social Sciences (Bombay), the Marwari Relief Society and the Ram Krishan Mission played an important role in the managing of the Kurukshetra Camp. The Ram Krishan Mission alone distributed 12 maunds of fresh milk and 100 tins of milk powder in the camp on a daily basis, see *Tribune*, 4 December 1947. Spread over 9 sq. miles it was planned for 2,00,000 people. It had two dispensaries and a 142-bed temporary hospital, and a separate Hospital for communicable diseases and also one for women.
245. Ibid., 12 November 1947.
246. *PT*, 7 October 1947.
247. *CMG*, 7 November 1947.
248. Ibid., 24 October 1947.
249. Ibid., 8 October 1947.
250. *CMG*, 17 and 19 October 1947.
251. Ibid., 4 November 1947.
252. Ibid., 13 November 1947.
253. *The Tribune*, 14 October 1947.
254. Ibid., 16 October 1947.
255. Ibid., 19 October 1947.
256. Extracts from ECM, 22nd Meeting, 10 October 1947, Item 2, MP, File 129; A small example could perhaps be given of how the Punjab government had indeed begun to function. A mob was reported to have attacked a Muslim train near Faridabad, nine Muslims were killed. But unlike on many earlier occasions troops of the 2 Madras Regiment cordoned of the train, recovered and restored all that had been looted and arrested a few of the killers, see *Dawn*, 17 October 1947.
257. *Statesman*, 13 October 1947; *Dawn*, 22 October 1947; *The Tribune*, 21 October 1947.
258. *Dawn*, 15 October 1947.
259. Ibid., 23 October 1947; *HT*, 12 October 1947.
260. *CMG*, 14 October 1947.
261. *The Tribune*, 20 October 1947.
262. *Dawn*, 18 October 1947.
263. Ibid., 24 October 1947.
264. Letter of S.K. Sen (Simla), *The Tribune*, 5 October 1947.
265. *HT*, 7 October 1947.
266. *Statesman*, 29 August 1947.
267. *Dawn*, 5 October 1947.

268. *HT*, 29 September 1947.
269. *Dawn*, 14 October 1947.
270. *Dawn*, 25 October 1947; *CMG*, 25 October 1947.
271. IOR Mss. Eur. F. 200/165. This is a long note by Lord Ismay titled 'The Indian Situation' and dated 5 October 1947.
272. *The Tribune*, 2 November 1947.
273. Ibid.
274. Ibid., 4 November 1947.
275. Ibid.
276. Ibid., 5 November 1947.
277. Ibid., 6 November 1947.
278. Ibid.
279. *Dawn*, 4 February 1947.
280. *The Tribune*, 5 November 1947.
281. Ibid., 7 November 1947.
282. *The Tribune*, 7 November 1947.
283. Ibid., 4 October 1947.
284. *PT*, 10 October 1947.
285. Ibid.
286. *The Tribune*, 3 November 1947.
287. *PT*, 15 October 1947.
288. *PT*, 10 October 1947.
289. *CMG*, 8 October 1947.
290. Ibid., 19 October 1947.
291. *The Tribune*, 8 and 10 November 1947.
292. Ibid., 8 November 1947; *Education Statistics*, pp. 8, 9, 10; Hoshiarpur, Amritsar, Jullundur had the largest number of unaided and partly aided schools managed by private organizations.
293. *The Tribune*, 14 November 1947.
294. Vakil, *Economic Consequences*, p. 134.
295. Mian Iftikharudin, Refugee Minister, West Punjab, *CMG*, 28 October 1947.
296. Prof. Darbara Singh, Khalsa College, Amritsar, *CMG*, 16 October 1947.
297. Ibid., 2 November 1947.
298. *HT*, 3 October 1947.
299. Ibid., 19 October 1947.
300. K.L. Gauba, *Inside Pakistan* , p. 13.
301. *The Tribune*, 2 November 1947; *PT*, 15 October 1947.
302. *The Tribune*, 13 October 1947.
303. *CMG*, 19 October 1947.
304. Ibid., *Tribune* 3 and 4 October 1947.
305. *Dawn*, 12 October 1947.
306. *CMG*, 4 November 1947; *CMG*, 28 September 1947.

307. *Dawn*, 8 October 1947; *PT*, 8 October 1947.
308. *PT*, 9 October 1947.
309. *CMG*, 24 October 1947.
310. *The Tribune*, 10 November 1947.
311. *CMG*, 13 November 1947.
312. *Dawn* 23 October 1947.
313. Ibid., 15 November 1947.
314. *CMG*, 16 November 1947.
315. *The Tribune*, 11 November 1947.
316. Ibid., 22 October 1947.
317. Ibid., 7 October 1947.
318. Ibid., 11 November 1947.
319. Ibid., 6 November 1947.
320. It is estimated that about 13,00,000 people who had shifted or were likely to shift were from urban areas in West Punjab. Assuming that even a fourth of them were inclined to register claims, the condition of the central office can well be imagined, also see *Tribune*, 16 October (editorial). With a view to estimating the value of property left behind by non-Muslims in Pakistan, the Government of India had opened a Registrar of Claims Office in Delhi to entertain claims. By end of July 1948 96,650 people had filed claims in excess of Rs. 10.26 crore in Delhi alone, the government believed it was greatly exaggerated and decided to close the office. In October 1948 a Census of evacuees was conducted, according to this a figure of Rs. 3,929 crore emerged as value of properties left behind. But this too was believed to be exaggerated. It was only in July 1950 that Displaced Persons Claims Act came into operation, see Vakil, *Economic Consequences*.
321. *HT*, 14 October 1947.
322. See letter from Gurmukh Singh Musafir to G.B. Pant, Premier UP where he pointed out that a marriage procession of Punjabis from Ambala was prevented from entering UP, *Tribune*, 29 October 1947.
323. Extracts from ECM, 16th Meeting, 24 September 1947, MP, File 131-B,
324. *HT*, 7 October 1947; *The Tribune*, 7 November 1947.
325. Extracts ECM, 17th Meeting, 26 September 1947, MP, File 131-B.
326. Ibid., 18th Meeting, 29 September 1947, MP, File 131-B.
327. *HT*, 12 October 1947.
328. *The Tribune*, 27 October 1947.
329. Ibid., 3 November 1947.
330. *HT*, 25 September 1947.
331. *The Tribune*, 21, 22 and 29 October 1947; *The Tribune*, 3 November 1947. There were a large number of stories of how 'local people' usually prowled around refugee camps at night—mostly to rob refugee families but also to sell eatable items at exhorbitant rates. Infact Lt.

Col. Lewis Collinson 2 Battalion Assam Regiment has made a note of how this repeatedly happened at the Karnal camp for Muslim refugees. Lloyd Jones Papers, Box IV, CSAS.

332. Vakil, *Economic Consequence of Divided India*, p. 27.
333. Ibid., p. 150.
334. Ibid., p. 160
335. MP, File 131-B.
336. Vakil, *Economic Consequences*, pp. 90, 108.
337. Capt. U.S. Dhillon, *The Tribune*, 4 November 1947.
338. Vakil, *Economic Consequences*, pp. 132, 146.
339. Some agreements were reached between India and Pakistan on the issue in a conference in December 1947 as part of the Inter Dominion Agreements. It was decided in this conference to have evacuees with Bank Accounts deposit their pass books with the D.G. Post and Telegraphs, who was to make a consolidated list and forward it to his counterpart in the other country. The same procedure was to apply to other savings certificates like NSS, Defence Savings Certificates, Post Office Five Year Certificates, etc. Vakil, *Economic Consequences*, p. 104. The same conference also took decisions with regard to pensions, pending bills, and a large number of other such issues.
340. *The Tribune*, 9 October 1947; C.P. Oberoi (Ambala), 21 October 1947.
341. Ibid., 13 October 1947.
342. Ibid., 21 October 1947.
343. *PT*, 10 October 1947; *PT*, 6 September 1947.
344. *The Tribune*, 9 November 1947.
345. Ibid., 16 November 1947.
346. Ibid., 19 November 1947.
347. Ibid., 9 November 1947.
348. *PT*, 18 October 1947.
349. *CMG*, 16 November 1947.
350. *The Tribune*, 15 November 1947.
351. Ibid., *Dawn*, 16 November 1947.
352. *The Tribune*, 15 November 1947; *Statesman*, 15 November 1947; *Times* (London), 15 November 1947.
353. *Dawn*, 16 November 1947; *The Pioneer*, 6 February 1948.
354. *Dawn*, 16 November 1947.
355. *Abhyudaya*, 24 November 1947.
356. *Dawn*, 16 November 1947.
357. Ibid., 15 November 1947.

7

Peace Returns to Punjab: A Story of Corruption and Greed

The ICS, IPS, IES and IFS, the spoilt children of the British bureaucracy whom the British have passed on to the present ministry and whom it has to use unfortunately as the chief instruments for the enforcement of its will are so intoxicated with power . . . they are driving the province to damnation . . . there is loot everywhere and the most revolting part of it is that the famished impoverished naked refugees are victimised.[1]

NEOGY'S STATEMENT IN THE CONSTITUION ASSEMBLY

K.C. Neogy, Refugee and Rehabilitation Minister, Government of India, in an important statement in the Central (Constituent) Assembly on 29 November (1947) regarding the exchange of population stated that the about 5,00,000 non-Muslims who were still in the western districts could be divided into three main categories: abducted women, the forcibly converted, and Harijans. The efforts to locate and evacuate the first two were yielding satisfactory results, but the evacuation of Harijans was more complex.[2] Neogy told surprised and shocked members of the Assembly that reports had mentioned that the Pakistan authorities were not only discouraging non-Muslim sweepers, *dhobis* and other sections involved in such work from moving to India but in some cases had even banned their evacuation.[3]

The day that Neogy referred to the problem of Harijan evacuation, Dr B.R. Ambedkar issued a press statement in New Delhi: 'It would be fatal for the Harijans whether in Pakistan or Hyderabad to put their faith in Muslims or the Muslim League. It has become a habit for the scheduled castes to look upon Muslims as friends merely because of their (Muslims) dislike for the Hindus. . . . The Muslim League will never give consideration to scheduled caste claims. I speak from experience. They should rather die then be converted.'[4] Interestingly within a few days of Dr Ambedkar's statement an MEO (India) spokesman told press reporters in Amritsar that a large number of scheduled caste Hindus who had earlier refused to be evacuated from West Punjab were now asking for assistance to be evacuated to India. The same spokesman also referred to how some scheduled castes who had been converted were also showing a keenness to move out of West Pakistan.[5]

DELHI CONGRESS LEADERS WANT REFUGEES KEPT OUT

In his statement, Neogy also explained to the House that refugees from West Punjab were tending to resettle in towns that were situated on main railway lines, mainly between Amritsar and Karnal, and that attempts were being made to persuade them to shift to tehsil and other towns where accommodation was still available. The influential Delhi Congressmen were so been to keep the refugees out of Delhi that they even managed a resolution by the DCC to the effect. Later, Krishan Gopal Dutt, MLA and General Secretary of the Central Refugee Welfare Board, reminded the Delhi Congress leaders that it was the Punjab that had paid the price for freedom and it did not behoove the DCC to demand that refugees be evicted from Delhi.[6] The Delhi administration had in fact even announced that refugees registered after 30 November 1947 would not be entitled to rehabilitation assistance in Delhi and also that ration card distribution to refugees had been stopped with effect from 10 January 1948.[7]

Neogy also stated in the Constituent Assembly that 10,000 tonnes of food grain was supplied in October and in November as well as 76,000 lbs. of medicine for refugee relief. Plans to disperse the refugees to places like Gwalior, Kota, Bharatpur, Indore, Bombay and even towns in Bihar and Orissa, had not taken off due to the unavailability of trains and the natural desire of Punjabis to stay as near to Punjab and their own communities. In fact, Neogy noted that the tendency of people from the West Punjab regions to concentrate mainly in East Punjab and Delhi was causing many administrative problems other than congestion. Refugees from Sind, he said, preferred Bombay, Rajputana, the Central Provinces and some central Indian states. He also pointed out that an effort was being made to contain the entire rural population of west Punjabis and other people of 'Punjabi extraction' within East Punjab and PEPSU.[8]

We have already noted how refugees from West Punjab in particular had been discouraged by the national leadership in Delhi from moving away from the East Punjab. This policy was possibly influenced by the view that since the refugees from West Punjab had seen extensive violence they were likely to carry their hatred and desire for revenge with them. It is of course difficult to say whether there was an element of truth in this, but all the same when Ch. Lehri Singh, the Minister-in-Charge of Rehabilitation in East Punjab said on 7 December that plans were being made 'to build new townships with electricity near the main railway line' and that land would soon be allotted to refugees at subsidized rates, the announcement was seen not only as a step to resettle refugees but also to ensure that they stopped overcrowding Delhi.[9] Delhi was naturally the desired destination of every West Punjab refugee who had been displaced from an urban or semi-urban area. But Delhi on its part had plans only for about 1,00,000 people. After a meeting on 22 November, Neogy said that about 50,000 refugees would be settled in the industrial areas of Delhi and another 50,000 in residential areas where the government had planned to build about 8,000 houses for the lower classes, about 700 for the middle and 100 for the upper sections of the refugee population.[10]

In another statement in the Constituent Assembly on 16 January (1948), Neogy mentioned plans for the expansion of Delhi and many towns in East Punjab.[11] Plans for four new, self-contained towns around Delhi were also announced a few days later.[12] Within East Punjab, too, there were regions where refugees from West Punjab were not 'quite' welcome. Surprisingly some of these towns—Simla and Solan, for example—were put on the non-refugee list because of pressure from some influential people.

Princely State Refuse Refugees

While the princely states of East Punjab generally agreed to take in the refugees some, however, like the representative of Jind said that 'Jind did not have the food nor the land for the refugees', and in any case the demands of the refugees could be met as 'they (the refugees) demand all sorts of facilities'. East Punjab Premier Bhargava, who was present in the meeting said that even Alwar and Bharatpur had offered to take refugees from Dera Ghazi Khan and about 40,000 acres of land had been earmarked for them.[13] But having said this, attention needs also to be drawn to an observation recorded by the Commissioner of Jullundur Division in a meeting of the Emergency Committee (8th Meeting) in Delhi on 22 September. The Commissioner reported that certain states—Kapurthala and even Patiala—had turned away many refugees even without a day's food.[14] The significance of this is that all along the ruling families of the states had been proclaiming in newspapers how much they had done for refugee families but the reality was quite the opposite.

REFUGEES—LOSE EARLY SYMPATHY

This issue of whether the refugee population was welcomed earnestly or merely out of sympathy needs to be looked into more carefully. To be fair it was not only in Delhi but in many other parts of the country as well that refugees from West Punjab faced the problem of acceptability. The reasons for this were many. According to Gobind Sahai, Chief Parliamentary Secretary, UP, the province had taken in almost 4,00,000 people from West Punjab by the end of 1947. Sahai also said that the UP government had absorbed about 30,000 of the refugees in the economy and about 40,000 were living in regular camps.[15] The impression that Sahai appears to having given was that refugees were welcome in UP. Unfortunately this was only half true.

On 18 January the *Statesman* published a long report in its UP 'newsletter' column which said that the influx of 4,00,000 refugees had raised feelings of 'regional chauvinism'. The story said that refugees from West Punjab were generally considered as outsiders. This feeling was aggravated by the enterprise and hard work of the people from the West Punjab, which only added to the sense of insecurity and loss of economic opportunity among the 'local' population. The report referred to the cash assets some refugee families had managed to bring out with which they had begun to increasingly grasp every available economic opportunity. The manner in which the refugee population took to economic enterprise often at the cost of the local population strained 'relations' between the new settlers and the original local residents.

In this context, the most important reason was the aggressive competitiveness of the refugees in trade and business. The report also said the 'local' population thought that the refugees from the West Punjab were not only 'loud' but often ignored 'local sentiments of the people'.[16]

A more or less similar view was recorded by Tek Chand. He said that in the beginning, as Hindu families began coming into the south-eastern districts, the 'local' Hindu population welcomed them and even extended help. But since the Muslims who left the area were mostly farmers, truck drivers, bullock-cart transporters, and those who came to take their place were usually small traders and shopkeepers a peculiar problem resulted. These traders began crowding the small towns and bigger villages with shops, wayside stalls, etc., and in doing so began to be perceived as threats to the original inhabitants. Also the displaced families (quite understandably) began to patronize only the traders who had come from the western districts.

Tek Chand has recorded another interesting reason for the early rift that developed between the families who came to settle from West Punjab and the local inhabitants. He notes that the displaced families had realized that to make their demands heard they would have to organize politically on a refugee and non-refugee basis, and in doing so had started asserting their right for adequate representation in local bodies, etc. This was perceived as another threat by people who were controlling such bodies. Tek Chand also noted 'that the refugees by nature were very accommodating—they accepted water and "lassi" even from Harijans and had no inhibitions in doing manual labour'.[17] All this must naturally have come as a surprise to many of the caste-ridden community leaders of the region.

Interestingly while the government reeled off figures of how the Congress government in UP was doing a great deal for the refugees, the same report pointed out that not a single refugee's name had figured in the list of 30 deputy superintendents of police and 200 sub-inspectors of police recruited in November and December 1947 in UP. But the increasing uneasiness came to the surface immediately following Gandhi's assassination. When the news of the assassination first reached Lucknow the identity of the assassin was still unknown. A large number of Hindu and Sikh refugees were assaulted in Lucknow by crowds who for some reason believed that the assassin was a West Punjab refugee.[18]

Muslim Refugees from East Punjab—*Bhagoras*

It is hardly surprising that the Muslims who vacated their ancestral homes in Delhi and East Punjab had to go through the same humiliating and embarrassing grind in cities like Lahore. The *Statesman's* special representative in Pakistan, in a long story said how there was plenty of sympathy on paper for the refugees and that people spent a great deal of their time in finding faults with the arrangements being made for them but genuine sympathy and assistance were had to come by. The refugees from East Punjab came to be widely termed as *bhagoras*, or those who deserted and ran away. In the Sind region things were as bad. For the local Sindi Muslim, all Muslim refugees were simply outsiders, and from this followed a host of other problems.[19]

PAKISTAN AUTHORITIES PLAYED FAIR

On 30 November, an official statement made by the East Punjab government said that as on date about 1,31,000 non-Muslims still awaited evacuation from West Punjab.[20] A week later Brigadier H.M. Mohite, Commander of India's MEO estimated that there remained about 50,000 Hindus and Sikhs in the NWFP and Bhawalpur. In the same statement Brigadier Mohite said the MEO had started winding up exercises and that the MEO office in Lahore was likely to close down some time in December.[21]

The figures given by Brigadier Mohite, differed slightly from those of Minister Neogy possibly because Mohite's statement was issued a few days earlier (26 November) and quoted by newspapers on 27 November and also because he gave figures that were linked to the MEO's work. But far more important than the difference in the evacuation figures is what Mohite had to say of his counterparts on the Pakistan side: 'I say without any reserve that on the whole the Pakistan authorities have played fair and we shall have little difficulty in getting the rest of our nationals out.'[22]

While people from both sides continued to cross the border in large numbers throughout the early part of 1948, the Government of India's Ministry of Relief and Rehabilitation announced the formal ending of the evacuation of Hindus and Sikhs on 4 December.[23] The Pakistan government rang down the curtain about ten days later. The figures released by the Government of India were mind-boggling—

8 million people had crossed both ways, i.e. from East to West and West to East. Gopichand Bhargava also formally announced the end of the exchange of population on 12 December, formally thanking the MEO: they have performed a task unparallel [*sic*] in world history.'[24]

The MEO of Pakistan issued a press release on 15 December 1947 saying that it had organized the evacuation of 20,50,000 Muslims between 20 October and 10 December, an average of almost 50,000 people per day.[25] The statement specifically appreciated the contribution of Brig. Mohite for the joint effort that came into operation after 20 October. On 17 December a second press note of the Pakistan MEO said: 'The Government of Pakistan wishes to thank the following people of India for the movement of Muslims from East Punjab—Maj. Gen. K.S. Thimayya; Brig. H.M. Mohite; K.S. Hinder, Maj. Gen. Rajinder Singhji, Y.K. Puri and Mridula Sarabhai for [her] role in recovering abducted women and giving them protection.' Brig. H.M. Mohite, Commander of India's MEO had also complimented officers in the Pakistan Army for their help in evacuating Hindus and Sikhs—Gen. B.W. Key (Lahore Area Commander); Brig. Mohd. Iftikhar Khan, Deputy Commander, MEO Pakistan and Brig. Stevens.[26]

The two-way traffic, as Ghazanfar Ali put it, had practically ended by the end of December 1947.[27] The last Muslim convoy comprising about 8,000 people, mainly Meos, was reported by *The Tribune* to have left Gurgaon in peace and without any problems en route on 4 December.[28] Its entry into Pakistan as the last convoy was naturally reported prominently. The *CMG* story, based on a Associated Press report, said: 'Friday 19 December marked the end of one of the saddest chapters in human suffering when the last Pakistan-bound foot convoy entered Sulemanki Head . . . beneath shades of months of misery one could unmistakably read the unbreakable spirit that has long been associated with the Meos.'[29]

PREDICTS WAR BETWEEN INDIA AND PAKISTAN

Tara Singh believed that war was the only way to solve the crisis that had erupted from the displacement of Hindus and Sikhs from Pakistan.[30] When he was asked what in his view would be the role of the British in such an eventuality, he remarked that he was certain that British sympathies would lie with Pakistan, but he believed they would not actively intervene. But it was the other issue raised by Tara Singh that was of greater significance. He said that if Jawaharlal

Nehru was convinced that Pakistan was responsible for the trouble in Kashmir and if he had proof to support his allegations he should open a front of conflict near Lahore and shift the focus from Jammu.[31]

Tara Singh's statement built up quite a hysteria, so much so Ghazanfar Ali even issued a formal statement: 'Pakistan does not want war with any country much less with India', and that Tara Singh's reference to war was only a hysterical outburst.[32] On the other hand, Zafarulla Khan, the Pakistan Foreign Minister said that relations between India and Pakistan had 'reached a level where rupture cannot be ruled out'.[33]

As the talk of war between the two dominions further intensified, it led to a panic exodus from the border town of Amritsar in the first week of January 1948. A report also said that as a result of the panic the normal daily proceeds of the Amritsar railway station, which were on an average about Rs. 12,000, had increased to over Rs. 26,000 per day in the first week.[34]

It may have been noticed that earlier in this text the effort has been to bring out the difference in the perception or rather understanding of the ground conditions that prevailed in Punjab among public figures in Punjab on the one hand and important national leaders who were as much concerned about Punjab but looked at the crisis in a more total perspective—that of India—on the other. Perhaps the most pronounced example of this is the manner in which there was in Punjab the talk of war with Pakistan and paradoxically, at about the same time, Gandhi in particular was appealing to Hindus and Sikhs to go back to their homes in the West Pakistan districts.

While the Akali and Congress leaders talked of war in Punjab and the border towns like Amritsar saw a panic exodus, Gandhi appealed to outgoing Muslim convoys to turn back and settle down again in the East Punjab. On a visit to Panipat he said that he had been made to understand that it was only the influx of refugees from the western districts that had put pressure on the Muslims and created conditions which made the existence of Muslims in Panipat impossible.[35]

Gandhi visited Panipat for the second time on 2 December. He was greatly pained to see that far from improving, things had only deteriorated.[36] Addressing a large gathering which included Muslims, he said that if Muslims were willing to stay and die in their houses, he 'would stay with them in Panipat'.[37] He wanted the people of Panipat to invite the Muslim, back to their homes and set an example for Pakistan, this, he said, would enable Hindus to go back to Pakistan.[38]

It is obvious that Gandhi was misinformed about the conditions in Lahore, because at about the time he was suggesting that normalcy had returned in Lahore, there were reports which said just the opposite. The *CMG* published a special report on 9 December, based on versions of many non-Muslim businessmen, mainly Hindus, who had gone back to Lahore and some other towns in the hope of restarting their businesses they soon returned to India realizing that there was practically no chance of such a possibility. The conditions were simply impossible, and in any case, most of the shops and other business premises had already been taken over by the West Punjab Rehabilitation Commission and had been reallocated.[39]

Atma Ram Chakwal wrote a letter to *CMG* saying that appeals by leaders like Ghazanfar Ali, etc., to non-Muslims to stay back were 'empty words'. He said: 'while some Pakistan leaders are issuing lengthy statements regarding their most friendly intentions towards minorities the officials on the spot seem to be doing all they can to enlarge the gulf between the two communities'. Ghazanfar himself admitted later that indeed his goodwill efforts (see Chapter 6) had failed because of the hostile situation that had developed between the two countries over the Kashmir valley.[41]

Gandhiji of course remained convinced till the end that there was always a chance, a possibility, of a day dawning when Hindus and Sikhs would be able to go back to their homes in Pakistan. Reacting to a question of when such a time would come, he said 'when the time was ripe he would accompany the first batch of Hindus and Sikhs when they returned to their homes in Pakistan'.[42] In fact, a part of the post-prayer address on new years day (1948) was devoted by Gandhi to the issue. He was reported to have said that mentally he could never accept a permanent exchange of population and wanted people to go back to their homes. It was this stand of Gandhi that led Master Tara Singh into a duel of words with Gandhi himself.

TARA SINGH DEMANDS MUSLIM LEAVE DELHI

As the bloodshed came to an end, the race to gain and regain influence, wealth and prestige began in 'earnest' across the towns and villages of Punjab. Names that had been associated with villages and localities in towns for generations were replaced overnight. The question of mixed localities did not arise as far as in most of the towns and villages on both sides of the border because the minorities had been completely removed. In Delhi, too, for the first time in its eventful history, mixed localities had completely disappeared from the city.[43] The situation was practically the same in Lahore. Zahid Hussain, Pakistan's ambassador to India praised Gandhi for his effort to restore confidence among the Muslims in Delhi. Speaking to reporters in Karachi he said, Gandhi was doing all he could, including getting mosques vacated of refugees settlers even in areas where there were no Muslims.[44]

But Master Tara Singh disapproved of this and said: 'Let Mahatma Gandhi pay more attention to the property of Hindus and Sikhs. It is not a popular government that pays more attentions to the rights of the disloyal than the loyal citizen.'[45] In the same statement he strongly attacked leaders who were appealing to Hindus and Sikhs to return to Pakistan: 'no Hindu and Sikh can be loyal to Pakistan', he said.

Around the same time that Tara Singh was publicly voicing his disapproval of those who wanted Muslims to stay on, another issue added to the tension—the banning of *kirpans* more than nine inch in length.[46] Gandhi raised the issue on 26 November, in response to a letter he had received from Sardar Sant Singh, MLA (Central), Lyallpur, and other Sikhs who had approached him to use his influence to remove the ban on the *kirpans* and had even quoted a judgement of the Privy Council which allowed freedom to carry *kirpans* of any sizes.[47] Gandhi's reaction was not only strong but of great distress: 'There was a time when my word was law . . . manners have changed with times . . . let the Sardar and every Sikh who wishes well not be carried away by the prevailing current . . . and help in ridding the great and brave community of madness, drunkedness and all vices that flow from it. Let them sheath the sword which they have flourished loudly and badly. . . . A *kirpan* ceases to be sacred when it goes into the hands of a unprincipled drunkard.' He also said the *kirpan* could be used only to defend innocent men and women, the old and children, and was to be used only against heavy odds. The Sikhs who indulges in drink and other vices had forsaken, he said, the right to use this *kirpan*.[48]

Master Tara Singh was very hurt by the manner in which the issue of the *kirpan* had been handled in Delhi and reacted angrily at a press conference in Bombay in the last week of November. He also commented on Hindu–Sikh relations when a reporter sought his comments on reports that the Sikhs were likely to seek a separate homeland in East Punjab: 'let everybody understand that relations between Hindus and Sikhs are so deep that neither of them can be used to crush the other'. He also said that it was all Pakistan propaganda sponsored to cause a rift between Sikhs and Hindus.[49]

Forced Occupation of Vacated Properties

Gandhi of course was not impressed by the talk of war and naturally saw no sense in the call of vacating Delhi of Muslims—abhorring the very idea. As if to put to rest the whole issue he narrated at the post prayer meeting (6 December) the experiences of his second visit to Panipat. He said he was deeply worried about the manner in which Muslim places of worship had been desecrated and properties forcibly occupied. He said Gopichand Bhargava and East Punjab Home Minister Swarn Singh while addressing the public meeting had given assurances that all mosques that had been converted to temples in East Punjab would be restored.[50] In Delhi too the problem of people forcibly occupying properties and places of worship had assumed alarming dimensions. Authorities in Delhi had to issue a warning to all such encroachers to vacate Mosques within a week failing which the police would cause forced eviction and also launch prosecution.[51]

Gandhi took up the issue once again in his post-prayer meeting on 7 January 1948 when he rebuked angrily people who had occupied properties of Muslims and continued to do so even after they had been allotted accommodation, merely to harass Muslims and 'squeeze them out to get Delhi cleared of Muslims'.[52] As reports continued to reach Gandhi of how conditions were being created in parts of Delhi, that is to make it impossible for Muslims to stay, he was reported to have said: 'If Delhi's Hindus and Sikhs and sufferers (refugees) from Pakistan are determined to rid themselves of Muslims they should say so boldly . . . the government should then declare itself incapable of affording protection to Muslims. . . .'[53]

Gandhi appears also to have advised Hindu and Sikhs refugees coming into Delhi to first seek the approval of the Muslim residents of a particular *mohalla* before they took possession of properties vacated by Muslims. This was an issue that was taken by *Panchjanya.*

It said it was unreasonable to think that only the Muslims had suffered, Hindus and Sikhs cannot be overlooked.[54]

The issue of vacated properties being forcibly taken over was not something that applied merely to Delhi and East Punjab. Muslim refugees were doing the same in West Punjab. In Delhi, however, it assumed a more serious dimension because no locality was completely empty of Muslims, unlike other big and small towns and villages of East Punjab where Muslims had been forced out almost to the last person. In Delhi, as the pressure of the incoming Hindu and Sikh refugees began to build, the refugees, who had seen extreme brutality and had undergone experiences which had changed their mental make-up drastically, were surprised to see that while houses were lying vacant in Muslim *mohallas* they and their families were having to face the extreme Delhi winter in tents which were just about tattered pieces of cloth. They saw no reason why Hindus and Sikhs should not move into houses that had been vacated by Muslim families who had left for Pakistan.

One of the major outbreaks of violence in Delhi followed an incident on 23 November 1947 when some Hindu and Sikh refugees tried to take possession of a house that had been vacated by a Muslim family. When the Muslim residents of the *mohalla* resisted the clash turned into a major incident.[55]

As we shall see in the next chapter, the problem of people coming in from the West Punjab and forcibly occupying vacated properties in Delhi was one that greatly bothered Gandhi. Almost coinciding with the 13 January fast of Gandhi, the Delhi government launched a crusade to requisition all vacant houses and even some big buildings.[56] It was widely agreed that a great part of the communal problem in Delhi was due to the scramble for housing and an early solution of the problem would greatly improve the communal situations. In fact, even as Gandhi was fasting, a large number of Sikhs took out an anti-government procession from Gurudwara Sisganj to Birla House. The police first used batons to disperse the procession and then arrested 27 people.[57]

But looking at the issue from another angle, the winter of 1947–8 was unusually harsh in the Punjab—with a great shortage of woollen clothing and tents what were refugees to do? V.N. Gadgil, Minister Works, told the Constituent Assembly that 88 private buildings had been requisitioned in Delhi, and that in Delhi alone 'refugees had forcibly occupied 700 government buildings'. He told the House that the government was trying not to use force to have the buildings cleared, but usually those who had occupied them were able to produce letters of recommendation from important political leaders including members of the Constituent Assembly. Things had reached a stage in Delhi, as the *Daily Milap* put it, that no accommodation could be allotted without paying a bribe, particularly in the areas of Daryaganj and Hauj Qazi. This was the main reason why large number of houses were lying unoccupied.[58]

A large number of complaints were recorded by aggrieved families who had shifted to Delhi in particular of how money and connections with Congressmen were all that was required to win house and shop allotments. P.S. Sodhbans, a chartered accountant who had left Lahore after his house was burnt down had managed to get possession of two rooms in the Dilbar Building, Original Road, Paharganj after obtaining the permission of the area magistrate. But after the Delhi government launched its campaign to vacate all Muslim properties that had been occupied by Hindu and Sikh refugees, Sodhbans too was asked to vacate the two rooms. He wrote numerous letters to the authorities concerned detailing the rampant corruption and the manner in which government officials were sub-letting parts of their official accommodation.'[59]

In the East Punjab too the situation was scarcely better. In Ludhiana, for example, the authorities had to face a serious demonstration when they tried to have occupied properties vacated. In this case it was a large number of women from the NWFP who came out on the streets, refusing to vacate the buildings they had occupied.[60] There were also reports of refugees refusing even to get off trains demanding that they be taken to their places of choice, which were usually the bigger and more important cities.[61]

On its part the government did initiate legal measures to protect evacuee properties. An ordinance was promulgated, which provided that property transfers after 15 August 1947 would not be accepted as legal until and unless new owners had made payment to the original owners by a process as laid down in law. Failing this, the property was to be restored to the original owners.[62] The East Punjab Evacuees (Administration of Property) Act came into effect on 1 January 1948.[63]

In the West Punjab and Karachi the situation was as bad. The Rehabilitation Department of West Punjab had to appeal to the people to reveal information about those who had forcibly occupied vacated properties. In Karachi things took a serious turn when a large number of house hunters who had been waiting in the blazing sun were roughly handled by a police officer, injuring one of them. When the officer refused to apologize, the mob of house seekers tore off his uniform and even snatched his revolver. The District Magistrate of Karachi admitted that there was rampant corruption in the house allotment procedures.[64]

A *CMG* editorial said 'People in every rank of life from the highest to the lowest found it impossible to resist the chance of a rich harvest while the sum of disorders shone, the result has been an all round lowering of moral values which persist.'[65]

The charges of corruption were directed essentially at those who were associated with the allotment of urban and rural properties, possession of goods, occupation of houses, receiving of claims. The story was the same on both sides but certainly far more common in Delhi and the East Punjab.

The issue took much of the Constituent Assembly's time in the first week of December. Members like Deshbandhu Gupta and Naziruddin Ahmed called for drastic action, Sardar Patel said he too had heard stories of widespread corruption but that part of the problem was that those who did not get houses or shops thought that those who did, did so by bribing officials. Patel said 1,224 cases had been investigated of which 750 had been sent for trial, out of which 407 had ended up in conviction and of these 407, 120 were on trial, departmental action had been recommended against 180, 145 had been dismissed from service.

Dr Syama Prasad Mookerjee had also spoken on the issue. Patel supported him by saying that drastic action was required and it was the collective responsibility of all sections of society.[66] So much was at stake that little could really be done to check the rampant looting that went on. Tek Chand was a leading barrister and well-known figure in the Lahore and Simla circles. He contributed an insightful article on how the vast majority of people were suffering: . . . the taste of the newly found freedom so far as the question of deliverance from government and official tyranny is concerned has been bitter and poignant . . . the harassment of the citizen at the hands of the power proud jacks (officers) in office . . . has become a grave public menace and a serious threat to fundamental rights.'[67]

Interestingly, the government of East Punjab had earlier decided to allot factories to evacuees on the basis of auctions, but then thinking that evacuees might not be able to compete in these auctions decided that henceforth a cabinet committee would make the final allotments.[68] On the face of it there was merit in the decision because many factory owning families that had shifted to East Punjab had indeed lost everything and they may have been unable to compete in open auctions. But what transpired as a result of this change in policy was that no sooner was the policy changed, than politicians and their rich friends began cornering prime factories and other commercial establishments vacated by evacuating Muslims.[69] In fact, Pratap Singh Kairon, the powerful Civil Supplies Minister, East Punjab, admitted that indeed there was widespread corruption in the allocation of properties and that the government was considering involving civilians in the process.[70]

Lehri Singh, another influential, minister in East Punjab had given a detailed statement to the press following a tour he had undertaken in the districts of Karnal, Gurgaon and Rohtak. The report quoted Lehri Singh as saying that officers remained surrounded by stooges, henchmen and agents and that there were a large number of cases where policemen had occupied prime properties and were not letting rightful allottees and genuine cases come near the premises. The report also quoted Lehri Singh as saying the situation was no better in Amritsar, Jullundur and Ludhiana.[71]

Ministers were aware of the problems which ordinary people were having to deal with; possibly they were keen to remedy things, but so many were the opportunities to get rich and so degenerated was the bureaucracy that there was little anyone could do to check them. As one Inderjit Bharti (Jagraon) complained, even the submission of a simple application to the office of the 'cloth' inspector entailed waiting for hours in a long queue and repeated visits because the officers were never on their seats.[72]

In an article by the *Organiser* Acharya Kriplani (Congress President) was cited as saying that the entire bureaucratic system had been taken over by people who had retained their old roots—education, culture, upbringing. The problem, Kriplani said, was that even though the British had left, a whole set of Indians had filled the gap and taken over from where the British had left-off.[73]

In the western districts, the *CMG* quoted the prominent Punjab Muslim League leader and Finance Minister of West Punjab, Mumtaz Daultana, as saying that 'corruption among government servants is widespread'.[74] A.Q. Niazi discussed in an article the 'havoc done by bribery . . . to the man on the street', and of how a considerable part of the money earmarked for refugees had found its way into the wrong pockets. Niazi also said that stamping out corruption would solve a great deal of the problems.[75] The West Punjab government's civil supplies department formed an eight-member committee to fight corruption under Mohammad Hussan Chatha, MLA. Chatha said: 'the evil which assumed alarming proportion during the war years has shown no signs of decreasing'.[76]

Some unlucky corrupt officers were caught and punished. Ikram ul Haq had worked as ADM Amritsar, before he joined his new posting as ADM Lyallpur. He was suspended from service after vast amounts of goods were recovered from his house.[77] The *CMG* gave details of the property recovered which included 11 truckloads of goods including sugar and kerosene and vast amounts of others valuables.[78]

The issue of corruption in the bureaucracy also attracted widespread attention in the sessions of the West Punjab Assembly. Fiery speeches were made by many members on the need to check the menace.[79] On 23 January the *CMG* reported that 171 policemen in West Punjab had already been suspended. The complaints against the police were far too many even in East Punjab, and of varying kinds. A sub-inspector of police posted in Gurgaon was reported to have made vast amounts by charging Rs. 10 to 50 per head for allowing fleeing Muslim families to board refugee evacuating trains.[80] Among the rare exceptions was Ch. Ram Singh, Superintendent of Police, Amritsar. By the end of November 1947, he had recovered looted goods worth Rs. 28,20,842 and had 11 policemen arrested and inquiries instituted against another 26.[81]

So widespread was the urge to make a quick buck that there was hardly any public dealing department that could claim to be 'clean'. The Railways suffered massive losses throughout the months that followed the partition of Punjab. While people increasingly travelled without tickets, railways employees contributed to the losses in booking of goods, and black marketing other services. Dr John Mathai told the Constituent Assembly that the Railways had suffered a loss of Rs. 2.5 crore in the period 15 August 1947 to 31 October 1947.[82]

LAND ALLOTMENT—WIDESPREAD CORRUPTION

The nexus between the rich and influential, the bureaucracy and the police was in a way natural in view of the huge stakes involved.

Whether it was the fertility and situation of the agricultural land to be allotted or the location of the business properties, the power of discretion that lay in the hands of the reallotment officials gave to the whole exercise a dubious character. For example, the Kamboj caste of the Sikhs are known even today to be the finest tillers of the soil,—people who literally live and die in their fields. A large number of these people were relocated in a fertile belt near Karnal, but later had to seek the intervention of Prime Minister Nehru himself to save their lands from influential people who tried to dispossess them by force. The petty patwari was perhaps the most influential official on both sides of the border. A person by the name L.H.K. wrote from Lyallpur that patwaris were charging between Rs. 150 to 300 merely to give physical possession of land that had been allotted to refugees. Extensive black marketing was reported in court agreement stamps and papers.[83] One Fazal Mahmood of Lyallpur said: 'I went to the Tehsil to seek a workable piece of land but soon learnt that the good lands are for the relations of Patwaris, Tehsildars and those with money-highest bidders.' The huge pressure on the patwari who was expected to provide the necessary records of the land to enable allotment and then to enable the allottee to take actual possession of the land can be better understood in terms of the number of families that were to be allotted land.[84]

Ishar Singh Majhel, the minister in charge of resettlement in East Punjab did not explain or counter the charges of corruption but said the whole exercise was unprecedented in its scope and dimensions, and there were bound to be flaws. Majhel put the number of persons resettled on the land at 17,00,000. He added: 'there has been very great pressure, some families had captured land to which they were not entitled, they were now being dislodged'. He also explained that a great part of the problem was because the princely states within East Punjab were not linked (till then) administratively with the East Punjab, as a result there was no planning or combined efforts.[85]

It can be stressed here that while displacement from places of business in urban areas was equally traumatic and ruinous, for the peasantry, however, the agony was many times worse. Rural households were built brick by brick over years of hard work—a small part being added from the minor savings that may have occurred in a crop season. In the West Punjab, agricultural abilities were years ahead in terms of technique and facility with fields being looked after like living souls. It is difficult for someone not born in a village to understand the intense attachment to the land even to the 'well' in the fields or the trees that grow near it or even the tree in the family courtyards, and the mental agony of leaving it all behind. Thus when the peasantry from the relatively more prosperous villages of West Punjab had to face not only the trauma of leaving behind ancestral lands and homes but also the corrupt and indifferent bureaucracy of East Punjab they were naturally shattered. To this was added the fact that the villages that were allotted to them in the East Punjab were hardly livable compared to the villages they had left behind. As a letter to the *Tribune* said: 'there is dust and dust every where . . . what we have been allotted can hardly be called villages'.[86]

THE CALL TO NATIONALIZE LANDS

The call for nationalizing the large landholdings and large business concerns of non-Muslims who vacated the western districts came from various people in Pakistan well before anyone spoke of it in East Punjab or in other parts of India. Ironically it was India that took up land reforms while Pakistan forgot all about it. A. Sahid Hussain wrote to *CMG* that the expectations of a large number of people had rested on Mian Iftikhar-ud-din when he was the Refugee Minister of West Punjab and had proposed the abolition of landlordism and *jagirdari* and the adoption of equitable agricultural landholdings.[87]

Mian Iftikhar-ud-din led the demand that Pakistan adopt a socialist path with regard to land reforms and pro-poor policies.[88] He addressed a huge public meeting at Islamia College, Lahore, where he called for 'a Peoples Pakistan', implying a wide-ranging socio-economic revolution: 'our struggle has just begun. Nepotism and jobbery are rampant in Pakistan on a scale far greater than the worst days of the British. We have to liquidate such people who are sucking the blood of the people.'[89] The demand for the nationalization of land in Pakistan had drawn considerable attention. Another section, however, said that only the lands that had been vacated by Hindus and Sikhs should be nationalized.[90]

Iftikhar-ud-din's call for land reforms had won many admirers for him, not just in the western districts but even in East Punjab. A staff reporter of *CMG* who had travelled in Amritsar district in the middle of December reported that many families had expressed support for him in the hope that if the West Punjab were to take up reforms in landholdings, the East might also follow.[91]

The urban areas of East Punjab, Premier Bhargava said would have to cater for about 15,00,000 extra people of whom about 5,00,000 were non-agriculturists.[92]

By the middle of February (1948), Bhargava said that over 2 million refugees had been settled, and of these about 15,00,000 had been settled on about 2 million acres of land. He said about 2,23,000 had been settled in the Punjab states with Patiala alone having taken in 1,23,000, another 50,000 had settled in Jodhpur.[93]

By the end of December the UP government, as mentioned as earlier, had its fill of refugees from West Punjab. Government spokesman Gobind Sahi also asked the Punjab government not to issue any more entry permits for UP which in any case, he said, were being procured by refugee families after paying a bribe of Rs. 5 per family.[94]

The pressure on prime properties in major towns like Simla can thus be imagined even though Simla for one had been declared a non-refugee town. 'Hot Cakes' was the title given to an article by P.N. Soni. He virtually blew the lid off the nexus of the rich and influential with the bureaucracy and the politicians that had cornered prime properties in Simla. He pointed out that one such allotment committee processed 4,000 applications in less than six hours. Soni said that a large number of trusting people had sent their applications by post, these applications he said were not even listed for consideration. He also said influential refugees 'who were friends relatives or attached to coat tails of members of the allotment committee' were allotted the prize shops: 'influential people coming in cars from Delhi got shops on the Mall and left Simla the same day . . . one such person even produced an application on the spot because the original was not on the file—he was allotted a shop on the Mall. Another person managed two shops in Delhi and another in Simla, in Lahore he had only one . . . the rich are getting richer the fat fatter.'[95]

Soni contributed a second article on the malpractices in the allotment of shops in Simla on 6 January (1948). He said while protesting applicants could do little more than march in protest on the Mall, one thing was certain that all the successful applicants were rich and influential.[96] The Deputy Commissioner of Simla, Kewal Singh Chaudhry, issued on 25 January 1948 a statement which the government thought was an answer to the large number of charges of malpractice and nepotism in the allotment of properties in Simla.[97] What Chaudhary said only added to the confusion. He said that there were

1000 genuine applicants for about 200 shops, with applications of a large number of people having been rejected on various grounds by the Committee. Interstingly he said that the principle guiding factor was that allottees should be men of status who could fit in well with the social status of Simla. The second factor that was kept in mind was that 'no one who at some time could prove a danger or was likely to be apathetic to the laws of sanitation and hygiene should be allotted a shop'.

One of the major problems in the resettlement exercise was that influential people not only grabbed the best properties but did so in different names. On 19 December the Director of Industries Punjab, Dr Sarin, reeled off a large number of figures of factories and workshops that had been vacated in East Punjab. He said that about 4,000 applications had been received for 65 registered factories and 525 other workshops situated mainly in Amritsar, Ludhiana, Jullundur and Ambala. Dr Sarin also added that about 850 registered factory owners and 2,000 workshop owners had come into East Punjab from the West.[98]

In the allocation of factories too there was rampant corruption and favouritism. Ved Prakash Khosla (Batala) complained in writing that factories were being allotted not on merit or previous ownership but only to those who had been able to bring out their money while fleeing West Punjab, and in any case, a large number of allotments were being cornered by the same people but under different names.[99] On paper the authorities concerned appear to have taken precautions, because they did withdraw the earlier notification of auctioning factories, but the committee that replaced the auction procedure was only worse. It was a small committee nominated by the East Punjab Cabinet which finalized the allotment.[100] Exactly the same thing happened in the allotment of factories and workshops as had happened in the allotment of commercial spaces in Simla.

While there were numerous stories of needless paperwork and red tape which made people run around even for small help, the major issue was the attitude of those who were entrusted with the task of handling the rehabilitation process: 'persons of the Department remain untouched by human misery . . . their style of work could not have been tolerated anywhere in the world'. A report in *The Tribune* revealed the numerous flaws that had derailed the resettlement process in East Punjab. It said there was a widespread feeling that allotments were being made in favour of one community at the cost of the other and that big landowners, in connivance with political leaders, were grabbing prime lands so much so that some Congress and Akali politicians were reported to have evicted genuine allottees from prime lands with the help of armed anti-social elements. The report also said that almost without exception every organization or meeting of refugees conveyed the view that politicians were indulging in loot and grabbing of properties and that they were responsible for the large number of false entries in property allotment records.[101] Officials of the Evacuee Property Office were reported to have embezzled a large amount money during the peak of the crisis.[102]

But then as reports of corruption filled up space in newspapers, on paper and on the face of it, rules framed for evacuee properties and abandoned goods were in force; for example, the rules framed for the management of evacuee property in Amritsar. A government statement called for applications by 30 November for allotments in Amritsar. It said every adult would be given 50 sq. ft. and every child 30 sq. ft. of covered area for residing. Cattle abandoned by Muslims would be given as *taccavi* loans to applicants or openly auctioned if no one came forward to take possession. Likewise agricultural implements, quilts, tools, beds left behind by Muslim evacuees would be given free.[103] But such rules were obviously only on paper and applicable mainly to those properties and goods that had not already been grabbed.

About a year later the East Punjab government, like other provincial governments, also contributed a statement to a booklet compiled by Dr R.V. Rajkumar on behalf of the Congress, which gave the figures of land available in East Punjab and how much had been allotted by 15 June 1948. It also same the figure of houses, shops and factories that also been allotted.[104]

The Refugee Transport Organization—an Exception

While the Rehabilitation Department and other organizations of East Punjab had come to be known for their inefficiency, the Refugee Transport Organisation was an exception. This organization was headed by Sita Ram and assisted by Gurcharan Singh and Ramanand Bhatia. It won extensive praise for its work, part of which was to transport refugees to places where they were to be resettled.[105] With about 275 buses at its disposal, it transported with relative efficiency about 5,000 people everyday. It had opened offices at important places along the Grand Trunk Road, where refugees seeking transport were to report everyday.[106]

TO CONTROL OR DECONTROL FOOD

For the vast majority of refugees who had crossed the border the second major problem was of food. To the prevailing shortage was added the manipulation of prices by black marketeering syndicates. So quickly and effectively did black marketeers manage to control the supply chains that virtually every single commodity—match boxes, sugar, salt, cloth, coal, kerosene, bus tickets, railway tickets, wheat *atta*—had parallel prices in the East Punjab and Delhi.[107]

We have seen earlier how it was believed that controls were adding to the problem and how Gandhi had on numerous occasions advised that controls must be ended. When the government lifted the control on sugar, for example there was a sudden spurt in its price. On 11 January 1948, *The Tribune* published different views on whether controls on food supply were good or bad. Dewan Anand Kumar, East Punjab University's Dean of University Instructions (DUI) said that controls must be removed because they had created a parallel line of corrupt bureaucracy. On the other hand, Justice Teja Singh of the East Punjab High Court said that in view of the circumstances the controls were required. His colleague Justice Falshaw was of the view that the public outcry was not much against the controls but against the fact that they bred extensive corruption.

Dr Rajendra Prasad, Food Minister, Government of India, was extremely distressed by how traders had manipulated markets, and that the government had not been able to foresee the possibility of black marketing. In a statement issued on 10 December, he warned that if decontrol failed the government would have no alternative other than tough controls. He said that in 1944, when rationing was introduced in the present form 26 million people were listed for ration supply, the number rose in 1945 to 52 million, in 1946 to 100 million, in 1947 to 171 million, and in 1948 December, he said, the number was about 148 million.[108]

Many members of the Constituent Assembly were against decontrol in food supply. Balkrishan Sharma said it was surprising that India was following the path of decontrolling food because the world trend was towards controlled economies: in this sense India was going against the economic current. Dr Rajendra Prasad, however, stated clearly that rationing and food control had created black markets and ghost ration cards was the root of the widely prevalent corruption in India. In any case, he said, even if there were risks, the risks in decontrolling were smaller.[109]

The control on the supply and distribution of cloth was lifted in East Punjab in the first week of February 1948. Traders in Amritsar, who had earlier suffered extensive losses, raced back into the trade, with reports stating that many of them had left for major centres like Ahmedabad and Bombay to place new orders. There were also demands that trade with Pakistan be allowed freely.[110]

FOOD SHORTAGE—EAST PUNJAB

Wheat and wheat flour were in extreme short supply in the eastern districts of Punjab and in most parts of India. The position was further aggravated by the failure of the West Punjab government to supply about 75,000 tonnes of wheat which it had earlier promised.[111] To this was also added the role of black market operations. The shortage of wheat had led Natha Singh, the Ration Controller, Amritsar to order shopkeeper's to mix 25 per cent barley in the wheat rations so as to conserve the stocks of wheat.[112]

As part of the Government of India's policy of decontrolling food grains, the East Punjab government on 9 February (1948) lifted the control on the price, sale and purchase of wheat.[113] While the government would continue to supply wheat through the food supply chain, it would not purchase, as had been the practice, all the production of Wheat that came to the market nor would there be an authorized distributor.[114] The government of East Punjab however notified that while the free sale and purchase of wheat would be permitted within Punjab, no food grain could be exported.[115]

West Punjab

A woman from Lahore complained in a letter that traders not only kept people waiting for hours but had now developed the ingenious technique of having high 'sale counters' in their shops so that customers could not see the exact weight of the goods they were purchasing.[116] Lahore was extremely short of milk as well, a fact that led to adulteration on a large scale, with milk selling for 12 annas a ser.[117] When a health official reprimanded a sweet shop corner for the unhygienic conditions and the quality of milk he was using, the witty Muslim refugee shopkeeper who had only recently settled in Lahore replied: 'if it did not kill people in Delhi surely it could do no harm to the robust Punjabi'.[118]

The West Punjab authorities did however do a better job with sugar and this even when Pakistan was extremely short of it. The government ordered that no *gur* was to be produced within 15 miles of the Gujranwala Sugar Mill, and that no sugar cane was to leave the districts of Lyallpur and Sheikhupura. But this of course did not mean that the black market was weaker in Pakistan, it was as organized and strong as in Delhi and East Punjab. Fazal Karim wrote: 'the irony of it is that nobody knows the current price of bajra, jowar, maize, etc. Bajra is selling at Re. 1 for four seers, but the farmer who produces it has been selling it to the middleman at Re. 1 for even 10 seers.'[119] Karim said that the prices of hundreds of other items including cotton and gold were being manipulated.[120]

On 28 October the *PT* carried a report by Zia-ul-Ishan Bakhary, which said to that the problem of black-marketing in Lahore could be traced to Muslim businessman who had been uprooted from Katra Jaimal Singh (Amritsar) in the March disturbances. These businessmen had brought up all the essential goods and were selling them at exhorbitant rates to retail shopkeeper.[121]

Newspapers in Lahore reported that a person who claimed to be a nephew of the senior West Punjab Congress leader and former finance minister, Bhimsen Sachar was arrested trying to smuggle large stocks of milk powder into India.[122] The huge stock had been purchased by a Delhi firm—Express Dairy Farms—from a military depot at Harbanspura. P.L. Jain, the company's representative in Lahore, had bribed railway officials to put stickers on the railway wagon, showing it was to go to Karachi.[123]

Mamdot *Kebabs*

Although Pakistan was extremely short of tea, tobacco, matchboxes, cloth and coal, its markets were, however, flooded with beef, which was at rates three to four times cheaper in roadside stall than in established shops—up to 4. The same report also said that roadside hawkers were selling stale meat in the form of *kebabs*, naming them after Liaqat Ali and Mamdot.[124]

The tendency to create shortages and then overcharge helpless people grew dramatically even as there were appeals to have black marketeers publicly flogged.[125] There was black marketing not only in food grain and other supplies but even in bus and train tickets so much so even the pedestrian *tonga* drivers did not miss an opportunity to make a few extra annas.[126]

As black marketing thrived across the towns and villages of Punjab in complete connivance with the bureaucracy and police, extensive business began to take place on the Pakistan side of the border near Amritsar. An unauthorized temporary *mandi* was flourishing with about 500 traders transacting business usually in excess of Rs. 5,00,000 a day.[127] Interestingly, on 20 December, *The Tribune* reported a statement made by the Deputy Commissioner of Amritsar, that no special permission was actually required to trade at Attari (the border point) and that the situation was just the same in the context of trade as it was before 15 August, but that the police had been instructed to ensure that the crowd was within limits. But the very next day the thriving trade on the border was brought to an abrupt end by orders of the deputy commissioners of Lahore and Amritsar. The smuggling *mandi* appears to have shifted to the Khemkaran area, from where large amounts of tea was smuggled into Pakistan.

INDIAN GOVERNMENT'S WASTEFUL EXPENDITURE

Even as the East Punjab government was struggling for more resources to provide some basic and elementary relief to millions of people who were crossing the province for shelter and food, amazingly it was still able to find the additional resources to pay the DA instalments of government employees.[128] In the Constituent Assembly, too, many members expressed their annoyance at the manner in which the government was spending on its officers. During the course of the debate, a member cited examples of how a vast amount of money was being spent on travel facilities for government servants. Most of such travel made no contribution to efficiency. He said the government of India was the 'largest tourist agency in the world'.[129]

In other examples of misplaced expenditure the budget allocated a large sum for the hiring of a police band. While teachers received a meagre salary, a senior officer of the Education Department was sent to the UK at huge expense for training.[130]

The point here is that while on the one hand people were in dire straits, the bureaucracy—the planners of financial expenditure—did not for a moment subordinate their personal interests when it came to increasing the DA or providing for special pays. These are small

It was widely believed that the conditions of anarchy that followed partition, particularly in Punjab, were partly because the bureaucracy had led the race in the loot, favour seeking and nepotism. A large number of positions came to be filled by discretion, personal acquaintance and nomination (*Shankar's Weekly*, 30 May 1948).

examples, but they point to the reasons of why ordinary people suffered as much as they did.

Om Prakash Mehta, President of the Refugee Teachers Association said that 6,000 teachers who had been working in non-government schools in West Punjab and had now shifted to the East had not been paid salaries for six months. He also said that it was difficult to believe that so much should be spent on upkeep of people who were already so well provided, while thousands of others were not even being given their basic due.[131]

ADJUSTMENT PROBLEMS ON BOTH SIDES

Guruanditta Mal Mahajan (Phagwara) complained that even after four months pension had not been paid to junior employees of the government who had moved from the West Punjab to the East.[132] Likewise there were a large number of government employees who for months did not receive their new posting orders, mainly because the Government of India believed that responsibility for absorbing all the employees of the government who had opted out of West Punjab lay with the East Punjab government.[133]

In the western districts the problem of adjusting government employees who had vacated the East Punjab and other parts lay mainly in the North-West Railway. Mirza Ibrahim, a union leader of the NWR, said that of about 52,000 railway employees who had opted for Pakistan, not more than 25,000 were likely to be absorbed. He added that the plight of the remaining was worsened 'by the indifference of the officers'.[134]

Then there were others who were not employees of the government but all the same lived on monthly salaries. One such category was the film industry. Lahore had been the heart of the film industry in India. All the five film studios of Punjab were situated in Lahore. Over 5,000 people were directly involved in film production and distribution-related work in Lahore. Partition had brought with it complete ruin for a large number of such families.[135] A letter from Simla appealed to the Government of India to absorb people of the trade in the Publicity Department of the government and the All India Radio, because a large number of such people had suddenly been reduced to penury.[136] A large number of such families ultimately moved on to Bombay, some also opened photo studios in Simla and other places.

Misuse of official positions was widely reported in 1947. This had greatly added to the problems of people displaced from the western districts. As noted Congress President Kriplani, for example, had received a large number of complaints against officials (*Shankar's Weekly*, 30 May 1947).

SURPLUS TEACHERS IN THE EAST TOO FEW IN THE WEST

The fact that educational activity at both school and college levels in pre-partition Punjab was to a great extent associated with non-Muslim communities was a blessing in disguise for the Muslim teachers who left East Punjab. A spokesman of the West Punjab Education Department said that of the 1,933 Muslim teachers who had migrated from the eastern districts, 1,878 had already been re-employed and of the 26 Islamia schools 16 had already been made functional in buildings vacated by non-Muslims.[137]

The authorities in West Punjab seemed to have realized that some of the schoolteachers did not even have money to pay for transport to their new places of posting, and therefore provided grants to such families, the amount being recoverable in small instalments over a long period of time.[138]

Schoolteachers who came into East Punjab were less fortunate. The main reason for this was that East Punjab was flooded with them and there were no schools or buildings.[139] But an equally important reason was the indifference and insensitivity of the authorities. Vishwanath wrote to *The Tribune* questioning the East Punjab government's decision to start a teacher's training college at Jullundur even though thousands of schoolteachers were desperately seeking re-employment in East Punjab.[140]

The situation with regard to college lecturers may have been less desperate yet even among them there was a sense of apprehension R.K. Bahl and Hansraj were lecturers in colleges in Lahore. They made an appeal to the government of East Punjab that it incorporate a provision in the recruitment rules that priority would be given to people who had been displaced from the western districts.[141] Interestingly, one reason given by them was that people who had gone through the agony of partition would make better teachers as they 'understood first hand the psychology of suffering'.[142]

Examinations and Promotions

Even though the situation was completely out of control, the school administration in East Punjab had been able to work out a timetable for the conduct of promotion examinations. On 10 December it was announced that the Matriculation examination would not be held as usual in March/April but from 1 September 1948, and that there would be no summer vacation in 1948. As for the 1949 Matriculation examination, it would be in the month of May, thereafter, that is, from 1950, the examination would be held as usual in March/April every year.[143]

The Senate of the East Punjab University had met at Jullundur on 30 November, with Bhargava presiding over the meeting. It resolved to provide some relief to examinees in view of the complete disruption of academic activity. Those candidates who put in three months of social service in the refugee camps would be exempted from appearing in one subject in the Matriculation, BA and BSc examinations in 1947.[144] For the MA examination, those appearing in 1947 would have no such provision, but those who were to appear in 1948 would be allowed to forego one paper out of six in lieu of three months of social service.[145] For medical students, however, things were not so easy. A large number of them demanded that the examination be postponed because most students had lost their books. Others demanded that they should be allotted to the Medical College at Aligarh and not sent to distant colleges across India as was being done.[146]

ABDUCTION OF WOMEN: DIMENSIONS OF THE CRISIS

It was only as things began to settle down that the picture regarding the abduction of women began to emerge.[147] 'Numerous are the social and economic problems that have arisen in the wake of the mass migration . . . but none has such wide repercussion as the problems of abducted women,'[148] observed Neogy, Minister for Rehabilitation. He also noted that 'this problem was nearest to Gandhiji's heart'.

While newspapers were flooded with stories of atrocities against women, *The Tribune* gave a graphic account of how some women had been abducted: 'Girl hunting is the most prominent feature of the holy war that Pakistanis are carrying on . . . it first started in Rawalpindi and Multan . . . all women were collected at one place . . . the young and beautiful would be lined up to be chosen . . . some would be stripped and paraded before being absorbed in the Pakistan underworld.'[149] Another report said that the MEO (India) with the help of the Pakistan army recovered 70 Hindu and Sikh girls from the land tenants of a single landlord, a MLA near Lyallpur.[150]

Indeed if there was any issue upon which both governments differed the least, it was the commitment to recover abducted women. A reference has already been made to the various difficulties which arose not only in recovering women but even more so in restoring them to their families. The problem drew repeated and frequent references in various meetings. The All India Congress Committee, for example, had met on 17 November 1947. The popular Socialist leader Jayaprakash Narayan, in spite of his differences with many Congress leaders, participated in this meeting and moved a resolution which read: 'During the disorders a large number of women have been abducted on either side and there have been forcible conversions on a large scale . . . every effort must be made to restore the women to their homes.'[151]

Under the guidance of Mridula Sarabhai a detailed strategy was worked out to speed the process. Women workers were appointed for each East Punjab district to assist Pakistan teams that were trying to locate abducted women. Likewise 32 Hindu and Sikh women were selected to go to Pakistan to make a similar search.[152]

According to an estimate about 25,000 Hindu and Sikh women still remained to be recovered from Pakistan. On the other hand, Ghazanfar Ali Khan had quoted a figure of about 50,000 Muslim women who were abducted in East Punjab. He also said that not more than 5,000 Hindu and Sikh women were abducted in West Punjab.[153] There is just no way to tell how correct or incorrect these figures were because both sides continued to release statements on a weekly basis of the number of women recovered.

The Tribune reported that most of the women being restored to

India by the West Punjab authorities were those who were not 'saleable'.[154] A day later *The Tribune* gave more details of how abducted Hindu and Sikh women were being 'exhibited in the bazars of Peshawar—Banu. Many of these women were from Mirpur, Rajouli, Kotli, Bhimber . . . [and] sold for up to Rs. 200'.

Both sides naturally highlighted the problems they encountered in the recovery expeditions, particularly those that were organized by army units. Maj. Ghulam Rasul of the 16 Punjab Regiment (Pakistan) filed a report which said that considerable problems were created in the course of his effort to recover abducted Muslim women, particularly in Amritsar. He said that while senior officers were generally helpful, the problem was at the lower level. In many villages he said abducted women were frightened by the villagers into keeping quiet. Major Rasul also reported that many Muslim women had been badly treated even in the refugee camps.[155]

Just as the West Punjab teams working for the recovery of abducted women charged the East Punjab authorities with not cooperating, similar reports were filed by East Punjab officials and social workers who were trying to recover abducted Hindu and Sikh women from West Punjab. A lady by the name of Sheela wrote to *The Tribune* that how authorities in Pakistan had denied access to Indian 'recovery of women' teams into areas of Rawalpindi and Jhelum where most such abductions had taken place. She said that Muslim women recovered in East Punjab should not be returned to West Punjab until the Pakistan authorities 'begin helping sincerely', and that 'as of now it is only one way traffic'.[156] Mrs Bhag Mehta was also associated with recovery of Hindu and Sikh women from West Punjab, mainly in the Lahore region. She too said that the West Punjab authorities were not only not cooperating but were not allowing recovery teams to proceed beyond Jhelum.[157]

Interestingly Mahatma Gandhi was against the deployment of the army in support of social workers in the recovery of abducted women. He shared this view with Rameshwari Nehru who, like Mridula Sarabhai, played an important role in the recovery work. Gandhi in fact suggested that the best way to recover Hindu and Sikh women was to restore the Muslim women that still remained in East Punjab; this he believed was bound to influence the Pakistan authorities to reciprocate.[158] In fact, this is exactly what Iftikhar Hussain Mamdot too believed. Speaking in the context of a special effort backed by both governments—'Abducted Women's Week'—at the end of February (1948), he said: 'The existence of abducted women in our country is a blot . . . Muslim women in East Punjab can be brought back only if abducted women in West Punjab are restored immediately'.[159]

The efforts of women workers like Sarabhai, Fatima Begum and Rameshwari Nehru yielded fairly good results though much of the recoveries took many more months. However, between 8 December 1947 and 25 January 1948, Sarabhai and Fatima Begum said that 1,576 abducted Muslim women and children had been recovered from East Punjab and about 1,218 Hindu and Sikhs women had been handed over by West Punjab authorities to India.

The problem of recovering the abducted women was only half the story, the more difficult one was of restoring the dignity of such women, convincing and canvassing with families to take 'back' the abducted women. Rameshwari Nehru noted that families often refused or were unwilling to accept the return of such women:

> No Hindu *Shastra* provides that those women who suffered because their men proved too weak to defend them should be despised . . . if anyone is to be condemned it is our Hindu society not the women . . . I request my brethren to rise above silly notions and superstitions and welcome these women with open arms.[160]

There were no doubt some reports of how some of the social groups and individuals involved in the recovery of abducted Hindu and Sikh women had organized events to welcome the women who were being returned to the East Punjab authorities.[161] Jatinder Singh in a letter to *The Tribune* made some insightful suggestions with regard to women who had been recovered and had no place to go because families had closed their doors on them: 'It is all very well to express generous sentiments but this will not do . . . honourable marriages will go a long way.' He suggested that a list be prepared of such women and given to reputed social organizations because if carefully handled a great many of such women could be remarried and resettled.[162] There are no figures available as to how many such women were actually resettled by marriage in the early months of 1948. Since abducted and restored Muslim women suffered the 'stigma' as much as the Hindu and Sikh women, authorities in West Punjab did try to initiate a plan that provided for the remarriage of such restored non-Muslim women.

About 300 Hindu and Sikh women who had been recovered in

Lahore area were temporarily housed in a part of the women's jail in Lahore. When Begum Ishq, the Superintendent of the women's jail announced that those women who wished to remarry should register their names, the women demonstrated violently saying that the authorities should not play with their sentiments and that the marriage proposals were only a ploy to misuse them.[163] *The Tribune* reported a similar incident from the women's jail in Jullundur.[164]

Some success, however, appears to have been achieved from the fairly good number of such women who had themselves registered in one of the marriage bureaus set up by the Government of India's Ministry of Rehabilitation in New Delhi.[165] Similar camps were opened in Amritsar and Kurukshetra. The Women's Home at Roshanara Road in Delhi was put under the able charge of Rameshwari Nehru.[166] A vocational training centre was also opened at Curzon Road (New Delhi).

Nehru shared his deep anguish on the plight of women who were recovered but had no place to go. I am told that sometimes there is unwillingness on the part of relations to accept the women back . . . the social customs that support their attitude must be condemned . . . relations should be proud to take them back.'[167] While inaugurating the Restoration of Abducted Women's Week, Prime Minister Nehru said: 'we may forget other things but this (abduction of women) will take a long time to forget'.[168]

As families shied away from taking back their women the government was once again burdened with an unexpected task: it had now to take care of not only the women and children who had lost all their menfolk but also those women whose families had closed their doors on them. The first of such camps was opened in Putilighar (Amritsar) in the Harikishan Khanna School, under the charge of Sita Devi, MLA.[169] Homes for such women were also started around the same time in Patiala, Simla, Ambala, Amritsar—they came to be known as Sewa Safiana.[190]

The West Punjab authorities too had to start a special camp for Muslim women who had lost all their men and found living in the regular camps difficult. In fact, a large number of such women were reported to be from well-provided families. The officials concerned were sensitive to the plight of these women and organized a special and separate home for them. This camp was opened in Bhawalpur House in Lahore and was managed by Begum Zubeda Shah.[171]

Thousands of abducted women had been recovered on both sides.

While some were scared that their families may not take them back, others feeling stigmatized and refused to cooperate with the authorities and social workers. However, there were heartening exceptions. Rajkarni, a Hindu girl had lost all male members of her family and like hundreds of other women, was abducted by raiders. Somehow Sain Jalal, a resident of Bhati Gate, Lahore, came across the girl and was able to rescue her. He looked after her until he could restore her to her grandfather, Dial Chand in Simla. When Rajkarni left Lahore, the local residents were seen weeping.[172]

Forced Conversion of Abducted Women

The Government of India even advertised appeals through newspapers, calling upon people and social organizations to join in the 'recovery of women', effort.[173] During the course of the 'Abducted Women's Week', one of the many articles and reports published by *The Tribune* dealt with the problem of families refusing to take back recovered women:

> The Hindu and Sikh families should . . . receive these unhappy women back into their homes and . . . not treat them as defiled creatures. . . . This is necessary because some recovered women have even tried to escape from recovery homes believing that . . . there is no place of honour for them in Hindu society. Did not Gandhiji say that such abducted women and forcibly converted women were as pure as gold.[174]

Gandhi had in fact spoken at great length on the forced conversion issue while addressing a gathering at Jesrah (Gurgaon): 'no conversion or marriage of a woman to a member of the opposite community could be recognised as valid on the plea of the consent of free will. It was abuse of the words to talk of free consent when terror reigned.'[175]

An interesting case of a Muslim family that converted to Hinduism and wanted to stay on in India but was forced to leave for Pakistan by other evacuating Muslims from Simla was taken up by the East Punjab High Court in dramatic circumstances. As the last convoy of about 800 Muslims, which included every single Muslim policemen in Simla, prepared to leave it was reported that two Muslim children whose parents had become Hindus were being forced by the Muslim policemen to go to Pakistan. A *habeas corpus* petition was filed on behalf of the converted Muslims parents in the High

Court by H.L. Bhagat, Advocate. The case was listed in the court of Justice Bhandari. It so happened that even as Bhagat was arguing the case he was informed that the train carrying the last convoy had left Simla and the children who had wished to stay on in Simla had been forcibly taken along. Justice Bhandari then ordered the District Magistrate Ambala and the Naib Tehsildar Kalka to intercept the convoy at Kalka and produce the children in his court.[176]

This was obviously a rare case because Muslims who changed their faith in 1947 were far less in comparison than the number of Hindus who had converted—the flow of conversions was almost always in favour of Islam. But there are a large number of unrecorded reports of Muslim families completely unwilling to evacuate from the East Punjab and of the local people wanting them to stay on.[177]

THE REFUGEE CAMPS—DECEMBER-JANUARY

It was Question Hour in the Constituent Assembly when K.C. Neogy, Minister Relief and Rehabilitation, informed the House of the number of people who had died in the Kurukshetra camp between 5 November 1947 and 24 January 1948. The House was stunned into silence when it heard of the comparative figures of deaths that had taken place in the Refugee Camp at Kurukshetra on the one hand and all the camps of Delhi put together on the other (see Table 7.1).[178]

The story was of course the same across the border. An Associated Press report from Lahore said that while exact figures were not available, over 5,000 people—Muslim refugees—had died because of intense cold in the refugee camps of Lahore, Kasur and Sulemankhi:

TABLE 7.1: DEATHS IN REFUGEE CAMPS—KURUKSHETRA AND DELHI

Case of death	Delhi Camp (all combined) (period 1 December, 1947 to 5 February 1948)	Kurukshetra Camp (period 5 November 1947 to 24 January 1948
Cholera	nil	98
Dysentery	nil	547
Small pox	1	288
Other diseases	82	2,288
Total	83	3,221

Source: *CMG*, 8 February 1947.

'unnoticed by their well off brethren whose heaters have overloaded the Lahore electric supply system thousands have died on frozen floors of camps and open pavements'.[179]

What could be more pathetic than to see people dying on an average of 65 per day of simple and treatable diseases like dysentery or because there was not enough protection against the intense north Indian winter, whereas less than a hundred miles away, in Delhi, the nation's leadership had the time, resources and above all the desire to celebrate the wedding of Princess Elizabeth, the future queen of England? C. Rajagopalacharya, Acting Governor-General, gave a grand reception in the ballroom of Government House (Rashtrapati Bhawan) which was tastefully decorated with the Union Jack and the Tricolour and was attended by Prime Minister Nehru, Sardar Patel and the entire cabinet.[180]

Some days later a person who had attended the grand function in the Government House in New Delhi wrote a letter, saying how shocked he was to see the lavish food, the varieties of wines and liquours: 'if this is Swarajya, it is high time Mahatma Gandhi realised that some of his comrades of yesterday are least equipped to give practical shape to the Independence of his conception. At government House one witnessed "Rum Rajya rather than Ram Rajya"'. The letter wondered how Rajagopalacharya, once a strong prohibitionist could have compromised his principles and been inclined to 'keep up such imperial traditions'.[181]

As people dismantled and used the wood of their precious bullock carts to keep themselves warm in the Muslim refugee camps in East Punjab,[182] the East Punjab government launched a campaign to collect clothing for the refugees.[183] Trees that were being cut down to widen the Grand Trunk Road between Amritsar and Delhi were given to the refugees for use as fuel.[184] The temperature in Simla touched freezing point on 21 December, creating severe cold-wave conditions in the entire East and parts of West Punjab.[185] The Rotary Club started a blanket fund at Ambala, another 30 truckloads, mainly of clothing but also some tea and salt, were contributed by the people of Calcutta.[186] The Pakistan government with fewer resources than India used funds from the Qaid-i-Azam Relief Fund to order 100,000 blankets from England for the Muslim refugees in its relief camps.[187]

At an all-India conference to discuss relief Nehru gave detailed figures of the clothes, blankets, quilts and tents which had been supplied by the end of November to the refugee camps in East Punjab, Kurukshetra and Delhi.[188] So large was the scale of the effort that there were bound to be problems. *The Tribune* reported the impressions of relief workers, of why their efforts were still not yielding the desired results. It was because the politicians were only trying to score points off each other, and the aid being given by the government of India often had parts missing.[189] For example, tents lay unused for many days because they were not accompanied by other attachments like ropes, hooks, etc.[190]

At a meeting in Kuldip Nagar (Ambala), attended by about 20,000 refugees almost every speaker said that they were pained and hurt by the manner in which the whole crisis had been created and later handled. The camps were all in an appalling state.[191] Mrs Trivedi, wife of the East Punjab Governor, had visited Ambala on 18 December. Seeing the extreme disorganization and the dilapidated state of the camp she initiated a move to choose two new sites for the camps—one at Gandhi Nagar near the Central Jail and the other in Jawahar Nagar near Mubarikpur village.[192]

The state of affairs that prevailed in most refugee camps in East Punjab was graphically portrayed in an article by R.L. Ahuja: appointed to look after these homeless wretches do not come until paid extra . . . the milk meant for the sick is managed by those who can pay for it . . . the bread is stolen by kitchen stewards, the woollens by those who are entrusted to distribute them . . . and if you (Gopichand Bhargava) were to treat us like this why did you drag us all the way, the enemies bullets would have solved the problems'. He added: 'it is maddening to watch the self complacency of our leaders'.[193]

There were many people, like Parmanand Soni who questioned the policy of merely running camps on such a large scale and not giving more urgent attention to the rehabilitation process:

> At the Panipat camp there are thousands of Muslims, they are unwilling guests—caught as we are in the maze of Gandhian philosophy, we sleep over the matter and our treasury is being emptied . . . I believe this expense can be avoided if rehabilitation plans are put into action, but . . . there are no plans. Meanwhile contractors . . . are getting richer.[194]

It needs to be emphasized that most of the complaints that flooded newspapers were against the manner in which the limited resources were handled. Everyone had something critical to say of the politicians and the bureaucracy, but almost always there was great praise for the army. As the work of evacuation neared completion, Giani Kartar Singh, and Dalip Singh issued a statement greatly complimenting the Indian Army: 'Human history has no parallel when 10 million people crossed borders in three months . . . most of the credit goes to the Army and its 4th Division commanded by Lt. Gen. Thimayya.' They also said that much of the confusion, filth and corruption that came to prevail in the camps could have been avoided if the camps too had been handed over to the army, particularly the control and distribution of food rations.[195]

Financial Commissioner Rehabilitation (East Punjab)—His Side

Ministers like Lehri Singh and even Majhel of the East Punjab government knew that a great deal of the resources provided for relief had been misused and that the rampant corruption had virtually derailed the entire exercise. But there were other problems that just had no answers—the indifference of the bureaucracy.

P.N. Thapar, the East Punjab Financial Commissioner, Rehabilitation, in a detailed report cited some of the problems that had seriously affected the relief effort. The Kurukshetra camp was planned to be the only one that would hold about 5,00,000 refugees for a longer period, to be served by transit camps like Attari, Amritsar, Khemkaran, Fazilka, Dera Baba Nanak. But the rush of refugees was too great and with not enough tentage they had to be scattered resulting in congestion and confusion. The erratic movement of trains and the lack of coordination between the governments of India and Pakistan added to the confusion.

Thapar also said that with the telegraph usually being non-functional, so much time, energy and resources were spent in trying to safely evacuate people that there was little time left for other work. He said that with the unsanitary conditions in the camps and the unavailability of medicine, he was surprised that no major epidemic had broken broke out.[187]

As things had began to settle down *The Tribune* started a debate that many of the problems could have been avoided if a more pragmatic view had been taken of the situation in Punjab by senior leaders in Delhi. Two editorials followed each other within a couple of days, which tried to explain the reasons for the chaos and anarchy that had prevailed in East Punjab. 'Sloth and Muddle in East Punjab' was the title of the first:

why are we witnessing disgusting sloth and muddle in East Punjab . . . in this post upheaval? It is not our intention to criticise our present cabinent . . . It has an indifferent master in New Delhi . . . when the top most leaders took the liberation movement to the highest pitch and raised the cry of Quit India they . . . did not know how to turn the victory to the advantage of the teeming millions. They still do not know how to do it. Those ICS, IPS and IES officers who continue to pay more attention to the creases on their trousers than their work or indulge in red tapism must be sacked on the spot.'[197]

A few days later *The Tribune* again said: 'we have often been constrained to point out in these columns how in its preoccupation with extensive idealism the Government at Delhi has failed on many occasions to take a practical view of things'.[198]

CORRUPTION IN THE CONGRESS

Newspapers across India announced the beginning of the last of the historic fasts by Gandhi on 14 January 1948 (see following chapter for deailts). *The Tribune* also highlighted the important reference Gandhi had made to something which had obviously been greatly bothering him. On 13 January Gandhi read out a letter he had received from an old friend in Andhra Pradesh—Konda Venkatappya. Essentially the letter dealt with how power had corrupted the Congress party: 'the one great problem apart from the political and economic issues . . . is the moral degradation into which men in Congress circles have fallen . . . a strict and honest officer cannot hold his position . . . false complaints are filed . . . people have begun saying the British government was better . . . they are cursing the Congress.'[190] With anguish Gandhi was reported to have said: 'just contemplate the rot that has set in'.[199]

Lionel Fielden was in New Delhi on 14 August 1947. He was a close friend of many of the senior Congress leaders including Rajagopalacharya, Patel, Nehru, Vijayalakshmi Pandit and Rajkumari Amrit Kaur, all of whom entertained him levishly. He has recorded his shock at the manner in which senior Congress leaders had adopted the British system: 'it did seem to me a little odd that the Congress party should be living more or less under the conditions of luxury and splendour which they were apt to criticise in the British'. Talking

Torch-uous Freedom!

Widespread shortage of food grain and famine-like conditions prevailed through many parts of East Punjab and Rajasthan in 1947–8, but this of course did not alter the ways of influential politicians. The semi-starved characters depict the plight of millions of ordinary people (*Shankar's Weekly*, 28 November 1948).

of issues that Gandhi had raised in his recent addresses he noted: 'Every revolutionary party is no doubt beset with difficulties when it comes to power. . . . But I was surprised to find so much criticism of it; the old accusations of nepotism and corruption and extravagance so familiar under the British Raj seemed no less violent under the Congress.'[200]

It could be said that the assessment of an Englishman was bound to be somewhat sweeping when the subject of review was the Congress. But interestingly, a file, part of the massive AICC Papers relating mostly to letters written to Acharya Kriplani, tells a similar story. On 15 November, A. Narayan Kamath wrote to Kriplani congratulating him for having resigned from the presidentship of the Congress. Kamath went on to accuse the Congress leadership particularly the Cabinet ministers for doing too much speech-making but remaining indifferent to problems: 'speeches of Mrs. Pandit in the UNO have no meaning for the common man who wants only food and cloth . . . the plain fact appears that with the advent of power the Congress members of the Cabinet have thrown away . . . the very body and people to which they owe their existence'.[201]

P.K. Ray in a similar letter highlighted the plight of the Hindus who had come from the East Bengal (Pakistan). He said that they 'were being treated like beasts', and the least that the Congress leaders—particularly Nehru—could do was to stop making too many speeches and 'do some work'. Similarly, R.L. Malhotra criticized the Congress for the 'complete' crisis and for failing to understand the true dimensions of the suffering.[202]

Mangal Sain Nasht also wrote to Kriplani saying that his thirty-year-old son, his son's wife and his own daughter had been killed. He then questioned Kriplani as to why plans had not been worked out for the population exchange, and why was it that the Congress leaders were still dwelling on 'sermonizing' rather than handling the crisis in a more assertive and focused manner. He said that prior to the transfer of power Nehru was often heard saying that he was helpless because he did not have real power, but almost three months later the situation was many times worse.[203]

The Congress was riding on the wings of new found-power, and because it had represented the political will of India against foreign rule it was naturally the inheritor of the power and prestige that came to be associated with ruling India. In the East Punjab the stakes were much higher because people with political influence were proving to be instrumental in the allocation of the vast properties evacuated by Muslims. With so much waiting to be grabbed—prime commercial and industrial properties, residential houses, agricultural lands with water and wells—the maddening lust for office witnessed by both East and West Punjab in the last month of 1947 was perhaps only natural.

The lust for political office reached its extreme when some Congress leaders objected to Congressmen who had migrated from West Punjab becoming members of Congress bodies and seeking office in the East Punjab Congress. Ugly scenes were witnessed, with Congressmen coming to loggerheads. This was because Congressmen in East Punjab did not want to share their own avenues for power. Many of these meetings saw party workers complaining that Congress MLAs were encouraging black marketing and favouritism in property allocations.[204]

To be fair, the stories of widespread corruption among Congress ranks were not limited to Punjab alone. As early as June 1947, Madan Mohan Malviya's paper *Abhyudaya* published an article which said that corruption had crept into the 'Congress from 1937 onwards and that it was bound to the power and privilege of the 'golden chairs'—offices of patronage—and that many smalltime Congressmen were terrorising the masses by wielding their Congress connection.[205] It also said that many Congressmen were getting rich by controlling the distribution of food grain and rationed cloth. The article also noted how some Congressmen were even trying to capture the control of some trade unions. A couple of months later an editorial noted: 'Congress is dead—bring it to life.'[206] 'The greatest danger to India is from Congressmen who quarelled among themselves . . . '. In this address Nehru even called upon Congressmen to accept a two-year truce of peace with other Congressmen.[207]

In Amritsar, the race for power had reached a comical level. Mohinder Gopal Singh, President of the Amritsar District Congress Committee had nominated 14 people from that part of Kasur, that had now come into Amritsar, to a committee of the Congress. A group of 20 'local' Congressmen were however opposed to any such move. When Mohinder Gopal refused to ignore the rights of the Kasur Congressmen, the 20 men walked out and formed a separate committee and elected Darshan Singh Pheruman their new President.[208]

At the higher level, another report said that a group of Legislative Assembly Members were working over time to manage berths in the

A depiction of how influential people managed wide-ranging favours from the state (*Shankar's Weekly*, 23 May 1948).

A disgusted Nehru looks on as a typical favour seeker wearing the popular Congress cap seeks a favour (*Shankar's Weekly*, 23 May 1948).

Aap ki Khidmat Men!

On the first anniversary of Gandhi's death, the *Shankar's Weekly* devoted a special edition to Gandhiji. This insightful representation depict how politicans projected themselves as Gandhians but in reality only used his name to seek favours, money and power (*Shankar's Weekly*, 30 January 1949).

Cabinet for Bhimsen Sachar, Giani Kartar Singh and Diwan Chaman Lal. The same report added that this was unlikely to succeed because an equally influential group of Congressmen was resisting this on the ground that Congress MLAs from the West Punjab districts had already been given their due allowances, memberships on committees and therefore could not be taken into the Cabinet.[209] Lehri Singh the outspoken East Punjab Minister was of course an exception in that he wanted all Hindu and Sikh MLAs from West Punjab to be reinstated in view of the fact that the people whom they represented had moved to East Punjab.[210] The possibility of this happening led to counter moves among other Congressmen, who naturally wanted the 'cake' to themselves. Hindu and Sikh MLAs who represented constituencies that had gone to the West Punjab part of Pakistan ironically appeared more welcome in Lahore than they were in the corridors of power in Simla. Things reached a stage where they had to collectively represent that they should also be given representation in various committees in East Punjab in which other MLAs were being nominated.[211]

On the other hand, the West Punjab political leaders appear to have been keen for Hindu and Sikh MLAs who had represented constituencies in West Punjab to attend the West Punjab Assembly session which was scheduled for 5 January 1948. The West Punjab Assembly met on 5 January 1948. Members who spoke on the occasion said it was unfortunate that members from the East Punjab had been unable to attend the session. Premier Iftikhar Hussain Mamdot told the House that Bhimsen Sachar had requested him to make some additional security and other arrangements to enable Hindu and Sikh Legislative Assembly Members from East Punjab to attend the session and that all arrangements had been made but he regretted that no guest had come.[212]

The national leadership of the Congress party ultimately yielded to the appeals of Hindu and Sikh MLAs who had represented constituencies that had now gone to West Punjab, to be nominated to the East Punjab Assembly. With the Governor-General's consent they were made regular members of the East Punjab Assembly.[213] By the end of January all such Hindu and Sikh MLAs had resigned their seats in the West Punjab Assembly.[214]

Once the issue of nominating the West Punjab Hindu and Sikh MLAs to the East Punjab Assembly had been resolved, the next and natural step was the demand for a separate quota of seats in the

Constituent Assembly for East Punjab. The Constituent Assembly took up the issue on 27 January (1948). While a similar demand for the new province of West Bengal was approved without much discussion, there was a serious difference of opinion with regard to the demand for seats by East Punjab. The issue was that while Bengal had demanded seats on the basis of the division—the new boundary—the East Punjab case was made on the basis of the exchange of population. Diwan Chaman Lal, for example, said that 2.25 million Hindus and 1.67 million Sikhs who had shifted to East Punjab were within their right to demand representation in the Constituent Assembly.[215]

Sikhs Discouraged from Entering West Punjab

Sachar's reference to security and conveyance in his letter to Mamdot to attend the Session was not out of place because in the preceding days (early December) there had been reports of even senior functionaries of the East Punjab government being harassed at the border by Pakistan officials. In one such incident senior police officers of East Punjab were unable to participate in an important meeting which was to take place in Lahore because the Pakistan officials on the border would not allow the armed escort accompanying the Indian officials to enter. Incidentally the escort comprised mostly Sikh policemen.[216]

But this apart, there had come into being by about the end of November an unofficial policy of discouraging as far as possible the entry of Sikhs into West Punjab so much so the Pakistan authorities had turned down the request of the Government of India to permit Sikhs to visit the holy shrine of Nankana Sahib on Guru Nanak's birthday, 26 November.[217] *Dawn* said that Sikhs had been advised by the Government of India not to visit Nankana Sahib in view of the tension and the possibility that it might jeopardize the lives of non-Muslims still awaiting evacuation in Pakistan.[218] Sardar Swarn Singh the East Punjab Home Minister however had been allowed to visit Nankana Sahib. He visited the shrine on Guru Purab along with Pir Ahsan-ud-din, the Commissioner, Refugee Movement West Punjab. Swarn Singh later said he was satisfied with the upkeep of the shrine.[219] Giani Kartar Singh had infact demanded that both governments should mutually resolve to protect each others shrines and that Nankana Sahib be given a status similar to the Vatican.[220]

MATTERS WITH PAKISTAN RESOLVED: PATEL

For both West and East Punjab, the burden was unbearable whatever its context—financial, housing, food, medicine, clothing. In the West, however, situation was far more critical because from the very beginning the Government of Pakistan had committed itself to an exceptionally high expenditure on defence—by 1949–50 defence absorbed almost 67 per cent of Pakistan's (current) revenue and nearly 50 per cent of the expenditure on capital accounts. In the case of East Punjab, however, the Indian government took up a great part of the burden.[221] By the middle of January 1948, Prime Minister Nehru said the government was spending about Rs. 1,00,000 per day on the refugee population. Naturally a great deal of this amount was spent on the refugees from West Punjab.[222]

To give an idea of the situation as it prevailed in March 1948 and the burden on the government in terms of merely managing the relief camps, it would be appropriate to look at some figures. In March 1948, for example, 6,66,000 people were housed in various camps in East Punjab, and even as late as February 1950, the number remained at around 1,35,000. By October 1949, close to 8,92,000 people had been accommodated in various kinds of dwelling units. The very character of East Punjab had as a result undergone a radical change because by the end of 1949, every fifth person in the province was a displaced person, mainly from West Punjab.[223]

Between the two countries a long list of problems relating to assets and other issues remained unresolved, those that were resolved took many more years. In the immediate sense, of course, some important decisions were made in late November and early December, resulting in newspapers carrying big headlines on 10 December—'Partition Issue Settled'.[224] Sardar Patel told Parliament on 9 December that a series of high level meetings in the 'past fortnight' both in Delhi and in Lahore had resolved 'all matters with Pakistan'. Among the issues settled, or as the negotiators believed at the time, were the division of the cash balance as on 14 August 1947, the division ratio of debt, the manner in which Pakistan would discharge its debt in India, division of military stores, the division of Sterling balances, the division of Ordinance factories and Railway assets, etc.

While agreements were reached, as the Home Minister said, on major issues, the applicable part of the agreements naturally brought up many more problems. One of these, the transfer of Rs. 50 crore from India to Pakistan, will be discussed in the next chapter. But others that remained unresolved and caused extensive problems in the East and West Punjab were questions relating to evacuee property. It is true that both the countries had agreed that ownership of vacated properties still rested with the original owners and that custodians were looking after the properties on their behalf. Zahid Hussain, Pakistan's Ambassador to India had said in a statement: 'How we deal with evacuee properties will largely influence the economic future of both the countries'.[225] However, at the ground level between the East and West Punjab the tangles were so complex that many cases look months and years to resolve—some remaining unresolved to this day. The question of banks, their safety vaults and the balances that remained was one such unresolved problem for refugees on both sides. Then there was the question of the movable and immovable assets of offices and other institutions which had to be divided at the provincial level. Water, electricity, records even chairs, tables and ceiling fans were there to be shared.

But to return to the issue of evacuee property, as early as 29 August 1947 the Joint Defence Council of both countries had met in Lahore and resolved to appoint custodians for evacuee property and not to recognize the illegal seizure of such properties. This was also officially stated by both sides on 3 September.[226] Both East and West Punjab issued ordinances and appointed custodians for evacuee property.

Between 3 September 1947 and January 1948 many meetings and conferences were held between the authorities of East and West Punjab, on the issue. In a meeting on 3 October, it was resolved that both should stay within the spirit of the 29 August agreement—a common policy for handling evacuee property. But once again, and for no given reason, the West Punjab government issued an ordinance on 1 December 1947. This ordinance provided confiscatory provisions and, more broadly, it took away the right of absentee owners to sell their properties and also provided that an owner of property—whatever its nature business or residence—could resume it only if he came back to reside in West Punjab. There being virtually no chance of those who had fled the western districts of returning, the 1 December 1947 ordinance virtually withdrew the rights of original owners who had become refugees over their property.[227] Having failed to make the West Punjab authorities revise their stand, the East Punjab government issued an ordinance (January 1948) to match the provisions of the West Punjab ordinances.

As time passed, mistrust and suspicion only increased, and in the context of banks and business related to it like, for example, the safe-keeping of valuables, handling and storage of currency, the mistrust caused great harm. K.C. Neogy while responding to a supplementary question by Pandit Balkrishan Sharma told the Constituent Assembly that as on 19 November 1947, even though the West Punjab authorities had not yet taken possession of the safe deposit vaults of the banks they had sent notices to managers that the opening of these vaults must begin by 20 November 1947, and if this was not done the government would take them over. The minister also told the House that Prime Minister Nehru had sent a strongly worded telegram to Pakistan's Prime Minister Liaqat Ali saying that conditions in Lahore were still not safe or conducive for managers to return and resume work in Lahore.[228] *Dawn* published a statement made on behalf of the West Punjab government that it had no intention of depriving any person of his valuables and even cited in its statement the version of a 'Hindu' Banker who was satisfied with safety of banks and vaults in Lahore.[229]

But this as subsequent events proved was only half the story. On 20 November (1947) a team of bank managers from Amritsar went to Lahore. As they tried to remove three truckloads of vaults from the National Bank a mob of 4000 people surrounded them and threatened violence if the vaults were removed. The situation was only diffused when senior officials intervened and had the trucks unloaded. Those who had come from Amritsar were individually searched. The crowd vented its anger against Deputy Commissioner Zafarul Hasan (who they belived) had given permission for the removal of the valuable.[230]

This incident could have turned serious because the crowd was heavily armed. The incident was taken up in the Constituent Assembly during Question Hour on 22 November, when Home Minister Patel said efforts were being made to safeguard bank assets.[231] The *CMG* in an editorial said it was unfortunate that the city had been held to ransom by a mob and that 'reasonable Muslims cannot deny the fact that deposits in the vaults were legally theirs (non-Muslims who had left) . . . if some Muslims had claims there were always courts of law for the purpose'.[232]

After the near disastrous incident of 20 November authorities in East Punjab decided to formulate a general policy. It announced that all those who wished to recover valuables from bank vaults in West Punjab would have to submit applications at Jullundur, which would then be forwarded to Lahore for permission.[233] It is another matter whether permission from either the authorities in the East or the West had any meaning in the face of an angry mob as the owner of the well-known shoe shop Bhalla Boot Shop (Anarkali) realized. He had gone to Lahore with due permission to recover some papers from his shop when a mob suddenly attacked and looted the shop. Some other shops in the area that were locked were also looted in the process.[234]

Contrary to the common perception that looting was the handiwork mainly of uprooted refugees, Gauba has recorded that this was not necessarily so in cities like Lahore:

> It cannot be said that the looting was the work of the newly uprooted refugees from East Punjab, nor the work of *goondas* or the police entirely. Persons considered well-to-do let themselves go to seize the easy property of neighbours, friends and erstwhile acquaintances. . . . A well-known Barrister organized a party and raided a foreign liquor shop. . . . A surgeon in Government service broke into a fellow practitioner's surgery and stole his entire surgical equipment.[235]

In the first week of December authorities in Lahore announced that Muslims who wished to open their bank lockers could do so with the permission of the Deputy Commissioner's office.[236] In the meantime the Inter-Dominion Conference (December 1947) also made things somewhat easier. Bank pass books could now be handed over to the Director Generals of Post Offices on both sides, who were asked to prepare consolidated lists, and to have accounts transferred by taking up the cases with their counterparts.[237] Some restricted provisions were also made for bank lockers to be operated by individuals. With regard to pension papers, the two governments had agreed that pending the transfer of papers both sides would release provisional pensions up to 31 March 1948. Both governments also decided to set up special bodies to deal with pensions, provident funds, salary accounts, etc.[238]

However, as was usually the case, the actual working of the agreements was dependent on how the officers concerned handled the cases that came up for their consideration. Even after agreements had been worked out with regard to bank vaults, *The Tribune* reported on 8 January that the West Punjab government had ordered that no bank locker owned by non-Muslims could be opened because 'after the Government of India refused to transfer Pakistan's share of cash balances the West Punjab authorities had decided to retain the lockers which it is estimated contained ornaments worth Rs. 10 crore'. A virtual repeat of the Lahore National Bank scene took place in Ludhiana when a party of Muslims who had come with an escort from Lahore to collect their valuables was surrounded by a mob of over 1,000 people. In this case, however, Muslims were permitted to collect their valuables mainly because of the timely and effective intervention by the Ludhiana police, which had to open fire to scare away the crowd injuring one Sikh in the process.[239]

Stories of how rich families buried their valuables in the ground in the hope of recovering them later were widespread in the months that followed partition. Many such treasures were recovered in later years by families who came to possess evacuated properties. This happened on both sides. One such report said that Naib Tehsildar Jaswant Singh who had gone to village Ajnala to conduct a survey of land noticed that a pit near a big Muslim haveli had been freshly filled with soil. When the pit was dug up, it yielded a rich haul of gold and silver.[240]

However, like everything else in the Punjab of 1947–8, problems which involved rich and influential families were usually resolved in dramatically quicker circumstances. Announcements were made in the third week of January 1948, that those who wished to withdraw their valuables from Lahore would be required to apply after which they would be informed of the date on which they would be escorted to Lahore. Some days later such applicants were asked to gather in a hotel at Amritsar from where they were to be taken under military escort to Lahore.[241] The group of 29 people who had tried to recover their valuables on 20 November in Lahore but had been forced to redeposit them by the violent crowd were informed by H.R. Nair, Secretary to Chief Liaison Officer, East Punjab Government, himself.[242]

HIGH COURT FURNITURE TO BE SHARED EQUALLY

As the administrative mechanism began to get some respite from the evacuation and relief effort, basic issues dealing with less important but essential details were taken up. Governor Trivedi presided over a meeting of the Punjab Partition Committee at Jullundur on 21 November 1947. Premier Gopichand Bhargava, Home Minister Swarn Singh and Chief Secretary M.R. Sachdev represented the East Punjab, while the West Punjab was represented by Shaukat Hayat and Chief Secretary Majid. The Committee resolved to refer unsettled matters like canal waters and waste land to the Arbitral Tribunal headed by Sir Petric Spens, where appeals were to be filed by 1 January 1948. It also decided to extend the period of an agreement that had earlier been reached with regard to sharing hydroelectric power up to 31 December 1947.[243]

The Committee further decided to divide the Lahore High Court library in the ratio of 60 per cent to East Punjab and 40 per cent to West Punjab, while the furniture of the High Court was to be divided equally. It was decided to refer the division of the movable assets of the Lahore Museum to a committee of experts. The statues of Sir Ganga Ram and Lala Lajpat Rai were to be moved to East Punjab. The Committee was however unable to amicably settle the distribution of the equipment of the Mayo and Wellington Hospitals of Lahore. The East Punjab was of course very keen that it be given its share of the equipment.[244]

The Partition Committee met once again exactly a month later.[245] However, no agreement could be reached with regard to the assets of the Lahore Museum. To this list of unsettled or unsettleable issues was added the question of the movable assets of the prestigious Lyallpur Agriculture College and the Engineering Colleges of Lahore and Rasul and also the Lahore Veterinary college.[246]

The Committee did, however, manage to resolve that original files and records in English be retained by West Punjab and the East be given copies of the files. But with regard to pension records, both the sides demanded to retain the originals. It was decided to refer the matter to the Arbitral Tribunal. The District Records and the miscellaneous were put to the share of East Punjab and the old Gazetteers were retained in West Punjab.[247] *The Tribune* came up with an editorial on the distribution of lesser known but extremely important assets that were movable. In the Constituent Assembly too many members had shared their concern for a careful distribution of various records, assets of newspapers, schools, cultural institutions. The editorial pointed out that Pakistan should reciprocate generously in the matter keeping in view the generosity shown by Indian in the distribution of financial assets.

The issue that took up most of the time of the Committee and remained unresolved was that of electricity. The extended date of the agreement that had been signed between East and West Punjab with regard to the sharing of electricity was to end on 31 December 1947. Some days later, Lehri Singh issued a statement giving reasons for why an agreement had not been reached between the two sides on the crucial issue: 'it is not true that Shaukat Hayat did not agree because we offered electricity at a reduced ratio. The fact is that the West Punjab government wanted electricity for at least three years. This we could not afford . . . it is common knowledge that before partition efforts were made to develop only the West Punjab districts. Our projects are incomplete how can we spare Electricity—it can be done only at the cost of East Punjab.' He also pointed out that West Punjab had already got in the division the vast network of irrigation canals.[248]

It is not clear as to when the electricity supply to West Punjab from the Jogendernagar power stations was disconnected but the shortage of electricity in West and East Punjab was becoming acute. In Ambala, for example, power was supplied only on alternate nights and people who had electric connections were not permitted to draw quotas of kerosene on their cards.[249] Lahore too was unable to meet the demand. According to a report the situation was aggravated because important and influential people had started withdrawing power directly from the lines, causing frequent breakdowns.[250]

EXCHANGE OF PRISONERS

Ever since the government of Punjab had partitioned itself operationally, the question of looking after prisoners who were expected to go to the other side had been a difficult one. With all the blood that had been shed it was only natural that prisoners who had the misfortune of being in jails on the wrong side of the border were mistreated. Finally on 7 January (1948) E.P. Katoch, Inspector General of Prisons East Punjab issued a statement that the exchange of prisoners between East and West Punjab would begin on 12 January and would be completed by 7 February.[251]

Even though the exchange of prisoners had been agreed to at the provincial level between the authorities of East and West Punjab, there was a problem when it came to the question of exchanging Muslim prisoners housed in Delhi. The issue was important enough to have drawn the Home Minister's attention even in the days following Gandhi's assassination. The West Punjab Premier, it appears from reports, was insisting that Muslim prisoners of Delhi also be included in the exchange between East and West Punjab. Patel took exception to this and was reported to have said that the question of exchanging Muslim prisoners did not arise—because if Muslims could remain in Delhi so could the prisoners. Patel was also reported to have said that Mamdot was linking the issue and delaying the transfer of Sikh and Hindu prisoners only because he was personally interested in the transfer of some Muslim prisoners from Delhi.[252]

This tough reaction of the Home Minister it appears was related to reports that an escort party that had gone to West Punjab to bring back Hindu and Sikh prisoners had had to come back empty-handed because the West Punjab authorities refused to hand over the prisoners unless Muslim prisoners in East Punjab jails were released first.[253] As both sides failed to find answers 1,600 Hindu and Sikh prisoners of the Lahore Central Jail went on a hunger strike—protesting against the poor conditions in the jail and the discrimination in the supply of clothing, food and medicine.[254]

CONGRESSMEN IN EAST PUNJAB TALK OF WAR

As discussed earlier, at a public gathering in Amritsar on 11 January 1948, Tara Singh had warned of a war with Pakistan 'in the near future' and demanded that Muslim vacate Delhi[255] The people of Amritsar had became accustomed to such talk, till to their surprise even East Punjab Congress leaders and ministers began talking the 'war language'. Premier Gopichand Bhargava, the mild Gandhian, was as different from Tara Singh as one could possibly imagine Swarn Singh was a man known to take things in his stride, cool, almost unflappable, always choosing words very carefully.[256] For such Congress leaders of East Punjab to break the party line, particularly as people were aware of how angry Nehru was with those who talked of war, was quite something. Premier Bhargava said: 'Who lives if East Punjab dies . . . brave sons defend your provinces . . . do not run away like cowards.'[257] Lehri Singh was his usual outspoken self: 'The government will defend you at all costs . . . we ministers will come out and participate in defence of the land.' Ishar Singh Majhel and Swarn Singh also added to the excitement 'those arms that strike you shall be cut to pieces . . . those eyes that look at you with evil intentions shall be torn away'. So great was the excitement that even the Deputy Commissioner of Amritsar, Narender Singh, joined the chorus: 'The border shall be defended at all costs . . . we shall smash the enemies head'.[258]

An outraged Nehru, while appealing for harmony assured refugees in Delhi of suitable accommodation and said he understood the suffering they had undergone but their suffering should not cloud their judgement. He clearly stated there was not the remotest chance of war, though India was prepared for it.[259] Nehru addressed a massive public meeting at Jullundur on 24 February 1948. As the issue had refused to die down, once again he not only said that 'such talk of war was childish' and that 'some prominent people have been talking of war . . . it should be the duty of the administration to prevent such wild talk.'[260]

Interestingly, however, more people tended to agree with what Congress leaders in Punjab and the Akalis like Tara Singh were saying—that war was imminent. This was also because of the many reports by officials, the army (MEO) and some social workers that they had been prevented from entering particular areas of Rawalpindi, Sialkot and Jhelum districts, where Pakistan was mobilizing its army units. Some reports said that district authorities were distributing arms licences.[261]

For Congressmen to talk of war with Pakistan was seen as an aberration. Two incidents possibly led them to do so. The first was an incident that occurred in Karachi. One hundred and eighty-four Sikhs had reached Karachi by train on the morning of 6 January (1948) and had then proceeded to the safety of a Gurudwara near Rattan Talao. It is not clear what happened but the Gurudwara was soon surrounded by a mob of 8,000 people who burnt it down and also killed a number of Sikhs.[262]

The Gujarat Railway Station Bloodbath

The second incident was far more serious. A trainload of non-Muslim refugees—among the last such evacuations—was attacked in the early hours of 12 January 1948 at the Gujarat Railway Station. The incident was the last in the chain of major attacks on trains that horrified the world in 1947. Describing the incident

Ghazanfar Ali, Pakistan's Minister for Refugees said: 'I cannot over stress my horror at what I have seen and heard . . . what we saw at Gujarat nauseated me'.[263] The *Keesings Contemporary Archives* has termed it as the 'worst outrage' and said that of 2,400 passengers 1,650 were killed.[264]

The first detailed report of the incident appeared only on 15 January, based on an official press release of the West Punjab government.[265] It said that in the early hours of 12 January a train carrying the last lots of non-Muslim refugees from Bannu arrived unexpectedly at Gujarat Railway Station. The railway staff at the station had received information regarding the arrival of the train only 15 minutes before it actually arrived. The train had been diverted to Gujarat for safety reasons and was not scheduled to stop. The report said that some people waiting at the station, not realizing that it was a refugee special, tried to board the train. Some women and children in the train panicked and began to scream for help. In the commotion the military escort was said to have used a hand grenade, which killed one person and injured some others on the platform. The commotion attracted a large crowd which attacked the train. There was firing from both sides. The Pakistan troops and police were reported to have intervened only at daybreak. The report said that 174 people were dead, this included 30 people from among those that attacked the train.

The Tribune's version (16 January), however, said that about 1,700 had been killed and that the attack was well planned and executed by Pathans. This report also added that the Liaison Officer of India was not given permission by the Pakistan authorities to visit the site. *The Pioneer* (15 January) said that about 2,000 to 3,000 Pathans had attacked the train which was escorted by 60 jawans of the Bihar Regiment. *The TOI* (14 January) version also said that hundreds of women were kidnapped and that grenades were freely used and also that the incident was one of the worst of such attacks.

The West Punjab authorities did however admit that a large number of passengers had fled in the darkness to nearby villages but fortunately most of them were later recovered. This official version also said that the villagers gave protection to about 600 people who had fled the train and handed over 245 children and 183 women within a couple of hours of the attack.[266]

In an editorial of 18 January, *The Tribune* said the Muslim military escort of the train was unable to act effectively because the attack was supported by the Pakistan army. The editorial said that there were 2,400 passengers in the train of whom 700 survived and reached India. It also referred to Gandhi's fast and said that in view of it the people of East Punjab must show restraint and patience, and not react to the attack.

THE CASH BALANCE TRANSFER—A MAJOR ISSUE

As sensational versions of the Gujarat 'bloodbath' swept across the towns, cities and refugee camps of East Punjab, fanning the flames of war, another cause of strife between the two countries emerged at about the same time. We have already noted that an agreement had been drawn between India and Pakistan whereby India was to transfer a sum of about Rs. 55 crore as Pakistan's share of the cash balance. But no sooner had this agreement been finalized than there was a demand from a cross-section of political opinions in India that it should not be transferred.

The Tribune once again took the lead by publishing an editorial as early as on 10 December (1947), 'Do not give cash to Pakistan'. The editorial said that the Government of India should not have committed to transferring the remaining part of the cash balance because Pakistan was bound to use it to fund its aggression in Kashmir.[267]

There was as many members of the Constituent Assembly said, merit in Saxena's motion with regard to the possibility of the money being used to fund the invaders in Kashmir. Prime Minister Nehru himself had earlier stated that the delay in the transfer of the cash balance had occurred because of the problem in Kashmir—which Pakistan had created.[268] A couple of days after Nehru had made the sensational charge against Pakistan, the firebrand Socialist Ram Manohar Lohia also called upon the government to reconsider its decision of transferring the cash balance and other assets because Pakistan was violating agreements that had been reached earlier.[269]

A day after Lohia had charged the Pakistan government with breach of faith, Ghulam Mohammad, the Finance Minister of Pakistan, while addressing a press conference in Karachi said: 'The Pakistan Government regards the Government of India's interference with the Reserve Bank of India not only as an unfriendly act but as an act of aggression.' He also said that the Government of India had directed the Reserve Bank of India not to credit the cash balance to Pakistan. As for the Kashmir issue, Mohammad said, it could not be linked to the terms and conditions of financial agreements that had been reached between the two countries.[270]

Sardar Patel's reaction to this statement first appeared as part of a small observation he made to a correspondent of the Associated Press of India on the morning of 10 January 1948. The Sardar was to leave for Jammu on the same day and said that he would issue a detailed statement on his return, but did say: 'I regret they have abused our generosity and are flinging baseless accusations.'[271] On his return from Jammu, the Sardar, accompanied by the Finance Minister, R.K. Shanmugan Chetty, addressed a press conference in Delhi on 12 January, and also released a statement explaining the Indian government's stand on the issue.[272]

While the press versions were based on the questions raised during the conference, the detailed statement traced the entire case, starting from the first meeting held in connection with Kashmir which was 'held in an atmosphere of hope, cordiality and goodwill'. In sum, however, the statement said the Rs. 55 crore cash balance being demanded by Pakistan was technically unsound because after Rs. 20 crore of the cash balance that had been credited to Pakistan on 15 August 1947, all other balances had automatically stood credited to the Indian dominion. 'There was therefore no balance of the old undivided Government of India with the Reserve Bank of India.'

But it was the second point made by the Sardar at the press conference that formed the headlines. He said there was an armed conflict on in Kashmir which 'was threatening to assume even more serious dimensions that will destroy every financial agreement . . . will endanger even other parts of the settlement like debt division, and the division of stores, etc.'. He also said goodwill was the basis of the agreement, and without goodwill agreements were bound to lose their significance.

The Sardar minced no words and made no effort to conceal how angry he was with the Ghulam Mohammad's statement. He said that Pakistan's Finance Minister was 'descending to the familiar art of bullying and blackmailing in order to gain the coveted ransom of Rs. 55 crore'. Patel also made it more than clear that the Kashmir conflict was likely to destroy the whole basis of the agreements that had been reached between the two countries. He also added that 'India was standing by the commitment' and that 'there was no time frame in the agreement.' 'We cannot be asked to make a payment of the cash balance when an armed conflict—dangerous in character is in progress.'[273]

Pakistan's official response to Sardar Patel's press conference came in the form of a statement by Prime Minister Liaqat Ali. He said the cash balance was Pakistan's and there was no way the issue could be linked to the conflict in Kashmir. The Pakistan government also said that the control of the cash balances (due to Pakistan) did not rest solely with the Reserve Bank of India but lay technically with His Majesty's Government for both dominions, and as such India alone could not take a unilateral decision.[274]

Millions of displaced Hindu and Sikh families across the plains of East Punjab felt that the transfer of the cash balance was grossly out of place, just as the Muslim families that had moved to the West believed that India by withholding the cash balances was trying to starve the infant Pakistan. The onset of an early and unusually extreme winter therefore saw distraught and traumatized families huddled around 'weak fires' in the small and big refugee camps on both sides linking their future with the cash balances. In any case, on both sides, the whole debate and the talk of agreements and peace made little sense. The past year had taught the ordinary Punjabi that the sword and the spear alone decided matters. Families had been slaughtered for small bags of grain, silver bracelets and more often just for nothing, and now when it involved Rs. 55 crore there was 'talk of peace'. Raj Kumar Dutta summed up the general sentiment as he saw it, from the eastern side of divided Punjab:

> The complacency of our leaders and administration in the face of grave provocation is astonishing . . . false pacifism and the tendency to give in will be our undoing . . . you cannot propose a gentleman's agreement to people who understand only violence . . . we are passing through *Kalyug* in which only those nations will survive who expect their citizens to safeguard their tradition and culture with their blood.'[275]

It is difficult, however, to state conclusively whether it was sheer complacency or a more trusting temperament which came from liberal democratic traditions of the Indian leadership, that enabled Pakistan's new rulers to open the tragic chapter of Kashmir in 1947. For Punjab—both East and West—the warlike conditions in Kashmir had other implications. As the conflict in Kashmir rapidly took the form and colour, particularly for India, that of the nation's honour, and quite rightly so, the painful and tragic story of Punjab's partition found itself relegated to the background. In a way the conflict in Kashmir and the conditions that followed swept aside the questions, that in more normal times would have been asked about the errors of judgement, and the haste that had pushed Punjab through 1947. And whatever little desire to seek answers for the Punjab tragedy that may have remained was extinguished by the tragic assassination of Mahatma Gandhi.

NOTES

1. 'Cries of Woes', *Tribune*, 18 November 1947; ibid., 21 November 1947; ibid., 13 December 1947; ibid., 21 November 1947; ibid., 11 December 1947; ibid., 3 December 1947.
2. *Dawn*, 30 November 1947; *The Tribune*, 30 November 1947.
3. *CMG*, 13 November 1947.
4. *The Tribune*, 30 November 1947.
5. *CMG*, 6 December 1947.
6. *The Tribune*, 16 January 1948; AICC Papers, File G-26, 1947–8, Part II.
7. *Statesman*, 8 January 1948.
8. Vakil, *Economic Consequences*, p. 87.
9. *The Tribune*, 8 December 1947; The building of these townships in particular and other buildings was delayed considerably, because steel, cement and bricks were not available. See statement of Gopichand Bhargava, who said that Rs. 2 crore had been earmarked but no material was available, *The Tribune* 15 January 1948.
10. Ibid., 23 November 1947.
11. *Statesman*, 17 January 1948.
12. Ibid., 27 January 1948.
13. *The The Tribune*, 5 December 1947.
14. IOR Mss. Eur. F 200/129, Viceregal Official Correspondence Files, Proceedings of ECM, 8th Meeting, 22 September 1947.
15. *Statesman*, 6 January 1948.
16. Ibid., 18 January 1948.
17. Tek Chand Memoir, Oral History Transcript, NMML.
18. *Statesman*, 17 January and 2 February 1948.
19. Ibid., 9 January 1948.
20. *The Tribune*, 1 December 1947.
21. Ibid., 9 December 1947.
22. *CMG*, 27 November 1947.

23. *The Tribune*, 5 December 1947.
24. Ibid., 6, 13 and 23 December 1947.
25. *CMG*, 16 December 1947.
26. Ibid., 18 December 1947.
27. *Times* (London), 1 January 1948.
28. *The Tribune*, 9 December 1947; also *CMG*, 16 December 1947.
29. *CMG*, 21 December 1947.
30. *The Tribune*, 5 December 1947; *CMG*, 4 December 1947.
31. Ibid. On 2 November 1947, *CMG* had carried a long report under a big headline 'Kashmir invasion sponsored or not'. The report said that sources in New Delhi were greatly worried and surprised with regard to reports that the 'raiders' in Kashmir were very well equipped and even had very good transport support—meaning that this could have happened only with support from the government of Pakistan. On 25 November 1947 Nehru made an important statement saying: 'we have sufficient evidence in our possession to demonstrate that the whole business of armed raids both in Jammu province and Kashmir was organised by high officials of the Pakistan government', see *CMG*, 26 November 1947.
32. *CMG*, 6 December 1947.
33. Ibid., 3 January 1948; *The Times of India*, 9 January 1948.
34. *The Tribune*, 12 January 1948; ibid., 25 November 1947; *CMG*, 16 and 18 December 1947.
35. *The Tribune*, 20 November 1947; *CMG*, 21 November 1947.
36. *CMG*, 4 December 1947.
37. Ibid., *The Tribune*, 4 December 1947.
38. *The Tribune*, 4 and 13 December 1947.
39. *CMG*, 9 December 1947.
40. Ibid., 19 November 1947.
41. Ibid., 14 December 1947.
42. *The Tribune*, 19 December 1947. After the restoration of normal conditions in India during 1948 a number of Muslims mainly from Sind returned to their homes in West UP and Delhi. They were mainly agriculturists and found the Sind system of irrigation inadaptable. As the number of Muslims returning to India, became very large, on 19 April 1948 the Government of India introduced a permit system and passed the 'Influx' from Pakistan Control Ordinance 1948, which provided that Government of India could forcibly evict Muslims who refused to go when ordered to do so. This was applicable only to West Punjab, see Vakil, *Economic Consequences*, pp. 81–2.
43. *CMG*, 25 November 1947; *The Tribune*, 26 November 1947.
44. Ibid., 25 November 1947.
45. *The Tribune*, 5 December 1947.

46. Ibid., 1 December 1947.
47. Ibid., 26 November; *CMG*, 27 November 1947.
48. *CMG*, 27 November 1947, *The Tribune*, 27 November 1947.
49. *The Tribune*, 1 December 1947.
50. Ibid., 7 December 1947.
51. Ibid., 30 November 1947.
52. Ibid., 8 January 1948.
53. *CMG*, 21 December 1947. Also see *Daily Milap* (Urdu), 21 January 1948 (NMML, Microfilm). Gandhi had said that those who wanted to vacate Delhi of Muslims were enemies of the country.
54. *Panchjanya*, no. 2, December 1947. A Hindi weekly started publication in December 1947, first from Lucknow, then shifted to Delhi. A.B. Vajpayee was its founder editor (NMML, Microfilm).
55. *Dawn*, 24 November 1947.
56. *The Tribune*, 16 January 1948.
57. *Daily Milap*, 17 and 18 January 1948.
58. Ibid., 18 January 1948.
59. AICC Papers, File G-26, 1947–8, Part II, Reel 123, Microfilm, NMML;
60. *CMG*, 19 December 1947.
61. *The Tribune*, 21 November 1947.
62. Ibid., 4 December 1947.
63. Ibid., 1 January 1948.
64. *Dawn*, 19 and 26 November 1947.
65. *CMG*, 20 November 1947.
66. Ibid., 6 December 1947.
67. Ibid., 18 January 1948.
68. Ibid., 2 December 1947.
69. Ibid., 13 December 1947.
70. Ibid., 27 December 1947. Such committees were later formed but since they had officials who headed them the problem remained, in fact possibly worsened. For example, see complaint against Harnam Singh, Tehsildar Jagraon, made by the Mazdoor Sangh to DC Ludhiana, saying that he had broken all rules in allocation of shops, AICC Papers, File G-26, 1947–8, Part II, letter dated 25 April 1948.
71. *CMG*, 26 November 1947.
72. Ibid., 17 January 1948.
73. *Organiser*, 16 October 1947.
74. *CMG*, 26 November 1947.
75. Ibid., 18 December 1947.
76. Ibid., 20 November 1947.
77. *The Tribune*, 14 December 1947.
78. *CMG*, 16 December 1947.
79. *Statesman*, 9 January 1948.
80. *CMG*, 27 November 1947.

81. Ibid., 2 December 1947; *The Tribune*, 10 December 1947; ibid., 30 November 1947.
82. *CMG*, 21 November 1947.
83. *The Tribune*, 23 November 1947.
84. Ibid., 6 December 1947. The Patwari is at the lowest rung of the hierarchy in the control and administration of land in India. While essentially his job is the maintenance of land records for a particular zone that normally comprises the lands owned by a few villages—the zone being known as Patwar. But the Patwari is also for the Deputy Commissioners a kind of 'Man Friday' a clog that can be used every where and must be handy with every kind of information regarding his Patwar. Universally corrupted across India for the fact that he issues all documents related to the ownership of land.
85. Ibid., 23 January 1948.
86. Ibid., 30 December 1947.
87. *CMG*, 21 November 1947; Spate Papers, Diary Entry, 29 July 1947, CSAS.
88. *CMG*, 25 and 28 November 1947.
89. Ibid., 2 December 1947.
90. Ibid., 23 November 1947.
91. *CMG*, 18 December 1947.
92. Ibid.
93. Ibid.; *The Tribune*, 23 February 1948.
94. *The Tribune*, 23 December 1947.
95. Ibid., 21 December 1947.
96. 6 January 1948. Similar complaints were also made with regard to allotment of shops in Amritsar, see for example, *The Tribune*, 10 February 1948.
97. Ibid., 26 January 1948. Also *Statesman*, 27 January 1948.
98. Ibid., 19 December 1947.
99. Ibid., 1 January 1948; ibid., 30 November 1947; AICC Papers, File G 26, 1947–8, Part II.
100. *The Tribune*, 2 December 1947.
101. Ibid., 5 and 6 January 1948.
102. *Daily Milap*, 24 December 1947.
103. *CMG*, 27 November 1947.
104. N.V. Rajkumar, *One Year of Freedom*, pp. 111–12.
105. *The Tribune*, 7 February 1948.
106. Ibid., 10 December 1947.
107. *The Tribune*, 15 January 1948.
108. Ibid., 11 December 1947.
109. Ibid.
110. *Statesman*, 9 February 1948.
111. *The Tribune*, 8 January 1948.

112. Ibid., 23 December 1947.
113. Ibid., 9 February 1948.
114. Ibid.
115. *The Tribune*, 13 February 1948.
116. *CMG*, 12 December 1947.
117. Ibid., 25 and 29 November 1947.
118. Ibid., 9 December 1947.
119. Ibid., 16 November 1947.
120. Ibid., 23 November 1947.
121. Gauba, *Inside Pakistan*, p. 187.
122. Sachar later denied having any such nephew. 'My brother's son obviously cannot be a Jain or Handa, he must be a Sachar', *CMG*, 18 December 1947.
123. Ibid., 16 December 1947.
124. *The Tribune*, 9 December 1947.
125. Ibid., 6 December 1947; ibid., 21 November 1947; ibid., 28 December 1947.
126. Ibid., 22 November and 25 December 1947; ibid., 24 November 1947; *CMG*, 16, 19 and 27 November 1947; ibid., 17 December 1947.
127. *CMG*, 16 December 1947. Also *The Tribune*, 14 December 1947.
128. *The Tribune*, 1 December 1947.
129. Ibid., 5 December 1947.
130. *Government of East Punjab Budget 1947–8*, pp. 2–3, New Expenditure Head 29: Police, Punjab Civil Secretariat Library, Chandigarh; ibid., New Head 37: Education, p. 30.
131. *The Tribune*, 28 December 1947.
132. Ibid., 25 December 1947.
133. Ibid., 1 and 3 December 1947.
134. *CMG*, 29 November 1947.
135. Ibid., 5 December 1947.
136. *The Tribune*, 1 January 1948.
137. *CMG*, 27 November 1947.
138. Ibid.
139. *The Tribune*, 2 December 1947.
140. Ibid., 12 December 1947.
141. Ibid., 3 December 1947.
142. Ibid.; *CMG*, 19 December1947.
143. *The Tribune*, 11 December 1947. West Punjab authorities were unable to declare the Matriculation results of 1947, because a large number of answer scripts had been destroyed and in many cases examiners having moved to East Punjab had not been able to submit the awards in time, *The Tribune*, 5 January 1948.
144. Ibid. 1 December 1948. Incidentally this meeting of the Senate was

much talked about for Mehar Chand Mahajan's stand against the appointment of Mr. Bhalla as the Registrar of the University. Mahajan said an advertisement should have been duly made. Premier Bhargava however said he had approved the appointment of Bhalla as a special case in view of the special circumstances even though Bhalla had infact earlier opposed his (Bhargava's) election to the Senate, see *The Tribune*, 3 December 1947.

145. Ibid., 17 December 1947.
146. Ibid., 12 December 1947; *Statesman*, 17 January 1948.
147. MP, Weekly Summaries, Week Ending 19 December 1947, File 190.
148. *The Tribune*, 19 and 21 February 1948, *Statesman*, 18 February 1948.
149. *The Tribune*, 22 January 1948.
150. Ibid., 6 January 1948.
151. *CMG*, 20 November 1947.
152. *The Tribune*, 20 December 1947. Also see Chapter 6.
153. *The Tribune*, 4, 9 and 20 December 1947; *CMG*, 25 November 1947; *Dawn*, 26 November 1947; *Statesman*, 14 January 1948.
154. *The Tribune*, 22 January 1948.
155. *CMG*, 9 December 1947.
156. *The Tribune*, 17 January 1948.
157. Ibid., 5 February 1948.
158. Ibid., 13 December 1947.
159. Ibid., 20 February 1948.
160. Ibid., 21 and 22 February 1948; *Statesman*, 20 February 1948.
161. *The Tribune*, 5 February 1948.
162. Ibid., 6 January 1948.
163. *CMG*, 4 February 1948.
164. *The Tribune*, 7 February 1948.
165. *Statesman*, 7 February 1948.
166. Ibid., 22 January 1948.
167. *The Tribune*, 17 January 1948.
168. *CMG*, 17 February 1948; *Times of India*, 17 February 1948; *Statesman*, 17 February 1948; *CMG*, 28 December 1947.
169. *The Tribune*, 22 November 1947.
170. Ibid., 1 December 1947.
171. *CMG*, 14 December 1947.
172. Ibid., 11 December 1947.
173. Ibid., 19 December 1947.
174. *The Tribune*, 23 February 1948.
175. Ibid., 22 December 1947; 11 January 1948.
176. Ibid., 24 November 1947.
177. For years and years I have heard stories from old men of my village (Lukhi—district Kurukshetra, Haryana) of how the Muslim families

were unwilling to leave and how the villagers mainly Rajputs wanted them to stay on. The village was surrounded by people from the Kurukshetra refugee camp and from the Thanesar city, who demanded that the Muslim families be handed over. For about 30 hours, the Rajputs of the village kept the crowd away, with not a single Muslim being hurt or robbed. When an Army detachment came to recover the families, about 50 Rajputs accompanied the families to the large Muslim convoy that was then passing from near Rajpura to ensure their safety. Village elders could not remember a time when the whole village, with all its rigid *purdah* customs came out to the last child to see of the Muslims on the day they left. In all the Muslims were merely about 200 people, but so much food was handed over to them that they could have fed a thousand more. Two bullock carts with the finest pair of bullocks were gifted to the departing families to carry the food.

178. Ibid., 8 February 1948; *CMG*, 7 December 1947.
179. *CMG*, 24 December 1947. For report on the death of Muslim refugees due to shortage of proper clothing see *Statesman*, 21 January 1948. Gauba has given an interesting table—appearing to be somewhat exaggerated no doubt but of interest all the same. He says close to 20,000 people had died of cholera in West Punjab alone, and another 5,000 were dying of other diseases on a weekly basis. The cholera figures were sourced to a statement by Iftikharudin and those of the week, to Ghazanfar Ali Khan, see his *Inside Pakistan*, pp. 257–8.
180. *CMG*, 21 November 1947.
181. Ibid., 2 December 1947.
182. Report of Brig. Stevens, Commanding Officer, Pakistan (MEO), *CMG*, 3 December 1947.
183. *The Tribune*, 21 December 1947.
184. Ibid., 8 December 1947.
185. Ibid., 22 December 1947.
186. Ibid., 2 and 11 December 1947.
187. *CMG*, 18 November 1947, *CMG*, 23 November 1947; 15 January 1948.
188. Ibid.; *The Tribune*, 20 January 1948.
189. *CMG*, 3 October 1947.
190. *The Tribune*, 3 December 1947.
191. Ibid., 24 November 1947.
192. Ibid., 20 December 1947.
193. *The Tribune*, 24 November 1947; ibid., 25 January 1948.
194. Ibid., 1 January 1948.
195. Ibid., 6 December 1947.
196. Ibid., 22 and 30 November 1947.
197. *The Tribune*, 19 November 1947.
198. Ibid., 14 January 1948.

199. *The Tribune*, 14 January 1948.
200. Lionel Fielden, 'Four Talks on Pakistan' this compilation of lectures delivered by Fielden over the BBC contains a chapter 'Congress and the People of India', see I.M. Stephens Papers, Box 20, CSAS. This business of lunches and dinners even as thousands were being slaughtered of course stands out. Interestingly Mountbatten noted in his inaugural Jawaharlal Nehru lecture (1968) at Cambridge, that of his 15 months stay in India as Viceroy and Governor General, 10 months were under Congress rule. During these months he notes that he hosted and attended thousands of lunches, dinners and tea parties, Mountbatten, *Jawaharlal Nehru Lecture 1968*, Cambridge, I.M. Stephens Papers, Box 19, CSAS.
201. AICC Papers, File G-19/1947–48, Reel 123, letter from A. Narayan Kamath to J.B. Kriplani, 15 November 1947; *Dawn*, 4 February 1947.
202. AICC Papers, File G-26/1947–48, Part II, letter P.K. Ray, 70 Serpintine Lane, Calcutta 14, 20 May 1948; R.L. Malhotra letter to General Secretary AICC, 1 April 1948; IOR Mss. Eur. D. 621/14, Wilfred Russel Diary.
203. AICC Papers, File G-19/1947–48, Reel 123, letter from Mangal Sain Nasht to Kriplani, 28 October 1947.
204. *The Tribune*, 8 January 1948.
205. *Abhyudaya*, June 1947.
206. Ibid., 20 October 1947.
207. *Indian Express*, 14 March 1948, Nehru Clippings 8787, Microfilm, NMML.
208. *CMG*, 10 December 1947.
209. Ibid., 17 January 1948.
210. See statement of Lehri Singh, *The Tribune*, 19 December 1947.
211. *The Tribune*, 25 December, Most of the committees to which these MLAs made a reference were the ones that dealt with evacuee properties and other rehabilitation work.
212. *Statesman*, 6 January 1948.
213. Ibid., 13 January 1948.
214. Ibid., 23 January 1948: ibid., 4 February 1948.
215. *Statesman*, 28 January 1948.
216. *The Tribune*, 7 December 1947.
217. *CMG*, 25 November 1947. Also *Dawn*, 26 November 1947.
218. *Dawn*, 26 November 1947; *The Tribune*, 4 December 1947, ibid., 15 January 1948.
219. *CMG*, 29 November 1947.
220. *The Tribune*, 23 December 1947.
221. Vakil, *Economic Consequences*, pp. 116–17.
222. *Statesman*, 24 January 1948.
223. Vakil, *Economic Consequences*, pp. 122, 145.

224. *CMG*, 10 December 1947; *The Tribune*, 10 December 1947.
225. *The Tribune*, 3 January 1948.
226. *CMG*, 4 September 1947; *Dawn*, 4 and 5 September 1947.
227. *CMG*, 3 December 1947.
228. Ibid., 19 November 1947.
229. *Dawn*, 20 November 1947; The *CMG*, 1 October 1947.
230. *CMG*, 21 November 1947; *The Tribune*, 22 November 1947.
231. *The Tribune*, 23 November 1947.
232. *CMG*, 22 November 1947.
233. *The Tribune*, 30 November 1947.
234. Ibid., 26 November 1947.
235. Gauba, *Inside Pakistan*, p. 12.
236. *CMG*, 5 December 1947.
237. In fact, on both sides bank officials were being over cautious. There were many reports of how managers were not allowing withdrawals on one pretext or the other even after the account holders had been duly verified. The specimen signature register was of course a big problem, as many banks had lost their registers, see for reports related to Bank settlements *The Tribune*, 21 November 1947; *Daily Milap*, 22 December 1947 and 26 December 1947; *Statesman*, 7 February 1948.
238. Vakil, *Economic Consequences*, pp. 104–5.
239. *The Tribune*, 8 January 1948.
240. Ibid., 13 December 1947.
241. *Statesman*, 24 and 28 January 1948; *Daily Milap*, 26 December 1947.
242. CMG, 18 February 1948.
243. *The Tribune*, 22 November 1947. The initial agreement had expired on 15 November 1947.
244. Ibid. As both sides wrangled over all kinds of issues, the Pakistan government some time later possibly to divert or dilute attention on claims that had been raised by the East Punjab authorities for proportionate share in the moveable assets of the Mayo and Willington Hospitals of Lahore demanded that Rs. 50,00,000 collected as donations by the late Dr. Ziaudin Ahmad, Vice-Chancellor of Aligarh Muslim University for the Medical College at Aligarh be transferred to Pakistan. Many people of course opposed such a demand because they said the large sum had been collected not merely from Muslims but all communities had contributed to the fund, see, *The Tribune* 18 January 1948; *The Pioneer*, 16 January 1948.
245. *CMG*, 24 December 1947.
246. *The Tribune*, 21 and 25 December 1947.
247. Ibid., The Punjab State Residency Records which as per an earlier decision were to be transferred to East Punjab, interestingly a Railway

Wagon (ND 37444) carrying these important records from Lahore disappeared enroute. No one had an answer as to how a whole wagon carrying such records could have disappeared, *The Tribune*, 2 December 1947.

248. *The Tribune*, 28 December 1947.
249. Ibid., 12 January 1948.
250. *CMG*, 29 January 1948.
251. *The Tribune*, 8 January 1948; *CMG*, 1 January 1948; *TOI*, 12 January 1948.
252. *The Tribune*, 7 February 1948.
253. Ibid., 21 January 1948.
254. *Daily Milap*, 24 January 1948.
255. *The Tribune*, 12 January 1948. For his earlier references to a possible war with Pakistan see *CMG*, 4 December 1947. For Tara Singh's demand on Nehru, that if he had proof, as Nehru had said he did, of Pakistan's involvement in the Kashmir trouble, he (Nehru) should open a war front with Pakistan on the Punjab border to decrease pressure on the valley, see *CMG*, 2 November 1947. For Nehru's statement that there was substantial proof that the raids in Kashmir were sponsored/ organised by Pakistan, see *CMG*, 26 November 1947; *Organiser*, 13 January 1948.
256. *The Tribune*, 16 January 1948; *CMG*, 15 January 1948; *Statesman*, 15 January 1948.
257. *The Tribune*, 16 January 1948.
258. Ibid.; *CMG*, 15 January 1948; *Statesman*, 15 January 1948.
259. *The Tribune*, 16 January 1948; *Statesman*, 20 January 1948.
260. *Statesman*, 25 February 1948.
261. *The Tribune*, 8 January 1948.
262. *CMG*, 7 January 1948.
263. Ibid., 15 January 1948.
264. Rosenberger and Tobin, *Keesings Contemporary Archives*, vol. 6, A 9051.
265. *CMG*, 15 January 1948; *Statesman*, 16 January 1948.
266. *CMG*, 15 January 1948.
267. *The Tribune*, 10 December 1947. Some of the tribal infiltrators who were arrested in Kashmir in mid-November (1947) were reported to be carrying American weapons, detailed maps, etc. There was also a report that said that two fully loaded ships carrying arms and ammunition had docked at the Karachi port. *Daily Milap*, 17 November 1947 for the report on the tribals; and 26 December 1947 for the report of ships carrying American weapons.
268. *TOI*, 3 January 1948.
269. *The Tribune*, 8 January 1948.

270. *CMG*, 9 January 1948.
271. Durga Das (ed.), *Sardar Patel's Correspondence* (hereafter *SPC*), vol. 6, Ahmedabad, 1973, p. 507; *Hindu* (Madras), 12 January 1948.
272. *SPC*, pp. 508–13, *CMG*, 13 January 1948; *Statesman*, 13 January 1948; *TOI*, 13 January 1948; *The Tribune*, 13 January 1948.
273. *SPC*, vol. 6, p. 511.
274. *TOI*, 16 January 1948; *The Tribune*, 16 January 1948.
275. *The Tribune*, 13 January 1948

8

Punjab in the Aftermath of Gandhi's Assasination

Each one of us who raised a hand against innocents is a culprit. . . . Gandhi's murder constitutes an attempt at the extinction of humanity.[1]

The entire city (Lahore) is shrouded in a pall of gloom and will go to the river at 4 p.m. and offer prayers.[2]

By the beginning of 1948, the issue of whether India should or should not transfer the cash balance of Rs. 55 crore to Pakistan clubbed with the invasion of Kashmir had displaced the stories of bloodshed and bestiality that had come out of Punjab. Both sides—India and Pakistan—entered into a war of words. Sardar Patel was clear that Pakistan had by sponsoring the conflict in Kashmir lost the moral and technical right to claim the cash balances.[3] Liaqat Ali, the Pakistan Prime Minister, said that there was no way Pakistan could be denied the cash balances.[4] He warned India against harming the cause of Pakistan and the Muslims.[5] Patel issued an ultimatum asking Pakistan to stop supporting the invaders in the valley and also stated that not an inch of land in the valley would be allowed to go to Pakistan.[6] As reports gave details of how India had launched a massive counter-attack in the valley to push out the invaders,[7] Patel added that India was being pushed towards a full-scale war.[8]

This was the background when Gandhi undertook the last of his historic fasts unto death on 13 January (1948). Across the plains of Punjab, which were also experiencing an unusually early and extreme winter, it was only natural for the fast to receive wide attention. There was widespread praise and appreciation for Gandhi and his cause, of harmony and peace among Muslims, and non-Muslims in the Pakistan press.

Firoz Khan Noon while speaking in the West Punjab Legislative Assembly said, 'Gandhiji was the greatest man the world has ever seen.'[9] Mian Iftikharuddin was reported to have said: 'Mahatma Gandhi's fast is symbolic of our failure to . . . cure the disease of cruelty and hatred and barbarity which threatens to undo what we have achieved'.[10]

The *CMG* published many letters from ordinary Muslims. While one Mohammad Khan appealed for peace to save Gandhiji's life, Abaid Ullah Khan said 'Gandhi's fast was a last resort . . . a noble act that has caused a stir across the world and made people realise the gravity of the situation.'[11] West Punjab Premier Mamdot issued another statement: 'Gandhi has made a powerful gesture to draw attention to . . . the growing feeling of ill-will on the part of the majority community towards the Muslims.'[12]

In East Punjab, the broader consensus was that the fast was also a sign of Gandhi being unhappy with the working and policies of the Government of India. The East Punjab cabinet met in Simla on 16 January and discussed the dramatic change that had suddenly taken place in the entire political scene following Gandhi's fast. Simla was flooded with posters: 'He lives for you—save him', with the cabinet having resolved, 'who lives if he dies?'[13]

GOVERNMENT OF INDIA REVERSES STAND ON CASH BALANCES

Gandhi had laid seven main conditions for ending his fast. These were stated in a press conference addressed by Maulana Azad on 17 January.[14] In sum the conditions were:

1. The annual fair of Khawaja Bakhtyar should be organized freely and without fear.
2. The 117 mosques that had been desecrated and converted to temples during the recent disturbances in Delhi should be restored immediately.
3. Muslims should have no fear and restriction in conducting business in markets like Karol Bagh, Subzi Mandi, Paharganj.
4. Hindus and Sikhs must have no objection and must not cause problems for those Muslim families who had fled to Pakistan during the riots, but now wished to return.
5. Muslims should be allowed to travel in trains without fear.
6. There should be no economic boycott of Muslims.
7. The houses and other properties vacated by Muslim families who

had gone to Pakistan from Delhi should not be occupied by non-Muslim refugees from West Punjab without the consent of the Muslim families living in this area.

Looked at carefully each of the seven main issues was only an attempt by Gandhi to restore the confidence of the Muslims who had been traumatized. None of the points even remotely referred to the transfer of the cash balance to Pakistan and, yet, for some reason, the common perception, particularly in East Punjab, was that Gandhi had undertaken the fast to force the Government of India relent on the issue and transfer the amount to Pakistan. This widespread view that the money was being transferred to Pakistan only because Gandhi wanted it so was the result to a great extent of the official statement released to the press on behalf of the Government of India. *The Pioneer*, said that while Gandhi did not make any mention of the cash balance transfer, the Government of India in its statement 'did not divest him of the inspiration for the step'.[15]

As newspapers continued to speculate on the reasons for the fast, the Government of India suddenly undertook a complete reversal of its earlier decision and ordered the Reserve Bank of India to credit Rs. 35 crore to Pakistan immediately. What followed was only natural. Speculative stories flooded the newspapers. The *Daily Milap* questioned the grounds on which the payment was withheld and then suddenly released without assigning any reason. It wanted to know what were the circumstances that had led to this change in policy.[16]

One report said that Nehru, Patel and Finance Minister Chetty had had a long meeting with Gandhi on 14 January, and that Patel had left Delhi for Bhavnagar early next morning, i.e. on 15 January. This report also said that some kind of agreement had been reached in the meeting with regard to the cash balances.[17] *The Tribune* gave a more detailed story based on information given by 'extremely reliable quarters'. The report said that it was common talk in Delhi that Sardar Patel had done some plain talking with Gandhi and had even offered to resign. It also said that the late-night decision of the government ran counter to the views and decisions of the Reserve Bank of India, which had also worked late into the night the same evening. The report added: 'it is also said that Gandhiji and Nehru were against the suspension of the cash balances'.[18]

Prime Minister Nehru was naturally the first to state that even though Gandhi had been consulted on the issue, the decision to transfer the cash balance to Pakistan had nothing to do with his fast. The Prime Minister also said: 'we have come to this decision in the hope that the gesture in accord with India's high ideals and Gandhiji's noble standards will convince the world of our earnest desire for peace'.

Interestingly, *TOI* also quoted Nehru as saying that the decision had been taken to transfer the money even though most cabinet members were of the same view as Sardar Patel, 'but that in view of the world's concern for Gandhiji's fast . . . we were searching for ways to reduce ill-will'.[19]

Gandhi was happy that the government had taken the initiative to reduce the tension. In a statement which it was read out on his behalf at the post-prayer meeting on 16 January, he 'wondered how Pakistan would reciprocate . . . the ways are many. If there is a will there is a way'.[20]

In Pakistan there was considerable enthusiasm and excitement with regard to the release of the cash balance. Ch. Nazir Ahmad and Syed Martab Ali, Directors on the Central Board of the Reserve Bank of India, were the first to express gratitude to Gandhi for his 'noble and herculean effort', although they also added that 'it would have been far better if the Indian dominion had come to its decision in a more graceful manner without putting Gandhiji's precious life at peril'.[21]

CMG's editorial on the 17 January 1948 said: 'As a result of Gandhiji's fast the Government of India has made a gesture towards Pakistan in its decision to implement its final agreement involving a sum of Rs. 55 crore. . . . More significant is the concern men of all communities have displayed in India at the risk to which Gandhiji has exposed himself in the interest of communal peace.'

The news that Gandhi had decided to end the fast was welcomed not only in New Delhi but even in Pakistan. Pakistan's High Commissioner even assured the Government of India that 'it (Pakistan) would do everything possible for peace'. Prime Minister Nehru addressed a public meeting specially organized to celebrate the ending of Gandhi's fast.[22] Even the *Organiser*, the leading platform for anti-Gandhi and anti-Congress viewpoints noted: 'All is well that ends well and in the context of Mahatma Gandhi's fast it is the best. The anxiety felt over the safety of his life is over.'[23]

Gandhi himself addressed an unusually large post-prayer gathering on 18 January, the day he ended his fast, in spite of the slight winter drizzle. Gandhiji spoke for sometime on the microphone, while the larger part of the address was read out by Sushila he said 'this is an auspicious day for me and it should be auspicious for you too . . . it is also the birthday of Guru Gobind Singh'.[24]

East Punjab's Reaction

East Punjab's reactions to the transfer of cash balances and the belief that the decision of the government of India was possibly linked to Mahatma Gandhi fast were not highlighted for as long as the fast continued. But once Gandhi had ended the fast there was a flood of attacks against the Government of India, essentially aimed at Nehru, Patel and even Gandhi. *The Tribune*, which for years had been the leader in forming public opinion said in a strongly worded editorial on 20 January:

> [W]e are sure that with the realisation of the aim that Gandhiji had set before himself so far as the protection of Muslim interests is concerned he will now devote his attention to securing justice for the Hindus and Sikhs of Punjab . . . we cannot help referring to one very serious result to which the fast and its aftermath have already led. It is the decision of the Union Government to pay at once to Pakistan a sum of Rs. 50 crore . . . it was only a few days ago that the Deputy Prime Minister (Patel) and Finance Minister (Chetty) had taken great pains to explain that India was right both in law and equity in the action that it had taken. . . . This quick change of face can not add to the prestige of the government.

Just a day after Gandhi had ended the fast another report stated that there was immense resentment against the government's decision to transfer the cash balance, not merely because of Kashmir or on emotional grounds but for technical reasons as well. Before the cash balance had been transferred to Pakistan, the East and West Punjab governments had jointly encashed securities worth Rs. 10 crore. The dispute, the report said, between the East and West Punjab was unresolved with regard to securities that were held by the Reserve Bank of India. The question of these securities should have been resolved before crediting the cash balances to Pakistan.

Another report from Jullundur said it was widely believed among financial circles in Amritsar and Jullundur that India had put itself at great risk in view of the debt liability of Pakistan towards India and that Pakistan was now certain to wriggle out of the debt commitment.[25]

The Punjab unit of the Hindu Mahasabha met in Amritsar on 19 January and resolved that the conditions set by Gandhi for ending the fast were one-sided and had clearly favoured Pakistan.[26] The Meerut unit of the Hindu Mahasabha resolved that just as Gandhi had demanded the restoration of the 117 mosques occupied by Hindu and Sikh refugees, all temples and other shrines which had been converted to mosques or otherwise desecrated must also be restored.[27] The UP unit of the Hindu Mahasabha took up the issue of Gandhi's fast by linking it to the cash balance transfer. Mahant Digvijaynath, President of the UP unit issued a statement saying that there was no doubt that the cash balances that had been transferred to Pakistan were bound to be used by Pakistan for funding the conflict in Kashmir.[28] The All India Hindu Mahasabha issued a statement on 20 January saying that Gandhi's fast had failed to achieve anything, the best example being that even after the cash balance had been transferred, there was still no change in Pakistan's policy with regard to Kashmir and other issues. Deshpande of the Hindu Mahasabha issued yet another statement (just a couple of days before Gandhi's assassination) that Gandhi's fast had served no purpose other than to simply strengthen Pakistan which had not curtailed its policy of sponsoring violence in the valley even while Gandhi was on his fast.[29]

In East Punjab, there was considerable surprise if not anger at the almost hurried and impulsive manner in which the cash balance had been credited to Pakistan, and most people were certain that it would be used to fund Pakistan's adventure in Kashmir. Vakil, the eminent economist, in his extremely important and authoritative work has given clear indications that from early 1948 itself, the Pakistan government had committed itself to extremely heavy and disproportionate expenditure on defence (see Chapter 7).[30]

The link between the transfer of the cash balance and Pakistan's heavy commitment to defence expenditure appears to have been a major reason for the widespread anger in East Punjab with regard to the conditions that Gandhi had set for ending the fast. It is true that the cash balance issue, as we have seen, was not even mentioned in the seven points, but it is the manner and timing of the government's decision to transfer the amount that immediately led people to believe that the government had only acted under directions and pressure from Gandhi.

The fast came to be seen more generally as a measure to make the

Indian government reverse its decision and release the payment. The profound irony of this mix-up was that the far greater objective of enabling Muslims to live in the homes they had lived in for generations, and to do so without fear and with freedom, was relegated to the background. To Gandhi, peace and coexistence, and in this case the right to freedom of existence for Muslims in Delhi, were only a part of the principles which had guided him throughout his life. What problem could anyone have had with most of the issues that Gandhi had raised in the context of his fast is hard to fathom. Organizing an age-old fair, restoring mosques, ensuring freedom to move and do business freely, asking Hindu and Sikh refugees to seek permission before moving into houses vacated by Muslim families in *mohallas* were simple issues, aimed only at restoring confidence and normalcy.

The issues raised by Gandhi were commonly considered as resolvable and as such there was no need for him to have taken such an extreme step. At least this was the widely held belief. Therefore, the actual reasons for the fast must have been, as it was generally believed, something else. This 'something else' came immediately to be linked to the transfer of the cash balance, by the timing and the manner of the actual transfer. With war-like conditions in Kashmir, and fresh memories of the Gujarat Station train killings, the anger in East Punjab against the government of India's decision seems understandable. In particular, the Akalis believed that the cause of India had been greatly harmed by the transfer of the money whatever the reason.

TARA SINGH ON GANDHI

On 24 January, Master Tara Singh issued what was possibly the most critical of statements on Gandhi's fast and its objectives.[31]

> Mahatmaji you did a great deal to serve the nation and country and both should be grateful to you and pay you the highest tribute. . . . But changes in time need changes in policy which you do not seem capable of making . . . the only practical course for you is to retire. . . . I request you not to interfere in government affairs as you do not have a realistic view . . . let Mahatmaji cease to be a super Prime Minister as he is now . . . at present even your prayers are dominated by your politics . . . is it not politics to appear non-sectarian.[32]

RELATION BETWEEN PATEL AND NEHRU STAINED

The government's complete reversal of policy on the issue of the cash balances must have been acutely embarrassing for Sardar Patel particularly after the tough stand he had taken on the issue in the preceding days.[33] As *The Pioneer* put it: 'the turn around has bewildered the public . . . while Sardar Patel proposes, Gandhiji disposes, thus is policy made and unmade in Delhi'.[34] The *Daily Milap* even quoted Patel as having said that it was unpractical to believe that India could be ruled the way Gandhi thought it should be. The report also quoted Patel as saying that many Muslims in India had still not broken their loyalties with the Muslim League, which was unfortunate particularly in the context of Kashmir.[35]

Before leaving Delhi on 15 January for Bhavanagar for an official visit, Patel wrote a letter to Gandhi, which left little unsaid:

> The sight of your fasting has made me disconsolate. It has set me furiously thinking. The burden of work has become so heavy that I feel crushed under it. . . . May be I have deteriorated with age and am no more any good as a comrade to stand by him (Nehru) . . . and (you) have again and again to take up cudgels on my behalf. This also is intolerable to me. . . . I know it is no time for argument. But since I can be of no help even in ending your fast I do not know what else there is for me to do.[36]

Patel's programme to leave Delhi, as just mentioned was not sudden because Nehru had referred to it in a letter as early as 11 January. In the letter Nehru had enclosed a copy of a note he had written to Gandhi about the serious differences that had developed between himself and Patel.[37] The basic differences which threatened to blow up related, in Patel's view, to the duties and functions of the prime minister 'I have', he said, 'found myself unable to agree with his conception of the Prime Minister's duties. That conception if accepted would raise the Prime Minister to the position of a virtual dictator, for he 'claims full freedom to act when and how he chooses.' There were also differences between them on economic matters and Hindu-Muslim relations.

The situation was serious enough for Gandhi to make references to it on two occasion. For example, on 13 January he said 'Patel should not be blamed for holding the view that the Muslim League cannot become a friend overnight.'[38] Gandhi's reference was obviously to a speech made by Patel in Lucknow on 6 January, when he spoke of the need for Muslims to express their loyalty openly to India. If they were unable to do so, they should leave, he said. Gandhi appears to have learnt of the speech on the same day itself. This hard hitting speech on the other hand had also got much praise. The *Pioneer* said in its editorial with reference to the Lucknow speech: 'The Sardar has fire in his belly and ice in his head.' The *Organiser* said it was 'one of the best and memorable speeches made in recent times.'[39]

It was only natural for Patel's speech to receive widespread attention in Pakistan. The *Daily Gazette* reported from *Dawn's* London office that Patel and Nehru had split and that Gandhi's fast was directly linked to the fallout between the two. The report also added that Gandhi was unhappy with Patel for charging the Muslims in India with not having spoken up against Pakistan on the Kashmir issue.[40]

For the first time perhaps Gandhi also discussed how most of the Muslim press had been praising Gandhi and Nehru but attacking Patel. He said this was wrong. 'Patel', he said, 'was still a valuable colleague though he was no longer a yes man as he was once affectionately nicknamed.'[41] The issue of 'Patel no longer being a yes man' was raised by a newspaper reporter. It had already been widely reported and there was also speculation that Gandhi was not happy with Patel and had lost faith in his policies. Gandhi's reply was that he was not happy with the way his 'simple statement had been interpreted', otherwise he would never have made, it he said. Gandhi also said: '. . . the Sardar had bluntness of speech but his heart was expansive enough to accommodate all . . . any one who can link the fast to the policies of the Sardar will hurt me more than the Sardar'.[42] He also said that 'no power in the world can separate Patel from me'.[43]

The issue refused to die down, leading Gandhi to refer to it yet again. On 20 January he said that 'there were no differences of views between Sardar Patel, Nehru and himself'.[44] Stories, however, continued to do the rounds of the corridors of power in Delhi in the subsequent days. 'Stories of acute differences between Nehru and Patel abound in Congress circles', as the *CMG* had earlier put it.[45]

Nehru suggested on 11 January that the two could possibly seek Gandhi's intercession, to talk out their differences.[46] Patel agreed to the suggestion: 'you can fix up with Bapu for a discussion any time that suits you. I shall be leaving for Bhavnagar on 15 January morning'.[47] In the meanwhile Gandhi, aware that 'his right and left hands' were rapidly distancing, suddenly decided to go on the fast leaving Nehru to tell to Patel on 13 January that their proposed meeting with Gandhi may not materialize because 'it would be improper to put an additional burden on him just now when he is fasting'.[48]

Many years later (1968), while delivering the inaugural Jawaharlal Nehru lecture at Cambridge, Mountbatten made a reference to the strained relations: 'indeed just before his assassination Gandhi had asked me to help him bring about a reconciliation. I told them both of his last wish as he lay there dead. They wept and embraced each other.'[49]

NEHRU WARNS COMMUNAL BODIES NOT TO OPPOSE THE GOVERNMENT

As government agencies in Delhi set out to implement the seven basic issues that Gandhi had put forth for ending the fast, the Delhi unit of the Hindu Mahasabha organized a big public meeting in Connaught Place on 27 January. The meeting was presided over by Deshpande, General Secretary of the All India Hindu Mahasabha. Almost every speaker who addressed the gathering opposed the conditions that Gandhi had laid to end the fast. Some speakers demanded that Muslims be asked to leave Delhi to make room for refugees from West Punjab. The general sentiment that prevailed was that Gandhi was concerned only about the Muslims and not the Hindus and Sikhs.[50]

Nehru was in Amritsar and its neighbouring areas on 29 January (1948). He was upset by Tara Singh's comments on Gandhi as well as the great enthusiasm that had been seen at the Hindu Mahasabha rally in Delhi on 27 January. In all the speeches he made on 29 January, there was one common theme—a warning to communal bodies not to oppose the government and if they wished to do so, 'they must come out in the open'.[51] As he had done on numerous occasions, Nehru warned of the danger from fascist forces. He also said that contrary to the widespread belief in Punjab, there was no chance of war with Pakistan.[52] The *Pakistan Times* referred to his emphasis against the RSS and the Hindu Mahasabha, which, the report quoted him as saying, had done great harm to India.[53]

Dr Rajendra Prasad also took up with Dr Syama Prasad Mookerjee his concern about some of the speeches that had been made in the Hindu Mahasabha meeting. He particularly drew Mookerjee's attention to the slogans that had been raised in support of Madan Lal, the man who was arrested for throwing a 'bomb' at Gandhi. A section of the large crowd had demanded the release of Madan Lal.[54]

As pressure to restrict the activities of the RSS and even the Akali Dal mounted one report said that the Congress had not banned the RSS because of apprehension that such an action would lead to a public agitation against the government. A *CMG* report from Jullundur said that the East Punjab government's plan to recruit 13,000 men and train them for specific tasks was in fact a step to build up an organization like the RSS—because that was the only way to counter its popularity. Iqbal's immortal composition *Sare Jahan se Achha* was chosen to be the banner song for this new outfit.[55]

That Congress leaders were having a lot of problems with the RSS was put in plain words by Sardar Patel. While the Prime Minister was known for his great dislike for the RSS, the Sardar had been charged with having a soft corner for the Hindu Mahasabha and possibly even for the RSS. Most of these charges as we have earlier seen, had been made by *Dawn*, which had frequently tried to draw a line between Nehru and Patel. Therefore, what Patel said in Lucknow came as a surprise to many keen observers—the *CMG*, for example, dedicated a full editorial to 'The Patel Surprise'. Patel warned the RSS that 'its activities have brought it in conflict with those who are in power in the Congress'. Patel also said that if they began to behave judiciously and in balance he could intercede on their behalf with the senior leaders in the Congress.[56]

EAST AND WEST PUNJABS MOURN GANDHI

Mahatma Gandhi's assassination shocked the world, but if there was a country and people that mourned his death as much if not more than India it was perhaps Pakistan. Every single office and business establishment in Pakistan was closed on the day following the tragedy.[57] As newspapers devoted complete editions to the tragedy quoting leaders of all levels, the *CMG* (31 January) spared two full pages for excerpts from John Gunther's book *Inside Asia*, in which Gunther said that Gandhi was the greatest Indian since Buddha.[58]

The West Punjab Muslim League directed all its units to organize 'befitting' memorial services. The *CMG* reported that schools and colleges were not only closed but that the only question in the hearts of the common Pakistani was, why had this happened. The *CMG* editorial itself gave an appropriate answer. 'Each one of us who raised a hand against innocents is a culprit . . . or has publicly or secretively entertained sympathy for such acts is a collaborator . . . Gandhi's murder constitutes an attempt at the extinction of humanity.'

Lahore and Karachi had come to a complete standstill, 'with faces ridden with genuine grief'. Every eye at the first memorial meeting at the Lajpat Rai Bhawan in Lahore was moist. The meeting had begun with the *Ram Dhun—Raghupati Raghav Raja Ram*. An aged Muslim who had come to the meeting to recite from the Koran was seen weeping hysterically.

The public meeting organized at the Islamia College Lahore, grounds was comparable in size to the first Independence Day' meeting—mammoth and almost unprecedented in size. The sea of humanity adopted exactly at 4 p.m. a condolence resolution—to coincide with the time of the cremation. It was presided by Alauddin Siddiqui, General Secretary of the West Punjab Muslim League.

A senior correspondent of the *CMG* who had mingled with the mammoth crowd at the memorial meeting at the Islamic College, Lahore said that thousands of Muslim refugees who had lost their all were openly weeping. When speakers while addressing the gathering talked of welcoming Hindus back into Pakistan the mammoth crowd roared and cheered in approval. The Islamia College staff and students also passed a separate resolution of 'great sympathy with the great Hindu community'.[59]

Karachi like Lahore was in deep grief. At the main memorial meeting at the Clifton beach, hymns from the *Bhagwadgita* and prayers in Sanskrit were recited along with verses from the Koran, to coincide with the time of the cremation in New Delhi. Karachi was a silent city on 31 January—there were no cars or vehicles on its roads, every shop and office was closed, people could be seen 'walking in silence'. At another large meeting in Karachi Major Yusuf Ismail said: 'The Muslims have lost a beloved guide and advisor.'[60]

In Simla over 1,00,000 men and women gathered on the Ridge to participate in the memorial meeting presided over by Sardar Kapur Singh, Speaker of the East Punjab Legislative Assembly. A long line of speakers were heard in pin-drop silence.[61] Fifty thousand people marched through the streets of Patiala. Every single town in East Punjab was reported to have organized well-attended memorial meetings.[62] In Amritsar the 4-mile-long memorial procession which started from Jallianwala Bagh reminded people of the only other time that people had grieved so much—the martyrdom procession of Bhagat Singh.[63] Srinagar witnessed for the first time in memory a complete *hartal* on 31 January. Every single town and village in Jammu & Kashmir had come to a complete standstill.[64] Ch. Hamid Ullah, President of the All Jammu & Kashmir Muslim Conference, said: 'He was the symbol of Hindu–Muslim unity and was held in very high regard . . . in Kashmir'.[65]

As politicians of all colours and creeds lined up across the subcontinent to pay tributes to Gandhi's memory, Mian Iftikaruddin, President of the West Punjab Muslim League, was in New Delhi to attend the funeral. In an exclusive meeting with a representative of *The Tribune*, he said: 'I have no hesitation in saying that in fact we are all the murderers of Gandhiji . . . because we did not help in his life's mission that was to unite people.'[66]

On 12 February, the end of the official mourning period, towns across East and West Punjab once again saw massive expressions of solidarity and grief. Over 2,00,000 people gathered on the banks of the Sutluj to witness the immersion. The 30-km. route from Jullundur to Phillaur along which the ashes were to be taken for immersion was covered with petals.[67]

Lahore and Karachi witnessed a complete *hartal* on 12 February. A letter from Lahore said: 'The entire city is shrouded in a pall of gloom and will go to the river at 4 p.m. and offer prayers.'[68] All newspaper offices in Pakistan were closed on 12 February.[69]

SETTLING POLITICAL SCORES

The world joined India in her hour of grief, in Delhi and East Punjab, however, the first political fallout of the tragedy had begun to manifest itself. On 1 February Hari Chand, the RSS *chalak* (principal organizer) of Delhi, issued a statement which said: 'it is a pity that some parties are trying to take advantage of this cowardly act and are associating the name of the RSS'.[70] The RSS *chalak* of Bombay had also categorically stated that: 'the persons arrested in Bombay have no connection with the RSS'. Hari Chand stated that the RSS had suspended all its activities like parades, etc., for thirteen days in memory of Gandhi.[71] L.B. Bhopatkar of the All India Hindu Mahasabha also issued a similar statement saying that 'it was unfair and unjust to condemn or penalise the Mahasabha for the act of any individual',[72] termed Gandhi's assassination as one of the 'most reprehensive acts in the history of the world'.[73]

In East Punjab, the RSS chief Rai Bahadur Badri Das condemned Gandhi's assassination and said that all organizational activity of the RSS stood suspended for the entire duration of the mourning.[74] Similar statements were used across the country on behalf of the RSS and the Hindu Mahasabha, stating mainly that it was unfair to hold the two organizations responsible for the actions of a handful of people. But the government of course had made up its mind; it was time to get even.

On 2 February about 2,000 youths organized a noisy demonstration near the Parliament complex. The slogan was 'ban the RSS and Hindu Mahasabha and drive out the enemies of Nehru'.[75] The following day an Amritsar report said that 'one particular group of leftists was trying to make capital out of the tragedy. At Amritsar, Jullundur and other places they took out a procession and held meetings crying blood for blood'.[76] This report said that some of the slogans raised by this small group of protesters were 'avenge Mahatma Gandhi's death'. The report added that the East Punjab government believed this was an organized attempt to create strife. As desperate attempts were made to guide or rather misguide the anger and sorrow of the people to settle political scores, Master Tara Singh in his first statement following the assassination made an earnest appeal for peace and restraint. He said that: 'Any attempt to avenge the murder would have disastrous and far-reaching effects.'[77]

Clashes between small groups of Communists and RSS activists were reported from other parts of India as well. A report from Bezwada said that the two had clashed on 31 January 1948, and one person was killed while thirty others were seriously injured. The incident was the result of statement made by P. Sundaraya, a Communist leader of the region, that: 'the Hindu Mahasabha, the RSS and Sardar Patel had planned to kill the Mahatma with a view to perpetuating fascist rule in India'.[78]

THE GOVERNMENT MUST RESIGN

A reporter of the *Statesman* who had talked to some members of the Central Assembly a couple of days after Gandhi's assassination filed a report saying that many members were of the view that the tragedy could have been averted if timely action had been taken. In this particular report, the criticism was surprisingly directed more at Prime Minister Nehru than at the Home Minister.[79] More generally it also said that many members felt that if the problems that followed partition, particularly the refugee-related issues, had been handled well and in time, the bitterness that 'hung' over Delhi could have been avoided.

In New Delhi, Jayaprakash Narayan, Dr Ram Manohar Lohia and Kamla Devi Chattopadhyaya jointly addressed a press conference on 3 February. They said that the Socialists were in support of banning communal organizations but at the same time the Communists must also be kept out of government because they had not contributed to the freedom struggle.[80] The three firebrand Socialists created a sensation in Congress circles and other centres of power in New Delhi by seeking the Nehru government's resignation, especially targeting Patel. Jayaprakash Narayan said that he had never doubted the ability of the Sardar, but 'he is now 74 years old and has got the work that even a 30 year old will find difficult to handle'.

The *Statesman* agreed with Jayaprakash's view with regard to the Communists: 'recognising that communal organisations were stout barriers to their progress. . . . They sow distrust and reap disorder.' With regard to the observations made by the socialists in the context of Patel, however, the *Statesman* said it was 'unfair'.[81]

The Sardar was hardly one to restrain his views. The Congress Legislative Party met for the first time after Gandhi's death on 4 February, soon after the Constituent Assembly had adjourned for the day as a mark of respect. Patel spoke extempore for about 40 minutes. This address, as one report put it, was regarded by many members as his best ever. The Sardar broke down twice and for the two minutes that he took each time to recompose himself, there was pin-drop silence. Speaking brilliantly he said that, 30 security men in plain clothes were present in the gathering of about 500 people on the day Gandhi was assassinated. He explained how the CID wing of the government had been greatly affected because over 80 per cent of its staff, which was Muslim or British, was no longer available and that work was being conducted with only 25 per cent of the strength of the staff.[82]

Patel then took up the sensitive issue of banning the Hindu Mahasabha. He said that such an action was not only against democratic principles but was bound to lay the Congress open to the charge of political vindictiveness. More importantly, he said that since even the Draft Constitution had already accepted the distinctive identity of the Muslims in India, the Hindu sentiment could not be ignored and that the need of the hour was to 'act firmly but with fairness', and to ensure that decisions were not taken under pressure from hysterical agitations.[83] He also talked of the good work the RSS had done during the disturbances, particularly in protecting women and children. He admitted that there were many 'fanatical and misguided elements in it'.[84] Notwithstanding the tone and content of Patel's references to the Hindu Mahasabha and the RSS, the Congress Legislative Party resolved to ban the RSS.[85] This resolution of course was only a formality. It is almost certain that the decision had already been taken by the time the Legislative Party was asked to resolve on it. Interestingly, the meeting also decided to study carefully the influence of the RSS in areas that were Congress strongholds.[86]

On 27 November *Dawn* had published a lengthy article titled 'Fascist Origins of Delhi–Punjab massacres'. The article started by noting that the Karachi office of *Dawn* had received information from an ex-RSS man who said that the massacres of Muslims in Punjab and Delhi were part of a plan to overthrow the Nehru government. To substantiate this charge the article referred to some of the statements Nehru was said to have made over the past few months against 'Hindu fascism'. He was reported to have said, for example, in Lucknow on 19 October that: 'a few groups in Punjab have made it their profession to murder people . . . not accidental but pre-planned'. The article then went on to cite a 'Hindu journalist' who told *Dawn* that there was little doubt that 'the trouble was planned by the RSS and the Akali Sikhs', and that the RSS 'wants its own men to hold important positions in East Punjab . . . it wants Bakshi Tek Chand as Governor and Rai Bahadur Badri Das as Premier . . . in Delhi the RSS and the Akalis are running a whispering campaign that Nehru and Azad be removed'.[87]

Possibly a coincidence but all the same it is interesting to note that just a day before *Dawn* charged the RSS and the Akalis with trying to capture power in Delhi and East Punjab, *The Tribune* had carried a hard-hitting editorial which said that Prime Minister Nehru was putting pressure on the East Punjab government to ban the RSS and the Akali Dal:

> Our staff representative at Jullundur is well informed and we are reluctant to doubt the authenticity and correctness of his report that Nehru wants the RSS and Akali Dal to be banned and disbanded and has issued a directive to

[T]he East Punjab Government . . . it is too bad to be true . . . it is the bounden duty of those who hold the reins of government in the province as representatives of the Punjabis to resist it with all their might . . . it is amazing that while the existence of far flung Muslim League organisations in India with their secret arsenals replenished do not cause the slightest irritation to Panditji—the existence of the RSS and the Dal which function as massive bullworks against internal Pakistani sabotage cause acute pain and anger to him. Need we remind Panditji that but for the gallant resistance offered by these national organisations thousands more of Hindu and Sikh women would have been raped and slaughtered . . . when the west Punjab Hindus and Sikhs were burning and bleeding and the cry of the millions of oppressed elicited no better response from outside than a cry in the wilderness would do . . . their (RSS & Akali Dal) valiant members cheerfully laid down their lives. . . . It might be true that some of them were involved in the disturbances. . . . But then they were no more than worse . . . what we want to emphasise is that the RSS and the Akali Dal are protectors of people and enshrined in the hearts of the people . . . Jinnah is building up his National Guard but Nehru instead of building up a powerful citizens defence force and absorbing the RSS and the Akali Dal is thinking of smashing it.[88]

That it was part of the broader political strategy of the Congress to hit at the RSS and the Akalis as things began to quieten down in Punjab is fairly clear. Interestingly it is only from around the end of September (1947) that senior Congressmen led by the Prime Minister began targeting the RSS.

It is also important to note that as reports speculated that senior Congressmen wanted to ban the RSS and the Akalis, there was no denial or contradiction from any senior Congress leader in Simla or in Delhi. That there was more to the so-called 'Congress Plan' to finish the RSS is clear from an address by Dr S. Radhakrishnan at an RSS camp in Rewa. After praising the RSS for its physical fitness, self-sacrifice and discipline, he appealed to them to refrain from criticizing and attacking Congressmen.[89]

In East Punjab, as the pressure mounted throughout December for some action against the RSS and the Akali Dal, the East Punjab government, possibly worried that any move to single out the two as 'communal forces—dangerous to India' might do more harm than good to the Congress, wisely decided to club them with other 'paper organisations'.[90] That the East Punjab authorities should have clubbed the formidable RSS and the Akali Dal with others like the Punjab Frontier Force, Congress Seva Dal and Gen. Mohan Singh's (INA) Desh Sewak Sena came as a surprise to many.

RSS IS BANNED

The order for banning the RSS was issued in the evening of 4 February (1948). The *TOI* quoting government sources said it was the first step towards combating 'forces of hate and violence'. The *CMG* said banning the RSS had been seriously discussed in government circles even in November 1947, but the view then was that the stage had not yet come for it to be banned as an organization.[91] The *Statesman* welcomed the ban in an editorial, adding that there were other organizations too that needed to be banned and that the ban must also be seen in the light of reports which said the RSS possibly had a hand in the killings of Muslims in Punjab.[92]

As violent agitations were organized against the RSS in many parts of India, the government sat back helplessly. *The Tribune* took up the issue in a powerful editorial.

On 6 February, *The Tribune* in an editorial 'Nehru Government must pause and ponder', strongly questioned the ban, and said that the move had clear political motives:

> [T]he Nehru government's position will be clearly questionable and untenable if it forges deadly repressive weapons and uses them freely against political parties and organisations which happened to be opposed to its national and internal policies and moves . . . we request the Nehru Government to pause and ponder . . . instead of attacking parties whose outlook is different from its own. . . .[93]

There were many others who believed like *The Tribune* that it was unfair to have pinned down only the RSS. Dev Das Gandhi's address on All India Radio on 6 February was reproduced by the *TOI* the following day: 'There are people in the RSS and the Hindu Mahasabha who would have given their lives to save Gandhi . . . this applies to a vast majority of them . . . there are no more than a handful of individuals who are guilty of the crime.'[94]

The *Organiser* naturally took up the fight on behalf of the RSS. It had all along been the main mouthpiece for its views against Gandhi and the Congress. Its press and office were the first to be sealed following the assassination. In its first issue in the post-assassination period, on 29 July 1948, it condemned the assassination and absolved the RSS. It called the assassination 'a misdeed of the undeserving sons of the land' and said that the 'evil and tragic day of Gandhi's assassination marks a new phase in our national life. On that day truthfulness, love and tolerance were dethroned and falsehood, lust and intolerance usurped their place.' A couple of months later, on 2 October, Gandhi's birthday, it devoted yet another editorial to the 'Father of the Nation', calling Gandhi the greatest and noblest son India had ever produced.[95] In the same editorial, the *Organiser* took issue with the Congress. 'Thousands of Hindu youth were arrested . . . who ever was found lacking in faith in Gandhi's policy of Muslim appeasement was taken to be an accomplice in his murder plot. Newspapers that were critical of the policy were treated as places where the conspiracy was hatched and sealed'. It also charged the Congress with failing to see that a few misguided youths were not representative of the RSS. But more interestingly, the editorial called upon the Congress to help in healing the wounds 'let us stand united'.[96]

The *TOI* also carried a long statement by Veer Savarkar, in which he condemned the killing in the strongest possible terms.[97] Dr Syama Prasad Mookerjee's first reaction to the assassination was 'The shot of the assassin not only vitally pierced through the mortal body but grievously struck the very heart of Hinduism.'[98] In a statement, he said that: 'the greatest Indian was done to death by a Hindu is a tragedy unparallel in history. That he was a member of the Hindu Mahasabha is a matter of shame and humiliation for every one connected with the Hindu Mahasabha.'[99]

Soon after Gandhi's assassination *Panchjanya* published an article without a byline but possibly it was written by the Bounding editor Atal Behari Vajpayee. It said that by killing Gandhi the assassin had in fact killed the soul of India—*yeh bharat ki atma ka patan hai*. The article said that the assassination was not only anti-India but had destroyed in a minute the system of values that had been nurtured for thousands of years and that even after having differences with him (Gandhiji) 'his presence was always conciliating'. The article called for a thorough investigation and justice.[100]

In East Punjab, even as RSS activists continued to defy the ban by taking out organized processions, many of its leaders went underground. A procession of young boys marched through the streets of Amritsar on 10 February protesting against the ban.[101] The challenging positions taken up by RSS volunteers in Amritsar in particular appear to have drawn Nehru's attention. He wrote to East Punjab Premier Bhargava on the issue on 11 February. Bhargava took great pains to explain that the government of East Punjab was committed to containing the RSS and there was no let up in the effort. He went on to assure Nehru that 'so long as I am at the helm of affairs I will not allow anything to be done which might lower the prestige of the Congress'.[102]

The government's decision to ban two other organizations, the Muslim League National Guard and the Khaksars was obviously an afterthought, resulting mainly from the charge that its reason for banning the RSS alone was because of the organization's popularity rather than the desire to combat the forces of 'hate'.[103]

Surprisingly, even though the police in East Punjab went overboard in hitting at the RSS, the total number of arrests by 10 February was merely 922.[104] There were many reports that referred to incidents of evidence being cooked up by the police to book families known to have links with the RSS. Lal Chand, a schoolboy, was caught pasting posters in Amritsar. Since the police could do little to the boy, a weapon was reported to have been planted in his home and the whole family was booked.[105] The UP government notified that any government official found to be associated with the RSS was likely to be dismissed.[106] The police was given an additional handle to hit at the RSS and its sympathisers by the Indian Criminal Law Amendment Act, which provided that all stores and buildings that housed its offices were to be declared as notified areas.[107]

The banning of the RSS formed a major part of the discussions that took place in the AICC meeting on 20–21 February in New Delhi. Jayaprakash Narayan wondered how the Congress could have banned the RSS and left the Akalis untouched. He said it was a surprise to see the Congress talking of combating communalism but retaining the Akalis as ministers in the Congress-led government in East Punjab. Jayaprakash supported the ban on the RSS but wondered how the government had come to know of the RSS follies only after Gandhi's assassination. This report also said that as he (Jayaprakash) spoke, not a word was uttered by any member in approval or disapproval with regard to his views.[108]

What Jayaprakash said had naturally stunned the Congressmen attending the AICC, more so when Congress had walked hand in hand with the Hindu Mahasabha and even sections of the RSS in East Punjab. Particularly during the period of disturbances, there was little to distinguish between the Congress and the RSS. Just a couple of months before the RSS was banned, East Punjab Premier Gopichand Bhargava had himself stated to Nehru that he had met Rai Bahadur Badri Das (chief of the East Punjab RSS) in mid-December to discuss Badri Das's appointment as Vice-Chancellor of the

(East) Punjab University.[109] But after Gandhi assassination, however, Bhargava not only did not appoint Das, he even went on to support the ban on the RSS itself.[110]

In a letter to B.G. Kher, Prime Minister of Bombay, Patel expressed not only his surprise but also his unhappiness at the tendency to exaggerate the 'role' of organizations like the RSS. 'you will recall that it was considered that the reports of the activities of organisations like the RSS were somewhat exaggerated and it was not necessary to take such a view of the matter'.[111] The day after the RSS was banned, Premier Bhargava sought direction from Sardar Patel as to what was to be done with some other 'private armies' in East Punjab—in this case the Desh Sevak Sena of INA General Mohan Singh.[112] Patel replied only on 9 February and asked Bhargava to first try to convince Mohan Singh to disband the Sena—if possible—by meeting him. As for the Akal Sena, Patel noted: 'I am afraid we shall have to take action against the Akal Sena.'[113]

As Congress premiers of provincial governments vied with each other to please the Congress high command, 'their over enthusiasm to weed out dangerous elements' sometimes crossed the line and was known also to get some of them in trouble. In line with policy the Bombay government had restricted the activities of the Rashtriya Seva Dal. The decision however angered Nehru who sought an explanation from Premier Kher. One reason for the ban possibly was it was under the control and influence of the Congress Socialists, who were Congressmen only in name, rarely losing an opportunity to hit at the Congress leadership. The Premier obviously believed that Nehru would be pleased. Nehru, however, advised Kher to reconsider the decision: 'I am rather worried at various developments which are isolating the Congress and Congress governments from a large body of public opinion.'[114]

While the Prime Minister seems to have been clear in his mind that voluntary organizations associated with the Congress need not be banned, Sardar Patel certainly had reservations about exempting them from the ban. He wrote to Dr Rajendra Prasad: 'it has been pointed out that it would be illogical to ban other volunteer organizations without banning the Congress volunteer organization. For the time being I have issued instructions to leave Congress volunteers organization and prohibit the activities of other political and communal volunteer organizations.'[115]

Jayaprakash Narayan's motion to remove representatives of communal parties in East Punjab and Delhi was surprisingly rejected by the AICC, even though there was no explanation forthcoming from any speaker in the Congress for how it could remain associated with one political party as it was in East Punjab, and at the same time ban an old and close ally of that party.[116] The question raised by Jayprakash Narayan essentially therefore was that while he had no objections to the banning of the RSS, if the government was genuinely committed to eradicating the politics of 'hate and division', it must in all fairness adopt the same approach to other parties as well.[117]

The Tribune's suggestion that there was much more to the banning of the RSS formed a major part of the proceedings of the first meeting (after Gandhi's assassination) of the Working Committee of the All India Hindu Mahasabha in New Delhi on 14–15 February. With L.B. Bhopatkar President of the Hindu Mahasabha, presiding a six-hundred-word resolution was passed which supported the government in its fight against 'terrorism and subversive activity', but it also said that in detaining people without charges and trials, as was happening following the ban on the RSS, the government had 'clearly opened itself to the charge of eliminating political opposition in the country'.[118]

NEHRU WARNS TARA SINGH

By the middle of February 1948, the political scene in East Punjab was ridden with suspicion and unease. The RSS, which had along with the Akalis and the Congress been an integral part of all the action now stood banned. The great Master and his following had mellowed, no doubt, but the future was unclear.

As the government's clampdown on the RSS continued, Master Tara Singh spoke on the banning of the RSS for the first time on 10 February. He said the government's effort must be to punish the culprits and not innocent people. If the RSS, he said, is undesirable it will die a natural death.[119] He also said that 'implicating innocent men and organizations will not please Gandhi's soul'.[120]

Around the same time that Tara Singh came out in part support of the RSS a small faction of the Akalis led by Udham Singh Nagoke (MLA) added another twist to the scenario: the possibility of the Akalis merging with the Congress and that 'there was no need of private armies in free India'.[121] Tara Singh had obviously been aware of the effort by some Congressmen to divide the Akali Dal and therefore ridiculed and refuted the talk of the Akalis merging with the Congress.[122] We need to go back about a month to understand why the love–hate relationship between Tara Singh and the Congress had finally snapped. Even though it is difficult to accept that Nehru could have ever imagined conceding a separate electorate for the Sikhs, reports indicate that by the beginning of January this is exactly what the Akalis had begun to believe. In fact, a report in the *TOI* even quoted the Prime Minister as saying, in response to the Akali demand that the 'reservation of seats in services and legislatures may possibly be conceded for a limited period of time'.[123]

Tara Singh in a fiery address at the Guru Ka Bagh in Amritsar on 11 January had called for the eviction of Muslim from Delhi and, of course, a war with Pakistan. It is clear that he was feeling betrayed, having returned from Delhi knowing that the possibility of a separate electorate for the Sikhs was now a closed chapter, even though the Akalis refused to give up on the issue. Then came the call to club the Akali Dal with the RSS and the demand for its ban as well.[124]

It was against this background that Giani Kartar Singh, President of the Shrimoni Akali Dal, issued a categorical statement, warning the Government of India. He said there was no truth in the reports that the Akali Dal had sought 15 days' time from Home Minister Patel to disband the Akali Dal. The Akali Dal, he said, had never been a military or even a semi-military organization and had never threatened peace and tranquillity: 'we warn the government that we will oppose any move to ban the Dal and no sacrifice is too great'.[125]

About a week after Giani Kartar Singh's 'tough' statement, a small section of politically active Sikhs who were obviously acting in alliance with Congress leaders in East Punjab and Delhi, formed a group, calling it the Nationalist Sikhs. The first demand they raised was that only people associated with the Congress should be allowed to hold office in the government in East Punjab and the Union Cabinet should also be immediately reconstituted and that representatives of 'communal' parties should be excluded in such a reconstitution.[126]

The Akalis however refused to give up and continued to insist that the Congress was backtracking on commitments it had earlier made. To the Akalis the 'sudden talk' of communal harmony was nothing but an attempt to sweep into irrelevance all the issues that they had fought for in the preceding months. They were surprised to see that

Congress leaders like Bhargava, who less than a month earlier had supported the Akali call for war with Pakistan, were now appealing to people not to be swayed by passion and sentiment.[127]

A great part of Akali thinking and politics had always been associated with passion, sentiment and emotion. Manipulation and political intrigue had never been their forte. For the second time in less than a year the Akalis were being pointed out as the 'black sheep'.

This was the kind of feeling that prevailed among senior Akali circles in the middle of February (1948) when yet again they decided to send a delegation to Delhi to remind the Congress leadership of promises the Akalis believed the Congress leaders had made. A delegation of senior Akali leaders including the Master himself, Giani Kartar Singh and Advocate Harnam Singh left for Delhi on 16 February. The main objective of the delegation was to remind the Congress leaders in Delhi of the promises they were supposed to have made earlier. That the delegation did not achieve any significant concession from the Congress leadership was obvious from the statement Tara Singh issued on his return to Amritsar. He called for separate electorates for the Sikhs, mainly on the grounds that no Sikh would be elected in joint electorates. He said the Congress had earlier promised to be sympathetic to this demand of the Akalis, but had backed out. He also said that: 'Congress had turned out the British but it had failed in maintaining India as a nation of Hindus, Muslims and Sikhs by accepting the two nation theory.' The immediate Congress response to Tara Singh's statement came from Darshan Singh, President of the District Congress Committee of Amritsar, who said that it would be suicidal for the Panth to come into confrontation with the Congress.[128]

NEHRU REJECTS DEMAND FOR SPECIAL WEIGHTAGE

Nehru was in Jullundur on 24 February (1948). In a public meeting attended by about 2,00,000 people he said the Akalis had been demanding weightage for the Sikhs: 'in this country weightage is not to be given to anybody. . . I may frankly tell you that to demand weightage is nonsense . . . weightage or special weightage can be given only by depriving others of their right. This cannot be done . . . if we once tried the wrong path there will be no end . . . we shall one day have to give up the dream of establishing democracy in India'.[129]

It is difficult to imagine that Nehru could ever have promised a separate electorate to the Sikhs, whatever the Akalis may have claimed. Therefore, what he said at Jullundur, even as the Akalis were leaving nothing unsaid, cannot be perceived as being anti-Sikh or even anti-Akali for that matter. That Nehru was by the end of February very unhappy with the situation in East Punjab is however quite clear, as we have also seen in his correspondence to Bhargava, but whether his disillusionment was with the Panth as a whole or a section of the Akalis it not clear.

In order to understand the complexity of the situation between the Congress and the Akalis in East Punjab it is nessasary to look at an extremely important Aide–Memoir recorded by Mountbatten. This note is quite aptly titled, 'Sikh Problem' and pertains to the period 1 January 1948 to 24 April 1948. Mountbatten and Nehru had over the years developed a deep trust and understanding. They consulted each other on every issue of any significance, so there is no possibility that Mountbatten's view on the Sikh problem were not known to Nehru, in all probability they may even have been influenced by Nehru. Mountbatten had noted: 'they (the Sikhs ignore orders of the provincial government and even the Central government, which is supine with regard to the Sikhs whom it obviously fears . . . the Sikhs are a threat not only to Hindustan but also to Pakistan'. Mountbatten also noted that the long association of the Sikhs with the armed forces had helped them during the disturbances.[130]

What is also significant in this important note is that Mountbatten has used the words 'they' and 'Sikhs', therefore not drawing a distinction between the Akalis and the Panth more broadly—in fact the word Akali does not figure at all in the note.

Nehru fortunately was more clearer on this—his dislike and suspicion was manifested for the Akalis, an irony in itself keeping in view the extent to which the Congress had played the Akali game in the pre-3 June Plan days to ensure that the Akalis accepted the Plan without too much of a fuss. Indeed by April 1948 much had changed with regard to Panthic politics in East Punjab—whereas in May/June 1947 the Sikhs guided by the Akali stars were the pivots of the partition plan chalked out by a handful of Congressmen and Jinnah with Mountbatten but by the beginning of 1948 they were treated with suspicion, almost disdain.

It is also of course rather difficult to say whether the situation in which the Akalis specifically and the Sikhs more generally found themselves in early 1948 was of their own making or the result of a plan followed by the Congress leadership—even as early as July 1947 there was talk in Lahore that the Congress was in fact acting to a plan which involved, first, handling the Muslim League and, then, taking care of the Akalis.

Attention has earlier been drawn to O.H. Spate, the Englishman who was specifically contracted by the Ahmadiya community to plead its case before the Punjab Bombay Commission. Spate made an interesting entry in his diary on 19 July 1947. Just as the Commission had settled down to start its proceedings, he noted that the 'Congress was using the Sikhs as the cats paw against the Muslim League and that Congress would deal with the Sikhs the moment they had dealt with the Muslim league.'[131]

The Congress leadership had had no serious problem with Akalis throughout July and August 1947. There were of course the occasional complaints against the *jathas* who were said to enjoy Akali support. In fact, even as late as October (1947) Nehru had no doubt with regard to Tara Singh's popularity among the Sikhs and believed that the Master's control was well established. Lord Ismay had minuted an extremely important 'India Situation' report on 5 October. He records the view that Nehru believed that the Sikhs were, by and large, amenable to Tara Singh with the exception of about 3,000 who were organized, violent and independent of Tara Singh.[132]

Much had changed between November 1947 and May 1948 in the perception of the Akalis towards the political crisis. The discontent had begun to simmer as time passed and the Akalis increasingly felt let down. The first indication of how unhappy leaders like Tara Singh were is evident in his statement soon after the Gandhi had ended his fast. The reaction of the Akalis to the banning of the RSS brought matters to a boil.

On 16 April (1948) Nehru wrote to Bhargava: 'certain speeches of Master Singh and Giani Kartar Singh published recently in the press have rather alarmed me.'[133] Nehru then shared with Bhargava a view he said he had formed on the basis of newspaper reports—that some Akalis were reported to have joined the Congress only to 'gain particular communal objectives'.[134] Ten days later Nehru wrote Dr Rajendra Prasad sharing his distress with the state of affairs in Punjab. 'It is a good thing that the Akalis are joining or have joined the Congress, provided of course that this is not some artificial step without any real meaning.'[135] Nehru's reference to the term 'artificial' possibly pointed to how the Akali Dal had allowed its 23 MLAs to join the Congress while retaining its identity.[136] Nehru of course had reason to be concerned with regard to what Tara Singh and Kartar Singh were actually stating rather than the 'ornamental' merging of some legislators with the Congress. Tara Singh was more than clear that the Akalis wanted real authority and power and could never accept being 'treated as orphans dependent on the Congress'.

A week later Nehru once again shared with Dr Rajendra Prasad his opinion of Kartar Singh. Nehru was greatly upset over the possibility of the Giani becoming a Minister in East Punjab. 'Quite apart from his past record of anti-national activities he is a person who is not desirable or reliable from any point of view. I think the reputation of the Congress will go down if we make him a minister. . . . As it is we are accused of being pure and simple opportunists'.[137] In spite of such reservations Giani Kartar Singh was included in the reconstituted cabinet on 11 June 1948.

There are two other letters that need attention in the context of Nehru's intrinsic suspicion, bordering on intense dislike, of Master Tara Singh in particular. On 20 May (1948) he wrote to Premier Bhargava referring to a declaration of a charter of Sikh rights made at the Golden Temple: 'They cannot have it both ways, i.e. fight the government as it is and cooperate with it gaining advantages'. Nehru had also said that some of the Akalis are 'amazingly irresponsible'.[138] The volume editors' note on this letter appears to suggest that Nehru was angry with something Tara Singh may have said in the recent past. The fact is that all the major points mentioned in the editors' note (on this letter) had been raised by Tara Singh during the previous six months: that the Government of India had made a mess of the rehabilitation policy, and that problems between the two—Pakistan and India—could be solved only by war, so Nehru's anger against Tara Singh, if it was for these reasons should have been there all along. Writing to Baldev Singh on 6 June (1948) Nehru had said: 'I am greatly worried at the intemperate and highly objectionable effusions of Master Tara Singh. I just do not see how the matter can be seriously considered when people like Tara Singh continue holding forth threats and preaching a gospel of intense communalism'.[139]

TARA SINGH'S POINT OF VIEW

But having said all this, if we pause for a moment and look at the state of the Sikhs from Tara Singh's point of view, we may possibly understand that with so much having been lost in terms of both life and property, the language used by him is understandable. With every single issue of significance having been decided in the Punjab in the previous six months by the might of the sword and the spear, to Tara Singh and his followers the sudden talk of high ideals of secularism and sacrifice appeared somewhat out of place. We have already noted the harsh words he had used even against Gandhi in the third of week of January. Inexcusable as it may seem, he was personally convinced that the only way to save lives in the Kashmir valley was to launch an offensive on the East and West Punjab border. After so much blood had flowed, the talk of war was no doubt repulsive to Nehru and he very rightly dismissed all such talk as 'absurd'.

Attention has already been drawn in considerable detail to the fact that a vast majority of the Sikh and Hindu population believed most of their problems were the result of hurried decisions, lack of a co-ordinated effort and, above all, the tendency of the Congress leaders to overlook the human aspect of the problem. It is necessary in this context, therefore, to understand that all the communal poison that some of the Akalis were charged with spreading was not because the Sikhs were 'inherently communal', but only because they believed the division of the Punjab—of India—was based on faith and religion and nothing else. The broader notion that partition was an abstract political decision—forgettable in the course of time was not acceptable to a vast majority of the people who had suffered it because, to them, it was not the result of a political decision taken by earnest, sincere and well-meaning leaders, but by people who had yielded to pressure and had been unable to cope with the crisis that they had themselves created.

To the ordinary Punjabi, the Sikh peasant in particular, partition had brought disaster. It is one thing to leave behind a business or a shop, but in leaving agricultural lands one leaves not only a piece of land but also a vast number of emotional bonds. If the Sikh peasant was more agonized than others it was only because he had brought into great fertility vast stretches of land with great physical effort, and just as the time had come for the new generation to enjoy the fruits of the labour of their fathers and grandfathers, they were uprooted. We have also noted at length how the Sikhs had begun expressing their deep concern and worry the moment the notional line that was to divide the Punjab was announced. The notional line, which came to be known as Sir Radcliffe's line, also deprived the Sikhs of the only thing they valued more than their lands—some of their most sacred shrines.

Tara Singh's 'intemperate and objectionable effusions', therefore, cannot be seen as merely the reactions of a communal mind that lacked the 'vision' of building a secular India and had no understanding of the 'concept of communal co-existence'. What is surprising is not the stand that Tara Singh had begun to take but the manner in which the Congress had forgotten that it was he and his colleagues who, by insisting that the Sikhs would come to India, created the basis for the great success story that the Indian part of Punjab went on to become.

As we have seen immense pressure was mounted on the Sikhs by the Muslim League and its loyal following in the media to reconsider their decision of choosing their new homeland in the Indian part of Punjab rather than in Pakistan. Other things apart, the Sikhs were repeatedly warned that they would certainly be reduced to an insignificant minority in the East Punjab.[140] It is important to understand Tara Singh not merely in the context of some of the statements he made with regard to the eviction of Muslims and later against the government of India but also in the fact that never did he or any of his important colleagues display anxiety, fear or apprehension that the Sikhs would be reduced to a minority in East Punjab. It must be remembered that even as late as November 1947, when Tara Singh was asked for his reaction to reports that the Sikhs were demanding a Sikh homeland within East Punjab, he had dismissed the speculation as absurd and ridiculous.[141]

A reporter of *The Tribune* who had travelled in some parts of Punjab soon after Gandhi's assassination and had met several Akali leaders pointed to the growing feeling among the Akalis—the demand for a new province within East Punjab, to be carved out on the basis of the Punjabi-speaking population.[142] The report also said the view among the Akalis was that the Sikh states of Patiala, Jind, Nabha, Faridkot and Kapurthala needed to be merged with the new province which should however exclude the East Punjab districts of Gurgaon and Rohtak. Thus, in less than two months—from 29 November 1947 to, say, the middle of February 1948—profound and far-reaching changes had occured within the broader Sikh and Akali politics in Punjab.

The peculiarity of the crisis was that the Akalis had now begun seeing their actions and statements as a means of seeking their rightful place—a province which the Sikhs could call their own, something that may even have been promised to them at some stage in the crucial pre-3 June Plan days by senior leaders in Delhi who were desperate to push the Plan through. But as things began to settle down and the Government of India began to find its feet, the tone and tenor of Delhi's reactions to the Akalis began to reveal a greatly hardened approach. 'I have read in the newspapers of the declaration about the charter of Sikh rights made recently at the Golden Temple,' Nehru, wrote to Bhargava, asking him also to warn Tara Singh and his followers that the Government of India did not approve of their activities that 'there would be endless trouble if he (Tara Singh and party) persists in them'.[143] Nehru was wrong. There was no 'trouble' that could possibly be worse than what the Punjab had undergone in 1947. The Akalis understood this better than anyone else.[144]

NOTES

1. *CMG*, 2 February 1948.
2. *The Tribune*, 14 February 1948; *The Pioneer*, 17 January 1948.
3. *Daily Milap*, 2 January 1948; *Statesman*, 13 January 1948; *CMG*, 13 January 1948.
4. *Daily Milap*, 24 December 1948; *TOI*, 16 January 1948.
5. *Daily Milap*, 1 January 1948.
6. Ibid., 7 January 1948.
7. Ibid., 12 January 1948.
8. Ibid., 14 January 1948.
9. *Tribune*, 14 January 1948.
10. *CMG*, 15 January 1948.
11. Ibid., 18 January 1948.
12. *Tribune*, 17 January 1948.
13. Ibid.
14. Ibid., 18 January 1948; *CMG*, 18 January 1948.
15. *The Pioneer*, 17 January 1948.
16. *CMG*, 17 January 1948, and *Daily Milap*, 18 January 1948.
17. *CMG*, 17 January 1948.
18. *The Tribune*, 20 January 1948.
19. *TOI*, 16 January 1948, also *CMG*, 17 January 1948; *HT*, 16 January 1948.
20. *Statesman*, 17 January 1948; also *Daily Milap*, 18 January 1948. *Milap*

reported Gandhi as saying that the transfer of the cash balance should be able to solve the Kashmir crisis. Also see *Leader*, 17 January 1948 for Gandhi's reference to Kashmir and the hope that it might now be solved.

21. *CMG*, 17 January 1948.
22. *The Tribune*, 20 January 1948.
23. *Organiser*, 22 January 1948.
24. Valmiki Choudhary (ed.), *Dr. Rajendra Prasad's Correspondence and Select Documents*, vol. 8, New Delhi, 1987, pp. 405–8.
25. Ibid., 26 January 1948.
26. *Statesman*, 21 January 1948.
27. Ibid., 24 January 1948.
28. *The Pioneer*, 18 January 1948.
29. *Daily Milap*, 21, 26 and 29 January 1948.
30. Ibid., 26 December 1947.
31. The author has included this statement with great reluctance, the intention being merely to convey the kind of sentiments that prevailed. It must be remembered that Tara Singh was not an armchair leader and no Sikh leader understood the pulse of the Panth better than him, no leader was even close in popularity and mass appeal.
32. *The Tribune*, 25 January 1948. In this statement Tara Singh had asked the Sikhs of Delhi 'not to address Gandhiji as "Bapu" because Guru Gobind Singh was their true Bapu'. This statement was possibly a reaction from Tara Singh to an observation made by Gandhi around the 19 or 20 January. Gandhi had said that those who wanted Delhi to be vacated of Muslims were enemies of the country. Since Tara Singh was the most vocal on this count a reaction followed. See *Daily Milap*, 21 January 1948, for Gandhi's statement.
33. *TOI*, 13 and 17 January 1948; *CMG*, 13 and 17 January 1948; *Daily Milap*, 31 December 1947; ibid., 2, 7, 12 and 14 January 1948; *HT*, 17 January 1948; Chapter 7.
34. *The Pioneer*, 17 January 1948.
35. *Daily Milap*, 19 January 1948.
36. *SPC*, vol. 6, Patel's letter to Gandhi, pp. 24–5.
37. Ibid., Nehru to Patel, 11 January 1948, p. 17.
38. *Statesman*, 14 January 1948.
39. *The Pioneer*, 7 and 8 January 1948; *Organiser*, 22 January 1948.
40. *Daily Gazette* (Karachi), 16 January 1948, Nehru Clippings, Microfilm, NMML.
41. *Statesman*, 14 January 1948; *Daily Milap*, 15 January 1948.
42. *Statesman* and *TOI*, 16 January 1948.
43. *Daily Milap*, 18 January 1948.
44. *Statesman*, 21 January 1948.
45. *CMG*, 6 January 1948.

46. *SPC*, Nehru to Patel, vol. 6, 11 January 1948, p. 17.
47. Ibid., Patel to Nehru, 12 January 1948, p. 21.
48. Ibid., Nehru to Patel, 13 January 1948, p. 24.
49. I.M. Stephens Papers, Box 21, CSAS.
50. *Statesman*, 28 January 1948. Incidentally it was in this meeting that the Hindu Mahasabha officially condemned the move for a plebiscite in Kashmir and also resolved to oppose it.
51. *Statesman*, 30 January 1948; *The Tribune*, 30 and 31 January 1948.
52. *HT*, 30 January 1948.
53. *PT*, 30 January 1948.
54. *Dr. Rajendra Prasad's Correspondence & Select Documents*, vol. 8, p. 48. Madan Lal was a refugee from Montgomery. On his arrest he had said he had not meant to harm Gandhi but to draw attention to the incorrectness of transferring the cash balances to Pakistan, see *Daily Milap*, 22 January 1948.
55. *CMG*, 31 December 1947.
56. Ibid., 9 January 1948.
57. *CMG*, 31 January 1948.
58. Ibid.
59. Ibid., 2 and 3 February 1948.
60. Ibid.
61. *The Tribune* 2 February 1948.
62. Ibid., 3 February 1948.
63. Ibid., 5 February 1948.
64. Ibid., 3 February 1948.
65. *CMG*, 2 February 1948.
66. *The Tribune*, 3 February 1948.
67. *The Tribune* 13 and 20 February 1948.
68. Ibid., 13 February 1948.
69. Ibid., 14 February.
70. *Statesman*, 2 February 1948.
71. *The Tribune*, 3 February 1948.
72. *Statesman*, 3 February 1948.
73. *The Tribune*, 4 February 1948.
74. Ibid.
75. Ibid., 4 February 1948.
76. Ibid., 5 February 1948.
77. Ibid.
78. *Madras Mail*, February 1948; *SPC*, vol. VI, pp. 28–9.
79. *Statesman*, 4 February 1948.
80. Ibid., 4 February 1948; *TOI*, 4 February 1948; *HT*, 3 February 1947.
81. Ibid., 5 February 1948.
82. *Statesman*, 5 February 1948; *The Tribune*, 5 and 6 February 1948.
83. Ibid.

84. *The Tribune*, 6 February 1948; Syed Azhar Husain Zaidi, *New Nazis*, I.M. Stephens Papers, Box 19, CSAS.
85. *Statesman*, 5 February 1948.
86. Ibid.
87. *Dawn*, 27 November 1947; *Peoples Age*, Bombay, 19 October 1947.
88. *The Tribune*, 26 November 1947. *The Tribune* as we have noted were old rivals.
89. *The Tribune*, 30 December 1947.
90. *The Tribune*, 5 December 1947; *CMG*, 4 December 1947; *The Tribune*, 25 December 1947.
91. *TOI*, 5 February 1948; *CMG*, 5 February 1948; also *Statesman*, 5 February 1948.
92. *Statesman*, 6 February 1948.
93. Ibid., 6 February 1948.
94. *TOI*, 7 February 1948.
95. *Organiser*, 29 July 1948; 2 October 1948.
96. Ibid., 29 July 1948.
97. *TOI*, 7 February 1948.
98. *Dr. Rajendra Prasad's Correspondence & Select Documents*, vol. 8, p. 415.
99. *CMG*, 7 February 1948; *The Pioneer*, 7 February 1948.
100. *Panchjanya*, vol. 6, Acc. no. 8998, Microfilm, NMML.
101. *The Tribune*, 7, 9, 10 and 11 February, 1948.
102. *SPC*, vol. 6, Bhargava to Nehru, 14 February 1948, pp. 39–40.
103. *Statesman*, 9 February 1948.
104. *The Tribune*, 13 and 19 February 1948.
105. *The Tribune*, 14 February 1948.
106. *TOI*, 7 February 1948.
107. Ibid., 20 February 1948.
108. *Statesman*, 21 February 1948.
109. *SPC*, vol. 6, Bhargava to Nehru; 14 February 1948, pp. 39–40.
110. Ibid.
111. *SPC*, vol. 6, Patel to Kher, 8 January 1948, p. 179.
112. Ibid., Bhargava to Patel, 5 February 1948, p. 35.
113. Ibid., Patel to Bhargava, 9 February 1948, pp. 35–6.
114. *SW*, vol. 6 (Second Series), Nehru to Kher, 11 April 1948, p. 43.
115. *SPC*, vol. 6, Patel to Dr Rajendra Prasad, 25 February 1948, pp. 42–3.
116. Ibid.
117. *Statesman*, 21 February 1948.
118. *TOI*, 16 February 1948; *Statesman*, 15 February 1948; *SPC*, vol. 6, Mookerjee to Patel, 8 February 1948, pp. 36, 37, 41.
119. *Statesman*, 11 February 1948.
120. *The Tribune*, 13 February 1948.

121. Ibid., 14 February 1948.
122. Ibid., 13 February 1948.
123. *TOI*, 7 January 1948.
124. *Statesman*, 21 February 1948.
125. *TOI*, 14 February 1948.
126. *Statesman*, 21 February 1948.
127. *The Tribune*, 14 February 1948.
128. *Statesman*, 26 February 1948.
129. *The Tribune*, 26 February 1948; Press Information Files, Microfilm, Reel 8787, NMM.
130. IOR Mss. Eur. F 200/144, India Viceregal Office Correspondence Files, 'Sikh Problem Part II', 1 January 1948 to 24 April 1948.
131. Spate Papers, Diary entry 19 July 1947, CSAS; Chapter IV.
132. IOR Mss. Eur. F 200/165, Note by Lord Ismay, 'India Situation Report', 5 October 1947.
133. *SW*, vol. 6 (Second Series), Nehru to Bhargava, 16 April 1947, p. 45.
134. Ibid.; The editorial note to this letter suggests that Kartar Singh had only wanted suppression of the Communists and not of the RSS. But we have already seen that Giani Kartar Singh's first reaction following the ban on the RSS that was issued and published by newspapers on 14 February 1948, was only an assertion that the Dal will not dissolve itself and will continue guiding the Panth. The idea that he wanted a ban on the Communists and the ban on the RSS to be removed appears over stretched. *TOI*, 14 February 1948.
135. *SW*, vol. 6 (Second Series), Nehru to Rajendra Prasad, 26 April 1948, pp. 47–8.
136. Ibid.
137. Ibid., 1 May 1948, p. 50.
138. Ibid., Nehru to Bhargava, 20 May 1948, p. 53.
139. Ibid., Nehru to Baldev Singh, 6 June 1948, p. 57.
140. *Dawn*, 12, 14 and 15 May 1947; *CMG*, 8 May 1947.
141. *The Tribune*, 1 December 1947.
142. Ibid., 7 February 1948.
143. *SW*, vol. 6 (Second Series), Nehru to Bhargava, 20 May 1948, pp. 53–4.
144. The Akalis got what they wanted when parts of south-east Punjab—the Ambala Division—was separated from other parts of East Punjab to form the new state of Haryana on 1 November 1966. The creation of Haryana was not merely the result of the demand for a Punjabi-speaking Punjab because there was an equally strong movement in the regions that came to form Haryana for seperation from the central districts of Punjab. The reasons were not merely language and cultural differences—but the economic and educational neglect of Ambala Division as well.

Glossary

achyut	:	Untouchable, a caste term.
Ahirs	:	A sturdy peasant tribe, legendry herdsman, found mainly in the south-east of Punjab—the Mewat region—large numbers are found in the armed forces.
annas	:	One-sixteenth of a rupee—no longer in use.
atta	:	Usually refers to wheat flour but also to other grains like maize, gram, barley, etc.
bahista	:	The literal meaning is heaven on earth. It was commonly used by Muslim League activists in their campaign to woo the Muslim masses to the cause of Pakistan in the 1940s.
barbadi	:	Destruction, or complete loss.
bania	:	A class of traders, shopkeepers. The term is usually used with reference to those of the Hindu faith.
Bhagora	:	The literal meaning is one who ran away. A term used across Pakistan for those Muslims who moved from India to Pakistan in 1947. Another term for *mohajirs*.
bhusa	:	Hay, a type of dry cattle fodder, made usually from the stalks of wheat and other grain.
biradari	:	Brotherhood, community—claiming common descent.
chalak	:	A person who controls/guides animal-drawn carriages—*tonga chalak*, bullock cart *chalak*, etc.
charpoy	:	A cot of strings or bands made from jute and coconut fibre or cotton. Nowadays the hands are of plastic. A common feature in rural households across India.
Chaudhri	:	A little prefixed to names; usually signifying an elevated superior status associated more commonly with ownership of land; also used as caste term.
chautha	:	The fourth day after death, associated with the conduct of religious ceremonies, prescribed, by scriptures—for peace of the departed soul.

crore : One hundred lakh—ten million.

dhaba : A wayside food stall, usually serving regional local food at cheap rates. A very common sight across India.

dharamshala : Boarding and lodging places, usually built along caste/community/religious lines, usually free or at very nominal rates for short durations. They are more commonly found at places of religious importance in India.

dhobi : Laundryman.

Dussehera : An important religious festival of the Hindus, signifying the victory of good over evil; associated with the epic *Ramayana*.

ghee : A cooking medium.

goondas : Anti-social elements

Gujjars : A sturdy peasant tribe renowned for their cattle-rearing abilities, found in scattered pockets across north India. In present times they have fallen back because of educational backwardness.

gur : An extract of sugarcane juice, a coarse and cheap form of unrefined sugar. Until a few decades ago, refined sugar was not affordable and most households in India, served *gur*.

guru : A leader highly regarded by a group of followers a spiritual adviser. In the present context, the Sikh Gurus.

hartal : A strike or ceasing of work, including the closure of markets, etc., usually as a form of mass protest.

haveli : A large residential building—usually older buildings owned by rich families.

jathas : Organized groups/bonds/squads. The reference here is to Sikh *jathas*.

Jats : A peasant tribe found mainly in the south-eastern parts of Punjab, Rajasthan and western Uttar Pradesh.

Jatstan : A homeland for the Jats. A term referring to the demand among a section of the Hindu Jats for a separate homeland.

Jat Sabha : An organized body of Jats which watches over the interests of the Jats.

ji : A suffix added to a name to pronounce reverence and respect.

kafir : One who does not believe in Islam. A negative

		expression used mainly by Muslims holding extreme views.
kirpan	:	A sword worn by the Sikhs as a symbol of faith and purity.
lakh	:	A tenth of a million, one hundred thousand.
lathis	:	A sturdy staff, usually of bamboo, carried by peasants across India.
mard-i-khuda	:	A man of God—a true believer of Islam.
masjid	:	A place of Muslim worship.
Mohajir	:	A derogatory term for Muslims who migrated to Pakistan following the partition of India. *See also bhagora*.
malkhana	:	A secured place in a police station or judicial complex where confiscated or disputed articles are normally stored.
mandi	:	A market where farmers sell their produce.
mela	:	A fair.
Meos	:	A sturdy Muslim peasant tribe found mainly in the region identified with them—Mewat.
mohalla	:	An urban neighbourhood.
morcha	:	An organized show of strength, protest, solidarity.
mullah	:	A Muslim preacher versed in the Koran, more commonly an interpreter of Islamic law.
murdabad	:	A negative term used to denounce, to show wish ill and disapproval.
numberdar/ lumberdar	:	An important intermediary position created by the colonial rulers to rule India—a kind of village headman representing the prominent agrarian tribe of the village.
pallabandi	:	A social norm which defined relations on caste and community lines, mainly in the Mewat region. The concept underplayed religion; its weakening was one of the main reasons for communal strife in Mewat.
panth	:	A following. Essentially a reference to the Sikhs' common objectives, culture, language, and religious belief.
paise	:	The lowest currency denomination—100 paise make a rupee.
pir	:	Muslim spiritual guide—sufi guide.
pugree/pagree	:	Money taken by a person for the understand to transfer the possession of immovable property. More commonly the word means a type of turban

		worn across India mainly by the peasantry, but an integral part of the Sikh dress code.
Ram rajya	:	A reference to the time and rule of Lord Rama of the epic *Ramayana*, signifying virtue, happiness for all and fairness.
Rupee	:	Indian currency.
rashtrabhasha	:	National language.
safedposh	:	Semi-official position created in rural India by the colonial rulers as part of their intermediary hierarchy at the village and group level falling between the *zaildar* and *numberdar/lumberdar.*
sajjada nashin	:	Successor to the spiritual authority of a sufi saint at his shrine; usually a lineal descendant of the saint.
shakar	:	Unrefined sugar extracted from sugarcane, a grade superior to the basic *gur*.
shuddhi	:	Purification or the reconversion of those who had left the fold of Hinduism.
taccavi	:	A short-term loan or relief given by the government to cultivators, usually in times of distress or natural calamity.
tola	:	A measure of weight, approximately 10 grams.
tonga	:	Horse-drawn cart, a common mode of transport across India even to this day.
turrah	:	A long extension of turban known as the *pugree* or *safa* which cover the neck. The *turrah* came to be referred as a negative term because it was a part of the police uniform in colonial Punjab—hence a sign of oppression. It was also more commonly associated with the feudal character of rural Punjab.
Ulema	:	A Muslim learned in Islamic religious sciences.
urs	:	The celebration of the death of a sufi saint, an annual fair at sufi shrines often attracting crowds from all communities.
zamindar	:	A landowner.
zindabad	:	An expression of support and approval, literally meaning long life.

Bibliography

NEWSPAPERS/NEWS PUBLICATIONS

Abhyudaya (Hindi, Allahabad)
Civil & Military Gazette (Lahore)
Daily Milap (Urdu, Lahore/Delhi)
Dawn (Lahore)
Eastern Times (Lahore)
Hindu Outlook (Delhi)
Hindustan Times (Delhi)
Janvani (Hindi, Benaras)
Pakistan Times (Lahore)
Panchjanya (Hindi, Lucknow)
The Pioneer (Lucknow)
Statesman (Delhi/Calcutta)
The Times of India (Bombay)
Times (London)
The Leader (Allahabad)
Organiser (Delhi)
The Tribune (Lahore/Simla)

MICROFILM, NMML

Mitra, N.N., *Indian Annual Register 1946–7* (relevant volumes).
Rosenberger, Walter and Herbert C. Tobin (eds.), *Keesings Contemporary Archives: Weekly Report of Important World Events*, vol. VI, 1946–8.

PRIVATE PAPERS/MEMOIRS (UNPUBLISHED)

Arthur, A.J.V., Papers, CSAS.
Attlee, Clement Papers, Microfilm, NAI.
Auchinleck, Claude, 'Plain Tales from The Raj', BBC Transcript, NMML.
Bhargava, Gopichand, Diary, 1947, Manuscript Section, NMML.
Brenden, P., Papers, CSAS.
Chandra, Prabodh, Memoir, Oral History Transcript, NMML.
Khosla, G.D., Papers, Manuscript Section, NMML.
Lloyd Jones, D.E., Papers, CSAS.
Majhel, Ishar Singh, Memoir, Oral History Transcript, NMML.

Moon, Penderel, 'Plain Tales From The Raj', BBC Transcript, NMML.
Mortan, Jack, 'Indian Episode: A Personal Memoir', Police Papers, IOR, British Library, London.
Muddie, Francis, Collection, IOR.
Peddie, John, Lt. Col., 'The Steady Drummer', Memoir, Imperial War Museum Reading Room, Kennington, London.
Reynolds, R.N.P., Papers, CSAS.
Rich, W.H.A., Papers, Police Papers, IOR.
Russel, Wilfred, Diary, IOR.
Sachar, Bhimsen, Memoir, Oral History Transcript, NMML.
Sarabhai, Mridula, Papers, Microfilm, NMML.
Spate, O.H.K., Papers, CSAS.
Stephens, I.M. Papers, CSAS.

MINUTES/RECORDS/REPORTS (UNPUBLISHED)

All Indian Congress Committee Papers, Reel 123, Microfilm, NMML.
Eustance, J.C., Note on Situation in Punjab—Lahore, IOR. Mss. Eur. D. 1065/1.
I.B. Meetings Proceedings, IOR L/PO/6/122(ii).
Indian Viceregal Official Correspondence Files, 'Sikh Problem Part II', IOR Mss. Eur. F. 200/141.
Information Deptt. Fortnightly Appreciation (IOR L/1/1/665).
Ismay, Lord, Indian Situation Report, October 1947, IOR Mss. Eur. F. 200/165.
Mountbatten, Earl Papers/Records. The collection at the NMML is on microfilm and comprises 30 reels. Many of these are also in the *TP* volumes. File 161-A is on microfilm, IOR. A large number of documents associated with Mountbatten have also been listed under different heads in the Notes.
Rees, Maj. Gen. T.W., Report, IOR L/MIL/17/5/4319.
Surveys of Policies of Newspapers in India, IOR L/1/332.
Transfer of Power Viceroys Plan, IOR L/PO/6/120(i) & 122(ii).
Viceroys Conference Papers, IOR 133, MP, File 161-A.
Viceregal Official Correspondence Transfer of Power Ceremonies, IOR, File 161-B, Reel 15557.
Viceroys Personal Reports, IOR L/PO/6/123.
Note: Documents that were not titled under special heads have not been listed here; they are listed only in the notes.

OFFICIAL RECORDS/DOCUMENTS (PUBLISHED)

Alana, G., *Pakistan Movement: Historic Documents*, Karachi, 1967.
Govt. of India, *Census of India—Punjab* 1921, 1931, 1941.

———, *Millions on the Move: The Aftermath of Partition.*

———, *Recovery & Restoration of Abducted Persons.*

Govt. of Pakistan, *The Partition of Punjab 1947: A Compilation of Official Documents*, National Documentation Centre, Lahore, 1993.

Govt. of Punjab (East), *Educational Statistics of Punjab 1947–8, 1949–50*, Publication no. 4 1952.

———, *Budget 1947–8.*

———, *Millions Live Again.*

———, *Orphans of the Storm.*

———, *Punjab Legislative Assembly Debates (1946).*

———, *Rural Rehabilitation in East Punjab.*

Jafri, S.Q.H., *Rare Documents*, Lahore, 1967.

Khalsa College, Amritsar, *Annual Report 1947–8, 1948–9.*

Mansergh, N.; E.W.R. Lumby, and Penderel Moon, *Constitutional Relations Between Britain and India: The Transfer of Power*, London, 1976–82, vols. 6 to 12.

Pirzada, S.S., *Foundations of Pakisan: All India Muslim League Documents, 1906–47*, 2 vols., Karachi, 1970.

Stewart, H.R. and Karan Rasul, *Farm Accounts in The Punjab 1926–7*, Board of Economic Inquiry, Punjab Rural Section Publications, no. 19, 1926.

LETTERS/CORRESPONDENCES—INDIVIDUAL (PUBLISHED)

Choudhary, Valmiki (ed.), *Dr. Rajendra Prasad's Correspondence & Select Documents*, vol. 8, Delhi, 1987.

Das, Durga (ed.), *Sardar Patel's Correspondence*, vol. 6, Ahmedabad, 1973.

Gopal, S. (ed.), *Selected Works of Jawaharlal Nehru*, Delhi, 1972–9.

Jafri, S.Q.H. and S.A. Bukhari (eds.), *Quad-i-Azam's Correspondence with Punjab Muslim League Leaders*, Lahore, 1977.

Mountbatten, Earl, *Time Only to Look Forward: Speeches as Viceroy & Governor General of India 1947–8*, London, 1949.

[*Note*: Some correspondence independent of the above has been listed only in the notes.]

RARE BOOKS (CONTEMPORARY)

Ansari, Shaukatullah, Dr., *Pakistan: The Problem of India*, Lahore, 1944, State Central Library, Hyderabad.

Bali, A.N., *Now It Can Be Told*, Jullundur, 1949, NMML.

Gandhi, M.K., *To The Protagonists of Pakistan*, Karachi, 1947, Royal Asiatic Library, Mumbai.

Gauba, K.L., *Inside Pakistan*, Delhi, 1948, Royal Asiatic Library Mumbai.

Kumar, N.V. Raj, *One Year of Freedom*, Delhi, 1948, Royal Asiatic Library, Mumbai.

Malik, D.M., *The Tragedy of Delhi*, Delhi, 1947, I.M. Stephens Papers, Box 19, CSAS.

Meharally, Yusuf, *A Trip to Pakistan*, Bombay, 1944, State Central Library, Hyderbad.

Talib, G.S., *Muslim League Attack on Sikhs and Hindus in Punjab 1947*, SGPC, Amritsar, 1950, CSAS.

Nanda, J., (B.R.), *Punjab Uprooted: A Survey of The Punjab Riots and Rehabilitation Programmes*, Bombay, 1948, rpt. Delhi, 2003 references are from the 1948 edition, NMML.

Setalvad, Chimanlal, *India Divided: Who Is To Blame For It?* Bombay, NMML.

Surlerl, Ziauddin Ahmad, *Wither Pakistan*, London: Eastern Publishers, State Central Library, Hyderabad.

West Punjab Govt., *RSS in Action*, Lahore, 1948, I.M. Stephens Papers, Box 21, CSAS.

———, *Sikhs in Action*, Lahore, 1948, I.M. Stephens Papers, Box 21, CSAS.

Zaidi, Azhar Husain, *New Nazis*, I.M. Stephens Papers, Box 19, CSAS.

ARTICLES IN JOURNALS/PERIODICALS/BOOKS/NEWSPAPERS

Ahmad, Ishtiaq, 'The 1947 Partition of Punjab: Arguments Put Forth Before The Punjab Boundry Commission By The Parties Involved', in Ian Talbot and Gurharpal Singh, *Region and Partition: Bengal Punjab and The Partition of The Sub Continent*, Oxford, 1999.

Bookspan, Shelly, 'History Historian and Visual Entertainment Media: Towards a Reapproachment', *The Public Historian*, vol. 25, no. 3 Summer 2004.

Boyce, D.G., 'Public Opinion and Historians', *History* 63, June 1978.

Chaudhry, Tapan Ray, 'Rereading Divide and Quit', *The Partition Omnibus*, Oxford, 2002.

Datta, V.N., 'Towards Freedom: Inside Story', *Symposia Paper 26, Indian History Congress*, 62nd Session, 2001.

———, 'Interpreting Partition', in Amrik Singh (ed.), *The Partition in Retrospect*, Delhi, 2002.

Gilmartin, D., 'Religious Leadership and The Pakistan Movement in Punjab', *Modern Asian Studies,* 13, 3, 1970.

Hasan, Mushirul, 'Introduction', *The Partition Omnibus*, Oxford, 2002.

Jeffrey, R., 'The Punjab Boundry Force and The Problem of Order August 1947', *Modern Asian Studies* 8, 4, 1974.

Jolly, Margaretta, 'The Letter as a Propaganda', in Bertrand Taithe and Tim

Thorton (eds.), *Propaganda Political Rhetoric & Identity 1300–2000*, Surrey: Sutton, 1999.

Lohia, Rammanohar, 'Partition and Its Nullification', *Mankind*, May 1971.

Majumdar, A.K., 'Writings on The Transfer of Power 1945–7', in B.R. Nanda (ed.), *Essays in Modern Indian History*, Delhi, 1980.

Menon, Ritu and Kamla Bhasin, 'Recovery Rupture and Resistance: Indian State and Abduction of Women During Partition', *Economic and Political Weekly*, 24 April 1993.

Mountbatten, Earl, *Jawaharlal Nehru Lecture*, Delivered at CSAS, Cambridge, 1968.

Pandey, Gyanendra, 'Hindus and Others: The Militant, Hindu Construction', *Economic and Political Weekly*, 28 December 1991.

———, 'Review of Writings on Communalism', *Economic and Political Weekly*, 15 October 1998.

Plane, Ann Marrie, 'Historian Behind The Corner', *The Public Historian*, vol. 25, no. 3, Summer 2003.

Talbot, Ian, 'Literature and Human Drama of The 1947 Partition', in Ian Talbot and Gurharpal Singh (eds.), *Region and Partition: Bengal, Punjab and the Partition of the Sub-Continent*, Oxford, 1999.

———, 'The Growth of The Muslim League in The Punjab 1937–46', *Journal of Commonwealth and Comparative Politics*, vol. 22, 1982.

Tinker, H.R., 'Jawaharlal Nehru at Simla, May 1947', *Modern Asian Studies*, 4, 4, 1970.

———, 'Pressure, Persuasion, Decision: Factors in the Partition of the Punjab August 1947', *Journal of Asian Studies*, vol. 36, no. 4, 1977.

Tanwar, R., 'Tradition Versus Modernity: A Study of The Failure of Muslim Peasant Leadership in Punjab', *Journal of The Pakistan Historical Society*, vol. XL, Part III, July 1992.

———, 'Origin of the Punjab National Unionist Party: Feudal Elite and Legislative Politics', *Journal of The Pakistan Historical Society*, XLIV, Part II, April 1996.

Vyas, Darshnik, 'Good Morning Kurukshetra', *Times of India*, 20 May 2004.

Yadav, K.C., 'The Partition of India: A Study of Muslim Politics in Punjab 1849–1947', *Punjab Past and Present*, vol. 18, 1 April 1983.

SELECT PUBLISHED WORKS

Ahmad, Jamil-ud-din, *Some Aspects of Pakistan*, Lahore, 1947.

Ahmad, K.S., *Politico-Regional Division of India*, Lahore, 1945.

Ali, I., *Punjab Politics in the Decade Before Partition*, Lahore, 1974.

Ambedkar, B.R., *Pakistan or Partition*, Bombay, 1945.

Attlee, C.R., *As It Happened*, London, 1954.

Barrier N.G. and P. Wallace, *The Punjab Press*, Michigan University, 1970.

Bhalla, Alok (ed.), *Stories About The Partition of India*, 3 vols., Delhi, 1994.

Bhattacharjee, A., *Countdown to Partition: The Final Days*, Delhi, 1997.

Birdwood, C.B., *India's Freedom Struggle: Role of Muslims and Sikhs*, Delhi, 1988.

Bolitho, H., *Jinnah: Creator of Pakistan*, London, 1957.

Brittain, V., *Pethick-Lawerence*, London, 1963.

Calvert, H., *The Size & Distribution of Land Holdings in Punjab*, Lahore, 1925.

———, *Wealth & Welfare of The Punjab*, Lahore, 1922.

Chandra, Bipan, *Communalism in Modern India*, Delhi, 1984.

Connell, J., *Auchinleck*, London, 1959.

Cowasjee, Saros and K.S. Duggal, *Orphans of The Storm: Stories on the Partition of India*, Delhi, 1995.

Darling, M.L., *Punjab Peasant in Prosperity and Debt*, 1st edn. 1925, rpt. New Delhi, 1977.

Das, Durga, *India: From Curzon to Nehru and After*, London, 1969.

Das, M.N., *Partition and Independence of India*, Delhi, 1982.

———, *Fateful Events of 1947: The Secret Game of Divide and Quit*, Delhi, 2004.

Davis, Emmet, *Press and Politics in British Western Punjab 1936–47*, Delhi, 1988.

Duggal, K.S., *Twice Born Twice Dead*, Delhi, 1979.

Dungen, P.H.M., *The Punjab Tradition*, London, 1972.

Duni Chand, *Ulster of India: An Analysis of The Punjab Problem*, Lahore, 1936.

Edwards, M., *The Last Years of British India*, London, 1963.

Farwell, Byron, *The Gurkhas*, London, 1984.

Ferguson, B., *Wavell: Portrait of Soldier*, London, 1961.

Freitag, Sandra, *Collective Action and Community: Public Arenas and The Emergence of Communalism in North India*, Delhi, 1990.

Gauba, K.L., *The Consequences of Pakistan*, Lahore, 1946.

Ghosh, Sudhir, *Gandhi's Emissary*, Boston, 1967.

Gilmartin, David, *Empire and Islam: Punjab and The Making of Pakistan*, Delhi, 1988.

Gunter, Barrie, *Media Research Methods, Measuring Audiences Reactions and Impact*, Delhi, 2000.

Hamid, A., *Muslim Separation in India*, Karachi, 1967.

Hansen, Anders Bjorn, *Partition and Genocide: Manifestation of Violence in Punjab 1937–47*, Delhi, 2002.

Hardy P., *The Muslims of British India*, Cambridge, 1972.

Hasan, Mushirul, *Nationalism and Communal Politics in India*, Delhi, 1991.

——— (ed.), *India's Partition Process, Strategy and Mobilisation*, Delhi, 1993.

———, *India Partitioned: The Other Face of Freedom*, 2 vols., Delhi, 1995.

Hassan, S.S., *Plain Mr. Jinnah*, Karachi, 1976.

Hodson, H.V., *The Great Divide: Britain India and Pakistan*, London, 1969.

Hugh, R., *Mountbatten: Hero of Our Time*, London, 1980.

Ikram, S.M., *Modern Muslim India and The Birth of Pakistan*, Lahore, 1977.

Isphani, M.A.H., *Quad-i-Azam: As I Knew Him*, Karachi, 1976.

Jalal, Ayesha, *The Sole Spokesman Jinnah: The Muslim League and The Demand for Pakistan*, Cambridge, 1985.

Jeffrie, C., *The Transfer of Power*, London, 1960.

Jinnah, M.A., *Muslim India Speaks*, Aligarh, 1942.

Johnson, Campbell, *Mission With Mountbatten*, London, 1951.

Kaul, Chandrika, *Reporting The Raj: The British Press & India 1800–1922*, Manchester, 2003.

Khairi, Saad R., *Jinnah Reinterpreted: The Journey from Indian Nationalism to Muslim Statehood*, Karachi, 1996.

Khan, Wali, *Facts are Facts: The Untold Story of India's Partition*, Delhi, 1987.

Khosla, G.D., *Stern Reckoning: A Survey of The Events Leading Upto and Following The Partition of India*, Oxford, Omnibus Edition, 2002.

Krishan, Y., *Mountbatten and The Partition of India*, Delhi, 1983.

Lippman, W., *Public Opinion*, New York, 1997.

Lohia, Rammanohar, *Guilty Men of India's Partition*, Allahabad, 1960.

Lumby, E.W.B., *Transfer of Power in India*, London, 1954.

Mahajan, M.C., *Looking Back*, Bombay, 1963.

Malik, I.A., *A Book of Readings on The History of The Punjab 1799–1947*, Lahore, 1970.

Mansergh, N., *Prelude to Partition: Concepts and Aims in Ireland and India*, Cambridge, 1978.

Mehta A. and A. Patwardhan, *Communal Triangle*, Allahabad, 1942.

Mehtar, M.A., *Whys of The Great Conflict*, Lahore, 1947.

Mehrotra, S.R., *Towards India's Freedom & Partition*, Delhi, 1979.

Moore, R.J., *Escape From Empire: The Attlee Government and The Indian Problem*, Oxford, 1983.

Moeller, Susan D., *Compassion Fatigue: How The Media Sell Disease Famine War and Death*, New York, 1999.

Moon, Penderel, *Wavell: The Viceroy's Journal*, London, 1973.

———, *Divide & Quit: An Eyewitness Account of The Partition of India*, Oxford, Omnibus Edition, 2002.

Moor, R.J., *Escape From Empire: The Attlee Government and The India Problem*, Oxford, 1983.

Mosley, L., *The Last Days of The British Raj*, London, 1961.

Mukerji, Hiren, *Was India's Partition Unavoidable*, Calcutta, 1987.

Mushid, Tazeem, *The Sacred and The Secular: Bengal Muslim Discourses 1871–1977*, Calcutta, 1995.

Nanda, B.R., *Essays in Modern Indian History*, Delhi, 1980.

Nagarkar, V.V., *Genesis of Pakistan*, Delhi, 1975.

Najjar, B.S., *Punjab Under The British Rule, 1849–1947*, 3 vols., Delhi, 1974.

Narang, G.C., *Plight of The Punjab Minorities Under The So Called Unionist Government*, Lahore, 1941.

Nawaj, Mumtaz Shah, *The Heart Divided*, London, 1969.

Nayar, B.R., *Minority Politics in Punjab*, Princeton, 1966.

Nehru, Jawaharlal, *An Autobiography*, Delhi, 1962.

Newman, W.L., *Social Research Methods: Qualitative and Quantitative Approaches*, Boston, 1994.

Noon, Firoz Khan, *From Memory*, Lahore, 1966.

Page, David, *Prelude to Partition: The Indian Muslims and The Imperial System of Control 1920-32*, Oxford, Omnibus Edition, 2002.

Pandey, Gyanendra, *The Construction of Communalism in Colonial North India*, Delhi, 1990.

———, *Remembering Partition*, Cambridge, 2001.

Parthasarthy, Rangaswami, *Journalism in India*, Delhi, 1989.

Philips, C.H., and M.D. Wainwright, *The Partition of India: Policies & Perspectives 1935–47*, London, 1970.

Philips, C.H. (ed.), *The Evolution of India and Pakistan 1857–1947*, London, 1962.

Prasad, B., *The Hindu Muslim Question*, Lahore, 1943.

Prasad, Rajendra, *Autobiography*, Delhi, 1957.

———, *India Divided*, Bombay, 1947.

Quereshi, S., *The Struggle For Pakistan*, Karachi, 1947.

Rai, S.M., *Partition of Punjab*, Delhi, 1985.

Rajput, Allah Baksh, *Punjab Crisis and Cure*, Lahore, 1947.

Randhawa, M.S., *Out of Ashes*, Delhi, 1954.

Saini, B.S., *Social and Economic History of Punjab*, Delhi, 1975.

Sayeed, K.B., *Pakistan: The Formative Phase 1857–1948*, London, 1968.

Seal, Anil, *The Emergence of Indian Nationalism: Competition and Collaboration in The Late 19th Century*, Cambridge, 1968.

Sharma, S.R., *Punjab in Ferment*, Delhi, 1971.

Sherwani, L.A. (ed.), *Pakistan Resolution to Pakistan*, Delhi, 1985.

Shah, K.T., *Why Pakistan? and Why Not?* Bombay, 1944.

Singh, Anita Inder, *The Origins of The Partition of India*, Oxford, Omnibus Edition, 2002.

Singh, H., *Punjab The Homeland of The Sikhs*, Lahore, 1945.

Singh, Harnam, *Sikh Memorandum on The Punjab Boundary Commission*, Lahore, 1947.

Singh, Kirpal, *Select Documents: Partition of Punjab 1947*, Delhi, 1991.

———, *The Partition of Punjab*, Patiala, 1972.

Singh, Khushwant, *Train to Pakistan*, New York, 1956.

———, *A History of The Sikhs*, vol. 2, Princeton, 1966.
Singh, Tara, *Why We Must Avoid A Civil War in India*, Lahore, 1946.
Smith, W.C., *Modern Islam in India*, London, 1946.
Sondhi, K., *Uprooted*, Delhi, 1977.
Spate, O.H.K., *India & Pakistan: General and Regional Geography*, London, 1954.
Stephens, Ian, *Horned Moon*, London, 1953.
———, *Monsoon Morning*, London, 1966.
Talbot, Ian, *Khizr Tiwana: The Punjab Unionist Party and The Partition of India*, Richmond, 1996.
———, *Punjab and The Raj: Provincial Politics and The Pakistan Movement*, Delhi, 1988.
———, *Freedoms City: The Population Dimension in The Pakistan Movement and The Pakistan Experience in N.W. India*, Karachi, 1995.
Talbot, Ian and Gurharpal Singh, *Region & Partition: Bengal Punjab and The Partition of The Sub Continent*, Oxford, 1999.
Tandon, P., *Punjab Century 1857–1947*, London, 1961.
Tanwar, Raghuvendra, *Politics of Sharing Power: The Punjab Unionist Party 1923–47*, Delhi, 1999.
Tinker, H., *Experiment With Freedom: India and Pakistan 1947*, London, 1967.
Trench, Charles Chevinix, *The Indian Army 1900–47*, London, 1988.
Tuker, F., *While Memory Serves*, London, 1950.
Tyabji, H.B., *Why Mussulmans Should Oppose Pakistan*, Bombay, 1946.
Vanden, P.H.N., *The Punjab Tradition*, London, 1972.
Wolpert, S., *Jinnah of Pakistan*, New York, 1984.
Yadav, K.C., *Elections in Punjab*, Delhi, 1987.
Zillmann, B. and J. Byrant (eds.), *Selective Exposure to Communication* New Jersey, 1985.
Zinkin, Taya, *Reporting India*, London, 1962.

Index